10th EAI International Conference on Body Area Networks (BODYNETS 2015)

Sydney, Australia
28 - 30 September 2015

ISBN: 978-1-5108-4178-9

Printed from e-media with permission by:

Curran Associates, Inc.
57 Morehouse Lane
Red Hook, NY 12571

Some format issues inherent in the e-media version may also appear in this print version.

Printed by Curran Associates, Inc. (2017)

For permission requests, please contact European Alliance for Innovation (EAI)
at the address below.

European Alliance for Innovation (EAI)
c/o Volha Shaparava , Dr
Publications
Via alla Cascata 56/D - 38123 Povo,
Trento - Italy

publications@eai.eu

Additional copies of this publication are available from:

Curran Associates, Inc.
57 Morehouse Lane
Red Hook, NY 12571 USA
Phone: 845-758-0400
Fax: 845-758-2633
Email: curran@proceedings.com
Web: www.proceedings.com

TABLE OF CONTENTS

Fall-MobileGuard: a Smart Real-Time Fall Detection System

Giancarlo Fortino, Raffaele Gravina*
Department of Informatics, Modelling, Electronics and Systems, University of Calabria
Via P. Bucci, cubo 41C, 87036 Rende (CS), Italy
g.fortino@unical.it, rgravina@deis.unical.it

***Abstract*—This paper proposes Fall-MobileGuard, a novel real-time non-invasive fall detection and alarm notification system. The proposed system, in particular, is able to recognize different types of falls and is based on a wearable inertial sensor node, equipped with a tri-axial accelerometer, worn at the waist and a personal mobile device. The detection method consists of two main processing blocks; the first is threshold-based trigger and is executed on the wearable sensor while the second includes posture classification and operates on the mobile device. Conversely to previous literature, we introduced multiple severity levels of detected fall events. The system is primarily intended for elderly people living alone or in retirements homes and supports alarm notifications of fall events over diversified channels, including social networks and automatic voice calls, according to the severity of the event. A comprehensive and well defined experimentation has been conducted, collecting in semi-controlled environment acceleration data from twenty subjects emulating falls and performing everyday life activities. Performance evaluation of our system has been carried out, resulting in 97% specificity, 83% sensitivity and 90% precision.**

Keywords*—Fall detection, wearable devices, cloud computing, BodyCloud.

I. Introduction

Automatic human activity detection in uncontrolled environments is an important component of many research studies. Non-invasive activity recognition systems may help to ensure the continuous monitoring of elderly and patients to increase their safety and provide better insights on their health status. Fall detection is a specific problem of this research domain attracting wide scientific interest; it is addressed with very diversified methodological and technological approaches.

More specifically, in this paper we introduce Fall-MobileGuard, a fall detection and alerting system based on a wearable motion sensor and a personal mobile device.

The main issues of a fall detection system based on wearable devices are related to the number of sensors, their position on the body and the accuracy of the system itself.

On the one hand, more sensors will result in more information available for the system, with more chances of better accuracy. On the other hand, however, a more complex system results in higher economic costs and comfort issues; users expects to use such systems seamlessly and in fact to conduct their daily life activities without any interferences.

This work hence proposes a method and a practical solution for real-time recognition of different types of falls which involves the use of:

- a single sensor node placed in comfortable, convenient location on the body (for example with a belt clip or in the trousers pocket);
- the SPINE open-source framework [1], [2] for flexible dynamic sensor node configuration;
- pattern recognition techniques to support fall detection algorithm;
- an Android smartphone that serves as end-user device.

The rest of the paper is structured as follows. Section II gives a classification of several type of falls and analyzes a wide plethora of related works, providing useful comparison tables. Section III describes in detail our fall detection method. In Section IV we present the Fall-MobileGuard, discussing the prototype and reporting performance evaluation results; the section also describes the experimentation activities we conducted. Finally, in Section V conclusive remarks are drawn and directions of future work are briefly outlined.

II. Background

Every year there are more than 30 million domestic accidents in the US only, predominantly affecting the elderly, with major consequences in terms of temporary and permanent disability, hospitalization and mortality. Among domestic accidents, falls represent the most common cause and it is estimated that one third of the population over the sixties has suffered at least one significant fall and among the elderly residing in retirement houses and medical centers, this percentage is even greater [3].

The fall event is usually caused by a complex interaction of personal and environmental factors and circumstances related to the simple daily activities. Falls can be caused by intrinsic factors (e.g. age-related changes, muscular and skeletal problems, and disorders that affect the normal operation vestibular, proprioceptive and visual cognitive mechanisms) and extrinsic factors (e.g. obstacles in the environment). Independent elderly

BODYNETS 2015, September 28-30, Sydney, Australia

DOI 10.4108/eai.28-9-2015.2261462

are typically less debilitated at physical level, but at the same time tend to be exposed to greater environmental factors that contribute to the risk of falling. Falls, especially for the elderly, have varied and complex implications [4]: about 20% of falls require medical intervention, 5-10% result to hip fracture (and 7% of elderly who suffered hip fracture eventually dies). Falls are also the second leading cause of head and spinal traumas. Finally, a very severe consequence of the fall is the fracture of the thigh bone that occurs in 0.6% of fall victims under 64 years, rising to 10.8% for people over 64, to 12.9% for people over 74 years and 14.2% for those above 79 years.

A. Fall taxonomy

Fall can be defined as a sudden and unexpected change of the body position in which static and dynamic balance mechanisms fail and the voluntary responses are inadequate to correct the lack of balance. Falls can be classified correctly only if all the different related factors are identified.

In Table I we report a wide, yet not exhaustive, classification of falls.

TABLE I. FALLS CLASSIFICATION

Fall	Description
Front-lying	From a standing position one falls toward the ground and keeps the lying position after the impact. This fall commonly happens when people lose balance or stumble.
Front-protecting-lying	From a standing position one falls to the ground by attenuating the fall with the arms, yet keeping the lying position after the impact.
Front-knees-lying	From a standing position one falls, landing initially on the knees and then lying on the ground.
Front-right/left	From a standing position one falls toward the ground assuming a side position.
Front-quick-recovery	From a standing position one falls toward the ground but quickly recovers the standing position after the impact. This type of fall often does not result in immediate significant consequences, although the risk of delayed implications should not be excluded.
Front-slow-recovery	From a standing position one falls toward the ground and slowly recover the standing position after the impact. In this type of fall, the person is able to stand up but presents some difficulties, possibly reporting traumas due to the impact with the ground.
Back-sitting	From a standing position one falls backward the ground ending in a sitting position.
Back-lying	From a standing position one falls backward to the ground ending in a lying position. This fall commonly occurs on slipper, wet floors. This type of fall more easily leads to significant consequences as the head is more exposed to impacts.
Back-right/left	From a standing position one falls backward to the ground ending up in a sideway lying position. This type of fall also can easily lead to serious injuries.
Right/left-sideway	From a standing position one falls sideways to the ground ending in a lying position without any ability to recover the standing posture.
Right/left-recovery	From a standing position one falls sideways towards the ground but quickly recovers the standing position after the impact.
Syncope	It is also known as fainting and consists of a short loss of consciousness and muscle strength followed by spontaneous recovery.
Rolling-out-bed	From a lying position one rolls out of bed falling to the floor. Falling out of bed is unfortunately a frequent event for the elderly.
Falling-from-stairs	Descending the stairs one stumbles and rolls down. This type of fall is extremely dangerous especially for the elderly due to bone fragility.

B. Related work

There are three major fall detection approaches based respectively on (i) image and video analysis, (ii) acoustic devices, and (iii) wearable devices. Systems based on video analysis capture images of human movement through one or more video devices (e.g. webcams or infrared cameras) and determine the occurrence of a fall by examining the variations of specific features of the image. Systems based on acoustic devices detect a fall through specific patterns in audio signals. Usually these systems are heavily influenced by environmental noise, particularly in open spaces, and therefore are typically supported with additional systems. Finally, systems based on wearable sensing devices allow to continuously and unobstructively acquire body motion data which are analyzed to detect (and report in real-time) fall events.

In this section we briefly outline the results of our study of the works related to the latter approach. We support in fact the idea of developing a fall detection systems that should be able to continuously monitor elderly so to favor them to carry out normal daily life activities (such as living independently, walking in their neighborhood, doing groceries). In addition, timely alerts to relative and caregivers should be issued upon the detection of any relevant fall, with the aim of avoiding worse situations.

It is worth noting that current mobile devices (such as commercial smartphones) integrate various sensors and are gaining always greater capabilities in terms of computing power, communication, and storage; as a consequence, we also analyzed works that use directly smartphones for sensing body movements. Being able to use uniquely the mobile device to realize a robust fall detection system has the significant advantage of not having to wear additional items (that are not easily accepted by the elderly); however, there are disadvantages too, mainly related to increased battery discharge of the device.

The following tables summarize the main aspects on the related work we analyzed; in particular, Table II contains information on the adopted sensors and their location on the body, Table III presents detection methods and algorithms, while Table IV synthesizes the obtained performance results.

Interested readers could also refer to recent and interesting surveys [5], [6] that discuss several works on fall detection and analyze the problem under various point of views.

TABLE II. SENSOR TYPES AND LOCATION ON THE BODY

Ref.	Wearable sensors	Smartphone sensors	Sensor location	Sensor type
[7]	X	-	waist	accelerometer
[8]	X	-	waist, head	accelerometer
[9]	X	-	head	accelerometer
[10]	X	-	chest, thigh	accel., gyroscope
[11]	X	-	chest, thigh	accel., gyroscope
[12]	X	-	chest	accelerometer
[13]	X	-	chest, thigh	accelerometer
[14]	-	X	waist	accelerometer
[15]	-	X	N/A	accelerometer
[16]	-	X	N/A	accelerometer
[17]	-	X	N/A	accelerometer
[18]	-	X	waist	accelerometer
[19]	-	X	waist	accelerometer
[20]	X	-	N/A	accel., barometer
[21]	X	-	waist	accelerometer
[22]	X	-	waist, back	accel., gyroscope

Regardless of the sensing device, most of the works found the waist to be the most suitable location to place the sensor [7], [8], [14], [18], [19], [21], [22], although a few others place the sensor on the chest [10], [11], [12], [13], or at the head [8], [9]. The use of a threshold-based approach to detect abrupt acceleration peaks is extremely common, while

TABLE III. METHODS

Ref.	Pre-filtering	Pattern recognition	Use of thresholds	Posture recognition
[7]	-	-	X	X
[8]	X	-	X	X
[9]	X	-	X	-
[10]	-	-	X	X
[11]	-	X	-	-
[12]	X	X	-	X
[13]	-	-	X	-
[14]	-	-	X	-
[15]	X	-	X	-
[16]	-	-	X	X
[17]	X	-	X	-
[18]	X	X	-	X
[19]	-	-	X	-
[20]	X	X	X	-
[21]	X	-	X	-
[22]	-	X	-	-

TABLE IV. PERFORMANCE EVALUATION COMPARISON

Ref.	Specificity	Sensitivity	Precision	No. of subjects
[7]	N/A	N/A	N/A	2
[8]	100%	95%	N/A	2
[9]	N/A	N/A	N/A	2
[10]	92%	91%	N/A	3
[11]	N/A	N/A	81%	8
[12]	N/A	N/A	84%	6
[13]	100%	95,5%	100%	20
[14]	N/A	N/A	N/A	15
[15]	N/A	N/A	95%	5
[16]	N/A	N/A	N/A	N/A
[17]	N/A	N/A	N/A	N/A
[18]	N/A	N/A	N/A	N/A
[19]	81%	77%	N/A	18
[20]	96%	96%	97%	-
[21]	100%	81%	90%	-
[22]	99%	97%	N/A	-

only few works also include posture recognition [7], [8], [10], [12], [16], [18]. Most of the related works are based on the use of accelerometer sensors (to detect body accelerations exceeding preset thresholds) and the detection of body postures (to contextualize acceleration peaks). However, carrying out a quantitative comparative analysis is not easy [23]. One of the main reason is that the set of analyzed actions referring to both the normal activities and the type of falls are not always indicated; secondly, the test sample (number and heterogeneity of participants to the experiments) is very variable and for some works very limited. Last, but not least, a problem that makes it difficult to perform a comparison among the various proposed solutions is the absence (in most cases as depicted in Table IV) of performance indexes, for instance in terms of sensitivity, specificity, and precision that would quantitatively characterize the achieved accuracy.

III. METHOD

The first phase of the development focused on the acquisition of accelerometer data during a series of (emulated) falls. To this purpose, we setup an experimentation in which twenty subjects were asked to wear a Shimmer2R sensor node [24] (which features an embedded tri-axial accelerometer) in their front pocket and to emulate a series of predefined falls (as described in section II.A).

Using the SPINE programming framework [1], [2], [25], [26], the wearable sensor was configured to continuously transmit over Bluetooth raw x, y, z acceleration data, setting the sampling rate to 40Hz. Data are received by the mobile coordinator device.

The first step of our detection method consists of a threshold-based trigger. Specifically, the raw acceleration signals are preliminarily scaled down around zero, then instantaneous (sample-by-sample) cross-axial energy, is computed as follows:

$$E_{tot} = x^2 + y^2 + z^2 \quad (1)$$

The choice of this function depends on its definition: the value of cross-axial energy depends on all three axes, therefore, regardless the nature of the fall and the orientation of the sensor, this value is expected to present a significant change. The plot in Fig. 1 shows the acceleration signals related a front-lying emulated fall. The plot in Fig. 2 shows the scaled acceleration signals corresponding to the fall event shown in Fig. 1. Finally, the plot in Fig. 3 shows the corresponding cross-axial energy signal.

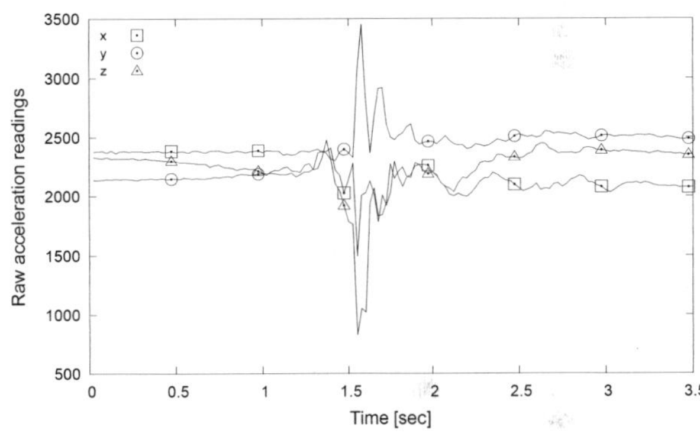

Fig. 1. Acceleration signals during a *front-lying* fall

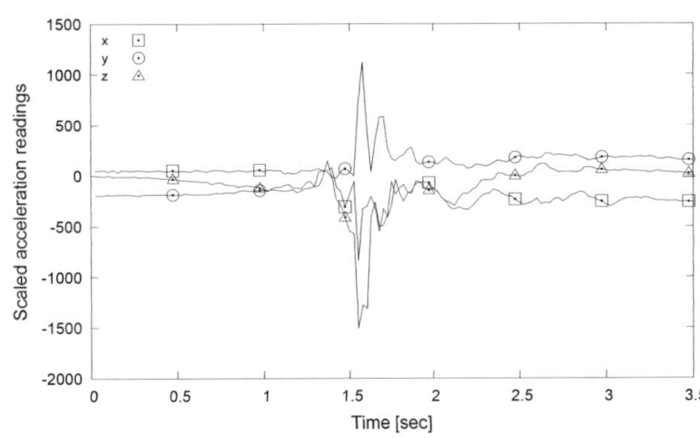

Fig. 2. Scaled acceleration signals

All these signal processing steps are executed online by the wearable sensor that checks if cross-axial energy exceeds the predefined threshold.

However, as previously examined [7], [8], [10], [12], [16], [18], solely relying on acceleration thresholds may induce the system to mis-detection errors, exchanging actual falls for normal physical activities and viceversa.

To avoid this problem, our recognition method is actually based on two main processing blocks. The first is performed directly on the sensor node, it has the purpose of detecting potential falls and is based on the threshold mechanism described so far; the second runs on the mobile device, includes a KNN algorithm for posture classification and determines whether the potential event actually corresponds to a fall.

Specifically, as the energy signal exceeds the predefined threshold, the wearable sensor node triggers an alarm to the smartphone which in turns starts the classification posture process to complete the detection procedure. Posture recognition is based on a binary classification of the current subject's posture, designed to simply detect *lying* and *not lying* status. The wearable node, in addition to the total energy, also computes and periodically transmits over Bluetooth the features useful for the classification (see Table V).

TABLE V. DATA COMPUTED AND TRANSMITTED BY THE SENSOR

Data type	Feature	Axis
Periodic	max	y
	min	y
Sporadic	cross-axial energy	x, y, z

To determine the actual subject's posture after the potential fall detection, we actually use a *m-out-of-n* classification decision. Determining the posture using a single classification immediately after the reception of the potential fall alarm may in fact introduce issues. For example, the person might stumble being able to recover the standing position right after: in this case, analyzing a single posture classification would generate a false positive. To address this issue, we analyze n posture classifications within 30 seconds after the potential fall event, and if at least m of them result equal to *lying*, then we can infer the subject has actually fallen. In addition, with the sake of allowing for more flexibility in reporting fall events, we introduce three different levels of alarm severity:

1) *Green* alarm: to indicate minor falls. The subject has fallen and recovers the standing position quickly.
2) *Yellow* alarm: to indicate major falls. The subject has fallen but slowly recovers the standing position.
3) *Red* alarm: to indicate critical falls. The subject has fallen and is unable to recover the standing position (the subject is unconscious and/or has reported major traumas).

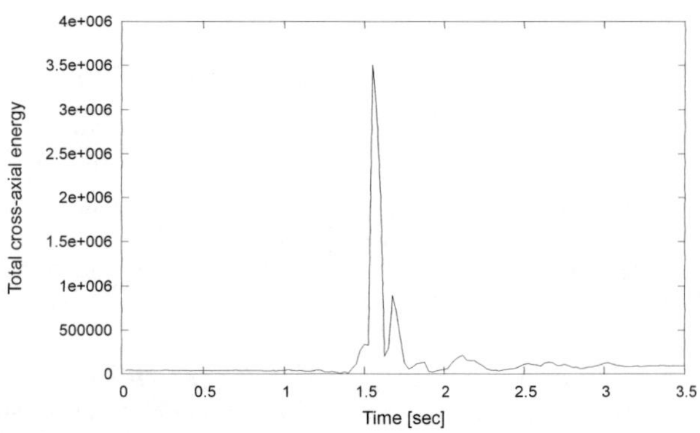

Fig. 3. Cross-axial energy signal

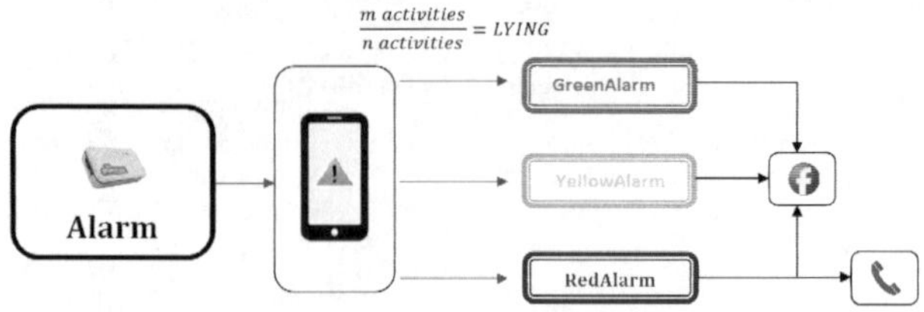

Fig. 4. Schematic diagram of our multi-level fall detection method

In Fig. 4 a simplified diagram of our multi-level fall detection method has been depicted. This fall detection modeling significantly improves the approach previously proposed in [27].

IV. FALL-MOBILEGUARD

Fall-MobileGuard is a smart fall detection system, implementing the method proposed in Section III. It is primarily intended for elderly who live alone or without continuous assistance and for patients with underlying medical conditions that raise the risk of falls. The system consists of an Android-based personal mobile device (e.g. a smartphone) that communicates via Bluetooth with a single Shimmer2R sensor node running the SPINE framework [1], [2], [25], [26]. The sensor can be worn with belt clips or placed in a pocket.

The end-user application runs on the smartphone and integrates a functionality to connect to Facebook. On the detection of any levels of fall, this feature allows to automatically write, on the user's personal wall as well as to predefined Facebook friends (e.g. relatives or caregivers), simple messages containing information about the detected event. Furthermore, it is possible to specify a list of preset phone numbers that are reached with an automatic emergency recorded voice message in case of red fall alarms (see Section III).

In addition, through the integration with BodyCloud [28], [29] platform, Fall-MobileGuard allows to keep an historic track of the fall events for diagnostic and prevention purposes. The underlying reasoning is that elderly people are often afraid (and ashamed) to report the happening of frequent fall episodes (unless they suffer immediate health consequences). In addition, with a system like Fall-MobileGuard, that does not rely on fixed infrastructures, the assisted user can be monitored in mobility and fall events can be detected and reported even when the user is outdoor, away from home.

It is worth noting that our system requires a 'one time' setup procedure (to connect to Facebook and to set the list of friends and emergency phone numbers), it features a very simple, intuitive user interface to launch the application, and does not involve any user interaction while running; the application indeed keeps operating in background as it is programmed as an Android *service*. This design choice gives more chances for the elderly, who are typically not familiar with electronic devices, to use the system in a seamlessly manner. Also, the use of a single sensor node requires quick wearing time and minimum maintenance (in practice, to only recharge the battery periodically).

Fig. 5. Participant to the experiment emulating a fall on the mattress

A. Experiments

Before evaluating the performance of the proposed system, it is necessary to define the scenarios in which it will eventually work. We therefore set the main body movements that are executed during our experiments:

1) emulated falls;
2) everyday life activities.

The experiments involved a sample of 20 participants with the following characteristics:

- *Gender*: M, F
- *Age*: 18÷58
- *Weight*: 50÷91 kg
- *Height*: 1.49÷1.92 m

During the test experiments, we collected accelerometer data from 340 emulated falls and 320 classification samples of everyday life activities.

Emulations have been performed for all types of falls described in Section II.A (except the fall from the stairs, to avoid obvious safety implications of the participants). In addition, since accidental falls can occur while performing daily life activities but at the same time certain activities could be misclassified as falls (if the recognition process is not robust enough), we decided to define the set of such most common activities and included them in our experimentation protocol. We reported the list of performed activities in Table VI.

In addition, we would stress that our system has been designed to detect falls as per the definition and the classification provided in Section II.A. Hence for instance, if the assisted subject collapses gradually on the ground or reaches a sitting position, the system will not issue an alarm as this situation goes beyond its specified capacity.

For guaranteeing the safety of the participants all the emulated falls have been performed on a mattress of size $190cm \times 80cm \times 18cm$, shown in Fig. 5. The thickness of the mattress plays a key role because if it is too thick, the measured acceleration patterns could not due to the fall itself but to bouncing effects after the impact with the mattress. Conversely, if the mattress is very thin, there are more chances to cause harm to the participants.

The mattress protects the participants and prevents direct impact with the ground. This allowed participants to the tests to emulate all the falls without any issues.

An interesting finding of the experiments is that the location we selected for the sensor did not cause discomfort to the participant during normal activities nor caused inconveniences upon falling. This is a matter of fundamental importance because the involved devices should not give impediment to the user and more important must be harmless in all situations.

TABLE VI. DAILY ACTIVITIES SUBJECT TO FALSE POSITIVE FALL DETECTIONS

Activity	Description
Lying-bed	from standing position to lying on the bed. Elderly often do not easily control their actions and they could perform abrupt movements trying to sit or lay down. The lying posture, which in this case is voluntary, could cause a false alarm if the resulting acceleration energy exceeds the threshold.
Rising-bed	from lying posture to standing position. While getting up, it is common to sit sideways to the bed and then to reach the standing position.
Sit-bed	from standing position to sit on the bed. This is also an activity of interest for us, as soft and elastic mattresses can generate abrupt movements.
Sit-chair	from standing position to sit on the chair. This is one of the most common and frequent everyday life activities.
Sit-sofa	from position position to sit on the couch or sofa. This activity is extremely common, too; if the system does not behave properly in this situation, the number of false positive fall detections caused would make the application totally useless.
Walking	walk forward. Walking is another basic and frequent activity, therefore, the system should not generate any false positive fall detections in this case.
Walking-back	walk backward.
Jogging	Although jogging and running are not among the most common activities carried out by elderly people, it is still important to analyze the behavior of the system in this situation. Running, in particular, can easily produce accelerations that exceed the threshold, therefore, in this case the posture classification module of the system is the key to avoid false positive fall detections.
Bending	from standing position one bends the trunk forward, keeping the legs straight.
Bending-pick-up	from standing position to bend down picking up an object from the ground. This action could cause abnormal body accelerations and the position temporarily assumed by the wearable sensor could trick the detection mechanism, but the system should still be able to handle the situation and avoid false alarm.
Trip-over	pick up an object from the ground while walking. Unlike the previous case, the object is grabbed without stopping to walk.
Stumble	while walking one stumbles but recovers the balance quickly.
Limp	walking forward with the aid of a crutch.
Squatting-down	from standing position to a crouched posture to standing again. Carrying out this activity can generate strong body accelerations and the crouched posture could mislead the system.
Coughing-sneezing	both coughing and sneezing cause abrupt movements of the upper body; in this case the location of the sensor plays an important role.

B. Performance Evaluation

Before discussing the obtained results, we give a definition of necessary terms:

- *True Positive* (TP): it consists of an actual fall event that the system correctly detects.
- *False Positive* (FP): it consists of a normal physical activity or action that the system exchanges for a fall.
- *True Negative* (TN): it consists of a normal physical activity or action that the system correctly does not exchange for a fall.
- *False Negative* (FN): it consists of an actual fall event that the system fails to detect.

We analyzed the performance of the system in terms of the following metrics:

$$sensitivity = \frac{TP}{TP + FN} \quad (2)$$

$$specificity = \frac{TN}{TN + FP} \quad (3)$$

$$precision = \frac{TP + TN}{P + N} \quad (4)$$

From the experiments related to the emulated falls, we get TP and FN values, while from the ones related to the everyday activities we calculate TN ed FP values. Specifically, we obtained the following values:

- TP = 282
- FN = 58
- TN = 311
- FP = 9

Hence, we can conclude that our system shows the following results:

- *specificity*: 97%
- *sensitivity*: 83%
- *precision*: 90%

V. Conclusions

In this paper we proposed an advanced method for automatic fall detection that features novel contributions and presented *Fall-MobileGuard*, a realtime fall detection system based on a single wearable sensor and an Android smartphone. The system is able to trigger fall events using different alerting modalities to allow for prompt emergency intervention if necessary. We described in detail our methodology and the prototype system. We discussed the experimentation setup and showed the obtained results. In particular, the proposed system has been tested on 20 subjects emulating several types of falls and performing normal activities, and it reached 97% sensitivity, 83% specificity, and 90% precision. Significant attention was dedicated to the related work which allowed us to have a clear view of strength and weakness of previous proposed approaches.

Ongoing works are currently devoted to remove the need for an external wearable sensor, using the accelerometer available on the smartphone. Future developments will focus on the extension of our approach, specifically defining a crowd-sourcing method based on our BodyCloud computing middleware to perform statistical analysis based on recorded fall events from multiple users. We also plan to introduce a different activity recognition method [30] as it appears promising to improve classification accuracy.

Acknowledgment

We would like to thank Marco Fucilla for his precious contribution to this work. This work has been partially supported by the LOCUBIRehab Project (Polo della Salute, Regione Calabria, CUP J24E07000400005). This work has been partially carried out in the framework of the open-source SPINE and BodyCloud Projects.

References

[1] G. Fortino, R. Giannantonio, R. Gravina, P. Kuryloski, and R. Jafari, "Enabling Effective Programming and Flexible Management of Efficient Body Sensor Network Applications," *IEEE Trans. on Human-Machine Systems*, vol. 43, no. 1, pp. 115–133, 2013.

[2] F. Bellifemine, G. Fortino, R. Giannantonio, R. Gravina, A. Guerrieri, and M. Sgroi, "SPINE: A domain-specific framework for rapid prototyping of WBSN applications," *Software Practice and Experience*, vol. 41, no. 3, pp. 237–265, 2011.

[3] CDC, "http://www.cdc.gov/homeandrecreationalsafety/falls/adultfalls.html," Jun. 2015.

[4] WHO, "http://www.who.int/mediacentre/factsheets/fs344/en/," 2015.

[5] R. Igual, C. Medrano, and I. Plaza, "Challenges, issues and trends in fall detection systems," *BioMed. Engineering*, vol. 12, no. 1, 2013.

[6] Y. Delahoz and M. Labrador, "Survey on fall detection and fall prevention using wearable and external sensors," *Sensors*, vol. 14, no. 10, pp. 19 806–19 842, 2014.

[7] J. Chen, K. Karric, D. Chang, J. Luk, and R. Bajcsy, "Wearable sensors for reliable fall detection," in *27th Int'nl Conf. of the Engineering in Medicine and Biology Society*, 2005, pp. 3551–3554.

[8] M. Kangas, A. Konttila, I. Winblad, and T. Jämsä, "Determination of simple thresholds for accelerometry-based parameters for fall detection," in *29th Int'nl Conf. of the IEEE Engineering in Medicine and Biology Society.*, 2007, pp. 1367–1370.

[9] U. Lindemann, A. Hock, M. Stuber, W. Keck, and C. Becker, "Evaluation of a fall detector based on accelerometers: A pilot study," *Medical and Biological Eng. and Computing*, vol. 43, no. 5, pp. 548–551, 2005.

[10] L. Qiang, J. Stankovic, M. Hanson, A. Barth, J. Lach, and Z. Gang, "Accurate, fast fall detection using gyroscopes and accelerometer-derived posture information," in *6th Int'nl Workshop on Wearable and Implantable Body Sensor Networks*, 2009, pp. 138–143.

[11] O. Ojetola, E. Gaura, and J. Brusey, "Fall detection with wearable sensors-safe (smart fall detection)," in *7th Int'nl Conf. on Intelligent Environments*, 2011, pp. 318–321.

[12] R. Jafari, W. Li, R. Bajcsy, S. Glaser, and S. Sastry, "Physical activity monitoring for assisted living at home," in *4th Int'nl Workshop on Wearable and Implantable Body Sensor Networks (BSN 2007)*, 2007, vol. 13, pp. 213–219.

[13] A. Bourke, J. O'Brien, and G. Lyons, "Evaluation of a threshold-based tri-axial accelerometer fall detection algorithm," *Gait & Posture*, vol. 26, no. 2, pp. 194 – 199, 2007.

[14] D. Jiangpeng, B. Xiaole, Y. Zhimin, S. Zhaohui, and X. Dong, "Perfalld: A pervasive fall detection system using mobile phones," in *8th IEEE Int'nl Conf. on Pervasive Computing and Communications Workshops*, 2010, pp. 292–297.

[15] G. Yavuz, M. Kocak, G. Ergun, H. Alemdar, H. Yalcin, O. Incel, and C. Ersoy, "A Smartphone Based Fall Detector with Online Location Support," in *Proceedings of PhoneSense 2010*, 2010.

[16] F. Sposaro and G. Tyson, "ifall: An android application for fall monitoring and response," in *Int'nl Conf. of the IEEE Engineering in Medicine and Biology Society*, 2009, pp. 6119–6122.

[17] M. Gökberk Ergün and M. Eray Koçak, "Implementing a Fall Detector and Location Presenter on a Smartphone," Tech. Rep., 2010.

[18] Y. He, Y. Li, and C. Yin, "Falling-incident detection and alarm by smartphone with multimedia messaging service (mms)," in *E-Health Telecommunication Systems and Networks*, vol. 1, no. 1, 2012, pp. 1–5.

[19] Y. W. L. Raymond and J. C. Alison, "Detection of falls using accelerometers and mobile phone technology," *Age and Ageing*, 2011.

[20] C. Wang, M. Narayanan, S. Lord, S. Redmond, and N. Lovell, "A low-power fall detection algorithm based on triaxial acceleration and barometric pressure," in *36th Int'nl Conf. of the IEEE Engineering in Medicine and Biology Society*, Aug 2014, pp. 570–573.

[21] P. Pierleoni, A. Belli, L. Palma, M. Pellegrini, L. Pernini, and S. Valenti, "A high reliability wearable device for elderly fall detection," *Sensors*, vol. 15, no. 8, pp. 4544–4553, 2015.

[22] N. Shibuya, B. Nukala, A. Rodriguez, J. Tsay, T. Nguyen, S. Zupancic, and D. Lie, "A real-time fall detection system using a wearable gait analysis sensor and a support vector machine (svm) classifier," in *8th*

Int'nl Conf. on Mobile Computing and Ubiquitous Networking, Jan 2015, pp. 66–67.

[23] N. Noury, P. Rumeau, A. Bourke, G. ÓLaighin, and J. Lundy, "A proposal for the classification and evaluation of fall detectors," *IRBM*, vol. 29, no. 6, pp. 340 – 349, 2008.

[24] Shimmer website, "http://www.shimmer-research.com," Jun. 2015.

[25] R. Gravina, A. Andreoli, A. Salmeri, L. Buondonno, N. Raveendranathank, V. Loseuk, R. Giannantonio, E. Seto, and G. Fortino, "Enabling Multiple BSN Applications Using the SPINE Framework," in *Int'nl Conf. on Body Sensor Networks (BSN 2010)*, 2010.

[26] SPINE website, "http://spine.deis.unical.it," Jan. 2015.

[27] R. Giannantonio, R. Gravina, P. Kuryloski, V. Seppa, F. Bellifemine, J. Hyttinen, and M. Sgroi, "Performance Analysis of an Activity Monitoring System using the SPINE Framework," in *3rd Int'nl Conf. on Pervasive Computing Technologies for Healthcare (Pervasive Health 2009)*, 2009.

[28] G. Fortino, D. Parisi, V. Pirrone, and G. D. Fatta, "BodyCloud: A SaaS approach for community Body Sensor Networks," *Future Generation Computer Systems*, vol. 35, no. 6, pp. 62–79, 2014.

[29] BodyCloud website, "http://bodycloud.dimes.unical.it," Jun. 2015.

[30] D. Mocanu, H. Ammar, D. Lowet, K. Driessens, A. Liotta, G. Weiss, and K. Tuyls, "Factored Four Way Conditional Restricted Boltzmann Machines for Activity Recognition," *Pattern Recognition Letters*, 2015.

A smartphone-centered wearable sensor network for fall risk assessment in the elderly

Andrea Mannini
Scuola Superiore Sant'Anna
The BioRobotics Institute
Pisa, Italy
+39-050883410
a.mannini@sssup.it

Angelo Maria Sabatini
Scuola Superiore Sant'Anna
The BioRobotics Institute
Pisa, Italy
+39-050883415
sabatini@sssup.it

ABSTRACT

Fall prevention is an important aspect to keep high the quality of life in aging. In this work, a wearable sensor network to automatically assess movement and its indicator for fall risk is proposed. The method is based on a smartphone linked to wearable devices. The proposed approach starts estimating the physical activity level using activity recognition algorithms running on the phone. Such estimation can be conducted by simply using the smartphone on its own. Activity recognition can also identify walking bouts to drive gait assessment tools using different sensing sources. In this regard a strategy to estimate stride-based gait stability indexes during ambulation was implemented. Waist and shank sensing nodes were involved in the computation of stride time, stride time variability, vertical acceleration variability and harmonic ratios. The proposed method can correctly recognize activity with a 95% accuracy within four classes. Ambulation in particular is recognized correctly in 97.2% of cases and gait stability indexes are then estimated capturing differences between controls and patients at high risk of falling.

Categories and Subject Descriptors

I.5.4 Computing methodologies: pattern recognition: applications
J.3 Computer applications: life and medical science: health
K.5.4 Computers and society: social issues: assistive technologies for persons with disabilities

General Terms

Algorithms, Measurement, Experimentation.

Keywords

Wearable sensor networks, fall risk assessment, gait stability, activity recognition.

1. INTRODUCTION

Falls are a major cause of death and injuries that can seriously limit independent living in the elderly. More than one-third of home-dwelling people aged over 65 years and two-thirds of those living in residential care fall each year at least once [1]; the trend for a person experiencing a fall is to fall again [2], which often leads to fear of falling, decreased mobility and independence [3].

Technologies to monitor body kinematics, ground reaction forces and electromyographic signals provide objective quantitative measures for fall risk assessment, but the associated equipment requires dedicated facilities, time consuming setups and its deployment in clinical practice is difficult [4]. Analyzing movement by means of wearable sensors is a widely developing research stream to improve effective usability of quantitative methods of fall risk assessment [4]. There is not yet a wide consensus on these methods, given that wearable sensor systems have not been validated thoroughly, using large datasets [5]. However, many studies are now pursuing this approach, involving typically inertial sensors (accelerometers and gyroscopes), the assumption is made that a wearable sensor system can efficiently capture and analyze quantitative mobility data that could help improve fall risk assessment, [4]. Postural sway, gait variability, gait stability, movement smoothness, walking speed and duration of a sit-to-stand transition are commonly considered quantities for fall risk assessment using wearable sensors [4]. In this regard, many works focus on the instrumented version of the timed-up-and-go (TUG) test [6], quantifying the various components of the test (sit-to-stand transitions, walk, turn, stand-to-sit transitions) [5, 7-9]. Most of studies based on wearable motion sensors focused on gait, given that most of falls occurs while walking and that, as said before, gait function is often compromised in individuals at high risk of falling [7, 10, 11].

In our opinion, fall risk has to be estimated with a multi-factorial approach to the analysis of movement data. The main solutions proposed in the literature tend, often, to propose standalone setups that address specific problems in isolation, such as estimation of physical activity level and gait assessment. The approach we intend to pursue here consists of casting these two aspects in a single, admittedly more complex problem. Accordingly, we attempt to move the first step in this direction by designing a wearable sensor network, which aims at jointly estimate several quantities potentially useful for fall risk estimation. As it is usual, different sensor placement sites can be helpful to address specific aspect of our overall problem: for instance, the shank is a good site for measuring temporal parameters of normal or pathologic gait, however, it cannot be chosen if the interest is for extracting useful indicators of walking stability (e.g., harmonic ratios); at the same time, the waist is widely considered to analyze the gait stability, but its usefulness to estimate reliably temporal parameters of gait is generally limited to normal gait. Of course, the availability of a body area network (BAN) may allow the different nodes to talk each other,

BODYNETS 2015, September 28-30, Sydney, Australia

DOI 10.4108/eai.28-9-2015.2261433

each of them being specialized in fulfilling specific computational tasks. The idea is that the information shared by the different BAN nodes could promote a better global knowledge about the human being that produces the observed movement data. Previous examples of BAN frameworks for human movement evaluation are in [12, 13]. In this work, two main problems related to fall risk assessment are discussed as an application niche for the proposed wearable sensor network: gait assessment and estimation of physical activity level through activity recognition. Activity recognition was performed directly on the smartphone that was used as the central node of the network. Activity information was also used for enabling gait stability assessment during walking bouts. A shank sensor was used for obtaining an accurate gait segmentation that drove stride-based gait stability indexes estimation using waist sensor data.

2. PROBLEM BACKGROUND

2.1 Activity recognition for fall risk estimation

The knowledge about the activity being performed throughout the day gives the clinicians an important tool for assessing the physical activity level and the mobility of patients. A lack of physical activity in elderly is known to be correlated with enhanced risk of fractures [14], cardio-vascular mortality [15], unhealthy body fat distribution [16]. There is not an unanimous consensus about the effects of physical activity in the elderly in relation to fall risk [17]. Intuitively, the positive relation between a physically active lifestyle and fall risk cannot be extended monotonically to all physical conditions in the elderly: a strong limitation of mobility would reduce the fall risk, despite the lack of physical activity. Moreover, exercising cannot reduce many fall risk factors such as those related to impaired vision or extrinsic risk factors (e.g., walking on slippery surfaces, improper footwear). However, the positive effect of improving physical activity on gait, strength and balance are known [17-20]. Several epidemiological studies evaluated the relationship between fall risk and inactive lifestyle in the elderly. In [19], 439 people aged 69-92 years were studied; a significant increase of fall risk was observed for those who did less than 75 minutes of activity per day, including walking, cycling, gardening, household activities and sports. Such basic activities nicely pair with those that are usually considered in automatic activity recognition methods, based on wearable sensors.

Automatically recognize the activity of a person using light-weight wearable sensors, allows estimation of his/her physical activity level, and to monitor its time evolution. Wearable inertial sensors are becoming very common to solve this particular problem, and commercial devices to this purpose start becoming available. Accelerometer-based activity monitors are capable of quantifying human motion, covering the range of acceleration amplitudes and frequencies required to measure human movement [21]. Moreover, their low power consumption, small dimensions, and light weight contribute to wearability and make long term activity monitoring practical. Although complex multi-sensor systems for a detailed activity recognition are becoming more practical [22], single-sensor systems may improve acceptability for long term studies, simplify study administration and lower cost and are therefore current practice in larger studies [23, 24]. Recently, single sensor solutions for activity classification are being implemented using sensors embedded in smartphones and smartwatches. First mobile health studies involving physical activity evaluation date back to early 2000s when mobile phone-based frameworks for vital signs and activity monitoring were proposed. The solution in [25] included a wearable accelerometer connected to the phone via Bluetooth to evaluate the posture and detect walking episodes. The phone was used to extend the communication between the user and a server where all the processing was done. In 2008, Hong et al suggested the possibility of using emerging devices, the smartphones, with embedded accelerometers as the platform for activity recognition research in the future developments of their method, [26]. In the same period, first implementation of activity classification in smartphones were presented: data were collected from body-worn sensors and classified using a smartphone [27, 28]. The high computational capabilities of current smartphones allow the implementation of online methods for recognizing daily activities. Some examples of this are the work by Del Rosario et al. [29], where a validation over both young and elderly users was done, the work by Antos et al, involving both activity recognition and smartphone localization [30], and the study by He and Li, where fall detection capabilities were also included [31]. Other smartphone based solutions for activity recognition are in [32, 33]. Many commercially available solutions and apps including simple activity recognition tasks are now being offered in application stores. Commercially available apps are based on inertial sensors or may rely on different sources such as network localization information from which the ambulation tasks are inferred. However, the vocabulary of recognized activities is limited and their level of accuracy is still perceived as approximate from final users.

2.2 Gait stability assessment for fall risk estimation

Gait is the most important human activity, and its assessment is often oriented to the evaluation of gait stability. This particular aspect is strongly related to fall risk assessment. Gait stability is a precondition for walking without falling: a decrease in the value of a gait stability index is generally associated to an increased risk of fall. Gait stability can be estimated using stability measures (direct methods) or studying foot kinematic trajectories (indirect methods). [10]. Some direct methods are based on the evaluation of Floquet multipliers [34, 35], Lyapunov exponents [36, 37] or Poincaré plot indexes [38, 39]. Gait variability is the most widely used feature in indirect methods proposed for gait stability estimation: variability is related to fall risk given that an increased variability may bring the dynamic state of a person closer to his/her limit of stability [10]. Other kinematic quantities that have been associated to gait stability are the foot clearance [37, 40], the step width [41, 42] and the double support time [43]. Several models to estimate fall risk indexes or to recognize faller from non-fallers using wearable sensors measurements has been proposed in literature, as reviewed in [4]. Of great interest are also the so-called harmonic ratios (HRs), for which a quite extensive literature exists to show their applicability in the analysis of abnormal gait [44, 45].

3. MATERIALS AND METHODS.

3.1 Wearable sensor network

The experiments of this paper were performed with three battery-powered barometric-inertial-magnetic measurement units we developed and named WIMU (wearable IMU, figure 1). Each

WIMU is endowed with a 32-bit ARM Cortex processor (NXP Semiconductors LPC1768) and a Bluetooth (BT) transceiver and is currently implemented in a version for data communication with an Android smartphone. The WIMU sensors are a digital tri-axial gyro (InvenSense ITG-3200, with range ± 2000 °/s), a digital tri-axial accelerometer (Bosch BMA180, with range ± 4g, where g = 9.81 m/s2 is the gravity acceleration), a digital tri-axial magnetic sensor (Honeywell HMC5843) and a digital barometric altimeter (Bosch BMP085, with resolution 1 Pa). Inertial sensor data were sampled at 50 Hz and on-board digitally filtered using a Butterworth second-order low-pass filter (cut-off frequency: 10 Hz); air pressure sensor data were sampled at 50 Hz in the ultra-low power mode (oversampling was not performed internally to the sensor) [27]. The sensor data, logged into the ARM memory, were transmitted to the smartphone via BT.

Figure 1. The WIMU sensing node.

We focused on a smartphone as the center of the wearable sensor network (figure 2). Smartphones are becoming pervasive devices, and their computational capabilities allow online processing to deal with many of the cited problems. In particular, our solution was tested on a Samsung Galaxy S3 (GT-I9300) device equipped with Android 4.3 operative system. We choose the smartphone Bluetooth connection capability to link the three WIMUs. The selected placement sites were shank, wrist and waist. WIMUs were fixed with elastic Velcro bands: the shank sensor was placed above the lateral malleolus, the waist sensor was placed in correspondence of the L3 vertebra and the wrist sensor was placed as it would be done for a wrist-watch. Actually, we did not use the wrist sensing source for this work. However, we included this site in the network to stimulate future developments involving a smartwatch. Accelerometers and many other sensing sources are embedded in smartphones and can then be processed for several fall risk assessment applications, giving the fourth placement site, (trousers pocket).

3.2 Activity recognition for fall risk estimation

In this work we adopted a previously validated offline method for activity recognition [46]. First, the automatic classification methodology was applied to an existing dataset for offline training and validation purposes, using a PC running Matlab (The Mathworks, Natick MA). Second, the testing phase of the algorithm was implemented on the smartphone. Even if there was not any reason preventing us from doing activity recognition using data from the shank or waist sensors, as we previously did in [46], we preferred here to implement a solution capable of running on the smartphone. In particular, the previously validated methodology was applied to data from the accelerometer embedded in the smartphone assuming that during its use the smartphone is stored in the user's trousers pocket.

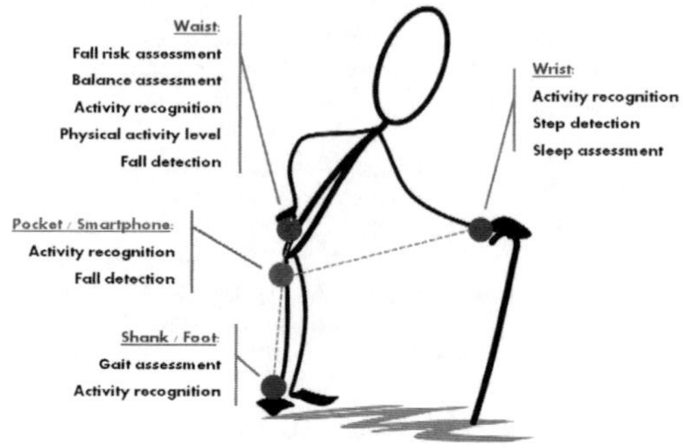

Figure 2. Sensor network placement sites and possible outcomes of sensor data processing.

The offline validation tests of the method were done using a previously available datasets [47]. In particular, data acquired using thigh-fixed sensors were considered from that dataset. This placement site slightly differs from the trousers front-pocket. However, previous literature confirms that features in time and frequency domain extracted from accelerometer magnitude data do not vary significantly when the sensor is moved within the same body region, including thigh [48]. During preliminary tests we observed that actually this was the case using the smartphone in the pocket. The only limitation to this was observed when the user wore very large trousers, which caused the smartphone to move unpredictably within the pocket. The dataset included data from 33 participants while doing a large set of activities grouped in four main classes: ambulation (including level, uphill, downhill on both treadmill and ground), cycling, sedentary activities (such as working at a desk) and a class named "others", which includes non-locomotion activities done in an upright position (such as sweeping and painting) [46, 47]. Time and frequency domain features were extracted by windowing the norm of the accelerometer data channels. Signals were windowed using 512-samples non-overlapping windows. The classifier chosen was a Support Vector Machine (SVM) with a radial basis function kernel [46]. The validation was conducted following a leave-one-subject-out strategy [46, 47].

After running offline validation tests, all the available data were used to train a general classifier, which was implemented in the smartphone. In the online testing phase, implemented using an *ad hoc* android application, 512-samples 90%-overlapping sliding windows were segmented and features were calculated from them. A soft-assignment classification strategy was then considered. A soft-assignment approach was preferred in the online test to allow discarding outputs from the classifier when the classification confidence was not acceptable. The soft-assignment was obtained by cascading a logistic regressor to the SVM classifier output.

3.3 Gait stability assessment for fall risk estimation

Data from 11 control subjects C (55±6.3 years old) and one 68 years old person (P) at high risk of fall were processed. Data were part of the preliminary studies we conducted for the IDONTFALL research project [49]. The tests consisted of instrumenting 30 meters walking bouts by using the described wearable sensor network. In particular, the shank and the waist sensor were considered in this part of the study. The test consisted of asking the person to walk along a 30-m long corridor: during tests data from the shank sensor were used for gait segmentation purposes, and segmented data from the waist sensor were processed to estimate parameters potentially useful for fall risk assessment. Gait segmentation was obtained by using the hidden Markov models (HMM) based strategy we previously validated and tested online in [50, 51]. HMM-based methods found application in this field because they improve results reliability, in the face of high inter-subject variability. The online version of our HMM-based gait segmentation algorithm was implemented in the shank sensing node to provide gait events time labels that drove the procedure for estimating stride-based HRs [51]. Segmentation information (toe-off and foot-strike events) from the shank, jointly with inertial sensor recordings from the waist were sent to the smartphone via BT. The set of parameters considered to describe gait stability were: stride time, stride time variability, expressed as coefficient of variation in %, root mean square (RMS) value of the component of vertical acceleration (gravity removed) and HRs of the three component of acceleration (medio-lateral, antero-posterior and vertical). Stride time information was derived from HMM based gait segmentation at the shank, by evaluating the time between consecutive foot-strike events. The vertical acceleration RMS was estimated using the complete acceleration trace acquired during the walking bouts. HRs were computed by submitting stride acceleration data to Fourier harmonic analysis, as described, e.g., in [44].

4. RESULTS AND DISCUSSION

4.1 Activity recognition

Some results for the leave-one-subject-out cross validation study are reported as a confusion matrix in Table 1. The algorithm confirmed to be effective in automatically recognizing activities using sensor information from a single placement site [46]. The overall recognition accuracy was 95%: the worst result was achieved for the "other activity" class (80.1%), where the amount of training data was smaller. Walking bouts were automatically recognized with 97.2% accuracy. This high accuracy justifies our initial intention to drive gait parameters estimation using activity recognition outputs.

Two screenshots of the online implementation are shown in figure 3. Classification results and *a posteriori* classification probabilities were reported online to the user. Notifications can be raised if the detected sedentary behavior lasts for more than a predefined time, which can be set by, e.g., the user or a therapist. A diary tool was also included to give the user an activity summary of the previous outputs from the classifier. Even though a quantitative test of outputs was not performed online yet, qualitatively the app showed correct classification for most of the tested windows. The availability of the *a-posteriori* classification probabilities, which were obtained as the result of the logistic regression, allowed us to add an additional "uncertain" class for those output showing uncertain classification output.

The battery consumption of the app was not negligible, given the high rate of accelerometer sampling (~100 Hz), however, the batteries of the tested phone (Samsung Galaxy S3, I-9300) using the app lasted for 12 hours. It is our plan to reduce the sampling rate to 40 Hz in future tests, given that offline tests indicated that this reduced sampling rate does not affect classification accuracy.

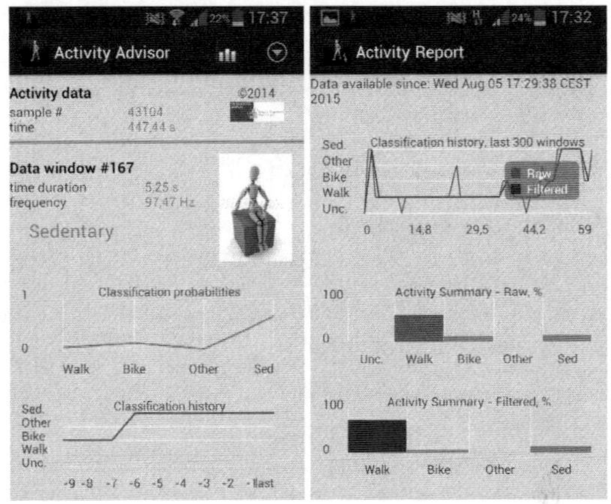

Figure 3. The Activity Advisor app for activity recognition using a smartphone.

Table 1. Confusion matrix for activity recognition

		Classified as			
		Ambulation (A)	**Cycling (C)**	**Other (O)**	**Sedentary (S)**
Actual label	**A**	**6615** (97.2%)	62 (0.9%)	51 (0.7%)	76 (1.1%)
	C	33 (1%)	**3167** (95.9%)	53 (1.6%)	48 (1.5%)
	O	24 (1%)	36 (1.4%)	**2002** (80.1%)	438 (17.5%)
	S	5 (0.1%)	41 (0.5%)	230 (3%)	**7506** (96.5%)

Table 2. Gait stability indexes

	ID	**Stride time**	**Stride time variab.**	**Vertical acc., RMS**	**HR ML**	**HR VT**	**HR AP**
C	1	1.05	1.04	2.77	1.84	2.38	2.95
	2	1.07	0.92	3.41	1.80	2.02	2.10
	3	1.22	2.13	1.58	2.01	2.29	2.26
	4	1.15	0.97	1.59	2.18	1.85	2.83
	5	1.11	2.52	2.10	1.72	2.89	3.35
	6	0.95	1.70	2.99	3.31	3.20	3.21
	7	1.08	0.82	2.51	1.69	1.95	1.48
	8	1.03	1.47	2.00	1.30	2.10	1.94
	9	0.93	1.91	3.07	3.03	3.54	2.71
	10	1.08	1.58	1.64	1.94	2.08	2.57
	11	0.96	2.58	2.14	1.63	3.08	3.32
	avg	**1.06**	**1.60**	**2.35**	**2.04**	**2.49**	**2.61**
P	*12*	*1.02*	*7.37*	*2.34*	*1.69*	*1.69*	*1.91*

4.2 Gait stability indexes

Results for gait assessment using shank and waist-mounted sensors are summarized in Table 2. It is worth noting that the values reported for the controls match closely normative values reported in the literature. It does not come as a surprise that the person known to be at risk of fall according to clinical screening (Tinetti scale score: 20 out of a maximum 28) exhibits a higher stride time variability and lower values of HR, which reflects a less regular and stable gait, according to the interpretation given to these parameters in the literature [43].

5. CONCLUSIONS

A body sensor network including a smartphone and three wireless sensing nodes has been proposed for the estimation of fall risk in the elderly with a multi-factorial approach. The proposed strategy involves the physical activity level estimation through activity recognition and gait stability assessment through gait spatio-temporal parameters estimation and signal harmonic ratios evaluation.

Concerning the activity recognition problem, we obtained a high accuracy online activity recognizer using a smartphone. This allowed raising a warning to the user if her/his activity does not fit the expected behavior during its use. The activity recognition output can be used in isolation from the rest of the processing or eventually, activity recognition output can drive other estimation such as the one proposed about gait stability assessment.

Concerning the fall risk assessment using measures of gait variability and symmetry, we are in the position to combine robust estimation of gait temporal parameters (even in conditions of pathologic gait), with a stride-based computational scheme that lead to estimate HRs with good precision.

In this work only few of the possible application of the proposed sensing network were reported. Many other applications such as gait spatial parameters analysis, pedestrian navigation, sleep monitoring, fall detection and so forth can be included, but their description is out of the scope of this paper.

6. ACKNOWLEDGMENTS

This work was supported by the Italian Ministry of Education and Research (MIUR) through the project (PRIN) "A quantitative and multi-factorial approach for estimating and preventing the risk of falls in the elderly people", and by the EC funded project I-DONT-FALL "Integrated prevention and Detection sOlutioNs Tailored to the population and Risk Factors associated with FALLs" (CIP-ICT-PSP-2011-5-297225). Fondazione Santa Lucia, IRCCS, Ethical Committee unanimously approved on June 28th, 2013 (Reference number: CE/AG4/PROG.409-29). The views expressed in this paper are not necessarily those of the I-DONT-FALL consortium. The authors would like to thank Prof. Intille, Prof. William H. Haskell and Dr. Mary Rosenberger for their work collecting and for sharing the original dataset for activity recognition validation.

7. REFERENCES

[1] Lord, S. R., Sherrington, C., Menz, H. B. and Close, J. C. *Falls in older people: risk factors and strategies for prevention*. Cambridge University Press, 2007.

[2] Rubenstein, L. Z. Falls in older people: epidemiology, risk factors and strategies for prevention. *Age and ageing*, 35, suppl 2 (2006), ii37-ii41.

[3] Walker, J. E. and Howland, J. Falls and fear of falling among elderly persons living in the community: occupational therapy interventions. *AmerJ Occupat Ther*, 45, 2 (1991), 119-122.

[4] Howcroft, J., Kofman, J. and Lemaire, E. D. Review of fall risk assessment in geriatric populations using inertial sensors. *J Neuroeng Rehabil*, 10, 1 (2013), 10-91.

[5] Shany, T., Redmond, S., Marschollek, M. and Lovell, N. Assessing fall risk using wearable sensors: a practical discussion. *Zeitschrift für Gerontologie und Geriatrie*, 45, 8 (2012), 694-706.

[6] Shumway-Cook, A., Brauer, S. and Woollacott, M. Predicting the probability for falls in community-dwelling older adults using the Timed Up & Go Test. *Physical Therapy*, 80, 9 (2000), 896-903.

[7] Scanaill, C. N., Garattini, C., Greene, B. R. and McGrath, M. J. Technology innovation enabling falls risk assessment in a community setting. *Ageing international*, 36, 2 (2011), 217-231.

[8] Greene, B. R., Doheny, E. P., Walsh, C., Cunningham, C., Crosby, L. and Kenny, R. A. Evaluation of falls risk in community-dwelling older adults using body-worn sensors. *Gerontology-Basel*, 58, 5 (2012), 472.

[9] Marschollek, M., Rehwald, A., Wolf, K., Gietzelt, M., Nemitz, G., Zu Schwabedissen, H. M. and Haux, R. Sensor-based fall risk assessment–an expert 'to go'. *Methods Inf Med*, 50, 5 (2011), 420-426.

[10] Hamacher, D., Singh, N., Van Dieen, J., Heller, M. and Taylor, W. Kinematic measures for assessing gait stability in elderly individuals: a systematic review. *Journal of The Royal Society Interface*, 8, 65 (2011), 1682-1698.

[11] Riva, F., Toebes, M., Pijnappels, M., Stagni, R. and van Dieën, J. Estimating fall risk with inertial sensors using gait stability measures that do not require step detection. *Gait & posture*, 38, 2 (2013), 170-174.

[12] Fortino, G., Giannantonio, R., Gravina, R., Kuryloski, P. and Jafari, R. Enabling effective programming and flexible management of efficient body sensor network applications. *IEEE Trans Hum Mach Syst*, 43, 1 (2013), 115-133.

[13] Jovanov, E., Milenkovic, A., Otto, C. and de Groen, P. C. A wireless body area network of intelligent motion sensors for computer assisted physical rehabilitation. *J. Neuroeng Rehab*, 2, 1 (2005), 6.

[14] Sorock, G. S., Bush, T. L., Golden, A. L., Fried, L. P., Breuer, B. and Hale, W. E. Physical activity and fracture risk in a free-living elderly cohort. *J Gerontol*, 43, 5 (1988), M134-M139.

[15] Ruigòmez, A., Alonso, J. and Antò, J. M. Relationship of health behaviours to five-year mortality in an elderly cohort. *Age and ageing*, 24, 2 (1995), 113-119.

[16] Visser, M., Launer, L. J., Deurenberg, P. and Deeg, D. J. Total and sports activity in older men and women: relation with body fat distribution. *AmerJ Epidemiol*, 145, 8 (1997), 752-761.

[17] Buchner, D. M., Cress, M. E., de Lateur, B. J., Esselman, P. C., Margherita, A. J., Price, R. and Wagner, E. H. The effect of strength and endurance training on gait, balance, fall risk, and health services use in community-living older adults. *The Journals of Gerontology Series A: Biological Sciences and Medical Sciences*, 52, 4 (1997), M218-M224.

[18] Brown, M. and Holloszy, J. O. Effects of walking, jogging and cycling on strength, flexibility, speed and balance in 60-to 72-year olds. *Aging Clin Exper Res*, 5, 6 (1993), 427-434.

[19] Stel, V. S., Smit, J. H., Pluijm, S. M. and Lips, P. Balance and mobility performance as treatable risk factors for recurrent falling in older persons. *J Clin Epidemiol*, 56, 7 (2003), 659-668.

[20] Liu-Ambrose, T. Y., Khan, K. M., Eng, J. J., Gillies, G. L., Lord, S. R. and McKay, H. A. The Beneficial Effects of Group-Based Exercises on Fall Risk Profile and Physical Activity Persist 1 Year Postintervention in Older Women with Low Bone Mass: Follow-Up After Withdrawal of Exercise. *J Amer Geriat Soc*, 53, 10 (2005), 1767-1773.

[21] Bhattacharya, A., McCutcheon, E. P., Shvartz, E. and E, G. J. Body acceleration distribution and O2 uptake in humans during running and jumping. *J Appl Physiol*, 49, 5 (1980), 881-887.

[22] Bao, L. and Intille, S. S. Activity recognition from user-annotated acceleration data. *Pervasive*, 301(2004), 1-17.

[23] Troiano, R. and Mc Clain, J. *Objective Measures of Physical Activity, Sleep, and Strength in U.S. National Health and Nutrition Examination Survey (NHANES) 2011-2014*. City, 2012.

[24] UK Biobank Coordinating Centre, Category 2 enhanced phenotyping at baseline assessment visit in last 100–150,000 participants, Addendum to mainstudy protocol, Stockport Cheshire, 2009..

[25] Chen, W., Wei, D., Zhu, X., Uchida, M., Ding, S. and Cohen, M. *A mobile phone-based wearable vital signs monitoring system*. IEEE, City, 2005.

[26] Hong, Y.-J., Kim, I.-J., Ahn, S. C. and Kim, H.-G. *Activity recognition using wearable sensors for elder care*. IEEE, City, 2008.

[27] Győrbíró, N., Fábián, Á. and Hományi, G. An activity recognition system for mobile phones. *Mobile Network Applicat*, 14, 1 (2009), 82-91.

[28] Bieber, G., Voskamp, J. and Urban, B. *Activity recognition for everyday life on mobile phones*. Springer, City, 2009.

[29] Del Rosario, M. B., Wang, K., Wang, J., Liu, Y., Brodie, M., Delbaere, K., Lovell, N. H., Lord, S. R. and Redmond, S. J. A comparison of activity classification in younger and older cohorts using a smartphone. *Physiol Meas*, 35, 11 (2014).

[30] Antos, S. A., Albert, M. V. and Kording, K. P. Hand, belt, pocket or bag: Practical activity tracking with mobile phones. *J Neurosci Method*, 231(2014), 22-30.

[31] He, Y. and Li, Y. Physical activity recognition utilizing the built-in kinematic sensors of a smartphone. *International J Distrib Sens Networks*, 2013(2013).

[32] Anguita, D., Ghio, A., Oneto, L., Parra, X. and Reyes-Ortiz, J. L. *Human activity recognition on smartphones using a multiclass hardware-friendly support vector machine*. Springer, City, 2012.

[33] Morillo, L. M. S., Gonzalez-Abril, L., Ramirez, J. A. O. and de la Concepcion, M. A. A. Low Energy Physical Activity Recognition System on Smartphones. *Sensors*, 15, 3 (2015), 5163-5196.

[34] Malatesta, D., Simar, D., Dauvilliers, Y., Candau, R., Borrani, F., Préfaut, C. and Caillaud, C. Energy cost of walking and gait instability in healthy 65-and 80-yr-olds. *J Applied Physiol*, 95, 6 (2003), 2248-2256.

[35] Granata, K. P. and Lockhart, T. E. Dynamic stability differences in fall-prone and healthy adults. *J Electromyog Kinesiol*, 18, 2 (2008), 172-178.

[36] Dingwell, J. B. and Cusumano, J. P. Nonlinear time series analysis of normal and pathological human walking. *Chaos: An Interdisciplinary J Nonlin Sci*, 10, 4 (2000), 848-863.

[37] Buzzi, U. H., Stergiou, N., Kurz, M. J., Hageman, P. A. and Heidel, J. Nonlinear dynamics indicates aging affects variability during gait. *Clin Biomech*, 18, 5 (2003), 435-443.

[38] Khandoker, A. H., Lai, D. T., Begg, R. K. and Palaniswami, M. Wavelet-based feature extraction for support vector machines for screening balance impairments in the elderly. *IEEE Trans Neural Syst Rehab Eng*, 15, 4 (2007), 587-597.

[39] Khandoker, A. H., Palaniswami, M. and Begg, R. K. A comparative study on approximate entropy measure and poincare plot indexes of minimum foot clearance variability in the elderly during walking. *J Neuroeng Rehab*, 5, 1 (2008), 4.

[40] Hausdorff, J. M., Edelberg, H. K., Mitchell, S. L., Goldberger, A. L. and Wei, J. Y. Increased gait unsteadiness in community-dwelling elderly fallers. *Archives of physical medicine and rehabilitation*, 78, 3 (1997), 278-283.

[41] Kang, H. G. and Dingwell, J. B. Separating the effects of age and walking speed on gait variability. *Gait & posture*, 27, 4 (2008), 572-577.

[42] Gabell, A. and Nayak, U. The effect of age on variability in gait. *J Gerontol*, 39, 6 (1984), 662-666.

[43] Hausdorff, J. M., Rios, D. A. and Edelberg, H. K. Gait variability and fall risk in community-living older adults: a 1-year prospective study. *Archives of physical medicine and rehabilitation*, 82, 8 (2001), 1050-1056.

[44] Doi, T., Hirata, S., Ono, R., Tsutsumimoto, K., Misu, S. and Ando, H. The harmonic ratio of trunk acceleration predicts falling among older people: results of a 1-year prospective study. *J Neuroeng Rehabil*, 10, 7 (2013).

[45] Kavanagh, J. J. and Menz, H. B. Accelerometry: a technique for quantifying movement patterns during walking. *Gait & posture*, 28, 1 (2008), 1-15.

[46] Mannini, A., Intille, S. S., Rosenberger, M., Sabatini, A. M. and Haskell, W. Activity recognition using a single accelerometer placed at the wrist or ankle. *Med Sci Sports Exerc*, 45, 11 (2013), 2193-2203.

[47] Mannini, A., Sabatini, A. M. and Intille, S. S. Accelerometry-based Recognition of the Placement Sites of a Wearable Sensor. *Pervas Mob Comput*, 21 (2015), 62–74.

[48] Amini, N., Sarrafzadeh, M., Vahdatpour, A. and Xu, W. Accelerometer-based on-body sensor localization for health and medical monitoring applications. *Pervas Mob Comput*, 7, 6 (2011), 746-760.

[49] Barban, F., Annicchiarico, R., Federici, A., Mazzù, I., Lombardi, M., Giuli, S. et al. ICT solutions to develop an effective motor and cognitive training to reduce risk of falls. The I-DONT-FALL project. Accepted for presentation. In *Proceedings of the Proc Internat Conf Information Communication Technologies for Ageing Well and e-Health* (Lisbona, Portugal, 2015).

[50] Mannini, A., Trojaniello, D., Della Croce, U. and Sabatini, A. M. Hidden Markov Model-Based Strategy for Gait Segmentation using Inertial Sensors: Application to Elderly, Hemiparetic Patients and Huntington's Disease Patients. In *Proc of the 37th Annual Internat Conf of the IEEE EMBS* (Milano, 2015)

[51] Mannini, A., Genovese, V. and Sabatini, A. M. Online Decoding of Hidden Markov Models for Gait Event Detection Using Foot-Mounted Gyroscopes. *IEEE J Biomedical Health Informat*, 18, 4 (2014), 1122-1130.

Feasibility of a low-cost platform for physiological recording in affective computing applications

Hamed Monkaresi, Rafael A. Calvo
School of Electrical and Information Engineering, The University of Sydney, NSW 2006, Australia
hamed.monkaresi@sydney.edu.au, rafael.calvo@sydney.edu.au

ABSTRACT
Physiological signals provide valuable information about human physical and mental states. For decades, sophisticated equipment has been used to measure them in health and psychological applications. More recently a variety of low-cost portable electronic devices and smart-phone applications are being used to measure physiological signals. The accuracy of these devices has not been evaluated in medical or practical affective computing applications. In this article, we evaluate a low-cost, Do-It-Yourself, and open-source device that can measure multiple physiological signals. The accuracy of this platform in measuring ECG signals has been examined and compared with a commercial psychophysiology system. In addition, we evaluate the feasibility of using this platform in affective computing applications.

Keywords
Electrocardiogram (ECG), Do-It-Yourself (DIY), Affect Detection, Portable Devices,.

1. INTRODUCTION
New devices for monitoring physiological signals are becoming mainstream consumer products. Most of the new smartphones are able to track heart rate and the activity of the user. Another set of wearable products such as Fitbit, Samsung Gear and the Apple watch can also be worn all day and night, even in the shower. Users can monitor their day to day activities and physiological changes in a low-cost simple way. Physiological signals were one of the first modalities explored in Affective Computing (AC) studies [1] due to the view that the human body produces different physiological patterns in response to each specific affective state. It is yet to be shown that wearable devices are accurate enough to be used in conjunction with AC techniques [2] to automatically detect emotions, stress and cognitive load in everyday situations.

2. METHODS AND MATERIALS
In this study, we developed an open-source software platform called JSiento [3] to receive, process and store physiological signals. The e-Health platform v2.0 [4] one of the popular open-source and low-cost platforms for measuring physiological signals was used in this study. The source code provided by the manufacturer for measuring ECG signals does not acquire the signals properly. There were a couple of issues embedded in the source code which made unwanted delays in sending data. We revised the source code and added a timer to measure and send the data every 4 milliseconds (250 Hz).

The BIOPAC MP150 system was used to acquire reference physiological signals at a sampling rate of 250 Hz. The BIOPAC measurements were used as the reference for our comparisons. The ECG features were extracted based on the important points on PQRST waveform and were used to classify participant's affective states. The main ECG features extracted are P-, Q-, R-, S-, and T-peaks, PQ, QS and ST segments, P-, Q-, and R-amplitudes and HRV. A variation of statistical features such as mean, median, minimum, maximum, range, etc. were extracted from the mentioned basic features.

3. EXPERIMENT
Twenty healthy participants volunteered to take part in this study (12 Females, 8 Males; mean age of 26.75 years). Two distinct sessions were recorded for each participant. In the baseline session, the ECG signals were recorded. The three electrodes from the e-Health platform were plugged on the participant's chest. The electrodes of the BIOPAC system were also placed next to the corresponding electrodes in almost the same area. A set of emotional images selected from International Affective Picture System (IAPS) database was shown to the participants in the AC session. Each image was shown for 10 seconds. Normative valence and arousal scores converted into binary scores. A vote classifier was used to combine the results achieved by four base classifiers with the average probability rule. Two sampling time windows were used for segmentation: image-level features were extracted from fixed 10-seconds time windows correspond to each image. Block-level features were extracted from larger time windows correspond to a group of images which had the same binary ratings.

4. RESULTS
Evaluating the Pearson r values for the signals recorded in the baseline sessions showed that 10 out of 13 ECG features had almost the perfect match with the reference values ($r > .90$, $p < .01$). The calculated HRV had also significant strong correlation with the reference values for the signals recorded in the AC session ($r_{\text{image-level}} = .94$, $r_{\text{block-level}} = 1$, $p < .001$). Compared to the image-level features, stronger agreements were observed for block-level features. The average Cohen's Kappa scores of .363 and .345 were obtained for valence detection using JSiento and the BIOPAC features respectively. The average Kappa scores of .150 and .196 were achieved for arousal detection for using JSiento and the BIOPAC features respectively. These accuracies were also comparable with similar physiology based affect detection systems [5] which showed the feasibility of using a low-cost and portable physiological sensing system in a practical AC application.

ACKNOWLEDGMENTS
Rafael Calvo and Hamed Monkaresi were supported by the LEADS project of the SSHRC, Canada. Rafael Calvo was supported by an ARC Future Fellowship.

REFERENCES
[1] R. Picard, E. Vyzas, and J. Healey, "Toward machine emotional intelligence: Analysis of affective physiological state," *IEEE Trans. Pattern Anal. Mach. Intell.*, vol. 23, no. 10, pp. 1175–1191, 2001.

[2] R. A. Calvo, S. K. D'Mello, J. Gratch, and A. Kappas, Eds., *The Oxford Handbook of Affective Computing*. New York: Oxford University Press, 2014.

[3] http://jsiento.poscomp.org/.

[4] http://www.cooking-hacks.com/documentation/tutorials/ehealth-biometric-sensor-platform-arduino-raspberry-pi-medical.

[5] S. Koelstra, C. Muhl, M. Soleymani, J. Lee, A. Yazdani, T. Ebrahimi, T. Pun, A. Nijholt, and I. Patras, "Deap: A database for emotion analysis; using physiological signals," *IEEE Trans. Affect. Comput.*, vol. 3, no. 1, pp. 18–31, 2012.

BODYNETS 2015, September 28-30, Sydney, Australia

DOI 10.4108/eai.28-9-2015.2261525

Noise Measurement via Human Body for Intra-body Communication

Yuki Hayashida[1], Mari Hasegawa[1], Akito Suzuki[1]
Mitsuru Shinagawa[1], Yuichi Kado[2], and Nozomi Haga[3]

[1]Faculty of Science and Engineering, Hosei University, 3-7-2, Kajino-cho, Koganei-shi, Tokyo, 184-8584, Japan
Phone: +81-42-387-6243
E-mail: yuki.hayashida.y8@stu.hosei.ac.jp

[2]Department of Electronics, Kyoto Institute of Technology, Matsugasaki, Sakyo-ku, Kyoto, 606-8585, Japan

[3]Faculty of Science and Technology, Gunma University, 1-5-1, Tenjin-cho, Kiryu-shi, Gunma, 376-8515, Japan

ABSTRACT

Intra-body communication has a serious problem with the noise via the human body. In this system, the noise via the human body is transmitted along the same path as a signal because of capacitance coupling among nodes. These are transmitted in a coordinate phase as common-mode, but the distinction between the signal and noise is difficult. We present an analysis of the noise from an approach to clarify the method of measurement. A measurement of the noise was done by assuming the noise source via the human body and an electric light. To determine the noise to maintain the influence in a signal electrode, we connected an additional electrode to a ground electrode. The noise level was almost unchanged. Thus, the noise was influenced more by the signal electrode than by the ground electrode in this measurement system.

Categories and Subject Descriptors

J.2 [**Computer Applications**]: PHYSICAL SCIENCES AND ENGINEERING– *Electronics, Engineering, Physics.*

General Terms

Measurement, Experimentation

Keywords

Intra-body communication, Noise transmission model, Common-mode noise, Capacitance coupling, Internet of Things, and Wearable and embedded transceivers.

1. INTRODUCTION

Intra-body communication [1] has been developed as a communication system to make our lives better. This is one of the key-communication systems for the looming period of the Internet of Things (IoT), in which all nearby things can access the Internet [2].

The concepts of this system are that the human body is used as a transmission path and that communication area is limited within the human body. The method of accessing the network can be achieved through natural human actions such as sitting on a chair or touching a door handle. Therefore, it is an intuitive and user-friendly interface [3]. The transmission path of intra-body communication is composed of capacitance coupling among nodes [4-9]. This system can be communicated through the human body even if you touch the transceiver through dielectrics such as clothes or shoes. The transceiver does not need to be touched directly. However, a problem with intra-body communication occurs with the transmission paths of the signal and noise. This system has two kinds of transmission paths of noise. One is noise via the human body from the electromagnetic environment [9-12]. The other is noise via the ground from the system's ground [5,6,9]. The transmission paths of the signal and the noise in this system are shown in Fig. 1.

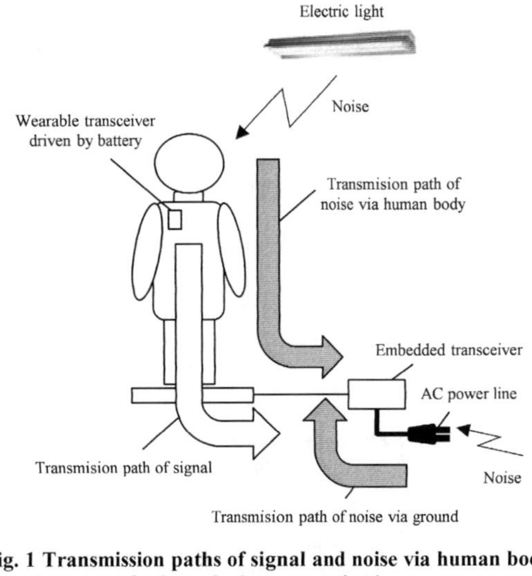

Fig. 1 Transmission paths of signal and noise via human body and via ground for intra-body communication

BODYNETS 2015, September 28-30, Sydney, Australia

DOI 10.4108/eai.28-9-2015.2261611

The focus in this system is that the signal and noise are transmitted in a coordinate phase as common-mode by capacitance coupling among nodes. When using wearable and embedded transceivers, a distinction between the signal and noise is difficult.

This system has been attracting attention for various kinds of applications [13,14], such as people who have a transceiver like an IC card transmit identification in touching a door handle, locking a door, and going through a ticket gate. Mainly, wearable and embedded transceivers are used in this system. A typical communication configuration for intra-body communication is shown in Fig. 2.

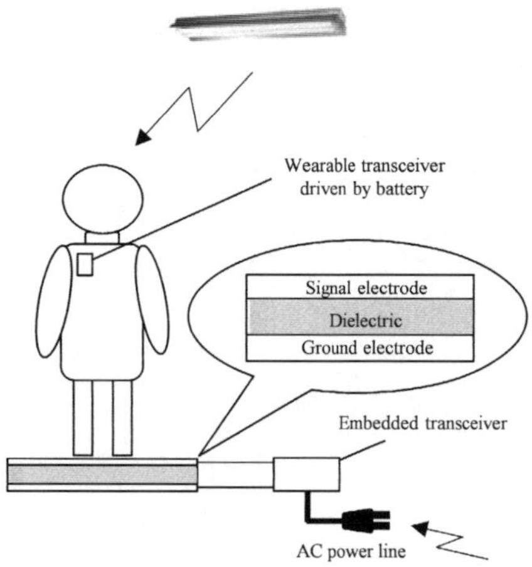

Fig. 2 Typical communication configuration for intra-body communication

Wearable transceivers have been attracting attention because people can use these transceivers every day. Watches, glasses, or bracelets can include them, for example. Wearable transceivers enable us to take care of certain activities without conscious effort. Embedded transceivers embedded in the surrounding environment such as door handles, walls, or floor mats are used for intra-body communication. Various kinds of applications between wearable and embedded transceivers have been reported for this system. [13,14].

A different driving method is used between wearable and embedded transceivers. The former is driven by a battery. It means that it is ungrounded and at a potentially floating state. The latter is driven by an AC power line. Embedded transceivers are just influenced from the ground because they are grounded. In previous work, the noise through the AC power line via the ground was the focus [5,6,9]. However, noise via the human body is a serious problem for intra-body communication [9,10]. Various kinds of noise sources are present in electric and electronic equipment, such as light fixtures, air conditioners, personal computers, televisions, and microwave ovens [5].

In this paper, we present our analysis of noise via the human body to clarify the method of measurement. As an antenna, electrodes composed of dielectrics sandwiched by signal and ground electrodes were used to consider the best transmission efficiency [5-7,9].

2. NOISE VIA HUMAN BODY

The problem of noise via the human body for intra-body communication is described herein. The main noise is electromagnetic noise emitted by a light fixture or peripheral electronic equipment [5]. In this paper, we regard an electric light installed in the ceiling as a noise source for intra-body communication. Therefore, we need to determine the noise spectrum of electric light and intra-body communication. An experiment using an electric light was conducted with a coaxial cable as an antenna that was brought close to the electric light. An experiment was also conducted using intra-body communication wherein a person stood on electrodes and was brought close to the electric light. The noise spectrums of the electric light and intra-body communication are shown in Fig. 3 when the electric light was on and off.

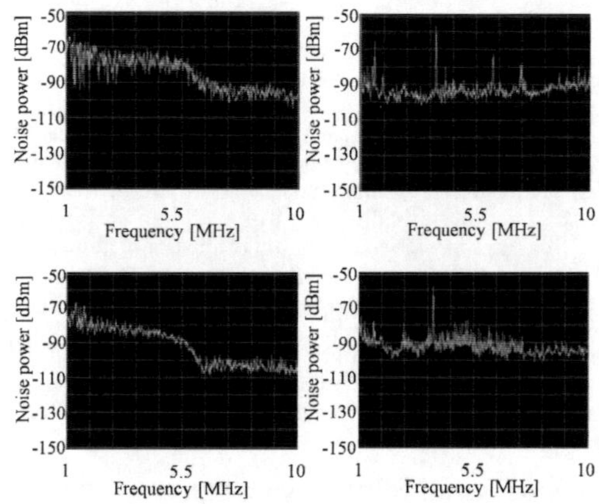

Fig. 3 Comparison of noise spectrum of electric light (a) "on" and (b) "off" and intra-body communication when electric light is (c) "on" and (d) "off"

(a) On	**(b) Off**
(c) On	**(d) Off**

The noise spectrum of electric light is shown (a) and (b) for on and off, respectively. The noise spectrum of intra-body communication is shown in (c) and (d) when the electric light is on (c) and off (d). A comparison of the noise spectrums (a), (b), (c), and (d) revealed them to be highly similar depending on the status of the electric light. Therefore, we regard the electric light as the noise source in intra-body communication.

Assuming a scene using wearable and embedded transceivers in Fig. 4, noise via the human body is transmitted along the same path as a signal because of capacitance coupling among nodes. Also, it is transmitted in a coordinate phase as common-mode. Therefore, a distinction between the signal and noise is difficult. Noise via the ground for the method of measurement and improvement has been reported in previous work [5,6,9]. We focus on the method of measuring noise via the human body.

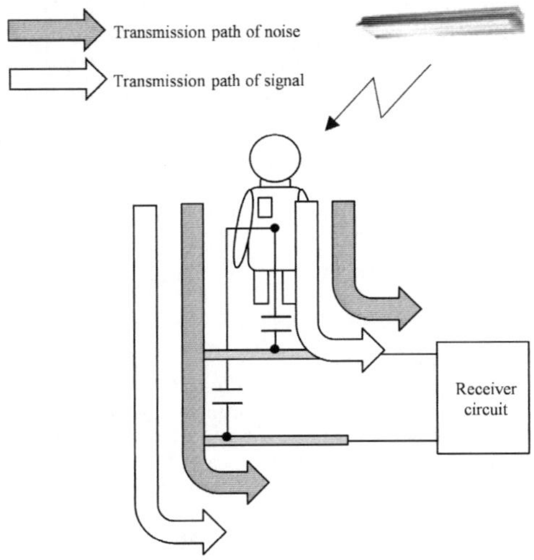

Fig. 4 Noise and signal transmitted as common-mode by capacitance coupling among nodes

3. NOISE MEASUREMENT SYSTEM

The basic model of noise in the transmission path has been reported [5,9]. Basically, two types of noise occur: differential-mode and common-mode noise.

A figure of a noise transmission model for intra-body communication [5,6,9] is shown in Fig. 5. The floor ground and power source ground are distinct from the earth ground because the electrical properties that each ground has is unknown. The distances d_{BS}, d_{SG}, and d_{GF} are defined by sandwiching foamed styrol as insulation plates. Impedance elements between each type of ground (Z_{CP}, Z_{PE}, Z_{FP}) are defined. The noise V_{CNF} via the floor ground was the focus in previous work [5,6,9]. In this paper, we focus on the noise V_{CNB} via the human body.

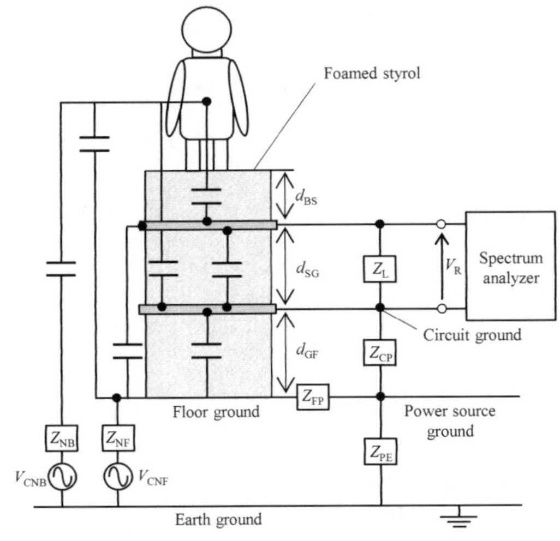

Fig. 5 Noise transmission model for intra-body communication

To measure the noise via the human body, we need to bring the human body close to the electric light and assume the noise source in a laboratory environment. Therefore, d_{GF} is changed by changing the thickness of the foamed styrol. Also, the measurement system must not be influenced by the ground. Therefore, the spectrum analyzer (Agilent N9340B) was driven by a battery. Electrodes composed of dielectrics sandwiched by signal and ground electrodes were used as the antenna to take impedance matching on the transmission path. If the distance between the signal and ground electrode is short, the characteristics of the noise may not be considered. Therefore, d_{SG} was fixed at 0.3 m to keep the influence in the signal electrode. A photograph of the experimental setup for the noise measurement is shown in Fig. 6.

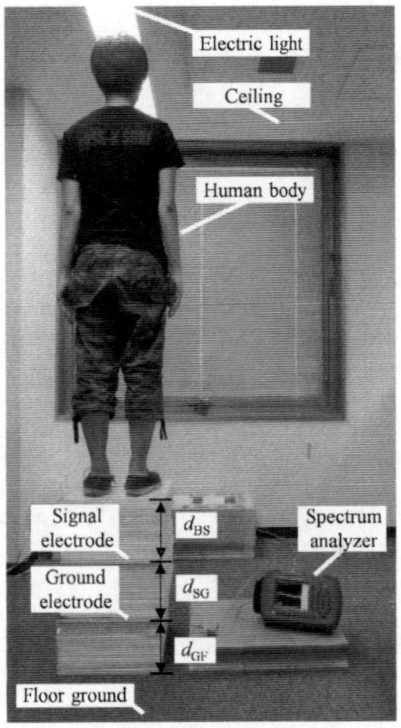

Fig. 6 Photograph of experimental setup for noise measurement

4. EXPERIMENTAL RESULTS

The height of the room in the laboratory environment and the person who participated were 2.6 m and 1.8 m, respectively. To measure the characteristics of intra-body communication, the measurement system needed to be regarded as high impedance. A non-inverting amplifier was connected just before the spectrum analyzer. To consider the characteristics of the noise via the human body, we paid attention to a certain frequency band where the noise level was notably different in Fig. 3: from 1.9 MHz to 2.8 MHz. d_{BS}, d_{SG}, and d_{GF} were fixed at 0.01 m, 0.3 m, and 0.01 m, respectively. d_{GF} was only changed by changing the thickness of the foamed styrol to bring the human body close to the electric light. When the electric light was on, the noise power was measured using the aforementioned setting shown in Fig. 7.

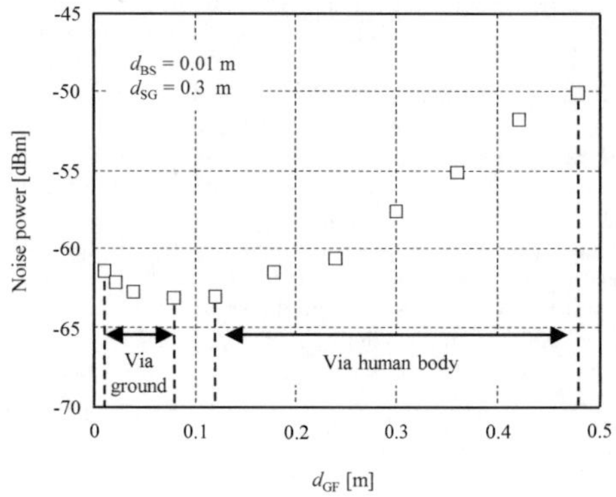

Fig. 7 d_{GF} dependence on noise power for intra-body communication

We divided d_{GF} into via ground and via human body. When via ground was considered (d_{GF} = 0.01 m - 0.08 m), this system was influenced more by the noise via the ground than by the noise via the human body. The noise level was gradually decreased by taking the impedance matching of the transmission path. And, when the electric light was off, the characteristics of the noise were also highly similar. When via human body was considered (d_{GF} = 0.12 m - 0.48 m), this system was influenced by the noise via the human body. This is because the human body was close to the electric light, and this system was influenced more by the noise via the human body than by the noise via the ground. We found that the kinds of noise influenced in intra-body communication were divided. Subsequently, to determine that the noise via the human body was influenced more by the signal electrode than by the ground electrode, we connected an additional electrode to the ground electrode. The measurement system of the additional electrode and the change in the noise level are shown in Fig. 8 and in Table 1.

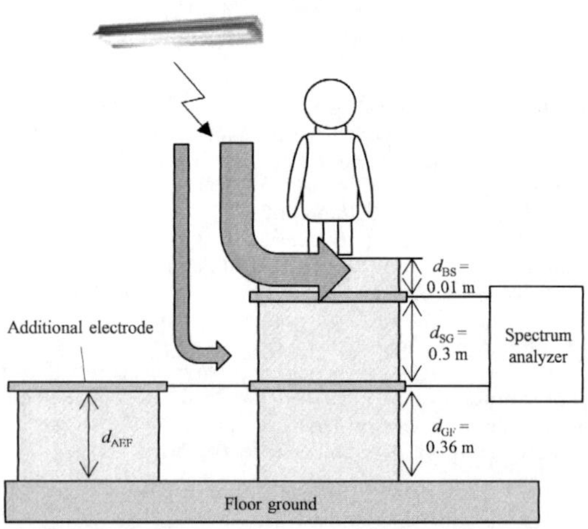

Fig. 8 Estimation system of noise level by additional electrode

Table 1 Change in noise level by additional electrode

d_{AEF} [m]	Without	0.01	0.02	0.04	0.08	0.12
Relative noise level [dB]	0	3.1	3.0	2.5	1.9	1.8

It has been reported that the noise transmitted as common-mode by connecting the additional electrode to the ground electrode decreased [5]. However, the noise level was almost unchanged even if d_{AEF} was changed. Therefore, the noise was not transmitted as common-mode. And this means that the noise was influenced more by the signal electrode than by the ground electrode in this measurement system.

5. CONCLUSION

The problem of the noise via the human body in intra-body communication was analyzed. The distinction between the signal and noise is difficult as these are transmitted as common-mode by capacitance coupling among nodes. We analyzed the noise from the approach of clarifying the method of measurement. In assuming the noise source via the human body with electric light, this finding indicates the measurement of the noise. We found the kinds of noise are different depending on the distance between the human body and the noise source. We connected an additional electrode to a ground electrode. The noise was found to be highly influenced by a signal electrode.

6. ACKNOWLEDGEMENTS

The authors would like to thank Hiroyuki Hatanaka, Yasuaki Takizawa, Yoko Yabe, and Yusuke Ido for their advice and help with the experiments.

7. REFERENCES

[1] T. G. Zimmerman. 1996. Personal Area Networks: Near-field intrabody communication. *IBM System.* J, 35 (3/4) 609-617.

[2] L. Atzori, A. Iera, and G. Morabito. 2010. Internet of Things: A survey. *Elsevier Computer Networks 54.* 2787-2805.

[3] Y. Kado and M. Shinagawa. 2010. AC Electric Field Communication for Human-Area Networking. *IEICE Trans. Electron.* E93-C, No. 3, 234-243.

[4] N. Haga, K. Saito, M. Takahashi, and K. Ito. 2012. Proper Derivation of Equivalent-Circuit Expressions of Intra-Body Communication Channels Using Quasi-Static Field. *IEICE Trans. Commun.* E95-B, No. 1, 51-59.

[5] M. Shinagawa, J. Katsuyama, K. Matsumoto, S. Hasegawa, R. Sugiyama, and Y. Kado. 2014. Noise analysis for intra-body communication based on parasitic capacitance measurement. *Elsevier Measurement 51.* 206-213.

[6] A. Sasaki, T. Ishihara, N. Shibata, R. Kawano, H. Morimura, and M. Shinagawa. 2013. Signal-to-Noise Ratio Analysis of a Noisy-Channel Model for a Capacitively Coupled Personal Area Network. *IEEE Trans. Antennas Propag.* 61, 390-402.

[7] R. Sugiyama, Y. Hayashida, J. Katsuyama, K. Matsumoto, Y. Ido, M. Shinagawa and Y. Kado. 2013. Signal Analysis of Wearable Transmitter for Intra-body Communication. *BodyNets. ICST* 449-452.

[8] T. Minotani and M. Shinagawa. 2014. Methods of Estimating Return-Path Capacitance in Electric-Field Intrabody Communication. *IEICE Trans. Commun.* E97-B, 114-121.

[9] Y. Hayashida, R. Sugiyama, Y. Ido, A. Suzuki, Y. Takizawa, M. Shinagawa, Y. Kado, and N. Haga. 2014. Capacitance Model of Embedded Transceiver for Intra-body communication. *BodyNets. ICST* 222-228.

[10] N. Haga, K. Motojima, M. Shinagawa, and Y. Kado. 2014. Received noise voltage of wearable transceiver in the presence of fluorescent lamps using high-frequency electronic ballasts. *IEICE. Electro. Express. Vol. 11, No. 21, 1-6.*

[11] Y. Namba, T. Morita, and K. Hirata. 2006. Numerical analysis of electromagnetic emission from lighting implement. *Int. Zurich Symp. Electromagn. Compat. 449.*

[12] R. Redl. 2001. Electromagnetic environmental impact of power electronics equipment. *IEEE. Vol. 89, No. 6, 926-938.*

[13] Y. Kado, T. Kobase, T. Yanagawa, T. Kusunoki, M. Takahashi, R. Nagai, O. Hiromitsu, A. Hataya, H. Shimasaki, and M. Shinagawa. 2012. Human-Area Networking Technology Based on Near-Field Coupling Transceiver. *2012 IEEE Radio & Wireless Sym. (RWS 2012),* 119-122.

[14] R. Nagai, T. Kobase, T. Kusunoki, H. Shimasaki, Y. Kado and M. Shinagawa. 2012. Near-Field Coupling Communication Technology For Human-Area Networking. *Journal of Systemics, Cybermetics & Informatics, Vol. 10, Issue 6,* p14.

Design and Simulation of a Low-Actuation-Voltage MEMS Switch

Yasser Mafinejad
School of Engineering
Deakin University
Waurn Ponds
Victoria 3216, Australia
ymafinej@deakin.edu.au

Abbas Z. Kouzani
School of Engineering
Deakin University
Waurn Ponds
Victoria 3216, Australia
kouzani@deakin.edu.au

Ladislau Matekovits
Department of Electronics and Telecomunications
Politecnico di Torino
Torino 10129 Italy
ladislau.matekovits@polito.it

ABSTRACT
This paper presents a low-actuation-voltage micro-electro-mechanical system (MEMS) capacitive shunt switch which has a very large bandwidth (4 GHz to 24 GHz). In this work, the isolation of MEMS switch is improved by adding two short high impedance transmission lines at the beginning and end of a coplanar waveguide (CPW). Simulating the switch demonstrates that a return loss (S11) is less than -26 dB for the entire frequency band, and perfect matching at 20 GHz in upstate position. A ramp dual pulse driver is also designed for reducing the capacitive charge injection for considering the reliability of the switch. The simulation results show that the shifting of voltage due to the capacitive charge is reduced by more than 35% of the initial value. Finally, the dynamic behavior of the MEMS switch is simulated by modal analysis and using CoventorWare to calculate the natural frequencies of the switch and its mode shapes. The switching ON and OFF time are 4.48 and 2.43 μs, respectively, with an actuation voltage of less than 15 V.

Categories and Subject Descriptors
C.2.1 [**Computer-Communication Networks**]: Network Architecture and Design – *wireless communication.*

General Terms
Measurement, Performance, Design, Experimentation.

Keywords
RF MEMS, switch, low-actuation-voltage, capacitive, shunt.

1. INTRODUCTION
The advancement of micro/nano electro mechanical systems (MEMS/NEMS) has enabled integration of MEMS switches and electronic devices on the same substrate in order to serve for low power consumption, high electrical isolation and ultra wide frequency band applications [1-4].

Radio frequency (RF) MEMS switches are categorized into four groups based on their types of actuation: piezoelectric, electro-thermal, electro-magnetic and electrostatic. The piezoelectric switch uses piezo materials such as AlN or PZT between two electrodes of beam or membrane [5]. The electro-thermal switch bonds material with different expansion coefficients to their beam [2, 6]. The electro-magnetic switch uses electro-magnetic force (EM). This force is created by applying a current element with in the magnetic field through the coil on top of the membrane. There is a very interesting EM RF MEMS switch proposed by Cho et al. [7] with an actuation voltage of 3V and a very high isolation bandwidth (-54 and -36 dB at 2 and 20 GHz respectively). The gap between transmission line and beam is 10μm. The fourth group is electrostatic (ES) switch. This type of switch is the most popular switch compared to other types of switches from the standpoints of fabrication, switching time, reliability and frequency bands. However, unlike the other types of switches which have the actuation voltage less than 15V, ES RF MEMS switches have a very high actuation voltage (>50V) [8].

Over the past decade, many researchers have demonstrated modular approaches to reduce the actuation voltage of electrostatic RF MEMS switches to be able to integrate them with electronic devices. Different methods have been used for reducing the actuation voltage of RF MEMS electrostatic MEMS switch. The first method for reducing the actuation voltage is to increase the electrostatic force. This can be done by using three states switches (ON, OFF and neutral) [9]. This type of switch consists of a beam which is anchored to a pillar at the middle while both ends are free. It also uses two separate voltage sources to provide negative and positive voltages. While voltages are applied to either of the electrodes, large positive deflection is then noticed on one side and smaller negative deflection with a large contact area is obtained on the other side. However, there are some issues with this method. Firstly, it uses the RIE etching instead of the wet etching, and also requires more fabrication steps than the normal MEMS switches for patterning pillars. Moreover, it requires two voltage sources which increase the power loss. The second method for increasing the force is a comb switch. It uses a comb driver which consists of stationary and movable fingers to provide a large electrostatic force. However, most of the reported RF MEMS comb switches have a DC contact and less capacitive contact. These are due to the deposition of dielectric on the side walls which limits the ON and OFF capacitance ratio. Moreover, the switching time for this type of switches is high due to the bulky and heavy comb drivers [10, 11]. The second method for reducing the actuation voltage is to reduce the spring constant. This can be achieved by movable

BODYNETS 2015, September 28-30, Sydney, Australia

DOI 10.4108/eai.28-9-2015.2261432

membrane and transmission line [12], or low spring constant. Although these techniques reduce the actuation voltage, they negatively affect the switching time [13]. The third method for reducing the actuation voltage is to use carbon nanotube (CNT) materials such as single wall carbon nanotube arrays for membrane [14, 15], multi wall carbon nanotube [16] or graphene [17, 18] instead of metal alloys. These types of switches are called RF NEMS carbon based switches [19] and have a very low actuation voltage due to the effect of van deer Waals force. The switching time of these switches is very low (ns) [20], but their fabrication process is extremely hard. There are only a few reports on RF parameters of NEMS switches.

The aim of this research work is to design a low ES actuation voltage (less than 15V) and also a very high isolation multipurpose switch with a very large bandwidth to cover the hiperlan mobile frequency till RF receivers of satellite communication. This method of design provides two main advantages compared to other methods: Firstly, it does not affect mechanical parameters of the switch such as switching time or spring constant. Secondly, it uses convenient fabrication processes which are used for MEMS switches such as soft lithography, wet etching and sputtering. It does not have any additional lithography process. We also propose a convenient electrical model for further analyzing the whole circuit. The validity of the electrical model is verified by simulation and analytical calculation.

2. PARAMETERS of MEMS SWITCHES

Any RF MEMS capacitive shunt switch consists of two essential parts: a transmission line and a bridge. The transmission line is a Coplanar Waveguide (CPW) or a microstrip line for transferring the signal from the input to the output of the switch. The bridge can be a fixed-fixed or a cantilever which are anchored to the ground. The performance of the switch depends on their RF parameters, mechanical parameters and reliability of the switch.

2.1 RF Parameters

The validity of the RF parameters of the switch is verified by the scattering parameters in the desired frequency band by the simulation or analysis of the electrical circuit model. The value of the lumped elements of the electrical model can be calculated through the physical structure of the switch or determined from the scattering parameter at the convenient frequencies. The parasitic element of the model cannot be easily neglected because the frequency band is extra wide (4-24GHz). The performance of the MEMS switches strongly depends on the ratio of capacitance at up and down state. At the up state position while the parallel switch is ON, the switch should be matched with input and output. The values of S_{11} equals or less than -10 dB providing acceptable matching at the input in the up-state position (Eq. (1)), and while the switch is OFF (down state), signal should not be transferred from the input to the output ($S_{21} \leq$ -10 dB) (Eq. (2)).

$$S_{11} \text{ (sup state)} = \frac{-j\omega C_{up} Z_0}{2 + j\omega C_{up} Z_0} \tag{1}$$

$$S_{21} \text{ (up state)} = \frac{1}{1 + j\omega C_d Z_0 / 2} \tag{2}$$

Another parameter which affects the RF performances of MEMS switches is the resistivity of material owing to the effect of the skin depth on the transmission line and the bridge. The thickness of the gold transmission line (TL) and bridge should be more than 2 µm and between 0.5-1 µm respectively.

2.2 Mechanical Parameters

The mechanical behavior of MEMS switches depends on the mode shapes and the frequencies of each mode. Modal analysis is used to predict the mode shapes and natural frequencies of each mode. This paper investigates a type of clamped-clamped beam. The dynamic model and natural frequency of MEMS switch for a fixed-fixed beam are given below. More information is provided in ref. [21-23].

$$\varphi_i(x)=A_i \cos(\beta_i x) + B_i \sin(\beta_i x) + C_i \cosh(\beta_i x) + D_i \sinh(\beta_i x) \tag{3}$$

where A_i, B, C_i, and D_i are calculated through the boundary conditions for a fixed-fixed beam and an is the frequency. The boundary condition for fixed-fixed MEMS switch is:

$$y = \frac{dy}{dx} = 0 \quad at\ x = 0 \quad , \quad y = \frac{dy}{dx} = 0 \quad at\ x = L \tag{4}$$

Therefore, the characteristic equation and natural frequency are:

$$\omega_n = \frac{\beta_n^2}{L^2}\sqrt{\frac{EI}{m}} \quad for \quad \beta_n = a_n = \frac{2n+1}{2}\pi \tag{5}$$

The switching times of MEMS switches is limited by the mechanical structure, and it is likely to keep the resonant frequency of MEMS switches less than the first natural frequency of MEMS switch. Although a high natural frequency may also lead to an increased switch-on time, the shape mode of the beam is not useful for RF MEMS switches. The relation between the switching time and the natural frequency of MEMS switch is given as bellow [24].

$$t_{ON}(pull-in\ condition) = 0.46 f_N^{-1} \tag{6}$$

$$t_{OFF}(pull-out\ condition) = 0.25 f_N^{-1} \tag{7}$$

The relation between gap and voltage source is shown in Figure 1. Increasing the actuation voltage ($V_{pull\text{-}in}$) makes instability and causes the upper electrode to snap down at $V_{pull\text{-}in}$. Electrostatic force relies on a voltage source and a capacitor between the TL and the membrane (Eq. (8)). The membrane still in down state until $V_{pull\text{-}out}$ due to the wan deer Waals force. The upper electrode is released at the pull out voltage because of the elastic force (Eq. (9)) [25-27].

$$V_{pull-in} = \sqrt{\frac{8k}{27\varepsilon_0 Ww} g_0^3} \tag{8}$$

$$V_{pull-out} = \sqrt{\frac{2k}{\varepsilon\varepsilon_0 Ww}(g_0 - g)\left(g + \frac{t_d}{\varepsilon_r}\right)^2} \tag{9}$$

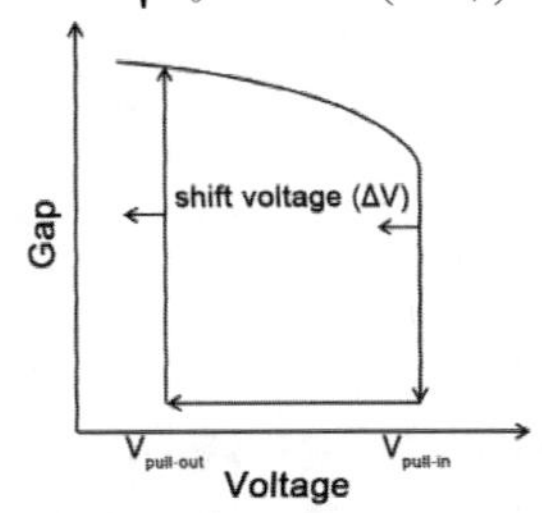

Figure 1. $V_{pull\text{-}in}$ and $V_{pull\text{-}out}$ of RF MEMS switches.

2.3 Reliability

The dielectric charging is the main failure mechanism in the lifetime of the electrostatically actuated capacitive RF MEMS switches. Due to the high actuation voltage required to actuate the switch, the electric filed across the dielectric can be higher than 10^8 V/m. This causes the charges to tunnel from the top and the bottom electrodes into the dielectric. With repeated ON-OFF cycles, charges gradually build up in the dielectric, which shifts the pull-in and pull-out voltages (Figure 1) [28-32]. The amount of the shifting voltage is given in Eq. (10).

$$\Delta V = \frac{qhQ}{\varepsilon_r \varepsilon_0} \tag{10}$$

where h is the distance between the bottom electrode and trapped charge sheet of density Q, q is electron charge and $\varepsilon_0\varepsilon_r$ is the permittivity of dielectric.

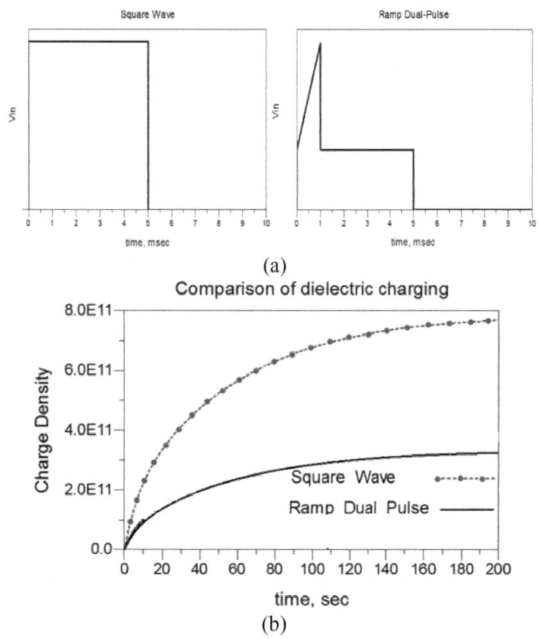

Figure 2. Comparison of charge effect of driver. (a) Pulse and RDP. (b) Comparing the amount of charge due to the effect of pulse.

This phenomenon becomes very critical at low actuation voltage because it shifts $V_{pull\text{-}in}$ and $V_{pull\text{-}out}$. This will cause the membrane to actuate by itself without any actuation voltage, or stuck the membrane at down state. In our previous work a new types of voltage driver was introduced to reduce the capacitive charge of MEMS capacitive switches. The ramp dual-pulse (RDP) actuation voltage increases with constant slope at the beginning of the ON period (Figure 2) instead of the pulse [33]. However, this will have a negative impact on the switching time of MEMS switches.

3. PROPOSED RF MEMS SWITCH

The structure of MEMS switch is given in Figure 3. It consists of CPW that include GaAs and 2 μm thick Au for providing a minimum insertion loss. Also, the bridge is a low spring constant folded flexure dual fixed with 0.7 μm thickness of gold. The top view and cross section of RF MEMS switch is shown in Figure 3.

3.1 RF Parameters

3.1.1 Design and Simulation of RF MEMS Switch for 4-24 GHz

The first step is to calculate the effective area between the 50Ω CPW (W=80 μm and G=60 μm) and a bridge. According to Eq. (1), the Cu should be less than 83 fF at 24 GHz. The parameters and values of the MEMS switch are given in Table I by using Eq. (11) and details in references [34, 35].

$$C_u = K\frac{\varepsilon_0 A}{g_0} \tag{11}$$

Table 1. RF MEMS switch parameters.

Parameter	Value
Membrane width (w)	185 μm
Membrane length (L)	220 μm
Signal line width (W)	120 μm
Gap between signal line and ground (G)	80 μm
Overlap area	185×120 μm²
CPW thickness	2 μm
Dielectric thickness	1000Å
Gap between TL and membrane (g_0)	2 μm
Bridge thickness	0.7 μm
HR silicon substrate constant (ε)	11.6
Fringing constant (K)	1.4

Figure 4 shows the simulation result of MEMS shunt switch according to the physical structure of MEMS switch with electromagnetic 3 dimension simulator (EM3DS). It can be seen that the MEMS switch provides a good isolation and insertion loss at up and down state (S_{11} and $S_{21} \leq$ -10 dB) for 4-24 GHz. The electrical model and values of RF MEMS switches are given in Figure 4(b). The simulation results by Genesys show a perfect agreement between the physical structure and lumped model at both up and down state position.

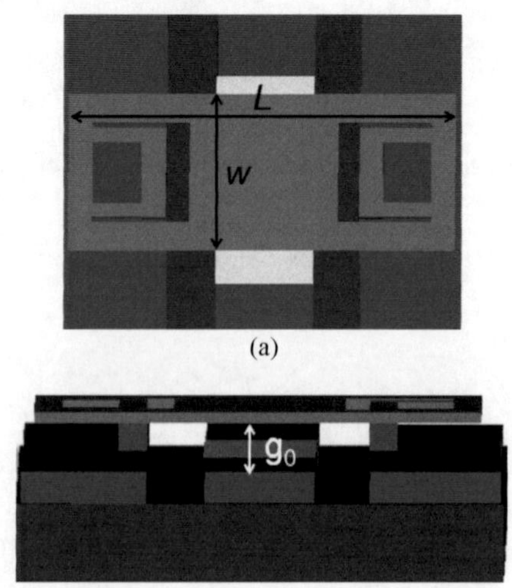

(b)

Figure 3. RF MEMS capacitive shunt MEMS. It consists of high resistivity (HR) silicon, Au CPW, SiN dielectric, anchor and folded beam. (a) Top view of the switch. L and w are the length and width of beam. (b) Cross section view of the switch. It consists of silicon substrate, CPW, SiN, anchor and dual fixed beam.

3.1.2 Improving Isolation of MEMS Switch

According to the previous discussion the most effective way for improving the isolation is to increase the gap or reduce the up state capacitance between transmission line and bridge. However, this increases the actuation voltage of MEMS switch. In this design we increase the isolation by providing a perfect matching between input and output. T matching is one effective method for cancelling the capacitance behavior of MEMS switch in order to make a resonant frequency at the entire frequency band.

The T match circuit consists of two transmission line (50 and 100 ohm). The 50 Ω transmission line is used for MEMS switch which we discussed earlier and high impedance transmission line for matching (L). The electrical circuit of switch at up state is shown in Figure 5. The length of short high impedance transmission line (SHITL) for Z_h=100 Ω can be calculated by Eq. (12).

$$\tan(\beta l) = \frac{Z_h^2 - Z_0^2 \pm \sqrt{\left(Z_h^2 - Z_0^2\right)^2 - \left(\omega C_u Z_h^2 Z_0\right)^2}}{\omega C_u Z_h^3} \qquad (12)$$

where Z_0=50 Ω, Z_h=100 Ω, C_u=0.11 pF, f=10 GHz. Two values are found for l but due to the variation of the phase shift along the transmission line, the shorter value is selected because it makes the circuit less sensitive to frequency band (l=230 μm). The scattering parameters show that this switch provides a very high isolation S_{11} less than -20 dB for the frequency of up to 24 GHz. Furthermore, there is a desirable matching at 20 GHz for S_{11} less than -32 dB. Also, the S_{11} and S_{21} down-state position for the switch are desirable for the frequency more than 4 GHz. The electrical circuit at up state is shown in Figure 5. The value of intrinsic C_{TL} and L_{TL} of high impedance transmission line is given in Eq. (13) and Eq. (14) (20 fF and 0.2 nH):

$$L = \frac{Z\beta l}{\omega} \qquad (13)$$

$$C = \frac{\beta l}{Z\omega} \qquad (14)$$

C_u for this MEMS switch consists of $2C_{TL}$ and C_{bridge} at up state. The value of electrical model of MEMS switch at up and down state is given in Figure 5. The simulation results by Genesys show a perfect agreement between the physical structure and lumped model in both up and down state position.

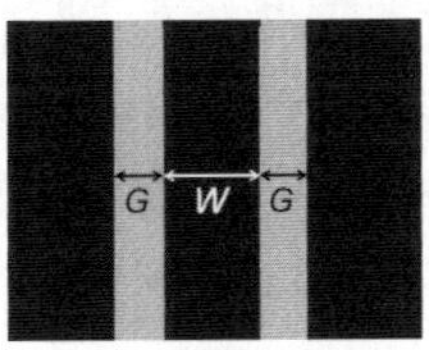

(a)

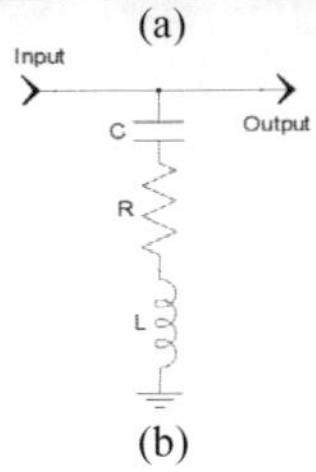

(b)

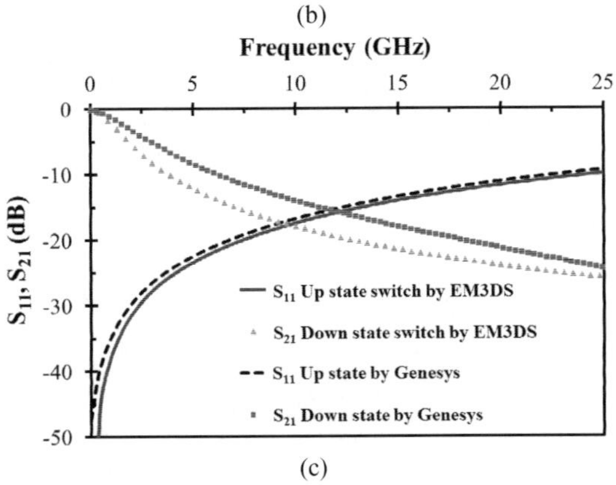

(c)

Figure 4. (a) A 50 Ω CPW, W is the wide of signal line and G is the gap between the signal and ground lines (80 and 60 μm respectively). (b) Lumped electrical models of MEMS capacitive shunt switch for both up and down state. C_u is 91fF, C_d is 2.87 pF, L is 4.3 pH and R is 0.04 Ω. (c) Comparing S_{11} and S_{21} for up and down states for both physical structure and electrical lumped model with EM3DS and Genesys.

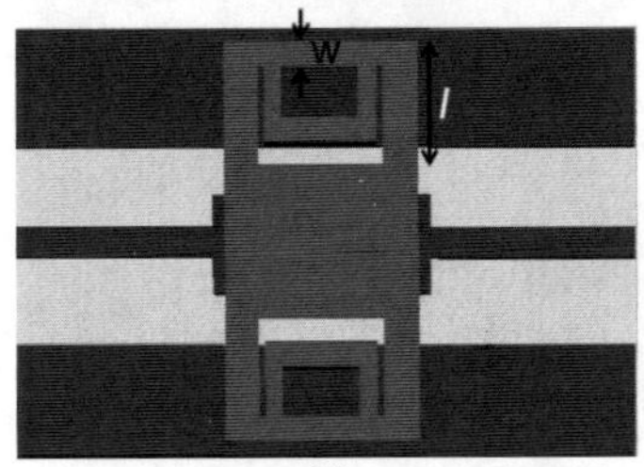

(a)

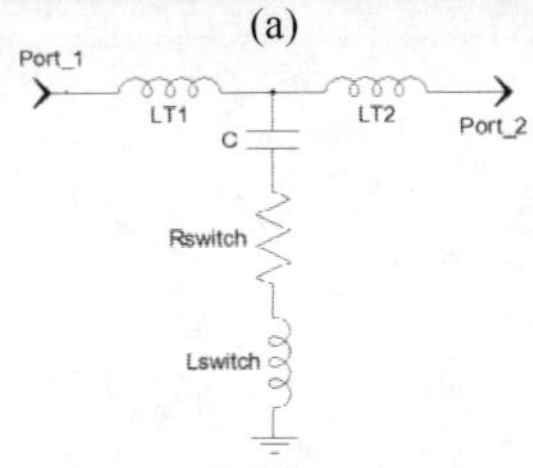

(b)

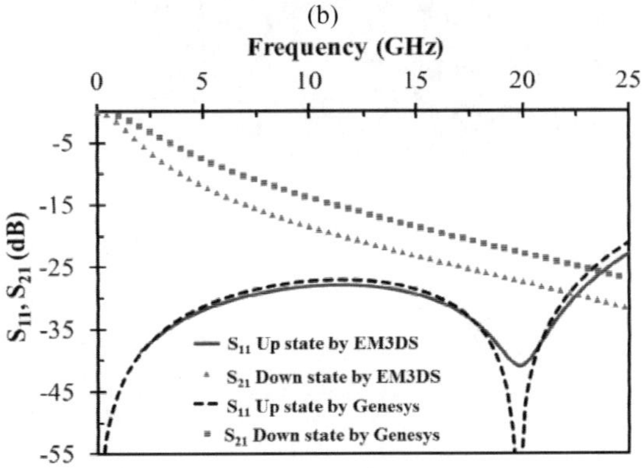

(c)

Figure 5. (a) Physical structure of MEMS switch with additional two short high impedance transmission lines. (b) Lumped electrical models of MEMS capacitive shunt switch for both up and down state. C_u is 131 fF, C_d is 3.5 pF, L is 4.3 pH and R is 0.04 Ω. (c) Comparing S_{11} and S_{21} for up and down state for both physical structure and electrical lumped model with EM3DS and Genesys.

3.2 Mechanical Parameters

The actuation voltage should be less than 15 volts; therefore the spring constant should be close to 24 N/m (Eq. (8)). The spring constant of the folded flexure MEMS switch is given in Eq. (15).

$$k = 2Ew\left(\frac{t}{l}\right)^3 \quad (15)$$

where E is Young's modulus (80 GPa), t is the thickness (0.7 μm), w is the width of truss 5 μm and l is 22.5 μm. As discussed, the beam has an infinite number of modes and it is very important to load the beam in the associated mode. The first three natural frequencies for this beam are simulated by CoventorWare and shown in Figure 6. As can be seen, the direction of the movement for the first resonant is suitable for the RF MEMS switch

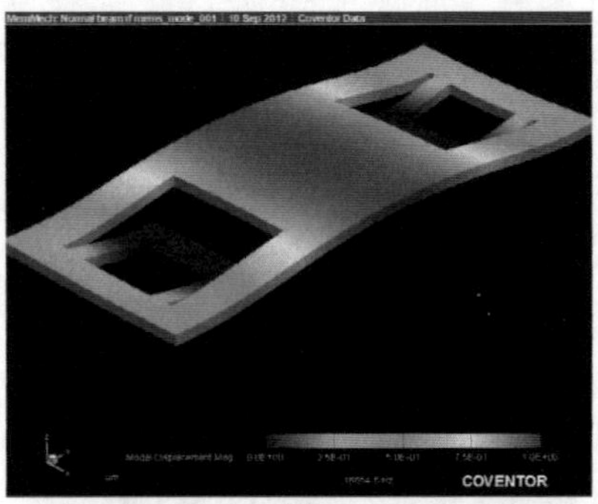

(a)

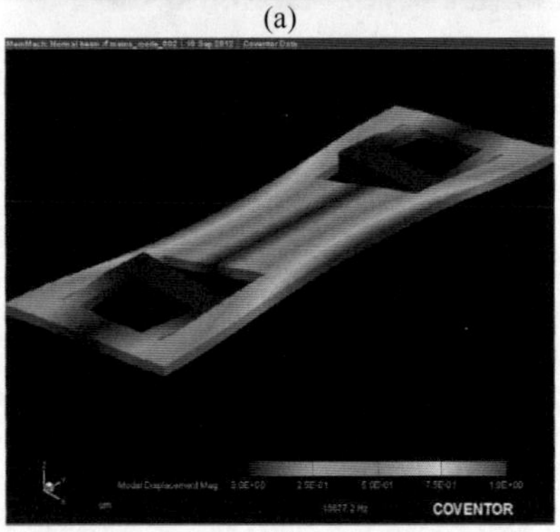

(b)

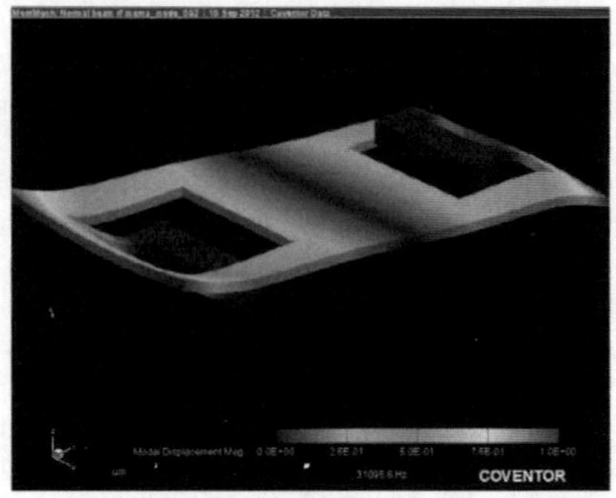

(c)

Figure 6 The first three natural frequency of the beam for the mass and k of 2.2×10^{-10} Kg and 24 N/m, respectively. (a) First mode natural frequency is 52567 Hz. (b) Second mode natural frequency is 58952 Hz. (c) Third mode natural frequency is 98148 Hz.

(52567 Hz) while the other modes does not provide overlap between the transmission line and bridge. Therefore, the mechanical parameters of MEMS switch should be calculated for this frequency. According to the Eq. (6) and Eq. (7), the switching ON and OFF time are 8.75 μs and 4.75 μs, respectively.

3.3 Reliability

Ramp dual-pulse is the method to enhance the lifetime of the switch. For this particular switch, the simulation result shows the comparison of actuation-voltage shift between a 100 Hz square actuation signal and a 100 Hz RDP actuation signal with equal duty cycles (Figure 2(a)). Figure 7 shows the compare the shifted C/V curve by square and RDP waveform. It is seen that the actuation voltage shifts is reduced from 2.6 to 1.3V.

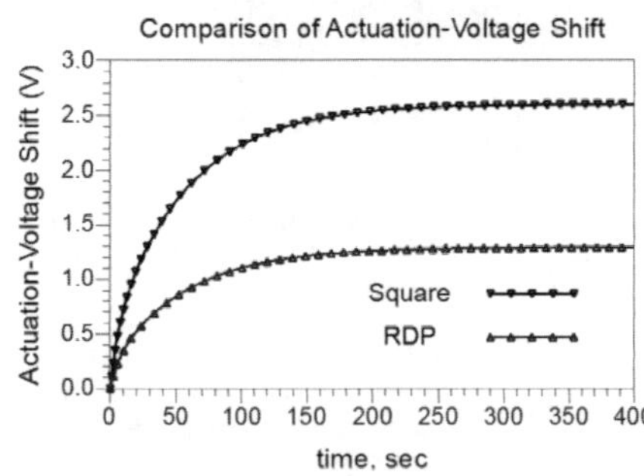

(a)

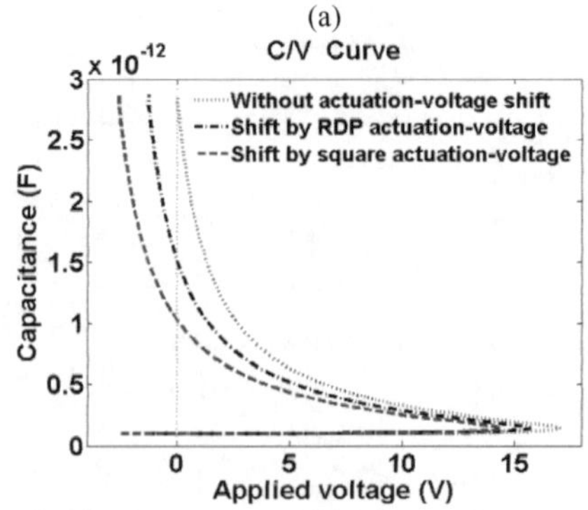

(b)

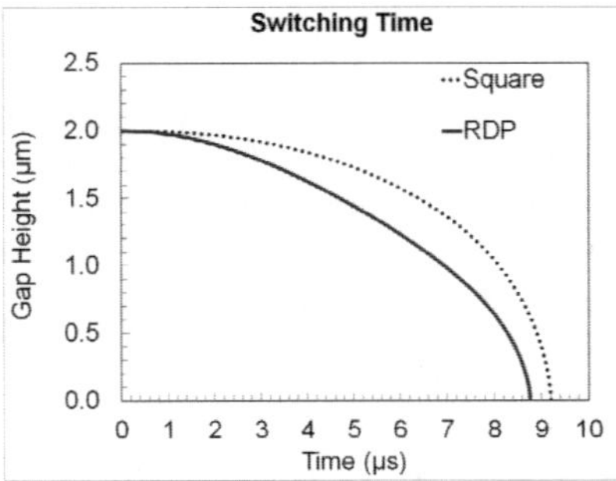

(c)

Figure 7. (a) Comparison of the actuation-voltage shift between square and RDP. (b) C/V curve shift by square and RDP actuation voltage. (c) Effects of the actuation signal waveform on the switching time.

Displacement is usually discussed in terms of some functions, such as time. This variable can be obtained using numerical integration from equations motion [36]. Figure 7c compare the time-domain response for the proposed switch under applied voltages which is gained by Mathematica and results are agrees well with CoventorWare. Square and RDP switching times are approximately 8.75 μs and 9.2 μs, respectively. In square waveforms, maximum voltage occurs immediately, whereas the RDP waveform gradually increases the actuation voltage, therefore the membrane reaches the contact later than the square waveform.

4. CONCLUSIONS

This paper explained in details how to design a low ES actuation-voltage MEMS switch for C-K band. Two short high impedance transmission lines were designed and included at both ends of the transmission line in order to improve the matching at the entire frequency band at the up-state. Simulations are carried out using ElectroMagnetic 3D Simulator (EM3DS) and CoventorWare to calculate the electrical and mechanical parameters. Return loss and isolation are better than 26 dB and 20 dB at both up and down states respectively. The calculated pull-in voltage was almost 15 V and the mechanical resonant frequency equaled 52 kHz. Moreover, the major problem on reliability of MEMS switches is due to the shifting voltage because of the accumulation of trapped charges on the dielectric. This failure is improved by applying a type of driver which generates a ramp dual-pulse. This driver can be easily implemented by electronic devices.

5. REFERENCES

[1] K.J. Park, S.M. Kang, H.S. Kim, C.W. Baek, T.K. Chung, Energy scavenging system utilising MEMS switch for power management, Electronics Letters, 48 (2012), 948-949.

[2] S. Zhang, W. Su, M. Zaghloul, Design and Simulation of a Thermally Actuated MEMS Switch for Microwave Circuits, International Journal of RF and Microwave Computer-Aided Engineering, 19 (2009), 492-501.

[3] P. Gammel, G. Fischer, J. Bouchaud, RF MEMS and NEMS Technology, Devices, and Applications, Bell Labs Technical Journal, 10 (2005), 29-60.

[4] G. Rebeiz, K. Entesari, I. Reines, S.J. Park, M. El-tanani, A. Grichener, A. Brown, Tuning in to RF MEMS, Microwave Magazine, IEEE, 10 (2009), 55-72.

[5] R. Guerre, U. Drechsler, D. Bhattacharyya, P. Rantakari, R. Stutz, R.V. Wright, Z.D. Milosavljevic, T. Vaha-Heikkila, P.B. Kirby, M. Despont, Wafer-Level Transfer Technologies for PZT-Based RF MEMS Switches, Journal of Microelectromechanical Systems, 19 (2010), 548-560.

[6] C.D. Nordquist, M.S. Baker, G.M. Kraus, D.A. Czaplewski, G.A. Patrizi, Poly-Silicon Based Latching RF MEMS Switch, Microwave and Wireless Components Letters, IEEE, 19 (2009), 380-382.

[7] I.-J. Cho, E. Yoon, Design and fabrication of a single membrane push-pull SPDT RF MEMS switch operated by electromagnetic actuation and electrostatic hold, Journal of Micromechanics and Microengineering, 20 (2010), 035028-035035.

[8] S. Gong, H. Shen, N.S. Barker, Study of Broadband Cryogenic DC-Contact RF MEMS Switches, Microwave Theory and Techniques, IEEE Transactions on, 57 (2009), 3442-3449.

[9] C.H. Kim, Mechanically Coupled Low-Voltage Electrostatic Resistive RF Multithrow Switch, Industrial Electronics, IEEE Transactions on, 59 (2012), 1114-1122.

[10] J. Park, E.S. Shim, C. Wooyeol, K. Youngmin, K. Youngwoo, C. Dong-il, A Non-Contact-Type RF MEMS Switch for 24-GHz Radar Applications, Journal of Microelectromechanical Systems, 18 (2009), 163-173.

[11] A.Q. Liu, M. Tang, A. Agarwal, A. Alphones, Low-loss lateral micromachined switches for high frequency applications, Journal of Micromechanics and Microengineering, 15 (2005), 157–167.

[12] A. Kundu, S. Sethi, N.C. Mondal, B. Gupta, S.K. Lahiri, H. Saha, Analysis and optimization of two movable plates RF MEMS switch for simultaneous improvement in actuation voltage and switching time, Microelectronics Journal, 41 (2010), 257-265.

[13] C. King Yuk, R. Ramer, RF MEMS Switch with low stress sensitivity and low actuation voltage, in: Antennas and Propagation Society International Symposium, 2009. APSURSI '09. IEEE, 2009, pp. 1-4.

[14] D. Acquaviva, A. Arun, S. Esconjauregui, D. Bouvet, J. Robertson, R. Smajda, A. Magrez, L. Forro, A.M. Ionescu, Capacitive nanoelectromechanical switch based on suspended carbon nanotube array, Applied Physics Letters, 97 (2010), 233508.

[15] M. Dragoman, A. Takacs, A.A. Muller, H. Hartnagel, R. Plana, K. Grenier, D. Dubuc, Nanoelectromechanical switches based on carbon nanotubes for microwave and millimeter waves, Applied Physics Letters, 90 (2007), 113102.

[16] S.W. Lee, D.S. Lee, R.E. Morjan, S.H. Jhang, M. Sveningsson, O.A. Nerushev, Y.W. Park, E.E.B. Campbell, A Three-Terminal Carbon Nanorelay, Nano Letters, 4 (2004), 2027-2030.

[17] M. Dragoman, D. Dragoman, F. Coccetti, R. Plana, A.A. Muller, Microwave switches based on graphene, Journal of Applied Physics, 105 (2009), 054309.

[18] K.M. Milaninia, M.A. Baldo, A. Reina, J. Kong, All graphene electromechanical switch fabricated by chemical vapor deposition, Applied Physics Letters, 95 (2009), 183105.

[19] M. Liaoa, Y. Koidea, Carbon-Based Materials: Growth, Properties, MEMS/NEMS Technologies, and MEM/NEM Switches, Critical Reviews in Solid State and Materials Sciences, 36 (2011), 66-101.

[20] M. Dequesnes, Z. Tang, N.R. Aluru, Static and Dynamic Analysis of Carbon Nanotube-Based Switches, Journal of Engineering Materials and Technology, 126 (2004), 230-237.

[21] D. Thorby, Structural dynamics and vibration in practice: an engineering handbook, Butterworth-Heinemann, 2008.

[22] S.S. Rao, Mechanical vibrations, Prentice Hall, Englewood Cliffs, 1995.

[23] R.P. LaRose III, K.D. Murphy, Impact dynamics of MEMS switches, Nonlinear Dynamics, 60 (2010), 327-339.

[24] S. Dutta, M. Imran, R. Pal, K.K. Jain, R. Chatterjee, Effect of residual stress on RF MEMS switch, Microsystem Technologies, 17 (2011), 1739-1745.

[25] G.M. Rebeiz, RF MEMS: Theory, Design, and Technology, New Jersey: John Wiley & Sons, 2003.

[26] M.I. Younis, Sensing and Actuation in MEMS, in MEMS Linear and Nonlinear Statics and Dynamics, Springer, New York, 2011.

[27] S. Lucyszyn, Advanced RF MEMS, Cambridge University Press, New York, 2010.

[28] W.S.H. Wong, L. Chean Hung, Longer MEMS Switch Lifetime Using Novel Dual-Pulse Actuation Voltage, Device and Materials Reliability, IEEE Transactions on, 9 (2009), 569-575.

[29] Y. Xiaobin, P. Zhen, J.C.M. Hwang, D. Forehand, C.L. Goldsmith, A transient SPICE model for dielectric-charging effects in RF MEMS capacitive switches, Electron Devices, IEEE Transactions on, 53 (2006), 2640-2648.

[30] W.M.v. Spengen, Capacitive RF MEMS switch dielectric charging and reliability: a critical review with recommendations, Journal of Micromechanics and Microengineering, 22 (2012), 074001-074023.

[31] Y. Huang, A.S.S. Vasan, R. Doraiswami, M. Osterman, M. Pecht, MEMS Reliability Review, Device and Materials Reliability, IEEE Transactions on, 12 (2012), 482-493.

[32] P. S. Sumant, N. R. Aluru, A. C. Cangellaris, A Compact Model For Dielectric Charging in RF MEMS Capacitive Switches, International Journal of RF and Microwave Computer-Aided Engineering, 19 (2009), 197-203.

[33] M. Zarghami, Y. Mafinezhad, A.Z. Kouzani, K. Mafinezhad, Low actuation-voltage shift in MEMS switch using ramp dual-pulse, IEICE Electronics Express, 12 (2012), 1062-1068.

[34] Y. Mafinejad, A.Z. Kouzani, K. Mafinezhad, A. Golmakani, Pi-shaped MEMS architecture for lowering actuation voltage of RF switching, IEICE Electronics Express, 6 (2009), 1483-1489.

[35] Y. Mafinejad, A.Z. Kouzani, K. Mafinezhad, H. Nabovatti, Design and simulation of a low voltage wide band RF MEMS switch, in: Systems, Man and Cybernetics, 2009. SMC 2009. IEEE International Conference on, 2009, pp. 4623-4627.

[36] V. Kaajakari, Closed form expressions for RF MEMS switch actuation and release time, Electronics Letters, 45 (2009), 149-150.

Bio-compatibility of metallic alloys for body-area communication systems

Ildiko Peter[1]
Department of Applied Science and Technology
Politecnico di Torino- Italy
+39 011 090 4670
ildiko.peter@polito.it

Mario Rosso[2]
Department of Applied Science and Technology
Politecnico di Torino- Italy
+39 011 090 4664
mario.rosso@polito.it

ABSTRACT

Mechanical behavior, biocompatibility in body environment and tissues and chemical stability are the most important requirements for the effective application of any bio-implant materials in the human body. Among the known metals and alloys, stainless steels, CoCr alloys and Ti and its alloys are the most widely used materials in such applications. In case of their use, one of the most important engineering approach is to guarantee insignificant biological stress to the human system and to maintain the whole integrity and functionality of the human being.

In this paper we pay our attention on the study of the properties of two types of metallic alloys: one of them is a modified CoCr alloy, while the second one is a new generation of TiNb based alloy. The first step of the study is related to the determination of the microstructural and mechanical behavior of the alloys and to assess their chemical stability by the evaluation of their corrosion resistance. The further step will be to evaluate and to control the interaction between the human body and the biomaterial inside the biological environment using an appropriate numerical model. In this way it will be possible to detect the presence of defects in the biomaterial, considering the surface chemistry and its topography, which can control this system leading to regulate in time an inappropriate interface avoiding the removal of the implant for the restoration. Furthermore, the results of such an investigation represent a good starting point in designing of intra-, inter-body or body-coupled printed implanted antennas, i.e., antennas located inside the body used to communicate with external base stations or between different nodes of a network.

Categories and Subject Descriptors

J. [Computer applications], J.3[**Life and medical sciences**]: Health, medical information system

K [**Computing Milieux**], K.4. [Computers and Society], K.4.2 [Social Issues]: - Handicapped *persons/special needs*

General Terms

Theory, Experimental results.

Keywords

Metallic biomaterials, CoCr alloys, Ti alloys, body environment, numerical simulation.

1. INTRODUCTION

Because of their excellent mechanical properties, good corrosion resistance and good biocompatibility, metallic alloys are usually employed for dental implants and orthopedic device production. In addition, they are desirable for some neuromuscular stimulation tools production, due to their good thermal and electric conductivity coming from the natural electron movement within the metal crystal system. Compared to polymeric, ceramic and composite based biomaterials, metals and their alloys have superior tensile and fatigue strength associated to a superior fracture toughness, good corrosion resistance and good biocompatibility [1, 2]. Usually, metallic alloys are exploited thanks to their structural functions in different parts of the human body to substitute the lost or unhealthy natural assembly and to repair them, but they do not have any bio-functionalities, like blood compatibility. The most important metallic biomaterials are stainless steel, CoCr based alloys and Ti and its alloys. In the case of stainless steel one can have localized corrosion and the release of metallic ions which could be dangerous for the human body. Actually, CoCr based alloys have acquired higher attention and compared to stainless steel as strength and corrosion resistance regards show superior features, but as from manufacturing point of view they are more expensive [3, 4]. For such alloys, Cr is a crucial constituent from corrosion resistance point of view and gives to the alloy intrinsic corrosion resistance, developing a passive chromium oxide layer. Cr and Mo act as solid solution strengthening elements and can modify the alloys thermal coefficient of expansion. Ni can amplifies the ductile properties of the Cr-Co metallic alloy and can stabilize the faced centred cubic structure which is favored due to its better tenacity of the Co-matrix, but at the same time, Ni is a potent allergen component and can cause higher hypersensitivity reaction compared to other metallic or ceramic materials used in such application. Inflammatory responses, associated to Ni-Cr alloy restoration subside when the alloys is removed and replaced with Ni-free materials [5, 6]. Actually, Ti and its alloys have been received much more attention and they show the best

BODYNETS 2015, September 28-30, Sydney, Australia

DOI 10.4108/eai.28-9-2015.2261434

biocompatibility between the metallic biomaterials. They reveal good fatigue resistance, excellent in vivo corrosion resistance due to the stable and rapidly forms passive oxide layer. In addition, the lower elastic moduli compared to other metallic biomaterial, guarantee less stress shielding avoiding bone atrophy and faster osseointegration. The development of close bone-to-implant apposition after short implantation periods result an important benefit for permanent bone-interfacing implants [7]. A standard Ti based alloy for orthopaedic implants is Ti6Al4V alloy, which has been firstly developed for aeronautic applications. Another alloy, widely used as bio-alloy is NiTi alloy, thanks to its unique super-elastic and shape memory properties. However, a lack of biocompatibility has been demonstrated with these alloys: Ni is very allergenic and can cause violent inflammatory reactions; in Ti6Al4V, Al ions released from implant are associated with long term health problems like neurological pathologies while V is also known to be cytotoxic. Moreover, the high Young's modulus of the Ti6Al4V alloy affects long-term practical performances due to the stress shielding effect. In the last period, new Ti alloys with $\alpha + \beta$ structure, without V were obtained: Ti6Al7Nb; Ti5Al2.5Fe; Ti6Al6Nb1Ta; Ti5Al3Mo4Zr. Since the β microstructure in Ti alloys shows a significantly lower modulus than the $\alpha + \beta$ one [8], there is a need for improvement in design for an ideal medical implant. Consequently, a new generation of low modulus β-Ti alloys, free of Ni, V an Al have been made with β-stabilizing and biocompatible elements such as Nb, Ta, Zr and Mo (alloys of super β-type - Ti13Nb13Zr and β-type Ti15Mo). Among the β-type Ti alloys, the biocompatible metastable βTi-Nb based alloys are very promising for biomedical applications. Indeed, these alloys have a low elastic modulus close to that of bone. On the other hand, an encouraging super-elastic behavior can be achieved due to the αmartensitic transformation (orthorhombic phase). Consequently, Ni-free alloys can also be designed for biomedical smart devices or orthodontic wires [9, 10]. A group of special β-Ti alloys with unique physical-mechanical properties and wide range of possibilities in medical applications are Gum alloys, belonging to the β-type Ti alloys and is basically expressed as Ti (Ta, Nb, V) + (Zr, Hf, O). Gum alloys reveal excellent mechanical behaviour at room temperature: an ultra-low Young's modulus (60-70 GPa) and a non-linear elastic behaviour, an extended elastic limit, ultra-high strength (> 1 GPa), superplastic-like deformability, Invar-like thermal expansion, and Elinvar-like thermal dependence of the elastic modulus. These properties provide numerous opportunities for Gum alloys application [11]. After their development in Japan, being the first alloy that combines extremely low elastic modulus with extremely high strength they became ideal candidate for medical implants able to withstand reasonably large loads, due to their special mechanical properties and with no hazardous elements in their chemical composition. Nb, Ta and Zr are now considered to be the safest, non-toxic and non-allergic alloying elements for Ti alloys, being demonstrated through research studies their higher cell viability, corrosion resistance, tissue compatibility and non-allergic properties. One of the alloys studied in the present paper is situated in the compositional system: Ti-Nb-Ta-Zr-O, and the other one is a CoCr-based alloy. Metallic implants made of biodegradable metals or their alloys, like Mg and its alloys, reveal some new biomedical features: after being implanted, they will gradually degrade, avoiding their elimination associated to an immediate reduction in health risks, costs and damaging [12]. Mg and its biodegradable alloys (AZ91, WE43, AM50, LAE442) appear to be the most promising candidate for the construction of temporary implants, including stents [13], since they can degrade naturally in the physiological environment by corrosion and the corrosion products of such implants have been well accepted by human organism: Mg2+ ions are the fourth most abundant cation in the human body and are stored mainly in bones. In this general framework, the study and the development of new alloy compositions and new production processes for medical device construction can be integrated by numerical investigation on the development of efficient production processes and/or on the model of the possible interaction between the biomaterial surfaces and the body environment. Such studies allow drastically reduction of the number of experimental tests and the probability of infections. Theoretically modelling, in many cases, one can avoid the removal of the implant, the cure of the diseases, which is very important for the patient and is beneficial from economical point of view.

The aim of the present paper is to provide, firstly, a general overview on the metallic biomaterials and their possible use in the human body focusing the attention on Ti enriched CoCr-based and TiNb-based alloys. In the further step we propose a possible model to evaluate and to control the interaction between the metallic biomaterial and the surrounding biological environment using an appropriate numerical model. In this way we will control the surface chemistry and its topography, which can control this system leading to correct in time the inappropriate interaction between the two elements avoiding the removal of the implant for the restoration. Additionally, the development of the radiating part, i.e., antenna of an intra-, inter-body or body-coupled system could directly benefit from the possibility to have a biocompatible conductor with good electric properties.

2. EXPERIMENTAL DETAILS

CoCr basic alloy enhanced by Ti (25.5%Cr, 6% Mo, 1% Si, 4% Ti, Co balance and the TiNb based alloy (Ti61.70, 30.50Nb, 4.80Zr, 2.80Ta, 0.20O) were produced by cold crucible levitation melting technique with induction heating system.. As reference material a commercially employed Wirobond®280 alloy (Co60.9, Cr25, Mo4.8, W6.2, Ga2.9) were used. The samples in as-cast state were prepared by traditional metallographic procedures and then were submitted to morphological and compositional analysis by Optical Microscope (OM, MeF4 Reichart-Jung) and by Scanning Electron Microscopy (SEM, Leo 1450VP) equipped with Energy-Dispersive X-ray Spectrometry (EDS, Oxford microprobe). X-ray technique (X-ray, PANanalytical tool with Cu kα wavelength of 1.5418 Å) was employed for phase identification. Mechanical properties were evaluated by hardness measurement performed on the polished samples using a force of 5 N for 15 s for each measurement. The corrosion behaviour of the alloys was evaluted by static immersion test according to the route specified in the Standard ISO 10271/2011 at 37°C (± 1°C). The samples were maintained in acid solution (7.5 ml lactic acid, 5.85 g NaCl, 300 ml H_2O di grade 2 purity, and 700 ml H_2O) at pH=7.4, simulating the oral cavity surroundings. The samples were monitored after the permanence in this biological solution for 28 days. As reference solution a biological solution maintained in the same condition with no any metallic alloy inside was used.

3. EXPERIMENTAL EVALUATION AND CHARACTERIZATION OF THE METALLIC BIOMATERIAL

The microstructural investigation, mechanical and corrosion resistance evaluation of the biomaterials considered for medical device production is directly correlated to the surface chemistry of the alloys and to their topography. The adhesion mechanism in the human body structure will be governed by these elements. For these reasons, in this paper we, firstly, experimentally characterize the metallic alloys and then we propose a theoretical study for the further evaluation of the interface created in the body between the metallic alloys and the adjacent atmosphere.

3.1 Morphological observation

The microstructure of the CoCr based alloy shows a non-homogeneous features, and according to the ternary equilibrium diagram, the presence of the solid solution (dark areas in the Figs.1) is shown with a casual disposition of the dendrites within the structure (light areas in the Figs. 1); in addition carbides (mostly $Cr_{23}C_3$, Cr_7C_3 and TiC_8) formation was identified. There is no evidence of continuous grain boundary carbides, which would be undesirable because negatively affect the ductility of the alloys. Ti, due to its high affinity to the carbon, easily reacts with the carbon inside the metal matrix and the residual unbound element is dissolved in the solid solution. In the case of the commercial alloy the growth of the dendrites occurs according to a particular direction as revealed in Figure 1a and the structure results more uniform compared to the experimentally produced and Ti enriched alloy (Figure 1b) where the segregation tendency is more accentuated and the dendrites appear larger with indefinite orientation. A typical pure equiaxed β grain microstructure for the TiNb alloy is reported in Figure 1c. The average β grain size is about 161 μm.

3.2 Mechanical behavior evaluation

The carbide development confers to the alloy high hardness improving the alloy wear and corrosion resistances. Hardness measurements have been performed with a standard Vickers pyramidal Figure 2 reports the obtained results. As expected, the Ti modified alloy shows the higher hardness due to the highest content of Cr and Mo carbides, compared to the reference metallic alloy with no any carbide formation. As concerns, TiNb based alloy there are no any presence of hard particles and the hardness values are lower than those obtained for the commercially used metallic alloy (there are only the presence of β-Ti in the composition) and confers to the alloy good workability.

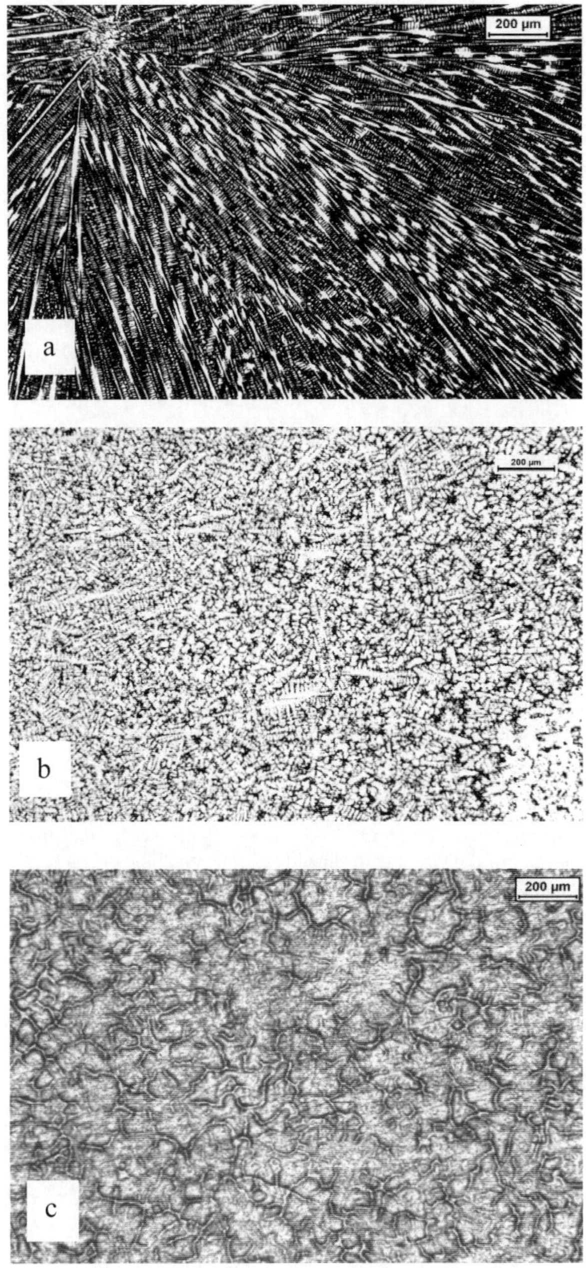

Figure 1: Optical micrographs of the alloys employed for the study: (a) Wirobond®280 alloy, (b) Ti enriched CoCr alloy and (c) TiNb alloy

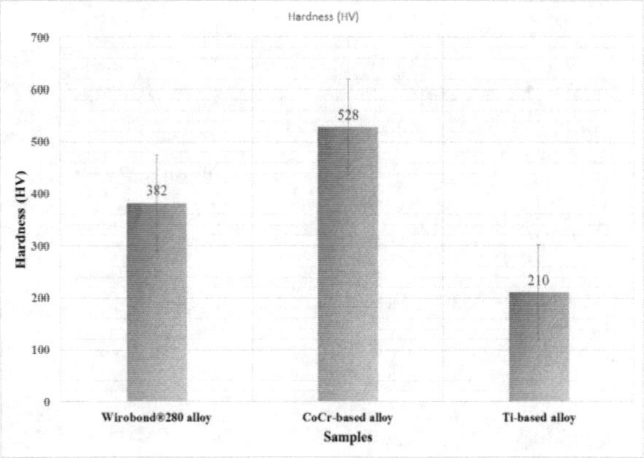

Figure 2: Vickers hardness measurement results for the alloys investigated

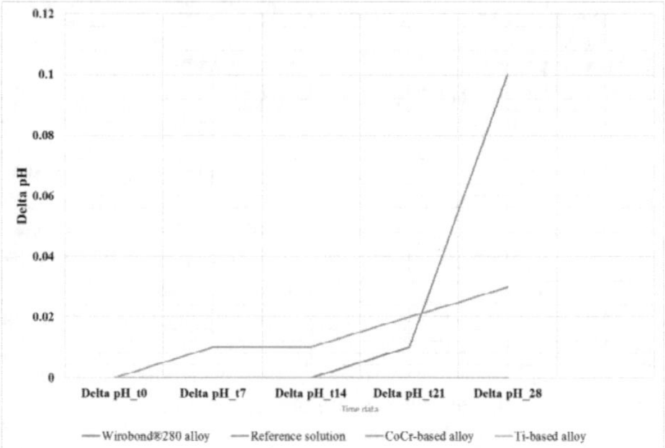

Figure 3: Variation of the pH value during 28 days of investigation

3.3 Corrosion resistance evaluation

As corrosion resistance regards, the samples have been surface-finished and then ultrasonically cleaned to remove any impurities and to avoid any possible contamination. The bottles used for the test have been disinfected. Each samples have been placed separately in the bottle and one bottle has been monitored containing only the solution. After a regular time, the weights of the samples have been measured and the pH values has been monitored. The alloys do not present any significant weight alteration after 28 days. During one week all tested materials maintain the initial pH value. No significant release of metallic ions has been detected even after 28 days, as reported in Figure 3. The result obtained has pointed out that the alloys conserve the condition requested: according to the Standard used for the test the deviation for the initial state could be only 1% and the experimentally widely fulfil this condition. The dissolution of the passive film developed on the surface of the alloy, with protective properties, has a very low rate and it is able to protect the alloy in such conditions, which simulates the oral cavity environment.

The morphological investigation pointed out that both experimentally metallic alloys are homogeneous as their structure concerns. They do not present on their surfaces inclusions, local depressions, in terms of dimples and cavities, which can favour the adhesion of the particles deriving from the biological environment. As their mechanical behaviour concerns, they are adequately resistant to withstand the mechanical solicitations and they do not present such a hardness that compromise their workability. It was observed that the alloys are corrosion resistant in a simulated human environment, since no important release of metallic ions has been detected for the period of 28 days. Based on the results obtained, the alloys show an adequate properties for biomedical purpose and the further step is to theoretically evaluate the possible parameters which can influence and can create the interaction between the biomaterial surfaces and the human body environment.

3.4 Analytical model description

In the case of the use of medical devices results very important to consider and to control the adhesion of different elements to the biomaterial surfaces. If adhesion occurs, this lead to the formation of a contagious layer on the medical devices and can conduct to the failure of the implant and diseases of the person. The adhesion is governed by different physical and chemical properties and is depends on the elements involved in the system: the substrate biomaterial and the biological environment. The hydrophobicity, hydrophilicity and the surface charge are the most important aspects in this context [14, 15]. The interaction energies governing the initial phase of the adhesion mechanism are mostly related to the attractive forces of Van der Waals (LW) type and the electrostatic double layer (EL) interactions, which can be either attractive or repulsive depending on the surface charge. These interaction energies can be generally described by the classical Derjaguin, Landau, Verwey, Overbeek theory (DLVO) [16], and can be used to evaluate the adhesion energy variations involved in the process as a function of the separation distance between the interacting surfaces. By comparing the different adhesion energy variation and by comparing them one can predict in order to compare predict if the adhesion is favorable or not for the elements combination and which elements has a positive or negative effect on the adhesion mechanism.

The influence of the chemical composition and of the surface topography on the adhesion of the various particles coming from the biological environment will be determined using the DLVO theory. The DLVO theory assumes that the interaction forces can be well approximated by the total energy of adhesion due to the interpenetration of the electrical double layer. The force F(h) among two units can be obtained using (1), considering a surface separation (h) and the free energy of the two units W(h) per unit area:

$$F\,(h) = 2\pi R_{eff} W\,(h) \qquad (1)$$

where the effective radius is given by (2)

$$R_{\text{eff}} = \frac{R_+ R_-}{R_+ + R_-} \quad (2)$$

Where R+ and R– are the radii of the two units involved in the considered process respectively.

Identifying the force between the materials, the interaction free energy is given by (3):

$$U(h) = \int_h^\infty F(h')\,dh' \quad (3)$$

DLVO theory assumes that the free energy per unit area can be well approximated by two additive contributions: Van der Waals and double layer interactions (4) :

$$W(h) = W_{\text{vdW}}(h) + W_{\text{dl}}(h) \quad (4)$$

Van der Waals forces are almost always present, and they result from the interactions of the rotating or fluctuating dipoles of the atoms and the molecules. This type of interaction can be modeled by (5)

$$W_{\text{vdW}}(h) = -\frac{H}{12\pi h^2} \quad (5)$$

where H is a constant and in most situations is positive. Typical values of H are 10^{-21} – 10^{-19} J. A slight decrease of H occur when the salt level of the solution increases. The model takes into consideration also the flatness of the substrate material (the surface roughness can reduce this interaction at smaller distances), important aspect for the considered application. In case of low salt level and for charged substrates the double layer interactions are important. The interaction free energy can be approximated by (6):

$$W_{\text{dl}}(h) = \frac{2\sigma_+\sigma_-}{\epsilon_0\epsilon\kappa}\exp(-\kappa h) \quad (6)$$

where σ+ and σ– are the surface charge densities per unit area of the two surfaces, ε0 is the permittivity of vacuum, ε the dielectric constant of water, and κ is the inverse Debye length. The last parameter is given by (7):

$$\kappa^{-1} = \left(\frac{k_B T \epsilon_0 \epsilon}{2q^2 N_A I}\right)^{1/2} = \frac{0.3\ \text{nm}}{\sqrt{I}} \quad (7)$$

where q is the elementary charge, NA is the Avogadro's number, I is the ionic strength, kB is the Boltzmann constant, and T is the absolute temperature. The second equality is approximatively valid for water at room temperature.

4. Conclusions and future directions

In this paper, we investigated two metallic alloys for biomedical applications in the human body. The morphological analysis evidenced that both metallic alloys are homogeneous with no any presence of inclusions or local depressions. In addition, they are sufficiently strong to survive the mechanical solicitations. From corrosion resistance point of view, the considered alloys fulfil the conditions required for the release of metal ions in the simulated biological solution. As future work, we will consider the experimentally achieved results and we will use them to theoretically investigate on the parameters of the surface features which control the adhesion mechanism between the metallic substrate and body environment. As any communication system, e.g., intra-, inter-body or body-coupled, requires reduced size antennas, e.g., printed, for communication between sensors/devices inside the body and external base station. The studied metals exhibit good electric properties as conductibility, etc. making them a good candidate for considering them as ground plane or radiative elements for example when flat printed antennas are employed. Using this approach, it would be possible to monitor the human vital functions by placing such devices in the different helpful positions on and near the human body with the possibility to communicate with each other with no any negative health effects for the person. The results of the study demonstrates that the using such alloys without any further coatings is possible. Such solution allows reduction of the cost and of the dimensions of the devices.

5. Acknowledgement

This research has been carried out within the European ManuNet Framework Programme "Load-bearing implants functionalized of superelastic alloys"- acronym ISA".

6. REFERENCES

[1] Ashby MF and Jones DR. Engineering Materials 1. An Introduction to their Properties and Applications, and 2. An Introduction to Microstructures, Processing and Design, Pergamon Press: London, 1980.

[2] R.Z. Valiev, R.K. Islamgaliev, and I.V. Alexandrov, Bulk Nanostructured Materials from Severe Plastic Deformation, Prog. Mater. Sci., 45 (2000) 103.

[3] Kurtz, S.M., Ong, K., Bozic, K.J., Greenwald, A.S., Prevalence of primary metal-on-metal bearings in the United State. In: AAOS 2011 Annual Meeting, American Academy of Orthopedic Surgeons, San Diego, CA, USA. 2011.

[4] Thomann, J. Uggowitzer, Wear- corrosion behaviour of biocompatible austhenitic stainless steel, Wear 239 (2000) 48-58.

[5] M. K. Lei, X.N. Zhu, In vitro corrosion resistance of plasma source ion nitrided austenitic stainless steels Biomaterials 2 641-647 2001.

[6] M. Browne, P.J. Gregson, Surface modification of titanium alloy implants, Biomaterials 15 894–898 1994. [41] Collings EW.,The physical metallurgy of titanium alloys, Ohio: ASM; 1984. pp. 321–354.

[7] Polmear IJ. Light alloys. In: Metallurgy of the light metals.Metallurgy and materials science series. London: Arnold; 1981. 239–278.

[8] M. Niinomi, Shape memory, Super Elastic and Low Young's Modulus Alloys, Biomaterials for Spinal Surgery, edited by Luigi Ambrosio and Elzabeth Tanner, Woodhead Publishing, 2012, ISBN: 9781845699864.

[9] S. Miyazaki, H.Y. Kim, H. Hosoda, "Development and characterization of Ni-free Ti-base shape memory and

superelastic alloys" Materials Science and Engineering: A, Volumes 438–440, 25 November 2006, Pages 18–24, doi:10.1016/j.msea.2006.02.054.

[10] Mitsuo Niinomi, "Recent research and development in titanium alloys for biomedical applications and healthcare goods", Science and Technology of Advanced Materials Volume 4, Issue 5, September 2003, Pages 445–454, doi:10.1016/j.stam.2003.09.002.

[11] Furuta, T., Kuramoto, S., Hwang, J., Nishino, K., & Saito, T. (2005). Elastic Deformation Behavior of Multi-Functional Ti–Nb–Ta–Zr–O Alloys. MATERIALS TRANSACTIONS, 46(12), 3001–3007. doi:10.2320/matertrans.46.3001.

[12] Li J, Song Y, Zhang S, Zhao C, Zhang F, Zhang X, et al., In vitro responses of human bone marrow stromal cells to a fluoridated hydroxyapatite coated biodegradable Mg–Zn alloy, Biomaterials 2010 31 5782–8.

[13] Kraus T, Fischerauer SF, Hanzi AC, Uggowitzer PJ, Loffler JF, Weinberg AM., Magnesium alloys for temporary implants in osteosynthesis: in vivo studies of their degradation and interaction with bone, Acta Biomater 2012 81230–8.Colloids Surf B Biointerfaces. 2009 Oct 1;73(1):1-9. doi: 10.1016/j.colsurfb.2009.04.030. Epub 2009 May 14.

[14] Derjaguin, B. (1939) A theory of interaction of particles in presence of electric double-layers and the stability of lyophobe colloids and disperse systems, Acta Phys. Chim., 10, 333-346.

[15] Derjaguin, B. and Landau, L. D. (1941) Theory of the stability of strongly charged lyophobic sols and of the adhesion of strongly charged particles in solutions of electrolytes Acta Phys. Chim., 14, 633-662.

[16] Bayoudh S., Othmane A, Mora L, Ben Ouada H., "Assessing bacterial adhesion using DLVO and XDLVO theories and the jet impingement technique", Colloids Surf B Biointerfaces. 2009 Oct 1;73(1):1-9. doi: 10.1016/j.colsurfb.2009.04.030.

Estimation and Tracking of Knee Angle Trajectory using Inertial Sensors and a Smartphone Application

Jaskaran Singh Grover
Systems Engineer, Intel Labs
457 Green Avenue
Amritsar, India 143001
009101835014824
groverjaskaran@gmail.com

Venkat Natarajan
Senior Research Scientist, Intel Labs
B-207 Brigade Palmsprings apts, JP Nagar 7th Ph. Bengaluru, India 560078
009108049530723
venkat.natarajan@intel.com

ABSTRACT

We demonstrate a practical solution to track the 2-D knee angle trajectory of a user in real-time using inertial sensors embedded in a wearable knee-band wirelessly coupled with a mobile device, by mathematically modeling the knee as a hinge joint. We show how the bias of gyroscopes can be automatically computed to eliminate manual calibration and combined with a computationally simple Kalman filter model for tracking the knee-angle on a power-constrained mobile device. Finally, we visualize the 2-D knee motion trajectory in real-time using an avatar on an Android phone.

Categories and Subject Descriptors

I.2.9 [**Artificial Intelligence**]: Robotics --- Kinematics and dynamics, Sensors.

General Terms

Algorithms, Measurement, Human Factors, Theory.

Keywords

Android, Flexion Angle, Motion Tracking, State Estimation

1. INTRODUCTION

Continuous motion trajectory tracking of the human body is an emerging frontier of research that has applications in healthcare, sports medicine, rehabilitation and yoga [1]. Advances in miniature and wearable inertial sensors have made it possible to quantify, track and characterize body motion in everyday ambulatory settings. In particular, gait analysis is used to treat individuals with medical conditions affecting their ability to walk [2]. In sports biomechanics applications, gait analysis improves limb movements of athletes to optimize and enhance their performance.

There are many advantages of using inertial sensors to track human motion compared to a camera-based optical marker system [3]. The miniature size of inertial measurement units (IMUs) enables measurement of full body kinematics by placing them at different joints and limbs, without causing hindrance to routine living. Inertial sensors do not require controlled laboratories like camera-based systems and can be deployed in real-world environments, thereby facilitating routine motion monitoring. Finally, inertial sensors consume low power which enables continuous motion tracking and monitoring for longer durations.

One promising application is continuous tracking of knee-joint motion and trajectory for rehabilitation. Consider a patient who is prescribed a sequence of exercise routines to rehabilitate a diseased knee. Therapy requires constant supervision by a physiotherapist which is not a practical long-term solution and is also infeasible in the home. However, using wearable inertial sensors coupled with a personal mobile device, the patient can track his motion in a home-setting, get continuous feedback on his performance, and regularly benchmark practice against a prescribed exercise regimen without therapist intervention. Such a system can also provide corrective feedback in real-time and can help restore ambulation for patients recovering from fractures and strokes [4].

2. PRIOR WORK

Prior studies have investigated knee angle tracking using inertial sensors assuming rigid-body motion for thigh and shank under conditions of 2-D and 3-D motion. Favre et. al. [5] integrated angular velocity data obtained from gyroscopes, and corrected the knee-angle estimation based on inclination data obtained from accelerometers gathered during rest or the constant-velocity motion period. Liu et. al [6] proposed a double sensor difference algorithm which requires two accelerometers mounted on a rigid board for one segment. Using data from accelerometers and magnetometers, they perform a 3D orientation study of the lower limb segments. Bennet et.al [7] proposed an extended Kalman filter model to calculate the walking distance and gait parameters by measuring knee angle using gyroscopes and accelerometer. Watanabe et. al. [8] use an error-state complimentary Kalman Filter to combine measurements from accelerometer and gyroscope to calculate an accurate estimate of the knee flexion angle. Sen Qiu et. al. [9] use triaxial accelerometer, magnetometer and angular rate sensors to calculate orientation quaternion of the shank to compute its 3D orientation while walking and transmit this data to an XBUS logger for data aggregation and communication to pc via Bluetooth. Liu et. al [10] propose a gait parameter measurement and a phase detection system. This approach uses data from thigh, shank and foot mounted inertial sensors and an 8 channel data recorder for logging and motion feature extraction algorithms on the PC. All these studies require a manual procedure for gyro bias estimation for input to the Kalman Filter. For example, Bennet et.al [7] used an average of gyroscope readings under static conditions to estimate the bias for an extended Kalman filter model to calculate knee motion parameters. Estimation of bias for a gyroscope is challenging, especially for low-cost sensors. Usually the user must manually calibrate the gyroscope by running static experiments, making the solution obtrusive and unattractive for routine use. Moreover, in a full-body motion-tracking wearable system, the user is

BODYNETS 2015, September 28-30, Sydney, Australia

DOI 10.4108/eai.28-9-2015.2261468

instrumented with many IMUs, each with a tri-axial gyro - rendering manual bias correction for multiple IMUs infeasible. A usable knee-trajectory tracking system must be autonomous and should not entail any manual calibration requirements. Prior art knee motion tracking solutions are not a good fit for ambulatory and automatic real-time trajectory tracking of body motion on a personal mobile device. They are either computationally demanding or require obtrusive user-calibration of the gyroscopes [9], or require a special data logger device with WiFi for data transmission and post-processing [9,10]. These data loggers and aggregators [9,10] are not viable for ambulatory tracking as they are cumbersome, unsuited for real-time feedback and expensive.

Although automated systems for real-time knee motion tracking using a personal mobile device are attractive, stringent constraints need to be met to realize a practical embodiment. These include a user-centric design with no manual calibration for IMU bias, a compact Kalman Filter implementation for power efficiency, real time data transmission and processing, efficient computation on a mobile device (e.g. phone or tablet), and rendering the knee motion trajectory in real-time on an avatar.

3. CURRENT WORK

In the present work, we demonstrate a user-friendly solution to track 2-D knee motion in real time on a mobile phone using IMUs. Our approach consists of: (i) a gyro bias estimation algorithm that is automatic and requires no user input whatsoever, (ii) a simplified Kalman filter for a mobile implementation that is ~2X faster than the conventional Kalman filter approach and (iii) an android application on a smartphone to track and visualize user's 2-D knee motion in real time. We can thus demonstrate a practical embodiment of a real-time knee-angle tracking solution on a mobile phone using wearable inertial sensors over Bluetooth Low-Energy.

3.1 Wearable System Configuration

For knee motion tracking, we capture the movements of the thigh and the shank independently, assuming each as a rigid body element. We instrument each segment, i.e. the thigh and shank, with an IMU as shown in Fig. 1.We also fabricated a conformal band that snugly wraps around the knee to resist motion artifacts. The band houses two IMU nodes as shown in Fig. 1. The thigh sensor node has a microcontroller and a battery that also supplies power to the shank sensor node, which is connected via a flexible interconnect. Each sensor node has an InvenSense® MPU-9150™ inertial measurement unit that consists of a tri-axis accelerometer, gyroscope, and magnetometer. We set the digital-output accelerometer to provide a full scale range of ±2g. We set the digital-output gyroscope to give a full scale range of ±250 deg/sec. Since we restrict the current study to 2D motion tracking, we do not use the magnetometer. The data from both IMUs is sampled by the microcontroller using the I2C interface every 50ms i.e. the sampling frequency is 20Hz. The microcontroller transmits the measured data to an android tablet/phone in real-time over a Bluetooth low energy (BLE) radio link. We evaluate our knee-motion tracking solution for walking, flexion and cycling activities performed by three users (N=3). We use a mechanical jig with a wooden robotic arm for ground-truth measurements and validation.

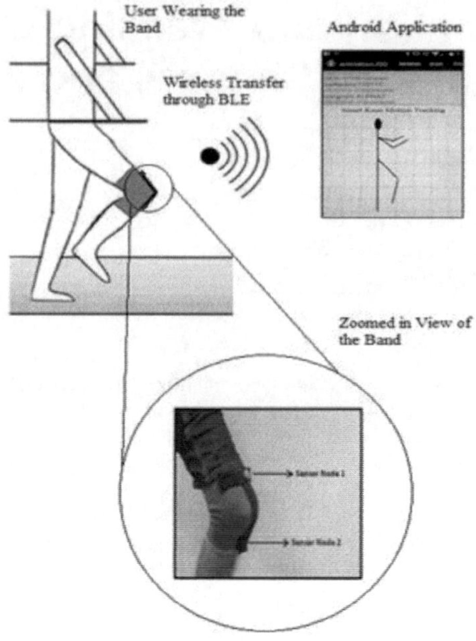

Figure 1 Wearable System Configuration

3.2 Mathematical Model for Knee Angle Estimation

To enable accurate tracking of knee motion, we must describe several parameters that relate to the instantaneous orientation of the user's limbs. An efficient mathematical model that relates these kinematic parameters to the measurements from the inertial sensors is the primary contribution of this work.

We use the instantaneous joint angles as motion parameters. Combining these angles with information about user's segment (thigh and shank) lengths, it is possible to extract rich gait parameters such as step length, stride length etc. In this study we limit our scope to estimating the joint angles using measurements from inertial sensors. However, this task is not trivial as inertial sensors are prone to random and systematic errors which are reflected in the parameters derived from them. Hence, our mathematical model must accurately predict joint angles in the face of this measurement uncertainty.

The random noise of the accelerometers contributes to jitter in the angle estimates and the non-zero bias of the gyroscope leads to integration drift which restricts accurate estimation of angles to barely few seconds. Thus, we need a sensor fusion algorithm, based on an underlying mathematical model for the system dynamics and measurement error, which can mitigate the measurement uncertainty of the accelerometer and gyroscope (i.e. noise and bias), and at the same time harness their complimentary properties (i.e. long-term and short-term stabilities respectively) to advantage so as to produce accurate motion parameters. One contribution of this work is a Kalman filter model for knee-angle estimation in our wearable system configuration. The dynamics of sensors are used to determine suitable process and measurement model equations that relate the unknown state (i.e. the angles) to the measurements.

Related studies have explicitly incorporated a bias variable as part of the Kalman state estimation vector because the gyro bias can be dynamically estimated as part of the Kalman filter. When this traditional approach to estimating bias is applied to the knee-angle estimation problem, it introduces a usability problem since gyro bias is calibrated manually a-priori. A second contribution of this work is a technique to dispense with the in-run bias estimation by pre-processing the sensor readings. This leads to a more efficient and usable implementation.

In the following section, we develop a conventional Kalman filter model for knee angle prediction for our wearable system configuration. We then describe a modified Kalman filter formulation which accurately estimates knee angle without including any bias terms in the state vector. This modified filter is simpler to implement, provides good accuracy and is well suited for a mobile implementation.

3.2.1 Conventional Kalman Filter Model with bias variable in state vector

We assume rigid-body motion of the knee and restrict this motion to the plane of walking only i.e. the sagittal plane. We ignore the coronal and transverse plane motions i.e. abduction/adduction and internal/external rotations since they do not significantly affect the knee flexion angle. We model the knee as a two-link revolute, i.e. a hinge joint with flexion as the dominant motion

Fig. 2 is a schematic representation of a user's lower limb and its stick model equivalent. In the figure, the line segment **A-S1-B-S2-C** is the geometric representation of the instantaneous orientation of the user's lower limb. The segments **A-S1-B** and **B-S2-C** represent the thigh and shank respectively. Point **A** represents the fixed hip joint and point **B** is the patella. Locations **S1** and **S2** represent the inertial sensor nodes on the thigh and shank respectively. Conceptually, segment **S1-B-S2** represents the wearable knee band embedded with the inertial sensors at coordinates **S1** and **S2**.

The instantaneous flexion angle between thigh and shank during dynamic motion is calculated as the internal angle $\angle ABC\,(180 - \theta_2)$ in Fig. 2. To estimate θ_2, we need to first obtain angles θ_1, which represents angle between thigh and vertical, and angle α, which represents angle between shank and vertical. The relationship between these angles can be geometrically deduced as below:

$$\theta_2 = \theta_1 - \alpha \tag{1}$$

In a conventional Kalman filter, the thigh angle θ_1 is first predicted using thigh gyroscope readings (location **S1**) and corrected by corresponding accelerometer readings. This approach enables one to take advantage of the long term stability of the accelerometer and the short term stability of the gyroscope.

A gyroscope sensor reports instantaneous angular rate of rotation about its sensitive axes. To find the absolute angle in any rotation, the gyro readings are integrated over the duration in which the rotation occurs from an initial reference orientation (2D motion). However, gyroscopes are affected by a bias error i.e. they give a non-zero rate even when stationary. As a result, the knee angles calculated using bias-prone gyroscope measurements are erroneous and increase linearly without bound, a phenomenon referred to as integration drift. Unless the bias is eliminated, the gyroscope cannot estimate knee angles accurately. Since the bias is a systematic error, a commonly used technique to estimate the bias is to sample several measurements over a stationary period and take their average.

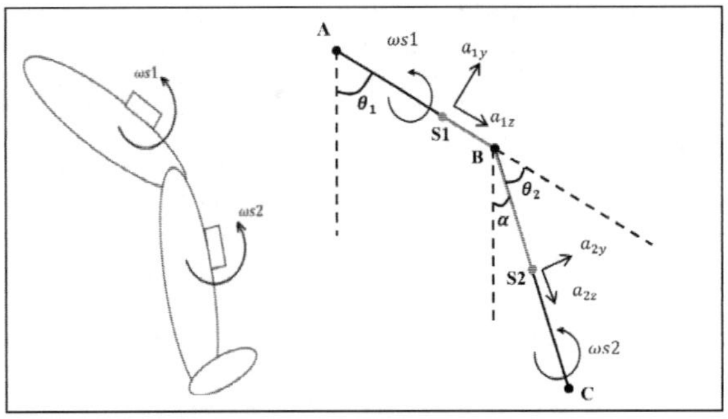

Figure 2 Schematic of the knee modeled as a hinge joint

Typically, the gyroscope is left stationary for a short duration, say a 20-second period (i.e. number of samples at 20Hz sampling = 400). The measured samples are averaged to give the bias value as in equation (2) below wherein ωs_i is the ith sample of angular rate measured by the gyroscope:

$$\beta = \frac{\sum_{i=1}^{N} \omega s_i}{N} \tag{2}$$

This static bias estimation process assumes that the bias remains constant over the run of the experiment and does not include drifts in bias caused due to thermal issues, random walk and other bias instability errors. The conventional Kalman Filter recursively corrects the gyro-bias errors by fusing it with an independent estimate of the knee angle derived from accelerometer measurements. The gyro bias is included as a separate variable in the conventional Kalman model and is updated at every time step of the experiment to account for major drifts. The Kalman filter recursively calculates the best estimate of the bias at each time step and computes the optimal trajectory that has the least error. The inclusion of the bias variable in the state vector is required for high accuracy trajectory tracking seen in many applications such as satellite, missile tracking. Since gyroscope bias values change from run to run, the bias estimation must be done every time before a user begins to track her motion i.e. before the knee angles can begin to be computed. This manual calibration is impractical for everyday use. In section 3.2.2, we demonstrate an automatic bias estimation algorithm that closes this gap.

3.2.1.1 Calculating thigh angle θ_1

We implement two Kalman Filters, one to estimate the thigh angle θ_1 and second, to estimate knee angle θ_2. We calculate θ_1 by fusing the thigh angles computed independently from gyroscope and accelerometer sensors. In Fig. 2, the gyro mounted in location **S1** provides angular rate $\omega s1$ and measures the rotation of the thigh about hip joint **A**. The sensitive axis of the gyro at location **S1** is the one that is perpendicular to the plane of rotation i.e. its x axis. By convention we assume counterclockwise rotations as positive. The gyroscope measured angular rate, $\omega s1$ can be written as a sum of the true angular rate of the thigh $\omega p1$ and a bias value specific to the gyroscope i.e. β_1 (3).

$$\omega s1 = \omega p1 + \beta_1 \tag{3}$$

We integrate $\omega p1$ to calculate θ_1 as in (4):

$$\theta_1 = \int \omega p1 \, dt \tag{4}$$

Substituting the value of $\omega p1$ from (3) in (4):

$$\theta_1 = \int (\omega s1 - \beta_1) dt \tag{5}$$

We implement integration procedure (5) in a discrete-time Kalman Filter [19-20] described later in equations (9-10). To obtain an independent estimate of thigh angle θ_1, we use the accelerometer as an inclinometer/tilt sensor [11]. Note that the accelerometer can be used as a tilt sensor only under the assumption of slow physical motion of the associated limb i.e. when the net magnitude of motion contributed acceleration is negligible. Referring to Fig. 2, note that a_{1y} and a_{1z} are the normal and tangential accelerations (with reference to thigh) reported by the accelerometer at location **S1**. These readings are relative to the sensor frame, i.e. the *local* reference frame that supports the inertial sensor. We calculate the angle $\theta_{1\,acc}$, defined as the thigh angle using an inverse tangent function (6):

$$\theta_{1_{acc}} = tan^{-1}\frac{a_{1y}}{a_{1z}} \tag{6}$$

The thigh angle $\theta_{1\,acc}$ is prone to noise because of the susceptibility of the accelerometer to impact and jitter. To eliminate this noise, we fuse the knee angle estimate from the accelerometer with that of the gyroscope (5) via a Kalman Filter. Consider the generalized state space representation of the Kalman Filter (7):

$$\boldsymbol{x_{k+1}} = A\boldsymbol{x_k} + B\boldsymbol{u_k} + w_k$$

$$\boldsymbol{z_k} = H\boldsymbol{x_k} + v_k \tag{7}$$

Wherein,

$\boldsymbol{x_k}$	is the state vector at time instant k
$\boldsymbol{u_k}$	is an input control vector
w_k	is the process noise
A	is the state transition matrix
B	is the input control matrix
$\boldsymbol{z_k}$	is the observation made at time instant k
H	is the measurement/observation matrix
v_k	is additive measurement noise

The Kalman Filter assumes that the process noise and measurement noise random processes w_k and v_k are uncorrelated, white-noise processes with covariance matrices Q and R. We can write:

$$E(w_k {w_k}^T) = \delta_{ij} Q$$

$$E(v_k {v_k}^T) = \delta_{ij} R$$

$$E(w_k {v_k}^T) = 0$$

$$E(v_k {w_k}^T) = 0 \tag{8}$$

where E is the expectation operator and δ is the Kronecker Dirac Delta Function $\delta_{ij} = 1$ when $i = j$, else $\delta_{ij} = 0$. Q is the process-noise covariance matrix and R is the measurement noise covariance matrix. The algorithm of the generalized Kalman Filter is shown in Fig. 3 [12].

We formulate the discrete time version of equations (3-5) that relate thigh angles θ_1, thigh gyroscope angular rate $\omega s1$ and bias β_1 below in equation (9). The time steps $k+1$ and k refer to the current and previous values of time step where $k \in \mathbb{N}$:

$$\theta_{1_{k+1}} = \theta_{1_k} + (\omega s1 - \beta_1)dt$$

$$\beta_{1_{k+1}} = \beta_{1_k} \tag{9}$$

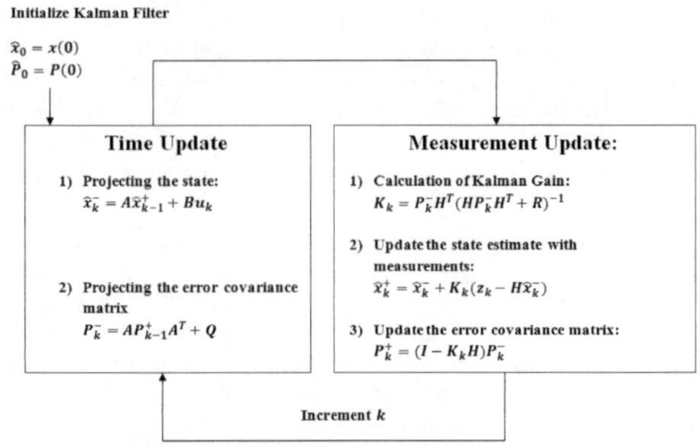

Figure 3 Kalman Filter algorithm

We rewrite above equations as a state space representation (10):

$$\begin{bmatrix}\theta_1\\ \beta_1\end{bmatrix}_{k+1} = \begin{bmatrix}1 & -dt\\ 0 & 1\end{bmatrix}\begin{bmatrix}\theta_1\\ \beta_1\end{bmatrix}_k + \begin{bmatrix}dt & 0\\ 0 & 0\end{bmatrix}\begin{bmatrix}\omega s1\\ 0\end{bmatrix}_k \tag{10}$$

This (eq. 10) defines the process model for the Kalman Filter to determine θ_1. Separately, we derive a *measurement* model (see eq. 7) for the knee angle $\theta_{1\,acc}$ using the accelerometer measurements. Based on (6), we can write:

$$z = \theta_{1_{acc}} = tan^{-1}\frac{a_{1y}}{a_{1z}} \tag{11}$$

Formulating equation (11) using the generic measurement model in (7), we find that:

- The measurement vector $z = \theta_{1\,acc}$
- The measurement/observation matrix $H = [1\ 0]$ such that $H * \boldsymbol{x} = [1\ 0] * \begin{bmatrix}\theta_1\\ \beta_1\end{bmatrix} = \theta_1$

We initialize *error covariance matrix* (12) $P_0 = L * I_2$ where I_2 the 2 x 2 identity matrix and L is a large number (1000 for our case). We choose this value empirically so that the Kalman filter iterations start with a high measurement uncertainty and converge towards reduced uncertainty as P gets recursively updated by the algorithm.

$$P = \begin{bmatrix}1000 & 0\\ 0 & 1000\end{bmatrix} \tag{12}$$

The off-diagonal terms of the error covariance matrix are zero as the state variables θ_1 and β_1 are uncorrelated. Likewise, *the process noise covariance matrix* Q (13) is a 2 x 2 block diagonal matrix [12-13]:

$$Q = \begin{bmatrix}\sigma_\theta & 0\\ 0 & \sigma_\beta\end{bmatrix} = \begin{bmatrix}10^{-4} & 0\\ 0 & 10^{-6}\end{bmatrix} \tag{13}$$

The parameters σ_θ and σ_β are r.m.s noise parameters of angle estimate using gyroscope and are empirically determined based on the noise susceptibility of θ on gyroscope angular rates. We selected and tuned these parameters for least error in our models [12-13]. Likewise, the *measurement noise covariance matrix* R in the generalized Kalman Filter in Fig. 3 represents the root mean square (r.m.s) of the noise in angles predicted using the accelerometer. Based on the measurement model, the R matrix contains a single element σ_r. Its value is the variance of the angles calculated using raw accelerometer measurements which, in our experiments was found to be to be 10^{-3}.

3.2.1.2 Calculating knee angle θ_2

We likewise estimate θ_2 by fusing the gyroscope and accelerometer readings via a Kalman Filter. Let $\omega s2$ be the angular rate reported by the gyroscope on the shank at location **S2.** In this case, the gyro at location **S2** reports the sum of the actual angular rates of the shank $\omega p2$ and thigh $\omega p1$. Furthermore, the shank gyro is corrupted by its own bias value β_2. Thus, we can express the sensor reported angular rate as (14):

$$\omega s2 = \omega p1 + \omega p2 + \beta_2 \qquad (14)$$

We integrate $\omega p2$ to calculate θ_2 as in (15):

$$\theta_2 = \int(\omega p2)dt \qquad (15)$$

$$\theta_2 = \int(\omega s2 - \omega p1 - \beta_2)\, dt \qquad (16)$$

Substituting the value of $\omega p1$ from (3) in (16) we have (17):

$$\theta_2 = \int(\omega s2 - \omega s1 - \beta_2 + \beta_1)dt \qquad (17)$$

The discrete time implementation of (17) is expressed as:

$$\theta_{2_{k+1}} = \theta_{2_k} + (\omega s2 - \omega s1 + \beta_1 - \beta_2)_k\, dt \qquad (18)$$

$$\beta_{2_{k+1}} = \beta_{2_k} \qquad (19)$$

We cast equation (19) in the state-space representation to comply with the Kalman filter model (7) below:

$$\begin{bmatrix}\theta_2\\ \beta_2\end{bmatrix}_{k+1} = \begin{bmatrix}1 & -dt\\ 0 & 1\end{bmatrix}\begin{bmatrix}\theta_2\\ \beta_2\end{bmatrix}_k + \begin{bmatrix}dt & 0\\ 0 & 0\end{bmatrix}\begin{bmatrix}(\omega s2 - \omega s1 + \beta_1)\\ 0\end{bmatrix}_k \qquad (20)$$

This completes the process model for θ_2. We now derive the *measurement model* for θ_2. We do not have a direct estimate of θ_2 from the accelerometer at location **S2** because θ_2 does not represent the tilt of the shank with respect to the vertical. The tilt of the shank with the vertical is denoted as α (Fig. 2) and is obtained in equation (21) from accelerometer readings a_{2y} and a_{2z} at location **S2** which represent normal and tangential accelerations (with reference to shank).

$$\alpha = tan^{-1}\frac{a_{2y}}{a_{2z}} \qquad (21)$$

Eq. 22 shows the relation between angles θ_1, θ_2 and α. We obtain angle θ_2 based on the readings of accelerometer at locations **S1** (i.e. θ_1) and **S2** (i.e. α).

$$\theta_{2acc} = \theta_{1acc} - \alpha_{acc} = tan^{-1}\frac{a_{1y}}{a_{1z}} - tan^{-1}\frac{a_{2y}}{a_{2z}} \qquad (22)$$

Thus, we obtain an independent estimate of angle θ_2 using θ_1 and α from the accelerometer. Referring to the Kalman Filter equation (7), we can see that:

- The measurement vector is $z = \theta_{2acc}$
- The measurement/observation matrix is $H = [1\ 0]$ such that $H * \boldsymbol{x} = [1\ 0] * \begin{bmatrix}\theta_2\\ \beta_2\end{bmatrix} = \theta_2$

The error covariance matrix, the process covariance matrix and measurement covariance matrix are initialized with the same values as in (12) and (13).

The conventional Kalman filter described above assumes that the bias is known a-priori, and uses it within the Kalman algorithm. This estimation procedure has the disadvantage of being user-unfriendly because it requires a manual calibration to determine the bias prior to use in the wearable system. In the next section, we overcome this limitation.

3.2.2 Kalman filter with automatic de-biasing

We formulate an alternate Kalman filter model in which we remove the gyro-bias variable from the state vector in Kalman filter. We automatically compute the gyro bias and subtract this estimate from the gyroscope measurements prior to using them in the Kalman filter. This approach reduces the dimension and computational complexity of Kalman Filter implementation and is a better fit for continuous trajectory tracking using constrained battery-powered device such as a phone. Despite the pre-processing overhead for de-biasing along with a simplified Kalman filter, the overall computational complexity is less than the conventional Kalman method, as we will demonstrate later.

Fig. 4 shows our automatic gyro bias estimation algorithm. It assumes that the bias is dominated by a static component (constant term) and variations due to drift and random walk errors are relatively small. This assumption would be appropriate in practice for non-critical daily tracking applications. We then approximate the bias using the DC component (constant term) of the Fourier transform of the gyroscope measurement under arbitrary activity. When the user initiates an activity, our algorithm uses the first 1000 gyroscope samples to estimate the bias. Every sample of the angular rates acquired after this window of 1000 samples is used for angle estimation in the Kalman filter. For longer duration activities, we envision that the bias may need to be automatically re-estimated periodically to compensate for any drift errors. Since the bias is computed in real time, we de-bias the gyro signal by subtracting the DC component from the raw measurements acquired subsequently. We have empirically validated our assumption on the nature of bias by demonstrating that our algorithm is able to predict knee angle trajectories accurately.

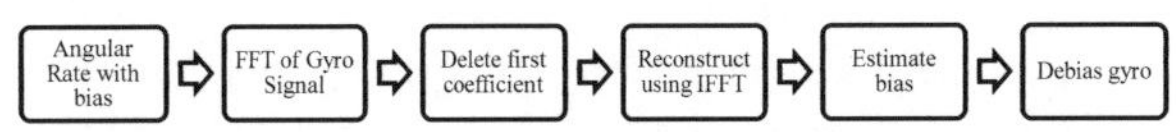

Figure 4 FFT based automatic gyroscope de-biasing algorithm

Using the de-biased gyroscope signal, we then formulate a Kalman filter that directly uses a clean gyro signal as input without any bias term in the state vector. The dimension of the state vector is now unity instead of two (in a conventional model), and the corresponding state transition, error covariance and process noise covariance matrices are of size 1x1 instead 2x2. The state estimation equations for the thigh angle are as follows:

$$\theta_{1k+1} = \theta_{1k} + \omega p1\, dt$$

$$z = \theta_{1acc} \qquad (23)$$

In this model, the state vector is $x = \theta_{1k}$, the state transition matrix is $A = 1$, the control input matrix is $B = dt$, the control input vector is $u = \omega p1$, the measurement vector is $z = \theta_{1acc}$ and the measurement/observation matrix is $H = 1$. Similarly, we formulate the shank angle model as follows:

$$\theta_{2_{k+1}} = \theta_{2_k} + (\omega p2 - \omega p1)_k dt$$

$$z = \theta_2 = \theta_{1acc} - \alpha_{acc} \qquad (24)$$

The state transition matrix A, the control input matrix B and the measurement matrix H are same as for θ_1 above. The state vector is $x = \theta_{2_k}$, the control input vector is $u = \omega p2 - \omega p1$ and the measurement vector is $z = \theta_2$.

This simplified Kalman Filter works for the auto de-biasing scheme because the actual bias value is always close to the in-run bias. Since the in-run bias is not updated at every time step in this approach (in contrast to the conventional Kalman Filter formulation, see section 3.2.1), the computed trajectory may not be optimal (in the Kalman sense) and will depend on the extent to which the in-run bias diverges from the actual bias. This approach, however, has that additional advantage that it allows periodic re-computation of the current in-run bias in real-time to correct drifts. If we were to instead use the static bias estimate (eq. 2) in this simplified Kalman filter formulation, the resultant angle estimate would progressively drift from reality. Furthermore, the use of static bias is impractical because the bias value cannot be dynamically updated on-the-fly in the middle of an activity.

4. RESULTS AND DISCUSSIONS

We first examine whether the bias can be approximated by the DC component of the Fourier transform of real-time gyroscope measurements for a user-friendly motion tracking design. Next, we assess the efficacy of our simplified Kalman filter model in comparison to the conventional Kalman filter for walking, flexion and cycling activities. Finally, we demonstrate automatic knee trajectory tracking using an avatar on a mobile phone use our modified Kalman filter algorithm.

To determine if our FFT algorithm is effective for gyro-bias estimation, we use static calibration bias as a reference (eq. 2). To assess whether the bias value is sensitive to activity type, we compute the bias for the three activities. To determine the right sampling window size for a reliable and consistent bias estimate, we also assessed the behavior of bias for different window sizes. In Fig. 5, the x-axis is the sample window size and the y-axis is the predicted bias estimate using the FFT method proposed in Section 3.2.2. The orange, blue and purple curves indicate FFT estimated bias values for flexion, walking and cycling activities. The static bias estimated using the standard averaging method is ~0.81deg/s which is indicated by green horizontal line in Fig. 5.

For a sampling window size greater than ~1000 samples, the bias estimate remains practically unchanged across the three activities. The bias for a 1000 sample window is within 5% of the static bias value. This result suggests that a good enough estimate of the bias can be calculated in real-time paving the way to a much improved user experience (since no manual calibration is required). At 20Hz sampling frequency, the 1000 sample window size corresponds to 50 seconds of measurement time, implying that the trajectory of the user should be tracked continuously 50s after the activity is initiated to automatically ascertain the gyro-bias. We now evaluate the effectiveness of our simplified Kalman filter formulation by comparing against the conventional Kalman filter model as a baseline. Fig. 6 shows the results of predicted knee angle trajectories for cycling, flexion and walking activities for a user. The graphs in Fig. 6 show the flexion knee angle i.e. $(180 - \theta_2$ in Fig. 3) against time for the simplified Kalman filter as well as for the convention Kalman filter. The static gyro bias value for the conventional model (refer to eq. 2) are 0.83 deg/s and -0.5 deg/s for the thigh and shank IMUs respectively.

The bias values automatically estimated by the FFT algorithm are 0.94 deg/s and -0.55 deg/s. For flexion and cycling, the angle predicted by our modified Kalman filter has a maximum- error of just 1.8 degrees relative to the conventional Kalman filter. For walking, the maximum error for the predicted angle is 3.7 deg. For vigorous activities, we expect this error to increase due to higher motion artifact in dynamic movements and increased sensor movement relative to the thigh/shank. For this set of experiments, our modified Kalman Filter model predicts the knee angle trajectory well and is an especially good fit for full-body tracking solutions that use multiple gyroscopes each needing calibration for bias.

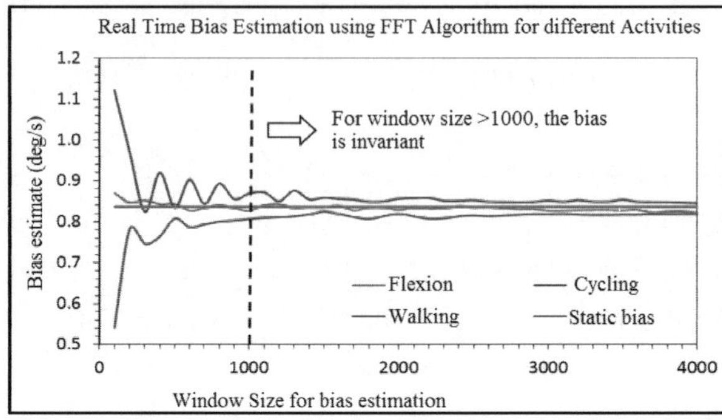

Figure 5 Sensitivity of estimated bias to sample window size

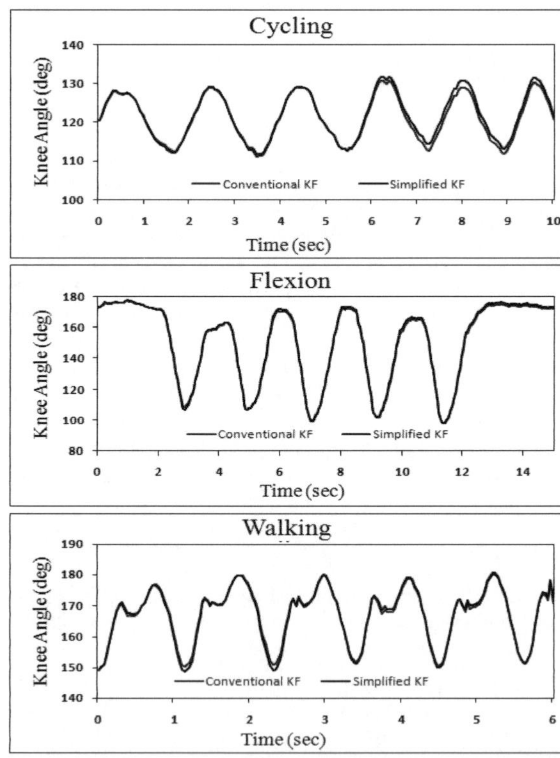

Figure 6 Knee angle profiles for cycling, flexion and walking

To quantify the computational benefits of our simplified Kalman filter model, we estimated the execution time in MATLAB (Table 1) and found that the simplified model runs ~2X faster than the conventional model without any significant loss of accuracy even when taking into consideration the de-biasing logic in the simplified Kalman filter algorithm. This demonstrates how knee angle can be tracked in real-time without any user calibration while simultaneously reducing computational load, enhancing battery life on a mobile device.

Table 1 Comparison of Conventional and Simplified KF models

Parameter	Conventional Kalman Filter	Our Simplified Model
Process Model	$\begin{bmatrix}\theta_1\\ \beta_1\end{bmatrix}_{k+1} = \begin{bmatrix}1 & -dt\\ 0 & 1\end{bmatrix}\begin{bmatrix}\theta_1\\ \beta_1\end{bmatrix}_k + \begin{bmatrix}dt & 0\\ 0 & 0\end{bmatrix}\begin{bmatrix}\omega s1\\ 0\end{bmatrix}_k$	$\theta_{k+1} = \theta_k + \omega dt$
Measurement Model	$z = \theta_{1acc}$ $H = [1\ 0]$	$z = \theta_{1acc}$ $H = 1$
State Vector Dimensions	2	1
Run time in MATLAB	2X	1X

Finally, we demonstrate automatic knee trajectory visualization via an avatar animation on a mobile-phone. Using the motion parameters estimated by the state estimation algorithm, we created an animation of the lower limb of the user in the sagittal plane. Figure 8 shows an avatar that tracks the knee-angle in real-time. To ensure a smooth rendering of the user's motion, the avatar gets updated every 50ms on the mobile phone.

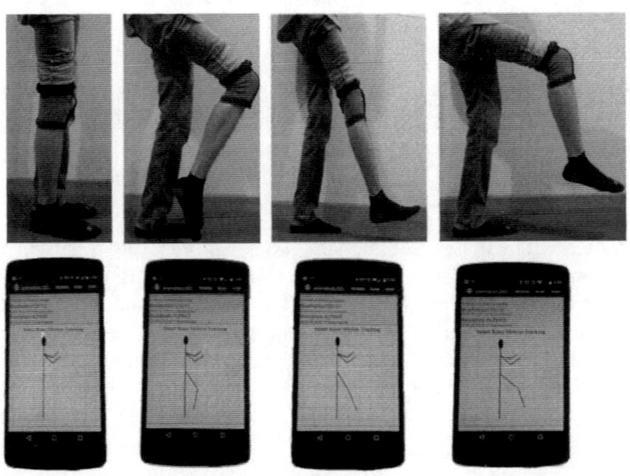

Figure 5 Snapshots of a user's leg and simultaneous motion tracking by our application.

This work has the following limitations: Our mathematical model is based on the assumption that the knee can be modeled as a perfect hinge joint, which, in reality, is not the case. Further, this model assumes that the anatomical axes and the axes of the sensor frame are perfectly aligned, which is not true. We have not quantified the errors resulting from such approximations. This requires the use of an optoelectronic camera based system as an independent ground truth to quantify the accuracy of our algorithms and calibration to account for the misalignment of sensor and anatomical axes. Further, this approach does not readily scale to other joints such as the shoulder because of these assumptions. We have not evaluated the suitability our technique for noisy signals under highly dynamic conditions such as those in sports monitoring applications.

5. CONCLUSIONS

We have demonstrated a practical embodiment of a real-time knee motion tracking solution on a phone using a smart wearable knee band instrumented inertial sensors. Our approach offers a user friendly alternative to a complex camera based motion tracking system. We achieve this by combining an automatic gyro de-biasing technique with a computationally efficient Kalman Filter algorithm.

6. ACKNOWLEDGEMENTS

The authors would like to thank Kumar Ranganathan, Manager and Principal Engineer, Intel Labs for his extensive support and guidance on the project.

7. REFERENCES

[1] Baker, Richard. "Journal of NeuroEngineering and Rehabilitation." *Journal of NeuroEngineering and Rehabilitation2006* 3, no. 4 (2005).

[2] Vito, L. D., Octavian Postolache, and Sergio Rapuano. "Measurements and sensors for motion tracking in motor rehabilitation." *Instrumentation & Measurement Magazine, IEEE* 17, no. 3 (2014): 30-38.

[3] Mayagoitia, Ruth E., Anand V. Nene, and Peter H. Veltink. "Accelerometer and rate gyroscope measurement of kinematics: an inexpensive alternative to optical motion analysis systems." *Journal of biomechanics* 35, no. 4 (2002): 537-542.

[4] Casamassima, Filippo, Alberto Ferrari, Bojan Milosevic, Pieter Ginis, Elisabetta Farella, and Laura Rocchi. "A Wearable System for Gait Training in Subjects with Parkinson's Disease." *Sensors* 14, no. 4 (2014): 6229-6246.

[5] Favre, J., R. Aissaoui, B. M. Jolles, O. Siegrist, Ja De Guise, and K. Aminian. "3d joint rotation measurement using mems inertial sensors: Application to the knee joint." *Valenciennes, France: ISB-3D* (2006).

[6] Kun, Liu, Yoshio Inoue, Kyoko Shibata, and Cao Enguo. "Ambulatory estimation of knee-joint kinematics in anatomical coordinate system using accelerometers and magnetometers." *Biomedical Engineering, IEEE Transactions on* 58, no. 2 (2011): 435-442.

[7] Bennett, Terrell, Roozbeh Jafari, and Nicholas Gans. "An extended kalman filter to estimate human gait parameters and walking distance." In *American Control Conference (ACC), 2013*, pp. 752-757. IEEE, 2013.

[8] Watanabe, Takashi, Hiroki Saito, Eri Koike, and Kazuki Nitta. "A preliminary test of measurement of joint angles and stride length with wireless inertial sensors for wearable gait evaluation system." *Computational intelligence and neuroscience* 2011 (2011): 6.

[9] Qiu, Sen, Yu Yang, Jijian Hou, Ran Ji, Huosheng Hu, and Zhelong Wang. "Ambulatory estimation of 3D walking trajectory and knee joint angle using MARG Sensors." In *Innovative Computing Technology (INTECH), 2014 Fourth International Conference on*, pp. 191-196. IEEE, 2014.

[10] Liu, Tao, Yoshio Inoue, and Kyoko Shibata. "Development of a wearable sensor system for quantitative gait analysis." *Measurement* 42, no. 7 (2009): 978-988.

[11] Pedley, M. "Tilt Sensing Using a Three-Axis Accelerometer, Freescale Semiconductor Application Note,(2013), n." *AN3461, rev* 5.

[12] http://cs.brown.edu/stc/education/course95-96/Kalman-Filters/kalman.html

Correlations between Inertial Body Sensor Measures and Clinical Measures in Multiple Sclerosis

Jiaqi Gong
Department of Electrical and Computer Engineering
Center for Wireless Health
University of Virginia
Charlottesville, VA, USA
jgong@virginia.edu

Matthew M. Engelhard
Department of Systems and Information Engineering
Center for Wireless Health
University of Virginia
Charlottesville, VA, USA
mme@virginia.edu

Myla D. Goldman
Department of Neurology
James Q. Miller MS Clinic
Center for Wireless Health
University of Virginia
Charlottesville, VA, USA
mdg3n@virginia.edu

John Lach
Department of Electrical and Computer Engineering
Center for Wireless Health
University of Virginia
Charlottesville, VA, USA
jlach@virginia.edu

ABSTRACT

Gait assessment using inertial body sensors is becoming popular as an outcome measure in multiple sclerosis (MS) research, supplementing clinical observations and patient-reported outcomes with precise, objective measures. Although numerous research reports have demonstrated the performance of inertial measures in distinguishing healthy controls and MS subjects, the relationship between these measures and the impact of MS on gait impairment remains poorly understood. In contrast, although clinical evaluation has limited variability in scores, it is meaningful and interpretable for clinicians.

Therefore, this paper investigates correlations between two inertial measures and three clinical measures of walking ability. The clinical measures are the MS Walking Scale (MSWS-12), the Expanded Disability Status Scale (EDSS), and the six minute walk (6MW) distance. The inertial measures are the double stance time to single stance time ratio (DST/SST) and the causality index, both of which have been proven effective in MS gait assessment in previous work.

28 MS subjects and 13 healthy controls were recruited from an MS outpatient clinic. Most correlations among measures were strong and significant. Experimental results suggested that combining all five measures may improve separability performance for tracking MS disease progression.

Categories and Subject Descriptors

G.3 [**Mathematics of Computing**]: Probability and Statistics–*correlation and regression analysis.*

General Terms

Algorithms, Measure, Performance, Experimentation, Human Factors, Theory, Verification

Keywords

12-item Multiple Sclerosis Walking Scale, 6-minute Walk, Inertial Body Sensors, Separability Enhancement

1. INTRODUCTION

Gait impairment is a common marker of disease progression in persons with multiple sclerosis (MS). MS is a chronic autoimmune disorder of the central nervous system (CNS) that results in neurologic impairment and functional disability over time, leading to decreased mobility, independence and quality of life. Gait performance is, therefore, an important outcome to assess severity of disease, disease progression, and therapeutic efficacy.

There are many measures of gait impairment that have been used in research and clinical practice. They can be divided into two groups: clinical measures and inertial measures from body sensors.

Clinical measures include assessments completed by patients and assessments completed by physicians or other care providers. Several clinical measures are routinely used to assess the impact of MS on mobility. These measures have been developed using standard methods of test construction and validated in community and hospital-residing samples of individuals with MS. For instance, the Expanded Disability Status Scale (EDSS) [1] is a physician-assessed composite score based on neurological examination of walking ability along with seven functional systems: pyramidal, cerebellar, brainstem, sensory, vision, bowel and bladder, and cognitive. The 12-item Multiple Sclerosis Walking Scale (MSWS-12) [2] is a patient-reported outcome questionnaire developed by a panel of experts that is used to assess the impact of MS on walking. Otherwise, measures from timed walk tests (25-ft or 6-min walk tests) such as gait speed, and distance walked are also widely used in MS clinics and research.

BODYNETS 2015, September 28-30, Sydney, Australia

DOI 10.4108/eai.28-9-2015.2261504

Gait measures using inertial body sensors are gaining popularity in MS research. The measures drawn from the walk tests and movement analysis include gait cycles and interactions among body parts. Although several studies have demonstrated the performance of inertial measures in distinguishing between healthy controls and MS subjects, the relationship between inertial measures and the impact of MS on gait impairment is not well understood. In contrast, although measures from clinical evaluation have limited variability in scores, their meaning is well-known to care providers, making them easy to interpret; relationships between them have been extensively studied; and they are known to be effective outcome measures when evaluating treatment or monitoring disease progression.

To understand the relationship between gait measures from inertial body sensors and the impact of MS on gait impairment, this paper further investigated the most recent and best validated measures of walking performance. Experimental results from 28 MS subjects recruited from a MS outpatient clinic and 13 healthy controls show separability enhancement in MS and illustrate the efficacy of the proposed analysis.

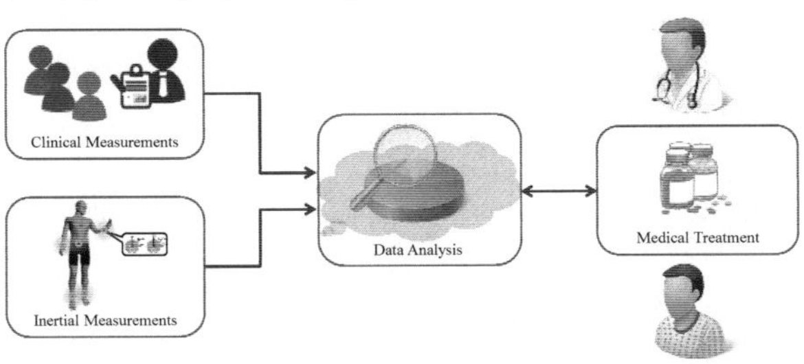

Figure 1. This paper further investigated the correlations between clinical measures including the 12-item Multiple Sclerosis Walking Scale (MSWS-12), Expanded Disability Status Scale (EDSS), and distance walked during 6MW, and two gait measures drawn from inertial body sensor data including the ratio between double stance time and single stance time (DST/SST) and the causality index, providing enhanced separability for tracking MS disease progression.

2. RELATED WORK

2.1 Clinical Measures

Validation of measures in clinics has been investigated in numerous studies. The EDSS has long been a popular outcome for validation, but research demonstrated that it was not sensitive to clinical change over a 9-month follow-up period, it was unresponsive to disease progression in moderate to severe disability, and it had limited variability in scores. Therefore, recently, another measure, MSWS-12, has gained popularity as an outcome measure partly based on its correlation to other objective measures.

McGuigan et.al [3] was the first attempt to validate the MSWS-12. Results from 149 patients illustrated that the psychometric properties of the MSWS-12 were excellent, and in particular the scale is responsive to change. Motl et al. [4] investigated the MSWS-12 scores of 133 participants based on confirmatory factor analysis and the experimental results demonstrated strong evidence of internal consistency. Motl et al. [5] further validated the MSWS-12 based on correlation with a physiological marker, the oxygen cost of walking. Pilutti et.al [6] also conducted further validation of the MSWS-12 using correlation analysis with spatiotemporal gait parameters such as gait speed, cadence, step length, and step time from 6MW. Sidovar et.al [7] mapped the MSWS-12 to the EuroQol 5-dimension (EQ-5D) in North American MS patients and proved the MSWS-12 scores also have strong correlation with EQ-5D scores.

Apparently, as described in [4], the MSWS-12 is the most recent and best validated patient-reported outcome for the effect of MS on walking ability, and plenty of experimental results from different research groups had proved it. However, the MSWS-12 appears to have variable sensitivity across the MS walking disability spectrum The traditional objective measures in clinics were based on manual measures, for instance, the patients followed instructions to walk in the clinic hallway, and then the doctors recorded the distance walked during each specified period and the total distance. We evaluated the characteristics of the 6MW in MS subjects and healthy controls and proved the strong correlation between objective measures from 6MW and subjective measures of physical impairment, including the MSWS-12 [10].

2.2 Inertial Measures from Body Sensors

In recent years, gait assessment using inertial body sensors is gaining more and more attention from MS researchers, because the sensors provide more precise and accurate measures than human observation and manual measures. Many methods for gait assessment based on inertial body sensors using gait cycle detection [8], gait pattern recognition [9], etc., had been reported in the literature. Often temporal gait features based on gait phase decomposition are used. These include gait speed [10, 11], stride length [12], joint angles [13], swing time [14], double stance time, single stance time [15] or other derived parameters [16].

Most recently, we proposed another novel view of the gait assessment based on using a causal model to describe and estimate the interactions among body parts [17]. Compared to other objective measures, this estimated representation of interactions among body parts, named as Causality Index, provides the best separability performance between the healthy controls and MS patients. This paper is the first attempt to validate the Causality Index based on the correlations with other measures, including EDSS, MSWS-12, gait speed, and other quantitative parameters from gait analysis.

Therefore, the main contributions of this paper are:

- A complementary validation of clinical measures including EDSS, MSWS-12 and distance walked during 6MW based on correlations with gait measures using inertial body sensors including the ratio between double stance time and single stance time (DST/SST) and the causality index.
- First attempt to validate the causality index drawn from inertial body sensors with other measures.
- Separability enhancement between MS subjects and healthy controls based on combined clinical and inertial measures.

Current measures for MS disease state assessment are generally based on clinical measures (e.g. MSWS-12, gait speed) separately. Based on the complementary results of this paper, we can say that combining the measures from clinical measures and inertial measures from body sensors has the potential to enhance the assessment of MS disease severity and progression.

3. METHODS

3.1 Participants

Participants (N = 41) were recruited from a MS outpatient clinic via telephone and e-mail messages from a member of the research team. This was followed by a screening for inclusion criteria that included a neurologist-confirmed diagnosis of MS; relapse free during the previous 30 days, ambulatory with minimal assistance, age between 18 and 65 years, and absence of risk-factors for undertaking strenuous physical activity (e.g., cardiovascular diseases, diabetes, hyperlipidemia, and hypertension). There were 60 individuals who underwent screening and 41 of those individuals satisfied inclusion criteria and volunteered for participation. All the measures including EDSS, MSWS-12 and 6MW data including gait speed, distance walked, and data from inertial body sensors were collected during a single clinic visit.

3.2 6MW Data Collection

The 6MW procedure followed Goldman's previous research [10]. We have left the details of this protocol to Appendix 1 of reference [10]. All the participants were assisted by the examiners to wear 5 inertial sensors, named "Technology-Enabled Medical Precision Observation (TEMPO) [21]", which contains 3 axes of accelerometers and gyroscopes on each sensor node for 6 degrees-of-freedom sensing, on the left/right wrists, left/right ankles and sacrum while completing the 6MW.

The distance walked was recorded in 1-minute epochs by a research assistant using a measure wheel. Subjects were asked to walk as far and as fast as possible (without running) up and down a 175-foot hallway. The inertial sensor data was wirelessly transmitted to a laptop for post-processing.

The inertial sensor sampling rate is 128Hz, sufficient to capture the frequency band of body motion while walking. The operator of the data collection system was required to make timestamp annotations in order to indicate the beginning and end of the walk.

132 data sessions were collected over 3 years and each subject performed at least one 6MW. All the data sessions were calibrated with recorded calibration parameters determined prior to data collection [18]. There is no general normalization in the data preprocessing. However, due to the technical issues of our custom data collection system and human factors in real-world deployment, 11 data session failed in the calibration process; 6 of them had too many dropped packets during wireless transmission to the laptop for data collection, 3 of them have timestamp errors due to system operator error, and 2 of them had lost calibration parameters in the calibration records. Finally, 36 data sessions were successfully collected from 13 healthy controls while 85 data sessions were successfully collected from 28 MS subjects.

3.3 Clinical Measures

The EDSS is used to categorize the severity of disability as mild (EDSS 0-2.5), moderate (EDSS 3.0-4.0), and severe (EDSS 4.5-6.5). In this pilot study, we did not recruit any participants with severe walking disability (EDSS $\geq$ 4.5).

MSWS-12 scores were collected every time the participant visited the MS outpatient clinic. We did not collect MSWS-12 scores from healthy controls; because they do not have any walking impairment due to MS, their score is 12, the minimum score.

Gait speed and distance walked during the 6MW were calculated based on the manual measures. However, based on the evaluation results of [10], we selected distance walked as the only one measure in next-step correlation analysis, because there is strong correlation (r=0.91) between gait speed and distance walked.

3.4 Inertial Measures from Body Sensors

Measures from inertial body sensors came from two types of gait assessment techniques; one is the temporal decomposition of the inertial sensor signals, such as stride length, single stance time (SST), swing time, and double stance time (DST); another is the causality estimation among the sensor signals which is used to represent the interactions among the body parts. This paper adopted two typical measures from inertial body sensors: Ratio between DST and SST (DST/SST) [16] and Causality Index [17].

3.5 Statistical Analysis

All analyses were performed using SPSS, version 19 (SPSS, Chicago, IL). Descriptive data are presented as mean and standard deviation. The differences in EDSS, MSWS-12, distance walked, causality index, and DST/SST across the 6MW tests were examined using one-way, within-subjects ANOVAs; disability measure (EDSS) was the within-subjects factor with three levels (healthy, mild, and moderate). The relationships between scores from the EDSS, MSWS-12, distance walked, causality index, and DST/SST across the 6MW tests were estimated using Pearson product-moment correlations (r) as the scores for all variables approximated a normal distribution with minimal skewness and kurtosis and had continuous measure properties. Cohen's guidelines of .1, .3, and .5 were used for judging the magnitude of the correlation coefficients as small, moderate, and large, respectively [19].

4. RESULTS

4.1 Bivariate Correlation Analysis

Table 1 presents a matrix of correlations among MSWS-12 scores, EDSS scores, distance walked, and other quantitative measures drawn from inertial sensor data including DST/SST index and causality index. Scatter plots of the stronger associations among the measures are provided in Fig. 1.

It is noteworthy that most of the correlations among these measures are significant and strong ($r>0.500$), except the associations between EDSS scores and quantitative measures drawn from inertial sensor data. This is because of the limited variability in the EDSS scores.

Distance walked during 6MW correlated significantly and strongly with causality index ($r = 0.822$, $p = 0.001$) and DST/SST index ($r = 0.748$, $p = 0.001$), while these two objective measures from inertial sensor data also correlated to each other significantly and strongly ($r = 0.772$, $p = 0.001$). MSWS-12 scores correlated significantly and strongly with distance walked during 6MW ($r=-0.678$, $p=0.001$). As we can see in Figure 2 (d-f), there is similar

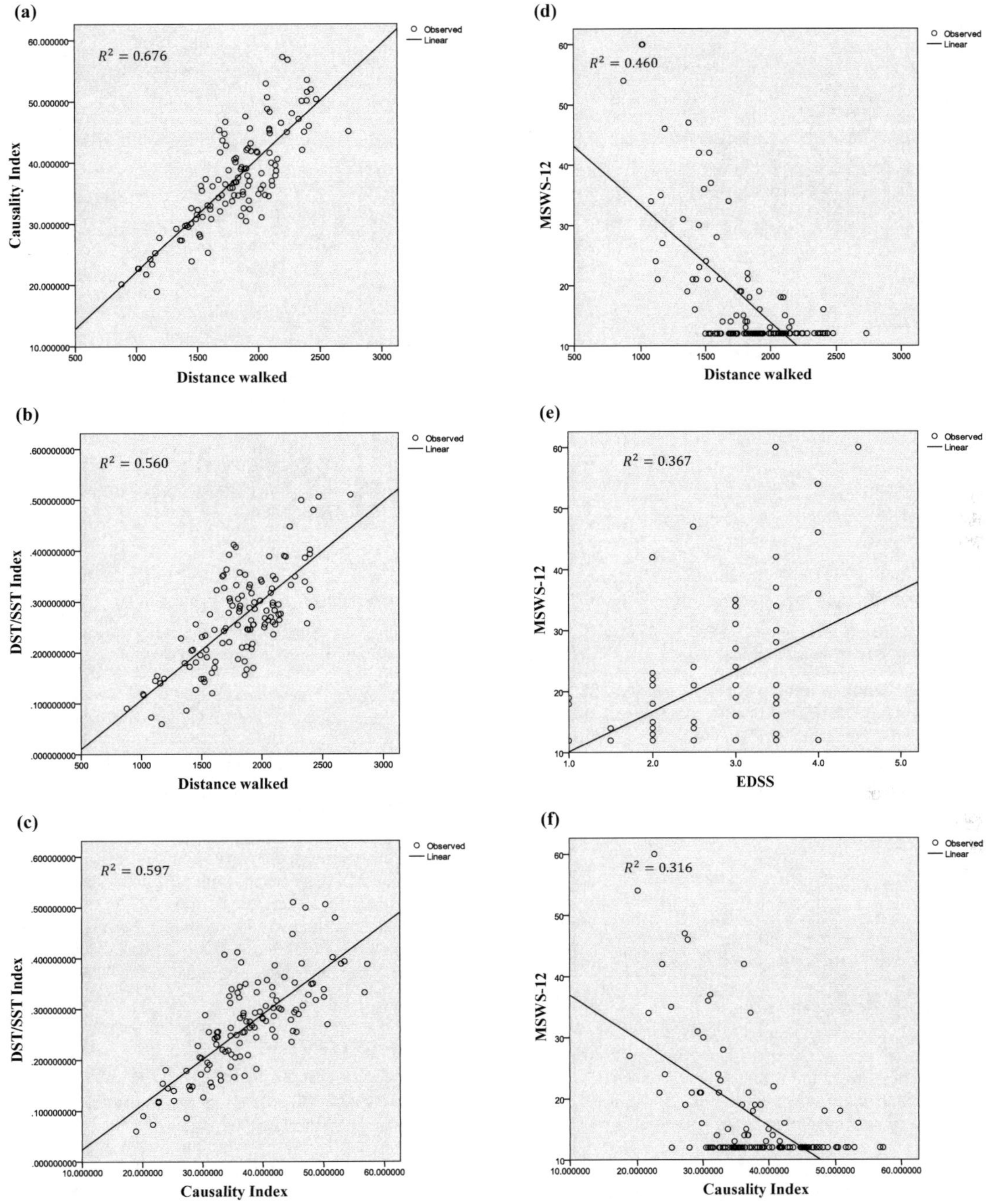

Figure 2. Scatter plot, linear trend-line, and squared multiple correlation (R2) for the stronger associations among the measures: associations between distance walked and (a) causality index, and (b) DST/SST index; (c) association between causality index and DST/SST index; and associations between MSWS-12 and (d) distance walked, and (e) EDSS, and (f) causality index. Apparently, the strongest association is the one between distance walked and causality index.

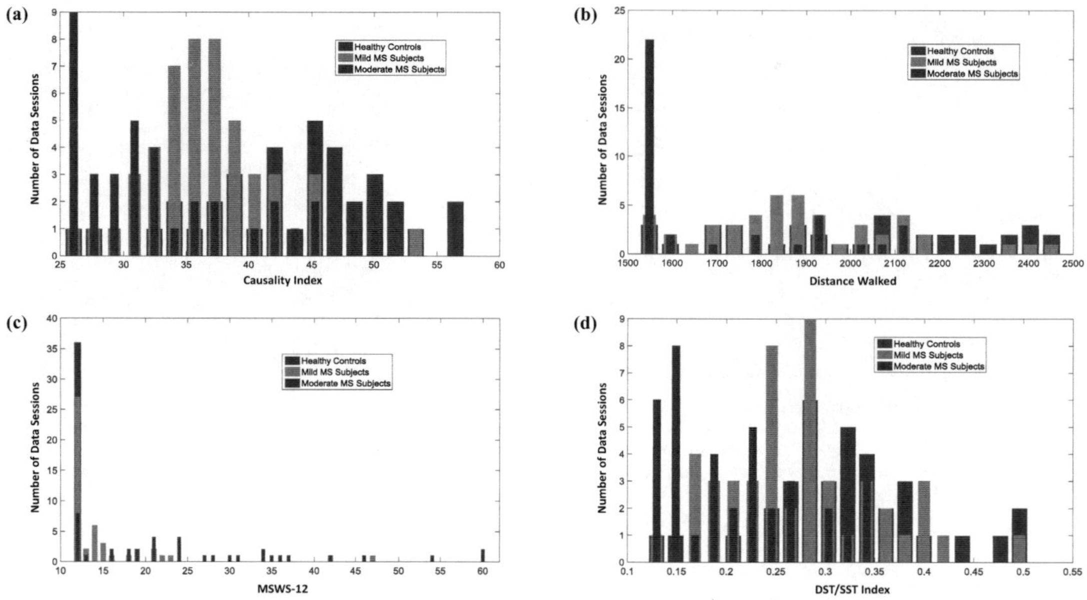

Figure 3. Distribution of (a) Causality Index, (b) Distance walked, (c) MSWS-12 scores, and (d) DST/SST index in three groups: healthy controls, mild and moderate MS subjects. The causality index distinguishes the three groups most clearly.

limited variability in MSWS-12 scores, impeding correlations between the MSWS-12 and other measures.

Table 1. Bivariate correlations among MSWS-12 scores, EDSS scores, distance walked, other quantitative measures drawn from inertial sensor data (causality index and DST/SST index)

Measure	1	2	3	4	5
1. MSWS-12	-				
2. EDSS	0.606	-			
3. Distance walked	-0.678	-0.510	-		
4. DST/SST index	-0.500	-0.358	0.748	-	
5. Causality Index	-0.562	-0.436	0.822	0.772	-

4.2 Separability Performance

A measure of walking ability can be used to provide assistance to doctors when evaluating and monitoring MS disease progression. This assistance comes from the ability of the measure to distinguish the within-subjects factors and then estimate the impact of MS in subjects. As we mentioned before, we use one-way, within-subjects ANOVAs using disability measure as the within-subjects factor with three levels (healthy (EDSS 0), mild (EDSS 0-2.5), and moderate (EDSS 3-4)). Our participants included 13 healthy controls, 17 mild MS subjects and 11 moderate MS subjects.

4.2.1 Separability for Three Groups

Figure 4 illustrates the analysis results of effect size from one-way, within-subjects ANOVAs. We adopted the MES toolbox V1.4 [20] as our analysis method, which provide appropriate effect size value rather than p value. The distributions of the measures are plotted in figure 3. As we can see, the distribution of the causality index better distinguishes between the three groups. Figure 4 shows the same results: causality index has the best effect size in separability of the three groups.

4.2.2 Combined Measures

Based on above analysis in correlations and separability, we selected MSWS-12 as the best validated subjective measure in clinics and the causality index as the measure with best separability performance. Combining the causality index and MSWS-12, Figure 4 shows that the combined index has the best separability performance and Figure 5 presents a better illustration of the separability among the three groups. As you can see, most of the moderate MS subjects are in the red area, most of mild MS subjects are in the blue area, while most of the healthy controls are in the black area. It is worth noting that there is a boundary in the plane which can be used to validate the data. This means it is less likely that any measures from a subject will fall outside the boundary.

5. DISCUSSION

The gait measures from inertial body sensors and clinical measures correlated to each other mostly strongly and significantly ($r>0.500$). This is consistent with the previous validation study of MSWS-12 scores and EDSS scores. This study shows not only the EDSS scores, but also MSWS-12 scores with limited variability. This limited variability greatly impacts the correlations with other measures and the ability to distinguish gait impairment due to MS. Therefore, although the MSWS-12 shows strong and significant correlations to other measures, it provides worse separability performance in experimental data. Figure 3 (c) presents its limited variability in scores.

Distance walked during 6MW is an outcome measure with growing application and utility in MS clinical research. Correlation analysis shows that gait measures using inertial body sensors have strong and significant correlation ($r = 0.822$, $p = 0.001$) with distance walked during the 6MW. This gives promising evidence that inertial body sensors can be a useful and convenient gait assessment tool for MS gait impairment. Otherwise, measures from inertial body sensors provide better separability (effect size = 1.26) in three groups in our experiments.

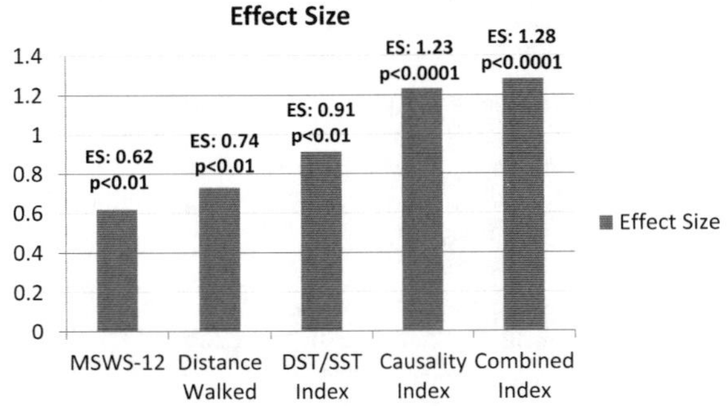

Figure 4. Analysis of effect size from one-way, within-subjects ANOVAs. The EDSS scores were used as the within-subjects factor with three levels (healthy, mild, and moderate). Combined index is a combination of the causality index and MSWS-12.

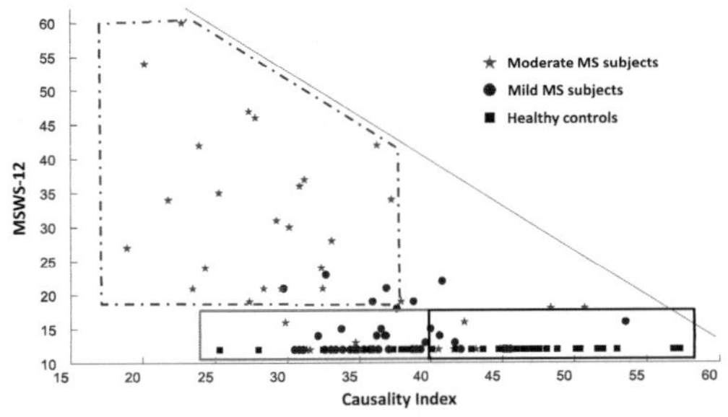

Figure 5. Causality index and MSWS-12 together provide better illustration of separability in three groups.

Strong evidence had been provided to prove the successful validation of causality index of inertial body sensors based on the obvious strong and significant correlations with MSWS-12, distance walked, and DST/SST index. Since the causality index is used to represent the interactions among body parts, we can say that the interactions among body parts can be a common measure to provide strong ability to distinguish three groups: healthy controls, mild MS subjects, and moderate MS subjects.

Combing the measures together is another promising method to enhance separability of MS among patients. Comparing to other measures, a simple data visualization combing causality index and MSWS-12 provided better illustration of separability for the three groups. Therefore, this preliminary result suggested that the information processing and integration between clinical and inertial measures will be next-step work in the near future since the importance of some information in the clinical measures is not well understood yet.

There are some limitations to this study. The first is the size of the sample. This study included three groups of 13 healthy controls, 17 mild MS subjects and 11 moderate subjects. However, the results are consistent with previous studies. Another limitation is the limited understanding of other effects on the 6MW. This study was conducted over a period of 3 years, and many potential issues that may affect the 6MW test were less well understood. A future study with a larger sample size will be needed to evaluate the impact of sample size on separability performance among MS subjects. Finally, there was no baseline assessment of fitness, exercise routine, or other impairment factors such as other pains or injuries. Therefore, it is possible that some of the differences between the groups could be due to level of fitness. This study shows that some MS subjects perform better in MSWS-12 and causality index. Future work should monitor and track energy expenditure in daily life to account for other impact factors, then explore the relationship between 6MW and gait impairment caused by MS.

6. Conclusion

This paper is motivated by the validation requirements of the most current measures from inertial body sensors for understanding the relationship between the gait measures from inertial body sensors and the impact of MS on gait impairment. Therefore, this paper further investigated the correlations between inertial measures from body sensors and measures in clinical evaluation then compared the separability performance of these measures. The experimental results suggested that combining the inertial and clinical measures provides better separability performance for tracking MS disease state and progression.

Future work will focus on larger validation studies for gait measures from inertial body sensors, optimal combination of inertial and clinical measures, and extraction of intuitional meaning for clinicians.

7. REFERENCES

[1] J. F. Kurtzke, "Rating Neurologic Impairment in Multiple Sclerosis an Expanded Disability Status Scale (EDSS)", Neurology, vol. 33, no. 11, pp. 1441-1444, 1983.

[2] J. C. Hobart, A. Riazi, D. L. Lamping, R. Fitzpatrick, and A. J. Thompson, "Measuring the Impact of MS on Walking Ability the 12-Item MS Walking Scale (MSWS-12)", Neurology, vol. 60, no. 1, pp. 31-36, 2003.

[3] C. McGuigan, and M. Hutchinson, "Confirming the Validity and Responsiveness of the Multiple Sclerosis Walking Scale-12 (MSWS-12)", Neurology, vol. 62, no. 11, pp. 2103-2105, 2004.

[4] R. W. Motl, and E. M. Snook, "Confirmation and Extension of the Validity of the Multiple Sclerosis Walking Scale-12 (MSWS-12)", Journal of The Neurological Sciences, vol. 268, no. 1, pp. 69-73, 2008.

[5] R. W. Motl, D. Dlugonski, Y. Suh, M. Weikert, S. Agiovlasitis, B. Fernhall, and M. Goldman. "Multiple Sclerosis Walking Scale-12 and Oxygen Cost of Walking." Gait & Posture, vol. 31, no. 4, pp. 506-510, 2010.

[6] L. A. Pilutti, D. Dlugonski, B. M. Sandroff, Y. Suh, J. H. Pula, J. J. Sosnoff, and R. W. Motl, "Further Validation of Multiple Sclerosis Walking Scale-12 Scores based on Spatiotemporal Gait Parameters", Archives of Physical Medicine and Rehabilitation, vol. 94, no. 3, pp. 575-578, 2013.

[7] M. F. Sidovar, B. L. Limone, S. Lee, and C. I. Coleman, "Mapping The 12-Item Multiple Sclerosis Walking Scale to

The Euroqol 5-Dimension Index Measure in North American Multiple Sclerosis Patients", BMJ Open, vol. 3, no. 5, pp. e002798, 2013.

[8] J. Rueterbories, E. G. Spaich, B. Larsen, and O. K. Andersen, "Methods for Gait Event Detection and Analysis in Ambulatory Systems", Medical Engineering & Physics, vol. 32, no. 6, pp. 545-552, 2010.

[9] S. J. Preece, J. Y. Goulermas, L. P. Kenney, D. Howard, K. Meijer, and R. Crompton, "Activity Identification using Body-Mounted Sensors—A Review of Classification Techniques", Physiological Measure, vol. 30, no. 4, pp. R1, 2009.

[10] M. D. Goldman, R. A. Marrie, and J. A. Cohen, "Evaluation of The Six-Minute Walk in Multiple Sclerosis Subjects and Healthy Controls", Multiple Sclerosis, vol. 14, no. 3, pp. 383-390, 2007.

[11] B. C. Kieseier, and C. Pozzilli, "Assessing Walking Disability in Multiple Sclerosis", Multiple Sclerosis, vol. 18, no. 7, pp. 914-924, 2012.

[12] C. L. Martin, B. A. Phillips, T. J. Kilpatrick, H. Butzkueven, N. Tubridy, E. McDonald, and M. P. Galea, "Gait and Balance Impairment in Early Multiple Sclerosis in the Absence of Clinical Disability", Multiple Sclerosis, vol. 12, no. 5, pp. 620-628, 2006.

[13] J. Favre, R. Aissaoui, B. M. Jolles, J. A. De Guise, and K. Aminian,"Functional Calibration Procedure for 3D Knee Joint Angle Description using Inertial Sensors", Journal of Biomechanics, vol. 42, no. 14, pp. 2330-2335, 2009.

[14] G, Chen, C. Patten, D. H. Kothari, and F. E. Zajac, "Gait Differences between Individuals with Post-Stroke Hemiparesis and Non-Disabled Controls at Matched Speeds", Gait & Posture, vol. 22, no. 1, pp. 51-56, 2005.

[15] R. Sacco, R. Bussman, P. Oesch, J. Kesselring, and S. Beer, "Assessment of Gait Parameters and Fatigue in MS Patients during Inpatient Rehabilitation: A Pilot Trial", Journal of Neurology, vol. 258, no. 5, pp.889-894, 2011.

[16] S. Chen, J. Gong, J. Lach, and M. D. Goldman, "Enhanced Multiple Sclerosis Gait Assessment using Inertial Sensors", Wireless Health Conference, Baltimore, MD, USA, Nov. 2013.

[17] J. Gong, J. Lach, Y. Qi and M. D. Goldman, "Causal Analysis of Inertial Body Sensors for Enhancing Gait Assessment Separability towards Multiple Sclerosis Diagnosis," The 12th International Conference on Wearable and Implantable Body Sensor Networks (BSN 2015), June 9-12, Boston, MA, USA.

[18] S. Chen, J. S. Brantley, T. Kim, and J. Lach, "Characterizing And Minimizing Synchronization and Calibration Errors in Inertial Body Sensor Networks", 5th International Conference on Body Area Networks, pp. 138-144, 2010.

[19] J. Cohen, "Statistical Power Analysis for the Behavioral Sciences", 2nd ed., Hillsdale, NJ: Lawrence Erlbaum Associates, 1988.

[20] H. Hentschke, and M. C. Stüttgen, "Computation of Measures of Effect Size for Neuroscience Data Sets", European Journal of Neuroscience, vol. 34, no. 12, pp. 1887-1894, 2011.

[21] A. T. Barth, M. Hanson, H. C. Powell, and J. Lach, "TEMPO 3.1: A Body Area Sensor Network Platform for Continuous Movement Assessment", The 6th International Workshop on Wearable and Implantable Body Sensor Networks (BSN 2009), pp. 71-76.

Posture Sensor: Cross Leg Detector at Knee Level

Gudi Siva Leela Krishna Chand, *Soo Young Shin
Department of IT Convergence Engineering, WENS Lab, Kumoh National Institute of Technology, Gumi, South Korea
Email: leelakrishnachand@gmail.com, *wdragon@kumoh.ac.kr

ABSTRACT
This paper presents a wearable posture device that can detect and alert when a person tries to attempt a cross leg at the knee level. Generally having a cross leg is considered as normal but if it is done regular then it can create large number of problems such as damaging the veins, increasing the blood pressure, temporary paralysis and sometimes long term numbness. The main problem is that we don't even realize that we are doing it. So, to overcome this problem, we have developed a prototype, that can alert the user. We have developed two types of prototypes where the first one is with feedback and other one is without feedback of our activity regarding cross leg.

KEYWORDS
Wearable device; Posture Sensor; Intel Edison

INTRODUCTION
Cross leg messes with the nerves as it cause more pressure on the peroneal nerve which is the major nerve in our leg that passes below our knee and along the outside of the leg. This pressure causes numbness and temporary paralysis of some of the muscles in our foot and leg. Cross leg was tested on forty two participants for 12min in [1]. It was shown that, it has increased the systolic blood pressure significantly by 6.7mmHg in the hypertensive patient and 7.9mmHg in the treated diabetics [2]. Till now in the market no devices are available to detect and alert if a person is having this kind of posture.

PROPOSED MODEL
We have proposed two models for our device. In the first method, our device alerts the user by vibrating. Also, user can see the feedback of his activity while in the second method the device just alert the user by vibrating. We have followed the principle of induction coupling which uses an electromagnetic field to transfer energy between two objects. Our prototype is as shown in the below Fig. 1.

Figure 1. Prototype of proposed cross leg detector with feedback

On the back of right knee, we have placed the coil with the vibrator along with our developed circuit using Intel Edison. On the other knee, we are adding a coil with a battery. When these two devices are coming near then the voltage is induced through an inductive coupling to the other side. So, when a person is trying to attempt a cross leg at the knee level then our device starts vibrating. While attempting cross leg, if the back of the knee of one leg is a little bit far then it starts to vibrate little and when it comes near or if it touches then it starts vibrating more. The amount of vibration and the time depends upon the transfer of energy through coupling. The Intel Edison calculates the number of times we have tried for cross leg. We can see the feedback of by connecting our mobile to Intel Edison. In the second method, the device gives vibrations without any feedback activity. So the size of the prototype became smaller as it is not going to use the Intel Edison. The device without feedback is of use and throw type. Our device with a cross leg with near and far along with feedback activity is as shown below in Fig. 2.

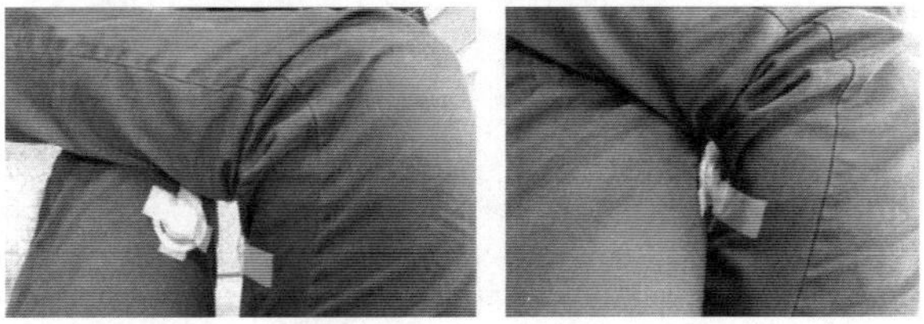

Figure 2. a) A bit far to have cross leg b) Near to have cross leg

CONCLUSION
Our prototype tries to avoid the cross leg at the knee level by alerting the user. It is going to help the user indirectly to prevent varicose veins, weakening or damaging the veins, causing numbness etc.

ACKNOWLEDGMENTS
This research was supported by the MSIP (Ministry of Science, ICT and Future Planning), Korea under the CITRC (Convergence Information Technology Research Center) support program (IITP-2015-H8601-15-1011).

REFERENCES

[1] Velthoven, Michelle Helena, Suzanne Holewijn, Gert Jan van der Wilt, Theo Thien, and Jaap Deinum. "*Does wave reflection explain the increasement in blood pressure consistently leg crossing ?.*" Blood pressure monitoring 19, No. 3 (2014). 129-133. DOI= http://onlinelibrary.wiley.com/doi/10.1111/j.1365-2702.2009.03148.x/full

[2] Pinar, Rukiye, Sıddıka Ataalkin, and Roger Watson. "*The effect of crossing legs on blood pressure in hypertensive patients.*" Journal of clinical nursing 19, no. 9-10 (2010): 1284-1288. DOI= http://journals.lww.com/bpmonitoring/Abstract/2007/06000/The_effect_of_crossing_legs_on_blood_pressure.9.aspx

BODYNETS 2015, September 28-30, Sydney, Australia

DOI 10.4108/eai.28-9-2015.2261509

Stretchable and Highly Conductive Carbon Nanotube-Graphene Hybrid Yarns for Wearable Systems

(Invited Paper)

Syed Muzahir Abbas[*‡], Javad Foroughi[§], Yogesh Ranga[*], Ladislau Matekovits[†], Karu P. Esselle[*], Stuart G. Hay[‡], Michael C. Heimlich[*], Farzad Safaei[⊥]

*Department of Engineering, Macquarie University, North Ryde, NSW 2109, Australia

[§]ARC Centre of Excellence for Electromaterials Science, University of Wollongong, Wollongong, NSW 2519, Australia

[†]Dipartimento di Elettronica e Telecomunicazioni, Politecnico di Torino, 24, C.so Duca degli Abruzzi, 10129 Torino, Italy

[‡]CSIRO Digital Productivity Flagship, PO Box 76, Epping, NSW 1710, Australia

[⊥]Information and Communication Technology Research Institute, University of Wollongong, Wollongong, NSW 2519, Australia

syed.abbas@mq.edu.au, foroughi@uow.edu.au, yogeshwar.ranga@mq.edu.au, ladislau.matekovits@polito.it, karu.esselle@mq.edu.au, stuart.hay@csiro.au, michael.heimlich@mq.edu.au, farzad@uow.edu.au

ABSTRACT

Carbon Nanotubes (CNTs) have emerged as potential candidates for replacement of conventional metals due to their significant mechanical, electrical, thermal properties and non-oxidizing abilities [1, 2]. The density of CNT composites is about five times lower than copper and around half that of aluminium. Moreover, their thermal conductivity is about ten times that of copper. With the above mentioned distinguishing features, CNTs have been of interest in medical, electronics and antenna applications [3]. CNTs are drawn into yarns by pulling and twisting them from CNT forests. Previously we have presented microwave characterization of CNT yarns [4]. Our results have shown that the CNT yarns exhibits frequency independent resistive behavior and is beneficial for wide-band applications such as ultra-wideband (UWB) and wireless body area networks [4].

Electrical conductivity of a CNT yarn depends on the properties, loading and aspect ratio of the CNTs. It also depends upon the twist angle and the characteristics of the conductive network. By doping or adding materials, such as gold, silver or NiCr, electrical conductivity of CNTs can by varied. In [5], highly conductive carbon nanotube-graphene hybrid yarns are reported. They are obtained by drawing vertically aligned multi-walled carbon nanotubes (MWCNT) into long MWCNT sheets. Then graphene flakes are deposited onto the MWCNT sheet to form a composite hybrid structure that is transformed into yarns by twisting. The electrical conductivity of these composite MWCNT-graphene hybrid yarns is over 900 S/cm. In this work, we have modeled this hybrid material as a potential data transmission line and compared it with a transmission line made out of copper on the same substrate. The results are tabulated in Table-I. They show a good agreement between copper based and composite MWCNT-graphene hybrid material based transmission lines.

The hybrid material is high conductive, flexible and stretchable. This makes it suitable to use as transmission lines and connecting wires in systems that require stretching and flexibility, such as wearable systems.

Keywords

Carbon nanotube, Graphene, Carbon nanotube-Graphene, Yarns, Hybrid yarns, Stretchable yarns, highly conductive yarns, Wearable.

BODYNETS 2015, September 28-30, Sydney, Australia

DOI 10.4108/eai.28-9-2015.2261421

Table I. Results of a hybrid CNT-Graphene yarn and copper wire at 2.5GHz when placed on a substrate to form a transmission line.

Structure	Impedance (Ω)	Phase of the transmission coeff. (Deg)
Copper strip-line	50	68.6
Hybrid CNT-Graphene strip-line	50	66.6
Copper Wire	130.5	103.4
Hybrid CNT-Graphene Yarn	131.8	101.7

REFERENCES

[1] G. W. Hanson, "Fundamental transmitting properties of carbon nanotube antennas," *IEEE Transactions on Antennas and Propagation,* vol. 53, pp. 3426-3435, 2005.

[2] M. Miao, "Electrical conductivity of pure carbon nanotube yarns," *Carbon,* vol. 49, pp. 3755-3761, 2011.

[3] S. Fan, "CNT Research: from Academic Wonder to Industrial Exploration," in *13th International Workshop on Computational Electronics (IWCE)*, 2009, pp. 1-4.

[4] S. M. Abbas, O. Sevimli, M. C. Heimlich, K. P. Esselle, B. Kimiaghalam, J. Foroughi, and F. Safaei, "Microwave Characterization of Carbon Nanotube Yarns For UWB Medical Wireless Body Area Networks," *IEEE Transactions on Microwave Theory and Techniques,* vol. 61, pp. 3625-3631, 2013.

[5] J. Foroughi, G. M. Spinks, D. Antiohos, A. Mirabedini, S. Gambhir, G. G. Wallace, S. R. Ghorbani, G. Peleckis, M. E. Kozlov, M. D. Lima, and R. H. Baughman, "Highly Conductive Carbon Nanotube-Graphene Hybrid Yarn," *Advanced Functional Materials,* vol. 24, pp. 5859-5865, 2014.

Foot Motion Measurement for Home based Rehabilitation Using Distributed Wearable Sensor

Zhelong Wang
Dalian University of Technology
School of Control Science and Engineering, Dalian City, China
+86-0411-84703624
wangzl@dlut.edu.cn

Sen Qiu
Dalian University of Technology
School of Control Science and Engineering, Dalian City, China
+86-0411-84703624
qiu@mail.dlut.edu.cn

ABSTRACT

This paper presents a wearable sensors based foot motion measurement method for rehabilitation applications. Two commercial wearable sensors were adopted with three measurement units fixed on feet. Quaternions were employed to represent three-dimensional orientation and a proportional-integral-filter (PIF) algorithm was used to calculate the quaternion derivative. Foot position and orientation were estimated and the effectiveness of the proposed method was validated on healthy subjects. Experimental results demonstrated that the proposed method is capable of providing consistent tracking of human foot without significant drift, with less than 0.5% position error, which matches that of Kalman based methods. The aim of this work is to allow therapists to make use of the biofeedback information to create biofeedback rehabilitation protocols, which can be used to monitor and evaluate rehabilitation progresses by the performance of patients doing prescribe corrective body movement and gesture. Moreover, this method could be applied to other cyclical activity monitoring.

Keywords

Body sensor network, inertial sensors, motion measurement, rehabilitation.

1. INTRODUCTION

Human gait is human behavior characteristics of lower foot coordination in the process of walking, involving personal exercise habits, health, gender, age, occupation and other factors, human gait detection is of great significance in many fields, for instance, in the domain of telemedicine, portable gait analysis equipment can reduce the need of long time monitoring by nursing staff. With regard to personal navigation, the pedestrian locomotion trajectory information can be achieved based on the calculation of wearable sensors in the absence of the position of the GPS system. The most important function of gait analysis tend to be medical rehabilitation application, gait analysis offers an easy manner to evaluate recovery process of human feet. In the past, the nurse in the hospital might collect the patient's vital signs data artificially three times per day, including body temperature, blood pressure and heart rate, etc. In the digital era of big data, we can collect much more physiological data per minute. More physiological data and details offer a better way to evaluate rehabilitation process, thereby to determine the following treatment priority accurately. According to the statistics of National Health Service (NHS), stroke occurs approximately 152,000 times a year in the UK and it is the third single largest cause of death. The damage caused by a stroke can be widespread and long lasting. Most patients suffer from foot movement disorder and need to have a long period of rehabilitation before they can recover their former independence. Fortunately sequela can be significantly alleviated by formal rehabilitation training, and reducing the need for therapy at hospital might lead to an optimal solution for therapy efficiency and expense issues. In literature, great interest has been drawn toward the development of home based rehabilitation schemes [1][2]. Bamberg et al.[3] developed a smart shoe for gait analysis using force sensitive resistors and IMU sensors. Sabatini [4] and Wang et al. [5] adopted wearable inertial sensor in walking distance calculation and walking pattern classification.

In this study, we use the inertial measurement unit in combination with wireless sensor networks (2.4GHz) and Ethernet network to set up a set of gait analysis system, the system directly measured the acceleration, angular velocity change and earth magnetic field in the process of walking. According to the characters of human movement, the raw sensor signals are filtered by both high pass and low pass filter to eliminate signal noise, filtered sensor data is then transmitted to a handheld device through the 2.4GHz wireless network and eventually delivered to PC by network cable. In the upper machine, the application software process the sensor data using the proposed gait analysis algorithm including digital filtering, threshold detection, sensor data fusion so as to obtain gait parameters, i.e. walking velocity, stride length, stride frequency, walking cycle and foot angle. An improved zero velocity update (ZUPT) algorithm [6][7] is used to eliminate the integral error step by step, make it suitable for different experimental scenarios.

The rest of this paper is organized as follows: Section 2 describes the components of the system and the algorithms used to estimate the gait parameters during walking; Experimental results are

BODYNETS 2015, September 28-30, Sydney, Australia

DOI 10.4108/eai.28-9-2015.2261463

given in Section 3; the potential applications of gait analysis are discussed in Section 4 and Section 5 concludes the paper.

2. SYSTEM OVERVIEW AND ALGORITHMS

2.1 Hardware Platform

The hardware platform of the measurement system is composed of two inertial sensor measurement nodes and a handheld device as shown in Fig.1. The sensor chips in measurement nodes are ADIS16448 (Analog Devices), including a tri-axial accelerometer, tri-axial gyroscope, and tri-axial magnetometer each.

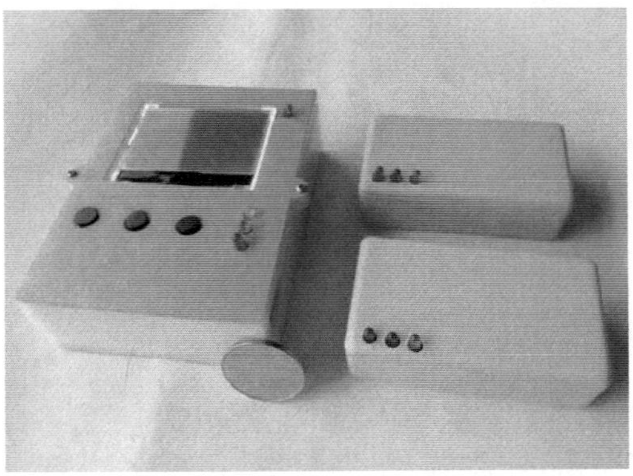

Fig.1. The profile of foot motion measurement system

The sensor performance specification is summarized in TABLE 1. The handheld device contains an ARM microprocessor and a 16Mega bit flash. Each sensor node is powered by 2000mAh lithium polymer battery, which enables the sensor node work more than 10 hours. The function of the handheld controller is data collection control and data transmission. The handheld controller is connected to computer via network cable and the communication between the handheld controller and inertial measurement nodes is 2.4GHz wireless. We chose cable to transmit data at the final step because we wanted to minimize the data loss. The sampling rate of the data collection system is 400Hz and the collected data are processed offline using MATLAB 2010a. The commercial (accurate, lightweight and non-invasive) sensor platforms like Shimmer, Xsens or X-IO IMU were not adopted by the authors because of the limited adjustability and the relatively lower sensitivity, which is not high enough to achieve high accuracy positioning. Meanwhile, the expandability of commercial sensor platforms is a challenge.

Table 1 THE PERFORMANCE OF ADIS16448

Parameter	Full Scale	Sensitivity	Bandwidth
Accelerometer	±18 g	0.833mg/LSB	330Hz
Gyroscope	±1000 °/s	0.04 °/s	330Hz
Magnetometer	±1.9gauss	142.9μgauss/LSB	25Hz

2.2 Algorithm Steps of Proportional-integral-filter

The specific algorithm steps of Proportional-integral-filter (PIF) proposed in this paper are as follows:

Step one, updating attitude estimation equation $\hat{R}$

$$\dot{\hat{R}} = \hat{R}\left(\Omega_y - \hat{b} + k_P \omega\right)_\times \tag{1}$$

$$\hat{R}(0) = \hat{R}_0 \tag{2}$$

Step two: Calculated bias correction $\hat{b}$

$$\dot{\hat{b}} = -k_I \omega \tag{3}$$

$$\hat{b}(0) = \hat{b}_0 \tag{4}$$

Step three: calculate the deviations between R_y and $\hat{R}$

$$\omega = vex\left(P_a\left(\tilde{R}\right)\right) \tag{5}$$

$$\tilde{R} = \hat{R}^T R_y \tag{6}$$

$$P_a\left(\tilde{R}\right) = \left(\tilde{R} - \tilde{R}^T\right) \tag{7}$$

Step four: let the error as the controller input, get the correction vector of rotating angular velocity

$$\delta\omega = \left(K_P + K_I T\right)e \tag{8}$$

Step five: Calculate the revised angular velocity vector

$$\hat{\omega} = \omega + \delta\omega \tag{9}$$

Step six: attitude updating based on quaternion

$$q = \left[q_1 \quad q_2 \quad q_3 \quad q_4\right]^T \tag{10}$$

$$\dot{q} = \frac{1}{2}\omega \otimes q \tag{11}$$

$$\omega = \left[\omega_x \quad \omega_y \quad \omega_z\right] \tag{12}$$

where Ω_y represents the skew symmetric matrix, $\hat{b}$ is constant bias, k_P and k_I are proportionality coefficient and integral coefficient of PI filter parameters, respectively; ω is measured value of gyroscope; Initial quaternion estimation q_0 can be obtained according to the accelerometer, and then a correction can be built through comparison with the relatively accurate attitude estimate $\hat{q}$ using the deviation between the two estimations. The correction is then used as an input variable of PI controller. Eventually, the output of PI controller is selected as a corrected value of gyroscope output angular velocity measurements ω, it is assumed that the sum of ω and $\delta\omega$ is more close to the true value of rotating angular velocity.

2.3 System Initialization and Alignment

When the subject is standing still on the ground, the gravity vector $[0, 0, g]^T$ is calculated as $[x, y, z]^T$ in sensor frame with rotation matrix. In the same time, the measurement value by accelerometer is $[a, b, c]^T$, we can get error vector $[e_x, e_y, e_z]^T$ by doing the vector product of $[x, y, z]^T$ and $[a, b, c]^T$. The rotation matrix can be corrected using this error vector. However, the correction can merely superpose the X-O-Y plane of sensor frame and ground frame. As for the rotating around the Z axis, i.e. the yaw angle, we can only rely on magnetometer to do further compensation. The measuring object of tri-axial magnetometer is the geomagnetic field with fixed magnitude in a relatively pure electromagnetic environment, the angle between the direction of the geomagnetic field and the horizontal plane is constant with regard to each location on the earth. The geomagnetic component in ground frame is denoted as $[u, v, w]^T$, the measurement value by magnetometer is $[l, m, n]^T$. Suppose the vector change to $[l', m', n']^T$ with the accelerometer compensation (coordinate system rotation), then there must be $u = \sqrt{l'^2 + m'^2}$ and $w = n'$.

Similarly, if we transform the treated vector $[l', m', n']^T$ to sensor frame, and do the vector product again to get error vector, then we can use the new error vector $[e_x', e_y', e_z']^T$ to correct the rotation matrix at the second time. In this way the yaw angle compensation is complete, and we have obtained a precise initial quaternion. Initial quaternion is used to describe the initial note orientation information, and the attitude change of an object can be gained by quaternions multiplication based on the initial quaternion. The theoretical value for the initial quaternion is $[1, 0, 0, 0]^T$.

After the initial alignment, the proposed method calculate the corresponding gait parameter step by step, the flowchart is shown in Fig.2. ZUPT represents the wildly used zero velocity updates algorithm, which is based on the fact that the foot swings to stance phase periodically during human locomotion and the foot is stationary in stance phase. Zero-velocity updates are well suited for limiting the error growth of a foot-mounted motion tracking, because the foot returns to a stationary state on a regular ground during ordinary gait cycle [6]. In this case, the information of when the foot has zero velocity is used to calibrate the accumulated errors since the last zero-velocity update. Then we are able to calculate step lengths and orientation at each detected step based on the results of ZUPT algorithm, so as to compute the absolute position and orientation of a subject during walking process. In literature, some approaches assume smooth walking on horizontal surfaces, while others are still valid for uneven terrain with complicated gait patterns. In this study, we assume the ground as horizontal and even.

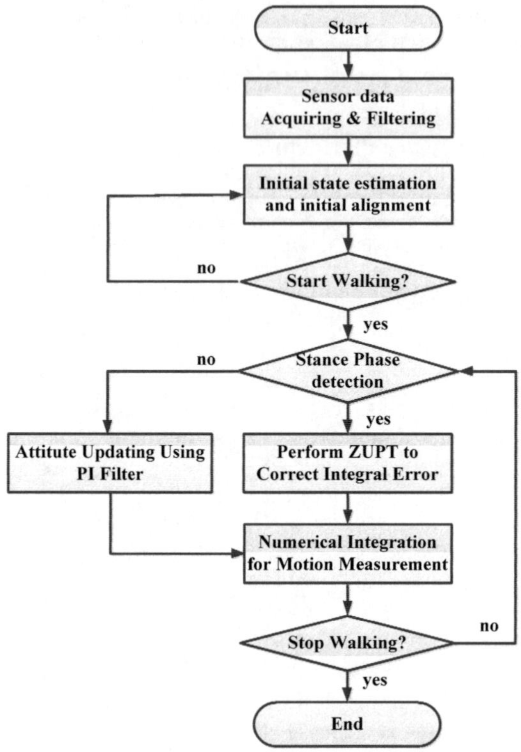

Fig.2. The flowchart of gait parameters estimation

3. EXPERIMENTAL RESULTS AND VALIDATION

To evaluate the effectiveness and accuracy of the gait analysis algorithm proposed in this paper, several experiments were carried out. The inertial measurement nodes were attached to the ankles using special elastic straps, and the data acquisition unit was held in hand by the subjects, as shown in Fig.3. We have studied the impact of the position of the sensors on the body and found that the ankle is an ideal position for sensor data acquisition. Four subjects participated in the experiments. In each walking trial, subjects were requested to stand still for 2~3 seconds before walking, and then walk forward in a straight line and rectangular route respectively at comfortable speeds. Fig.4. shows the sensor data collected during a ten steps straight line walking trials. Each 'peak' denotes a maximum value of angular velocity during walking, the total number of 'peak' equals the step number of the whole walking process.

3.1 Orientation and Position Estimation

It is always required to get motion information in ground frame (G) rather than sensor frame (S). However, the WEARABLE sensor merely output data in its own sensor frame. Hence the key is to transform the sensor frame acceleration into the ground frame and eliminate the gravitational acceleration $\vec{g}$:

$$a(t) = N_S^G(t) \cdot a_S(t) - \vec{g} \quad (13)$$

$$N_S^G = \begin{bmatrix} 1-2q_2^2-2q_3^2 & 2(q_1q_2+q_3q_4) & 2(q_1q_3-q_2q_4) \\ 2(q_1q_2-q_3q_4) & 1-2q_1^2-2q_3^2 & 2(q_2q_3+q_1q_4) \\ 2(q_1q_3+q_2q_4) & 2(q_2q_3-q_1q_4) & 1-2q_1^2-2q_2^2 \end{bmatrix} \quad (14)$$

$$v(t) = \int a(t)\,dt \quad (15)$$

$$p(t) = \int v(t)\,dt \quad (16)$$

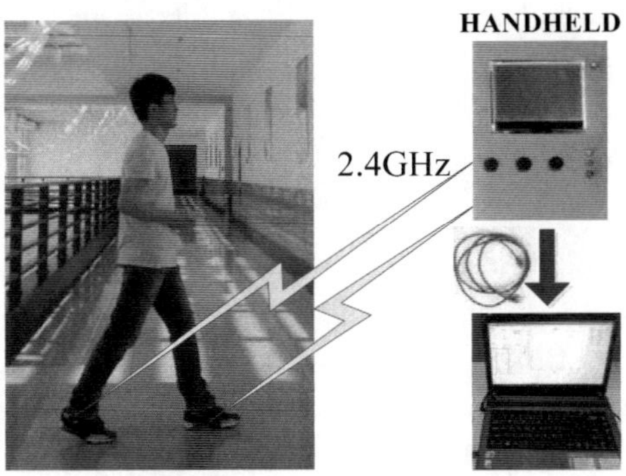

Fig.3. Sensor attachment and sensor data acquisition

3.2 Stance Detection

In literature, gait cycle is divided to two phases [6][8], four phases [9] or even more. It does not matter when it comes to velocity and position estimation by numerical integration of inertial sensor data. Since we only care about when the foot is swing in the air or stand steady on the ground. We tend to integrate the forward acceleration to obtain travelled distance and correct the integral error when we detect the foot is at rest on the ground. The key is to divide the sensor data into observation windows based on the detected peaks, followed by detecting stance phase using the proposed threshold. In this case, false stance detection shown in Fig.4 can be avoided accordingly.

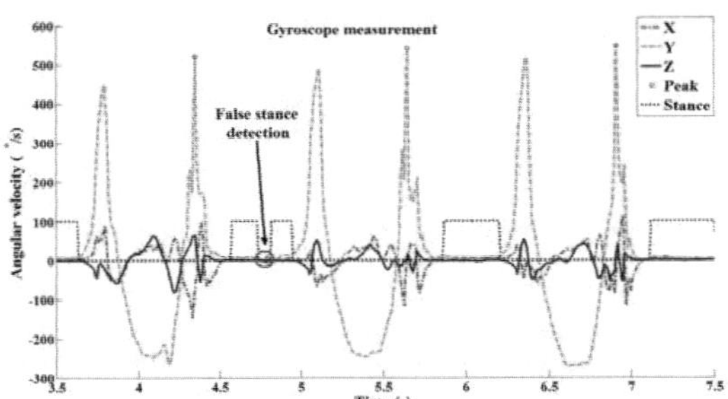

Fig.4. False detection of stance phase

The heel-strike movement is normally selected as the beginning of a stride. Under normal circumstances, accelerometer and gyroscope measurement can be used to detect stance phase. The stance phase lasts from Foot-flat to Heel-off and corresponds to about 25% ~35% of the gait cycle [9]. It was reported that the gyroscope readings are more reliable to detect the two main phase [6]. In our study, a phase detection algorithm based on peak-peak detection and an adaptive threshold is applied to gyroscope data to determine the stance phase [11]. Experimental results have shown that no false stance detection occurred throughout the trials.

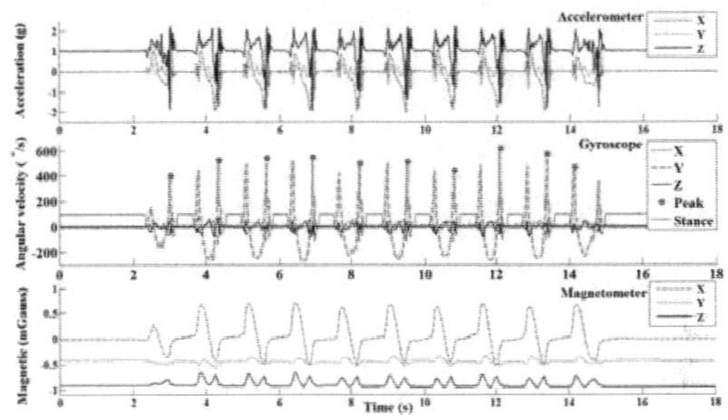

Fig.5. Sensor data during straight line walking

3.3 Position Estimation Error analysis

In level walking trials, the stride length L in horizon plane can be calculated as:

$$L(i) = \sqrt{p_x(i)^2 + p_y(i)^2} \quad (17)$$

where p_x and p_y represent position values in x-axis and y-axis, respectively. Table 2 shows the experimental results of distance estimation of rectangular route walking using proposed method. The subject was asked to walk along the rectangular route from the origin for one lap, two laps and four laps, respectively. Note that all the steps are correctly detected, i.e. our system can be used as a reliable pedometer. The percentage error of total distance is not more than 0.5%, which matches or even exceeds Kalman Filter based method [12] [13] [14].

Table 2. EXPERIMENTAL RESULTS OF TOTAL DISTANCE ESTIMATION

Trials	Total Step Num/Truth	Distance	True Distance	Distance % Error
One lap (CW)	28/28	21.63 m	21.68 m	0.23%
One lap (CCW)	30/30	22.18 m	22.27 m	0.40%
Two laps	47/47	40.67 m	40.73 m	0.15%
Four laps	85/85	73.85 m	74.13 m	0.38%

It should be note that the subjects were not walking exactly along the rectangle route, in this case, the actual walking distance for four laps is not expected to be 4 times the distance of one lap. As for the number of steps, even the same subject might perform diverse step numbers during several experiments.

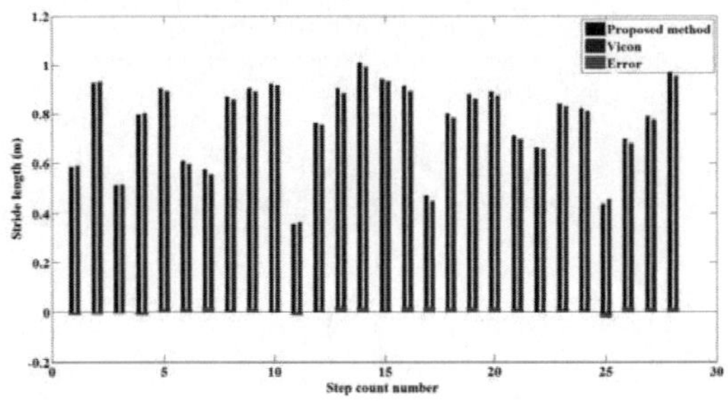

Fig.6. Error analysis of stride length estimation in compare with ground truth

In literature, nearly all the researchers merely focus on the total travelled distance error; it is worth noting how the error changes during the trials. Fig.6 illustrates a specific analysis of step size error during the one lap clockwise walking trial. VICON, a commercial motion tracking system is used to provide ground truth and validate the accuracy of the proposed method. There are 28 steps totally, the maximum error exists on 13rd step with 0.0212m, the mean error is 0.0077m and the standard deviation is 0.0087m. Fig.7 indicates the corresponding frequency histogram, kernel density estimation and normal distribution fitting. As we can see from the statistical analysis, the position estimation algorithm is feasible and effective, and the errors are well controlled.

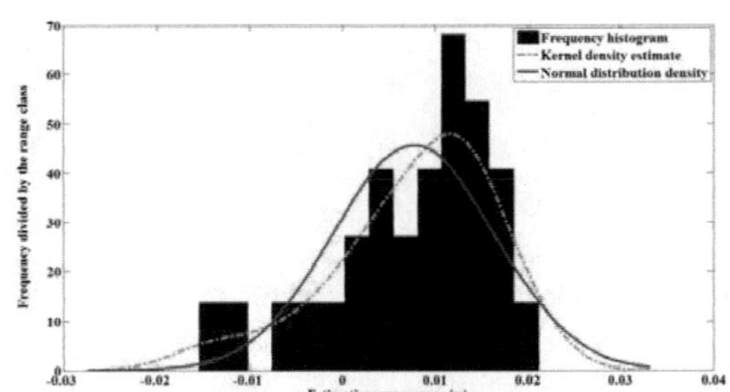

Fig.7. Error statistics of stride length estimation

4. DISCUSSION

In fact, most of individuals have some degree of bow-leg or knock-knee, which then lead to the outside of the heel contact with the ground first while walking or running. This assumption can be confirmed with excessive abrasion on the outside of our shoe's heel. It can be noted that at the beginning of each step, there is a negative abduction-adduction angle which means twist inward of knee as shown in Fig.8.

The foot rolls in and the weight is applied to the foot when the corresponding foot contacts with the ground after heel-strike. In the case that the ankle acts as a connect joint, the foot rolling in causes inward twist of the ankle (ITA), which often results in ankle sprains and pain. This causes pain at the bottom of the foot such as plantar fasciitis.

In the same way, the ITA causes the shank to twist inward, which causes damage to the ligaments and cartilage of the knee. This may leads to chronic knee pain and injuries. Up again, the inward twist of the knee (ITK) causes an inward twist of the thigh and hip, which causes a forward pelvis tilt which strains the lower back, this in turn leads to lower back injuries and chronic pain. Fig.8 illustrates the above mentioned physiological explanations of lower limbs pain. Therapists may come to a better understanding of the pathogenesis and rehabilitation process from the joint information of the patients. In conclusion, an accurate estimation of foot angle can be useful for rehabilitation therapy.

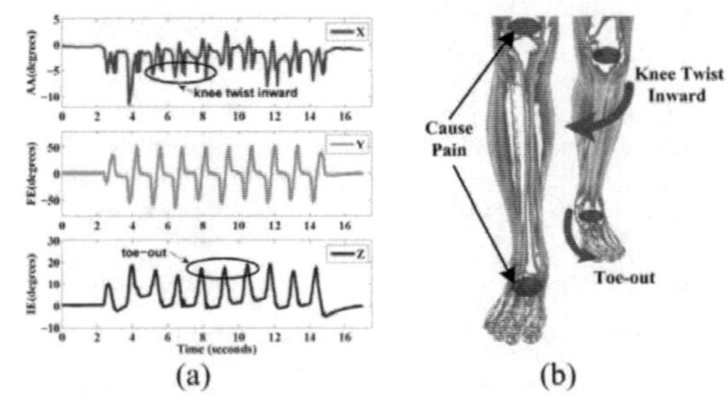

Fig.8. Physiological explanations of lower limbs pains. (a) foot angle during normal walking, (b) the relationship between lower limbs pains and foot angle.

The rapid developing BSN technologies [15][16] have provided new solutions of foot motion analysis, which offers us another way to monitor our health conditions, it might one day become as relevant as blood pressure as an indicator of overall health, however, it still take time to see how useful it is to doctors and patients. Significant impact of wearable technology on medical services may be far-reaching, including improve the nursing standard, reduced healthcare costs, improved employee health and wellness, and better support for networked society.

5. CONCLUSION

In this paper, foot motion data collected by wearable sensors were analyzed using the proposed method. The experimental results show that our method is effective, which is validated by the ground truth. And the results are comparable or even better than similar research work [4][9]. Furthermore, the proposed method has the potential to be applied in in clinic treatments and exercise rehabilitations. The barometric sensor will be integrated in the system to strengthen the estimation of vertical position component. Future work is underway to evaluate both healthy and pathological subjects at a wider movement range. We aim to set up a training database for the sake of facilitating related research of rehabilitation treatment.

6. ACKNOWLEDGMENTS

This work was supported by National Natural Science Foundation of China under Grant no.61174027, Fundamental Research Funds for the Central Universities (DUT15ZD114) and the State Key Laboratory of Robotics, Shenyang Institute of Automation. The authors would like to express their thanks to these funding bodies

7. REFERENCES

[1] Zhou, H., & Hu, H. "Human motion tracking for rehabilitation—A survey," Biomedical Signal Processing and Control, 3(1), pp.1–18. 2008.

[2] Lambrecht, J. M., & Kirsch, R. F. "Miniature low-power inertial sensors: promising technology for implantable motion capture systems," IEEE Transactions on Neural Systems and Rehabilitation Engineering, 22(6), 1138–47. 2014.

[3] S. J. M. Bamberg, A. Y. Benbasat, D. M. Scarborough, D. E. Krebs, and J. a. Paradiso, "Gait analysis using a shoe-integrated wireless sensor system," IEEE transactions on information technology in biomedicine. vol. 12, no. 4, pp. 413–23, Jul. 2008.

[4] Sabatini, A. M., Martelloni, C., Scapellato, S., & Cavallo, F. "Assessment of walking features from foot inertial sensing," IEEE Transactions on Biomedical Engineering, 52(3), 486–494. 2005.

[5] Wang, Zhelong, Qiu, Sen, Cao, Zhongkai and Jiang, M. "Quantitative assessment of dual gait analysis based on inertial sensors with body sensor network. Sensor Review," 33(1), 48–56. 2013.

[6] Skog, I., Händel, P., Nilsson, J.-O., and Rantakokko, J. "Zero-velocity detection --- an algorithm evaluation," IEEE Transactions on Bio-Medical Engineering, 57(11), 2657–2666, 2010.

[7] Z. L. Wang, H. Y. Zhao, S. Qiu, and Q. Gao (2015), "Stance phase detection for ZUPT-aided foot-mounted pedestrian navigation system," IEEE/ASME Transactions on Mechatronics, In Press, DOI:10.1109/TMECH.2015.2430357.

[8] Yun, Xiaoping, et al. "Estimation of human foot motion during normal walking using inertial and magnetic sensor measurements," IEEE Transactions on Instrumentation and Measurement, vol.61 no.7, pp. 2059-2072. 2012.

[9] Pappas, I. P. I., Popovic, M. R., Keller, T., Dietz, V., & Morari, M. "A reliable gait phase detection system," IEEE Transactions on Neural Systems and Rehabilitation Engineering, 9(2), 113–125. 2001.

[10] Skog, Isaac, J-O. Nilsson, and P. Handel."Evaluation of zero-velocity detectors for foot-mounted inertial navigation systems," 2010 International Conference on Indoor Positioning and Indoor Navigation (IPIN), 2010.

[11] Wang, J., Lin, C., Yang, Y. C., & Ho, Y. "Estimation Algorithms Using Gait Phase Information," IEEE Transactions on Biomedical Engineering, 59(10), 2884–2892. 2012.

[12] Qiu, S., Yang, Y., Hou, J., & Ji, R. "Ambulatory estimation of 3D walking trajectory and knee joint angle using MARG Sensors," Fourth International Conference on Innovative Computing Technology (INTECH), 191 – 196. 2014.

[13] Suh, Y. S., Ro, Y. S., & Kang, H. J. "Quaternion-Based Indirect Kalman Filter Discarding Pitch and Roll Information Contained in Magnetic Sensors," IEEE Transactions on Instrumentation and Measurement, 61(6), 1786–1792. 2012.

[14] Sabatini, A. M. "Kalman-filter-based orientation determination using inertial/magnetic sensors: observability analysis and performance evaluation," Sensors (Basel, Switzerland), 11(10), 9182–206. 2011.

[15] Giancarlo Fortino, Roberta Giannantonio. Raffaele Gravina, Philip Kuryloski, Roozbeh Jafari: "Enabling Effective Programming and Flexible Management of Efficient Body Sensor Network Applications," IEEE Transaction on Human-Machine Systems 43(1): 115-133. 2013.

[16] N. Raveendranathan, S. Galzarano, V. Loseu, R. Gravina, R. Giannantonio, M. Sgroi, R. Jafari, and G. Fortino. "From modeling to implementation of Virtual Sensors in Body Sensor Networks," IEEE Sensors Journal, Vol.12, No.3, pp. 583-593, Mar. 2012.

Securing the Timestamping of Sensor Data from Wearable Healthcare Devices

Muhammad Siddiqi†, Gerard Hager†, Vijay Sivaraman†, Sanjay Jha*
†School of Electrical Engineering and Telecommunications
*School of Computer Science and Engineering
†*the University of New South Wales, Sydney, Australia
{m.siddiqi@student., g.hager@student., vijay@, sanjay@cse.}unsw.edu.au

An ageing population, coupled with increasing prevalence of chronic diseases, is placing unsustainable demands on current healthcare systems. Home-based medical monitoring, supported by wearable sensors for heart-rate, ECG, blood pressure, blood glucose, blood-oxygen saturation, etc., has the potential to alleviate the growing burden on hospitals. Timestamping data from such sensors accurately is important for correlating and reconstructing events of medical significance, and to increase trust in the context associated with the data. Unfortunately, reliable timestamping is non-trivial, and cannot be left entirely to the sensor (too resource constrained), the gateway (can be tampered by user), or the datalog server (too far from the medical device).

Timestamps on data from medically-approved wearable devices available in market can be easily altered. For example, with the Fora Diamond Cuff BP, we found that we could tamper the timestamps of measurements simply by changing the time on the smartphone clock while taking the blood pressure. We could similarly tamper with timestamps of readings from the Withings Pulse O_2 device. Even in the case when the app keeps its own clock (rather than the smartphone's clock), it is relatively easy to tamper the timestamp by hacking the app using tools such as Apktool, Androguard, Cydia, Clutch, Hopper, and iRET. We used Apktool to decompile, modify, and recompile the Android apps for the iFora BP [1] and Withings heart-rate [2] devices, and these modifications are detected neither by the device nor by the data logging servers.

Wearable sensors, although reliable, cannot timestamp data independently as their local clock is relative to their boot time and does not know the absolute time; further, they are resource constrained and cannot run time synchronization protocols like NTP. Smartphone apps cannot be trusted to timestamp data reliably, as they can be hacked (shown above). Servers are too far removed from the wearable sensors, and unpredictable network latencies make the timestamping inaccurate; moreover, data might arrive to the server in bursts due to buffering in device or the smartphone app. We propose a new solution to the timetamping problem.

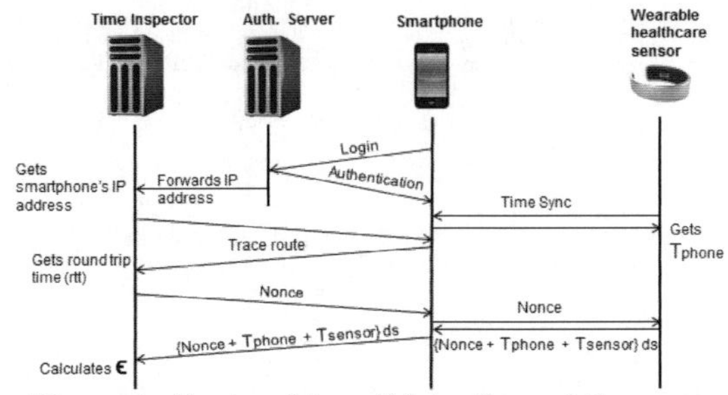

Figure 1: Protocol to validate time of the sensor

Our solution allows the device to obtain absolute time from the smartphone (to ensure accuracy), but uses a validation server (called Time Inspector) that periodically checks the accuracy of the timestamps. This solution allows the validation to be an optional add-on, and can be customized to trade-off the timetamp reliability against resource usage, to match the requirements of the deployment scenarios. The Time Inspector sends a cryptographic *nonce* (at a chosen interval) to the sensor, to which the sensor responds with a digitally signed response including its local clock value T_{sensor} and the global time value T_{phone} last taken from the smartphone. Based on the response the server calculates the time difference ϵ between the sensor's view of global time $\{T_{phone} + T_{sensor}\}$ and its own view of global time T_{server}, compensated for the network latency $\mu_{rtt}/2$. The latency is approximated by using traceroute to identify the router closest to the smartphone and then measuring latency via several ping requests. The mean μ_ϵ and standard deviation σ_ϵ of the time difference $\epsilon = \{T_{server} - (T_{phone} + T_{sensor} + \mu_{rtt}/2)\}/(\mu_{rtt}/2)$ are calculated from repeated responses to *nonce* challenges, and are used to quantify the trustworthiness of the timestamps from the sensor.

Our work[1] shows that medical timestamps are easily tampered at the smartphone, and develops a new overlay solution that can be used to increase confidence in timestamps associated with medical data.

Keywords

mHealth, wearable, provenance, timestamp, security

1. REFERENCES

[1] A modified clone app of iFora BP for research purposes. `https://github.com/sidz81/iFora-BP`.

[2] A clone app of Withings for research purposes. `https://github.com/sidz81/Withings`, June 2015.

[1]This work is funded by Australian Research Council's Discovery Grant DP150100564.

BODYNETS 2015, September 28-30, Sydney, Australia

DOI 10.4108/eai.28-9-2015.2261552

Subthreshold Energy Harvesters Circuits for Biomedical Implants Applications

Meriam Gay Bautista, Eryk Dutkiewicz, Michael Heimlich
Macquarie University, New South Wales, Australia
meriam.bautista@students.mq.edu.au,
eryk.dutkiewicz@mq.edu.au, michael.heimlich@mq.edu.au

ABSTRACT

This paper reviews the state-of-art of the subthreshold level design energy harvesters for powering biomedical implants. Power consumption and lifespan are crucial requirements for the electronic circuitry of implantable systems. In order to meet these challenging requirements, a design for an energy harvester that operates in a subthreshold level offers a promising solution.

Categories and Subject Descriptors

B.7.1 [Integrated Circuits] advance technologies, VLSI, simulation

General Terms

Design, theory, documentation, simulation

Keywords

Biomedical applications, energy harvesting, implantable devices, low power, subthreshold design

1. INTRODUCTION

Implantable medical devices are essential because of their direct impact on human lives, health and safety. The concept of energy harvesting from the human body for implant devices has gained a new relevance. As mentioned in [1], the energy harvesting technology enables monitoring of patients who are outside the clinical environment. To address the social needs of the increasing population of aging people with chronic long term health conditions and ensure their safety, recent research aims to develop technologies with low power requirements, higher energy efficiency, improved power management and improved sensor technology that will be able to monitor vital signs, communicate wirelessly, and will be implantable, biocompatible and self-powering. Therefore, it is important to use an implantable human energy harvester, as this would be an efficient alternative source of energy to continuously supply power to implant devices [2]. Since available power is a critical requirement for implantable devices to increase their lifespan, recent research on biomedical implants microsystems has focused on continued down scaling of electronic circuitry to achieve ultra-low power consumption [3]. Due to its ultra-low power consumption and high energy efficiency subthreshold level design has gained interest in the area of low lower design circuits, such as for biomedical implants. Subthreshold design enables wide-range dynamic voltage scaling by allowing circuits to operate in near/subthreshold voltages. Design requirements for implantable circuits include a minimal footprint or the surface area size of the integrated circuit implants and circuit operation must be at a very low power. In order to achieve the low power operation, subthreshold level operation of MOSFETS offers a promising solution.

This paper views self-powered biomedical implants from a systems perspective by reviewing both the energy created by the harvesting subsystem and the power needed by implant's electronics.

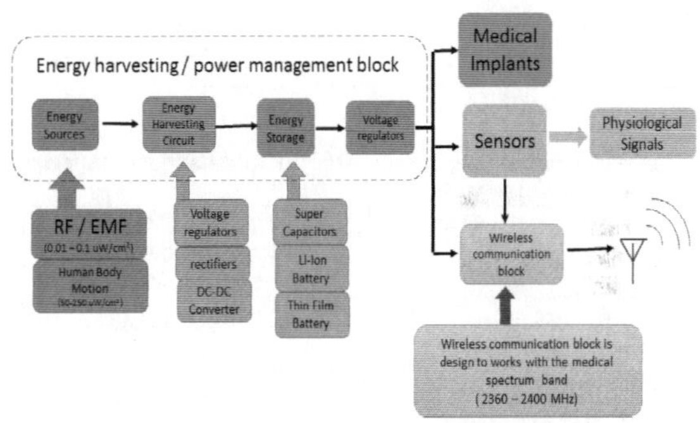

Fig. 1: Block diagram of Energy Harvesting subsystem

2. ENERGY HARVESTING SUBSYSTEM

An energy harvesting subsystem as depicted in Fig.1 is designed to harvest energy from the human body, Radio frequency and electromagnetic fields can provide source regulated voltages to the rest of the sub-circuits. The human body itself is also a potential source of energy. These source can be harvested in particular from the kinetic and thermal energies of the human-body [4].

Ambient radio frequency energy is a free flowing energy that can be collected and converted to dc power. It is an attractive approach due to its potential to provide power indefinitely. [5] For short ranges it is possible to harvest small amounts of energy from a typical WiFi transmitting power level of 50 to 100mW.

The power management block includes the front end harvesting circuit that is able to convert energy either in AC or DC to a regulated DC output. An energy storage super capacitor

BODYNETS 2015, September 28-30, Sydney, Australia

DOI 10.4108/eai.28-9-2015.2261402

and voltage regulators need to be designed to meet the specific voltage required by an implant sub-circuits.

Table 1 reports average values of power required to supply some implantable medical devices [4]. As depicted in the table the power consumption is in the range of 8uW to 5mW. Table 2 depicts amounts of kinetic energy from body motion and the expected generated electrical energy. [6]

If harvest energy levels are realized as shown in Table 2, in the range of, 6.9mW to 1000mW for mechanical energy and 1.2mW to 170mW in its equivalent electrical energy, then it is possible to meet the required power consumption of the implantable devices in Table 1. With this, designing an in-body harvester is possible and it will extend the lifespan to the implant device.

Since several types of implants devices perform real-time monitoring of physiological signals, to be able to communicate wirelessly opens the possibility to perform at-home monitoring [7]. Wireless powering and communication has the advantage of reducing the size, complexity and power consumption of implantable devices without sacrificing robustness and functionalities. [8]

Table 1. Power consumption of different implantable medical devices. [4]

Implantable Device	Power consumption
Cochlear	5.16mW
Drug Pump	400uW
Neuro-stimulator	50uW
Muscle stimulator	1.3mW
Pacemaker	8uW

Table 2. Kinetic Energy from Body Motion and the expected generated electrical energy. [6]

activity	Mechanical	Electrical	Electrical energy per movement
Blood flow	930mW	160mW	0.16J
Exhalation	1000mW	170mW	1.02J
Breath	830mW	140mW	0.84J
Fingers type	6.9-19mW	1.2-3.2mW	226-406uJ

3. SUBTHRESHOLD LEVEL DESIGN

Improvements in semiconductor technology in developing a low-cost, very low-power and energy efficient system designs have been the foundation in making information technology ubiquitous today. Scaling down the design size and power consumption of electronic equipment has recently encouraged researchers to find alternative ways to design it in a near/sub threshold level.

Subthreshold level operation is designed to have a supply voltage that is less than the typical threshold of the transistor. Operating at this modified supply voltage limits the performance of the system, but it is still acceptable given its substantial advantage in energy efficiency.

In order to achieve high performance, transistor sizes are aggressively scaling down, this increases the subthreshold leakage current, gate leakage, and reverse-biased source substrate and drain-substrate junction band to band tunnelling (BTBT) current increases. [9]

As shown in the Fig. 2, dynamic voltage dominates with higher power supply voltages in many of today's circuit designs. Note that leakage energy occurs when the circuit is not changing operational states, while the dynamic energy occurs in the circuit's switching mode, as the internal nodes are charging and it varies as the square of the supply voltage. Power is related to the supply voltage, reducing the voltage results in the reduction of power and energy consumption of the system. Fig. 2 also illustrates the region of operation for near/subthreshold design.

The tendency to reduce energy consumption at a cost of lower speed is suited for energy constrained applications such as wearable devices, implantable devices, and energy scavenging applications where lifespan extended and lower power consumption is the primary concern. Therefore, subthreshold level circuit designs offer promising solutions.

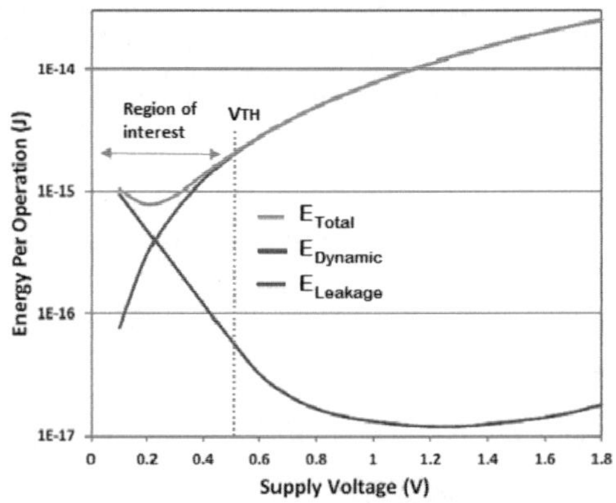

Fig. 2 Energy as a function of supply voltage

As the process technology continues to scale down, decreasing the supply voltage result an increase in subthreshold leakage current, as depicted in fig. 2. Thus, many of today's research is working on developing a circuit techniques to reduce the subthreshold leakage current in both dynamic and static mode in order to minimize the total power consumption of the system.

The expression for the total energy is given below;

$$E_{Total} = E_{Dynamic} + E_{Leakage} \quad (1)$$
$$= \propto \cdot n \cdot E_{switch,inv} + P_{Leak} \cdot t_d \quad (2)$$
$$= \propto \cdot n \cdot \left(\frac{1}{2} \cdot C_s \cdot V_{dd}\right) + (n \cdot V_{dd} \cdot I_{Leak}) \cdot (n.t_p) \quad (3)$$

where n is the number of stages, $E_{switch,inv}$ is the switching energy of a single inductor, P_{Leak} is the total leakage power of the entire inverter chain, t_d is the delay of the inverster chain, Cs is the total switched capacitance of a single inverter, I_{Leak} is the leakage current of the single inverter and t_p is the delay of a single inverter.

Fig. 3-4, show the distribution of power consumption levels of some of the reported subthreshold designs in mW (Fig. 3) and μW (Fig.4) respectively, against the year of publication. In there we can see a considerable scatter. The dotted red line shows a linear forecast of the trend over the years. As the process technology is scaling down, the power requirement is also shrinking down, thus, designing a low-power, low energy and more efficient circuit can be made possible, using subthreshold techniques.

Previous research has shown that optimizing process technology for subthreshold level operation can improve IC energy efficiency. However, for higher operating frequencies, devices need to be redesigned and optimized, as operating in the strong inversion region may not produces optimum results in the subthreshold region. Thus, there is much future research work to be done in the area of subthreshold architecture design. [9]

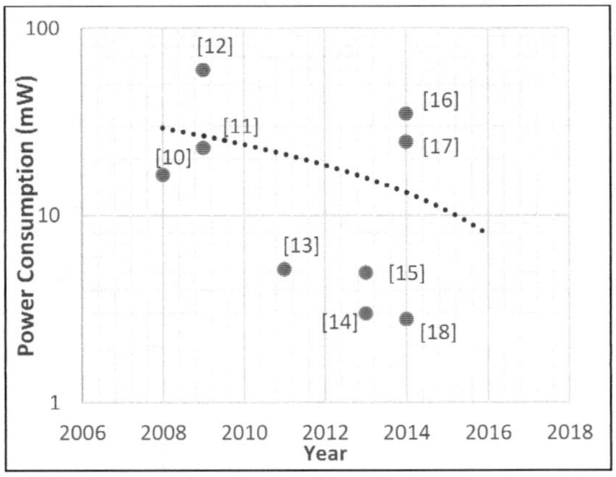

Fig. 3. Comparison and linear forecast of power consumption (mW) of some subthreshold designs presented in literature [10] – [18]

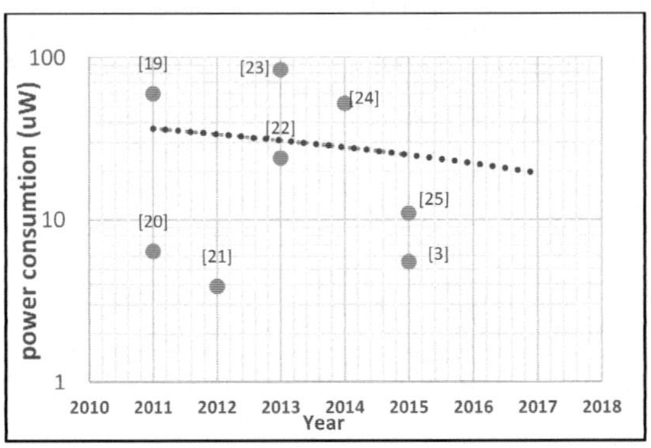

Fig.4 Comparison and Linear forecast from power consumption (μW) of some subthreshold designs presented in literature [3], [19] – [25].

4. RELATED STUDIES

In paper [26] by B.Zhai, et al, they presented the energy optimization for sensor processor and that subthreshold-voltage design offers an energy-efficient sensor network. They proposed a subliminal processor that is fully functional from a nominal supply voltage of 1.2 down scaled to 200mV. The processor attains maximum efficiency of 2.6pJ/instruction at 360mV with operating frequency of 8.33 kHz and concluded that tunning of the operating frequency is also an important factor aside from tuning the input voltage.

A.Yakovlev, J.Hoon et.al, [27] demonstrated a wirelessly powered transceiver design for implantable devices through a porcine heart tissue with the total power consumption of 10.7μW. The prototype consist of a rectifier, regulator, demodulator, modulator, controller and sensor interface. The forward link achieves 4 to 20 Mbps with 0.3pJ/Bit at 4Mbps and the backlink is 2 Mbps at 0.7 pJ/bit.

In [28], P.J Grossman, et,al. used a simulated-based approach to demonstrate the benefit of subthreshold-optimized transistor for logic gates to reduce the energy of the design circuit and achieved 57% percent energy efficiency improvement. Summary of the significant output from related studies id shown in table 3.

Table 3. Summary of the significant output form related studies.

Ref.	parameter	Efficiency
[26]	Vsub = 360mV	2.6pJ /instruction
[27]	Power = 10.7μW	Uplink = 0.3pJ/bit Downlink = 0.7pJ/bit
[28]	Vin = 0.3 to 0.6V	57% efficiency improvement

5. SUBTHRESHOLD MOSFET CHARCTERISTICS

Subthreshold voltage characteristics of MOSFET devices can be harnessed and utilized in the nano power region, allowing a wide possibility of using repeatable circuits through redesigning in a subthreshold level. An energy harvesting circuit, for example, which is of interest in today's field of research and innovation, sees the potential of subthreshold level design for nano power operation.

The expression for Subthreshold leakage current is given below;

$$I_{DS} = K \cdot e^{(Vgs-Vth)\frac{q}{nkT}} \cdot \left(1 - e^{-Vds\cdot\frac{q}{kT}}\right) \quad (4)$$

where k: function of technology, V_{GS}: gate-to-source voltage, V_{DS}: drain-to-source voltage, V_{th}: threshold voltage, q: electron charge, k: Boltzman constant, T: temperature, n: nonlinearity constant 1~2, (kT/q = 0.0259).

Considering the behavioural characteristics of the MOSFET in the subthreshold region for analog applications. Fig. 5 illustrates the I_{ds} vs. V_{gs} characteristic curve of NMOS and the region of operation for the subthreshold operation. The region at the condition where $V_{gs} < V_{th}$ is said to be that the device is cut off, and no current flows or current is said to be wasted. However, when the MOSFET is switched off, there is still power behind the gate below the threshold, and so the gate is not really completely off in most cases. It is found out that for values of V_{gs} smaller than but close to Vth, a small drain current flows to the device. In this subthreshold region the operation of the drain current is exponentially related to V_{gs}.

In subthreshold conduction, the transition from the ON state to the OFF state is gradual. This can be seen more clearly when Ids is plotted on a logarithmic scale as shown in Fig. 5, where I_d is expressed as;

$$I_d = \exp\left(\frac{q\,Vgs}{nkT}\right) \quad (5)$$

This is generally the channel-source pn junction current. Some electrons diffuse from the source into the channel when this pn junction is forward biased.

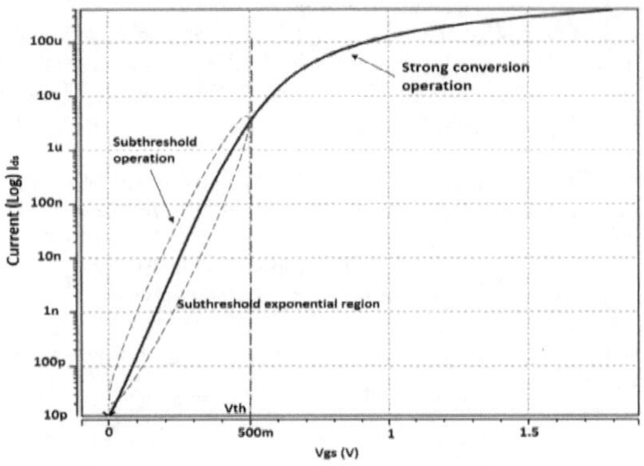

Fig. 5. I_{ds} vs. V_{gs} Characteristic Curve

The possibility to reduce the energy consumption at the cost of lower speed offers a solution to the following application in which the subthreshold level design is applicable. For energy constrained applications such as medical devices (like pace-maker, cochlear implants, wearable computing implants), wireless sensors, and energy harvesting circuits in which lower power consumption and extended battery lifetime is of concern, subthreshold circuits may be a good alternative. [9]

Fig. 6 illustrates the Ids vs, V_{ds} subthreshold output characteristics curve of nmos with varying V_{gs} from 0.2 to 0.5.

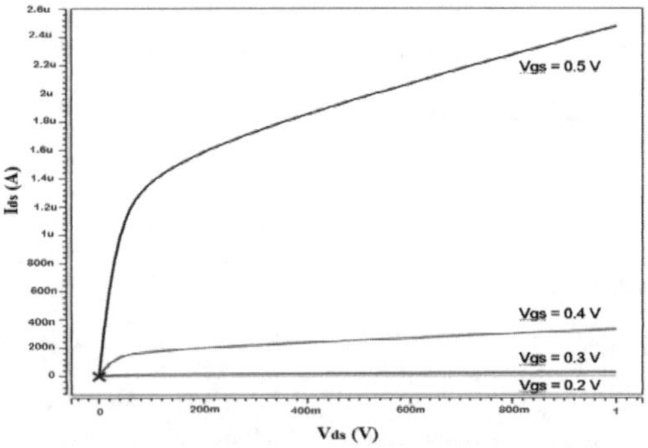

Fig. 6 Ids vs. Vds output characteristic curve varying Vgs

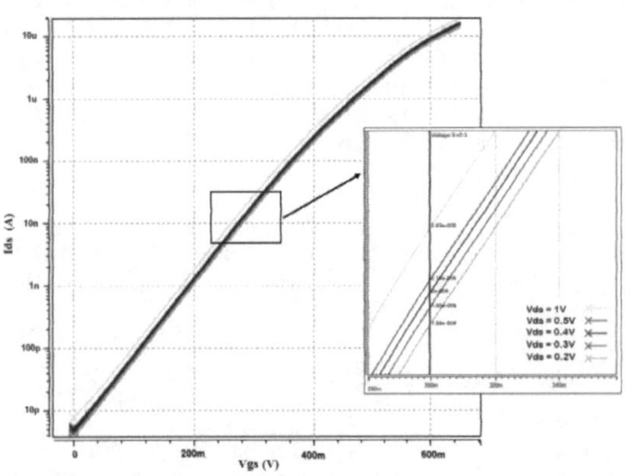

Fig. 7. Ids vs Vgs characteristic curve varying Vds

Table:2. Summary of Ids vs Vgs Value at Vgs=300mV

@Vgs= 300mV	
Vds = 1V	Ids = 28.3nA
Vds = 0.5V	Ids = 21.4nA
Vds = 0.4V	Ids = 2nA
Vds = 0.3V	Ids =18.5nA
Vds = 0.2V	Ids = 16.8nA

Table:3. Summary of Ids vs Vds Value at Vds=400mV

subthreshold region: Vgs < Vth ; Vth = 530mV @Vds = 400mV	
V_{gs} = 600mV	I_{ds} = 8.88uA
V_{gs} = 500mV	I_{ds} = 1.82uA
V_{gs} = 400mV	I_{ds} = 239nA
V_{gs} = 300mV	I_{ds} = 20.4nA
V_{gs} = 200mV	I_{ds} = 1.29nA
V_{gs} = 100mV	I_{ds} = 78pA

Fig. 7 shows the subthreshold current as a function of the sun-threshold voltage, for 0.18 CMOS technology. The typical value of V_{th} is 530mV. When V_{gs} is equal to 500mV the current Ids is equal to 1.82μA; when the value of V_{gs} is equal to 400mV, the current Ids decreases to 239nA. A further reduction of V_{gs} to 300mV drops the current Ids by another order of magnitude to about 20.4n; and when V_{gs} is equal to 200mV, Ids is equal to 1.29nA. This shows that when V_{gs} is less the V_{th} there is still a current flowing through the device. A subthreshold level design will utilize this amount of current available in order to reduce the power consumption. The subthreshold voltage may vary from 200mV to 500mV, a drop of 100mV in the input voltage causes a drop of 1000 times in the drain of the source current Ids. Thus, it is important to have a precise control in the gate threshold and subthreshold voltage level in the circuit. Table 2 shows the summary of I_{ds} vs. V_{gs} when V_{gs} is set to 300mV and table 3 shows a summary of I_{ds} vs V_{ds} is at 400mV

The subthreshold slope factor or the subthreshold swing is defined to be the inverse slope of the log (I_d) vs. V_{gs} a characteristic in the sub threshold region, which is usually give as:

$$S_s = \ln(10)\frac{kT}{q}\left(1 + \frac{C_d}{C_{ox}}\right) \qquad (6)$$

where, C_d is the depletion layer capacitance, Cox is the gate oxide capacitance, and kT/q is the thermal energy divided by the elementary charge.

6. CONCLUSION

Energy harvesting subsystems offer an alternative approach to supply power to implantable biomedical devices with the scaling of the process technology that reduces the chip area and improves performance. This also offers an opportunity to develop electronic circuitry that is low-power, low-voltage and has a reduced power consumption, through redesigning and optimization of the circuits in the subthreshold level.

Subthreshold design offers a promising solution in the semiconductor road map in developing a very low-power consumption energy harvester that is suited to biomedical implant applications.

Based on trends in both energy harvesting and subthreshold design, it is reasonable to conclude that a cross-over point will occur in the next five years. This will create an opportunity, from a systems perspective, of a self-powered implantable device.

The ability to operate in the subthreshold region is imperative for unlocking the benefit of nano power devices and driving the innovation in energy harvesting and other fields.

7. REFERENCES

[1] "Energy Harvesting form Human Power: a Roadmap to new research challenge", The Energy Harvesting Network, March 2011, http://eh-network.org/files/human_power.pdf..

[2] N. Fadhil, D. Saver, P. Patra, " Energy harvesting using Nano Scale Dual Layers PVDF Film for Blood Artery", Systems, Applications and Technology Conference (LISAT), 2013.

[3] N. T. Trung, P. Hafliger, "A Submicrowatt Implantable Capacitive Sensor System For Biomedical Application", IEEE Trans on Circuits and System. Vol. 62, No. 2, Feb. 2015.

[4] A. Cadei, A. Dionisi, E. Sardini, et, al. "Kinetic and Thermal Energy harvesters for implantable medical devices and biomedical autonomous sensors" Measurement Science and Technology, Nov. 2013,

[5] S. Gomos, J. Fernandes, E. Gultepe, et al., "Ultra-Small Energy harvesting Microsystem for Biomedical Application", 44th European microwave Conference, 2014,

[6] Z. L. Wang "Triboelectric Nanogenerator as New Energy Technology and Self-powered Sensors - Principles, Problems and Perspective", Faraday Discussions, Vol. 176, 2014.

[7] D. Halperin, T. Kohno T, T.S. Heydt-Benjamin T S, K. Fu et al., "Security and Privacy for Implantable Medical Devices" IEEE Pervasive Computing, Vol. 7, Issue 1, 2008.

[8] A. Yakovlev, S.Kim, A.Poom " Implantable Biomedical Devices Wireless Powering and Communication" IEEE Communication Magazine, April 2012

[9] R. Vaddi, S. Dasupta and R. P. Agarwar, " Device abd Circuit design Chanllenges in the Digital Subthreshold for Ultralow-Power Applications", VLSI Design Vol. 2009, Article 283702.

[10] Z.X.Pei, W.Hua et al., "Low power integrated circuits for wireless neural recording applications", IEEE Asia Pacific Conference Circuits and Systems, 2008. APCCAS 2008.

[11] M. Bennati; F. Thei, "A Sub-pA $\Delta\Sigma$ Current Amplifier for Single-Molecule Nanosensors", IEEE ISSCC 2009,

[12] G. Ferrari, F. Gozzini et al. "Transimpedance Amplifier for High Sensitivity Current Measurements on Nanodevices", IEEE Solid states circuits, 2009.

[13] J,. Zhao, Lei Yao et al. "A wireless power management and data telemetry circuit module for high compliance voltage electrical stimulation applications" IEEE Solid States Circuits, 2013.

[14] S. Y. Lee, J. Hua et al., "A low-power 13.56 MHz RF front-end circuit for implantable biomedical devices" IEEE Trans on Biomedical Circuits and System, 2013.

[15] H. M. Lee, M. Ghovanloo, "A high frequency active voltage doubler in standard CMOS using offset-controlled comparators for inductive power transmission", IEEE Trans on Biomedical Circuits and Systems, 2013.

[16] M. Crecentini, M. Bennati, "Ultra Low-Noise Electrophysiology Amplifier on a Chip", IEEE Trans on Biomedical Circuits and System, 2014.

[17] Y. Lu, W. H. Ki, "A 13.56 MHz CMOS active rectifier with switched-offset and compensated biasing for biomedical wireless power transfer systems", IEEEE Trans on Biomedical Circuits and Systems, 2014.

[18] W. M. Chen, H. Chiueh, et al., "A fully integrated 8-channel closed-loop neuralprosthetic CMOS SoC for real-time epileptic seizure control" IEEE Journal on Solid State Circuits. 2014.

[19] J. H. Lu, M. Inewicz et al., "A Low-Power, Wide-Dynamic-Range Semi-Digital Universal Sensor Readout Circuit Using Pulsewidth Modulation", IEEE journal on Sensors, 2011.

[20] F. Zhang, A. Mishra et al, "A Low-Power Multi-band ECoG/EEG Interface IC" , IEEE Custom Integrated Circuits Conference, 2011.

[21] S. Sano, Y. Takahashi, et al., "A sub-1 V 3.9 bandgap reference with a inaccuracy of 0.34% from 50 to using piecewise-linear-current curvature compensation", VLSIC 2012.

[22] M. Pons, J. L. Nagel, et al., "Ultra Low-Power Standard Cell Design using Planar Bulk CMOS in Subthreshold Operation", 23rd PATMOS, 2013,

[23] N. Nizza, M. Dei, et al. "A Low-Power Interface for Capacitive Sensors With PWM Output and Intrinsic Low Pass Characteristic", IEEE Trans on Circuits and Systems, 2013.

[24] T. Nguyen, L. Fernandez et al., "An Energy-Efficient Implantable Transponder for Biomedical Piezo-Resistance Pressure Sensors", IEEE JSEN, 2014

[25] YYakovlev,A. Jang, J.H, ect. " An 11 Sub-pJ/bit Reconfigurable Transceiver for mm-Sized Wireless Implants" IEEE trans on Biomedical Circuits and systems. Issue 99, Jan. 2015

[26] B.Zhai, S.Pant, L. Nazhandi et.al. " Energy-Efficient Subthreshold Processor design" IEEE Trans on Very Large Scale Integration (VLSI) System, Vol. 17, No, 8 Aug. 2009

[27] A. Yakovlev, J.Hoon , et al. " An 11μW Sub-pJ/bit Reconfigurable Transciever for mm-sized wireless implants" , IEEE Trans on Biomedical circuits and system. 2015

[28] P.J. Grossman,S.A Vitale, et al. " Energy Efficiency benefit of Subthrehold-optiomized transistor for Digital Logic. IEEE 2014

[29] M. Salas, White paper, " SubThreshold Design - A Revolutionary Approach to Eliminating Power", VP Marketing, Ambiq Micro -December 22, 2014

[30] J.Kao, S.Narenda, A.Chandrakasan "Subthreshold Leakage Modeling and Reduction Technique" Computer Aided Design, ICCAD, Nov. 2002

Design and Analysis of a Wireless Nanosensor Network for Monitoring Human Lung Cells

Eisa Zarepour, Najmul Hassan, Mahbub Hassan, Chun Tung Chou
School of Computer Science and Engineering, University of New South Wales, Sydney, Australia
Email:{ezarepour, nhassan, mahbub, ctchou}@cse.unsw.edu.au

Majid Ebrahimi Warkiani
Laboratory of Microfluidics & Biomedical Microdevices, School of Mechanical and Manufacturing Engineering
University of New South Wales, Sydney Australia
Email:m.warkiani@unsw.edu.au

ABSTRACT

Thanks to nanotechnology, it is now possible to fabricate sensor nodes below 100 nanometers in size. Although wireless communication at this scale has not been successfully demonstrated yet, simulations confirm that these sensor nodes would be able to communicate in the terahertz band using graphene as a transmission antenna. These developments suggest that deployment of wireless nanoscale sensor networks (WNSNs) inside human body could be a reality one day. In this paper, we design and analyse a WNSN for monitoring human lung cells. We find that respiration, i.e., the periodic inhalation and exhalation of oxygen and carbon dioxide, is the major process that influences the terahertz channel inside lung cells. The channel is characterised as a two-state channel, where it periodically switches between good and bad states. Using real human respiratory data, we find that the channel absorbs terahertz signal much faster when it is in bad state compared to good state. Our simulation experiments confirm that we could reduce transmission power of the nanosensors, and hence the electromagnetic radiation inside lungs due to deployment of WNSN, by a factor of 20 if we could schedule all communication only during good channel states. We propose two duty cycling protocols along with a simple channel estimation algorithm that enables nanosensors to achieve such scheduling.

Keywords: WNSNs, Nanoscale communication, Health monitoring systems, Nannosensors, communication protocols.

1. INTRODUCTION

Recent advancements in nanotechnology has made it possible to fabricate sensor nodes below 100 nanometers in size using various types of novel materials. These nanosensors have extra-ordinary sensing capabilities and can sense a range of information at molecular level. For example, it is now possible to fabricate supersensitive nanoscale sensors that can measure chemical compounds in concentrations as low as one part per billion [12]. Medical researchers are already considering use of nanoparticles for targeted delivery of drugs to infected cells within human body [3, 14]. When sensing is combined with these nanoparticles, they can also collect a range of valuable cell-level data for early detection of diseases. Wireless communication for such nanosensors will be a key enabler for such cell-level data collection from human body.

Although wireless communication at nanoscale has not been successfully demonstrated yet, recent simulation studies confirm that these nanosensors may be able to communicate in the terahertz band using graphene as a transmission antenna [7]. Following this development, in this paper, we present the design of a WNSN for monitoring human lung cells. The WNSN continuously measures important cell-level data inside lung cells and send them back to the Internet using terahertz communication.

The success of such WNSN will critically depend on the ability of the nanosensors to communicate reliably with other nanosensors to forward the data to a sink, which can directly communicate with a macro-scale receiver outside human body, such as a skin-patch. Electromagnetic radiation inside lungs due to wireless communication is another important consideration for such deployments. Hence, communication reliability must be achieved with as little transmission power as possible, which will minimise radiation. These requirements cannot be met without good knowledge of the channel characteristics. Thus the primary focus of this paper is to characterise the terahertz channel inside human lung.

It has been shown that terahertz is highly susceptible to molecular absorption, which can be characterised using radiative transfer theory [6, 18]. Essentially, this theory says that the amount of signal absorption will depend on the types of molecules are present in the channel, as different molecules have different absorption capabilities. We use this theory to study the characteristics of terahertz communication channels that may be encountered in human lungs. We have found that the respiration process is the major factor that influences the terahertz channel inside lung cells. The channel periodically switches between good state (i.e., bit error rate in the channel is low) and bad state (i.e., bit error rate is high) due to significant cyclic variations in the concentration of carbon dioxide in the channel. Using real res-

BODYNETS 2015, September 28-30, Sydney, Australia

DOI 10.4108/eai.28-9-2015.2261516

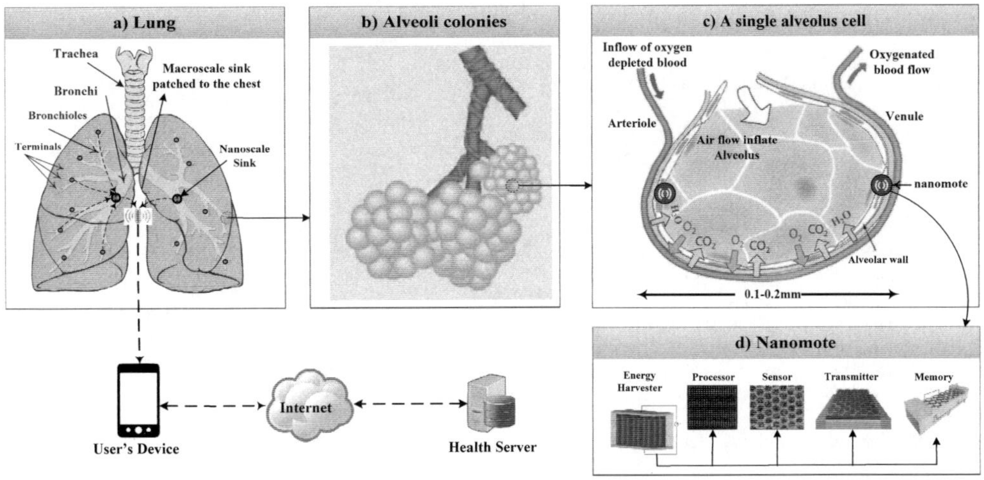

Figure 1: A schematic architecture of the proposed lung monitoring system via WNSN.

piratory data, we have shown that these channel variations are significant. More specifically, it takes 20x less power to communicate reliably if all communications are scheduled only during good channel states, which appear once in every 3 seconds, compared to the case when nanosensors communicate randomly at any time. Therefore, we propose duty cycling as a solution for nanomotes to smartly transmit only when the channel is good. Finally, we propose simple channel estimation algorithms that enable the nanosensors to achieve such scheduling.

The rest of the paper is structured as follows. The proposed WNSN for lung monitoring is presented in Section 2. The terahertz channel inside lung cells is analysed in Section 3 followed by the proposed duty cycling protocols in Section 4. We present simulation results in Section 5 and conclude the paper in Section 6.

2. PROPOSED WNSN FOR LUNG MONITORING

WNSNs are expected to sense and control important physical processes right at the molecule level delivering unprecedented performance improvement of medical, industrial, biological, and chemical applications [1, 17]. There are some indications that show WNSNs can potentially be deployed inside human body for different purposes such as health monitoring and targeted drug delivery systems [1, 3].

It is well-known that by monitoring the composition of the exhaled air, many diseases such as asthma, bronchiectases and even lung cancer can be detected at the very early stage of development [11]. For example, volatile organic compounds (VOCs) in breath are recently found as a novel biomarker that can provide precise information for quick diagnosis of the lung cancer [15].

In this work, we demonstrate using WNSNs to remotely monitor human lung at the molecular level. We first describe the lung structure followed by the proposed WNSN-based architecture for remote lung cell monitoring.

2.1 Lung Structure

The human lung is the organ of respiration, composed of a pair of large, spongy organs optimized for gas exchange between the blood and the air (Figure 1.a). Air enters the body through the nose or mouth and passes through the pharynx, larynx, and trachea. The trachea is a tube that connects the larynx to the bronchi of the lungs. Just before reaching the lungs, the trachea then splits into the left and right bronchi. Many small bronchioles branch off from the bronchi. The bronchioles further branch off into many tiny terminal called bronchioles. Terminal bronchioles are the smallest air tubes in the lungs and terminate at the alveoli of the lungs, a colony of lung smallest cell that is called alveolus (Figure 1.b).

Alveolus cells are the functional units of the lungs that permit gas exchange between the air in the lungs and the blood in the capillaries of the lungs that have surrounded each alveolus cell (Figure 1.c). A thin layer of connective tissue underlies and supports the alveolar cells. The respiratory membrane is formed where the walls of a capillary touch the walls of an alveolus. At the respiratory membrane, gas exchange occurs between the air and blood through the extremely thin walls of the alveolus and capillary.

Upon inspiration, the intra-alveolar pressure change around 5-6 mmHg within one respiration cycle due to relaxation of the intercostal muscles and diaphragm. Due to the same reason, the radii of an alveolus periodically varies between about 0.1 mm to 0.2 mm. We will later use these variations to harvest energy for our nanomotes.

Now we describe our proposed WNSN-based architecture for real-time monitoring of human lung cells.

2.2 Proposed Architecture

The proposed system aims to measure and report few markers that can help to detect the lung-related diseases. We target sparse sampling from several alveoli colonies that have been selected across both left and right lungs. For this purpose, we propose a hierarchical WNSN-based solution which includes four levels that has been depicted in Figure 1.

At the lowest level, we assume that we can deploy two nanomotes within each targeted alveolus cell to collect data from the cell. We refer to these nanomotes as '*nanocollectors*'. Nanocollectors can be attached to the cell walls by using some bioengineering techniques such as atomic force microscopy or some form of artificial bacteria [9]. Each nanocollector has been equipped with a nanoscale energy harvester [5] to harvest energy from pressure variation and cell wall movement during the respiration cycle ; a nanosensor [16] to measure the target markers in the exchanged gases; a nanomemory [13] to save the detected marker; a nanoprocessor [4] to run the required algorithm and a nanotransmitter [7] to transfer the recorded markers wirelessly to a nanoscale remote station. A schematic of the proposed nanocollector has been depicted in Figure 1.d.

In the next level, two nanoscale remote stations would be deployed in the central point of both left and right lungs that are able to receive signal from many nanocollectors. These nanoscale sinks which will be referred as '*nanosinks*' have similar modules to nanocollector except they do not have any sensor but instead have an extra energy harvester that can scavenge energy from RF waves. Nanosinks can transmit the received data from the nanocollector to the next level which is a macroscale sink (*macrosink*) that has been patched to the external skin of the chest in a proper position that minimizes the distance between macrosink and the nanosinks. The macrosink then transmit the received data from nanosinks to the user device that could be a mobile phone or a personal computer. The data would be processed by a spacial software on the device and the results would be displayed on the user's device monitor. For further analysis or to keep the person's record on a cloud, the data could be remotely transferred to a health server via Internet.

2.3 Powering of nanomotes

The nanocollectors can use a piezoelectric nanogenerator to either harvest energy from the motion due to alveolus cell movement or pressure variation during the respiration process. According to the literature up to few pW (10^{-12}) can be harvested from motions of human organs using a flexible piezoelectric nanogenerator of one square micron size [5].

The nanosinks need more power as they need to collect data from many nanocollectors and transmit data to the macrosink. RF energy harvesting might be an option for nanosink, i.e. macrosink feed the nanosinks via wireless RF transmissions.

3. IN-VIVO THZ CHANNEL MODELLING

The small antenna size dictates that nanomotes operate over very high frequencies, namely the terahertz band [1, 7]. As terahertz band is the resonance frequency of molecules, communication in this band is severely affected by molecular absorption noise and attenuation.

Radio communication is affected by the chemical compositions of the medium in two different ways in the terahertz band. First, radio signal is attenuated because molecules in the channel absorb energy in certain frequency bands. Second, this absorbed energy is re-radiated by the molecules which creates noise in the channel. We assume that the radio channel is a medium consisting of N chemical species $S_1, S_2, ..., S_N$. The effect of each chemical species S_i on the radio signal is characterised by its molecular absorption coefficient $K_i(f)$ of species S_i at frequency f. The molecular absorption coefficients of many chemical species are available from the HITRAN database [2].

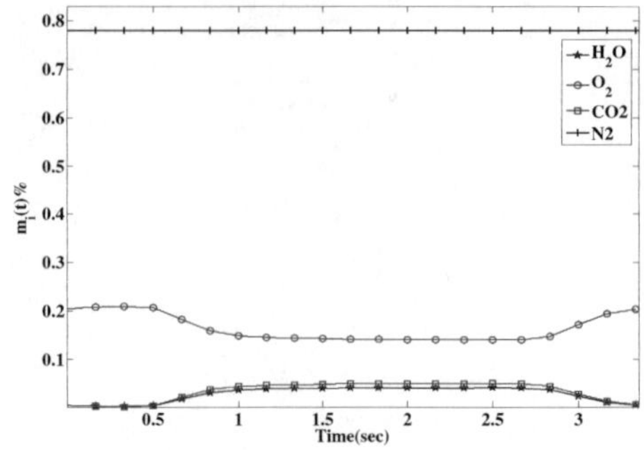

Figure 2: Alveoli gas composition during one respiration cycle.

In this section, we aim to characterise the THz communication within human body based on radiative transfer theory presented in [6].

3.1 Human lung as the communication medium

As we mentioned in previous section, the quality of communication in WNSN is strongly affected by the composition of the communication medium. It is then important to identify the composition of the medium. In the proposed architecture in Section 2, we have three mediums including communication between nanocollectors within one alveolus cell; between nanocollectors and nanosinks; and between nanosink and macrosink. It this paper, we focus only on the first medium, i.e. communication within alveolus cells, which is the most challenging medium due to the dynamic nature of its composition arising from the respiration process. The communication between nanocollectors is mainly affected by the exchanged gases in the membrane of the alveolus cells which is modulated by the human respiratory system. In addition, the blood circulatory system circulates the blood through the body; carrying oxygen to the cells; collecting the excess water and CO_2 which has been produced during cell respiration; and carries them to the alveolus cells in the lungs (Figure 1.c). This process affects the composition of the alveolus cells. Table 1 shows the composition of the in/exhaled air. While less than 0.04% of the inhaled air is CO_2, the exhaled air is composed of 4-5 CO_2.

Table 1: The composition percentage of exhaled and inhaled air [10].

	N_2	O_2	CO_2	H_2O	Others
Inhaled air	78	21	0.05	< 1	< 0.1
Exhaled air	78	13-16	4-5	3-5	< 0.1

Figure 3 shows the variation of the mole fraction, i.e. ratio of CO_2 during the respiration process in 10 second that contains 3 full respiration cycles for an adult person which

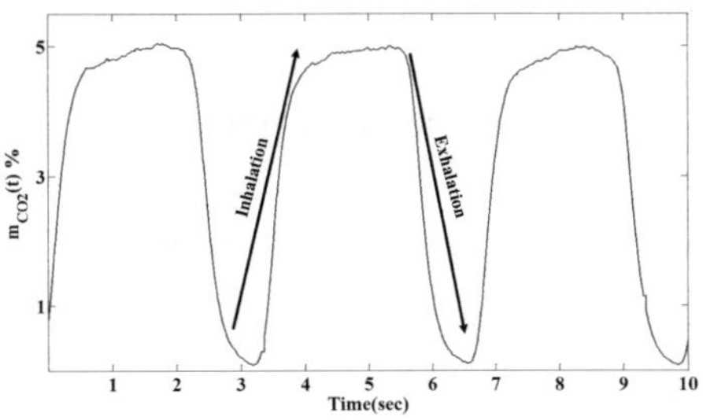

Figure 3: Variation of the CO_2 during the respiration in 10 second that has been experimentally measured [8].

has been obtained by real measurement [8]. It shows that CO_2 mole fraction fluctuated between 0.05-5 %. It starts at 0.05 at the beginning of inhalation and raises to around 5% at the end of inhalation. It drops again to 0.05 at the end of exhalation. Similar pattern has been observed in all respiration cycles. We use the data of Table 1 and the respiration data of the same person to simulate the gas exchange in the alveolus cell. Figure 2 shows the concentration (mole fraction) of different molecules during the gas exchange process in alveolus cell. As it can be seen, the composition of alveoli as our wireless medium is variable over time causing a time-varying WNSNs.

In the next section, we show how this variation in the composition of the medium can affect the quality of communication over the terahertz band.

3.2 Time-varying WNSN

We consider a radio channel in a medium which has time-varying chemical composition. Let $m_i(t)$ be the mole fraction of chemical species S_i in the medium at time t. The medium absorption coefficient $K(t, f)$ at time t and frequency f is a weighted sum of the molecular absorption coefficients in the medium:

$$K(t, f) = \sum_{i=1}^{N} m_i(t) \times K_i(f) \tag{1}$$

where $K_i(f)$ is the absorption coefficient of molecules i at the frequency f.

As we discussed in Section 3.1, Figure 2 shows the evolution of different molecules during the gas exchange process within one alveolus cell.

The attenuation at time t, frequency f and a distance d from the radio source is given in [6]:

$$A(t, f, d) = e^{K(t,f)d} \times \left(\frac{4\pi f d}{c}\right)^2 \tag{2}$$

where c is the speed of light. The molecular absorption noise, $N_{\text{abs}}(t, f, d)$, which is due to the re-radiation of absorbed radiation by the molecules in the channel, is given by [6]:

$$N_{\text{abs}}(t, f, d) = k_B T_0 (1 - e^{-K(t,f) \times d}) \tag{3}$$

where T_0 is the reference temperature 296K and k_B is the Boltzman constant.

Let $U(t, f)$ be the power spectral density of the transmitted radio signal at time t and frequency f. The signal-to-noise ratio (SNR) at time t, frequency f and distance d is:

$$\text{SNR}(t, f, d) = \frac{U(t, f)}{A(t, f, d) N_{\text{abs}}(t, f, d)} \tag{4}$$

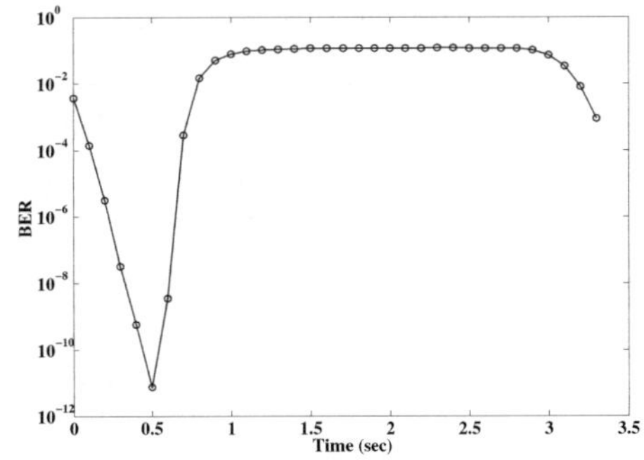

Figure 4: BER during one respiration cycle.

3.3 Channel simulation

Now, we are ready to analyse the quality of communication within alveolar. We first calculate the SNR based on the procedure of Section 3. We then use Pulse Amplitude Modulation (PAM) to calculate the Bit Error Rate (BER). Figure 4 shows the BER of the medium in one respiration cycle. It shows the BER fluctuated over time as the medium is mainly affected by gas exchanged process.

In the next section, we introduce two smart communication protocols that can duty cycle the nanomote to smartly wake-up and transmit when the BER in the channel is low.

4. BIO-INSPIRED DUTY CYCLING COMMUNICATION PROTOCOLS

In Section 2, we described how a WNSN can be used to monitor the lung biomarkers at the molecular level for early detection of the related diseases. We also showed in Section 3 that the quality of communication (BER) among nanomotes is variable over time, which is due to variation in the composition of the medium that is modulated by the human respiratory system. There are two approaches to provide reliable communication in such time-varying WNSN's channel. First, nanomotes can use a constant high transmission power to overcome the worst possible absorption in the channel. This approach can guarantee a target BER in the channel but it wastes the power when the channel's absorption is low which is not appropriate for resource restricted nanomotes. The second approach is dynamic power allocation [19] in which the nanomotes continuously adjust their transmission powers proportional to the channel's state, i.e. absorption coefficient while maintaining a low overall power budget.

Although dynamic power allocation can improve the reliability of communication, compared to the constant power allocation approach, it is more appropriate for applications that need to collect real-time data samples at a very high rate. However, in our proposed lung monitoring system, we do not need to collect continuous samples, instead the system requires to collect data at a low frequency, e.g. every few seconds. We therefore aim to design duty cycling protocols that smartly take advantage of the respiration information to transmit only when the channel's absorption is low. We will explain this protocol in the next Section.

4.1 Smart Sleep & Wake-up Protocol (SSW)

The aim of this section is to design a smart duty cycling protocol that allows nanomotes to intelligently stop transmitting when the absorption in the channel is high and only resume data transmission when the channel is good, i.e. the absorption is low. We refer to this protocol as smart sleep and wake-up (SSW) protocol. Let assume each respiration cycle $C(x)$ contains N discrete time slots:

$$C(x) = \{t_{x_1}, t_{x_2}, t_{x_3}, \ldots, t_{x_N}\}$$

Then, $T_x = t_{x_N} - t_{x_1}$ is the duration of the respiration cycle. The wake-up period for respiration cycle $C(x)$, $\Delta T_W(x)$, define as the time slots that the channel has the lowest possible absorption during a given respiration cycle of $C(x)$:

$$\Delta T_W(x) = t_{x_i} \in C(x) \text{ and } \bar{K}(t_{x_i}) <= \eta \times \Gamma(x); \eta => 1 \quad (5)$$

where $\bar{K}(t)$ is the average absorption coefficient of the channel at time t that can be obtained from integration of Equation 1 over transmitter's bandwidth, $\Gamma(x)$ is the minimum average absorption coefficient in the channel over $C(x)$ and $\eta > 1$ is a design parameter. The sleep period of the nanomotes over cycle x, $\Delta T_S(x)$ would simply be:

$$\Delta T_S(x) = C(x) \setminus \Delta T_W(x)$$

Now, we explain how nanomotes can practically estimate $\Delta T_W(x)$ for a given respiration cycle of $C(x)$. As we described in Section 2, we have two nanocollectors in each alveolus cell. Both nanomotes run algorithm 1 for T_x second to calculate $\Delta T_W(x)$:

Algorithm 1: Wake-up intervals calculation.

$\chi = \emptyset$
while $t < T_x$ **do**
  Transmit an estimation packet.
  Measure the received SNR from the counterpart nanocollector and label it as γ_t.
  $\chi = \chi \cup \gamma_t$
  $t = t + \Delta t$ which $\Delta t > 1ms$
$\Delta T_W(x) = t \in T_x$ and $\gamma_t <= \eta \times min\{\chi\}$

SSW can offer the best sleep & wake-up cycle but it needs nanomote to know the exact duration of each individual respiration cycle, $C(x)$ and also the exact values for channel absorption or SNR over the entire cycle. For a given person, the average respiration rate depends on the age, gender, health condition and the activity that person is doing. Hence, the respiration cycle time, $C(x)$ can be approximated for a given person in a given health and activity condition. Nevertheless, continues real-time measuring of the SNR in the channel is not practical for resource restricted nanomotes as it will exhaust their limited energies and also might affect their functionalities. In the next section, we therefore propose a practical protocol that can approximate the wake-up and sleep cycles based on only the real measurements from only one respiration cycle.

4.2 Extended Smart Sleep & Wake-up Protocol (ESSW)

Let assume that we can obtain the wake-up and sleep period for one respiration cycle via algorithm 1, $\Delta T_W(x)$. The extended SSW (ESSW) tries to extend this information to obtain the wake-up and sleep periods for all other respiration cycles.

Although for a given person p in a given condition, the exact period for each individual respiration cycle, $T_{p,x}$, is different but our investigation shows that the average period, $\bar{T}_p$ has a small variance (less than 5%) which means it can be used as a good estimation for each individual cycle time. The wake-up period for other next respiration cycles would be:

$$\Delta T_W(x+i) = \Delta T_W(x) + i \times \bar{T}_p \quad (6)$$

where $\Delta T_W(x)$ is the calculated wake-up period for cycle x and $\bar{T}_p$ is the average period for respiration cycles of the person p that can be obtained from the respiratory rate of the person.

Although the respiration period for a given person can be considered as fixed but if user changes his activity, e.g. starts walking prior to running, then the respiratory rate and as a result the cycle periods will change. Nanomotes therefore need to re-calibrate their $\bar{T}_p$ parameter to have a realistic estimation for the wake-up/sleep periods. The estimation of period in different activities and re-calibration process is left for future work.

5. RESULTS

This section aims to study the performance of the smart communication protocols proposed in Section 4. A good protocol is the one which provides a higher reliability for a given power budget. We compare two proposed protocols , SSW and ESSW against a *default* power allocation policy that use a constant power allocation all the time.

5.1 Methodology

We consider a single hop communication between two nanomotes that are communicating within an alveolus medium over a distance equal to 0.2mm. We extract the respiration data from CapnoBase database [8] for an adult person with respiratory rate of 18 breaths per minutes for 30 second that includes 9 respiration cycles, each around 3.32 second (T_x). Then, we follow the same steps as in Section 3.3 to simulate the gas exchange process in alveolus cells in each of 9 cycles, i.e. we extract the mole fractions of different molecules to calculate $K(t)$. Then, in order to implement SSW protocol, we follow the algorithm 1 with $\eta = 2$ to calculate the wake-up periods for all 9 cycles $\Delta T_W(x_1), \ldots, \Delta T_W(x_9)$. We also use the first wake-up period, $\Delta T_W(x_1)$ to approximate other 8 wake-up periods from equation 5 for ESSW. Finally, we use the WNSN's channel modelling described in Section 3 to calculate SNR and BER for each protocol/cycle.

For each protocol/cycle, we conduct 30 sets of experiments, each with a different nominal power levels, P_{nominal} that is ranging from 10^{-19} to 10^{-17} W that are equally spaced. For default power allocation, each nanomote uses P_{nominal} as the transmission power all the time. For other

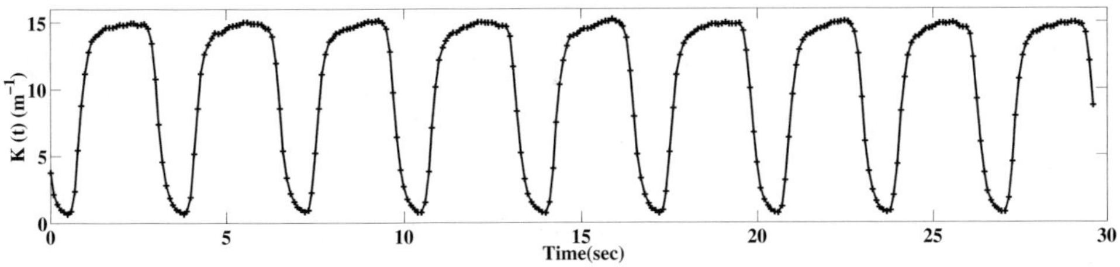

(a) Average absorption coefficient of the channel

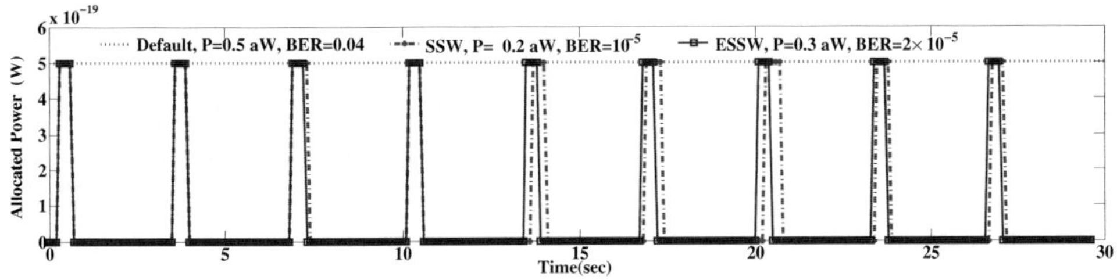

(b) Power allocation via default, SSW and ESSW.

Figure 5: Channel status and power allocation via different protocols within alveolus medium over 9 respiration cycles (nominal power equal to 0.5 aW).

policies, nanomote use P_{nominal} only during the wake-up periods and use $P_{\text{nominal}} = 0$ during the sleep period, i.e. don't transmit. The average allocated power over each cycle via each protocol therefore would be P_{nominal} for default protocol and $\frac{\Delta T_W(x)}{T_x} \times P_{\text{nominal}}$ for SSW and ESSW. Note that $\Delta T_W(x)$ for SSW and ESSW might be slightly different due to estimation error.

5.2 Results

Figure 5.a illustrates the $\bar{K}(t)$ over 9 respiration cycles. It shows that absorption coefficient of the alveolus channel varies between 1 and 15 m^{-1}. Figure 5.b shows the typical power allocation via 3 different protocols over the 9 cycles for a nominal power equal to 0.5aW (0.5×10^{-18}). As it can be seen, the SSW can successfully capture the moments that absorption is low in the channel. ESSW which uses the wake-up period of the first cycle to estimate other wake-up periods is also relatively close to the SSW. While default protocol uses 0.5 aW to provide BER of only 0.04, SSW and ESSW can improve the BER to 10^{-5} and 2×10^{-5} by spending almost half of the power that default protocol has used.

Figure 5 shows the results for a given nominal power. Now, let investigate the performance of proposed protocols when nanomotes use different nominal powers. Figure 6 shows the power/BER trade-off for different protocols. It shows that for a given power budget, the SSW can significantly improve the BER of the default protocol by few orders of magnitudes. On the other hand, for a given BER, SSW and ESSW reduce the required power by a factor of averagely 20 and 18, compared to the default protocol. We hypothesize that this lower performance of the ESSW is due to the variation in the respiration times, T_x which has been considered fixed in equation 5.

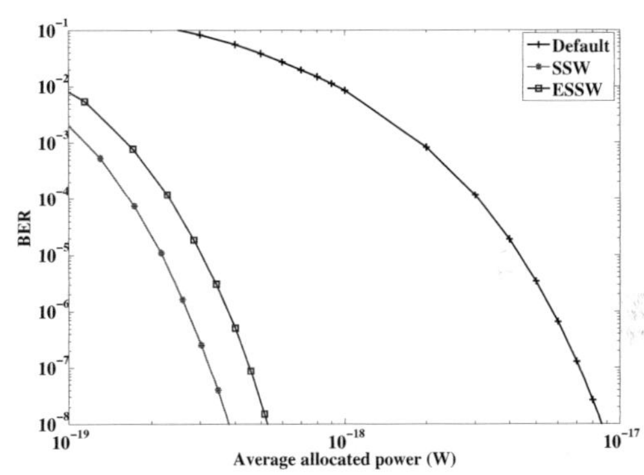

Figure 6: Achievable BER via different protocols as a function of average allocated power for the alveolus medium.

As the SSW and ESSW only transmit over a fraction of respiration cycle, it might negatively affect the channel capacity. So, we use the Shannon capacity formula [6] to calculate the average achievable channel capacity for different protocols over one respiration cycle that has been presented in Figure 7. Although SSW and ESSW have a relatively long sleep cycle, which means their capacities are zero, but they performs better than default protocol as their average SNR over wake-up period is significantly higher than the average SNR of the default protocol over the entire cycle. For fair comparison, we consider zero capacity for SSW and ESSW during the sleep cycles.

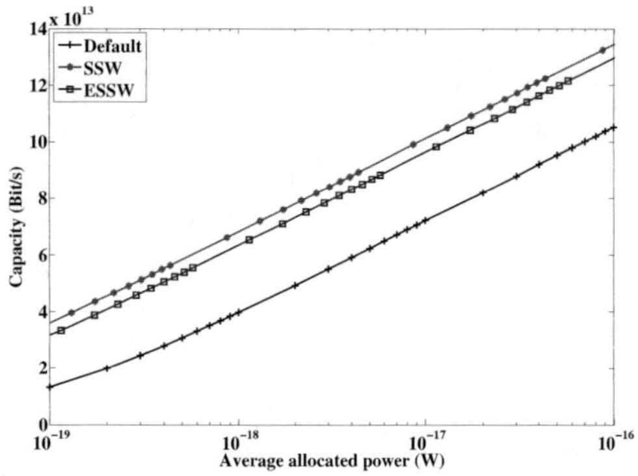

Figure 7: Capacity of different protocols as a function of average allocated power in alveolus medium.

6. CONCLUSION

We have presented the concept of a WNSN for monitoring human lung cells. Using radiative transfer theory, we have studied the characteristics of terahertz communication channels that may be encountered in human lungs. The key finding is that the respiration process is the major factor that influences the terahertz channel inside lung cells. The channel periodically switches between good and bad states due to significant cyclic variations in the concentration of the exchanged gases in the human lung. Using real respiratory data, we have shown that these channel variations are significant. More specifically, it takes 20x less power to communicate with a low BER less than 10^{-6} if communication is restricted to good channel states than the case where this restriction is not enforced. Given that good channel states cyclicly reappear once every 3 seconds, the power saving, which directly reduces the electromagnetic radiation in lung cells, can still support high frequency monitoring. We have further shown that it is possible for nanosensors to accurately detect and predict the timings of good and bad channel states, making the power saving viable.

7. REFERENCES

[1] I. F. Akyildiz and J. M. Jornet. Electromagnetic wireless nanosensor networks. *Nano Communication Networks*, 1(1):3–19, Mar. 2010.

[2] Y. L. Babikov, I. E. Gordon, and S. N. Mikhailenko. "HITRAN on the Web ", a new tool for HITRAN spectroscopic data manipulation. In *The proceeding of the ASA-HITRAN Conference*, Reims, FRANCE, 2012.

[3] F. Dressler and S. Fischer. Connecting in-body nano communication with body area networks: Challenges and opportunities of the internet of nano things. *Nano Communication Networks*, 6(2):29 – 38, 2015.

[4] M. Fuechsle, J. a. Miwa, S. Mahapatra, H. Ryu, S. Lee, O. Warschkow, L. C. L. Hollenberg, G. Klimeck, and M. Y. Simmons. A single-atom transistor. *Nature nanotechnology*, 7(4):242–6, Apr. 2012.

[5] G.-T. Hwang, M. Byun, C. K. Jeong, and K. J. Lee. Flexible piezoelectric thin-film energy harvesters and nanosensors for biomedical applications. *Advanced Healthcare Materials*, 4(5):646–658, 2015.

[6] J. Jornet and I. Akyildiz. Channel modeling and capacity analysis for electromagnetic wireless nanonetworks in the terahertz band. *IEEE Transactions on Wireless Communications*, 10(10):3211–3221, 2011.

[7] J. Jornet and I. Akyildiz. Graphene-based plasmonic nano-antenna for terahertz band communication in nanonetworks. *Selected Areas in Communications, IEEE Journal on*, 31(12):685–694, December 2013.

[8] W. Karlen, S. Raman, J. M. Ansermino, and G. A. Dumont. Multiparameter respiratory rate estimation from the photoplethysmogram. *IEEE transactions on bio-medical engineering*, 60(7):1946–53, 2013.

[9] S. Lenaghan, Y. Wang, N. Xi, T. Fukuda, T. Tarn, W. Hamel, and M. Zhang. Grand challenges in bioengineered nanorobotics for cancer therapy. *Biomedical Engineering, IEEE Transactions on*, 60(3):667–673, March 2013.

[10] W. J. P. D. Marshall and S. K. Bangert. *Clinical chemistry*. Edinburgh ; New York : Mosby, 5th ed edition, 2004. Includes index.

[11] P. J. Mazzone, X.-F. Wang, Y. Xu, T. Mekhail, M. C. Beukemann, J. Na, J. W. Kemling, K. S. Suslick, and M. Sasidhar. Exhaled breath analysis with a colorimetric sensor array for the identification and characterization of lung cancer. *J Thorac Oncol*, 7(1):137–142, Jan 2012.

[12] J. Riu, A. Maroto, and F. Rius. Nanosensors in environmental analysis. *Talanta*, 69(2):288–301, 2006.

[13] E. U. Stutzel, M. Burghard, K. Kern, F. Traversi, F. Nichele, and R. Sordan. Data storage: A graphene nanoribbon memory cell. *Small*, 6(24):2821–30, 2010.

[14] G. von Maltzahn, J.-H. Park, K. Y. Lin, N. Singh, C. Schwppe, R. Mesters, W. E. Berdel, E. Ruoslahti, M. J. Sailor, and S. N. Bhatia. Nanoparticles that communicate in vivo to amplify tumour targeting. *Nat Mater*, 10(7):545–552, Jul 2011.

[15] C. Wang, R. Dong, X. Wang, A. Lian, C. Chi, C. Ke, L. Guo, S. Liu, W. Zhao, G. Xu, and E. Li. Exhaled volatile organic compounds as lung cancer biomarkers during one-lung ventilation. *Sci. Rep.*, 4, Dec 2014.

[16] C. R. Yonzon, D. a. Stuart, X. Zhang, and A. D. McFarland. Towards advanced chemical and biological nanosensors-An overview. *Talanta*, 67(3):438–48, 2005.

[17] E. Zarepour, A. A. Adesina, M. Hassan, and C. T. Chou. Innovative approach to improving gas-to-liquid fuel catalysis via nanosensor network modulation. *Industrial and Engineering Chemistry Research*, 53(14):5728–5736, 2014.

[18] E. Zarepour, M. Hassan, C. T. Chou, A. Adesina, and M. Ebrahimi. Reliability analysis of time-varying wireless nanoscale sensor networks. In *the proceedings of 15th IEEE Conference on Nanotechnology (IEEE-NANO)*, Rome, Italy, July 2015.

[19] E. Zarepour, M. Hassan, C. T. Chou, and A. A. Adesina. Power Optimization in Nano Sensor Networks for Chemical Reactors. In *the proceedings of ACM International Conference on Nanoscale Computing and Communication*, Atlanta, Georgia, USA, 2014.

Gait Parameters Change Prior to Freezing in Parkinson's Disease: A Data-Driven Study with Wearable Inertial Units

Maria Laura Ferster, Sinziana Mazilu, and Gerhard Tröster

Wearable Computing Laboratory
ETH Zürich, Switzerland
{mazilus, troester}@ife.ee.ethz.ch

ABSTRACT

Freezing of gait (FoG) is a motor impairment among patients with advanced Parkinson's disease which is associated with falls and has a negative impact on a patient's quality of life. Wearable systems have been developed to detect FoG and to help patients resume walking by means of rhythmical cueing. A step further is to predict the FoG and start cueing a few seconds before it happens, which might help patients avoid the gait freeze entirely.

We characterize the gait parameters continuously with up to 10-12 seconds prior to FoG, observe if and how they change before subjects enter FoG, and compare them with the gait before turns. Moreover, we introduce and discuss new frequency-based features to describe gait and motor anomalies prior to FoG. Using inertial units mounted on the ankles of 5 subjects, we show specific changes in the stride duration and length with up to four seconds prior to FoG on all subjects, compared with turns. Moreover, the dominant frequency migrates towards [3, 8] Hz band with up to six seconds prior to FoG on 3 subjects. These findings open the path to real-time prediction of FoG from inertial measurement units.

Keywords

prediction, wearable sensors, Freezing of Gait, Parkinson's disease, gait parameters, motor impairment analysis

1. INTRODUCTION

Parkinson's disease (PD) is a neurological degenerative disorder with a worldwide prevalence of 16.1 million people [16], characterized by rigidity, tremor, reduced movement range and walking difficulties. A common symptom in PD is the so-called *freezing of gait* (FoG), an impromptu incapacity to walk [19], despite the intention of the subject to do so. Patients have the impression that *their feet are glued to the ground* [19] and loose control over their gait. FoG is transient and last for a few seconds up to 1-2 minutes [19]. It is the main cause of falls [3] and mortality in PD [6].

There is no cure at the moment for PD, medication being used to milden or temporary release the symptoms. FoG is one of the least responsive to the medical treatment. However, clinical studies suggest that subjects with FoG respond positively to rhythmical external cues, by exiting FoG and resuming natural gait [5, 18]. Continuous cueing wears of with time [18], thus rhythmic stimulation is given only during FoG and few seconds after, until the patient re-establishes the gait. On-body wearable sensors are used to detect the onset of FoG in real-time [11], and to start temporary rhythmical cueing upon gait freeze [2]. While such systems might be beneficial in shortening the FoG duration [2], they cannot help the user to avoid freeze, since they need at least some hundreds of milliseconds to react to the existent FoG [11]. A step further would be to predict that freeze episodes might happen in the next few seconds and start cueing, thus helping subjects to maintain natural gait and avoid the FoG altogether.

Plotnik and colleagues [21] suggest that FoG is a result of multiple gait impairments, that develop over time, decreasing the gait performance up to the point of freezing. We follow this hypothesis and aim to characterize whether there are specific changes in the gait properties during the transition from normal walking to freeze, and are different to gait variability before other walking events such as turns.

We contribute the following:

(1) We use data collected from inertial measurement units (IMU) mounted on both ankles of 5 subjects with PD and FoG, and extract gait features such as stride length and stride duration. Given the motor anomalies of the parkinsonian gait, we propose features to capture the postural control variability such as the stance phase percentage, or features to describe the coordination and symmetry of the gait such as the duration ratios between left and right limbs.

(2) Moreover, we introduce and discuss new frequency-based features to assess the gait prior to FoG, such as dominant frequency, dominant frequency amplitude and the inverse of the dominant frequency slope of the acceleration data. These features are a quantification of the gait quality.

(3) We report a constant variation of features with few seconds prior to FoG, the most common being the changes in stride duration, stride length, dominant frequency and the inverse of the dominant frequency slope.

To our knowledge, our study is the first to target a continu-

BODYNETS 2015, September 28-30, Sydney, Australia

DOI 10.4108/eai.28-9-2015.2261411

ous monitoring of gait parameters in the transient between walking and FoG, and compare it with the gait changes before turns. The motivation is the real-time prediction of such episodes using data from wearable sensors.

Our work is structured as follows: In Section 2 we survey the clinical observations of FoG patterns and the use of wearable sensors to describe the gait.We describe our dataset in Section 3, and our experimental framework in Section 4. In Section 5 we present and discuss the features and the potential of predicting FoG by observing trends in the gait properties. We conclude our work in Section 6.

2. RELATED WORK

In the following we review the literature *(1)* on clinical observations regarding gait patterns correlated with FoG, and *(2)* on the use of wearable sensors for gait analysis.

Clinical observations of gait patterns prior to FoG. The FoG pathogenesis is not understood at the moment [19, 10]. Nonetheless, there are several gait impairments associated with PD and FoG [12, 23] with respect to a healthy person's gait. Among gait anomalies which might contribute to FoG are the stride length reduction [4], step festination [10], deteriorations in rhythmic control [4, 8] and in step-to-step time variability [8], or the reduction of the cadence [4, 10]. Plotnik et al. [20] show that the impairments in left-right coordination are associated with the presence of FoG, while Yogev et al. [26] finds that gait asymmetry is increased in people with PD and FoG. Prior to freezing, subjects experience postural instability, which might be compensated by an increased time in which both feet are on the ground [17]. Yet, these evidences are found by comparing groups of subjects with FoG with groups of healthy subjects and people with PD, but who did not experience FoG. Different from prior studies, we focus on observing changes in the gait during the transient period before the FoG episode. These changes, if any, will open the direction of real-time prediction of gait freezing.

To the best of our knowledge, only Nieuwboer and colleagues [17] use gait characteristics to analyze the relation between walking pattern and the gait prior to FoG. The study focuses on the relation between cadence and stride length during normal walking, gait festination, pre-stop, and prior to freeze periods. However, it takes into account only three strides for each of the four groups of walking, for subjects which are in the OFF medication state. Different and in extension to [17], we analyze the gait during the whole transient period from normal walking up to the initiation of FoG or until the initiation of a turn, and extend the number of analyzed gait features. In addition, we use data from patients in ON medication, which makes it more difficult to extract the gait parameters [10], but is more realistic for the case of out-of-the-lab FoG prediction setting.

Wearable sensors and features for gait analysis. Wearable sensors are used to distinguish kinematic properties, with applications in sports [22], or in healthcare sector for clinical diagnosis or rehabilitation [25]. A wide range of sensors are used to extract gait properties, such as inertial measurement units [22, 25], reflective markers [17] or pressure insoles [4, 8, 20], usually attached on the lower body.

Characterizing Parkinsonian gait with accelerometers is more complex than in case of healthy subjects, due to the disease nature, which manifests into a large spectrum of motor anomalies [24]. Han and colleagues [7] propose an algorithm based on the a comparation of the standard deviation of each accelerometer data axis with a threshold to distinguish between stance and swing phases in PD. In our work, we use data from 3D wearable accelerometers and gyroscopes attached to the ankle to characterize the parkinsonian kinematics prior to the freezing episodes.

In a previous work, we study the change of time-series features and of unsupervised extracted features from acceleration in DAPHnet dataset [2], in the period prior to FoG events [13]. Although some vary prior and during FoG, such features seem to have limitations in capturing the gait variations prior to FoG, a reason being the unlabeled walking context in the dataset. Gait variability can be represented also using acceleration frequency-based features like the Amplitude [psd], width [Hz] and slope [psd/Hz] of the dominant frequency [Hz]. Weiss et al. [24] show that a larger width and a lower amplitude of the dominant frequency on the locomotion band [0.5, 3] Hz is directly related to the stride-to-stride variability and a relative less consistent gait pattern in PD patients compared with healthy people. We extend these frequency-based features to the total power band of locomotion and freeze [0.5, 8] Hz [15] and propose the inverse of the dominant frequency slope to analyze the spectrum prior to FoG compared with walking and gait prior to turns.

3. DATASET

To observe whether gait properties change prior to gait freeze, we extract features from a subset of subjects from Cupid dataset. Cupid [14] was collected with the purpose to describe and characterize FoG from a multimodal sensing perspective, i.e., IMU, skin response, electrocardiogram. Participants performed a clinical protocol in a lab-setting, designed to provoke FoG and simulate daily-life scenarios at-home, as for example tasks including passing narrow corridors, turnings, or walking with cognitive load.

We use the information provided by the wearable IMU attached on both ankles of the subjects, sampling synchronized 3D acceleration, 3D rotation, and 3D magnetometer data at 128 Hz. Data streams from the 2 IMU are synchronized with videos used to provide FoG labels by two clinicians. They considered the moment of the arrested gait pattern, i.e., stop in alternating left-right stepping, as the start of FoG, and the instant when the patient resumed a regular gait pattern as the end of it. Besides FoG, clinicians labeled the start of other walking events, i.e., gait initiation, turns, stops.

From the 18 participants, 7 did not experience freeze during the protocol, while 4 of them had less than 6 FoG, and for two subjects most of FoG happened similar in a chain reaction – freeze events were few seconds apart from each other during walking. We use data from the 5 participants which had more than 10 FoG episodes during the protocol. Included subjects are between 49 and 89 years old, with a disease duration ranging from 3 to 14 years, representing a wide range of PD stages in terms of Hoehn and Yahr score (II to IV) [9]. Subjects were in the ON medication state during protocol, as we aimed for a realistic representation of the usual daily-life setting.

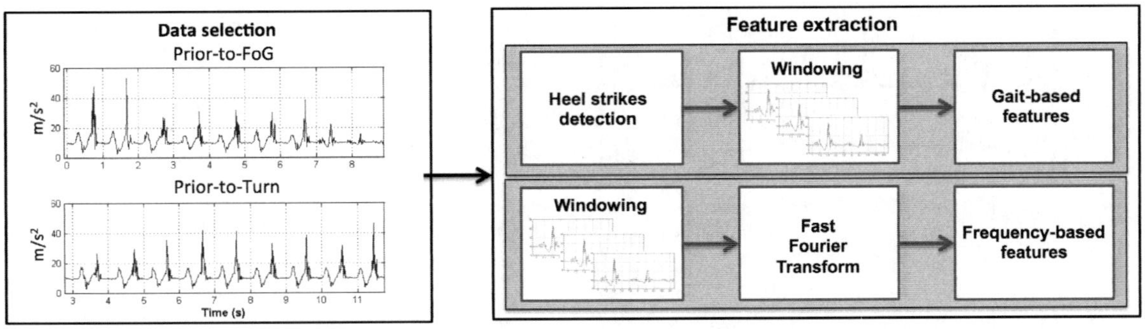

Figure 1: The data analysis framework: In the first phase we select the IMU data from *prior-to-FoG* and *prior-to-turn* sessions for each of the 5 subjects. Then, for each session we follow different procedures in case of the two types of features: (1) For gait parameters, we perform a heel strike detection, then we separate the session into 2 seconds non-overlapping windows. From each window we the extract the features. (2) For frequency features, we separate the session into 4 seconds overlapping windows, with a window-overlapping step of 2 seconds, on which we perform a Fourier Transform, and extract the frequency properties.

4. EXPERIMENTAL SETTING

In the following, we describe the methodology and the features we extract from IMU to observe whether there is a transition of the gait towards FoG.

4.1 Methodology

Figure 1 contains the main steps of our experimental setting: We first consider for each of the 5 subjects only the FoG events during turns and straight line walking. For the FoG during gait initiation, no prior information about the gait degeneration could be extracted, as patients were sitting or standing. Then for each freezing episode, we consider the walking IMU data just prior to it in a straight line, which does not contain any other gait event, such as stop walking, turns or other FoG. We call this period as the *prior-to-FoG session*. To have enough prior-to-FoG information, we keep only sessions which have at least 4 seconds of straight line walking prior to FoG. This duration was selected as a trade-off between having a statistical relevant number of prior-to-FoG sessions, and to have enough information to characterize the gait before FoG.

Similarly to the *prior-to-FoG* sessions, we consider for each subject an equal number of *prior-to-turn* sessions: Walking data prior to a turn is selected in the same manner as prior to a FoG. We use these *prior-to-turn* information in order to observe whether the gait features before a FoG change in a different manner than before an usual turn.

In a second step, we follow different procedures for the two types of features we extract from the IMU: (a) gait-based features, and (b) frequency-based features. In case of (a) gait properties, for each *prior-to-FoG* and *prior-to-turn* session, we detect the gait cycles from the IMU raw data. A gait cycle is defined as the difference between two consecutive heel strike time of the same leg. The heel strike is the moment in which the heel touches the ground and is represented by a maximum peak on the accelerometer magnitude data [22, 25, 1]. In the parkinsonian gait, the heel strike is often confused with the start of the swing phase, due to the walking abnormalities of the disease [25]. In order to avoid false heel strike detection, we use the gyroscope signal to

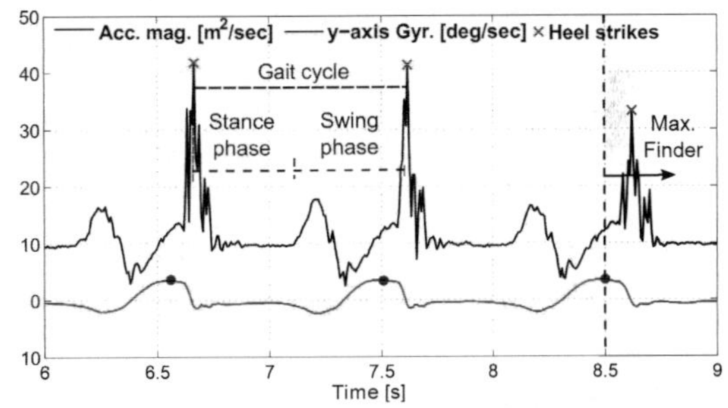

Figure 2: The procedure to detect the heel strike using accelerometers and gyroscopes: First we detect the ending of the swing phase represented as a peak in the gyroscope information. Then we look in the next period of acceleration data to detect the peak in acceleration corresponding to the heel strike.

detect the end of the swing phase, and thus to differentiate between the swing peak and the heel strike as in Figure 2: We first detect the ending of the swing phase represented as a peak in the y-axis gyroscope, and then we look in the next period for a maximum peak detection over the accelerometer magnitude data, which represents the heel strike. However, in some of the sessions the subjects experience the so-called *foot drop*, in which the swing phase is no present and can not be detected prior to FoG. These result in false detection or even no detection of the heel strike. In these rare cases, we manually set the heel strike.

Once the gait cycles are extracted, we separate each session of data in non-overlapping windows of $N_{window} = 2$ seconds. A full gait cycle lasts for 1-1.5 seconds, thus a window of 2 seconds is enough to capture it and to extract the gait parameters as detailed in Section 4.2.

In case of the (b) frequency features, we first separate each session of raw IMU data in overlapping windows of $N_{window} = 4$ seconds with an overlapping step of $N_{overlapp} = 2$ seconds. We choose the window length as a trade-off between

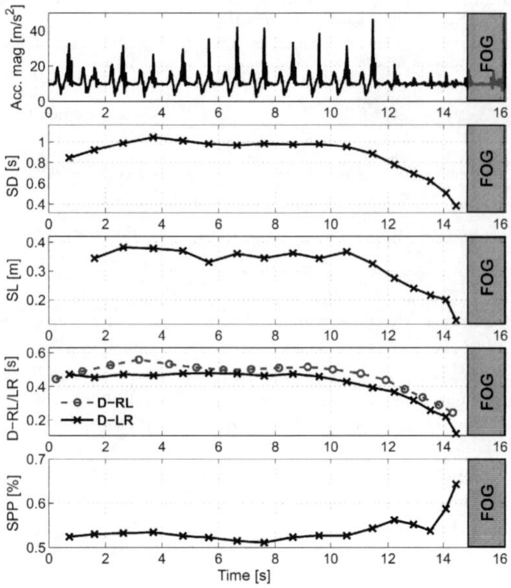

Figure 3: A *prior-to-FoG session*, expressed in raw data from acceleration and from gait parameters. We observe that with 2 and 4 seconds prior to FoG, the stride duration, stride length and both D-RL and D-LR decrease, while SPP increases. However, the gait features tend to remain constant during straight line walking (up to 10 seconds).

the latency of observations related to the upcoming FoG and the FFT estimation error. On each window we perform a Fast Fourier Transformation (FFT) on the magnitude vector extracted from the raw 3D acceleration data. We then compute the frequency features detailed in Section 4.3.

4.2 Gait Features

We extract the following gait-based features:

(1) Stride duration (SD): The time between two consecutive steps of the same limb. We compute SD as the time difference between two consecutive detected acceleration peaks of the same leg.

(2) Stride length (SL): The covered distance between two consecutive steps of the same limb. We consider SL as the double integration of the acceleration signal according to the sampling rate, between two consecutive acceleration peaks of the same limb.

(3) Right-Left Duration (D-RL)/ Left-Right Duration (D-LR): The time between a right heel peak and the consecutive left heel peak (D-RL), or the left heel and the consecutive right heel peaks (D-LR). Both D-RL and D-LR, are a measure of the bilateral coordination and the gait asymmetry/rhythmicity of the patient.

(4) Stance Phase Percentage (SPP) [%]: The time in which the foot is in contact with the ground over the whole stride duration of the same limb. D-RL can be considered as the time the left foot is in contact with the ground (stance time) and the time the right foot is in the air (swing time). The relation between D-LR and the stride duration of the right leg gives the stance phase percentage of the right leg. This feature is a measure of the postural control in PD [26].

As an example, in Figure 3 we plot the raw acceleration data from a prior-to-FoG session, together with the extracted gait features. In the first 10 seconds, there are no high variations in the gait features. However, with 2 to 4 seconds prior to FoG, the SD, SL, D-RL and D-LR abruptly decrease, while the stance phase percentage increases.

4.3 Frequency-based Features

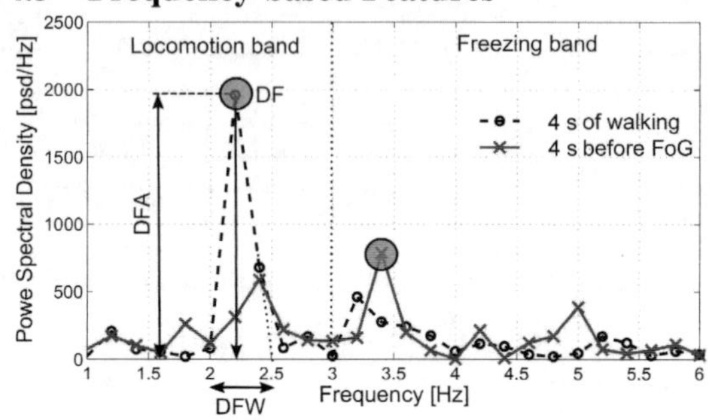

Figure 4: The acceleration's power spectral density between [1, 6] Hz, from a 4-second window just prior to FoG, and from a 4-second window during mere walking, from the same *prior-to-FoG* session. The three frequency features are different just prior to FoG, compared with walking: DF migrates to [3, 8] Hz freeze band, while its amplitude decreases, and the relation width-amplitude increases prior to FoG.

Most of the energy during walking in healthy subjects concentrates over [0.5, 3] Hz range around a dominant frequency and with a high amplitude. FoG episodes are related with gait asymmetry, suggesting variations of the walking frequency, while the energy might spread over a larger range of frequencies. Therefore a decrease in the dominant frequency amplitude and an increase in its width might be an indicator of gait symmetry variations [24]. Moreover, the SD is directly related to the walking frequency. Hence, a reduction of the stride duration might be also related to an increase of the dominant frequency.

We propose the following frequency features to characterize the gait variability prior to FoG:

(1) Dominant Frequency (DF) [Hz]: The frequency with the highest energy in the [0.5, 8] Hz band, which sums both normal gait and FoG frequency bands.

(2) Dominant Frequency Amplitude (DFA) [psd]: Corresponds to the power of the dominant frequency.

(3) Inverse of the Dominant Frequency Slope (IDFS) [Hz/psd]: The relation between the dominant frequency width (DFW) and the DFA where the DFW is the frequency range of the DF obtained through the extension of the DF's slopes.

Figure 4 shows the power spectral density with respect to the frequency, on a 4 seconds window of straight line walking acceleration, and on the 4 seconds window just prior to a FoG episode, for the same subject. We observe that with 4 seconds just prior to FoG the dominant frequency migrates

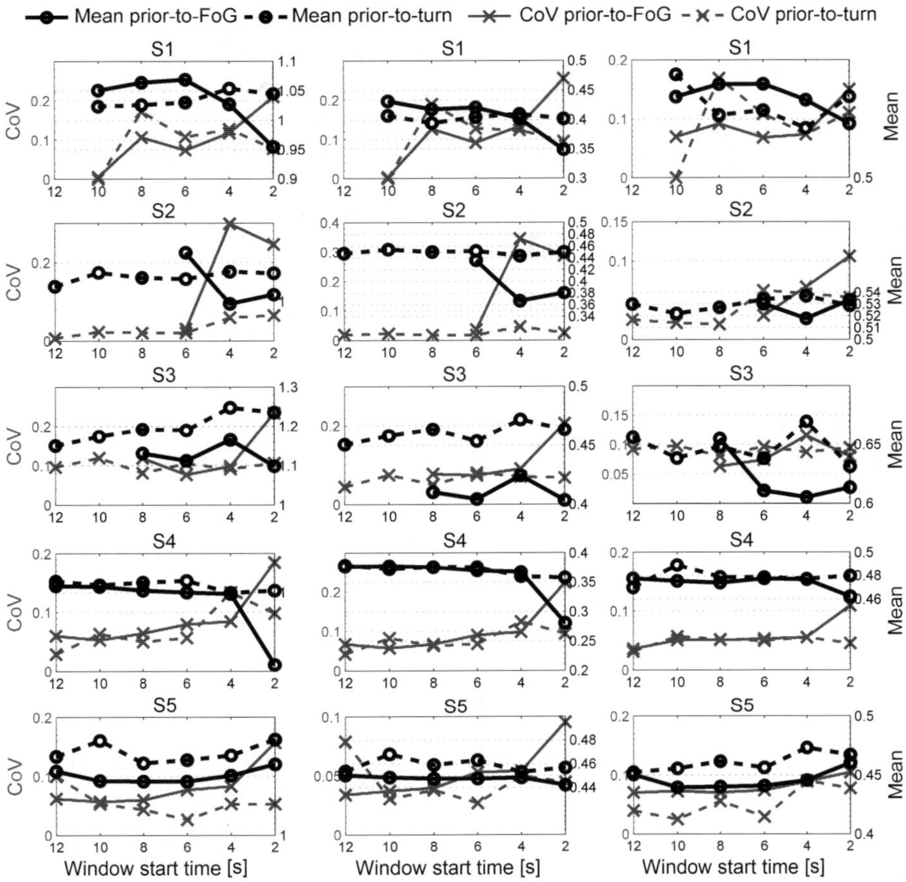

(a) SD (s) (b) SL [m] (c) SPP [%]

Figure 5: The mean and CoV values in case of stride duration, stride length, and stance phase percentage for the two different types of walking sessions, in each of the 5 subjects data. The numbers of the time axis represent the time difference between the start of FoG and the start of the window from which features were computed. For example, 2 seconds means that features were computed in the data window that started with 2 seconds prior-to-FoG, 4 seconds – in the window which started with 4 seconds prior to FoG, and so on.

to the so-called freeze band, being higher than 3 Hz, while in case of the 4 seconds window of normal walking, the DF is in the range of the gait movement [0.5, 3] Hz. Moreover, the DFA decrease just prior to FoG, compared with walking.

5. ANALYSIS AND DISCUSSION

To observe whether there are general trends in gait and frequency features prior to FoG, for each of the 5 subjects, we compute statistics such as mean, standard deviation, and the coefficient of variation overall the *prior-to-FoG* sessions. The statistics are computed for each synchronized window, as for example in windows which start 2 seconds prior to FoG, or start with 4 seconds prior FoG, and so on. The coefficient of variation (CoV) is defined as the ratio of the standard deviation to the mean, and in our case is a measure of how much dispersed are the the values of a specific feature in a window. To determine if the changes in the features are specific prior to FoG, we apply the same methodology for the features in each window from all *prior-to-turn* sessions of the same subject. In the following, we discuss our findings with respect to the two categories of features extracted.

5.1 Gait Features Trends prior to FoG

Figure 5 shows the CoV and mean statistics for each of the 5 subjects, in case of SD, SL, and SPP gait features. We will discuss further the results for each of them:

Stride duration. Clinical literature relates FoG with a decrease of in the SD [4, 17, 10] in subjects with FoG compared with subjects without FoG or healthy ones. We observe from Figure 5 that for all the 5 subjects, the CoV increases just prior to FoG, showing a higher dispersion of the stride duration in windows starting with 2 to 4 seconds prior to FoG. While for the rest of the walking session, the CoV values tend to have constant values across all windows (except in case of S2, on which we did not have sessions longer than 6 seconds *prior-to-FoG*). Moreover, when compared with *prior-to-turn* information, we observe that the CoV values tend to be constant across all the window times, except in case of S4, where the CoV also increases prior to turn, but the variation is smaller than in the case of FoG.

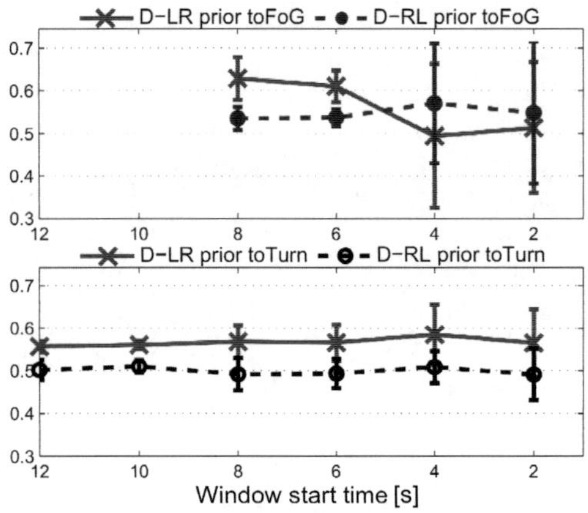

Figure 6: The variation of D-LR and D-RL features in case of prior-to-FoG and prior-to-turn sessions for S2. The values on the time axis follow the same convention as in Figure 5. For walking prior to turn, their average values and the ratio remains constant, and in windows starting with 4 seconds before FoG the D-LR decreases, while D-RL stays constant, suggesting gait asymmetry just prior to FoG.

Even if the CoV always increases in windows with few seconds prior to FoG, the SD follows different trends across datasets: For the first 4 subjects, the mean stride duration decreases with 2-4 seconds windows prior to FoG, with an overall average values between 0.1-0.2 seconds, while for S5 SD slightly increases with approx. 0.05 seconds, but also this happens in the periods prior to turns. In case of S3, even if the SD decreases with 2 second prior to turn, first it increases with up to 0.1 seconds with 4 seconds before turns.

Stride length. The same observations as for SD are present also in case of the SL feature: The CoV increases for all 5 subject in data up to 4 seconds of data before FoG, suggesting a high dispersion of the stride length values prior to FoG. SD and SL are directly related: In case of S1, S2 and S4 the mean of SL decreases with an average between 0.1 and 0.05 m in the windows starting 2 to 4 seconds just before FoG, compared with all the rest of walking. However, in case of S5 the mean stride length also slightly decreases with approx. average of 0.02 m, even if the SD increases, in this case suggesting stepping hesitation that might cause an eventual FoG. For all subjects SL tends to remain constant prior-to-turns.

For S3 and S5, even if prior to FoG the SL changes only slightly, when comparing *prior-to-FoG* SL with *prior-to-turn* SL values, we observe that constantly all over the session the SL prior to turn is lower than in the case of mere walking with turns (with up to 0.05 m for S3 and a constant 0.02 m in case of S5). The same observation holds in the case of SD feature for both subjects.

Stance Phase Percentage. Unlike the previous SD and SL features, the SPP CoV do not follow a clear trend. However, the stance phase percentage varies for S1–S4 patients, in windows starting with 2 seconds (S4) up to 6 seconds (S1 and S3) prior to FoG. SPP is a measure of the postural control, gait asymmetry and rhythmicity. Thus, the variation of SPP prior to FoG, as in case of S1, S3 and S4, suggest that the subjects loose the postural control just prior to FoG, compared to prior to a turn. However, for S1 and S3 the SPP also changes prior to turns, but opposite to the case of FoG sessions. In case of S5, the SPP is constant across time windows, but it is constantly lower than in case of sessions with mere walking and turns. This suggests that for this subject there is an anomaly of walking defined by all three SL, SD and SPP features which might be a cause of FoG, but over long sessions of time.

LR/RL Limb Durations. D-RL and D-LR features are a measure of the gait symmetry. In healthy subjects, D-RL and D-RL tend to have similar values during walking, expressing a symmetrical gait. In case of *prior-to-turn* session, all subjects tend to have constant ratio for D-RL/D-LR times. In case of *prior-to-FoG* data in S2 and S3, this ratio tends to change and also to have larger ranges towards 2 to 4 seconds before FoG, as shown also in Figure 6 for S2: In case of turns the D-RL/D-LR tends to remain constant, while in case of FoG, there is a variation in D-RL feature from data window starting 4 seconds prior to freeze. This suggests an asymmetry between the left and right limb prior to FoG, which might cause the freeze. However, for the other 3 subjects, this ratio is similar as in the case of turns.

5.2 Frequency Features Trends prior to FoG

In case of the three frequency features, the CoV for each window of walking does not show any significant differences in case of *prior-to-FoG* and *prior-to-turn* sessions in any subjects datasets, except for S2. However, In Figure 7, we plot the mean and standard deviation for the three frequency features in *prior-to-FoG* and *prior-to-turn* data. We observe that the dominant frequency tends to increase in windows starting 4 up to 6 seconds prior to FoG for all subjects. In case of S1, S2 and S4 the DF even migrates from the *normal gait band* of [0.5, 3] Hz to the *freezing band*, being higher than 3 Hz, with a higher variation of the feature values across sessions, compared with the mere walking.

In case of the IDFS feature, it increases in windows starting 4 to 6 seconds prior to FoG, compared with periods of normal walking preceding turns for all subjects. S1, S2 and S3 are particular cases, as DFA is constantly lower in sessions ending with a FoG, than compared with the walking sessions with turns, pointing towards a walking anomaly which lasts longer and might cause eventually a FoG. In this case the cueing can be given when this anomaly is observed, as it can help patients to ameliorate the gait.

5.3 Discussion

Table 1 contains a summary of our results regarding the gait variability before FoG, outlining the most informative features across all five subjects.

Stride length, stride duration and the stance phase percentage show significant variations prior to FoG for 4 out of 5 subjects. Moreover, these changes are not present during mere walking prior-to-turns sessions. These significant

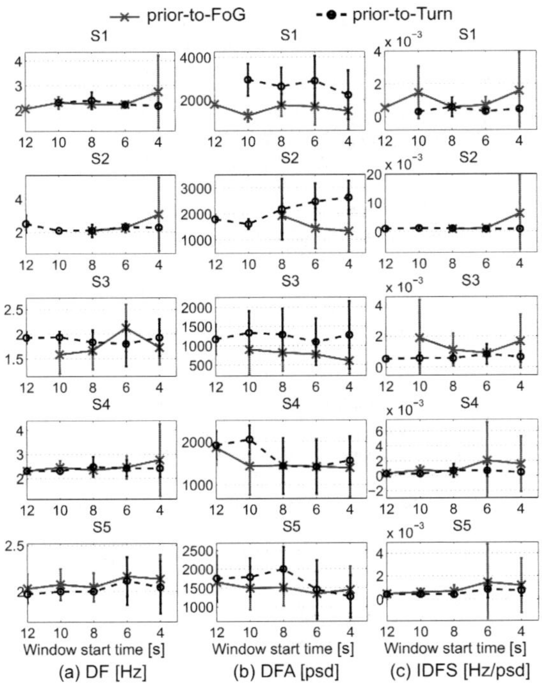

Figure 7: The average and standard deviation across all 5 subjects, for the three frequency features in case of *prior-to-FoG* and *prior-to-turn*. The time axis follows the same convention as in Figure 5.

changes can be observed on average in windows starting 2 to 4 seconds before FoG. In case of S5, even if there are not significant changes in these 3 features with few seconds before FoG, in case of *prior-to-FoG* sessions the average values for SD, SL, and SPP are constantly lower than in case of *prior-to-turn* sessions.

These characteristic trends of the SD, SL and SPP prior to FoG open the direction of predicting such freeze episodes with seconds before they are about to happen for S1–S4, and even help the subject correct the anomalous gait which will lead eventually to FoG, as in case of S5. Moreover, these observations are based on periods which transition from mere walking towards FoG, thus making possible a real-time prediction of such freezing episodes.

From the frequency features, the dominant frequency and the inverse of the dominant frequency slope increase in all of 5 subjects with 4 up to 6 seconds prior to FoG and the DF migrates towards the [3, 8] Hz band for 3 out of 5 subjects, which describes the FoG event.

All the other gait features such as D-RL/-LR and frequency features such as DFA are informative and helpful for FoG prediction, but are dependent and specific to some subjects. This suggests that there are anomalies of the gait with few seconds prior to FoG which announce the freeze, but these anomalies are subject specific. For building a model of FoG-prediction, we would need to take into account different

Table 1: Informative features across subjects

Feature	S1	S2	S3	S4	S5
Gait parameters					
SD	✓	✓	✓	✓	no
SL	✓	✓	✓	✓	no
SPP	✓	✓	✓	✓	no
D-(RL)	no	✓	✓	no	no
Frequency features					
DF	✓	✓	✓	✓	✓
DFA	✓	✓	✓	no	no
IDFS	✓	✓	✓	✓	✓

sets of gait and frequency features for each subject: Stride length, stride duration, dominant frequency, and the inverse of the dominant frequency slope seem to be a common set, on which specific features such as DFA or SPP can be added, depending on the gait anomalies of the subject, as for example for S5 the gait hesitation prior to FoG, or gait asymmetry in case of S2.

In this study, we used data from patients in the ON medication state, which might milden the overall gait variations prior to FoG. However, we were able to observe changes in the gait prior to freeze even in these realistic setting, which gives the possibility to predict FoG with a wearable system in a daily-life out-of-the-lab setting, where patients follow their regular PD treatment.

All the gait and frequency features to characterize the gait prior to FoG were extracted from wearable IMU mounted on the ankle of the subjects. There are already wearable systems which use information from on-body attached IMU to detect FoG in real-time and to start cueing to support the user to exit FoG and resume walking [11, 2]. Such systems can be extended with gait features and methods to predict FoG, given that the same information is used for both tasks.

6. CONCLUSION

We analyze the gait in the transient period between walking and freezing of gait in Parkinson's disease, and compare it with periods prior to other walking events such as turns. Our motivation is to find specific gait characteristics which change prior to FoG, thus enabling the idea of predicting in real-time FoG with few seconds before, in order to help the subject avoid the upcoming event.

We use inertial measurements unit mounted on both ankles of 5 PD subjects with freezing of gait. We compute gait-related parameters used to monitor the gait in sports and healthcare such as stride length and stride duration. Moreover, we propose specific gait and frequency features to catch the Parkinsonian gait characteristics, such as stance phase duration, dominant frequency of gait, or the inverse of the dominant frequency slope.

Our results suggest that stride length and stride duration significantly changes in all of 5 subjects, and on 4 of them in data starting with 2 up to 4 seconds prior to FoG. The dominant frequency also tends to migrate to the [3, 8] Hz band for 3 subjects with 4 up in data windows starting up 6 seconds prior to FoG and the inverse of the dominant frequency slope increase in the information starting with 4 up to 6 seconds prior to FoG compared with prior-to-turn sessions for all subjects. All other features capture specific gait characteristics prior to FoG, although are subject-dependent.

These evidences suggest that gait and frequency parameters from IMU might be used to predict FoG with few seconds before it happens. However, these findings are preliminary, due to the limited number of subjects in the experiments. For future work, we consider to increase the number of subjects, and to compare prior-to-FoG to other gait contexts, such as prior-to-stop periods.

7. REFERENCES

[1] K. Aminian, B. Najafi, C. Büla, P. Leyvraz, and P. Robert. Spatio-temporal parameters of gait measured by an ambulatory system using miniature gyroscope. *Journal of Biomechanics*, 35:689–99, 2002.

[2] M. Bächlin, M. Plotnik, D. Roggen, I. Maidan, J. M. Hausdorff, N. Giladi, and G. Tröster. Wearable assistant for Parkinson's disease patients with the freezing of gait symptom. *IEEE Transactions on Information Technology in Biomedicine*, 2010.

[3] B. R. Bloem, J. M. Hausdorff, J. Visser, and N. Giladi. Falls and freezing of gait in Parkinson's disease: A review of two interconnected, episodic phenomena. *Movement Disorders*, 19:871–884, 2004.

[4] R. Chee, A. Murphy, M. Danoudis, N. Georgiou-Karistianis, and R. Iansek. Gait freezing in Parkinson's disease and the stride length sequence effect interaction. *Brain*, 132:2151–2160, 2009.

[5] S. Donovan, C. Lim, N. Diaz, N. Browner, P. Rose, L. Sudarsky, D. Tarsy, S. Fahn, and D. Simon. Laserlight cues for gait freezing in Parkinson's disease: an open-label study. *Parkinsonism & Related Disorders*, 17:240–245, 2011.

[6] P. Gray and K. Hildebrand. Fall risk factors in Parkinson's disease. *Journal of Neuroscience Nursing*, 32(4):222–228, 2000.

[7] J. Han, H. Jeon, and K. Park. Gait detection from three dimensional acceleration signals of ankles for patients with parkinson's disease. *Proc. International Special Topic Conference on Information Technology in Biomedicine*, 2006.

[8] J. Hausdorff, J. Schaafsma, Y. Balash, B. A.L., T. Gurevich, and N. Giladi. Impaired regulation of stride variability in Parkinson's disease subjects with Freezing of Gait. *Experimental Brain Research*, 149:187–194, 2003.

[9] M. Hoehn and M. Yahr. Parkinsonism: onset, progression and mortality. *Neurology*, 50(2):318, 1998.

[10] R. Iansek, F. Huxham, and J. McGinley. The sequence effect and gait festination in Parkinson disease: contributors to freezing of gait? *Mov Disorders*, 21:1419–1424, 2006.

[11] E. Jovanov, E. Wang, L. Verhagen, M. Fredrickson, and R. Fratangelo. deFOG: A real time system for detection and unfreezing of gait of Parkinson's patients. In *Engineering in Medicine and Biology Society. Annual International Conference of the IEEE*, pages 5151–4, 2009.

[12] S. Lord, K. Baker, A. Nieuwboer, D. Burn, and L. Rochester. Gait variability in Parkinson's disease: an indicator of non-dopaminergic contributors to gait dysfunction? *J Neurology*, 258:566–572, 2011.

[13] S. Mazilu, A. Calatroni, E. Gazit, D. Roggen, J. M. Hausdorff, and G. Tröster. Feature learning for detection and prediction of freezing of gait in Parkinson's disease. In *Machine Learning and Data Mining in Pattern Recognition*, pages 144–158, 2013.

[14] S. Mazilu, E. Gazit, U. Blanke, D. Roggen, J. M. Hausdorff, and G. Tröster. Engineers meet clinicians: augmenting Parkinson's disease patients to gather information for gait rehabilitation. In *Proceedings of the 4th Augmented Human International Conference*, pages 124–127. ACM, 2013.

[15] S. Moore, H. MacDougall, and W. Ondo. Ambulatory monitoring of freezing of gait in Parkinson's disease. *Journal of Neuroscience Methods*, 167:340–348, 2008.

[16] W. Muangpaisan, A. Mathews, H. Hori, and D. Seidel. A systematic review of the worldwide prevalence and incidence of Parkinson's disease. *Journal of the Medical Association of Thailand*, 94(6):749–55, 2011.

[17] A. Nieuwboer, R. Dom, W. De Weerdt, et al. Abnormalities of the spatiotemporal characteristics of gait at the onset of freezing in Parkinson's disease. *Movement Disorders*, 16:1066–1075, 2001.

[18] A. Nieuwboer, G. Kwakkel, L. Rochester, D. Jones, et al. Cueing training in the home improves gait-related mobility in Parkinson's disease: the RESCUE trial. *Journal of Neurology, Neurosurgery and Psychiatry*, 78(2):134–140, 2007.

[19] J. G. Nutt, B. R. Bloem, N. Giladi, M. Hallett, F. B. Horak, and A. Nieuwboer. Freezing of gait: moving forward on a mysterious clinical phenomenon. *Lancet Neurolology*, 10:734–744, 2011.

[20] M. Plotnik, N. Giladi, and J. Hausdorff. Bilateral coordination of walking and freezing of gait in Parkinson's Disease. *European Journal of Neuroscience*, 27(8):1999–2006, 2008.

[21] M. Plotnik, N. Giladi, and J. Hausdorff. Is Freezing of Gait in Parkinson's Disease a result of multiple gait impairments? Implications for treatment. *Parkinson's Disease*, 2012.

[22] C. Strohrmann, H. Harms, C. Setz, and G. Troester. Monitoring kinematic changes with fatigue in running using body-worn sensors. *IEEE Transactions on Information Technology in Biomedicine*, 16(5):983–990, 2012.

[23] J. Vandenbossche, N. Deroost, E. Soetens, J. Spildooren, S. Vercruysse, A. Nieuwboer, and E. Kerckhofs. Freezing of gait in Parkinson Disease is associated with impaired conflict resolution. *Neurorehabil Neural Repair*, 25(8):765–773, 2011.

[24] A. Weiss, S. Sharifi, M. Plotnik, J. van Vugt, N. Giladi, and J. Hausdorff. Towards automated, at-home assessment of mobility among patients with Parkinson Disease, using a body-worn accelerometer. *Neurorehabil Neural Repair*, 25(9):810–818, 2011.

[25] A. Willemsen, F. Bloemhof, and H. Boom. Automatic stance-swing phase detection from accelerometer data for peronel nerve stimulation. *IEEE Transactions on Biomedical Engineering*, 37(12):1201–8, 1990.

[26] G. Yogev, M. Plotnik, C. Peretz, N. Giladi, and J. Hausdorff. Gait asymmetry in patients with Parkinson's disease and elderly fallers: when does the bilateral coordination of gait require attention? *Exp Brain Res*, 177(3):336–346, 2007.

Support Vector Machines for Young and Older Gait Classification using Inertial Sensor Kinematics at Minimum Toe Clearance

Braveena K. Santhiranayagam
Institute of Sport, Exercise Science and Active Living
College of Sport and Exercise Science
Victoria University,
Melbourne, Australia
braveena.santhiranayagam@live.vu.edu.au

Daniel T. H. Lai
College of Engineering and Science
Victoria University
Melbourne, Australia
daniel.lai@vu.edu.au

Rezaul K. Begg
Institute of Sport, Exercise Science and Active Living
College of Sport and Exercise Science
Victoria University,
Melbourne, Australia
rezaul.begg@vu.edu.au

ABSTRACT

The present study investigates the inertial sensor kinematics obtained at a critical toe-control event, Minimum Toe Clearance (MTC), to classify different age groups. Fourteen young and fourteen older adults performed treadmill walking at their preferred walking speed, wearing a shoe-mount inertial sensor unit measuring tri-axial acceleration and tri-axial angular velocities. Three dimensional (3D) position-time data was obtained using high accurate motion capture system. MTC timing within a gait cycle (MTC_{Time}), calculated using 3D motion capture data, was used to extract inertial sensor kinematics at MTC event. Mean and standard deviation of three inertial sensor acceleration features and three angular velocity features were compared between young and older individuals using t-tests. Young adults' mean anterior-posterior acceleration was greater than older adults (p=0.002). Further, standard deviations (SD) of all three accelerations and angular velocity about medio-lateral axis were greater in Older adults. The inertial sensor kinematics obtained at MTC_{Time} were able to classify young and older adults gait with 91.2% accuracy using a Support Vector Machine (SVM) classifier. The findings of the present study suggest that by employing SVM techniques, a portable inertial sensor system could be used to identify gait degeneration due to ageing and has the potential for wider applications in gait identification for falls-risk minimization.

Keywords

inertial sensor, accelerometer, gyroscope, minimum toe clearance, support vector machine

1. INTRODUCTION

As people age, their risk of falling increases and the consequences of a fall are more serious. Worldwide the population aged more than 60 was estimated to be 688 million in 2006 but is projected to grow to almost two billion by 2050 [9]. From a biomechanical perspective, falls during locomotion result from different destabilizing events such as tripping, slipping and loss of balance. Of these falls-related biomechanical events, tripping accounts for more than 50% of falls [13] and a high association between tripping frequency and falling was reported in community-dwelling older adults [10].

Tripping results directly from unsuccessful toe-ground clearance, primarily during the swing phase of a gait cycle. Previous research, therefore, focused on examining the lower limb swing-phase trajectory control, represented by a biomechanical event during the mid-swing phase of the gait cycle, Minimum Toe Clearance (MTC) of young and older populations to understand the ageing effects [2, 6, 8]. Low toe-ground clearance at MTC (MTC_{Height} ~10-20mm) in addition to high foot velocity (~4.60 m/s) and a single-foot base of support poses a significant hazard to locomotion. Failure to adequately compensate surface height variability by adjusting clearance at MTC, increases tripping risk. Older adults maintained their mean MTC_{Height} similar to young individuals' [2, 8] but their MTC_{Height} dispersion, characterized by either the standard deviation (SD) or inter quartile range (IQR) are greater than the young. This greater stride-to-stride variability in MTC_{Height} observed in older adults, increases the chances of toe-ground contact while walking [1, 2, 8].

Automated recognition of gait degeneration is the first step in developing different falls-risk minimization applications in the older, such as early identification of risky gaits, active intervention to modify the risky gaits, and monitoring the progress of treatment outcomes. The present study investigates accelerometer and angular velocity measurements obtained from a portable, compact and light-weight inertial sensor system to automatically classify young and older adults' gait using Support Vector Machines (SVM). MTC, as a cyclic event, has two physical characteristics, MTC_{Height},

BODYNETS 2015, September 28-30, Sydney, Australia

DOI 10.4108/eai.28-9-2015.2261579

Figure 1: Rigid body marker set up and inertial sensor attached to distal end of the shoe. The axes of inertial sensor unit were marked in yellow. The battery pack and data transmission unit was attached to the shank.

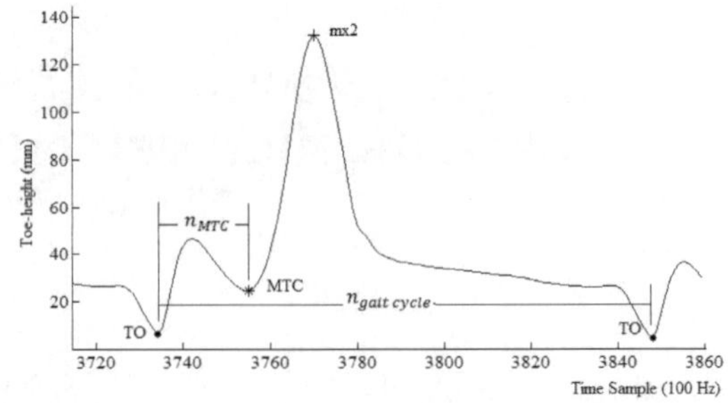

Figure 2: Toe-height over time for a typical gait cycle with an MTC event. At toe-off the toe breaks the contact with the ground and enters into the swing phase and at mx2 toe reaches the maximum vertical clearance. MTC_{Time} is calculated using n_{MTC}, number of samples from TO event to MTC and $n_{gaitcycle}$, number of total samples within the gait cycle, defined from one TO to the consecutive TO event.

as discussed above and timing of MTC event, i.e., time of MTC event occurrence within the gait cycle (MTC_{Time}). Mills et al. [8] used MTC_{Time} to analyse the lower limb joint angles at the MTC event to further understand swing phase biomechanics. Mills et al. [8] reported that older adults displayed less stance hip extension, greater swing hip flexion and less stance hip adduction at MTC_{Time} than the young. Further, greater MTC variability observed in older was mostly correlated with swing stance ankle adduction-abduction variability, whereas, for young MTC variability was mostly correlated with ankle plantar-dorsiflexion variability [8]. While it is reasonable to suggest that kinematics obtained from inertial sensor signals at MTC_{Time}, would indicate greater variability in older adults, no previous study has analysed inertial sensor signals at MTC_{Time}.

2. EXPERIMENTAL METHODS

The experiment was conducted in the Victoria University Biomechanics Laboratory, Melbourne, Australia. Fourteen young healthy adults and fourteen older adults aged 65+ with the ability to perform everyday walking for 30 minutes without a walking aid and having no orthopaedic, respiratory and cardiac conditions were recruited. Older adults also underwent following screening tests: (i) timed up and go ($<$ 13.5 secs [5], (ii) visual acuity ($>$ 6/12) and (iii) contrast sensitivity (Melbourne edge test $>$ 6/15 [7]. A wireless foot-mount sensor module was employed with 6 degrees of freedom (DOF) consisting of an accelerometer - ADXL345 and a gyroscope- ITG3200 to measure the distal foot linear accelerations and angular velocities (Figure 1 A). The ultra low-powered tri-axis accelerometer had a $\pm$16g capacity in full-scale, a sensitivity of 31.2 LSB/g and a maximum 3200 Hz bandwidth. The ITG3200 16 bit digital gyroscope had a sensitivity of 14.375 LSBs/sec and a full-scale range of $\pm$2000 $^{\circ}$/sec. The sensing unit was powered by a Sony Ericsson BST-41 Li-Polymer rechargeable Battery with an energy capacity of 1500 mAh that could transmit 100 Hz data wirelessly for approximately 11 hours. The embedded onboard system was implemented on a Freescale Semiconductor MCU (8-bit MC9S08SH8) and Bluetooth 2.0/EDR communications were used to (Sena ESD200/210) transfer the sensor data to a computer. A Matlab GUI was written to communicate and store data from the sensor units.

2.1 Data Collection

All participants completed informed consent procedures approved by the Victoria University Research Ethics Committee. A safety harness was worn while walking on the motorized treadmill. A rigid body comprising 3 infra-red emitting diodes was attached to the distal end of the right shoe and an imaginary marker was digitized at the lowest distal extremity of the shoe to represent the toe with respect to the rigid body (Figure 1). The three-dimensional (3D) coordinates of the markers were tracked relative to a three dimensional lab-based reference system. The horizontal plane of the global coordinate system was the treadmill deck surface, with the anterior-posterior axis directed in line with the treadmill belt motion. Custom built shoe-mount sensor unit was also attached to the distal end of the right shoe and a laptop was used to collect wirelessly transferred inertial sensor signals.

Participants' preferred walking speed (PWS) on the treadmill was determined by first increasing the treadmill speed until the participant reported the speed to be uncomfortably fast (fast limit). It was then decreased until reported to be uncomfortably slow (slow limit). The mean of three fast and three slow limits was considered as PWS. When required, participants were given 10-15 minutes familiarization before determining PWS. Participants walked at PWS for 5 mins. In first and last 30 s of the trial, participants did not walk, and the standing duration was used to sync 3D motion capture and foot-mount sensor data (Figure 3).

2.1.1 3D motion capture data

Position-time data from the Optotrak 3D motion capture system was exported to Visual3D (C-motion, Canada) analysis software and the raw data were first interpolated to compensate any occluded signals using a window of up to 10 frames (0.1s). A 4th order zero-lag Butterworth Filter

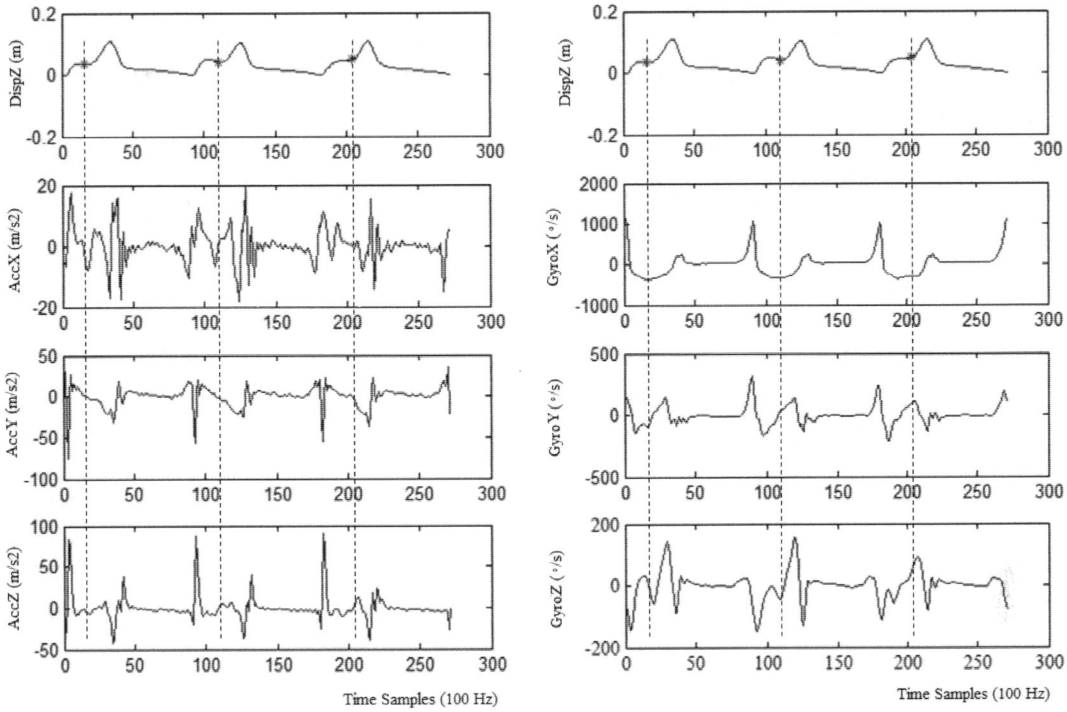

Figure 3: Time synchronized 3D motion capture vertical toe-displacement signals and corresponding tri-axial accelerometers and tri-axial gyroscopes obtained from a typical young participant for 3 complete gait cycles. * denotes MTC event in 3D motion capture data.

with a cut-off frequency of 12 Hz was then applied to toe displacement data. Conditioned data were saved as text files for further processed using in-house developed MATLAB v7.2 scripts (The Mathworks, Natick, MA, USA).

MTC is found in the characteristic vertical displacement trough between Toe-off (TO) and mx2 (Figure3). Once MTC was identified within the 3D motion capture data, MTC_{Time} was calculated as a percentage of total number of samples within a gait cycle using the formula:

$$MTC_{Time} = \frac{n_{MTC}}{n_{gaitcycle}} * 100 \quad (1)$$

where n_{MTC} is number of samples from a toe-off (TO) event to MTC, and $n_{gaitcycle}$ is number of total samples within the gait cycle, defined from one toe-off to the consecutive toe-off event (Figure 2).

2.1.2 Inertial Sensor Signal Processing

Three dimensional acceleration measurements obtained from the IMU were respectively foot acceleration along the medio-lateral axis (AccX), anterior-posterior axis (AccY) and longitudinal axis (AccZ) (Figure 3). Foot angular velocity about the medio-lateral axis (AngVelX), anterior-posterior axis (AngVelY) and longitudinal axis (AngVelZ) were measured using gyroscope. Both accelerometers and gyroscopes signals were high-pass filtered forward and reverse using a 2nd order Butterworth filter (cut-off frequency 1 Hz [6]) to ensure zero phase shift and to remove any sensor drift. Voltage outputs (V) of the IMU sensor were converted to SI (Standard-International) units using sensitivity scaling factor:

- Accelerometer (acc): $9.812 * V_{acc} * 31.2/1000$
- Gyroscope (gyro): $V_{gyro}/14.375$

Toe-off event in the inertial sensor signals were represented by the maximum medio-lateral toe angular velocity [11]. Inertial sensor signals and 3D positional data were then synchronised using toe-off events. Calculated MTC_{Time} was then used to extract inertial sensor kinematics. In gait cycles which did not show an MTC event, participant-specific mean MTC_{Time}, calculated over multiple gait cycles which showed an MTC event, was used to extract inertial signal kinematics for further analysis.

2.2 Data Analysis

Mean and standard deviation (SD) were calculated for each inertial signal kinematics (3 accelerometer signals and 3 gyroscope signals) extracted at MTC_{Time} for both Young and Older separately. Six mean and six SD values between Young and Older were statistically compared using t-test with significance set at .05.

2.2.1 *Support Vector Machine (SVM)*

Support vector machines (SVMs) [14,15,17] are binary classifiers based on Vapnik's structural risk minimisation theories [17] which achieves a trade-off between empirical risk (training set error) minimisation (ERM) and regularisation to avoid the problem of overfitting. Moreover, by using the kernel trick the SVM is able to overcome the so-called curse of dimensionality [3,4,12,16].

The SVM approximates the relation between input parameters $\mathbf{x} \in \mathbb{R}^{d_L}$ and class labels y using a function of the form:

$$g(\mathbf{x}) = \mathbf{w}^T \boldsymbol{\varphi}(\mathbf{x}) + b$$

where $\boldsymbol{\varphi} : \mathbb{R}^{d_L} \to \mathbb{R}^{d_H}$ is the feature map into a d_H - dimensional *feature space* given a-priori, $\mathbf{w} \in \mathbb{R}^{d_H}$ the weight vector and $b \in \mathbb{R}$ the bias. Given a training set of N pairs $(\mathbf{x}_i, y_i)$ the weight vector $\mathbf{w}$ and bias b are chosen to solve the primal training problem:

$$\begin{aligned} &\min_{\mathbf{w},b} R(\mathbf{w}, b) = \tfrac{1}{2}\mathbf{w}^T\mathbf{w} + \tfrac{C}{N} \sum_{i\in\mathbb{Z}_N} \xi_i \\ &\text{such that:} \quad \mathbf{w}^T \boldsymbol{\varphi}(\mathbf{x}_i) + b \le y_i + \xi_i \;\forall i \in \mathbb{Z}_N \\ &\qquad\qquad\quad \mathbf{w}^T \boldsymbol{\varphi}(\mathbf{x}_i) + b \ge y_i - \xi_i \;\forall i \in \mathbb{Z}_N \\ &\qquad\qquad\quad \xi_i \ge 0 \;\forall i \in \mathbb{Z}_N \end{aligned} \tag{2}$$

The first term in the cost R is a regularisation term included to minimise overfitting, while the second term is a measure of empirical risk (i.e. training set error). The parameter $C \in \mathbb{R}^+$ controls the trade-off between risk minimisation and regularisation.

In practice, rather than solving the primal (2) directly the dual form of (2) is solved [15], namely:

$$\begin{aligned} &\min_{\boldsymbol{\alpha}} Q(\mathbf{w}, b) = \tfrac{1}{2} \sum_{i,j\in\mathbb{Z}_N} K_{ij}\alpha_i\alpha_j - \sum_{i\in\mathbb{Z}_N} \alpha_i \\ &\text{such that:} \quad -\tfrac{C}{N} \le \alpha_i \le \tfrac{C}{N} \;\forall i \in \mathbb{Z}_N \\ &\qquad\qquad\quad \sum_{i\in\mathbb{Z}_N} \alpha_i y_i = 0 \end{aligned} \tag{3}$$

where $K_{ij} = K(\mathbf{x}_i, \mathbf{x}_j)$ and $K(\mathbf{x}, \mathbf{y}) = \boldsymbol{\varphi}^T(\mathbf{x}) \boldsymbol{\varphi}(\mathbf{y})$ is the kernel function.

The trained machine may be written in terms of the dual variables as:

$$g(\mathbf{x}) = sgn(\sum_{i\in\mathbb{Z}_N} \alpha_i K(\mathbf{x}_i, \mathbf{x}) + b)$$

In the present study the inertial sensor signal features extracted at MTC_{Time} were normalized to zero mean, unit variance (subtract the mean, divide by the SD) before testing with Support Vector Machine (SVM) to classify Young and Older gaits. Data from both young and older participants were randomized and one third of data was used to as the training set and the rest was used to test the model performance. Linear, and Gaussian RBF with g = 1e-3, 3e-3, 1e-2, ..., 100, 300) were examined. All the extracted inertial sensor features were used for classification and then only the inertial sensor signals which showed significant difference between the Young and the Older in the t-tests were used for classification.

1. Linear kernel: $K(\mathbf{x}, \mathbf{y}) = \mathbf{x}^T\mathbf{y}$.
2. RBF kernel: $K(\mathbf{x}, \mathbf{y}) = \exp\left(-\frac{1}{\sigma}\|\mathbf{x} - \mathbf{y}\|^2\right)$ (where $\sigma \in \mathbb{R}^+$).

Table 1: Mean and SD of inertial sensor kinematics obtained at MTC_{Time} for Young and Older adults. * denotes significant difference between Young and Older adults

Inertial Sensor Feature at MTC_{Time}	Young	Older	p
AccX mean	-1.23	-1.59	0.682
AccY mean	2.17	0.36	0.002*
AccZ mean	-0.22	-0.77	0.376
GyroX mean	-324.94	-297.62	0.150
GyroY mean	41.27	34.66	0.678
GyroZ mean	1.18	-0.28	0.953
AccX SD	2.08	2.73	0.006*
AccY SD	1.07	1.92	0.005*
AccZ SD	1.69	2.15	0.014*
GyroX SD	14.60	23.39	10^{-3}*
GyroY SD	20.17	20.12	0.984
GyroZ SD	24.56	28.09	0.168

3. RESULTS

Figure 3 shows time synchronized 3D motion capture vertical toe-displacement data and inertial sensor signals obtained from foot-mount sensor system. Table 1 presented mean and SD of 3 accelerometer features and 3 gyroscope features extracted at MTC_{Time} for Young and Older separately. Only one mean was different between Young and Older, i.e., AccZ, sagittal planar vertical acceleration, was significantly greater in Young than Older. Standard deviations of all three acceleration signals and angular velocity about medio-lateral axis (GyroX) of Older were significantly greater than the Young (Figure 4). Other inertial sensor signals distributions characterised by mean and SD were not different between Young and Older.

When only the features that showed statistical differences were fed into the SVM classifiers, the best classification accuracy was obtained with linear kernel was 52.65% and with RBF 83.6%. Gaussian RBF Kernel g was 0.9. When all six inertial sensor kinematics were used the accuracy improved to 92.1% with the RBF kernel.

4. DISCUSSION

The present study examined the inertial sensor kinematics obtained at MTC_{Time} for both young and older. As older adults generally show greater variability in gait related biomechanical parameters such as stride-width, stride length, and most importantly MTC, it was expected that

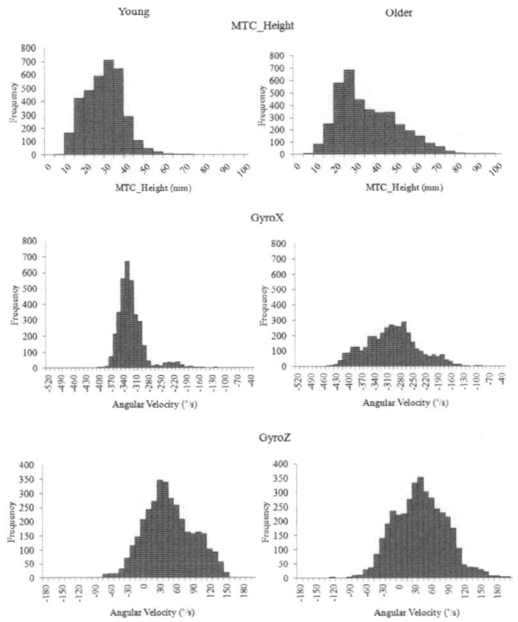

Figure 4: MTC_{Height} distribution of Young and Older and a sample of distribution with (GyroX) and without (GyroZ) a significant different between the age groups

the inertial sensor kinematics obtained at MTC_{Time} should also reflect such age-related biomechanical differences.

The study revealed that four of six inertial sensor kinematics obtained at critical toe-trajectory control event, MTC, were different between young and older, characterised either by mean or SD. Acceleration in the anterior-posterior axis (AccY) was significantly lower for Older than Young. The effect on anterior-posterior inertial kinematics could be possibly due to walking speed different between Young and Older. Older adults (0.46 m/s) walked slower than the Young (0.53 m/s), however the difference in walking speed was not significantly different (p=0.07). The greater AccY at MTC_{Time}, therefore, was not only due to walking speed difference, but also possibly due to ageing effects. Variability of all three acceleration measurements obtained at MTC_{Time} was significantly greater for Older than the Young. Further, variability of angular velocity about medio-lateral axis was also greater for Older. In consistent with literature, MTC_{Height} distribution showed in Figure 4 also revealed greater variability in Older adults than Young. Greater variability in inertial sensor kinematics at MTC_{Time} revealed reduced precision in low-limb trajectory control. The present study, therefore suggests that the three dimensional acceleration measurements and medio-lateral gyroscope reading at MTC_{Time} could be used to differentiate older and young gaits. In the present study MTC_{Time} was calculated using 3D motion capture to extracted kinematics at critical toe-trajectory control event, MTC. In future work, however, MTC_{Time} could be obtained directly from intertial sensor kinematics by detecting the 2nd peak (minimum) medio-lateral angular velocity, GyroX (Figure3). Further, in the future study, different classifiers such as Naive Bayes and logistical regression could be compared against SVM with cross-validation scheme.

The SVM classification with RBF kernel outperformed linear SVM classifier in differentiating young and older gaits using these inertial sensor kinematics obtained at MTC_{Time}. The SVM was, however, performing better when all six features were fed into the system than using only the features which showed statistically significant difference between young and older adults.

5. CONCLUSION

The present study showed that the inertial sensor kinematics obtained at MTC_{Time} were characteristically different between young and older adults. Further the study demonstrated that these inertial sensor kinematics at MTC_{Time} could be used to automatically classify young and older adults' gait with the aid of SVMs. These findings are significant in suggesting that the inertial sensors could be employed in clinical or research studies to differentiate older gaits in a non-laboratory setup while performing everyday tasks.

6. REFERENCES

[1] R. S. Barrett, P. M. Mills, and R. K. Begg. A systematic review of the effect of ageing and falls history on minimum foot clearance characteristics during level walking. *Gait & Posture*, 32(4):429–435, 2010.

[2] R. Begg, R. Best, L. Dell'Oro, and S. Taylor. Minimum foot clearance during walking: Strategies for the minimisation of trip-related falls. *Gait & Posture*, 25(2):191–198, 2007. doi: 10.1016/j.gaitpost.2006.03.008.

[3] N. Cristianini and J. Shawe-Taylor. *An Introductino to Support Vector Machines and other Kernel-Based Learning Methods*. Cambridge University Press, Cambridge, UK, 2005.

[4] R. Herbrich. *Learning Kernel Classifiers: Theory and Algorithms*. MIT Press, 2002.

[5] M. B. V. Iersel, R. P. C. Kessels, B. R. Bloem, A. L. M. Verbeek, and M. G. M. Olde Rikkert. Executive functions are associated with gait and balance in community-living elderly people. *The Journals of Gerontology Series A: Biological Sciences and Medical Sciences*, 63(12):1344–1349, 2008.

[6] D. T. H. Lai, R. Begg, and M. Palaniswami. Svm models for diagnosing balance problems using statistical features of the mtc signal. *International Journal of Computational Intelligence & Applications*, 7(3):317, 2008.

[7] S. R. Lord and J. Dayhew. Visual risk factors for falls in older people. *Journal of the American Geriatrics Society*, 49(5):508–515, 2001.

[8] P. M. Mills, R. S. Barrett, and S. Morrison. Toe clearance variability during walking in young and elderly men. *Gait & Posture*, 28(1):101–107, 2008. doi: 10.1016/j.gaitpost.2007.10.006.

[9] W. H. Organization. Who global report on falls

prevention in older age, 2007.

[10] M. J. Pavol, T. M. Owings, K. T. Foley, and M. D. Grabiner. Gait characteristics as risk factors for falling from trips induced in older adults. *Journals of Gerontology - Series A Biological Sciences and Medical Sciences*, 54(11):M583–M590, 1999.

[11] A. M. Sabatini, C. Martelloni, S. Scapellato, and F. Cavallo. Assessment of walking features from foot inertial sensing. *Biomedical Engineering, IEEE Transactions on*, 52(3):486–494, 2005.

[12] J. Shawe-Taylor and N. Cristianini. *Kernel Methods for Pattern Analysis.* Cambridge University Press, 2004.

[13] C. Sherrington, S. R. Lord, and C. F. Finch. Physical activity interventions to prevent falls among older people: update of the evidence. *Journal of Science & Medicine in Sport*, 7(1 Supplement):43–51, 2004.

[14] A. Smola. Regression estimation with support vector learning machines. Master's thesis, Technische Universität München, 1996.

[15] A. Smola and B. Schölkopf. A tutorial on support vector regression. Technical Report NeuroCOLT2 Technical Report Series, NC2-TR-1998-030, Royal Holloway College, University of London, UK, October 1998.

[16] I. Steinwart and A. Christman. *Support Vector Machines.* Springer, 2008.

[17] V. Vapnik, S. Golowich, and A. Smola. Support vector methods for function approximation, regression estimation, and signal processing. In *Advances in Neural Information Processing Systems*, volume 9, pages 281–187. MIT Press, 1997.

Using Cloud-assisted Body Area Networks to Track People Physical Activity in Mobility

Giancarlo Fortino[†], Raffaele Gravina[†,1], Wenfeng Li[°], Congcong Ma[°]
[†] Dept. of Informatics, Modelling, Electronics and Systems, University of Calabria, Rende, Italy
[°]Dept. of Logistics Engineering, Wuhan University of Technology, Wuhan, P.R. China
g.fortino@unical.it, rgravina@deis.unical.it, liwf@whut.edu.cn, macc@whut.edu.cn

***Abstract*—This paper describes a novel BSN-based integrated system for detecting, monitoring, and securely recording human physical activities using wearable sensors, a personal mobile device, and a Cloud-computing infrastructure supported by the BodyCloud platform. An integration with a smart-wheelchair system is also presented. BSNs are a key enabling technology for the revolution of personal-health services and their integration with Cloud infrastructure can effectively supports the diffusion of such services in our daily life. Many of these personal-health systems - regardless of their final aim - are based, use or are supported by contextual information on user's physical activity (body posture, movement or action) being performed. This work, hence, aims at providing a basic physical activity service that is capable of supporting personal, mobile-Health applications with real-time activity recognition and labeling both on the personal mobile device and on the Cloud.**

Keywords*—activity recognition, cloud, BSN, wearable sensors

I. Introduction

Body Sensor Networks (BSNs) [1] are Wireless Sensor Networks (WSNs) specifically tailored for monitoring human physiological signals. BSNs and their related smart wearables are demonstrating to play a disruptive role in several human-centric applications, such as mobile-Health, e-Fitness and e-Sport, mass events/trends detection and management. BSNs involves smart wearable sensor devices - heterogeneous in terms of form factors, sensing, computation and communication capabilities - that are designed to acquire physiological signals such as electrocardiogram (ECG), heart and respiratory rate, limb and full-body movements, body temperature, blood oxygenation, glucose level, and electromyography (EMG). In addition, such signals are processed to obtain indirect measurements and infer high level information that are used to build diversified non-invasive, 24/7 application services, including activity monitoring, early detection of heart conditions, emotion detection, neuro-degenerative disease monitoring.

Although these technologies are quickly taking place in the market and in our daily life, their actual potential is still partially uncovered. Particularly referring to community-awareness and crowd-sourcing opportunities, there is the need to deal with management of a large number of cooperative and non-cooperative BSNs, which is a hot research topic today. Indeed, enabling pervasive systems based on large communities of users represents a critical success factor for these technologies. The massive amount of data and information that BSN networks can generate at different layers, require efficient, scalable, distributed and interoperable platform for their collection, secure storage, and management. Such tasks simply cannot be achieved relying on the limited resources provided by the BSN alone.

With the aim of providing a solution to this complex task, we have realized, and released in open-source, the SPINE (Signal Processing in Node Environment) framework [2], [3], [4], [5] (a software platform to support BSN sensing and processing management) and BodyCloud [6], [7], [8], a Cloud computing infrastructure tightly integrated with BSN-based platforms, which enables several important functionalities in this context, such as:

- heterogeneous wearable sensing through personal mobile devices acting as local coordinators;
- scalability in terms of processing power for diverse medical analysis;
- scalability in terms of physiological signals collection and data storage;
- global access to processing and storage functionalities;
- simple and authenticated sharing of results.

SPINE is a software framework for the design and fast prototyping of Wireless Body Sensor Network (BSN) applications. It enables efficient implementations of signal processing algorithms for analysis and classification of sensor data through libraries of processing functionalities, and includes an application-level communication protocol too.

BodyCloud is a Software-as-a-Service (SaaS) platform for real-time storage, online and offline management of human vital signs and other physiological sensory signals. Additionally, BodyCloud includes mining functionalities to enable high-level decision-support from sensory data generated by the users' BSNs.. Although our framework is independent from MAC or network stacks, adopting specific solutions can help obtain high performance and reliable communications [9].

BODYNETS 2015, September 28-30, Sydney, Australia

DOI 10.4108/eai.28-9-2015.2261424

We adopted our technologies to realize several e-Health services [10], [11], [12], so showing their effectiveness and flexibility.

In this paper we describe another application of the BodyCloud middleware: an advanced human activity monitoring system, namely *Activity-aaService*, extending our previous work [13].

Activity-aaService is a full-fledged hardware/software system to support real-time, non-invasive human activity recognition and monitoring. It also features an accurate and advanced step-counter component. It uses two wearable motion sensors and a personal mobile device where a graphical application provides instantaneous feedbacks to the user; in addition, when Internet connectivity is available, data are also sent to a cloud back-end that serves as long-term, multi-user data storage and processing. Finally, a web-based interface gives remote access to such information at authenticated and authorized users.

In addition, we integrated Activity-aaService with a smart-wheelchair system.

The rest of the paper is structured as follows. Section II discusses related work on BSN-based human activity recognition and monitoring. Section III focuses on the proposed physical activity application service. In Section IV an advanced step-counter algorithm is proposed and described in detail. Section V describes the integration of Activity-aaService with a smart-wheelchair system. Finally, in Section VI conclusive remarks are drawn and directions of future work are briefly outlined.

II. RELATED WORK

Automatic physical activity monitoring has attracted tremendous interest and the topic is being studied under very diversified point of views. The problem is addressed with different approaches in terms of sensor types and recognition strategies. One of the most relevant and cited work is [14]. Here, several supervised learning algorithms are used and evaluated to detect physical activities using accelerometer data from sensors placed on different body locations. In [15], authors compared the activity classification accuracy by varying the number and the location of sensor nodes on the human body. In [16] an activity recognition system based on just a single motion sensor node worn at the waist is proposed. In [17], authors investigate the benefits of dynamic sensor selection to achieve the best trade-off between power consumption and activity recognition accuracy and propose an activity recognition method that is associated with an underlying run-time sensor selection scheme. In the last years, thanks to the significant improvements of commercial smartphones (particularly in terms of sensing opportunities), many researchers [18], [19] are highlighting the convenience of implementing physical activity monitoring uniquely relying on users' mobile phones, so to significantly improve user acceptance and reduce economic costs. Interesting surveys on human activity recognition have been published too [20], [21]. For broader reference, interested readers can consult additional interesting survey works on the e-Health domain [22], [23].

III. ACTIVITY-AASERVICE

Activity-aaService takes advantage of the related work targeting a better trade-off among classification accuracy, wearability, power requirements, and programming complexity. It is able to recognize both postures (lying down, sitting, and standing still) and a few movements (walking, running and jumping); furthermore, it includes a convenient guided procedure to extend its recognition capabilities with user-defined activities. Finally, it embeds a simple yet effective accidental fall detection widget that uses the activity classification to determine if a person is unable to stand up after having fallen. Our system uses two wearable accelerometer sensor units based on the Shimmer2R [24] platform (with a pre-installed instance of the SPINE framework) and an Android-based personal mobile device (e.g. a commercial smartphone or tablet) where most of the service logic is actually running. The end-user mobile application is hence written in Android and programmed atop the SPINE-Android framework and assisted by the BodyCloud middleware. Sensor nodes and mobile device communicate over standard Bluetooth.

In particular, BodyCloud has been used for integrating the service with a web application dashboard. Using BodyCloud, all relevant activity-related data are sent to a BodyCloud-based back-end along with time and geo-localization (when available and if granted by the user) references. In addition, with the intent of providing a degree of flexibility in terms computing power demand of the service on the mobile device, we chose to implement three different modes of operation, that can be selected upon application launch.

1) *Full Cloud*: the mobile application will only collect the raw data, and send this straight to the cloud. The cloud will then do all needed processing (i.e. feature extraction and classification).
2) *Mix Cloud*: the mobile application will be responsible for raw data collection and feature extraction. These features will then be sent to the cloud for classification.
3) *Full Local*: all processing will be done on the mobile device. Specifically, raw data collection, feature extraction, and feature classification. The cloud is therefore used only for long-term storage and graphical visualization of statistics (see Fig. 1).

In particular, to reduce network usage, the last operating mode is programmed to communicate with the cloud only after transitions between an activity/posture and another.

According to the BodyCloud programming paradigm based on XML scripting, we defined the following entities for the Activity-aaService:

- The ActivityMonitoring group, which represents the group of monitored users.
- The RawAccelerationDataFeed, FeatureDataFeed, and ActivityDataFeed modalities. These modalities reflect the three different operating modes described above.
- The ActivityMonitoring workflow, which models a three sequential nodes workflow able to read body motion data collected by the reader node, extract the features out of it, and apply the activity classification

TABLE I. POSTURE/MOVEMENT RECOGNITION ACCURACY.

Sitting	Standing	Lying	Walking	Falling
96%	92%	98%	94%	100%

algorithm. Note that this workflow is specifically activated when Activity-aaService runs in "Full Cloud" mode.

- The Activity View, which is used to model the we-based graphical representation of the various activities being performed by the user (currently a simple pie chart for statistics visualization).

The activity recognition relies on a classifier that takes accelerometer data features (max, min and average; see above) and recognizes the movements defined in a training phase. A K-Nearest Neighbor (KNN) classifier [25] has been chosen for recognition. The significant feature set has been identified using an off-line sequential forward floating selection algorithm [26]. Experimental results have shown that, given a certain training set, the classification accuracy is not much affected by the K value or the type of distance metric. This is because our target activity classes present high inter-class correlation as well as high inter-class separation. Therefore, K set to 1 and the Manhattan distance are used as parameters of the KNN-based classifier.

The overall recognition accuracy (see Table I) reached by the recognition system is considerably high, reaching an average value of 97%. The ground truth used to measure the system accuracy has been obtained by manual, online annotation of the actual activities being performed. In synthesis, during system evaluation, we asked subjects to wear our system and to freely perform any of the four target activities in a laboratory setting (a $150m^2$ room furnished with desks, sofas, chairs). We enabled a dedicated panel on the mobile application with a radio button to let us selecting the actual activity being performed by the subject and we programmed the application to store activity classification outputs on file a simple CSV file with two label columns, one for the actual activity (as indicated using the radio button) and the other for the activity classified by the system. Finally, we analyzed offline this file by counting the number of recorded classifications for each activity and comparing each estimated activity class against the corresponding ground truth value, so to detect classification errors. Therefore, the accuracy percentage of a given activity is obtained as the number of correct classifications divided by the total number of samples recorded on the file for that activity.

Fig. 1 depicts a statistics web-based dashboard of the activities performed by the user. The time period for statistics generation can be freely selected by the user. Specifically, the dashboard currently consists of a pie chart indicating the time percentage spent for each performed activity. If a certain activity is not performed at all within the selected time interval, it will not be show in the chart. In addition, a table reports the same information as the pie chart plus the total time spent (expressed in days.hours.minutes.seconds) within the selected time interval.

IV. STEP-COUNTER ALGORITHM

This section describes an innovative step-counter algorithm, whose main design requirements are the followings:

- Use of accelerometer data from a body worn sensor;
- Energy and computation efficient design to support embedded implementations;
- Use of a single sensor node, placed on the waist;
- General-purpose algorithm, to fit walking patterns of healthy people as well as elderly and/or people with disabilities;
- No need for user-specific calibration;
- High average accuracy (*precision*).

This algorithm has been integrated in Activity-aaService to provide additional information to the user and caregivers, allowing for accurate step detection and distance covered.

Several real walk data on different subjects have been collected and studied before starting the algorithm design. Subjects were asked to walk naturally, and to increase/decrease the walking speed occasionally. In particular, a single three-axis accelerometer sensor node was placed on the waist while recording. The sensor has been sampled at 40Hz.

Preliminary conclusions from this analysis include that:

- Off-line downsampling to 20Hz showed that the signal is still well characterized;
- Lateral acceleration presents a poor SNR (Signal-to-Noise Ratio) as the waist swing during walking is heavily influenced by noise;
- Frontal (horizontal) and vertical acceleration present very useful signals; they looks roughly sinusoidal, because the waist is interested by vertical accelerations/decelerations when the feet hit the ground, and by horizontal accelerations/decelerations when the body swings frontally while walking;
- Horizontal acceleration signal is generally less affected by noise than the vertical acceleration signal.

A number of step detection approaches were considered and evaluated, eventually converging to the proposed solution. To simplify the development, debugging, and evaluation, the implementations have been initially programmed in *Matlab*. Only *integer-math* computations were used, so allowing for a more straightforward embedded implementation (as the target embedded platform is based on a micro-controller with no hardware support for floating point operations).

A very simple "*fixed threshold-range*" technique has been studied at the beginning. The thresholds were empirically determined. In this approach, a step is detected if the instantaneous raw acceleration stays within the defined range. To remove multiple detections of the same step, the algorithm sleeps for the shortest "step-time", measured from the available observations. Although the algorithm is very simple, it showed high precision ($>$ 90% in lab experiments) while applied to healthy people, regardless the gender, weight, height, and

Fig. 1. The main dashboard of the Activity-aaService web-app module.

walking speed. However, when applied to elderly people, results were significantly poorer, with almost no steps detected. Intuitively, that is due to less pronounced movements of walking elderly people that lead to lower accelerations of the waist.

An enhanced algorithm followed a different approach. Rather than defining *a priori* the threshold range, it is possible to determine the best threshold for the monitored subject by running a search algorithm that requires a set of walking data of that subject, the number of steps inside that recording, and the required accuracy. The threshold search is performed iterating the step-counter algorithm previously described on the walking data, with a decreased threshold (initially set to the upper accelerometer scale value) at each iteration and comparing the number of detected steps against the actual number. The search stops when the required accuracy has been reached or the number of detected steps exceeds the actual number, and the threshold found is returned. This implementation performs overall better than the first one, but requires a training phase and the manual counting of the steps during the training. If the counting is incorrect and/or during the recording a significant number of data packets get lost, the threshold search can be compromised.

The first algorithm does not recognize effectively the steps of elderly people. On the other hand, the second algorithm needs a preliminary training phase. Furthermore, they both work on the raw accelerometer data.

To overcome these limitations, a third algorithm has been defined, borrowing some ideas from the previous ones. At the same time, additional real walk data have been recorded from hospitalized subjects (elderly and people with motor disabilities).This latter algorithm attempts at detecting steps by identifying the decreasing segment (*falling edge*) which corresponds to the last fraction of a step movement.

A step is characterized by time constraints (i.e. it cannot be "too" fast or "too" slow). However, walk patterns vary from people to people and even for the same person it might change from time to time; hence, the amplitude and slope of the acquired signal can vary significantly.

To simplify the pattern recognition, the raw acceleration is first processed with a *smoothing filter* which removes the high frequency components. Then, it looks for local maximums. When a local max is found, it looks for a local minimum. After the local min is found, the candidate segment (i.e. a potential step) is also identified. Two features are then extracted and used to determine whether the candidate belongs to a real step or not. The candidate is classified as *step* if (i) it has an acceleration drop within a certain range (specified by a "*tolerance*" parameter around a threshold), and (ii) its time duration is within a certain interval. More specifically, the pre-processing is a 9-point windowed smoothing filter using Gaussian kernels. Because they are applied to a digital signal, the sum of the kernels must be 1. However, because the algorithm works on integer-math, they have been scaled so that decimal factors are removed.

The following Gaussian kernels have been selected:

- { *5*, *30*, *104*, *220*, *282*, *220*, *104*, *30*, *5* }

The threshold is coarsely initialized, but it is automatically adapted while steps are recognized. In particular, it is continuously updated with the average of the last 10 acceleration drops that were classified as steps.

Since the threshold is just coarsely initialized at the beginning and because even following steps can occasionally present significant variance in their vigor, the updated threshold is

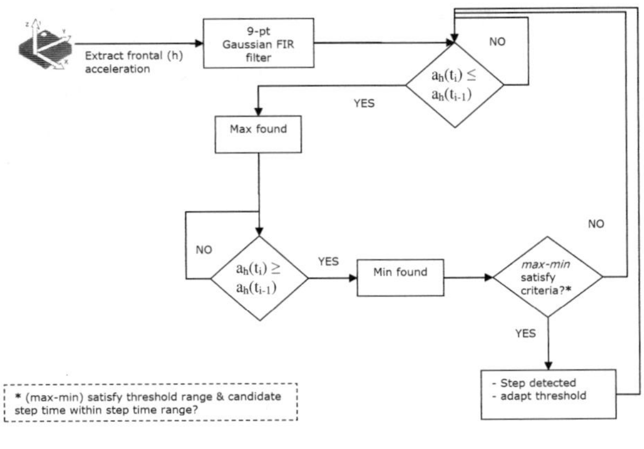

Fig. 2. Block diagram of the step-counter algorithm.

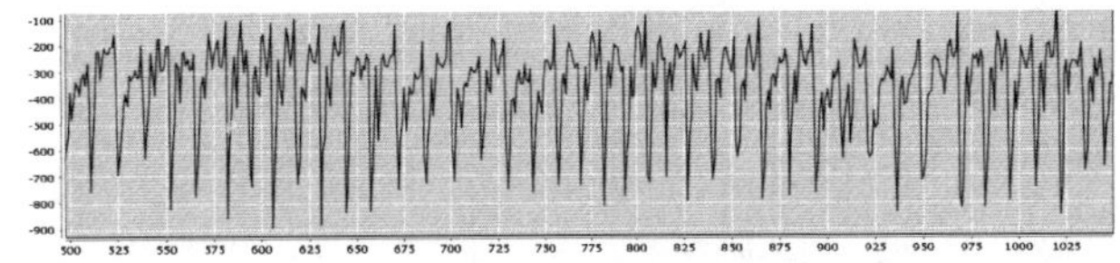

Fig. 3. Raw Data of the frontal (horizontal) acceleration of the waist during normal walking.

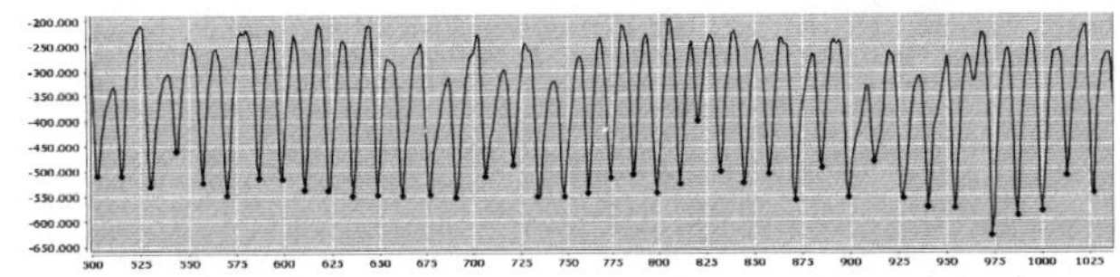

Fig. 4. Result of the Gaussian filtering of the data shown in Figure 3.

adjusted with parametric coefficients to specify the amplitude range in which a candidate must fall.

Finally, to reduce "false positive" recognitions, e.g. due to sudden shocks or slow tilts of the sensor, the time elapsed between the local max and min (which it is simply determined as the product between the number of samples composing the segment and the sampling period) must be longer than the "*minimum step time*" and shorter than the "*maximum step time*". Both values have been determined empirically from the available observations. In particular, based on the available walking data, the following values have been identified:

- *minimum step time* = 350*ms*
- *maximum step time* = 2000*ms*.

Fig. 2 shows the block diagram of the proposed algorithm.

The proposed algorithm has been initially evaluated on the computer using Matlab, and eventually implemented on a wireless sensor node running SPINE. For this application, the node-side of SPINE has been extended with the proposed algorithm. Every time the node detects a step, it communicates to its coordinator the total number of steps taken so far (this to avoid counting errors in case of lost packets). On the coordinator side, only minor additions were required.

As a running example of the algorithm, Fig. 3 shows the raw data of the frontal waist acceleration during normal walking of a healthy subject, sampled at 20Hz. The "end" of each step (which then brings to the beginning of the following one with the other foot), corresponds roughly to the sharp lower spikes in the plot.

Fig. 4 shows instead the result of the Gaussian filtering; the small black dots in Fig. 4 correspond to the points where the step-counter algorithm has detected steps. It is worth noting that although the strength of the steps sometime change significantly, the algorithm still detects properly all the steps.

The proposed step-counter algorithm has been tested on several subjects, from healthy young people to elderly and/or with motor disabilities. An experimentation consisting of 40 walking sessions from 8 healthy subjects (both males and females, with different height and weight) and 6 hospitalized subjects (with post-stroke disabilities, walking using crutch or wheels walkers, or simply elderly) has been carried out and our step-counter obtained an average precision of 91%.

The worst under-estimation was 27%, while the worst over-estimation was 18%. It is worth noting, however, that the subjects were not video recorded during their walking data collection; hence, it was sometimes difficult to validate the number of reported steps (manually counted by direct observation during walking) in each experiment. Furthermore, we detected limited packet loss that caused discrepancy between the number of reported steps and the recorded ones.

In conclusion, the main contribution of the proposed algorithm is the ability to provide a good estimate of the steps taken by people with disabilities and/or using crutch or wheels walkers. To the best of our knowledge, this is the only system being able to work properly for the latter category of users.

V. Integrating Activity Monitoring on a Smart Wheelchair

A non-motorized wheelchair has been enhanced with four main functionalities: wheelchair overturn detection, activity recognition, body posture recognition, and location tracking. Activity recognition is carried out with our BSN-based system described in Section III, while we designed a customized hardware platform for supporting the other functionalities.

This platform is composed of a sensor module, a signal processing module and a wireless communication module. The signal processing module is based on Arduino, it features low energy consumption, high sampling rate and high processing capabilities. The wireless communication module uses Bluetooth to support full interoperability with Activity-aaService. The sensor module uses accelerometers and pressure sensors to detect wheelchair overturns and user posture on the wheelchair cushion, as described in detail in the next subsections.

A. Overturn Measurement

To detect wheelchair overturns we equipped the smart-wheelchair system with a three-axis, low-power capacitive micro machined accelerometer (Freescale MMA8451). We sample the accelerometer at $f_s = 20Hz$, we compute the instantaneous cross-axial acceleration signal energy as follows:

$$E_{tot} = \sqrt{a_x^2 + a_y^2 + a_z^2} \quad (1)$$

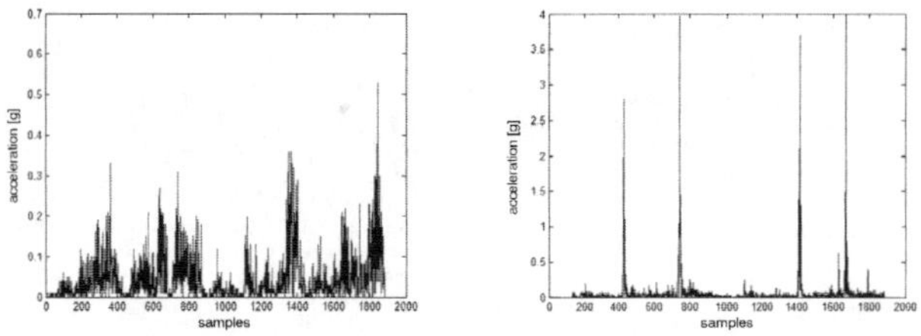

Fig. 5. Wheelchair operating regularly (left) and during four overturn events (right).

and we eventually compute second-by-second averaged E_{tot} values. Finally, we perform a threshold-based wheelchair overturn detection over the absolute value of the difference between consecutive E_{tot} values. Specifically, we extract another feature, Ev (signal energy variation), calculated as follows:

$$Ev_t = |E_{tot,t} - E_{tot,t-1}| \tag{2}$$

The threshold value has been obtained empirically, by monitoring acceleration data of our smart wheelchair moving regularly and occasionally let overturn intentionally (see the plots depicted in Fig. 5).

From Fig. 5, we can see that overturns determine Ev values significantly higher than 1.5g; it is therefore appropriate to set the Ev threshold to 1.5g to detect wheelchair overturn events.

B. Body Posture Measurement

Wheelchair users might feel uncomfortable to retain the same sitting posture for a long time; yet they might have difficulties to change posture. In addition, sitting on the wheelchair for long periods might lead to serious illness such us sores.

We instrumented our wheelchair with a smart cushion [27] that can measure pressure applied by the body weight from multiple points. Specifically, three pressure sensors are placed respectively on the two side and the center of the cushion. We adopted a Force Sensing Resistor (FSR) pressure sensor produced by Interlink Electronics. It is ultra-thin, lightweight, and highly accurate. Its size is approximately $45x38mm$. This FSR can sense applied force anywhere in the range of $100g - 10kg$ ($g = 9.8N/kg$). This pressure sensor is very convenient for our purposes as it can be easily embedded into the cushion textile or foam filling, as shown in Fig. 6. The cushion also includes a 3-color LED indicator and a speaker.

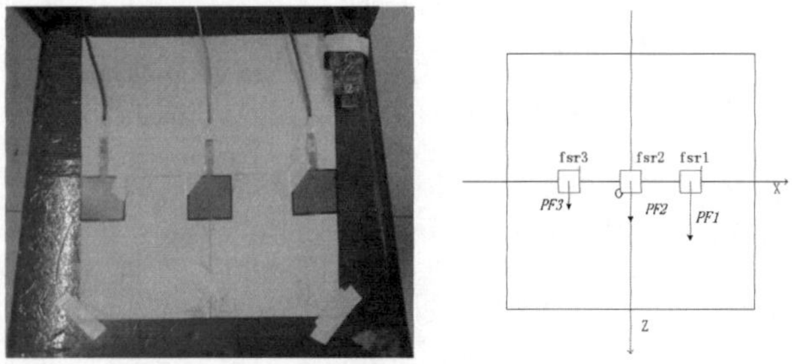

Fig. 6. Smart cushion equipped with FSR pressure sensors (left) and representation of pressure sensors data in coordinate system (right).

TABLE II. WHEELCHAIR USER'S POSTURE RECOGNITION ACCURACY.

No one Sitting	Sit straight	Lean to left	Lean to right
100%	98%	96%	95%

The smart cushion is placed on the chair and it is unobstructive for users. When the user sit on the chair, pressure sensory data are collected by the smart cushion and sent to processing module to recognize whether the user is comfortably sit or leans on a side. The user can set a sitting time alarm and when it is reached, the indicator light will change the color and a sound warning is played.

According to the pressure distribution among the three FSR sensors determined by the body weight, we can analyze the sitting posture, detecting whether the user is sitting upright or swinging from side to side. To perform such analysis, we set the FSR sensors sampling rate at $f_s = 20Hz$. The output of each pressure sensor is an integer number in the range of [0, 1023]. When the user is not sitting, the output value is zero; the pressure value increases as more weight insists on the sensor. We extract the feature vector of pressure sensor $F_{pr} = [PF1, PF2, PF3]$ and use a Support Vector Machine (SVM)-based classifier to detect four different body postures. Experiments have been carried out in a laboratory setting with 10 subjects having different height and weight and the results of the performance evaluation are reported in Table II.

C. User location tracking

The smart wheelchair communicates via Bluetooth with the user's personal mobile device where a customized version of Activity-aaService is running so to integrate the information coming from the wheelchair and take them in account. An useful functionality that has been implemented directly on the mobile device regards user's geo-localization, as shown with the screenshot in Fig. 7. We know that, if the wheelchair user is in danger (e.g. in case of wheelchair overturn), it is better to know his/her location accurately to give immediate rescue. For this purpose, we use the geographic coordinates provided by the assisted GPS sensor of the mobile device. When the system detects a dangerous situation, user's location is recorded and sent remotely to relatives and caregivers (see Fig. 1).

VI. CONCLUSIONS

In this paper we presented Activity-aaService, a hardware/software system to support real-time, non-invasive human activity recognition and monitoring that is based on the SPINE framework and the BodyCloud middleware. The service can run stand-alone on a personal mobile device, but can also be connected to a cloud back end so to enable remote access to collected data. Another significant contribution of this work is an advanced step-counter algorithm that has been integrated in Activity-aaService to allow for accurate step detection on healthy users and most notably on users with several types of motor disabilities, obtaining an average precision of 91%. Finally, we proposed an integration of Activity-aaService with a smart-wheelchair system to better assist and monitor wheelchair users. The smart wheelchair is able to detect and report to the cloud overturns, specific user sitting postures,

Fig. 7. Activity-aaService customized with user's geo-localization panel.

and geo-localization. Ongoing works are currently devoted to improving our system to monitor not only users individually, but to jointly infer mobility and activity patterns of those they usually interact with (such as family members, friends, and collaborators). We in fact believe that combining BSN data with large-scale awareness can represent a drastic improvement to current (standalone) m-Health systems. Finally, we plan to introduce a different activity recognition method [28] as it appears promising to improve classification accuracy.

Acknowledgment

This work has been partially supported by the joint bilateral Italy/China project ''Smart Personal Mobility Systems for Human Disabilities in Future Smart Cities" (N. CN13MO7) and the LOCUBIRehab Project (Polo della Salute, Regione Calabria, CUP J24E07000400005). This work has been partially carried out in the framework of the open-source BodyCloud Project.

References

[1] M. Chen, S. Gonzalez, A. Vasilakos, H. Cao, and V. C. Leung, "Body area networks: a survey," *Mobile networks and applications*, vol. 16, no. 2, pp. 171–193, 2011.

[2] G. Fortino, R. Giannantonio, R. Gravina, P. Kuryloski, and R. Jafari, "Enabling Effective Programming and Flexible Management of Efficient Body Sensor Network Applications," *IEEE Trans. on Human-Machine Systems*, vol. 43, no. 1, pp. 115–133, 2013.

[3] F. Bellifemine, G. Fortino, R. Giannantonio, R. Gravina, A. Guerrieri, and M. Sgroi, "SPINE: A domain-specific framework for rapid prototyping of WBSN applications," *Software Practice and Experience*, vol. 41, no. 3, pp. 237–265, 2011.

[4] N. Raveendranathan, S. Galzarano, V. Loseu, R. Gravina, R. Giannantonio, M. Sgroi, R. Jafari, and G. Fortino, "From Modeling to Implementation of Virtual Sensors in Body Sensor Networks," *IEEE Sensors J.*, vol. 12, no. 3, pp. 583–593, 2012.

[5] SPINE website, "http://spine.deis.unical.it," Jan. 2015.

[6] G. Fortino, G. D. Fatta, M. Pathan, and A. Vasilakos, "Cloud-assisted body area networks: state-of-the-art and future challenges," *Wireless Networks*, 2014.

[7] G. Fortino, M. Pathan, and G. D. Fatta, "BodyCloud: Integration of Cloud Computing and Body Sensor Networks," in *Proc. of the IEEE 4th Int'nl Conf. on Cloud Computing Technology and Science*, 2012.

[8] BodyCloud website, "http://bodycloud.dimes.unical.it," Jan. 2015.

[9] E.Kartsakli, A.Antonopoulos, A.Lalos, S.Tennina, M. D. Renzo, L.Alonso, and C. Verikoukis, "Reliable MAC Design for Ambient Assisted Living: Moving the Coordination to the Cloud," *IEEE Communications Magazine*, vol. 53, no. 1, January 2015.

[10] G. Fortino, D. Parisi, V. Pirrone, and G. D. Fatta, "BodyCloud: A SaaS approach for community Body Sensor Networks," *Future Generation Computer Systems*, vol. 35, no. 6, pp. 62–79, 2014.

[11] G. Fortino and R. Gravina, "Rehab-aaService: A Cloud-based Motor Rehabilitation Digital Assistant," in *Proc. of the 2nd Workshop ICT for improving Patient Rehabilitation Research Techniques Workshop - REHAB 2014 (PervasiveHealth 2014)*, 2014.

[12] R. Gravina, A. Andreoli, A. Salmeri, L. Buondonno, N. Raveendranathank, V. Loseuk, R. Giannantonio, E. Seto, and G. Fortino, "Enabling Multiple BSN Applications Using the SPINE Framework," in *Proc. of Int'nl Conf. on Body Sensor Networks*, 2010.

[13] G. Fortino, R. Gravina, and W. Russo, "Activity-aaService: Cloud-assisted, BSN-based system for physical activity monitoring," in *9th IEEE Int'nl Conf. on Computer Supported Cooperative Work in Design (CSCWD 2015)*, 2015.

[14] L. Bao and S. Intille, "Activity Recognition from User-Annotated Acceleration Data," *Pervasive 2004, LNCS 3001*, pp. 1–17, 2004.

[15] U. Maurer, A. Smailagic, D. Siewiorek, and M. Deisher, "Activity recognition and monitoring using multiple sensors on different body positions," in *Proc. of the Int'nl Conf. on Body Sensor Networks*, 2006.

[16] N. Ravi, D. Nikhil, P. Mysore, and M. Littman, "Activity recognition from accelerometer data," in *Proc. of the 17th Conf. on Innovative Applications of Artificial Intelligence*, 2005.

[17] P. Zappi, C. Lombriser, T. Stiefmeier, E. Farella, D. Roggen, L. Benini, and G. Troster, "Activity recognition from on-body sensors: accuracy-power trade-o by dynamic sensor selection," in *Proc. of the European Conf. on Wireless Sensor Networks*, 2008.

[18] D. Anguita, A. Ghio, L. Oneto, X. Parra, and J. Reyes-Ortiz, "Human Activity Recognition on Smartphones using a Multiclass Hardware-Friendly Support Vector Machine," in *Proc. of the 4th Int'nl Conf. on Ambient Assisted Living and Home Care*, 2012.

[19] M. Shoaib, "Human Activity Recognition Using Heterogeneous Sensors," in *Proc. of the ACM UbiComp Conference*, 2013.

[20] L. Chen, J. Hoey, C. Nugent, D. Cook, and Z. Yu, "Sensor-Based Activity Recognition," *IEEE Transactions on Systems, Man, and Cybernetics, Part C: Applications and Review*, vol. 42, no. 6, pp. 790–808, 2012.

[21] O. Lara and M. Labrador, "A Survey on Human Activity Recognition using Wearable Sensors," *IEEE Communications Surveys & Tutorials*, vol. 15, no. 3, pp. 1192–1209, 2013.

[22] E.Kartsakli, A.Antonopoulos, A.Lalos, S.Tennina, M. D. Renzo, L.Alonso, , and C.Verikoukis, "A Survey on M2M Systems for mHealth: A Wireless Communications Perspective," *Sensors Journal*, vol. 14, no. 10, pp. 18 009–18 052, 2014.

[23] G. Acampora, D. Cook, P. Rashidi, and A. Vasilakos, "A Survey on Ambient Intelligence in Healthcare," *Sensors Journal*, vol. 101, no. 12, pp. 2470–2494, 2013.

[24] Shimmer website, "http://www.shimmer-research.com," Jan. 2015.

[25] T. Cover and P. Hart, "Nearest neighbor pattern classification," *IEEE Transactions on Information Theory*, vol. 13, pp. 21–27, January 1967.

[26] P. Pudil, J. Novovicova, and J. Kittler, "Floating search methods in feature selection," *Pattern Recognition Letters*, vol. 15, no. 11, pp. 1119–1125, November 1994.

[27] C. Ma, W. Li, J. Cao, S. Wang, and L. Wu, "A Fatigue Detect System Based on Activity Recognition," in *Proc. of Int'nl Conf. on Internet and Distributed Computing Systems*, 2014.

[28] D. Mocanu, H. Ammar, D. Lowet, K. Driessens, A. Liotta, G. Weiss, and K. Tuyls, "Factored Four Way Conditional Restricted Boltzmann Machines for Activity Recognition," *Pattern Recognition Letters*, 2015.

Metallic Plasmonic Nano-antenna for Wireless Optical Communication in Intra-body Nanonetworks

Mona Nafari
Department of Electrical Engineering
University at Buffalo,
The State University of New York
Buffalo, NY, USA
monanafa@buffalo.edu

Josep Miquel Jornet
Department of Electrical Engineering
University at Buffalo,
The State University of New York
Buffalo, NY, USA
jmjornet@buffalo.edu

ABSTRACT

Nanonetworks consist of nano-sized communicating devices which are able to perform simple tasks at the nanoscale. Nanonetworks are the enabling technology for unique applications, including intra-body health-monitoring and drug delivery systems. In this paper, metallic plasmonic nano-antennas for wireless optical communication in intra-body nanonetworks are modeled and analyzed. More specifically, a unified mathematical framework is developed to investigate the performance in reception of gold-based nano-dipole antennas. This framework takes into account the metal properties, i.e., its dynamic complex conductivity and permittivity; the propagation properties of Surface Plasmon Polariton waves on the nano-antenna, i.e., their confinement factor and propagation length; the antenna geometry, i.e., length and radius, and the antenna fundamental resonance frequency, and it can be utilized to obtain the plasmonic currents on the nano-antenna generated by an incident EM filed. In addition to numerical results, the analytical models are validated by means of simulations with COMSOL Multiphysics. The developed framework will guide the design and development of novel nano-antennas suited for wireless optical communication in intra-body nanonetworks.

Categories and Subject Descriptors

C.2.1 [**Computer-Communication Networks**]: Network Architecture and Design—*Wireless Communication*; H.1.1 [**Models and Principles**]: Systems and Information Theory—*Information Theory*

General Terms

Theory

Keywords

Nanophotonics, Plasmonics, Nano-antenna, Nanonetworks

1. INTRODUCTION

Nanotechnology is providing the engineering community with a new set of tools to design and manufacture novel nanoscale devices, which are able to perform simple tasks, such as computing, data storing, sensing and actuation. The integration of several of these nano-devices into a single entity will enable the development of advanced nanoscale machines. By means of communication, nanomachines will be able to organize themselves in networks, or nanonetworks, and complete more complex tasks in a distributed fashion [1]. For example, a collection of nanomachines distributed within the human body or traveling with the blood stream could serve as the basis of novel *in-vivo* health monitoring systems. Among others, nanomachines could be able to transmit their sensing information in a multi-hop fashion to a gateway or sink, or coordinate between them in case that a joint response to an event is needed.

There are several technologies that could potentially enable the communication between intra-body nanosensors. Among others, molecular communication, which is based on the exchange of molecules to transmit information, has been thoroughly investigated for several years [2]. This mechanism is naturally used by cells to exchange information and to coordinate their actions, and could be enabled by means of synthetic biology. However, the very low achievable data rates in molecular communications could drastically limit the usefulness of nanonetworks. Another very relevant technology is the utilization of ultrasonic communication, based on the utilization of very high frequency acoustic waves [20]. However, for the time being, the size and power limitations of ultrasonic acoustic transducers pose a challenge in their integration within cell-sized nanomachines.

From the electromagnetic (EM) perspective, the miniaturization of a conventional metallic antenna to meet the size requirements of a nanomachine would theoretically result in very high resonance frequencies. For example, according to classical antenna theory, a one-micrometer-long metallic antenna would radiate at approximately 150 THz. This is only true if the material of the antenna building components is assumed to be a Perfect Electrical Conductor (PEC), i.e., a material with infinite conductivity. However, at the aforementioned frequencies, metals no longer behave as PEC [23]. On the contrary, the conductivity of metals such as gold or silver [17]; metamaterials, i.e., engineered materials with rationally designed arrangements of nano-structured building blocks [5]; as well as nanomaterials such as graphene [21], is a frequency-dependent complex magnitude.

BODYNETS 2015, September 28-30, Sydney, Australia

DOI 10.4108/eai.28-9-2015.2261410

The material conductivity affects the way in which a current wave propagates in the nano-antenna. In particular, the global oscillations of electrical charge in close proximity to the surface of the antenna building components, i.e., within the so called penetration depth, results into the excitation of a confined EM wave at the surface of the antenna. This peculiar EM wave is commonly referred to as a Surface Plasmon Polariton (SPP) wave. The frequency at which SPP waves are excited depends on the material conductivity of the antenna building components. For example, graphene supports the propagation of SPP waves at frequencies as low as in the THz band (0.1-10 THz) [22], whereas in noble metals such as gold or silver, SPP waves are only observed at several tens of THz and above [23].

In this work, we are interested in designing plasmonic nano-antennas able to efficiently operate *in-vivo*, i.e., directly in contact or inside the human body. It is well-known that the propagation of EM waves inside the human body becomes more challenging as the frequency increases, mainly because of the absorption by biological tissues with a high content of water as well as fat, melatonin or hemoglobin, among others [12]. For example, intra-body communication at THz-band frequencies enabled by graphene-based plasmonic nano-antennas [15] would suffer from very high absorption from water molecules [14].

For this, we advocate for the use of the near-infrared (NIR) or optical window for communication in intra-body nanonetworks. This is the frequency range between 225 THz and 460 THz (or, equivalently, from 650 nm to 1350 nm in terms of wavelength). In this window, the absorption of EM radiation by biological tissues is very small, in the order of 0.01 m^{-1} [12], or four orders of magnitude lower than the absorption at THz-band frequencies [19]. Moreover, plasmonic nano-devices at optical frequencies have already been utilized for *in-vivo* applications. For example, many of the biological nanosensors developed to date exploit the behavior of plasmons in nanomaterials and nano-particles [6, 8].

Within this context, the field of optical nano-antennas has been gaining momentum. Among others, in [4, 18], the state of the art in plasmonic nano-antennas for optical frequencies based on noble metals is described in detail. In [7], the propagation properties of SPP waves on nanowires are analyzed by taking into account the radial boundary condition along the nano-antenna. Then in [11], the impact of the nano-antenna caps is also taken into account. More recently, in [9], the nano-antenna fields are characterized, starting from the estimated propagation constant of SPP waves on nanowires obtained by means of experimental measurements. Despite all these results, a unified framework able to relate the material properties, the SPP wave behavior and the nano-antenna performance is missing.

In this paper, we model and analyze the performance of metallic plasmonic nano-antennas for intra-body optical communication. More specifically, we develop a unified mathematical framework to investigate the performance in reception of gold-based nano-dipole antennas. This framework relates the metal properties (conductivity and permittivity), the SPP wave propagation properties (confinement factor and propagation length), the antenna geometry (length and radius), and the antenna fundamental resonance frequency and can be utilized to obtain the plasmonic current in the nano-antenna generated by an incident EM filed. In addition to numerical results, we validate our analysis by

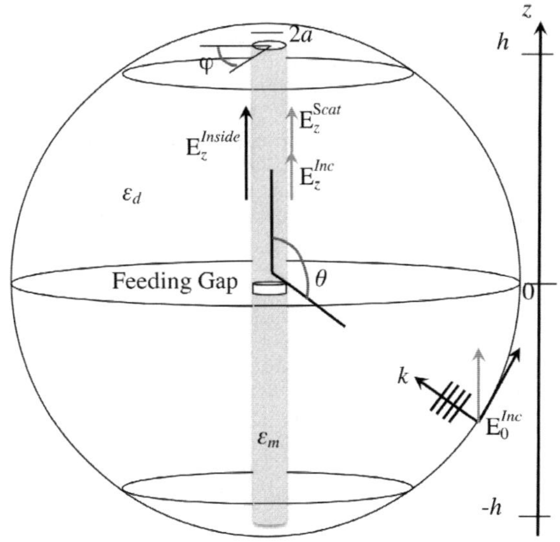

Figure 1: Plasmonic nano-dipole antenna considered in our analysis.

means of simulations with COMSOL Multi-physics.

The remainder of this paper is organized as follows. In Section 2, we review the fundamental working principle of a plasmonic nano-antenna, describe the conductivity model utilized in our analysis and analyze the SPP wave propagation properties. Then, in Section 3, we formulate the EM fields on and inside the antenna, and obtain a semi-closed form expression for the plasmonic current in the nano-antenna. The numerical and simulation results are presented in Section 4, and the paper is concluded in Section 5.

2. PLASMONIC NANO-ANTENNA MODEL

2.1 Working Principle

The plasmonic nano-antenna design considered in our analysis is shown in Figure 1. The nano-antenna consists of two identical metallic arms with a feeding/receiving gap in between. The working principle of the nano-antenna is as follows. Due to space constraints, we focus on its functioning in reception, but the same behavior holds in transmission due to the antenna reciprocity principle [3]. Then, in particular,

- Consider an incident plane wave with polarization parallel to the plane defined by the nano-antenna long axis and the direction of the wave propagation. Following the notation in Figure 1, in our analysis we are interested in the incident electric field component parallel to the z-axis, E_z^{Inc}, which is given by:

$$E_z^{Inc}(r,z) = E_0^{Inc}(r)\sin\theta e^{j(k_0\cos\theta)z} = E_{||}^{Inc}(r)\, e^{jk_{||}z}, \quad (1)$$

  where E_0^{Inc} stands for the field strength, k_0 refers to the wave vector, and θ is the angle of incidence. When E_z^{Inc} irradiates the nano-antenna, it excites the free electrons within the antenna penetration depth. The electronic response of the nano-antenna to an EM field is determined by the conductivity of its building material. In Section 2.2, we describe the conductivity model for metals that we utilize in our analysis.

- At the interface between the antenna metallic arms and the surrounding medium, longitudinal SPP waves that propagate along the z-axis are excited. The SPP wave vector, k_{spp} is mainly determined by the antenna geometry, namely, the antenna arm radius and length, as well as on the real and imaginary part of the material conductivity. In Section 2.3, we deduce the dispersion equation for SPP waves on the antenna and analyze their propagation properties as functions of the material conductivity and antenna geometry.

- To enhance the detection of the incident EM wave, we are interested in designing a plasmonic resonant cavity. In Section 3, we analyze the nano-antenna in reception, by starting from the formulation of the electric field incident to the antenna, scattered by the antenna and propagating inside the antenna.

2.2 Optical Conductivity Model for Metals

The conductivity of metals at optical frequencies is a complex magnitude. There are many analytical models for the conductivity of metals and, in our analysis, we utilize the well-established Drude model [13]. Accordingly, the metal complex conductivity, σ, or similarly, its complex permittivity, ε_m, can be written as functions of the angular frequency, $\omega = 2\pi f$, as follows:

$$\begin{aligned} \sigma(\omega) &= -j(\varepsilon_m(\omega) - \varepsilon_\infty)\varepsilon_0\omega \\ &= -j\omega\varepsilon_0\left[-\frac{\omega_p^2\tau_D^2}{1+\omega^2\tau_D^2} + j\frac{\omega_p^2\tau_D}{\omega(1+\omega^2\tau_D^2)}\right], \end{aligned} \tag{2}$$

where ε_0 is the vacuum permittivity, ε_∞ is 1 for metals [16], ω_p stands for the plasma wave frequency, and τ_D is the electron relaxation time.

In this paper, we consider the use of gold (Au) to build the nano-antennas [13] with values of $3.3 \cdot 10^{-14}$ s and $13.8 \cdot 10^{15}$ rad/s for ω_p and τ_D, respectively. In Figure 2, the real and imaginary parts of the relative permittivity for gold are shown as functions of frequency. The absolute value of real and imaginary part of permittivity in higher frequencies tends to decrease which considerably affects propagation of SPP waves, as we show in the next section.

2.3 Surface Plasmon Polariton Wave Dispersion Equation

In this section, we analytically study the propagation properties of SPP waves in the nano-antenna, by taking into account both its geometry and the complex conductivity of its building material. More specifically, we are interested in characterizing the complex SPP wave vector k_{spp}. The real part of the wave vector,

$$Re\{k_{spp}\} = \frac{2\pi}{\lambda_{spp}}, \tag{3}$$

determines the SPP wavelength λ_{spp}, as well as the confinement factor k_{spp}/k_0. The imaginary part, $Im\{k_{spp}\}$, determines the SPP decay or, inversely,

$$L = \frac{1}{2Im\{k_{spp}\}}, \tag{4}$$

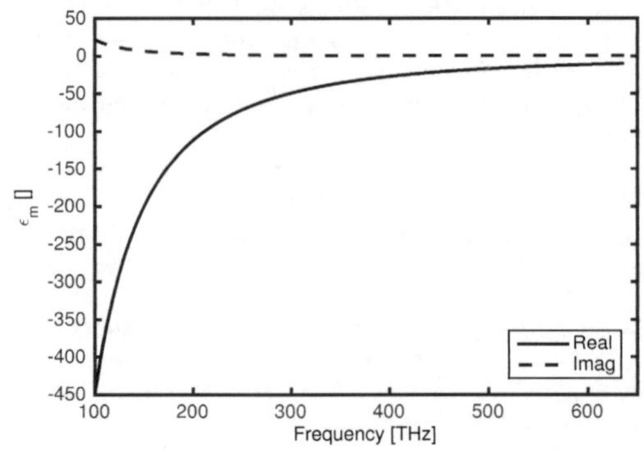

Figure 2: Real and imaginary parts of the relative permittivity for gold as functions of frequency.

determines the SPP propagation length, which is defined as the distance at which the SPP field strength has decreased by a value of $1/e$.

As mentioned before, when the antenna is illuminated by an incident plane wave, axially symmetrical SPP modes are excited on the antenna. In particular, for the design of an efficient antenna, we are interested in the propagation properties of Transverse Magnetic (TM) SPP wave modes [3]. To obtain k_{spp}, we need to solve the dispersion equation for SPP waves on the nano-antenna arms. We assume that the electric field $\vec{E}$ and magnetic field $\vec{H}$ on the antenna have the following form [7]:

$$E_r(r,z) = E_r(r)\, e^{jk_{spp}z}, \tag{5}$$

$$E_z(r,z) = E_z(r)\, e^{jk_{spp}z}, \tag{6}$$

$$H_\phi(r,z) = H_\phi(r)\, e^{jk_{spp}z}. \tag{7}$$

Starting from the Maxwell's equations in their differential form and taking into account that for an axially symmetrical mode $\frac{\partial E}{\partial \phi} = 0$ and $\frac{\partial H}{\partial \phi} = 0$, the following equations can be written:

$$E_r(r,z) = \frac{-j}{\varepsilon k_0}\frac{\partial H_\phi(r,z)}{\partial z}, \tag{8}$$

$$E_z(r,z) = \frac{j}{\varepsilon k_0}\frac{1}{r}\frac{\partial(rH_\phi(r,z))}{\partial r}, \tag{9}$$

$$H_\phi(r,z) = \frac{-j}{\mu_0 k_0}\left(\frac{\partial E_r(r,z)}{\partial z} - \frac{\partial E_z(r,z)}{\partial r}\right), \tag{10}$$

where $\varepsilon = \varepsilon_m$ is the relative permittivity of the region $z < h$ or $r < a$ and $\varepsilon = \varepsilon_d$ is the relative permittivity of the region $z > h$ or $r > a$, $k_0 = \omega/c$ refers to free-space wave vector and c is the speed of light. By taking the z derivative of (7), the radial component of the electric field can be written as:

$$E_r(r,z) = \varepsilon^{-1}\frac{k_{spp}}{k_0}H_\phi(r,z). \tag{11}$$

By substituting (11) into (10) and taking again the z derivative of (7), the magnetic field can be written as:

$$H_\phi(r,z) = \frac{-jk_0\varepsilon}{k_{spp}^2 - k_0^2\varepsilon}\frac{dE_z(r,z)}{dr}. \tag{12}$$

Finally, by substituting (12) into (9), the following equation for E_z is obtained:

$$\zeta^2 \frac{d^2 E_z(r,z)}{d\zeta^2} + \zeta \frac{dE_z(r,z)}{d\zeta} - \zeta^2 E_z(r,z) = 0, \quad (13)$$

where $\zeta = p_{m,d} r$ and $p_{m,d} = \sqrt{k_{spp}^2 - k_0^2 \varepsilon_{m,d} \mu_0}$ [7]. The solution of (13) for $E_z(r,z)$ has the form of $I_0(p_m a)$ in the metal and $K_0(p_d a)$ in the surrounding dielectric, where $I_n(.)$ and $K_n(.)$ are the generalized Bessel functions of first and second kind of order n. Substituting them into (12), and using the relations $\frac{dI_0(p_m r)}{dr} = p_m I_1(p_m r)$ and $\frac{dK_0(p_d r)}{dr} = -p_d K_1(p_d r)$, the solution of $H_\phi(r,z)$ can be determined. In particular, by taking into account the need for continuity in $E_z(r,z)$ and $H_\phi(r,z)$ at the surface of the antenna, i.e., at the interface between the surrounding dielectric and the metal, $r = a$, the following dispersion equation is obtained:

$$\frac{K_0(p_d a) I_1(p_m a)}{K_1(p_d a) I_0(p_m a)} = -\frac{\varepsilon_d p_m}{\varepsilon_m p_d}, \quad (14)$$

which can only numerically be solved. Ultimately, k_{spp} depends on the angular frequency ω, the cylinder radius a and the relative permittivities $\varepsilon_{m,d}$ of the metal and the surrounding dielectric. In Figure 3(a), the confinement factor (3) for gold-based nano-antennas is shown as a function of frequency and for different nanowire radius. The confinement factor increases as the frequency increases. It can also be seen that increasing the radius leads to a slow increase with frequency and, oppositely, the thiner the wire, the faster the confinement factor increases with frequency. Similarly, in Figure 3(b), the SPP wave propagation length (4) is shown as a function of the frequency. Ultimately, the smaller the radius, the higher the confinement factor is but the shorter the SPP propagation length becomes.

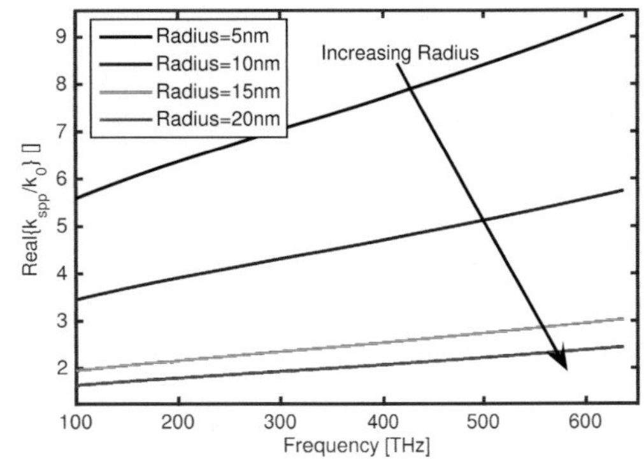

(a) Confinement Factor

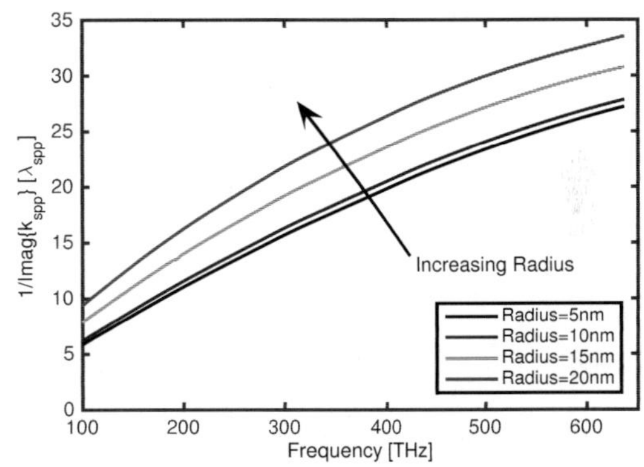

(b) Propagation Length

Figure 3: Propagation properties of SPP TM modes on gold nanowires.

2.4 Effective Resonance Length

Besides the boundary condition imposed in the radial direction, there is another boundary effect that alters the propagation of SPP waves on the nano-antenna: the caps at the two ends. SPP waves travel along the wire length l with a propagation constant k_{spp} and suffer a reflection at the two caps. To incorporate such effect in the analysis, the reflection coefficient $\mathcal{R}$ at the cap needs to be computed.

Following the methodology introduced in [11], by taking into account the boundary condition at the cap, we can write:

$$E_r(r, z = h^-) = (1 + \mathcal{R}) \frac{Re\{k_{spp}\}}{\omega \varepsilon_0 \varepsilon} F(r), \quad (15)$$

$$H_\phi(r, z = h^-) = (1 - \mathcal{R}) F(r), \quad (16)$$

with

$$F(r) = \begin{cases} \frac{I_1(p_m r)}{I_1(p_m a)}, \varepsilon = \varepsilon_m & \text{if } r < a, \\ \frac{K_1(p_d r)}{K_1(p_d a)}, \varepsilon = \varepsilon_d & \text{if } r > a, \end{cases} \quad (17)$$

and

$$E_r(r, z = h^+) = \int_0^{+\infty} t(\eta) \frac{\sqrt{k_0^2 \varepsilon_d - \eta^2}}{\omega \varepsilon_d \varepsilon_0} J_1(\eta \mathcal{R})\, d\eta, \quad (18)$$

$$H_\phi(r, z = h^+) = \int_0^{+\infty} t(\eta) J_1(\eta \mathcal{R})\, d\eta, \quad (19)$$

where $J_1(.)$ is the first order Bessel function of the first kind. To solve the reflection coefficient $\mathcal{R}$, first we should find t. Hence by using the orthogonality property of Bessel functions of the first kind, (18) is equated to (15), both sides multiplied by $J_1(\eta r) r$ and then integrated from 0 to ∞ over r to have:

$$t(\eta) = (1 + \mathcal{R}) \frac{\eta a \varepsilon_d Re\{k_{spp}\}}{\varepsilon_0 \omega \sqrt{k_0^2 \varepsilon_d - \eta^2}} [A_1(\eta) + A_2(\eta)], \quad (20)$$

where

$$A_1(\eta) = \frac{p_m I_2(p_m a) J_1(\eta a) + \eta I_1(p_m a) J_2(\eta a)}{I_1(p_m a) \varepsilon_m (\eta^2 + p_m^2)} \quad (21)$$

and

$$A_2(\eta) = \frac{p_d K_2(p_d a) J_1(\eta a) - \eta K_1(p_d a) J_2(\eta a)}{K_1(p_d a) \varepsilon_d (\eta^2 + p_d^2)}. \quad (22)$$

For the magnetic field H_ϕ, (19) is equated to (16). By multiplying both sides by $\frac{F(r) r}{\varepsilon}$ and following the same rule for ε depending on z and r, then integrating from 0 to ∞ over r, the final result would be:

$$\mathcal{R} = \frac{1 - G}{1 + G}, \quad (23)$$

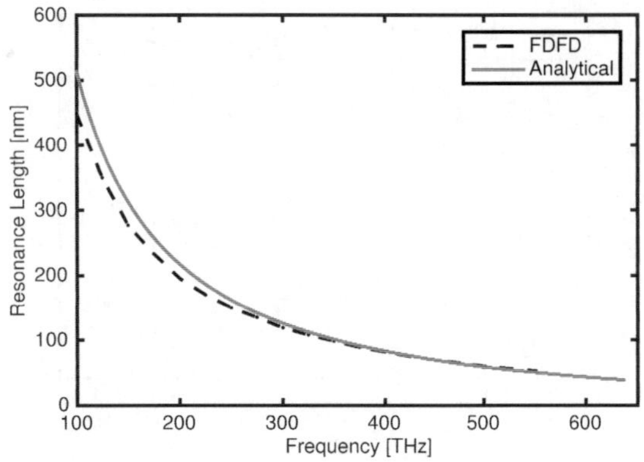

Figure 4: Resonance length of a gold-based plasmonic nano-antenna as a function of frequency (radius a=5 nm).

where G is given by:

$$G = \frac{\int_0^{+\infty} \frac{2\eta\varepsilon_d Re\{k_{spp}\}}{\sqrt{k_0^2\varepsilon_d-\eta^2}}[A_1(\eta)+A_2(\eta)]^2\, d\eta}{\frac{I_1(p_m a)^2-I_0(p_m a)I_2(p_m a)}{\varepsilon_m I_1(p_m a)^2} - \frac{K_1(p_d a)^2-K_0(p_d a)K_2(p_d a)}{\varepsilon_d K_1(p_d a)^2}}. \tag{24}$$

Finally, the resonances of the nanowire can be calculated by considering the propagation of the surface plasmon along the nanowire and reflection at two caps as [11]:

$$l = \frac{n\pi - \varphi}{Re\{k_{spp}\}}, \tag{25}$$

where n is the resonance order, φ is the phase of the reflection coefficient $\mathcal{R}$ calculated from (23), and k_{spp} is the wave vector calculated by (14). As before, this can only be numerically solved. In Figure 4, the resonance length for gold-based nano-antennas is shown as a function of frequency. The length of a resonace optical nano-antenna is shorter than what an ideal PEC antenna would require to resonate at the same frequency, due to the large confinement factor of SPP waves in gold nanowires. In the same figure, the numerical results obtained by solving (24) are compared with that of running Finite-Differences Frequency-Domain (FDFD) simulations with COMSOL Multi-physics, for validation purposes.

3. PLASMONIC NANO-ANTENNA PERFORMANCE IN RECEPTION

In reception, we are interested in characterizing the plasmonic current generated at the nano-antenna as a result of the incident EM wave. In order to determine the plasmonic current, we follow the conventional vector potential approach [3], but contrary to classical antenna theory for PEC antennas, we take into account that there is an electric field inside the antenna, within the penetration depth, which is the SPP wave that propagates with k_{spp}.

At the nanowire surface, the following boundary condition between the plasmonic field inside the nano-antenna, the incident field on the nano-antenna and the scattered field by the nano-antenna needs to be satisfied:

$$E_z^{Inside}(r,z) = E_z^{Inc}(r,z) + E_z^{Scat}(r,z). \tag{26}$$

To simplify our analysis, we make the assumption that the nanowire is effectively very thin and, thus, the current density J_z, the vector potential A_z and the electric field inside the antenna E_z^{Inside} depend only on z but not on r, i.e.,

$$J_z(r,z) \approx J_z(z), \tag{27}$$

$$A_z(r,z) \approx A_z(z), \tag{28}$$

$$E_z^{Inside}(r,z) \approx E_z^{Inside}(z). \tag{29}$$

The field inside the nano-antenna E_z^{inc} in (26) is related to the current density through the material conductivity, i.e.,

$$J_z(z) = \sigma(\omega) E_z^{Inside}(z) \tag{30}$$

where σ represents conductivity given by (2).

The incident field E_z^{Inc} in (26) on the nano-antenna surface is given by (1).

From [10], the scattered field by the nano-antenna, E_z^{Scat} in (26), can be written as

$$E_z^{Scat}(a,z) = \frac{jc^2}{\omega}\left(\frac{\partial^2}{\partial z^2} + k_0^2\right)A_z(a,z), \tag{31}$$

where

$$A_z(z) \approx \frac{\mu_0}{4\pi}\bar{Z}J_z(z), \tag{32}$$

and $\bar{Z}$ is the characteristic impedance of the wire, given by

$$\bar{Z} = \frac{4\pi}{(\varepsilon_m - 1)(k_{spp}^2 - k_0^2)}, \tag{33}$$

where ε_m is the metal permittivity given in (2) and k_{spp} is the SPP wave vector obtained from (14).

By combining (30), (31), (32), (33), and (1) in (26), the following inhomogeneous differential equation is obtained:

$$E_{||}^{Inc}e^{jk_{||}z} + \frac{jc^2}{\omega}\left(\frac{\partial^2}{\partial z^2} + k_0^2\right)\frac{\mu_0}{4\pi}\bar{Z}J_z(z) = \frac{1}{\sigma(\omega)}J_z(z). \tag{34}$$

Then, as analytically shown in [10], the total current in the nano-antenna J_z can be written as the combination of the following terms

$$J_z(z) = J_{||}e^{jk_{||}z} + J_{\pm p}e^{\pm jk_{spp}z}, \tag{35}$$

where $J_{||}e^{ik_{||}z}$ is induced by the illuminating field along the wire and $J_{\pm p}$ refers to two counter-propagating plasmonic current densities propagating with propagation constant k_{spp}.

By combining (35) and (34), an expression for $J_{||}$ can be found:

$$J_{||} = \sigma(\omega)\frac{(k_{spp}^2 - k_0^2)}{k_{spp}^2 - k_{||}^2}E_{||}^{Inc}. \tag{36}$$

By considering the role of the wire end caps as a hard boundary and the vanishing total current density, an expression for $J_{\pm p}$ is obtained as:

$$J_{\pm p} = -J_{||}\frac{\sin((k_{spp} \pm k_{||})h)}{\sin(2k_{spp}h)}, \tag{37}$$

where $h = \frac{l}{2}$ and l stands for the length of wire given by (25). Finally, by combining (37) and (36), the plasmonic current density can be obtained as a function of the incident field E_z^{inc}. As before, this can only be numerically done.

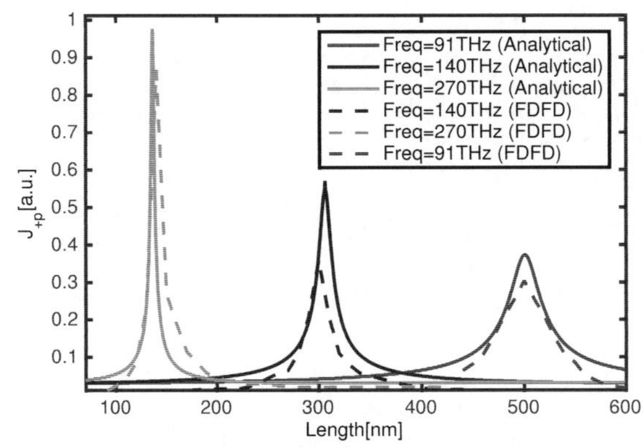

(a) J_{+p} vs nano-antenna length

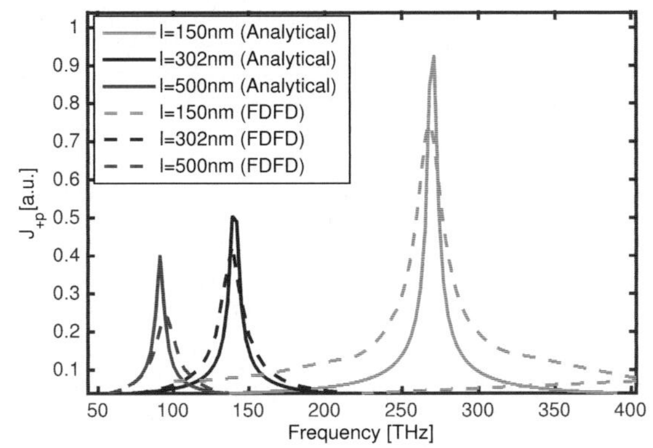

(b) J_{+p} vs frequency

Figure 5: Plasmonic current density on a gold-based nano-antenna as a function of frequency and length (radius a=5 nm).

4. NUMERICAL AND SIMULATION RESULTS

In this section, we numerically investigate the behavior of optical nano-antennas in reception. In this section, we consider gold-based nano-antennas with 5 nm radius and varying length. On the one hand, we numerically solve the plasmonic current density $J_{\pm p}$ given by (37), which depends on its turn on the SPP wave propagation constant k_{spp}, resonant length l and material conductivity σ parameters given by (14), (25) and (2), respectively. On the other other hand, we utilize COMSOL Multi-physics to validate our results by means of FDFD simulations, in which the only required initial parameter is the material conductivity σ.

In Figure 5(a), the plasmonic current density is shown as a function of the nano-antenna length l for three different illumination frequencies, namely, 91 THz, 140 THz and 270 THz. Clear resonances can be observed when the length is approximately 500 nm, 302 nm and 150 nm, respectively. The z-component of the current density and its maximum is taken from analytically produced data and FDTD simulations for different length and frequencies are performed for validation purposes. There is good agreement between the numerical and the simulation results. As expected, the high confinement factor of SPP waves in gold results into significantly smaller nano-antennas when compared to ideal PEC antennas at the same frequency.

Similarly, in Figure 5(b), the plasmonic current is shown as a function of the frequency of the incident EM field, for different nano-antenna lengths. The longest dipole (500 nm) exhibits the weakest response while the shortest nanowire (140 nm) exhibits the strongest response. Multiple resonances can be observed for each nano-wire length, but we are mainly interested in the fundamental resonance frequency.

5. CONCLUSIONS AND FUTURE WORK

In this paper, we have developed a unified mathematical framework to analyze the performance in reception of plasmonic nano-antennas in reception. Starting from the dynamic complex conductivity of the nano-antenna building components, we have formulated the dispersion equation for SPP waves in nanowires and obtained the SPP wave propagation properties and nano-antenna fundamental resonance length by taking into account also the impact of the nanowire caps. We have then analytically derived an expression for the plasmonic current in the nano-antenna when irradiated by an incident EM wave. The analytical models have been then validated by means of FDFD simulations with COMSOL Multi-physics. The developed framework can be utilized to guide the design and development of novel nano-antennas suited for wireless optical communication in intra-body nanonetworks. As part of our future work, we will extend our analysis to the nano-antenna in transmission, and we will also compare the nano-antenna performance, both in transmission and in reception, when utilizing different materials.

6. ACKNOWLEDGMENTS

This work was supported by the U.S. National Science Foundation (NSF) under Grant No. CBET-1445934.

7. REFERENCES

[1] I. F. Akyildiz and J. M. Jornet. Electromagnetic wireless nanosensor networks. *Nano Communication Networks (Elsevier) Journal*, 1(1):3–19, Mar. 2010.

[2] I. F. Akyildiz, M. Pierobon, S. Balasubramaniam, and Y. Koucheryavy. The internet of bio-nano things. *IEEE Communications Magazine*, 53(3):32–40, 2015.

[3] C. A. Balanis. *Antenna theory: analysis and design.* John Wiley & Sons, 2012.

[4] P. Biagioni, J.-S. Huang, and B. Hecht. Nanoantennas for visible and infrared radiation. *Reports on Progress in Physics*, 75(2):024402, 2012.

[5] A. Boltasseva and H. A. Atwater. Low-loss plasmonic metamaterials. *Science*, 331(6015):290–291, 2011.

[6] A. G. Brolo. Plasmonics for future biosensors. *Nature Photonics*, 6(11):709–713, 2012.

[7] Q. Cao and J. Jahns. Azimuthally polarized surface plasmons as effective terahertz waveguides. *Optics express*, 13(2):511–518, 2005.

[8] I. Choi and Y. Choi. Plasmonic nanosensors: Review and prospect. *IEEE Journal of Selected Topics in Quantum Electronics*, 18(3):1110–1121, 2012.

[9] J. Dorfmüller. *Optical Wire Antennas: Near-Field Imaging, Modeling and Emission Patterns*. PhD thesis, Citeseer, 2010.

[10] J. Dorfm§ller, R. Vogelgesang, R. T. Weitz, C. Rockstuhl, C. Etrich, T. Pertsch, F. Lederer, and K. Kern. Fabry-pérot resonances in one-dimensional plasmonic nanostructures. *Nano letters*, 9(6):2372–2377, 2009.

[11] R. Gordon. Reflection of cylindrical surface waves. *Optics express*, 17(21):18621–18629, 2009.

[12] S. L. Jacques. Optical properties of biological tissues: a review. *Physics in medicine and biology*, 58(11):R37, 2013.

[13] P. B. Johnson and R.-W. Christy. Optical constants of the noble metals. *Physical Review B*, 6(12):4370, 1972.

[14] J. M. Jornet and I. F. Akyildiz. Channel modeling and capacity analysis of electromagnetic wireless nanonetworks in the terahertz band. *IEEE Transactions on Wireless Communications*, 10(10):3211–3221, Oct. 2011.

[15] J. M. Jornet and I. F. Akyildiz. Graphene-based plasmonic nano-antenna for terahertz band communication in nanonetworks. *Selected Areas in Communications, IEEE Journal on*, 31(12):685–694, 2013.

[16] G. Kristensson, S. Rikte, and A. Sihvola. Mixing formulas in the time domain. *JOSA A*, 15(5):1411–1422, 1998.

[17] A. Mohammadi, V. Sandoghdar, and M. Agio. Gold, copper, silver and aluminum nanoantennas to enhance spontaneous emission. *Journal of Computational and Theoretical Nanoscience*, 6(9):2024–2030, 2009.

[18] Q.-H. Park. Optical antennas and plasmonics. *Contemporary physics*, 50(2):407–423, 2009.

[19] G. Piro, K. Yang, G. Boggia, N. Chopra, L. Grieco, and A. Alomainy. Terahertz communications in human tissues at the nano-scale for healthcare applications. *IEEE Transactions on Nanotechnology*, 14(3):404–406, 2015.

[20] G. E. Santagati, T. Melodia, L. Galluccio, and S. Palazzo. Ultrasonic networking for e-health applications. *IEEE Wireless Communications*, 20(4), 2013.

[21] T. Stauber, N. M. R. Peres, and A. K. Geim. Optical conductivity of graphene in the visible region of the spectrum. *Physical Review B*, 78:085432, Aug. 2008.

[22] A. Vakil and N. Engheta. Transformation optics using graphene. *Science*, 332(6035):1291–1294, 2011.

[23] P. R. West, S. Ishii, G. V. Naik, N. K. Emani, V. M. Shalaev, and A. Boltasseva. Searching for better plasmonic materials. *Laser & Photonics Reviews*, 4(6):795–808, 2010.

Energy Harvested IEEE 802.15.4 Wireless Body Area Network

Thien D. Nguyen
School of Electrical Engineering
and Computer Science
The University of Newcastle, Australia
ducthien.nguyen@uon.edu.au

Jamil Y. Khan
School of Electrical Engineering
and Computer Science
The University of Newcastle, Australia
jamil.khan@newcastle.edu.au

Duy T. Ngo
School of Electrical Engineering
and Computer Science
The University of Newcastle, Australia
duy.ngo@newcastle.edu.au

ABSTRACT

With the increasing demand of wireless body area network (WBAN) for patient monitoring systems, it is necessary to develop efficient energy management systems to either prolong node battery replacement time or to develop batteryless WBAN nodes. In this paper, we introduce an energy harvesting WBAN architecture that combines the energy harvesting system and an adaptable duty cycle adjustment algorithm ABSD (*Adaptive Beacon Order, Superframe Order and Duty cycle*) to prolong a WBAN node battery lifetime. The paper presents an energy harvesting model to show the effectiveness of human body motion based energy harvester. The paper further analyses the performance of a multi-patient and energy harvested WBAN using our proposed adjustable duty algorithm known as ABSD. The paper also presents several initial simulation results.

Keywords

Energy harvesting, human body motion, WBAN, IEEE802.15.4, adjustable duty cycle

1. INTRODUCTION

Wireless Sensor Networks (WSNs) have attracted a wide range of disciplines where close interactions with the physical world objects are essential. The distributed sensing capabilities and ease of deployment provided by a wireless communication paradigm make WSNs an important component of our daily lives. WSNs are deployed in a variety applications ranging from medical to military, and from home to industry. The recent development of IEEE 802.15.4-based Wireless Body Area Networks (WBANs) is promising as a cost effective approach to a patient monitoring system.

Energy efficiency (EE) is a main critical issue for the mass deployment of WSNs and WBANs. One of the key problems for the mass deployment is powering the sensor and router nodes due to use of limited energy source such as the battery. Frequent replacement of batteries for WBAN nodes could cause severe patient inconvenience. Even though many research have been studied and developed in layers of Physical (PHY), Data Link and Network to minimize energy consumption of a battery-powered node to prolong the lifetime of sensor nodes, the lifetime is still bounded and finite, thus limiting deployment of WBAN nodes for mass deployment.

To address the problem of finite node lifetime, energy harvesting (EH) is an alternative approach for field deployable WSNs as well as WBANs. EH refers to the capability of extracting energy from the surrounding environment, such as: kinetic energy (human body motion, mechanical vibrations, wind and wave), thermal energy (solar power, temperature variations), wireless transfer energy, and RF radiation energy. Energy from diverse sources are converted into electrical energy which could be either used directly to power sensor nodes or stored for later use. The EH techniques allow sensor nodes to recharge during the network operation to reduce the operational cost, also avoiding network downtime. EH networks allow fixed battery-less operation [11], thus making it very important for a sustainable *"near-perpetual"* WSN operability [2, 11]. Therefore, Energy-Harvesting-based WSNs (EHWSNs) architecture has been attracting a significant attention.

In recent year, the potential for human-powered energy harvesting has been gaining attention and considered as an effective approach for powering sensor nodes or devices [6]. In principal, human-powered energy harvesters or microgenerators will harvest energy from human body motions/activities or body heat. These sources could provide unlimited energy over an infinite period of time, however, only very limited amount of energy can be obtained at any particular time. The generated levels of power from these motions are different. Experimentally, sprint walking and motion have been considered as a major source of energy [12, 3, 9, 16] when it can generate up to $1630(mW)$ compared to $81(\mu W)$ during a sleep period [3]. In [12], Buren et. al introduced a map of major body motions (as shown in Fig. 1) during walking that could be considered as potential energy sources, such as: leg motions (ankle, knee, and hip motions), shoulder and elbow joint motion during arm swings, heel strikes and center of mass motion. These locations are set into two groups, namely *"upper body"* (locations 2 - 6) and *"lower body"* (locations 7, 8, 9). Significantly, the lower body locations yield around four times more power than the upper body locations [12].

This paper aims to consider the issue of energy efficiency of an energy harvested IEEE 802.15.4-based WBAN under variable traffic conditions. Here, the source of energy harvesting is from human motion. Our main contribution is to

BODYNETS 2015, September 28-30, Sydney, Australia

DOI 10.4108/eai.28-9-2015.2261429

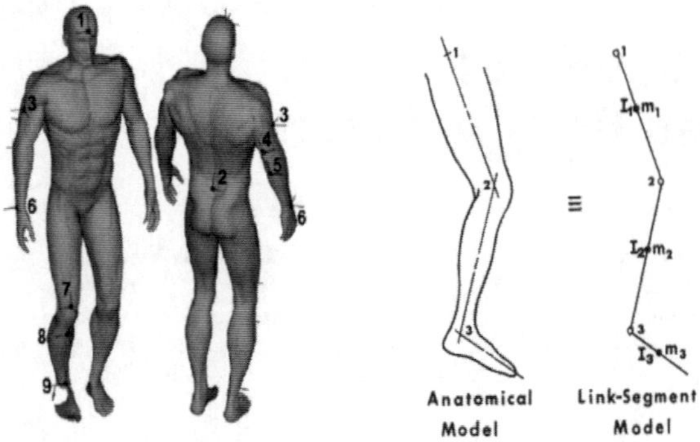

Figure 1: Major body locations for analyzing human movement [12, 13].

propose a combination between an adaptive packet transmission protocol and a human motion-based energy harvesting technique to enhance the EE. This paper also presents the battery lifetime performance for variable traffic load conditions for a multi-patient monitor scenario.

The rest of this paper is organized as follows. Section 2 provides an overview of the existing studies of human motion energy harvesting techniques. Section 3 introduces the IEEE 802.15.4-based WBAN and its traffic characteristics. The combination between an adaptive packet transmission protocol and a selected human motion energy harvesting technique is proposed in Section 4. Numerical results from OPNET and MATLAB based simulation models in terms of energy harvesting and battery lifetime performance will be presented in Section 5. Section 6 concludes the paper.

2. HUMAN MOTION AND RELATED WORKS

Biomechanical energy harvesting from human motion is emerging as a promising clean alternative to electrical power supplied by batteries for portable electronic devices. In principal, the idea of harvesting energy from human body motion is based on converting the mechanical energy (including positive and negative muscles work) that can be derived from the body within each motion to electrical energy [13, p.143].

To harvest energy from the human body motions, force-driven generators and inertial (or vibration-driven) generators can be used [12]. In the first generator, a mechanical energy will be converted by an direct application force. Meanwhile, the inertial generator is a mixed electromechanical system. Here, the mechanical energy will be transformed into electrical energy using the inertia of a moving mass within the generator frame combined with electric/magnetic field, or piezoelectric materials.

There are a number of research studies have investigated the human motion energy harvesting. In [14], based on the force-driven generator, Xie and Cai developed an in-shoe magnetic harvester that could be embedded in a shoe to scavenge mechanical energy from human foot strike during daily activity for conversion into electricity. In this work, a special trapezoidal sliding mechanism and gear train are used for transforming a low-speed linear motion into a high-speed rotation for a generator, which yields a relatively high power output for low-frequency footsteps. This motion then is sent to a microgenerator to produce electricity. By doing this, the harvester could generate an approximately 1W of output power during normal walking condition.

In [12], Buren et. al., compared the optimal performance of these different architectures including Velocity-damped resonant generator ($VDRG$), Coulomb-damped resonant generator ($CDRG$) and Coulomb-force parametric generator ($CFPG$), using actual measured acceleration waveforms from nine locations on the body of walking human subjects. Authors measured average harvested energy at different locations on the body when a person was walking on a treadmill for a given period of time. This is the first model which allowed to determine which body location could provide the most power as well as which generator architecture is best suited to which body location. However, the measured values of harvested energy are suitable for aconsistent walk. This is the main limitation in the work.

To overcome the above practical limitation, Zhang and Seyedi [16] consider the statistical characteristics of harvested energy as subject performs normal daily motions, develop stochastic models for human motion energy harvesting in human-worn wireless devices.

By combining the deployment of velocity-damped resonant generator ($VDRG$) structure and the use of wearable devices (at the four body locations: left ankle, left wrist, right wrist, and waist), named *Alive Heart and Activity Monitor*, human-motion accelerations are measured and then converted to electrical energy. Models provided in this study enable realistic analysis and simulation of wearable communication systems with human motion energy harvesting.

Different from [16], Merrett et. al, [6] consider the effect on harvestable power of generator location (five locations on the body, such as: elbow, wrist, waist, knee and ankle), human activities and take into account the effect of generator orientation and its relation with the other parameters. Authors also propose 2-DOF (Degree of Free) generators in order to examine whether these 2-DOF generators do increase the output power of energy harvested as well as do improve a generator's tolerance to orientation variation and different activities. Experiments and substantial analysis show that 2-DOF generators do not provide significantly greater output power. However, factors of rotation and misalignment which have significantly affected energy harvested, can be reduced using the 2-DOF generator.

3. OVERVIEW OF IEEE 802.15.4-BASED WBANS

3.1 Overview of IEEE 802.15.4 Standard

This standard defines the specifications of PHY and MAC layers for low-rate wireless personal area networks (LR-WPANs)[1]. The standard supports both star and peer-to-peer topologies, which can operate in both non-beacon-enabled and beacon-enabled modes.

Fig. 2 depicts the IEEE 802.15.4 superframe structure for the beacon-enabled mode. The frame is delimited by beacon slots sent by the coordinator, which divides the superframe into 16 slots of equal duration. The superframe is defined by the *Beacon Interval (BI)* and the *Superframe Duration (SD)* which are controlled by the *Beacon Order (BO)* and the *Superframe Order (SO)*, respectively. The *BI* refers to the time duration between two consecutive beacons, and it consists of an active and an inactive period. The active period is

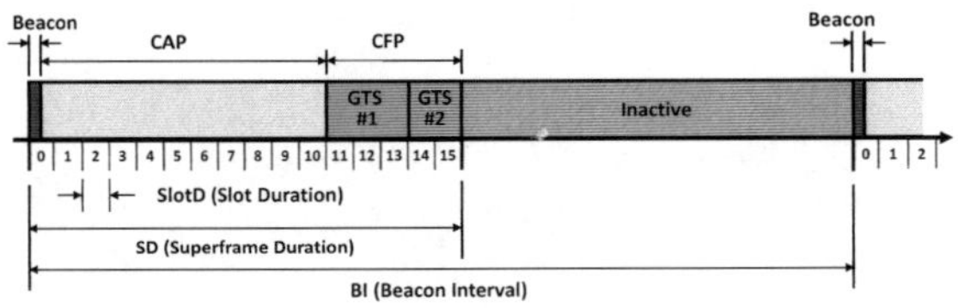

Figure 2: The IEEE 802.15.4 superframe structure for the beacon enabled mode.

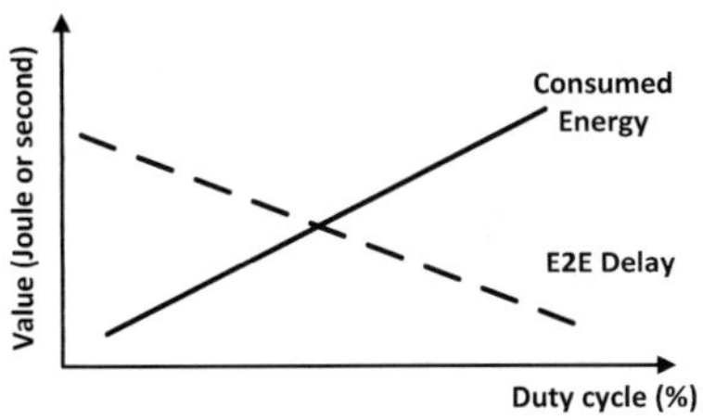

Figure 3: Consumed energy and E2E delay versus duty cycle [15].

further divided into a contention access period *(CAP)* and an optional contention free period *(CFP)*. Any sensor node intending to transmit a packet during the *CAP* must compete with others using the slotted CSMA/CA mechanism. After this period, nodes are able to enter the inactive mode to conserve their energy.

The values of *BI*, *SD* and duty cycle *(DC)* are determined by the following relations:

$$BI = aBaseSuperframeDuration \times 2^{BO}(symbols), \quad (1a)$$

$$SD = aBaseSuperframeDuration \times 2^{SO}(symbols), \quad (1b)$$

$$DC = SD/BI = 2^{SO-BO}, \quad (1c)$$

where $0 \leq SO \leq BO \leq 14$.

The duty cycle control has long been used in a wide variety of battery-operated devices and networks to save the energy and thus extend a network lifetime. Selecting an appropriate *DC* value is important because this does not only affect the energy consumption, but also the QoS parameters [15]. As seen from Fig. 3, with a lower *DC* value, sensor nodes spend more time in the inactive period to save their energy. And meanwhile, the costs for transmission (i.e, delay and packet losses) could sharply increase because of a higher contention level in the network. Therefore, a trade-off between the EE and QoS requirements needs to be maintained.

3.2 Overview of WBAN

An IEEE 802.15.4-based WBAN is a special purpose of WSN and it is composed of multi wireless body sensor nodes which are responsible for sensing physiological parameters on the patient body, such as electrocardiography (EKG), electroencephalogram (EEG), temperature, blood pressure or heart beat. These parameters are then transmitted to a Central Coordinator Unit (CCU) via wireless communication links before sending to remote monitoring stations (or health telemonitoring centers) to process and evaluate [4, 5]. The CCU also controls sensor node's data transmission.

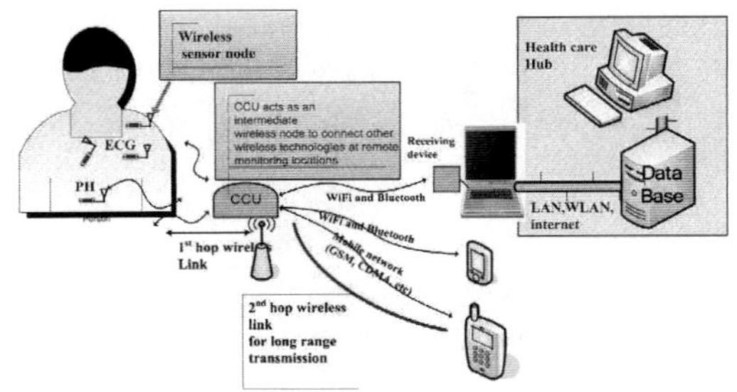

Figure 4: A typical model of WBAN [4]. © Springer

Note that, due to the variations of practical physiological conditions of a patient, the data rate, sample rate and sample size at sensor nodes could be varied. This causes these signals to appear as a periodic or a random (non-periodic) signals. For instance, if a patient develops an abnormal heart condition, then the heartbeat sensor can generate a non-periodic signal [4]. Thus, effectively adapting with these changes is one of important requirements for WBAN protocols, particular the media access control (MAC) layer.

Basically, WBAN-communications follow the standard of IEEE 802.15.4 [1] which is originally designed to support wireless personal area networks (WPANs) operating in short range (on or in the human body area) and on low data rates. The main purpose of this is to provide an efficient low-power and low-complexity communication. A typical WBAN model is illustrated in Fig. 4.

The sensed physiological parameters from sensor nodes (as shown in Table 1) in a WBAN can be divided into two main categories of information, including: regular and emergency. In the emergency case, the information has to be transmitted immediately to the remote monitoring stations to produce an alert signal. In such the case, the value of transmission delay will be minimized. In practical, *reliability (i.e., packet losses rate, data throughput, jitter)* and *latency* are the utmost important requirements and they strictly depend on the design of physical (PHY) and Data Link (MAC sublayer) layers [4, 5].

4. ENERGY EFFICIENCY IN AN IEEE 802.15.4 WBAN

In this section, we will focus on the issue of energy efficiency in an IEEE 802.15.4 WBAN under the variable load conditions. To do that, there is a combination between an adaptive packet transmission algorithm and human motion energy harvesting technique using the inertial generator as described in [12, 16].

4.1 An Energy-Avare Packet Transmission Algorithm

From Fig. 3, the energy management is ineffective if the duty cycle remains in the high range for a longer period (*i.e.*, 50% - 100%). In practical, the duty cycle of 50% could allow a node to save up to 50% of consumed energy.

In our earlier work, we reported some preliminary results on enhancing energy efficiency in an IEEE 802.15.4 WSN using our preliminary algorithm, namely *ABSD (Adaptive Beacon Order, Superframe Order and Duty cycle)*[7]. This algorithm allows to adapt the value of *DC* according to the offered load conditions via simultaneously adjusting the BO and SO values. A more detailed description of this algorithm can be found in [7].

The total consumed energy at a node is given by [7]:

$$E = E_{listen} + E_{tx} + E_{rx} + E_{sleep}, \tag{2}$$

where E_{listen} is the energy consumed during the listening period, E_{tx} is the energy for transmitting a data packet and its associated control overhead, E_{rx} is the energy used for successfully receiving a transmitted data packet and its associated control overhead, and E_{sleep} is the energy consumed during the sleeping period.

From [7], E in (2) can be explicitly rewritten as (3):

where:

t_{CCA} is the CCA duration and t_{idle} is the idle time,

t_{tx} is the time for transmitting a packet of $L(bits)$ at a data rate of $R(Kbps)$,

t_{sleep} and I_{sleep} are the time required and the current drawn by the radio in the sleeping mode, respectively,

t_{rx} is the time required to receive successfully a packet at the coordinator at the rate of R,

I_{tx} is the current consumed in the transmitting mode, I_{rx} is the current in the receiving mode,

U is the battery voltage.

4.2 A Human Motion Energy Harvesting Technique

As mentioned in Section 1 and Section 2, *"lower body"* locations are the main sources of energy for energy harvesting. Thus, in this paper, we explore the option of generating energy during activities that are performed naturally throughout the day, with particular emphasis on walking and *"lower body"* locations (Hip, Knee and Ankle) as shown in Fig. 5.

With these assumptions, when a person walks, forces or moments at these three locations will be generated. In this case, the human motion (i.e., walking) can be considered as a kinetics model. Based on this model, we can determine the forces, total moment of force values of ankle, knee, and hip joint during a motion. Based on an anatomical model, a link segment model and a free body diagram as illustrated in Fig. 5, combined with the Newton's Third Law, Newton's equations and Euler's equations [13], values of vertical force (F_y), horizontal forces F_x and moments (M) at the Hip, Knee and Ankle are determined as follows:

For the Ankle:

$$F_{Ax} = m_3 a_x, \tag{4a}$$
$$F_{Ay} = m_3 g + m_3 a_y, \tag{4b}$$
$$M_A = I_3 \alpha + F_{Ax} d_y + F_{Ay} d_x. \tag{4c}$$

For the Knee:

$$F_{Kx} = m_2 a_x - F_{Ax}, \tag{5a}$$
$$F_{Ky} = m_2 g + m_2 a_y + F_{Ay}, \tag{5b}$$
$$M_K = I_2 \alpha + F_{Ax} d_y + F_{Ky} d_x + F_{Kx} d_y + F_{Ky} d_x + M_A. \tag{5c}$$

For the Hip:

$$F_{Hx} = m_1 a_x - F_{Kx}, \tag{6a}$$
$$F_{Hy} = m_1 g + m_1 a_y + F_{Ky}, \tag{6b}$$
$$M_H = I_1 \alpha + F_{Hx} d_y + F_{Hy} d_x + F_{Kx} d_y + F_{Ky} d_x + M_K. \tag{6c}$$

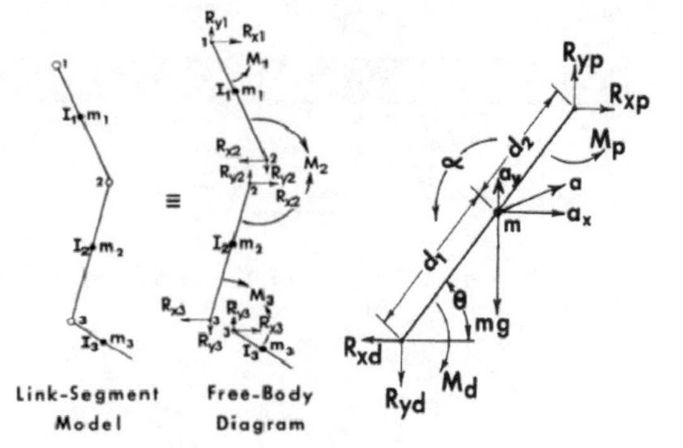

Figure 5: Link-segment and free-body model [13].

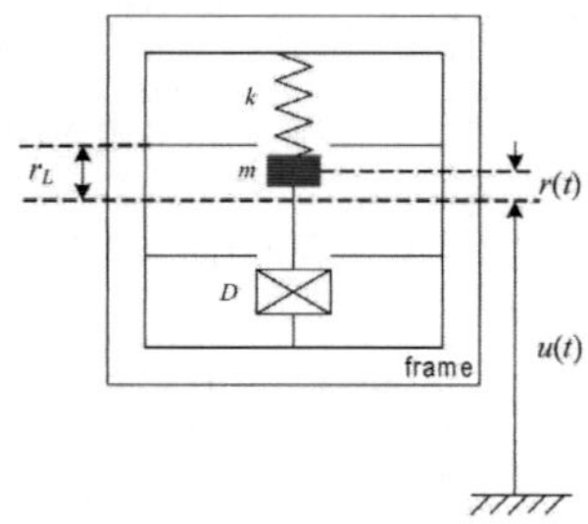

Figure 6: Model of vibration-driven power generator [12, 16].

where m is the mass, a is acceleration of segment, d is the distance, α is angular acceleration of segment and I is moment of inertia.

In this paper, we assume that a velocity damped resonant generator (VDRG) is used [12, 16]. The VDRG is a resonant generator with a magnetic internal mass moving inside a frame as illustrated in Fig. 6. The internal mass will be linked with the external frame by a spring and is damped by a force proportional to its velocity. The movement of the mass in an electromagnetic field will generate the harvestable power. Here, $u(t)$ is the absolute position of the external frame, and $u(t)$ is the second integral of $a(t)$. From [16], we have:

$$m\ddot{r}(t) = -kr(t) - D\dot{r}(t) - ma(t), \tag{7}$$

where k is the spring constant, D is the proportionality factor between the damping force and the velocity of the internal mass.

The Laplace transform between the mass-to-frame position $R(s)$ and the frame acceleration $A(s)$ is:

$$\frac{R(s)}{A(s)} = -\frac{1}{s^2 + \frac{D}{m}s + \frac{k}{m}}, \tag{8}$$

and the harvested power is given by:

$$p(t) = -f(t)\dot{r}(t) = D\dot{r}^2(t). \tag{9}$$

4.3 Battery Model for WBAN Sensor Node

$$E = \left\{((1+N)I_{tx} + I_{rx})\frac{L}{R} + (2^{BO} - 2^{SO})I_{sleep} + (2 \times t_{CCA} + t_{idle})I_{listen}\right\} U. \quad (3)$$

Table 1: Physiologic data characteristics [4].

Physiologic Parameter	Parameter range	Maximum frequency (Hz)	Inter-arrival time (sec)	Payload/Sample (bits)	Data (*Kbps)*
Blood flow	1-300 ml/s	20	0.025	12	0.48
ECG signal	0.5-4 mV	250	0.002	12	6
Respiratory rate	2-50 breaths/min	10	0.05	12	0.24
Blood pressure	10-400 mmHg	50	0.01	12	1.2
Blood pH	6.8-7.8 pH units	2	0.25	12	0.048
Body temperature	32-40 ^{o}C	0.1	5	12	0.0024

As mentioned in Section 1, extending the lifetime of nodes is known as an extremely important task in battery-powered systems, particular in WBAN and WSN. In practical, these battery-powered systems and devices always require an appropriate battery model. In this work, we utilize a battery model based on a Kinetic model, namely Kinetic Battery Model (KiBaM). KiBaM is an intuitive battery model, which was originally developed to model chemical processes of large lead-acid batteries by a kinetic process [8]. To use and deploy battery for sensor nodes in this work, we adopt the KiBaM for nickelmetal hydride (NiMH) battery as described in [8].

In this work, to store the harvested energy from the human motion, we use a rechargeable NiMH battery. In order to achieve a high recharging performance, state of charge (SOC) of batteries should be monitored. Depending on an actual SOC, the decision for battery recharging will be proposed to ensure there is enough energy to maintain normal operation of sensor nodes.

5. SIMULATION RESULTS

We develop a simulation model using MATLAB to determine the amounts of harvested energy from three different locations on the human leg (Hip, Knee and Ankle) during a walking. A set of data for a normal walking simulation is obtained from [13]. Also, the mathematical model of a energy consumption at a WBAN node as shown in (3) is performed in MATLAB environment. Simulation parameters are summarized in the Table 2.

Fig. 7 illustrates the generated values of forces and moment of force at three different locations on the human leg during his walking. According to the Dempster's Body Segment Parameters [10, p.65], the differences among the ratio of *segmental mass/total mass* at the segments of foot (ankle to ball of foot), leg (knee to ankle center) and thigh (hip to ankle center) (0.0145, 0.0465 and 0.1, respectively) are not significantly. During the period of 45-minute walking, the total harvested energy at the points of Hip, Knee and Ankle are approximately 1.1(*Joule*), 0.3(*Joule*) and 0.9(*Joule*), respectively. As can be seen from this Figure, the generated values of forces, moments, particular the harvested energy at these points are quite the same and suitable with reported values in [12].

Later we use an OPNET model to simulate a bursty traffic source for different IEEE 802.15.4 WBAN sensor nodes that transmit packets to the CCU using the superframe structure. In the simulation, the variations of the incoming traffic load under three typical values of interval packet per node (i.e, 0.5, 2 and 3 *packet/s/node*) and their distributions are shown in Fig. 8(a). The simulated scenario represents a multi-patient monitoring system. This figure shows that for different packet interval time, the offered traffic load varies with time. In addition, the load variability increases with the increasing traffic load. For a multi-patient WBAN, the traffic rate could vary depending on the physiological parameters observed.

Table 2: Simulation parameters and QoS requirements.

	Parameter	Symbol	Value
Sensor Node MICAZ	Receive	$I_{rx}(mA)$	19.7
	Transmit (0dBm)	$I_{tx}(mA)$	17.4
	Idle Listening	$I_{listen}(mA)$	0.02
	Sleeping	$I_{sleep}(mA)$	0.001
	Voltage	$U(V)$	2.7-3.3
Traffic	Packet arrival time (s)	λ	0.3-10
	Traffic ($packet/s$)	$1/\lambda$	
	Distribution	$Poisson$	
	Packet size ($bits$)	L	1,024
	No. of ReTx	N_{max}	3
Human walking	Body weight (kg)	M	70
	Speed (m/s)	v	1
	Gravity (m/s^2)	g	9.8
No. of patient			6
Ni-MH battery	Voltage (V)		1.25

Fig. 8(b) describes the relationship between a remaining energy in the battery at sensor node and packet. As seen, the remaining energy decrease with an increase in incoming traffic load.

As mentioned earlier, managing the state of charge of battery is an important task. In Fig. 9(a), at the initial stage, the battery state of charge (SOC) is 100%. It means that battery is full-charged and there is no need a charging at battery. During the sensor node's operation, nodes will use this energy to transmit or receive data and communicate with the CCU. Thus, the energy in sensor node's battery decreases quickly. If there is no harvester, the remaining energy continuously declines. In the case when SOC value

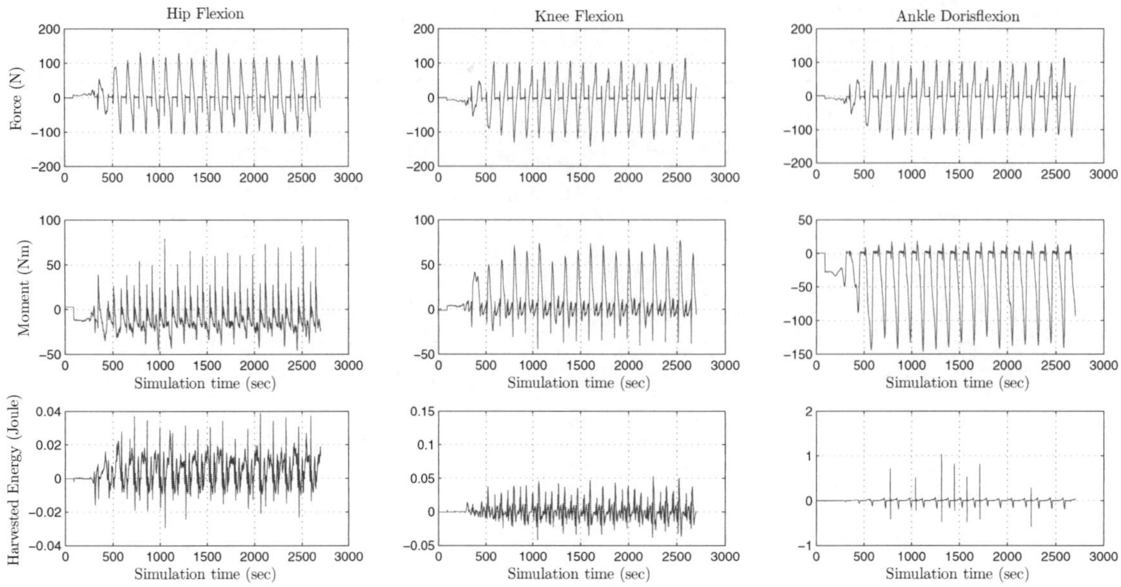

Figure 7: Force, Moment and Harvested energy at Hip, Knee and Ankle.

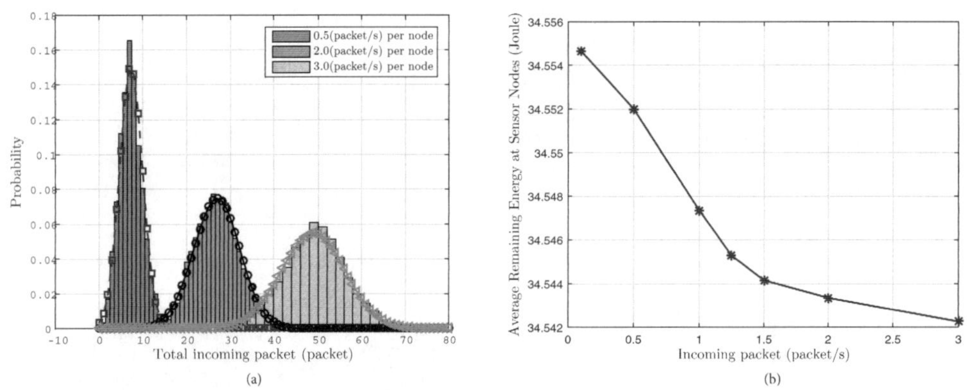

Figure 8: Incoming traffic at the CCU & Relationship of the Remaining Energy and Incoming traffic.

is equal or lower than 10%, the main operations of sensor nodes (transmitting, receiving) will be stopped and nodes will enter into the sleeping state and wait for batteries re-charging.

With an energy harvester, when the remaining level of energy in battery (or SOC value) reaches 50%, the battery will be re-charged. The amount of harvested energy will be charged into the battery and the remaining energy will start increasing. The more the amount of harvested energy is, more energy will be re-charged in battery. Fig. 9(b) shows that with the human motion energy harvester, the battery can extend their lifetime from the time of 1500(sec) to more than 2700(sec). Clearly, the energy harvester has a significant improvement on the lifetime of battery. This leads to an extension in the lifetime of sensor nodes.

Note that, in this simulation, battery charge level performance was obtained for the MATLAB by using the energy characteristics of IEEE 802.15.4 nodes obtained from an OPNET model when a patient monitoring system was simulated using 6 WBAN nodes. Also, for space limitation detail of the OPNET model is not provided.

6. CONCLUSION

The paper analyzed the performance of an energy harvested IEEE 802.15.4 WBAN using the proposed ABSD energy efficient packet transmission technique. The work used two simulation models to obtain the performance data of the WBAN. Initially, an OPNET based discrete event model was developed to measure the performance of the ABSD packet transmission technique. The OPNET model generated energy usage profiles of WBAN nodes for different traffic intensities. The energy usage profile was utilized

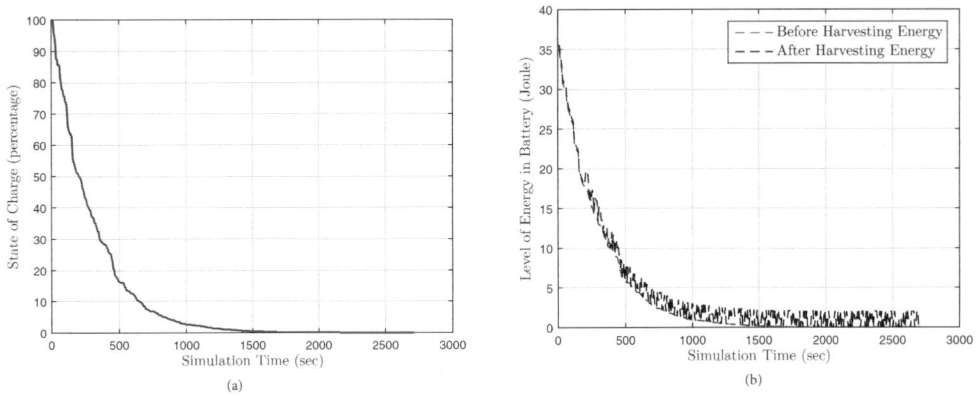

Figure 9: Battery state of charge and energy harvesting.

in the MATLAB model to compute the battery lifetime by linking the energy profile of WBAN nodes with the energy scavenging model. This a unique approach used in this work to measure energy efficiency with realistic network operating parameters and an energy scavenging model which takes account of human body movements and physiological traffic characteristics. As shown in the previous section that a body energy harvested network could significantly prolong a battery or energy source lifetime.

Energy efficient WBAN hardware can be designed by using other form energy storage devices such as the super capacitor which could act as an energy buffer and potentially provide WBAN support to patients or athletes without replacing the energy source at all. The energy scavenging model can be further extended to power up wearable devices either for standalone or for networking applications. This work will be further extended to develop a combined OPNET model by incorporating the MATLAB energy scavenging module. Such a combined model will allow us to analyze the performance a WBAN for different traffic and applications scenarios.

7. REFERENCES

[1] IEEE Draft Standard for Local and Metropolitan Area Networks Part 15.4: (lr-wpans) amendment to the MAC sub-layer. *IEEE P802.15.4e/D6.0 (Revision of IEEE Std 802.15.4-2006)*, Aug 2011.

[2] H. Chen, Y. Li, J. Rebelatto, B. Uchoa Filho, and B. Vucetic. Harvest-then-cooperate: Wireless-powered cooperative communications. 2015. to appear.

[3] M. Hannan, S. Mutashar, S. Samad, and A. Hussain. Energy harvesting for the implantable biomedical devices: issues and challenges. *BioMedical Engineering OnLine*, 13(1), 2014.

[4] J. Khan, M. Yuce, G. Bulger, and B. Harding. Wireless body area network (WBAN) design techniques and performance evaluation. *Journal of Medical Systems*, 36(3):1441–1457, 2012.

[5] Y. Kim, S. Lee, and S. Lee. Coexistence of zigbee-based wban and wifi for health telemonitoring systems. *IEEE Journal of Biomedical and Health Informatics*, PP(99), 2015. to appear.

[6] G. Merrett, H. Huang, and N. White. Modeling the effect of orientation on human-powered inertial energy harvesters. 15(1):434–441, Jan 2015.

[7] T. D. Nguyen, J. Y. Khan, and D. T. Ngo. An energy and QoS-aware packet transmission algorithm for IEEE 802.15.4 networks. In *Proc. of PIMRC'15*, Hong Kong, China, 2015. to appear.

[8] V. Rao, G. Singhal, A. Kumar, and N. Navet. Battery model for embedded systems. In *VLSI Design, 2005.*

[9] R. Riemer and A. Shapiro. Biomechanical energy harvesting from human motion: theory, state of the art, design guidelines, and future directions. *Journal of NeuroEngineering and Rehabilitation*, 8(1), 2011.

[10] G. Robertson, G. Caldwell, J. Hamill, G. Kamen, and S. Whittlesey. *Biomechanics and Motor Control of Human Movement, 4th-Ed.* Human Kenitics, 2014.

[11] M. Tentzeris, A. Georgiadis, and L. Roselli. Energy harvesting and scavenging. 102(11), Nov 2014.

[12] T. von Buren, P. Mitcheson, T. Green, E. Yeatman, A. Holmes, and G. Troster. Optimization of inertial micropower generators for human walking motion. 6(1):28–38, Feb 2006.

[13] D. A. Winter. *Biomechanics and Motor Control of Human Movement, 4th Edition.* John Wiley & Sons Ltd, 2009.

[14] L. Xie and M. Cai. An in-shoe harvester with motion magnification for scavenging energy from human foot strike. *IEEE/ASME Transactions on Mechatronics*, PP(99):1–1, 2015. to appear.

[15] O. Yang and W. Heinzelman. Modeling and performance analysis for duty-cycled MAC protocols with applications to s-mac and x-mac. 11(6):905–921, Jun 2012.

[16] S. Zhang and A. Seyedi. Statistical models for harvested power from human motion. *IEEE Journal on Selected Areas in Communications*, 33(8):1667–1679, Aug 2015.

Mobility Independent Secret Key Generation for Wearable Health-care Devices

Girish Revadigar[*†], Chitra Javali[*†], Hassan Jameel Asghar [†],
Kasper B. Rasmussen, and Sanjay Jha[*]
{girishr,chitraj,sanjay}@cse.unsw.edu.au; hassan.asghar@nicta.com.au;
kasper.rasmussen@cs.ox.ac.uk

[*]School of Computer Science & Engineering, UNSW Australia, Sydney, AUSTRALIA
[†]National ICT Australia (NICTA), Australian Technology Park, Sydney, AUSTRALIA
Dept. of Computer Science, University of Oxford, Oxford, UK

ABSTRACT

Security in Wireless Body Area Networks (WBAN) is of major concern as the miniature personal health-care devices need to protect the sensitive health information transmitted in wireless medium. It is essential for these devices to generate the shared secret key used for data encryption periodically. Recent studies have exploited wireless channel characteristics, e.g., received signal strength indicator (RSSI) to derive the shared secret key during random body movement of subject wearing devices. However, in the absence of node mobility, these schemes have very low bit rate capacity, and fail to derive keys with good entropy, which is a big threat for security.

In this work, we study the effectiveness of combining dual antennas and frequency diversity for obtaining uncorrelated channel samples to improve entropy of key and bit rate in static channel conditions. We propose a novel mobility independent RSSI based secret key generation protocol – iARC for WBAN. We conduct an extensive set of experiments in real time environments on sensor platforms used in WBAN to validate the performance of iARC. iARC has 800 bps secrecy capacity and generates 128 bit key in only 160 ms.

Categories and Subject Descriptors

C.2.0 [**General**]: Security and protection; C.2.1 [**Network Architecture and Design**]: Wireless communication

General Terms

Security, Design, Protocol, Experimentation

Keywords

Body Area Networks, Physical layer security, Secret key generation

1. INTRODUCTION

One of the remarkable outcomes of rapid development in wireless technology is the emergence of a new paradigm for personalized health care, sports and fitness applications, known as Wireless Body Area Networks (WBAN). Several wearable devices like FitBit Flex, JawBone's Up, and Nike+ FuelBand [1] are gaining popularity in the healthcare sector. According to a recent survey from ABI Research, wearable device revenues are expected to grow more than USD $6 billion by 2018 [3].

Although technological advancement has lead to wireless capability of body-worn devices, there are a number of security threats that these devices may face, for example, eavesdropping of confidential data and injection of malicious commands which can cause adverse effects on a person's health. Since WBAN devices handle sensitive health information, securing them against such attacks is a major challenge.

As WBAN devices are resource constrained, the complex traditional cryptographic key establishment schemes would not be feasible. Instead, the devices need lightweight security mechanisms that are fast and reliable. The secret keys used by these devices to encrypt the data must be generated dynamically and renewed periodically to avoid the threat of compromise and privacy leakage.

Recent studies [4, 17] have shown that the wireless link characteristics, for e.g., Received Signal Strength Indicator (RSSI) can be exploited to generate shared symmetric keys. RSSI based security schemes are well suited for WBAN devices as it can be easily measured by every device directly from the received packet without the need of special hardware. The existing schemes [4, 17] for secret key generation in WBAN are dependent on the channel randomness caused due to node mobility during the body motion of a subject wearing devices. It has been shown that keys with good entropy and high bit rate can be generated during the activities involving sufficient body movements. However, in the absence of node mobility the existing schemes will have very low bit rate and low entropy, in which case an eavesdropper can easily reproduce the same key by observing the channel [13]. This poses a major security threat. It is worth noting that, in real-time applications such as hospital scenarios or remote-health monitoring systems in home/office environments, one cannot expect the patient/person to be always mobile. Indeed, many static channel cases like person sitting in a position without much body movement (e.g.,

BODYNETS 2015, September 28-30, Sydney, Australia

DOI 10.4108/eai.28-9-2015.2261446

person at home/workplace), or sleeping on a bed (e.g., in home or critical care sections/wards of hospitals) are quite common, in which case the existing schemes cannot be used.

Thus, there is a need for a robust and lightweight secret key generation scheme which is independent of node mobility to make WBAN resilient against possible threats.

The security issues related to WBAN discussed above are the motivation for our work presented in this paper. We present an RSSI based shared secret key generation scheme which involves a novel approach for inducing artificial randomness in the wireless channel using dual antennas and frequency diversity to yield keys with sufficient entropy even under static channel conditions. Our proposed scheme is lightweight and suitable for deployment in real world applications.

Although multiple antenna architectures have been extensively used in complex wireless systems like WiFi with Multiple Input Multiple Output (MIMO) capability, they have not been used in WBAN devices with small form factor. MIMO systems allow simultaneous reception of an incoming packet on all the antennas of the receiver node. Typically, WBAN devices are resource constrained without MIMO capability, hence, the protocols available for WiFi cannot be directly applied to WBAN. Our scheme demonstrates the use of multiple antennas effectively for shared secret key generation without adding extra cost to power consumption.

We have validated our system using real sensor platforms used in WBAN applications by conducting an extensive set of experiments in different real-time environments.

To summarize, **our contributions** are as follows:

- We propose iARC – a novel, lightweight, RSSI based secret key generation scheme for WBAN which *induces artificial channel randomness* by employing dual antennas and frequency diversity for generating keys with good entropy in the absence of node-mobility.
- We propose a multiple bit extraction algorithm to reduce the number of packets exchanged during key generation and overall time taken for generating shared secret keys.
- We demonstrate experimentally that, iARC achieves the highest bit rate of 800 bps with high bit agreement between the two legitimate body-worn devices, and generates 128 bit key in 160 ms, which is faster by an order of magnitude compared to existing mobility based schemes.

To the best of our knowledge, the work presented in this paper is the first mobility independent physical layer based secret key generation mechanism for resource constrained devices of WBAN. We have evaluated the randomness of keys generated by our proposed protocol using NIST [10] entropy test. The keys generated by our protocol pass the NIST test with entropy in the range: 0.92 to 0.99.

The rest of the paper is organized as follows. In Section 2 we discuss related work. Section 3 presents our system model and Section 4 explains our protocol design. Section 5 describes detailed evaluation of the proposed protocol and results. In Section 6, we provide the security analysis, and in Section 7 we present conclusion and future work.

2. RELATED WORK

Recently, security mechanisms based on RSSI have been proposed for Wireless Body Area Networks. Authors in [6] have studied key generation in dynamic channel condition and achieved 2 bps bit rate in a simulation environment. Researchers in [4, 17] have shown that the body-worn devices can generate secret keys during dynamic channel conditions caused due to the body movement of subject wearing the devices. The scheme in [4] has a bit rate of 0.24 bps and requires 15-35 minutes to generate a 128 bit key. Additionally, the work employs Savitzky-Golay filter and windowing to select a subset of RSSI samples and discard the remaining. The scheme in [17] has the bit rate of 8.03 bps. One of the major drawback of existing schemes [4, 17] is that, in case of a stable channel, the above schemes will have very low bit rate and fail to derive keys with sufficient entropy. Researchers in [7] have proposed a protocol for key generation between non-reachable nodes with the help of a trusted relay in mobile environments.

The most recent protocols closest to our work are SeAK [8] and DLINK [14]. SeAK has been proposed for secure device pairing during the bootstrapping phase of WBAN. SeAK exploits the spatial separation of dual antennas to perform authentication and initial key generation with a nearby device (< 10-15 cm) aligned to one of its antennas prior to on-body deployment. In DLINK, an off-body base station exploits spatial separation of antennas for decorrelating the successive channel samples in mobile environments. In contrast, iARC is for session key renewal for the wearable devices after on-body deployment and is independent of antenna separation and device alignment.

To the best of our knowledge, the scheme presented in [18] is the only one to investigate secret key generation in static channel conditions. The authors have studied the effect of channel hopping to yield channel variation in static cases. It has been demonstrated on single antenna sensor platform that the basic channel hopping can provide a good source of correlated randomness at the two parties. However, as the channel decays very slowly in static cases, only a limited amount of meaningful information can be derived. On the contrary, in our work, we study the effectiveness of combining frequency diversity and random switching of dual antennas to obtain uncorrelated channel samples, and how this improves the bit rate, quality of secret keys, and bit agreement in static channel conditions.

3. SYSTEM MODEL

3.1 Assumptions

We assume that all the WBAN devices operate in 2.4 GHz. There is one on-body Control Unit (CU) and one or more wearable devices (D) which are in line of sight with the CU. The CU is equipped with two omni-directional antennas A1 and A2 having different features, whereas the devices have single antenna. The CU employs a pseudo-random number generator (PRNG) to generate a random bit string $r \in \{0,1\}^{128}$ used for antenna selection. Only the CU knows the random antenna switching algorithm and the initial secret random seed of 128 bits, i.e., $s \in \{0,1\}^{128}$ required for the PRNG. We assume that the WBAN devices are authenticated and are not compromised. We consider static channel conditions only.

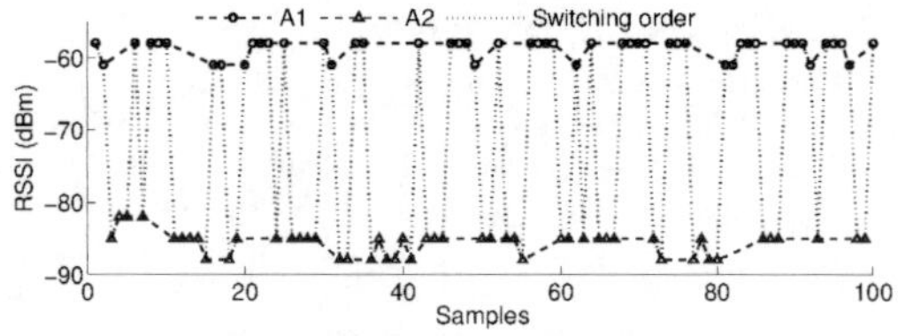

(a) RSSI samples measured by A1 and A2 on a single channel

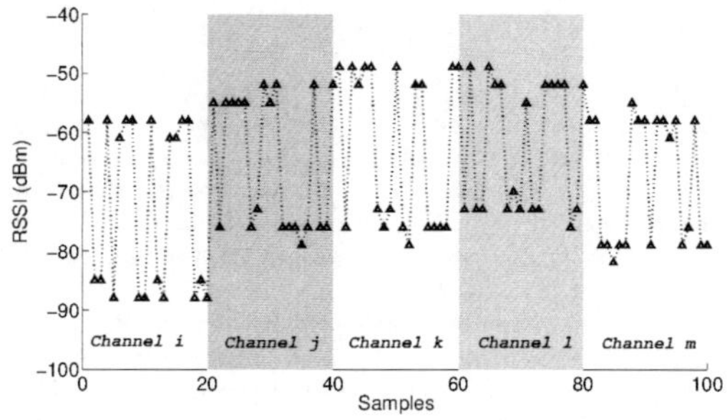

(b) RSSI samples measured by A1 and A2 with antenna switching and dynamic channel hopping

Figure 1: The CU induces artificial channel randomness by effectively combining random antenna switching and dynamic frequency hopping.

3.2 Threat model

We consider the presence of one or more off-body adversaries located away from legitimate devices at a distance more than half the wavelength (i.e., 6.25 cm) of radio signal being used. The adversaries may be either in line of sight (LOS) or non-line of sight (NLOS) to the WBAN devices. We consider both passive and active adversaries. A passive eavesdropper can capture the packets exchanged between the CU and D and attempt to extract the secret key. Eavesdroppers can have single or dual antennas. Active attackers can jam the channel, or cause man-in-the-middle (MIM) attack. It is assumed that the adversaries have same radio capability as the WBAN devices to sample the wireless channel and are aware of the secret key extraction mechanism.

4. PROTOCOL DESIGN

4.1 Inducing artificial channel randomness

Our design is based on the wireless signal propagation characteristics. As the distance between two wireless devices communicating with each other increases, the radio signal strength degrades because of fading and multi-path effects. However, the channel characteristics will be unique and highly correlated between the two devices due to reciprocity property [11]. Our system uses dual antennas and frequency diversity for inducing artificial channel randomness required for secret key generation [12,13]. The following subsections describe the steps involved in detail.

4.1.1 Employing dual antennas

In static channel conditions, for a fixed distance between the CU and D, suppose that the CU uses a single default antenna, i.e., either A1 or A2 during channel sampling, then the observed variation in the RSSI samples will be as shown in Fig. 1a. The successive RSSI samples measured on a single antenna will be highly correlated and hence secret keys with good entropy and high bit rate cannot be obtained. Our design aims to extract uncorrelated successive channel samples. Thus, the CU employs dual antennas for channel sampling and randomly switches between the two.

In order to decide the antenna switching pattern, iARC employs a PRNG used in [15]. This PRNG is a cryptographically secure, NIST recommended random number generator which uses AES as the block cipher [16]. An initial secret random seed s required for the PRNG is generated offline and stored in the non-volatile memory of the CU.[1] This seed is updated every time the PRNG is run for subsequent key generation. As 128 bit keys are used in WBAN [2], we use a 128 bit seed, i.e., $s \in \{0,1\}^{128}$. The CU employs random antenna switching for channel sampling based on the random bit string $r \in \{0,1\}^{128}$ generated by the PRNG. The CU uses antenna A1 or A2 for probe exchange based on the order in which bit 0 and 1 appear in r respectively. An example of variation in the RSSI samples after antenna switching is shown by the dotted line in Fig. 1a.

4.1.2 Exploiting frequency diversity

iARC exploits frequency diversity by employing our novel *dynamic frequency hopping* scheme, which is explained in detail in Section 4.2.3. Our scheme adopts frequency hopping for two important reasons, primarily to avoid the leakage of useful information to the adversary, and second, to bring additional randomness in the samples collected [18]. In our design, the total number of probes N required for key extraction is divided into a number of sub blocks, and each sub block key is derived in a different channel. In each channel, the CU performs random antenna switching as explained in previous Section 4.1.1 for channel sampling. As there are 16 channels available in 2.4 GHz, when each sub block key is generated in a different frequency channel, the RSSI samples collected in different channels will be shifted based on the channel spacing, i.e., the current channel and new channel after hopping. This further improves the randomness of the samples as shown in Fig. 1b and hence the secret key bits. The center frequency F_c (MHz) of each channel in 2.4 GHz is given by

$$F_c = 2405 + 5(\eta - 11) \quad (1)$$

where $\eta = \{11, 12, \ldots, 26\}$ is the channel number.

4.2 Key generation process

The secret key generation process consists of following different steps: (i) Channel sampling, (ii) Quantization, and (iii) Dynamic frequency hopping.

In iARC, the total number of probes N required for key generation is divided into B number of multiple sub blocks of equal length and each sub block key k_{sb} is derived in a different channel. The final secret key K is obtained by the concatenation of all the sub block keys as:

$$K = k_{sb1} \parallel k_{sb2} \parallel \cdots \parallel k_{sbB} \quad (2)$$

The CU and D perform channel sampling, quantization

[1]In commercial devices, this seed can be placed at the time of manufacturing.

and frequency hopping repeatedly until the total number of probes N required for key generation are exchanged.

4.2.1 *Channel sampling*

During channel sampling, both the CU and D exchange multiple probe and response packets and measure the RSSI of incoming packet. The device D sends a `Key_Renewal_Req` packet to CU to initiate the key renewal process. The CU transmits a total of N number of `Probe_Packet` at an interval of t ms by adding an index number i in the payload to track successful packet reception, where $i = \{0,\ 1,\ \ldots,\ N\text{-}1\}$. Let X and Y denote the set of RSSI captured by the CU and D respectively. Once the probe packet is received, D measures the RSSI y_i and immediately transmits a `Response_Packet` by placing index i of the last received `Probe_Packet` in the payload. After receiving the `Response_Packet`, the CU checks if the index i of payload matches the value in the last probe packet transmitted, and if it matches, the CU measures the RSSI x_i of the packet. The CU uses the same antenna, i.e., either A1 or A2 for sending a probe packet and receiving the corresponding response packet with the same index i. After successful packet exchange for a particular index i, i is incremented and the CU may use the same antenna or switch to another antenna for the next probe packet transmission based on the random string r. If the CU does not receive any reply from D within timeout interval t_o, it retransmits the probe packet with the index i. D updates y_i with the RSSI of latest packet.

4.2.2 *Quantization and multiple bit extraction*

Once the CU and D have RSSI samples collected on a particular channel, they perform quantization and bit extraction process to generate the sub block key k_{sb} as below:
(i) Suppose n is the number of bits to be assigned per sample, then divide the whole range of RSS available for the devices into L levels - $l_1, l_2, \ldots, l_L$, arranged in the highest to lowest order, such that $L = 2^n$.
(ii) Each level l is assigned a code word c of n bits, i.e., $c \in \{0,1\}^n$, e.g., for binary coding and $n = 3$, the levels can be coded as 000 (l_8) to 111 (l_1).
(iii) Categorize all the RSSI samples collected into two separate groups corresponding to packets exchanged on antenna A1 and A2. Calculate the mean of the samples in each group to decide their level l in the quantization process.
(iv) Each sample in the group is assigned the code word corresponding to level l assigned to the mean, and the sub block key k_{sb} is constructed.

As we have used devices with RF230 radio, the RSS of packets exchanged are in the range of 0 to -100 dBm.

4.2.3 *Dynamic frequency hopping*

After quantization, the CU and D consider lowest of RSSI levels obtained to decide the next channel to hop as per the following equation:

$$\text{New\_Channel} = ((\text{Cur\_Channel} - 11 + f) \bmod 16) + 11 \quad (3)$$

where $f = i$, the lowest RSSI level (l_i) obtained in the quantization scheme. For instance, for 3 bits/sample assignment, the whole RSSI range is divided into 8 equal levels - l_1 to l_8. If the current channel is 26 and the lowest RSSI level obtained for the mean of samples is l_4(4th level), then the next channel to hop is calculated as:
New_Channel = ((26 - 11 + 4) mod 16) +11 = 14.

4.3 Theoretical analysis

4.3.1 *Improvement in entropy and bit rate*

The entropy of final secret key is dependent on the entropy of channel samples (i.e., RSSI). The *estimated entropy* of channel samples can be calculated by the following equation:

$$E = -\sum_{\tilde{h}} p(\tilde{h}) \log_2 p(\tilde{h}) \quad (4)$$

where $p(\tilde{h})$ is the probability of occurrence of channel sample $\tilde{h}$ in the captured samples. As per our protocol, all the RSSI collected on a particular antenna on each channel will be assigned a unique n bit code word though the individual samples may show little fluctuation around the mean value. The *estimated entropy* gives an upper bound on the number of bits that can be assigned per sample during quantization. This is explained in detail as follows:
(*i*) *CU with one antenna and a single channel:* Let the symbol s_1 denote the individual channel sample captured. The resulting set of channel samples S consists of same symbol s_1, i.e., $S = \{s_1\}$. The maximum *estimated entropy* E_{max} will be: $-((1)log_2(1)) = 0$, which means that any one bit arbitrary value e.g., bit 1 can be used to encode s_1. Thus, the resulting secret key also will have entropy $= 0$.
(*ii*) *Effect of frequency hopping:* If the CU uses single antenna and two channels, e.g., 11 and 20, then all the individual RSSI of each channel can be mapped to symbols s_1 and s_2 respectively. Now $S = \{s_1,\ s_2\}$, and $E_{max} = 1$. Thus, s_1 and s_2 can be assigned 1 bit code, e.g., 0 and 1 respectively. Hence, the resulting secret key will also have entropy > 0, compared to previous case depending on the occurrence of s_1 and s_2. Similarly, for 3 channels, $S = \{s_1,\ s_2,\ s_3\}$ and $E_{max} = 1.58$. Thus, 2 bits are required to encode each symbol s_1, s_2 and s_3. This further improves the entropy of final key and bit rate. Hence, for C different channels, S = $\{s_1,\ s_2,\ s_3,\ \ldots,\ s_C\}$ and E_{max} also increases which means that more bits can be assigned.
(*iii*) *Effect of dual-antennas with frequency hopping:* From our experimental results we have noticed that using single antenna and frequency hopping though helps to get more symbols in S, it spans nearly 25-35% of the total RSSI range available for the devices. This limits the maximum bit rate and key entropy that can be achieved. Thus, in order to exploit complete RSSI range available for the devices, we employ another antenna on the CU. Now, consider the case of the CU having two antennas. If we consider both the antennas of the CU as identical, then they must be separated by atleast half the wavelength of radio signal being used, i.e., 6.25 cm for 2.4 GHz. As iARC is designed for miniature WBAN devices, we place both the antennas very close to each other without any gap in between. With this setup and frequency hopping we get $S = \{s_1,\ s_2,\ s_3,\ \ldots,\ s_C\}$, which has no improvement compared to the CU with single antenna, as both the antennas are placed very close, they measure nearly the same RSSI while operating on same channel [11]. Thus, we have selected two omni-directional antennas with different features such that even when placed close to each other, the difference in RSSI measured on both the antennas in a same channel should be more than atleast the total range of RSSI covered by a single antenna by frequency hopping. By carefully selecting a pair of antennas which satisfy this condition, we can obtain double the number of symbols compared to single antenna case i.e., $S = \{s_1,\ s_2,\ s_3,\ \ldots,\ s_C,\ s_{C+1},\ s_{C+2},\ \ldots,\ s_{2C}\}$. This dra-

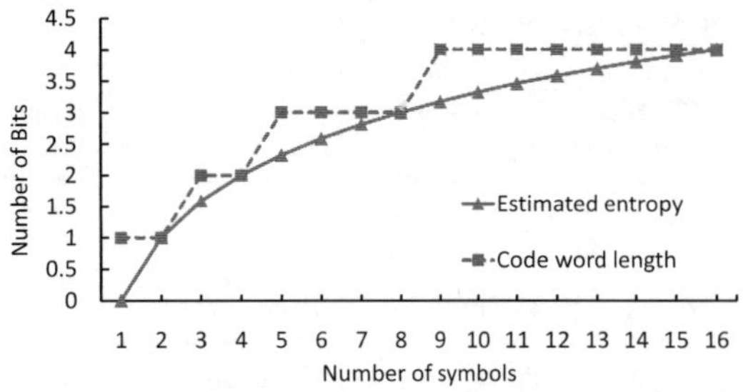

Figure 2: As the number of symbols increase, E_{max} and code word length also increase which improves the secret bit rate.

matically improves the maximum *estimated entropy* of channel samples and the secret key rate.

As there are 16 channels available in 2.4 GHz, the RSSI measured on few channels may have similar values as other channels [18]. Based on our experimental results, maximum 4 bits can be assigned per symbol (i.e., RSSI obtained on each channel on one antenna). Thus iARC dramatically improves *estimated entropy* of the channel samples (and hence the key entropy), and also the secret bit rate. Fig. 2 shows the theoretical estimation of maximum *estimated entropy* and code word length for increasing number of symbols in channel sample set S.

4.3.2 *Improvement in bit agreement*

In our scheme, the code to be assigned for each RSSI is decided based on the quantization level in which the 'mean' of all RSSI occur. Thus, practically when the RSSI samples are captured on the CU and D on a particular channel, though the RSSI are not exactly same, but the mean values calculated for both the devices occur in the same quantization level. This guarantees high bit agreement.

In rare cases due to sudden spikes in RSSI or for other reasons, the minimum of RSSI mean calculated on the CU and D for deciding the channel hopping may not be same, in which case the two devices may hop to different channels instead of hopping to same channel. In such cases, the devices notice if they do not get any probe/response packet on that particular channel. Thus, they can immediately terminate the key generation process and start from the beginning from the same channel as before. This ensures both the CU and D follow same channel hopping as well as both generate keys with high bit agreement.

5. EVALUATION AND RESULTS

We have used Opal sensor boards [9] to implement the CU and eavesdroppers with dual antennas. Iris motes, one of the commercial off-the-shelf (COTS) sensor platform were used for wearable devices D and eavesdroppers with single antenna. All the devices were operating in 2.4 GHz. TinyOS environment was used to program both the platforms. One of the major challenges in our design was to operate Opal in a controlled dual antenna mode. To achieve this, we have incorporated software modifications to the RF231 radio's low-level device driver layer of TinyOS. More details are available in our technical report [13].

We have validated the performance of our proposed key

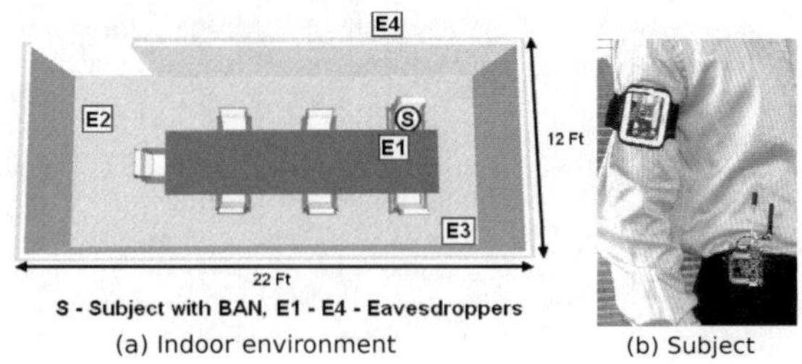

Figure 3: Experimental set-up.

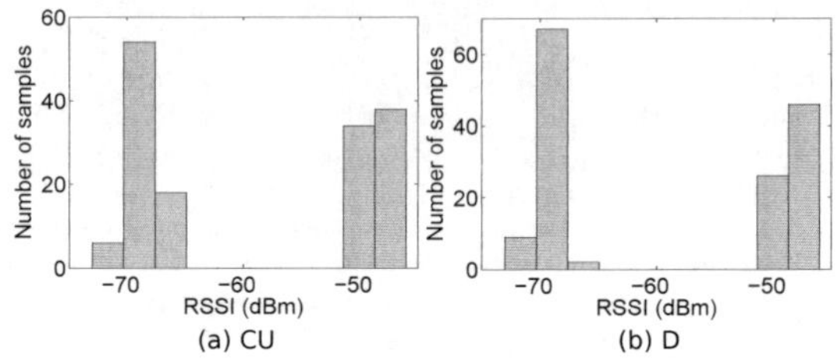

Figure 4: The histogram of RSSI samples collected by the CU and D on a single channel show same level l in the quantization process.

generation mechanism in different indoor environments, e.g., a medium sized conference room, cafeteria, and in a large room with multiple cubicles. In all these tests the performance of our protocol was nearly the same. In all these experiments the emphasis was to verify how our protocol performs in a static deployment scenario, e.g., a subject wearing the CU (on the waist) and a body worn device D (on the right arm) as shown in Fig. 3b sitting on a chair without any body movement.

5.1 Analysis of key extraction

Let us examine the shared secret key extraction mechanism between the CU and D by considering one of the data set from our experiments. For illustration purposes we provide the details of the experiments conducted in a conference room as shown in Fig. 3a. We had placed multiple eavesdroppers at different positions inside as well as outside the conference room (E1 was placed on the table). Fig. 4 shows the histogram of RSSI samples obtained by the CU and D on channel 26 during channel sampling in one of the experiments. We can notice that the total number of RSSI samples lying in the same range/quantization level l at both the legitimate devices are equal. Thus, both the CU and D follow same frequency hopping pattern for subsequent channel sampling. Both the CU and D derive secret keys with very high bit agreement when the size of the level selected by both the devices satisfies the requirement of the protocol.

Fig. 5a shows the secret bit rate of iARC for various probe intervals t and $n = 1$ to 4 (recall that n is the number of secret bits to be assigned per sample) in different indoor environments. In each environment, experiments were conducted for different inter packet intervals t, i.e., 100 ms, 50 ms, 10 ms, and 5 ms for the key generation. For each setting, we conducted 25 experiments with $N = 250$. Based

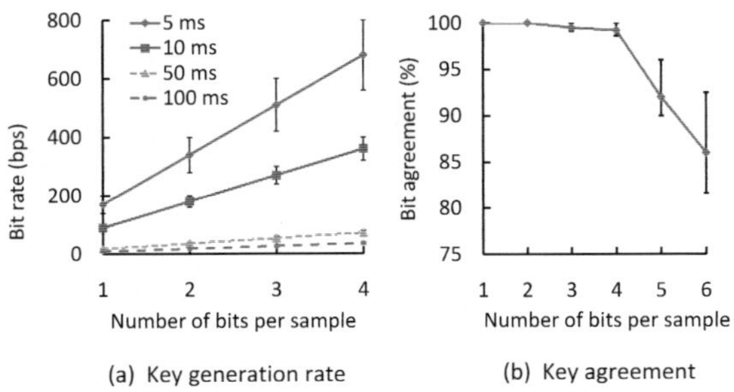

Figure 5: Performance analysis of iARC.

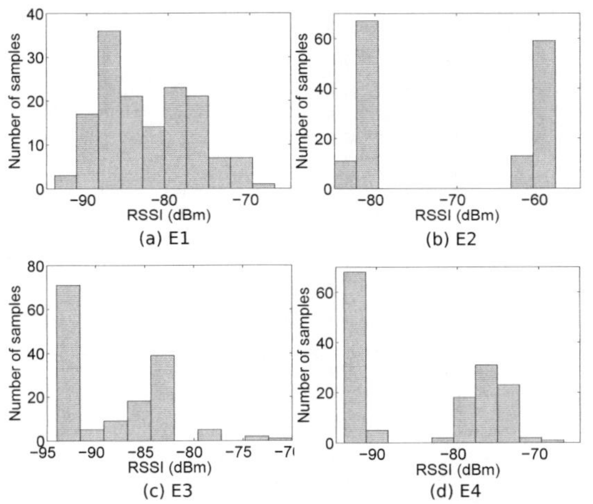

Figure 6: The histogram of RSSI samples measured by different eavesdroppers show different levels in the quantization than those of the CU and D.

on our observations, assigning 3 or 4 bits per sample is appropriate as it results in high entropy $\approx$ 0.92 to 0.99 and highest bit agreement as shown in Fig. 5b. However, the bit assignment $n > 4$ resulted in bit mismatches at the CU and D, and hence we have used 3 and 4 bit assignment scheme in all our tests. Thus, the maximum bit rate that can be achieved using our proposed protocol is 800 bits per second. Our protocol requires only 160 ms and 32 probe exchanges to generate a 128 bit key, which is nearly 100 times faster compared to the most recent scheme in WBAN [17].

We have performed the NIST [10] entropy test to check the randomness of keys. For $n = 3$ and 4, the keys generated by our protocol pass the NIST test with entropy varying from 0.92 to 0.99, which proves that our design is suitable to be employed in practical applications.

5.2 Secret key bits vs antenna switching

One might be interested to know whether learning the antenna switching pattern helps to guess the bits of final key. As explained in Section 4.1.1, iARC employs random antenna switching based on the random string $r \in \{0,1\}^{128}$ generated by PRNG. Thus, before channel sampling r is known only to the CU. Once the CU and D start exchanging probe/response packets, the RSSI value of packets exchanged depends on the distance between the CU and D and also on the channel being used. In iARC, since the final key is divided into multiple sub blocks and each sub block of the key is extracted in a different channel, the CU will not have any prior knowledge about the bits of final key. This is because, each RSSI sample is assigned 3 or 4 bits based on its level l in the quantization process. The final key K is extracted by the concatenation of the bit strings derived in each channel. Thus, the final key K is independent of r.

Table 1: Mutual information between the CU and different nodes for various probe intervals.

Device type		Mutual information (bits)		
		$t = 250$ ms	$t = 50$ ms	$t = 5$ ms
Single antenna				
	D	0.9235	0.9393	0.9279
	E1	0.0587	0.0147	0.0513
	E2	0.0766	0.0261	0.0156
	E3	0.0010	0.0816	0.0179
	E4	0.0449	0.0402	0.0029
Dual antenna				
	E1	0.0621	0.0253	0.0718
	E2	0.0545	0.0182	0.0491
	E3	0.0797	0.0374	0.0183
	E4	0.0358	0.0144	0.0216

6. SECURITY ANALYSIS

6.1 Estimation of shared randomness between the CU and D

The main factor influencing the performance of key generation is the shared randomness which can be quantified by computing the Mutual Information (MI) [5] by using channel estimates (i.e., RSSI). A large mutual information implies more shared information between the two parties. From Table 1 it is clear that MI between the CU and D is ≈ 1 bit, which shows that the CU and D have enough shared randomness to generate robust keys.

6.2 Passive adversary

Consider Fig. 6 which shows the RSSI samples captured by different eavesdroppers during channel sampling when all the parties (CU, D and eavesdroppers) were operating on the same channel (channel 26). It can be noticed that the RSSI samples in all the sub figures lie in different range/levels than those of the CU and D in Fig. 4. From Fig. 6 we can notice that the RSSI samples captured by the eavesdropper E2 situated in line-of-sight (LOS) with CU/D are well separated in two different ranges, similar to the CU/D, but will have different RSSI levels l in quantization process. On the other hand, for the adversaries which are in non-line-of-sight (NLOS) with the WBAN devices, RSSI values are scattered at various levels due to multi-path effect of the indoor environment on radio signal. Even if the eavesdropper succeeds to capture some of the initial packets exchanged between the CU and D, she cannot follow the *dynamic frequency hopping scheme* used by CU/D, which is dependent on the level of RSSI mean obtained. Thus, the eavesdroppers fail to capture subsequent packets exchanged by the CU and D and hence cannot reproduce the same key as CU/D.

In order to analyze the security in the presence of eavesdroppers with dual-antennas, we repeated the static channel experiments by replacing Iris motes used as eavesdroppers by Opal boards. More details are presented in our report [13]. Table 1 shows that the mutual information obtained by eavesdroppers is very minimal and is close to 0 in contrast to the high mutual information between the CU and D. It should be noted that, any attempt by the adversary to process the received signal would further reduce the MI, hence *collusion attack* is not possible [13]. Thus, the eavesdroppers cannot derive the same key as CU/D.

6.2.1 *Brute force attack*

It is important to analyze whether an adversary can guess the channel samples and reproduce the key by using her partial channel observations. As the eavesdropper has no information about the RSSI levels obtained by the CU/D and also the order in which the samples are captured on different antennas of CU, she can use her computational capabilities to reproduce the key by guessing the RSSI levels of channel samples to all possible options. However, the probability of an eavesdropper reproducing the same key as CU/D depends on the key length. Considering the 3 bits/sample assignment scheme, if the number of probes or samples exchanged is 1, then the probability of Eve cracking the key is 0.125 (i.e., 1/8). For a 128 bit key, the probability of Eve guessing the same key is very low $= 1.469 \cdot 10^{-39}$ ($\approx 2^{-129}$). Similarly, if 16 levels are used for quantization (4 bits/sample), then the Eve's probability to reproduce the key is as low as $2.93 \cdot 10^{-39}$ ($\approx 2^{-128}$), which is negligible.

6.3 Active adversary

In case of MIM attack, the CU and D can use information about RSSI of previous packets exchanged between the two when they detect a suspicious packet with large RSSI deviation, and discard if it is not within the expected range [13]. If channel jamming is encountered, the CU and D employ frequency hopping to continue key generation [13].

7. CONCLUSION AND FUTURE WORK

In this paper, we have presented a novel protocol – iARC, an RSSI based secret key generation scheme for wearable devices which is independent of node mobility. iARC protocol employs dual antennas and frequency diversity for inducing artificial randomness in the channel. Our experimental results reveal that the combined effect of dual antennas and frequency diversity improves performance of key generation by an order of magnitude as compared to the existing schemes [4, 17]. iARC substantially reduces the number of packets exchanged and the time required to derive the secret key in stable channel conditions. iARC generates 128 bit key with very high bit agreement in just 160 ms with a secrecy capacity of 800 bps. The keys generated by our protocol pass the NIST test for approximate entropy, which suggests that our scheme is suitable for practical applications.

Another possible direction to induce artificial randomness is to vary the power levels of transceivers. Designing such a scheme would require significant changes in the software stack and should be supported by the sensor platforms which we would like to explore in our future work.

8. ACKNOWLEDGEMENT

This work is partially supported by Australian Research Council Discovery grant DP150100564.

9. REFERENCES

[1] Comparison of wearable devices. http://allthingsd.com/. Accessed: 01-June-2015.

[2] IEEE 802.15 WPAN Task Group 6 (TG6) Body Area Networks. http://www.ieee802.org/15/pub/TG6.html. Accessed: 01-June-2015.

[3] Wearable device revenues to grow to USD 6B in 2018. http://mobihealthnews.com. Accessed: 01-June-2015.

[4] S. T. Ali, V. Sivaraman, and D. Ostry. Zero Reconciliation Secret Key Generation for Body-worn Health Monitoring Devices. In *ACM WiSec*, 2012.

[5] T. M. Cover and J. A. Thomas. *Elements of Information Theory.* John Wiley, 1991.

[6] L. W. Hanlen, D. Smith, J. A. Zhang, and D. Lewis. Key-sharing via Channel Randomness in Narrowband Body Area Networks: Is Everyday Movement Sufficient? In *BodyNets*, 2009.

[7] C. Javali, G. Revadigar, M. Ding, and S. Jha. Secret Key Generation by Virtual Link Estimation. In *Proc. EAI International Conference on Body Area Networks (BodyNets)*, 2015.

[8] C. Javali, G. Revadigar, L. Libman, and S. Jha. SeAK: Secure Authentication and Key Generation Protocol based on Dual Antennas for Wireless Body Area Networks. In *RFIDsec*, 2014.

[9] R. Jurdak, K. Klues, B. Kusy, C. Richter, K. Langendoen, and M. Brünig. Opal: A Multi-radio Platform for High Throughput Wireless Sensor Networks. *IEEE Embedded Systems Letters*, 3(4):121–124, Nov 2011.

[10] NIST. *A Statistical Test Suite for Random and Pseudorandom Number Generators for Cryptographic Applications.* 2010.

[11] T. S. Rappaport. *Wireless Communications: Principles and Practice* . Prentice Hall PTR, 2001.

[12] G. Revadigar, C. Javali, H. Asghar, K. Rasmussen, and S. Jha. iARC: Secret Key Generation for Resource Constrained Devices by Inducing Artificial Randomness in the Channel. In *ACM ASIACCS*, 2014.

[13] G. Revadigar, C. Javali, H. Asghar, K. Rasmussen, and S. Jha. Secret Key Generation for Body-worn Devices by Inducing Artificial Randomness in the Channel. *Technical Report UNSW-CSE-TR-201506, UNSW Australia*, 2015.

[14] G. Revadigar, C. Javali, W. Hu, and S. Jha. DLINK: Dual Link Based Radio Frequency Fingerprinting for Wearable Devices. In *IEEE LCN*, 2015.

[15] M. Rostami, A. Juels, and F. Koushanfar. Heart-to-Heart (H2H): Authentication for Implanted Medical Devices. In *ACM CCS*, 2013.

[16] S. S Keller. NIST-Recommended Random Number Generator Based on ANSI X9.31 Appendix A.2.4 Using the 3-Key Triple DES and AES Algorithms. *NIST Technical report*, 2005.

[17] L. Shi, J. Yuan, S. Yu, and M. Li. ASK-BAN: Authenticated Secret Key Extraction Utilizing Channel Characteristics for Body Area Networks. In *ACM WiSec*, 2013.

[18] M. Wilhelm, I. Martinovic, and J. B. Schmitt. Secret Keys from Entangled Sensor Motes: Implementation and Analysis. In *ACM WiSec*, 2010.

Secret Key Generation by Virtual Link Estimation

Chitra Javali[*†], Girish Revadigar[*†], Ming Ding[†], and Sanjay Jha[*]
{chitraj,girishr,sanjay}@cse.unsw.edu.au; ming.ding@nicta.com.au
[*]School of Computer Science & Engineering, UNSW Australia, Sydney, AUSTRALIA
[†]National ICT Australia (NICTA), Australian Technology Park, Sydney, AUSTRALIA

ABSTRACT

In recent years, researchers have explored using unique radio propagation characteristics between two devices for extracting symmetric keys. However, the state-of-the-art has the following limitations: (i) paying more attention to only when the two devices are in communication range, and (ii) generating keys only when the devices are in motion. Secret key generation for devices which are not in communication range and for stationary nodes is quite a challenging task. In this paper, we study the feasibility of generating secret keys between two devices which do not possess any direct link with the help of a trusted relay. We propose and implement our protocol using off-the-shelf commercially available resource constrained devices suitable for health-care applications which are a vital part of pervasive networks. We conduct an extensive set of experiments in an indoor environment for various scenarios involving stationary and mobile nodes. Our results show that the key generation rate increases by 20 times compared to the existing mechanisms using the same sampling frequency. We analyse the mutual information shared between the legitimate devices and eavesdroppers and our results reveal that, when at least any two of the three legitimate devices are mobile, an eavesdropper cannot obtain sufficient useful information to guess the shared keys.

Categories and Subject Descriptors

C.2.0 [**General**]: Security and protection; C.2.1 [**Network Architecture and Design**]: Wireless communication

General Terms

Security, Algorithms, Design, Experimentation

Keywords

Body-to-body communication, Physical layer security, Secret key generation,

1. INTRODUCTION

The ability of connecting machines to machines, machines to infrastructure has gradually evolved over the past few years and recently was given a prominent name known as pervasive networking. All the devices involved in this ecosystem sense, gather enormous amount of data, and process them into constructive actions. Furthermore, connecting all the smart devices brings people, data, and objects together. Cisco has predicted that there will be 50 billion connected devices by 2050 [1]. Pervasive networking also extends to smart wearable devices which measure the vital physiological data of a person, and forward it to the hospital for remote patient monitoring.

For future smart health-care applications, it is envisaged that the body-worn devices will be capable to seamlessly communicate with smart wireless devices embedded in the infrastructure (body-to-infrastructure), and body worn device of another person (body-to-body) for efficient acquisition of health related data. Body-to-body communication can also be exploited to reduce the bandwidth of the base stations in mobile networks. Secure data communication is paramount in such scenarios. The most naive method for secure communication, is to employ secret keys pre-stored in the devices by the manufacturer. However, a node is easy to be compromised in pervasive networks and this may result in key extraction by an attacker. As the devices e.g., body-worn sensors are resource constraint, it is not feasible to deploy traditional computationally complex cryptographic security mechanisms. In particular, the devices are required to exchange information securely and efficiently without security mechanisms being an overhead or requiring additional features. To improve security, the secret keys used by the devices must be generated and renewed dynamically.

Finding alternatives to heavy weight cryptographic algorithms for key generation has been an active research area. One of the approach is to extract secret keys by exploiting the unique wireless channel characteristics between two devices within communication range [8, 13]. Secret key generation for reachable nodes in body area networks has been extensively studied in [6, 10–13]. However, it is not practical to assume that two devices always possess a direct link. For instance, if two devices, Alice and Bob intend to communicate but are not within range, then it is not feasible to extract secret keys between these two devices using existing mechanisms, which only focus on single hop direct links [8]. In addition, recent work has paid more attention to secrete key generation only when the devices are in motion. However, extracting keys when the devices are station-

BODYNETS 2015, September 28-30, Sydney, Australia

DOI 10.4108/eai.28-9-2015.2261448

ary is still an open problem. In order to address the above challenges, we devise a scheme to extract secret keys from spatio-temporal characteristics of wireless channel between two legitimate unreachable and/or stationary devices, with the help of an intermediate trusted node acting as a relay.

Note that authors in [14] have also considered secret key generation based on radio propagation characteristics, where two legitimate parties communicate through a trusted relay. This work employs physical layer methods such as amplify and forward (AF) and amplify and forward with artificial noise (AF with AN) to perform key generation through simulation. However, these schemes have the following drawbacks: (i) in the conventional AF method, an adversary is able to obtain information about the secret key from the signal transmitted by the relay, and (ii) the maximum secret key capacity achieved is very low i.e., 1.3 bits/time slot from simulation results. Researchers in [7] have studied by simulation that usage of relay increases the key rate. The scheme employs traditional packet forwarding at the relay which involves considerable number of packet exchanges not feasible for resource constrained devices.

In this paper, we study how accurately a source node, say Alice, can estimate the virtual/unseen channel link between the intermediate node Relay and destination node Bob, in order to extract secret keys from wireless channel characteristics. To be precise, Alice predicts the unseen channel link between Relay-Bob and estimates the end-to-end link characteristics between itself and Bob. Our proposed scheme has the following benefits compared to prior research: (i) secret keys can be generated, even though the source and destination are not within communicating range, (ii) despite the fact that one/two transceiver(s) may be stationary, they can still generate secret keys between them with good entropy, and (iii) compared to the traditional scheme where a relay just acts as an information passing node, our scheme employs a smart relaying protocol leveraging Network Coding (NC) concept, which reduces the number of time slots required and helps to achieve 33% throughput improvement.

We believe that this work is the first to investigate the feasibility of key extraction exploiting received signal strength (RSS) characteristics and NC concept in real time environment when two nodes are communicating via a relay. The rest of the paper is organised as follows: Section 2 provides an overview of the assumptions of our system model. In Section 3 we first present secret key generation between two legitimate devices within communication range, and then we explain the traditional scheme of extracting keys with the help of relay. In the third part we propose our algorithm. Section 4 presents experimental results and security analysis, followed by concluding remarks in Section 5.

2. ASSUMPTIONS

We assume that the two legitimate transceivers - Alice and Bob are not within communicating range. In other words, they do not possess any direct link. A trusted node acts as a Relay between the two legitimate devices[1]. All the nodes communicate in the same frequency spectrum and the multipath fading channel is modelled as Rayleigh fading. The channel sampling time T for all the legitimate nodes for a single probe exchange is less than the channel coherence time T_{ch}. T_{ch} is defined as the fraction of time during which the channel parameters do not vary. The reciprocity of the channel holds true, i.e., the channel characteristics between Alice-Relay is identical to that of Relay-Alice and the same is valid for the channel between Bob and Relay when sampled within T_{ch}. Similar to existing schemes in physical layer security, we assume passive eavesdropper (Eve), who cannot jam, interfere or modify the signals transmitted between the legitimate nodes. The position of Eve is more than half a wavelength (λ) of the carrier frequency being used from any of the legitimate nodes. Eve can overhear all the transmissions of the legitimate nodes and is aware of the secret key extraction algorithm. We also assume that the noise at Alice, Bob, Relay and adversaries are independently identically distributed (i.i.d) complex Gaussian random variables with zero mean and a variance of σ^2.

[1]Note that if we do not assume Relay as a trusted node, active attacks such as man-in-the-middle (MITM) and Byzantine attack are possible. Security against active adversaries is a separate research problem which we intend to study in our future work.

3. ALGORITHM

Secret key generation exploiting wireless channel characteristics consists of two phases, i.e., (a) channel sampling phase, and (b) key extraction phase. In the first phase, the legitimate parties exchange multiple probes and estimate the channel between them. Phase (b) comprises of converting the channel estimates into secret bits which we present in the next section.

In this section, we first provide an overview of secret bit extraction between two legitimate parties within communication range, and then a traditional scheme to extract keys with the help of a Relay when the two authenticated devices are not within communication range. In the third part, we propose our scheme of extracting the secret keys with the help of Relay that has potential advantages compared to the traditional scheme.

3.1 Secret key generation between two legitimate nodes

Let us first review the basic algorithm of key generation between two devices Alice and Bob. Alice transmits a signal x_{AB} to Bob. The received signal at Bob at time instant i is:

$$y_B(i) = h_{AB}(i)x_{AB}(i) + n_B(i). \tag{1}$$

Similarly, Bob immediately transmits a signal x_{BA} to Alice and the received signal at Alice at time instant j is:

$$y_A(j) = h_{BA}(j)x_{BA}(j) + n_A(j). \tag{2}$$

Eve overhears all the transmissions between Alice and Bob, and her channel estimates can be written as:

$$y_{AE}(i) = h_{AE}(i)x_{AB}(i) + n_E(i) \tag{3}$$

$$y_{BE}(j) = h_{BE}(j)x_{BA}(j) + n_E(j) \tag{4}$$

where $h_{AB}(i)$ and $h_{BA}(j)$ are the complex channel fading coefficients associated with the channels Alice-Bob and Bob-Alice respectively, whereas $h_{AE}(i)$ and $h_{BE}(j)$ are the fading coefficients between Alice-Eve and Bob-Eve. $n_B(i)$, $n_A(j)$, $n_E(i)$ and $n_E(j)$ are the complex Gaussian noise random variables. If $(j - i) < T_{ch}$, then due to channel reciprocity between Alice and Bob, $h_{BA} \approx h_{AB}$. Let $\mathbf{Y}_A = \{y_A(1), y_A(2), \ldots, y_A(m)\}$ and $\mathbf{Y}_B = \{y_B(1), y_B(2), \ldots, y_B(m)\}$ be the set of consecutive signals measured at Alice and Bob for $i = \{1, 2, \ldots m\}$ at different time instants. After sufficient number of samples are exchanged between the two

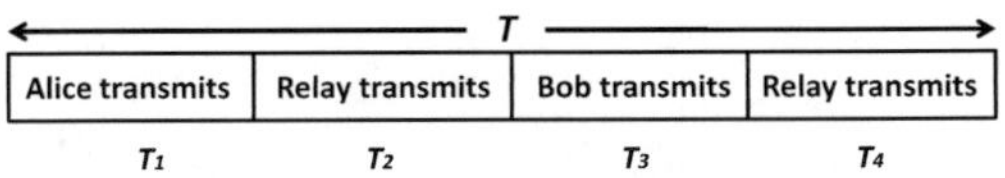

Figure 1: Traditional scheme for secret key generation requires 4 time slots.

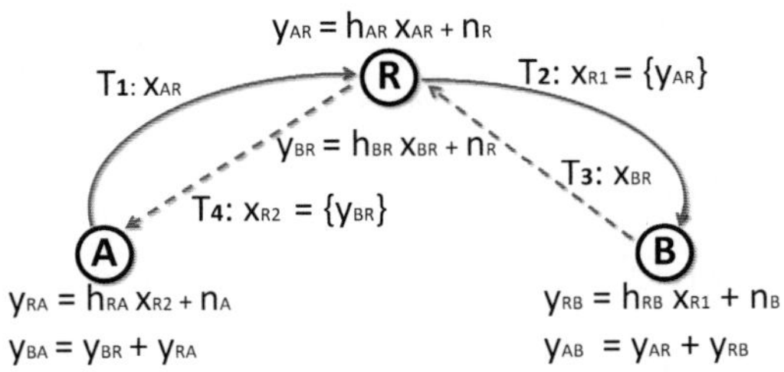

Figure 2: Traditional scheme for secret key generation protocol.

nodes, secret bits are generated by performing level-crossing or quantisation algorithm [8].

If Eve is located at a sufficient distance $> \lambda/2$ from Alice and Bob, then the signals received by Eve will be uncorrelated with those of the two legitimate parties. This is due to the fact that in a Rayleigh fading model representing a rich-scattered indoor environment, the correlation between wireless channel fading coefficients decreases rapidly with distance d and follows the zeroth-order Bessel function of the first kind J_0, given by $J_0(2\pi d/\lambda)$ [4].

3.2 Traditional scheme

In this scheme, for key generation between unreachable nodes Alice and Bob, the Relay acts as a packet forwarder. The time slot for the three devices is as shown in Fig. 1 and the protocol is depicted in Fig. 2. All the channel estimates are measured within T_{ch}. The received signal by Relay, when Alice transmits a known probe x_{AR} is:

$$y_{AR} = h_{AR}x_{AR} + n_R. \tag{5}$$

The relay then forwards the estimated response y_{AR} in the probe x_{R1} to Bob in time slot T_2. Bob receives the signal:

$$y_{RB} = h_{RB}x_{R1} + n_B. \tag{6}$$

Bob extracts y_{AR} and computes the total channel link estimation as:

$$y_{AB} = y_{AR} + y_{RB}. \tag{7}$$

In the next time slot T_3, Bob transmits a known probe x_{BR} to Relay, so as Relay is aware of the link between itself and Bob:

$$y_{BR} = h_{BR}x_{BR} + n_R. \tag{8}$$

Relay again appends y_{BR} to the probe x_{R2} being sent to Alice. In the last time slot, Alice performs the same operation as Bob in order to obtain the total link between itself and Bob:

$$y_{BA} = y_{BR} + y_{RA}. \tag{9}$$

As Eve is at a distance $> \lambda/2$, she will receive uncorrelated signals with respect to the legitimate devices, as explained in previous subsection. However, irrespective of Eve obtaining the uncorrelated signals, she can easily overhear the probes transmitted by the Relay to Alice and Bob that have the measured estimates appended in the probe. As a result, Eve can easily obtain the end-to-end link between Alice and Bob and hence also the secret key generated between the legitimate nodes. In the following subsection we propose our protocol which has three advantages when compared to the traditional scheme: (i) conceal the wireless channel characteristic information from the eavesdropper, (ii) increase the throughput, and (iii) extend the applicable range of the key generation scheme.

3.3 Proposed scheme

Alice, Bob and Relay communicate within T_{ch}. The total time T is divided into 3 time slots T_1, T_2 and T_3 during which Alice, Bob and the Relay transmit known probes respectively as shown in Fig. 3. The proposed protocol is as shown in Fig. 4. Reducing the number of time slots from 4 (as in traditional scheme) to 3 improves the throughput by 33%. This achievement in throughput has been well studied by researchers in [15]. Alice transmits x_{AR} to the Relay in the time slot T_1. The received signal at the Relay is:

$$y_{AR} = h_{AR}x_{AR} + n_R. \tag{10}$$

In the second time slot T_2, Bob transmits x_{BR} to the Relay and the received signal at the Relay is:

$$y_{BR} = h_{BR}x_{BR} + n_R. \tag{11}$$

Relay computes the value:

$$\Delta = y_{AR} - y_{BR} \tag{12}$$

and broadcasts a signal $x_R = \{\Delta\}$ i.e., value Δ appended in the probe. By obtaining Δ value, Alice and Bob estimate the end-to-end link in the following manner:
Alice receives the signal

$$y_{RA} = h_{RA}x_R + n_A \tag{13}$$

and extracts Δ value from x_R and obtains the link between Relay and Bob by:

$$y_{BR} = y_{RA} - \Delta. \tag{14}$$

Alice estimates the end-to-end channel link i.e., Alice-Bob by:

$$y_{BA} = y_{RA} + y_{BR}. \tag{15}$$

Similarly, Bob also estimates the end-to-end link by computing the following:

$$y_{RB} = h_{RB}x_R + n_B \tag{16}$$

$$y_{AR} = y_{RB} + \Delta \tag{17}$$

$$y_{AB} = y_{AR} + y_{RB}. \tag{18}$$

The channel estimates, $y_{BA} \approx y_{AB}$ as these are measured within T_{ch}. Alice and Bob exchange multiple samples through the Relay to estimate the virtual link between them for extracting secret bits.

The eavesdropper receives the signals transmitted by Alice and Bob respectively as:

$$y_{AE} = h_{AE}x_{AR} + n_E \tag{19}$$

$$y_{BE} = h_{BE}x_{BR} + n_E. \tag{20}$$

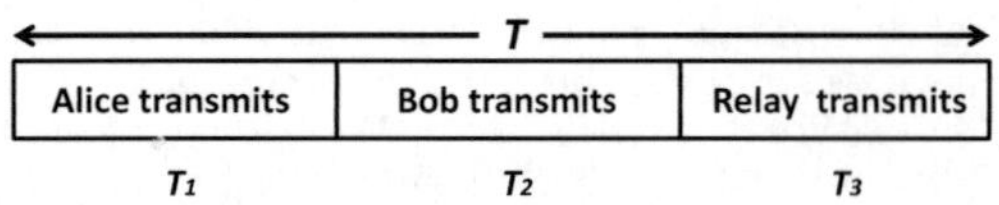

Figure 3: Time slots allocated to three legitimate nodes in our proposed scheme.

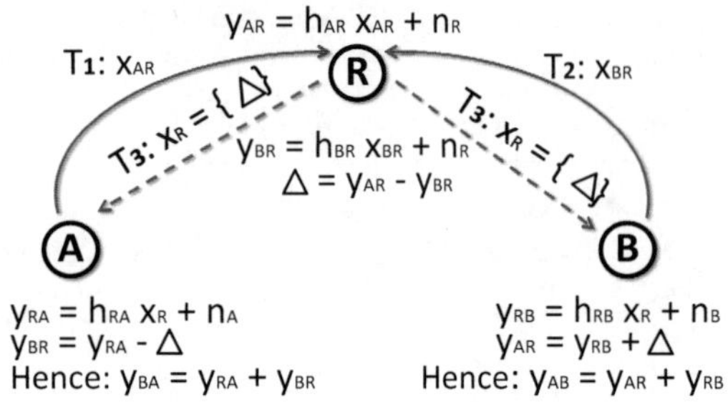

Figure 4: Proposed protocol for secret key generation leveraging NC scheme.

Eve is more interested in the Δ value computed by the Relay which is required to estimate the end-to-end link. The received signal by Eve when Relay transmits the packet is:

$$y_{RE} = h_{RE}x_R + n_E. \tag{21}$$

Let us analyse two eavesdroppers, Eve1 and Eve2 who follow Alice and Bob's operations respectively. Both the adversaries extract the value Δ from the estimated measurement y_{RE}. Considering the scenario for Eve1, similar to Eq. (14), she subtracts Δ value from the channel estimate y_{AE} (Recall that y_{AE} is Eve1's estimated channel measurement when Alice had transmitted to Relay in time slot T_1) giving:

$$\hat{y}_{BR} = y_{AE} - \Delta \tag{22}$$

which Eve1 assumes to be the identical channel measurement (that Alice has obtained) between Bob and Relay. It should be noted that $y_{AE} \neq y_{RA}$ as Eve1 is present at a different location than that of Alice. As explained in Section 3.1, the fading coefficients received by two receivers with respect to a transmitter are entirely independent, as the fading process decorrelates rapidly for distance $> \lambda/2$. As y_{AE} and y_{RA} are entirely different estimates, it follows that $\hat{y}_{BR} \neq y_{BR}$. In the next step Eve1 adds y_{AE} and $\hat{y}_{BR}$ (similar to Eq. (15)) which gives her a different value than that of Alice/Bob:

$$\hat{y}_{BA} = y_{AE} + \hat{y}_{BR}. \tag{23}$$

Even if we consider the case of Eve2 who follows same operations as those of Bob, Eve2 will not be able to obtain similar estimated values as Alice/Bob. The above explanation of Eve1 also holds for Eve2 as well.

4. EXPERIMENTAL EVALUATION

In our experimental set-up, all the devices communicate in the same channel and frequency band of 2.4 GHz. We implemented the proposed protocol on Iris motes having RF230 radio in TinyOS environment. Alice, Bob and the Relay execute the protocol described in Section 3.3. The

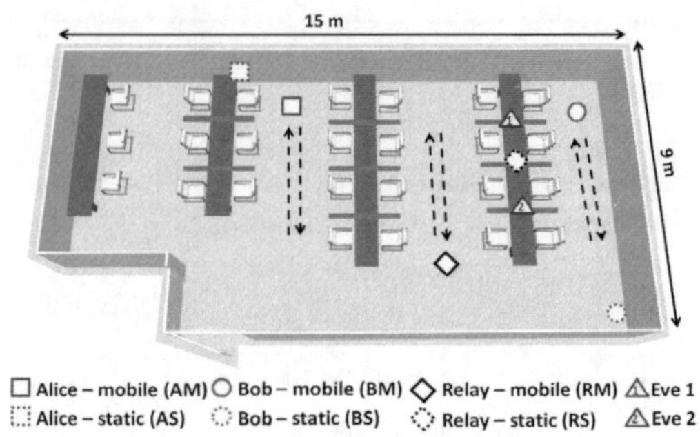

Figure 5: Floor plan of experimental set-up in an indoor environment.

Table 1: Various experimental scenarios with nodes as mobile and stationary

Expt	Stationary			Mobile		
	Alice	Relay	Bob	Alice	Relay	Bob
AMRMBM	·	·	·	✓	✓	✓
ASRMBM	✓	·	·	·	✓	✓
AMRMBS	·	·	✓	✓	✓	·
AMRSBM	·	✓	·	✓	·	✓
ASRSBM	✓	✓	·	·	·	✓
AMRSBS	·	✓	✓	✓	·	·
ASRMBS	✓	·	✓	·	✓	·
ASRSBS	✓	✓	✓	·	·	·

floor plan of an indoor environment and experimental set-up are as shown in Fig. 5. The two eavesdroppers, Eve1 and Eve2 were placed at a distance of 0.1 m each, on either side of the Relay. Eve1 performs operations similar as Alice and Eve2 as that of Bob. Both the eavesdroppers measure the received signal strength indicator (RSSI) from Alice and Bob and also the corresponding Δ value from the Relay. We validated our protocol for several scenarios i.e., when all the legitimate nodes are stationary, or either one/two of them is/are stationary, and also when all are mobile as shown in Table 1. For experiments involving mobile nodes, the devices Alice, Bob and Relay were worn on the right arm of 3 different subjects and for stationary scenarios, the nodes were placed on a table. Each scenario was repeated 15 times and each experiment was conducted for 5-10 minutes.

In each of the mobility based scenarios, the subject(s) was/were moving at a speed of 0.5 m/s back and forth. The rate at which the channel varies can be represented by the maximum Doppler frequency (f_d). In an indoor environment, for the carrier frequency 2.4 GHz; $f_d = v/\lambda = (0.5 \times 2.4 \times 10^9)/(3 \times 10^8) = 4$ Hz, which gives $T_{ch} = 250$ ms. The transmission of packets for one round of channel estimation i.e., Alice-Relay; Bob-Relay and broadcast of the packet from Relay to Alice and Bob, was performed within T_{ch}.

Another important part in our protocol is synchronisation of the legitimate devices. As Relay being the node which is in communication range with Alice and Bob, it initially sends a *START* packet to both the devices indicating the time slots during which each of the devices need to transmit their packets. Time slot available for each of the legitimate devices spans to a maximum of 20 ms.

4.1 Bit extraction

The transmission of packets between Alice-Relay; Bob-Relay and broadcast of the packet from Relay is one channel estimation, and hence considered as one sequence. As mentioned in Section 3, in the first phase of secret key generation, all the three legitimate devices (Alice, Bob and Relay) exchange a total of N number of packet sequences. Next, in the second phase, the samples collected by the legitimate devices (Alice and Bob) are passed through a moving average filter i.e., similar to a low-pass filter which results only in small scale fading variations. The resultant channel samples are mapped to binary bits by employing level crossing algorithm. The samples are encoded based on the following:

$$Q(x) = \begin{cases} 1 & \text{if } x > q_+^u \\ 0 & \text{if } x < q_-^u \end{cases}$$

where $q_+^u = (mean(U^m) + \alpha \times std\_dev)$ is the upper threshold, and $q_-^u = (mean(U^m) - \alpha \times std\_dev)$ is lower threshold. $U^m \in \mathbf{Y}_A$ and $U^m \in \mathbf{Y}_B$ for Alice's and Bob's samples respectively. std_dev is the standard deviation and α is selected to control the quantizer thresholds [8].

For our experiments, we set $\alpha = 0.5$. The samples that occur within the thresholds are discarded and do not contribute to secret bits. After bit extraction, there may be bit discrepancies in the extracted keys generated at the two nodes. This is due to the multi-path effects in an indoor environment [4]. In such a case, Alice and Bob exchange error-correcting messages to achieve 100% identical strings [3]. Later, Alice and Bob perform privacy amplification by using methods like universal hash functions to overcome the information leaked in error-correcting phase [2].

Once we have the binary strings of the secret bits, we quantify the bits extracted by the legitimate devices by the following four metrics:

(i) *Entropy* - The randomness of the generated secret bits is evaluated by entropy. Higher the randomness, more is the entropy of the key. Keys need to possess sufficient entropy to prevent it from being predicated by an attacker. The entropy value ranges from 0 to 1 for binary strings.

(ii) *Bit Agreement* - It is defined as the ratio of number of matching bits of the keys at the two parties to the key length. This metric should be high with regard to the device pair of Alice and Bob.

(iii) *Secret Bit Rate* - It is the number of shared secret bits generated per unit time and is measured in bps.

(iv) *Mutual Information (MI)* - MI(Alice:Bob) quantifies how much information does Bob's secret bits reveal about Alice's secret bits. MI is measured in bits and value is 0 when two extracted secret bit strings are statistically independent. More the MI between Alice and Bob, there is less uncertainty in Alice knowing about Bob's secret bits or Bob knowing about Alice's secret bits.

First let us analyse the performance of our scheme between the two legitimate devices Alice and Bob in all experimental scenarios.

4.2 Performance Analysis of Alice-Bob

4.2.1 All nodes are mobile - AMRMBM

In this scenario, we have all the three nodes Alice (A), Bob (B) and Relay (R) moving back and forth as shown in Fig. 5. Here the two channels A-R and R-B vary randomly and as observed from Fig. 6a, the RSSI values estimated by Alice and Bob for the end-to-end link have high amount of variation, i.e., about 20 dBm. Due to the reciprocity property of wireless channels, the two end devices indicate high correlation in the estimated links. Mobility of the nodes also adds value to the randomness of the samples measured, which helps to achieve keys with good entropy. From Fig. 7a, we observe that the bit agreement is about 95%-97% between Alice and Bob.

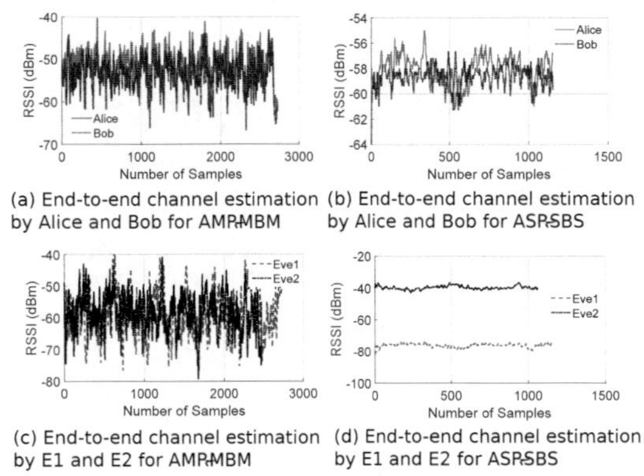

(a) End-to-end channel estimation by Alice and Bob for AMRMBM (b) End-to-end channel estimation by Alice and Bob for ASRSBS

(c) End-to-end channel estimation by E1 and E2 for AMRMBM (d) End-to-end channel estimation by E1 and E2 for ASRSBS

Figure 6: The channel estimations of Alice and Bob have high correlation. The eavesdropper's channel estimations vary from those of legitimate nodes.

4.2.2 One node is stationary - ASRMBM, AMRMBS, AMRSBM

For the case of ASRMBM, which features Alice as stationary and Relay and Bob mobile, the channel R-B varies randomly (due to mobility of Relay and Bob). The channel A-R also has varying RSSI values due to the movement of the Relay. The same explanation also applies to the other two scenarios AMRMBS and AMRSBM of having two mobile channel links. Though this scenario has one of the nodes as stationary, we observed that the entropy of the keys is as good as the scenario when all nodes are mobile. The bit agreement between Alice and Bob is about 96%-99% for all the 3 scenarios in this case as observed from Fig. 7a.

4.2.3 Two nodes are stationary - ASRSBM, AMRSBS, ASRMBS

Let us consider the case of ASRSBM. Here, as Alice and Relay are stationary, the channel between them has a minimal amount of variation, whereas since Bob is mobile, the channel link between R-B has higher fluctuation. Fig. 8a shows Alice's observations of the channel A-R. As Alice and Relay are static, we observe that RSSI variation is only about 1-2 dBm from the mean value. In contrast, from Fig. 8b we can observe that due to the movement of Bob, the estimated channel by Alice between R-B varies from -78 dBm to -64 dBm. Alice and Bob evaluate the end-to-end link between them, the net result is the corresponding sum of the RSS measurements of A-R and R-B. Fig. 8c shows that the end-to-end variation is from -135 dBm to -148 dBm for Alice, which shows the channel changes fast enough to extract secret keys. The same explanation holds good for AMRSBS. In case of ASRMBS, two nodes Alice and Bob are stationary and Relay is mobile, it has two varying channel links because of the movement of the Relay in between

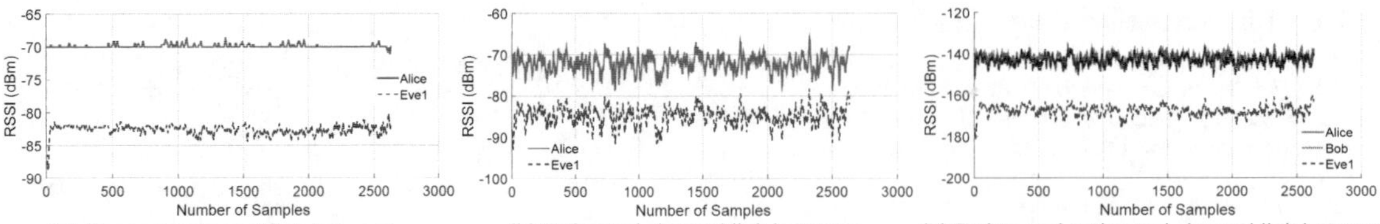

(a) Measured channel link between Alice - Relay
(b) Estimated channel link between Relay - Bob
(c) End-to-end estimated channel link between Alice - Bob

Figure 8: Channel estimation by Alice and Eve1 when two of the legitimate nodes i.e., Alice and Relay are stationary: ASRSBM.

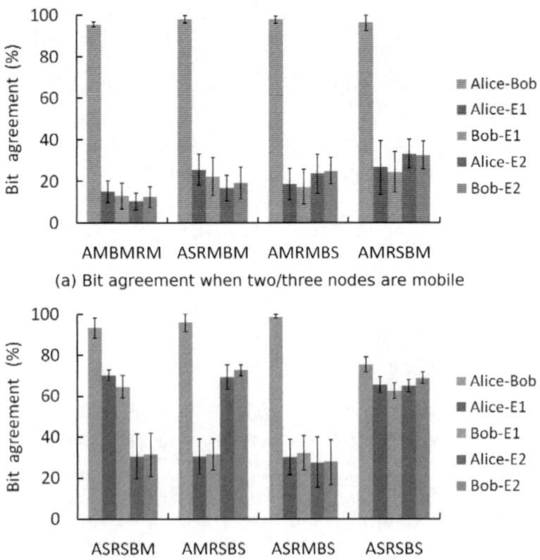

(a) Bit agreement when two/three nodes are mobile
(b) Bit agreement when two/three nodes are stationary

Figure 7: Bit agreement of all the devices for various scenarios.

the two nodes. This makes guessing the secret key difficult for the adversaries. Bit agreement is about 93%, 95% and 98% for ASRSBM, AMRSBS and ASRMBS respectively as seen in Fig. 7b.

4.2.4 *All nodes are static - ASRSBS*

From Fig. 6b, we notice that the channel estimations between Alice and Bob are not highly correlated and the RSSI values vary with very minimal deviation which is about 2-3 dBm. This minimum degree of variation produces secret key bits with a low entropy [5]. In this case, the bit agreement on an average is only 76% as observed from Fig. 7b due to the fact that in static scenarios, uncorrelated noise component at the two ends and multi-path effects will have strong influence on the signal variation [4]. Most of the bits are discarded as they do not contribute to the randomness of the channel which reduces the bit rate.

We have evaluated the randomness of the bits generated in all experiments by using NIST entropy test [9]. Our results reveal that, when all the nodes are stationary the entropy is ≈ 0.45, whereas for all other scenarios with at-least one node as mobile, the entropy ranges from 0.8965 to 0.9810. Note that the net RSSI measured at either end of the devices

Table 2: Mutual information (in bits) for various experimental scenarios.

Expt.	MI(A:B)	MI(A:E1)	MI(B:E1)	MI(A:E2)	MI(B:E2)
AMRMBM	0.8798	0.0233	0.0211	0.0143	0.0333
ASRMBM	0.7831	0.0625	0.0522	0.0416	0.0619
AMRMBS	0.8331	0.0818	0.0717	0.0523	0.0624
AMRSBM	0.8659	0.0851	0.0866	0.0569	0.0430
ASRSBM	0.7665	0.5601	0.5265	0.2318	0.2076
AMRSBS	0.7516	0.2518	0.2952	0.5931	0.6052
ASRMBS	0.7239	0.1012	0.0918	0.1100	0.0822
ASRSBS	0.6899	0.5999	0.5554	0.5988	0.6031

may not be valid RSS values, as different radios have specific range of RSSI. For example, RSSI ranges from -91 dBm to -10 dBm for RF230 radio and for CC2420 it varies from -100 dBm to 0 dBm. In our scheme the main goal is that the two devices which do not communicate directly must come to a common key agreement with the help of a relay by estimating the virtual channel link at the other side. Table 2 shows the MI between all the devices in various experimental scenarios. We can see that the MI between Alice and Bob is from 0.8798 to 0.689. The MI is lowest when all legitimate nodes are stationary. We evaluated the bit rate and observed that, on an average it varies from 24.32 bps to 18.8 bps for the cases which have at least one channel link as mobile. The bit rate reduces by 60%-70% for all static channels (ASRSBS).

4.3 Security Analysis

The two eavesdroppers Eve1 and Eve2 capture packets from all the 3 nodes, and moreover are very curious about the packets transmitted by the Relay, as Relay is the device which receives packets from both Alice and Bob, subtracts the two received RSSI and then appends the value Δ in the probe to broadcast.

4.3.1 *All nodes are mobile - AMRMBM*

As all the nodes are mobile, due to the inherent property of unique spatio-temporal characteristics, both eavesdroppers receive uncorrelated samples with respect to the legitimate devices. The RSSI samples of Eve1 and Eve2 vary in a different pattern than those of Alice and Bob as observed from Fig. 6a and 6c. The bit agreement of Eve1 and Eve2 ranges from 10% to 20% w.r.t Alice/Bob as seen from Fig. 7a. From Table 2, the MI observed for Eve1 and Eve2 is too low compared to Alice and Bob, which indicates that not much useful secret key bit information can be obtained when all nodes are mobile.

4.3.2 *One node is stationary - ASRMBM, AMRMBS, AMRSBM*

As this scenario has two varying channel links, it is not feasible for either Eve1 or Eve2 to obtain similar set of RSSI as those of legitimate devices. All the cases in this scenarios have eavesdropper's bit agreement of only 12%-39% with Alice/Bob as shown in Fig. 7a. The MI is < 0.1 for Eve1 and Eve2 with Alice and Bob as observed from Table 2. This scenario is as good as having all the nodes as mobile.

4.3.3 *Two nodes are stationary - ASRSBM, AMRSBS, ASRMBS*

We shall divide this case into two different scenarios: (i) ASRSBM, AMRSBS and (ii) ASRMBS. Let us consider (i) ASRSBM, we know that as it has only one node as mobile, it leads to only one mobile link and one stationary link. The channel estimation by Eve1 for the link A-R and R-B is as shown in the Fig. 8a and 8b respectively. As the channel A-R does not have large random changes, Eve1 can easily predict the channel link from A-B. We observe from Fig. 7b, that the bit agreement of Eve1 with Alice/Bob when the channel A-R varies minimally is about 58%-70%, whereas Eve2 following Bob's operation cannot exactly predict the secret bits. Hence the bit agreement of Eve2 with that of Alice/Bob drops to about 30%. Similarly for AMRSBS scenario, Bob is stationary which is an advantage for Eve2 and she can predict the extracted keys by about 65% to 70%. From Table 2 the MI is also high for Eve1 with Alice/Bob for ASRSBM scenario and Eve2 for AMRSBS. In (ii) ASRMBS experimental scenario there are two mobile channel links, thus both the eavesdroppers have low key agreement and MI with the legitimate devices.

4.3.4 *All nodes are static - ASRSBS*

Comparing Fig. 6b and 6d, we observe that the correlation of eavesdroppers is less than that of Alice and Bob. Though Alice and Bob are stationary, adversaries RSSI values differ as they are located at a distance greater than $\lambda/2$ [8]. Bit agreement of Eve1 and Eve2 with Alice and Bob ranges between 58%-68%. By observing Table 2, it can be noticed that Eve1 and Eve2 though individually might have MI less than Alice/Bob, their combined MI can reveal more information about the keys between Alice-Bob compared to other scenarios. In such cases, privacy amplification mechanisms [2] can be employed to strength keys between Alice-Bob.

5. CONCLUSION AND FUTURE WORK

We have proposed and implemented physical layer based secret key generation protocol for wireless nodes which are not in communication range. Our protocol employs a trusted relay between two unreachable legitimate devices and can generate secret keys with good entropy even when one/two of the three devices are stationary and achieves a throughput improvement by 33% compared to the traditional scheme. We have implemented our protocol on devices with small form factor applicable for health-care applications and conducted an extensive set of experiments to evaluate the performance. Our results reveal that we can achieve a bit agreement of about 95%-99% when all/one/two of the three nodes are mobile. The MI of the legitimate devices ranges from 0.8798 to 0.689, which is comparatively higher than the MI measured by the adversaries. In our future work, we intend to consider an untrusted relay in place of the trusted one, which can also collude with an eavesdropper in order to extract or manipulate the information exchanged between legitimate devices. The proposed protocol can also be extended for multi-hop scenario which is a challenging and interesting topic.

6. ACKNOWLEDGEMENT

This work is partially supported by Australian Research Council Discovery grant DP150100564.

7. REFERENCES

[1] Cisco: The Internet of Things, Whitepaper April 2011.

[2] C. H. Bennett, G. Brassard, C. Crepeau, and U. M. Maurer. Generalized Privacy Amplification. *IEEE Transaction on Information Theory*, 41(6):1915–1923, 1995.

[3] G. Brassard and L. Salvail. Secret-Key Reconciliation by Public Discussion. EUROCRYPT, pages 410–423. Springer-Verlag New York, Inc., 1994.

[4] W. C. Jakes. *Microwave Mobile Communications*. Wiley, Hoboken, NJ, 1972.

[5] S. Jana, S. N. Premnath, M. Clark, S. K. Kasera, N. Patwari, and S. V. Krishnamurthy. On the Effectiveness of Secret Key Extraction from Wireless Signal Strength in Real Environments. In *Proc. ACM MobiCom*, 2009.

[6] C. Javali, G. Revadigar, L. Libman, and S. Jha. SeAK: Secure Authentication and Key Generation Protocol based on Dual Antennas for Wireless Body Area Networks. In *Proc. RFIDsec*, 2014.

[7] L. Lai, Y. Liang, and W. Du. Cooperative Key Generation in Wireless Networks. *IEEE Journal on Selected Areas in Communications*, 30(8):1578–1588, 2012.

[8] S. Mathur, W. Trappe, N. Mandayam, C. Ye, and A. Reznik. Radio-telepathy: Extracting a Secret Key from an Unauthenticated Wireless Channel. In *Proc. ACM MobiCom*, 2008.

[9] NIST. A statistical test suite for random and pseudorandom number generators for cryptographic applications. 2010.

[10] G. Revadigar, C. Javali, H. Asghar, K. Rasmussen, and S. Jha. iARC: Secret Key Generation for Resource Constrained Devices by Inducing Artificial Randomness in the Channel. In *Proc. ASIACCS*, 2014.

[11] G. Revadigar, C. Javali, H. Asghar, K. Rasmussen, and S. Jha. Mobility Independent Secret Key Generation for Wearable Health-care Devices. In *Proc. BodyNets*, 2015.

[12] G. Revadigar, C. Javali, H. Asghar, K. Rasmussen, and S. Jha. Secret Key Generation for Body-worn Devices by Inducing Artificial Randomness in the Channel. *Technical Report UNSW-CSE-TR-201506, UNSW Australia*, 2015.

[13] G. Revadigar, C. Javali, W. Hu, and S. Jha. DLINK: Dual Link Based Radio Frequency Fingerprinting for Wearable Devices. In *Proc. IEEE LCN*, 2015.

[14] T. Shimizu, H. Iwai, and H. Sasaoka. Physical-Layer Secret Key Agreement in Two-Way Wireless Relaying Systems. *IEEE Trans. Information Forensics and Security*, 6(3):650–660, 2011.

[15] S. Zhang, S. C. Liew, and P. P. Lam. Physical-Layer Network Coding. In *Proc. ACM MobiCom*, 2006.

Signal Interference Analysis Model In Near-Field Coupling Communication

Shin Hasegawa
Kyoto Institute of Technology
Matsugasaki Sakyo - ku
Kyoto, Japan

Ibuki Yokota
Kyoto Institute of Technology
Matsugasaki Sakyo - ku
Kyoto, Japan

Masaki Ishida
Kyoto Institute of Technology
Matsugasaki Sakyo - ku
Kyoto, Japan

Hitoshi Shimasaki
Kyoto Institute of Technology
Matsugasaki Sakyo - ku
Kyoto, Japan
shimasaki@kit.ac.jp

Yuichi Kado
Kyoto Institute of Technology
Matsugasaki Sakyo - ku
Kyoto, Japan
kado@kit.ac.jp

Mitsuru Shinagawa
Hosei University
3-7-2, Kajino-cho, Koganei-shi
Tokyo, Japan
m.shina@hosei.ac.jp

ABSTRACT
Near-field coupling communication (NFCC) is a technology that uses the surface of the human body as a transmission path. To suppress the radiation signal from the human body, NFCC devices use a carrier frequency of less than 10 MHz. Because the radiation signal has the potential to disturb the other NFCC links, the radiation signal from other devices needs to be suppressed to ensure stable NFCC links. This paper describes our investigation of the interfering mechanism in NFCC systems to put the systems into practical use, such as at a ticket gate in the train station. We measured interference signal losses depending on the distance between two phantoms, regarded as human bodies. Based on the experimental and simulated results, an equivalent circuit of the signal interference was proposed. From the interference analytical model, we identified the capacitance that caused the interference problem and found that weakening the effects of this capacitance was important to achieve a stable NFCC link.

Categories and Subject Descriptors
B.4.1 [**INPUT/OUTPUT AND DATA COMMUNICATIONS**]: Data Communications Devices – *Receivers, Transmitters.*
B.4.2 [**INPUT/OUTPUT AND DATA COMMUNICATIONS**]: Input / Output Devices -*Channels and controllers*

General Terms
Measurement, Design, Reliability, Experimentation, Security, Human Factors, Standardization

Keywords
Near-field coupling communication, Electrically isolated measurement, Path/Signal loss, interference problem.

1. INTRODUCTION
Wireless body area networks (WBANs), which are technologies that support safety and convenience, have attracted attention. For example, WBANs are utilized as convenient new applications in various areas such as medical information, security, and payment systems. Near-field coupling communication (NFCC) is a technology that uses the human body as a data transmission path in the MHz band (i.e., below 10 MHz) and has the convenience of wireless communication and high secrecy by suppressing the radiation from NFCC devices. This communication technology is included in body-channel communication (BCC), which uses the human body as the communication channel to transmit electric signals [1]–[4]. The NFCC system consists of two types of transceivers worn on the body (wearable TRX) and those embedded in equipment or the environment (embedded TRX) [5]. The main advantages of NFCC using a 6.75-MHz frequency are the short radial distance and the establishment of a "touch and connect" intuitive form of communications. (Figure 1).

We should consider the interference problem so as to put the systems into practical use, such as at a ticket gate in the train station. In particular, the radiation signal from other NFCC devices must interfere with the main signal, as shown in Figure 2. The interference signal from other NFCC devices needs to be suppressed to achieve stable communication in crowded places, such as a train station. In this paper, a communication model of signal interference is mainly discussed. The interference signal loss was evaluated while changing the distance between phantoms, which were regarded as human bodies, by using both experiments and simulations. A simplified equivalent circuit was designed and compared with the experimental results we obtained. From these results, we found the main factor of signal interference.

BODYNETS 2015, September 28-30, Sydney, Australia

DOI 10.4108/eai.28-9-2015.2261485

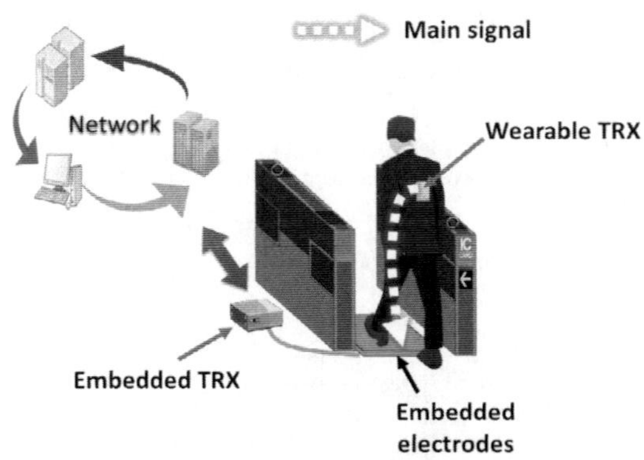

Figure 1. Hands-free ticket gate system using near-field coupling communication.

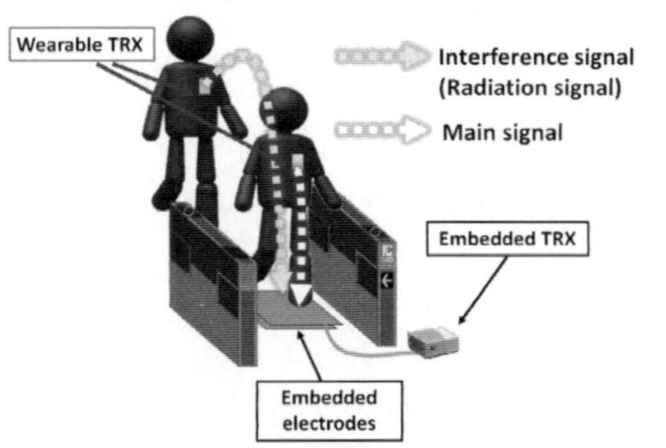

Figure 2. Signal interference in ticket gate system.

2. MEASUREMENTS SYSTEM

2.1 Battery - Powered TX

We developed a battery-powered TX to reduce the signal path enhancement by electrically connecting to a signal generator [6, 7]. The battery-powered TX includes a direct digital synthesizer (DDS) oscillator. It generates a sinusoidal wave. Figure 3 (a), (b), and (c) shows the internal circuits, a block diagram of the TX, and the external shape. To eliminate the effect of a voltage drop in a lithium ion battery, we connected the regulator to the battery. The frequency of the sinusoidal wave can be modified from 50 Hz to 20 MHz by 1 Hz increments. The dimensions of the TX were 85 x 54 x 6.5 mm. The electrodes in the TX were 70 x 50 mm each. The signal voltage of the TX changes 1 to 2 $V_{p\text{-}p}$ while changing its frequency. The output impedance was 50 Ω.

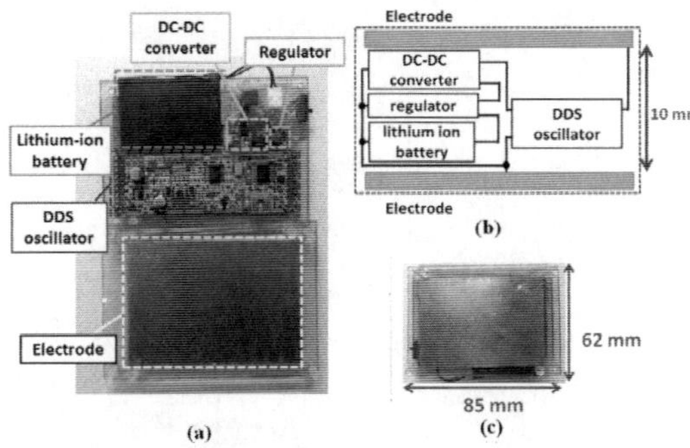

Figure 3. (a) Internal circuit of battery-powered TX, (b) block diagram of battery-powered TX, and (c) external shape of wearable TRX.

2.2 Phantoms

Phantoms, ones having the same electrical characteristics as the human body, were used in our experiments to obtain reproductive results constantly. Figure 4 shows a photograph of a phantom. Its outer shell is a polyvinyl chloride (PVC) pipe. The dimensions of the pipe were a diameter of 250 mm, a thickness of 8 mm, and a height of 1800 mm. The pipe was filled with salt water, the conductivity of which was adjusted to 0.6 S/m at 6.75 MHz (Human body: 0.6 S/m) [8]. The water level was 1500 mm. The relative permittivity of the water was 80. Figure 5 shows the experimental system and the results for evaluating the surface propagation of the main signal. The tendency of the surface propagation of the main signal in the phantom was almost the same as that in a human body. We also experimentally found that the electrical characteristics of the phantom were equivalent to those of the human body from the view of the antenna function for receiving radiation signals from other transmitters.

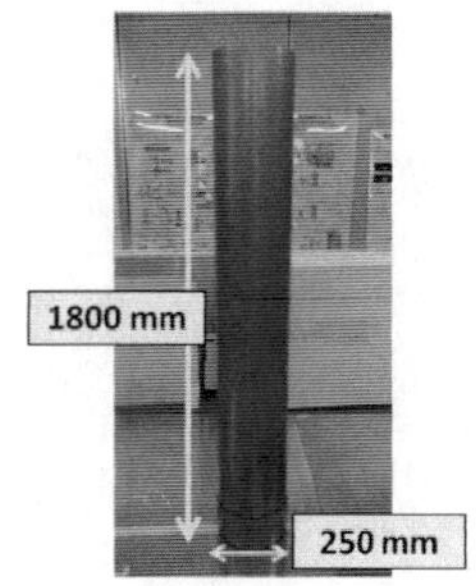

Figure 4. Photograph of phantom.

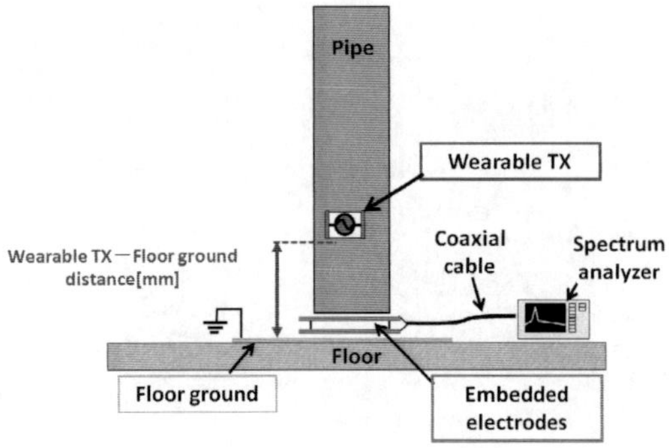

(a)

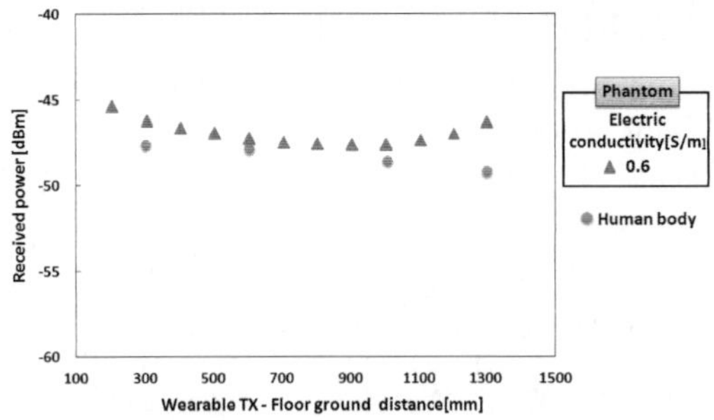

(b)

Figure 5. (a) experimental system to evaluate surface propagation of main signal (b) results of experiment.

3. EXPERIMENTS AND RESULTS

We assumed a situation where a human stands on the embedded electrodes of a ticket gate and where another human wearing a wearable TRX stands behind the first human. We defined the phantom standing on the embedded electrodes as phantom 1 and the other phantom wearing a wearable TRX and standing behind phantom 1 as phantom 2. The human body is regarded as a conductor under 10 MHz. Therefore, the model was composed of seven conductors, such as a signal electrode (#1) and a ground electrode (#2) of the wearable TRX, a floor ground (#3), an embedded lower electrode (#4), an embedded upper electrode (#5), phantom 1 (#6), and phantom 2 (#7), as shown in Figure 6. We call this the signal interference model. Figure 7 shows the schematic of our experimental system. Phantom 1 and 2 were the same as the phantom shown in Figure 4. The battery-powered transmitter generates a sinusoidal wave at 6.75 MHz. We measured the received interference voltage with embedded electrodes while changing the distance between phantom 1 and 2. The embedded electrodes were connected to a measurement instrument, and its dimensions were 350 x 350 mm. An 8-mm-thick polyethylene plate was inserted between the electrodes. The floor ground was connected to the power source ground of the AC resource, which was distinguished from the earth ground and measured to be 2000 x 3000 mm. We evaluated the interference signal loss, which was represented by the ratio of the received interference voltage to the transmitted interference voltage defined as

$$\text{interference signal loss} = -20 \times \log\left(\frac{\text{received interference voltage}}{\text{transmitted interference voltage}}\right)\ [\text{dB}] \quad (1).$$

Figure 8 shows the interference signal losses that were calculated from the experiment results. The closer the distance between phantom 1 and 2 became, the stronger the interference signals were. These results revealed that the signal interference depends on the distance between phantom 1 and 2.

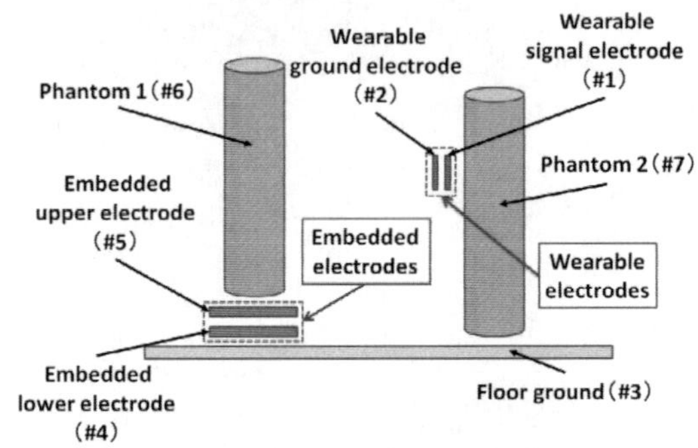

Figure 6. Signal interference model using seven conductors.

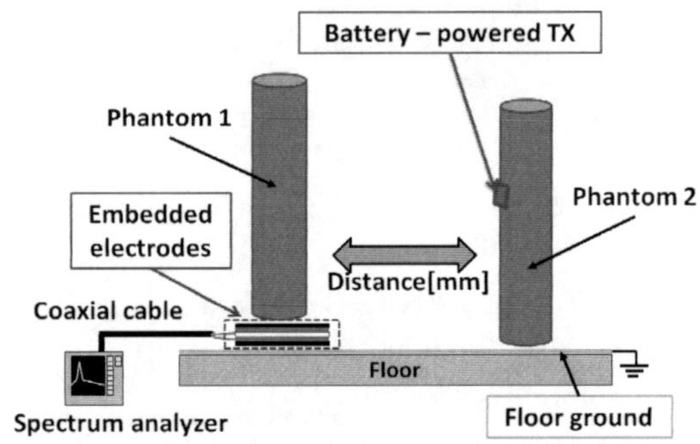

Figure 7. Schematic of experimental system.

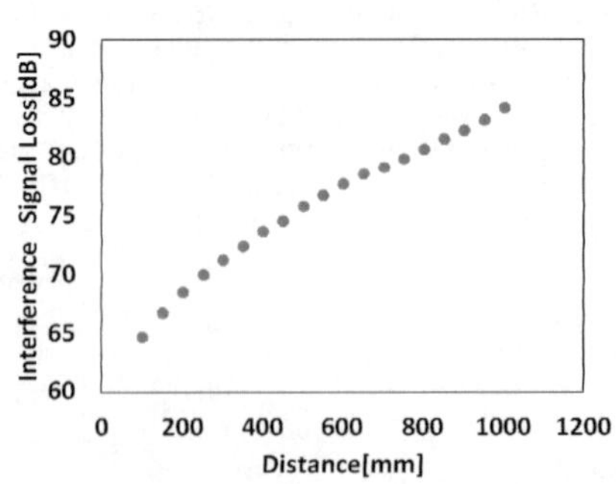

Figure 8. Interference signal loss according to distance between phantom 1 and 2 in experiment.

4. SIMULATION

4.1 Equivalent circuit

An equivalent circuit of signal interference model is represented by capacitances because conductors are capacitively coupled with each other in the NFCC system [9, 10]. The capacitances between seven conductors were calculated in the 3D electromagnetic field simulation. Figure 9 shows the structures for the simulation. The materials of the conductors were set to copper in the simulation. As shown in Figure 10, these capacitances were applied to the lumped-parameter equivalent circuit for the signal interference model. The conductors shown in Figure 6 are represented as nodes in the equivalent circuit. Figure 11 shows the simulation results of the capacitances according to the change in the distance between phantom 1 standing on the embedded electrodes and phantom 2 wearing the TX.

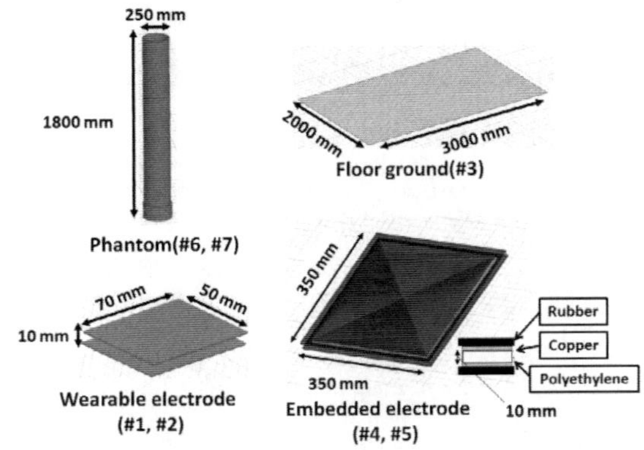

Figure 9. Structures in electromagnetic field simulation.

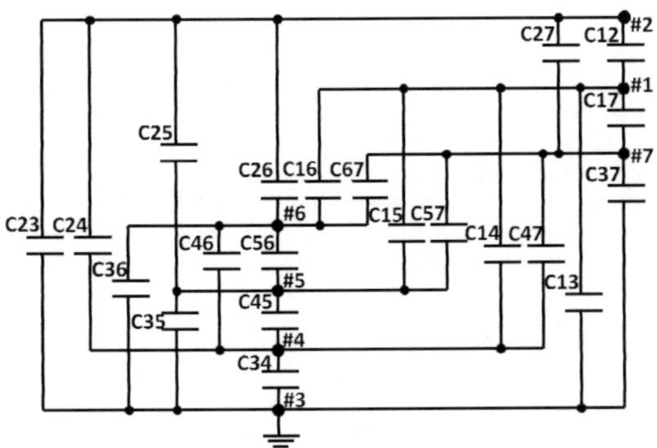

Figure 10. Lumped-parameter equivalent circuit.

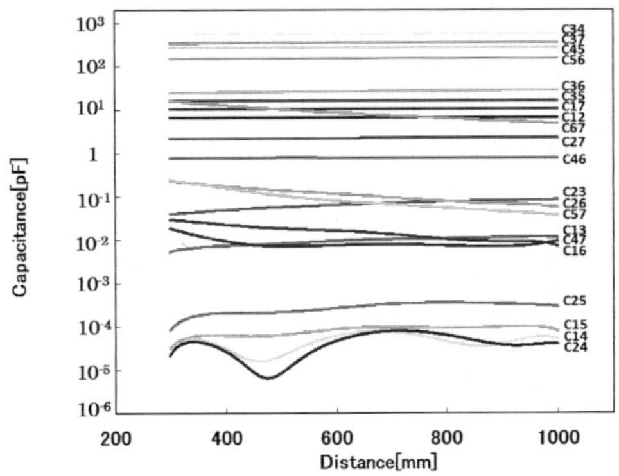

Figure 11. Dependence of capacitance values between seven conductors on the distance between phantom1 and 2.

4.2 Simplified equivalent circuit

We analyzed the mechanism of the signal interference in the simplified equivalent circuit to find how to suppress it. The simplified circuit was designed in consideration of the capacitance change due to the differences in the distance between phantom 1 and 2. We calculated the capacitances between each of the nodes in the equivalent circuit with the 3D electromagnetic field simulator. With these simulation results, we simplified the original circuit as follows. We omitted C_{13}, C_{14}, C_{15}, C_{23}, C_{24}, C_{25}, C_{47}, and C_{57}, which were below the capacitances 1 pF because they were smaller than other capacitances. But C_{26} was not omitted because it was one of the capacitances which comprised the main interference signal path of the equivalent circuit. We also omitted C_{35} because the value of C_{35} was much smaller than the value of the series of C_{34} and C_{45}. In addition, we continuously omitted C_{46} because the value of C_{46} was much smaller than the value of the series of C_{45} and C_{56}. Simplified circuit A was proposed with all these omissions. We also obtained a further simple equivalent circuit, which is named simplified circuit B. Simplified circuit B consists of only C_{12}, C_{17}, C_{26}, C_{35}, C_{37}, C_{45}, and C_{56} representing the main interference signal path. Figure 12 shows the equivalent circuits of simplified circuit A and B.

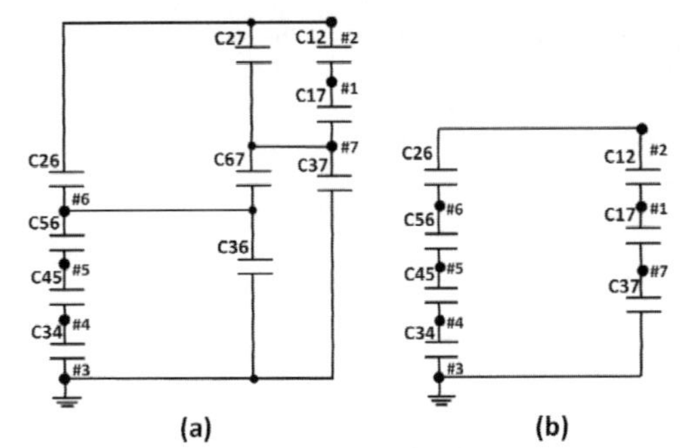

Figure 12. (a) simplified circuit A and (b) simplified circuit B.

4.3 Evaluation of simplified circuits

We calculated the signal transmission for each of the original equivalent circuit and simplified circuit A and B with the circuit simulation software (LTspice: Linear Technology). With the calculated results, we evaluated the interference signal losses by the equation (1). When we evaluated the interference signal losses of the simplified circuit B, the equation (1) was expressed as

$$\text{interference signal loss} = -20 \times \log\left(\frac{\frac{Z_0}{Z_0 j\omega C_{45}+1}}{\frac{1}{j\omega}\left(\frac{1}{C_{17}}+\frac{1}{C_{26}}+\frac{1}{C_{34}}+\frac{1}{C_{37}}+\frac{1}{C_{56}}\right)+\frac{Z_0}{Z_0 j\omega C_{45}+1}}\right) = -20 \times \log\left(\frac{Q}{Z_{26}+P}\right)\ [\mathrm{dB}]. \quad (2)$$

The angular frequency is ω. The embedded electrodes (#4 and #5) are connected to a spectrum analyzer, and its input impedance is $Z_0 = 50\ \Omega$. The impedance of the capacitive coupling C_{26} is $Z_{26} = 1/j\omega C_{26}$. The impedances Q and P are expressed by Z_0 and the capacitances other than C_{26}. On the other hand when we evaluated the interference signal losses of the simplified circuit A, the equation (1) was expressed as

$$\text{interference signal loss} = -20 \times \log\left(\frac{Z_{26}+R}{S{Z_{26}}^2+TZ_{26}+U}\right)\ [\mathrm{dB}]. \quad (3)$$

Here, the impedances R, S, T and U are given by Z_0 and the capacitances other than C_{26}. Figure 13 shows the interference signal losses that were calculated from the original equivalent circuit and simplified circuit A and B. The experimental results are also shown in Fig. 13. To estimate the validity of simplified circuit A and B, we calculated the residual errors between the results of the original circuit and each result of the simplified circuits; moreover, we extracted the square root of the errors. Figure 13 shows that the tendency of simplified circuit A was qualitatively similar to the tendency of the experimental results. Also, the residual error of simplified circuit A was within 1 dB. These results revealed that the accuracy of simplified circuit A was high. On the other hand there was a large difference of 3.8 dB between the experiment and the calculation using circuit B. From these results, we proposed simplified circuit A as a signal interference analysis model.

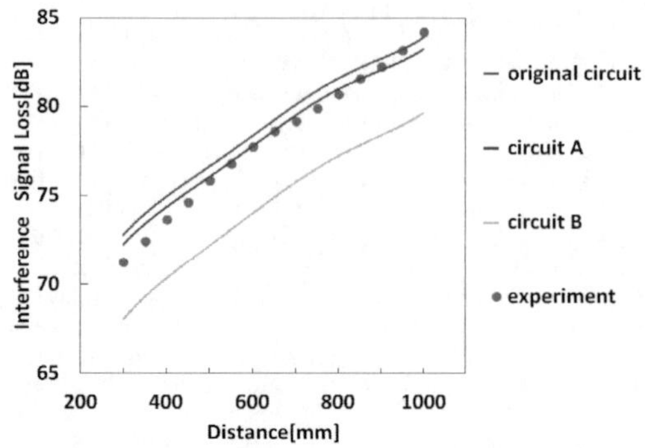

Figure 13. Interference signal loss according to distance between phantom 1 and 2.

4.4 Main factor of signal interference

We considered the main factor of the signal interference from simplified circuit A. The main interference signal path of simplified circuit A consists of C_{12}, C_{17}, C_{26}, C_{35}, C_{37}, C_{45}, and C_{56}. The capacitances C_{12}, C_{17}, C_{35}, C_{37}, C_{45}, and C_{56} are small changes due to the distance between the two phantoms. However, capacitance C_{26} depends on the distance between the two phantoms. The experimental results revealed that the interference signal in the model depends on the distance between the two phantoms. These revealed that capacitance C_{26} was the main factor in the signal interference.

Figure 14 shows the interference signal losses of simplified circuit A of the original and half and one-tenth parts of the value of C_{26}. The S/N ratio of the NFCC system needs 20 dB to establish stable communication. This condition is equivalent to the condition where the ratio of the main signal loss to the interference signal loss is 20 dB in Figure 14. The main signal loss level of 72.5 dB is also shown in the figure. This value was the simulated result when the height of the wearable TRX was 1150 mm on the phantom. The interference signal loss should be larger than 92.5 dB to establish stable communication. Therefore, we defined the distance that the interference signal loss level was equal to 92.5 dB as the interference distance. The interference distance means the threshold distance to establish stable communication in the NFCC system. The interference distances of the original, half, and one-tenth parts of value were 1900 mm, 1300 mm, and 300 mm, respectively. These results revealed that the interference distance was shortened by reducing C_{26}. We also found that the capacitive coupling C_{26} of ground electrode (#2) of the wearable TRX and phantom 1 (#6) need to be weakened to suppress the signal interference. For example, we suggest placing auxiliary conductor plates on both sides of the ticket gate system shown in Fig. 2. The plates are connected to the floor ground and terminate a large part of the radiation signal from the ground electrode (#2) of the wearable TX. This means that the plates weaken the coupling capacitance of C_{26}.

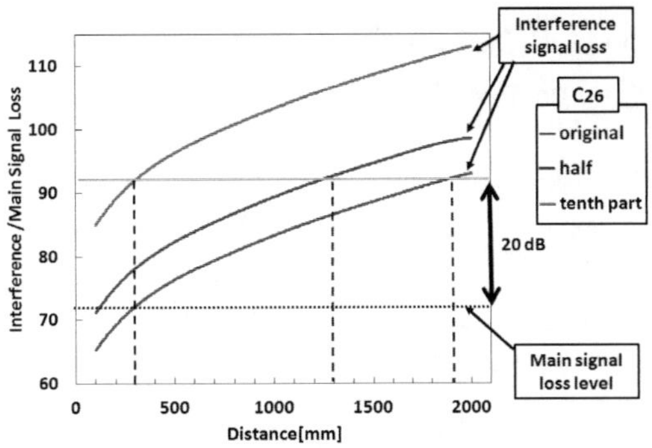

Figure 14. Effect of interference signal loss by varying C_{26}.

5. CONCLUSIONS

We investigated the interfering mechanism in NFCC systems to mitigate the interference problem. We measured interference signal losses depending on the distance between two phantoms and proposed an equivalent circuit of the signal interference as an analytical model. From the model, we identified the main factor of signal interference, which was the capacitive coupling C_{26} between phantom 1 (#6) and ground electrode (#2) of a wearable TRX. To design a stable NFCC link, we need to weaken the coupling capacitance between of C_{26}.

ACKNOWLEDGMENTS

Part of this work was supported by a Grant-in-Aid for Scientific Research (A) 23246073 from the Ministry of Education, Culture, Sports, Science and Technology of Japan.

REFERENCES

[1] T. G. Zimmerman. 1996. Personal Area Networks: Near-field intrabody communication. *IBM System.* J, 35(3/4) 609-617.

[2] N. Cho, J. Yoo, S. J. Song, J. Lee, S. Jeon, and H. J. Yoo. 2007. The Human Body Characteristics as a Signal Transmission Medium for Intrabody Communication. *IEEE Trans. Microwave Theory and Techniques.* 55, 1080-1086.

[3] A. Fazzi, S. Ouzonov, and J. v. d. Homberg. 2009. A 2.75mW Wideband Correlation-Based Transceiver for Body-Coupled Communication. *IEEE ISSCC.* 204-205.

[4] J. Bae, H. Cho, K. Song, H. Lee, and H. J. Yoo. 2012. The Signal Transmission Mechanism on the Surface of Human Body for Body Channel Communication. *IEEE Trans. Microwave Theory and Techniques.* 60, 582-593.

[5] Y. Kado, T. Kobase, T. Yanagawa, T. Kusunoki, M. Takahashi, R. Nagai, O. Hiromitsu, A. Hataya, H. Shimasaki, and M. Shinagawa. 2012. Human-Area Networking Technology Based on Near-Field Coupling Transceiver *2012 IEEE Radio & Wireless Sym.* (Santa Clara, California, USA, January, 2012). 119 - 122.

[6] M. Ishida, T. Nakamura, M. Nozawa, N. Watanabe, Y. Kado, and M. Shinagawa. 2014. MHz-Band RF Signal Propagation Characteristics on Human-Equivalent Phantom for Intra-body Communication. *EuCAP 2014.* 2284-2288.

[7] M. Ishida, T. Nakamura, M. Nozawa, N. Watanabe, Y. Kado, and M. Shinagawa. 2014. MHz-Band RF Signal Propagation Characteristics on Human Body for Intra-body communication. *I2MTC 2014.* 797-801.

[8] SGabriel, R.W.Lau and C.Gabriel. 1996. The dielectric properties of biological tissues: Ⅱ.Measurements in the frequency rage 10 Hz to 20 GHz. *Phys. Med. Biol.* 41, 2251-2269.

[9] N. Haga, K. Motojima, M. Shinagawa, Y. Kado. 2014. System of equations describing charges of multiple conductors immersed in electrostatic fields. *IEICE Electronics Express.* 11, no. 19.

[10] Y. Hayashida, R. Sugiyama, Y. Ido, A. Suzuki, Y. Takizawa, M. Shinagawa, Y. Kado, and N. Haga. 2014. Capacitance Model of Embedded Transceiver for Intra-body Communication. *BODYNETS 2014.* 222-228.

A Dual-channel Routing Protocol for Wireless Body Area Networks

Sobia Omer
Department of Engineering
Faculty of Science and Engineering,
Macquarie University
Sydney, Australia
sobia.omer@students.mq.edu.au

Rein Vesilo[1], Eryk Dutkiewicz[2]
Department of Engineering
Faculty of Science and Engineering,
Macquarie University
Sydney, Australia
[1]rein.vesilo@mq.edu.au
[2]eryk.dutkiewicz@mq.edu.au

Qi Zhang
Department of Engineering,
Aarhus University
Denmark
qz@eng.au.dk

ABSTRACT

Wireless Body Area networks (WBANs) are a subset of wireless sensor networks that interconnect miniaturized nodes with sensor or actuator capabilities in, on, or around a human body. WBANs can operate over a number of different frequency bands such as MICS (Medical Implant Communications system), 2.4 GHz ISM (Industrial Scientific and Medical), UWB (Ultra Wideband), HBC (Human Body Communications) bands. Most WBANs utilize only one of these wireless bands for routing, network access, etc. Fading conditions can result in poor network performance in terms of node energy and throughput. With recent interest in multi-band devices for WBANs such as multi-band antennas and transceivers effective utilization of multiple bands requires an equally effective routing protocol. In this paper we develop a multi-channel extension to the Ad Hoc on Demand Distance Vector (AODV) routing protocol for use in multi-channel WBANs that chooses the next hop channel that has the best Received Signal Strength Indicator (RSSI) value. Our extensions to AODV were implemented by modifying the single-band Castalia model built on the OMNeT++ network simulator. We compared our dual channel AODV protocol with RSSI channel selection against a dual channel AODV with random channel selection and single channel AODV. Our simulation experiments showed that in terms of packet delivery dual channel AODV with RSSI performs equally with single channel AODV but with a lower overhead of AODV control packets, better routing stability and slightly better energy per bit efficiency.

General Terms

Keywords

Wireless Body Area Network, Routing, Multi-channel, AODV Castalia

1. INTRODUCTION

Wireless Body Area (WBAN) technology utilizes wireless communications to interconnect miniaturized devices with sensor or actuator capabilities in the space of a human body [1]. These devices, especially designed for the human body, may be placed on the body surface, worn on clothing or implanted, and are able to communicate regular and critical physiological parameters to the rest of their infrastructure. For medical applications, WBANs used for medical monitoring, medical intervention and patient management in the clinic, at-home and out-of-home promise greater patient convenience and mobility and improved outcomes at lower cost. Key requirements for WBAN applications include low power consumption (because the battery capacity in each node is limited), low latency and high reliability of communications. The IEEE 802.15 Task Group 6 (TG6) communication standard [2] was released in 2012 for low power devices and operation on, in, or around the human body including physical layer and medium access control (MAC) components. WBANs are distinguished from other kinds of networks such as wireless sensor networks, ad-hoc networks and wireless mesh networks by their stringent requirements and their particular channel characteristics. A comprehensive review of WBANs is given by [3].

To date, most WBANs have utilized a single wireless band for communication that can be either narrowband wireless (including MICS (Medical Implant Communications system) and ISM (Industrial Scientific and Medical) bands), UWB (Ultra Wideband) wireless or the HBC (Human Body Communications) band. However, there has been an increasing interest in multi-channel[1] communication for WBANs to improve robustness, connectivity and performance. Most research to date on multi-channel WBANs has been on developing the core enabling technologies such as antennas, radio system architectures and simple protocols for link data transfer. Examples include the following: [4] developed a 433/868 MHz dual-band node with the aim of alleviating the effects of congestion and failure on reliability and QoS. [5] developed a wireless device that used an alternative HBC link if the main RF link (ISM) became unreliable or blocked; [6] developed an on-body repeater for implant (MICS) to external communication (2.4 GHz); [7] developed a dual-band device that used UWB for data transmission and narrowband communications to receive control signals in order to avoid the complexity of a UWB receiver in a small WBAN device. Dual-band antenna designs for WBAN applications have been reported by [8] [9] [10] and others.

To obtain the most out of these developments to support WBAN applications over a full WBAN network of devices including a Body Network Controller (BNC) requires the development of routing protocols and MAC protocols that are tailored towards multi-channel operation. In this paper we focus

[1] In the terminology used in the research literature some authors refer to multi-band capability and others refer to multi-channel capability. Our paper does not rely on the distinction.

BODYNETS 2015, September 28-30, Sydney, Australia

DOI 10.4108/eai.28-9-2015.2261430

on the development of a multi-channel routing protocol. Most research to date on WBAN routing protocols has been for single band communications. To the authors' knowledge, this paper is one of the first to investigate multi-channel routing protocols for WBANs.

A multi-channel WBAN device may use a single radio or multiple radios. The device may also have a single antenna or multiple antennas. A simple device architecture is to use multiple radios with each radio having its own antenna as it avoids the complexity of switching between radios. This was the approach used in the paper because it was the easiest way to incorporate multiple channels into a simulation model, although in practice there is an additional cost and size involved with multiple radios and antennas. We also used separate MAC modules for each band to avoid the problem of two nodes trying to find a common channel to send and receive data – the rendezvous problem. Our work thus concentrated mostly on the routing protocol.

We developed a multi-channel version of the Ad hoc On-Demand distance Vector (AODV) routing protocol [11] and tested it using the Castalia WBAN simulation model [12] that is built on the OMNet++ simulation platform [13]. A key aspect of our protocol is the development of a channel selection algorithm that chooses which channel to use between two nodes. We used the hop count metric to determine the best route. We tested our protocol using simulation over two channels in the ISM 2.4 GHz band (2.400~2.485 GHz). Simulation results showed that our multi-channel AODV protocol gave comparable, if not better, performance to single channel AODV in terms of packet delivery but with less AODV control messages needing to be sent, better routing stability and slightly better energy efficiency.

Section 2 describes related work on multi-channel routing. Section 3 describes the WBAN system. Section 4 describes our proposed multi-channel AODV protocol. Section 5 describes the Tunable MAC protocol that we used in our simulations. Section 6 describes the WBAN wireless channel models used. Section 7 presents the result of our simulation experiments along with discussion. Section 8 presents conclusions.

2. RELATED WORK

Routing protocols can be classified into three categories, proactive, reactive, and hybrid, depending on how the source finds a route to the destination. In proactive protocols, all routes are computed before they are really needed, while in reactive protocols, routes are computed on-demand. Hybrid protocols use a combination of proactive and reactive methods. Comprehensive reviews of WBAN routing protocols have been conducted by [14] and [15], that include temperature based routing, cluster-based routing, cross-layer routing, cost-effective routing and QoS based routing using proactive and reactive approaches.

Multi-channel routing protocols have been used previously in other kinds of networks such as wireless mesh networks and ad-hoc networks. In [16] they have proposed a multi-channel version of AODV called CA-AODV. In this protocol, if the source did not yet have a channel to transmit on it randomly picked a channel from the set of all available channels. Any node that received a Route Request (RREQ) packet selected a channel that none of its previous k-hop neighbors had selected. The RREQ message conveyed the node ids and channel numbers that its k preceding nodes were using. This method of channel selection may be practical in wireless mesh networks that have many channels available but in WBANS there is usually a small number of channels available so the approach is less practical there. In [17] they have developed a multi-hop routing protocol to operate over an ad-hoc 802.11 network with nodes equipped with multiple 802.11 NICs with the aim of improving performance when deployed in a wireless mesh network. They developed a distributed channel allocation algorithm that used only local traffic load information. In [18] a review of multi-channel MAC protocols and proposed a multi-channel MAC protocol called MMAC. They compared parallel rendezvous, dedicated control channel and split phase multi-channel MAC protocols. They noted that switching penalty could be an important factor in multi-channel MAC protocols that use frequency hopping. Sometimes routing functions have been combined with MAC channel functions such as in opportunistic routing. Opportunistic routing has been extended to the multi-channel case by [19].

3. WBAN SYSTEM

IEEE802.15 TG6 have categorized four scenarios for WBAN communication: on-body to on-body, on-body to around-body, in-body to on-body, and in-body to in-body. This paper focuses on the on-body to on-body scenario. A typical placement of WBAN nodes on the human body is shown in Figure 1. We assume the WBAN consists of K dual-channel nodes as shown in Figure 2. Each node has two antennas with each antenna supporting broadcast communication over a separate frequency channel to other nodes.

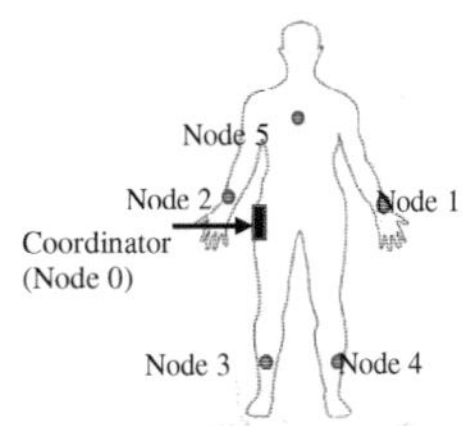

Figure 1: WBAN on a human body

The structure of a dual-channel node is shown in Fig. 3. It consists of an Application module, a Communication module and a Resource Manager. The Application module is the source and sink of all application data transmitted. For data monitoring applications the Application module sends sensor data (source) to the BNC (Sink). The Communication module supports the transmission of data between nodes and consists of one Routing Module, two MAC modules and two Radio modules. The Routing module implements the dual-channel AODV protocol developed in the paper.

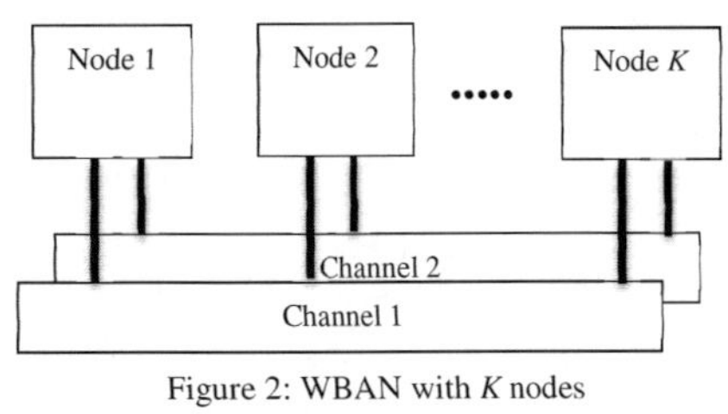

Figure 2: WBAN with K nodes

The two MAC modules each contain an instance of a single band MAC protocol module. In this paper, the MAC protocol used is the Tunable MAC implemented in Castalia. Each of the two radios is a single band radio with a separate wireless connection to separate Wireless channel modules. The Radio module not only transmits and receives signals, accepting signals whose signal strength is above the radio receiver sensitivity, but also provides RSSI (Receive Signal Strength Indication) and LQI (Link Quality Indication) information about channels to higher layer modules.

Each Wireless module operates in a different frequency channel and is responsible for broadcasting wireless signals to other nodes. In the Castalia simulator the wireless channel module implements a channel model to determine received signal levels. The Resource Manager module's main function is to keep track of energy usage in a node and control node start-up and shutdown.

4. MULTI-CHANNEL AODV PROTOCOL

In this paper, we extend AODV to the multi-channel case. We first describe how single-channel AODV operates before describing our extensions to the multi-channel case. AODV is an on-demand (reactive) routing protocol that determines routes for transmission only if a node needs to deliver packets to target nodes, thus reducing excessive consumption of network bandwidth and energy [20]. It supports both unicast and multicast packet transmissions even for nodes in constant movement [21]. Hence, in the presence of human body movements, AODV responds very quickly to topological changes that may affect active routes.

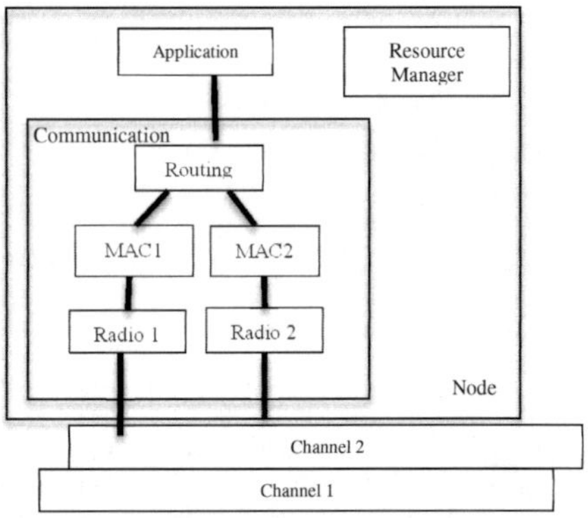

Figure 3: Dual-channel Castalia node structure

Suppose an AODV source node (source) has application data to send to an AODV destination node (destination). If the source has an active route to the destination it just begins sending the application data using AODV DATA packets to the next hop node in its routing table. If it does not have an active route to the destination, it initiates a route discovery process by broadcasting a Route Request (RREQ) message for that destination. When that RREQ message is received at an intermediate node, a next hop entry back towards the source is created in the intermediate node's routing table using the immediate source of the RREQ message as the next hop back towards the source. If the receiving node has not received this RREQ message before, is not the destination and does not have a current route to the destination, it rebroadcasts the RREQ message. If the receiving node is the destination or it already has an active route to the destination, it generates a Route Reply (RREP) message that is unicast in a hop-by-hop fashion back to the source using the previously stored next hop information in the node routing table. An intermediate node responding in such a way reduces the number of messages sent in the network. As the RREP propagates back towards the source, each intermediate node creates a next hop entry in the routing table towards the destination using the immediate source of the RREP message as the next hop towards the destination. When the initial source receives the RREP message, it records the next hop to the destination in its routing table, records that there is an active route to the destination, responds to the RREP message with an RREP Acknowledgment (RREPACK) message that is sent to the destination, and it begins sending data to the destination using DATA packets. Each time a node receives an RREP message the node updates its routing table if the RREP message indicates a route with less hop counts to the destination has been found.

As data flows from the source to the destination, each node along the route updates the timers associated with the routes to the source and destination. If a route has not used for some period of time, a node cannot be sure whether the route is still valid. A route expiry timer times-out and the node removes the route from its routing table. If data is flowing and a link break is detected, a Route Error (RERR) message is sent to the source of the data in a hop-by-hop fashion. When the source receives the RERR, it invalidates the route and re initiates' route discovery if necessary.

When RREP messages are received by a node it regularly broadcasts HELLO messages so that its neighbor nodes are aware of the node's continued presence. If a node fails to receive several HELLO messages from a neighbor, a link break is detected.

4.1 MULTI-CHANNEL AODV

A number of modifications were made to extend AODV to make it into a multi-channel routing protocol. The first modification was to incorporate channel selection so that when a node has a packet to send to a given destination and needs to send a RREQ message it first selects a channel over which to broadcast the RREQ message. To implement this we record RSSI values for all channels on which the node receives incoming packets. New RSSI values overwrite previous values. Each channel also has a max_time parameter that specifies the maximum amount of time that an RSSI value is maintained for the channel. If all channels (two channels in our case) have valid RSSI values then the channel with the largest RSSI value is selected. If one or more RSSI values is out of date then a channel is selected at random.

The second modification was to include in the routing table entry for a given destination the next hop channel along with the address of the next hop node. When an RREQ message is received the immediate preceding node address and incoming channel are stored as the next hop node address and the next hop channel back to the source in the routing table. Later, when the matching RREP message is received this next hop address and next hop channel are used to forward the RREP back to the source. Also the immediate source address and incoming channel of the RREP message are stored as the next hop address and next hop channel for forwarding packets and messages to the destination. Later, when a route has been established all DATA packets are unicast using the next hop next hop address and next hop channel information stored in the routing table.

AODV retransmits RREQ messages if an RREP message has not been received in a given time. We modified the RREQ retransmission queue such that the selected channel a RREQ was transmitted was stored with message so that the RREQ message could be retransmitted on the same channel as previously. For HELLO message we needed to manage each channel separately and each channel has its own HELLO expiry and refresh timers.

5. WBAN MAC LAYER PROTOCOLS

We utilised the Castalia provided Tunable-MAC (TMAC) protocol that normally operates over a single band using a single radio. In our dual-channel system we deployed two Tunable MAC modules, one for each frequency channel. TMAC was designed for broadcast communications and does not include acknowledgements and RTS and CTS control packets. It is a contention based protocol utilising the CSMA (Carrier Sense Multiple Access) mechanism for transmissions. The advantages of a contention based MAC protocol are its simplicity, its infrastructure-free ad-hoc feature and good adaptability to traffic fluctuation especially for low load. It is tunable in the sense that persistence and back-off policies can be adjusted. TMAC can be configured to transmit trains of beacon packets to support wake-ups and duty cycle management. The two packet types used by TMAC are DATA for data transfer and BEACON for beacon broadcasting.

6. WBAN WIRELESS CHANNEL MODEL

At channel bandwidths typical of narrowband BAN systems, the radio channel has been shown to be essentially slow and flat fading, with an insignificant amount of inter-symbol interference from multipath effects. On-body narrowband RF signal transmission in an anechoic chamber without any posture change or movement is primarily by creeping waves over the body surface and line-of-sight transmission, if it exists. Posture change causes small scale fading as waves interact with irregular body structures and in homogenous dielectric structures. Outside of the ideal anechoic environment additional multipath signal transmission occurs due to reflection, scattering and diffraction from the surroundings that causes additional small-scale fading.

The IEEE 802.15.6 standard defines a number of different scenarios for communication. Channel models for these different scenarios are given in [22] [23] and include: CM1 (implant-to-implant), CM2 (implant-to-surface or external), CM3 (body surface –to body surface or external). Overviews of these models are given in [24]. These models are based on probability distributions whose parameter values have been determined by measurements and physical modeling.

The work by [25] and [26] challenges a number of assumptions used in channel modeling. [26]. In particular show that posture changes of human bodies can cause temporal correlations and that many of the WBAN probability models are inaccurate. They proposed a more empirically based model and this has been included in Castalia. In this model, the body is divided into regions called cells using similar concepts to the virtual coordinate system developed by [27]. There may be more than one node in a cell. Each source-destination cell pair has a given path loss. When a transmission instance from one cell to another occurs the actual signal loss is the sum of the cell-to-cell path loss plus a fading loss whose value is determined by a random look-up from a look-up table whose values have been determined from measurement studies. Castalia also includes a mobility model that supports simple movement of nodes that involves recalculation of node positions and of path losses.

7. RESULTS

We implemented in Castalia a dual-channel version (using channels 1 and 2) of the multi-channel AODV routing protocol we proposed in Section 4.1. Implementing this in Castalia required significant modifications to the existing C++ and network description (.ned) files in the single channel model to add the extra node modules needed (second MAC and second Radio) and implemented the extra multi-channel AODV routing protocol functions into the Routing module.

We considered a network of 6 nodes (0-5) placed on the body front as shown in Figure 1. The sink (BNC) was the node 0 and nodes 1 to 5 transmitted data to that node only. Node 0 did not send any data to the other nodes. We used the 2.4 GHz IEEE 802.15.4/Zigbee-ready CC2420 RF transceiver provided in Castalia. The key simulation parameters used are shown in Table 1. The radio parameters has been derived from the Teleos Mote Datasheet [28]. We have set the radio to IDEAL modulation in Castalia and used the additive interference collision model.

Table 1. Simulation Parameters

Module	Parameter and Data Value
Application	20 packets per second, 100 byte payload + 30 byte overhead (application data rate is 20.8 kbps)
Routing	RREQ retries = 2 RREQ rate limit = 10 per sec Active route timeout = 6 sec
Tunable MAC	Default parameters (Constant backoff time, one transmission attempt)
Radio	Sensitivity: -100 dBm Noise floor: -110 dBm Transmit power: 0 dBm
Wireless Channel	Bandwidth 20 MHz, Data rate: 250 kbps Modulation type: BPSK Temporal model, static nodes
Initial energy	18720 J (2 x AA batteries)

To determine the effect of multi-channel AODV by itself we disabled the mobility module in Castalia and compared the performance between the single channel AODV (SCH) over channel 1, dual channel AODV using RSSI channel selection (DCH RSSI) and dual channel AODV with random channel selection (DCH Rand).

The simulation duration was set to 1400 seconds. Figure 4 shows, for each node, the numbers of packets sent by the application module in a node to the application module in node 0 and the number of packets received by node 0. The labels on the x axis identify the source node of packets. The top plot in the figure is for SCH, the middle plot is for DCH Rand and the bottom plot is for DCH RSSI. Since the simulation was configured for constant packet rate in the application layer all simulations sent around the same number of packets (140,096). The figure shows that SCH and DCH RSSI achieved almost the same packet delivery levels (SCH: total received = 137,687 packets, mean per node= 22,948 packets; DCH RSSI: total received = 138,987 packets, mean per node= 23,165 packets) whereas DCH Rand delivered less packets (total received = 123,192 packets, mean per node= 20,532 packets). If anything, DCH RSSI is slightly better than SCH.

Figures 5 and 6 show the number of AODV DATA packets sent on channels 1 and channel 2, respectively. In a groups of bars above a source node each bar is for a different destination nodes (0-5, left-to-right) (Figure 7 illustrates this the best).

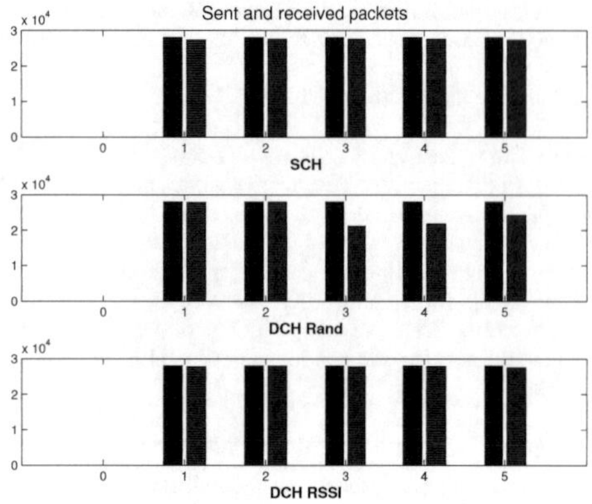

Figure 4: Numbers of application packets sent to node 0 (left bar) and received by node 0 (right bar) for each node for SCH, DCH Rand and DCH AODV.

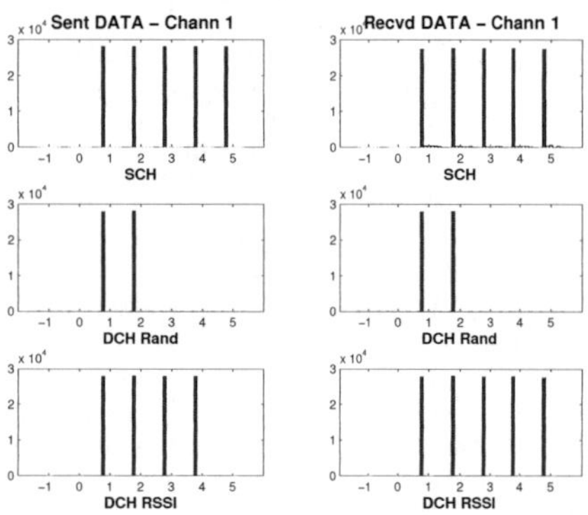

Figure 5: Sent and received AODV DATA packets on Channel 1

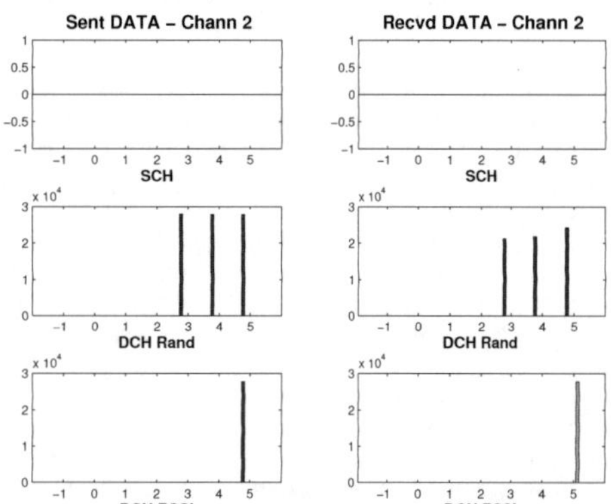

Figure 6: Sent and received AODV DATA packets on Channel 2

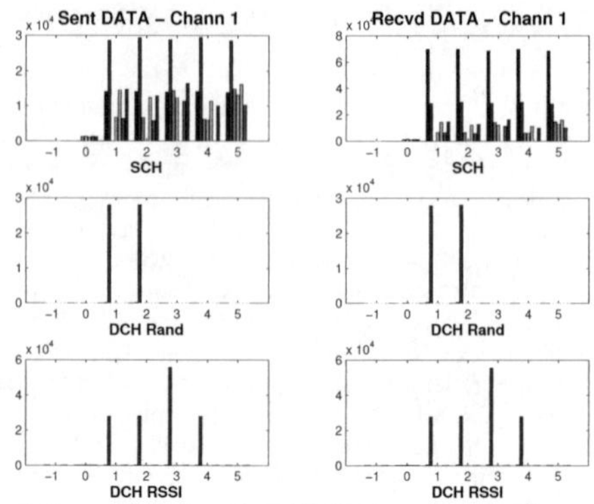

Figure 7: Sent and received MAC DATA packets on Channel 1

To understand how the dynamics of the different forms of AODV affected performance we conducted detailed analyses for each node of the number of AODV messages and packets sent and received.

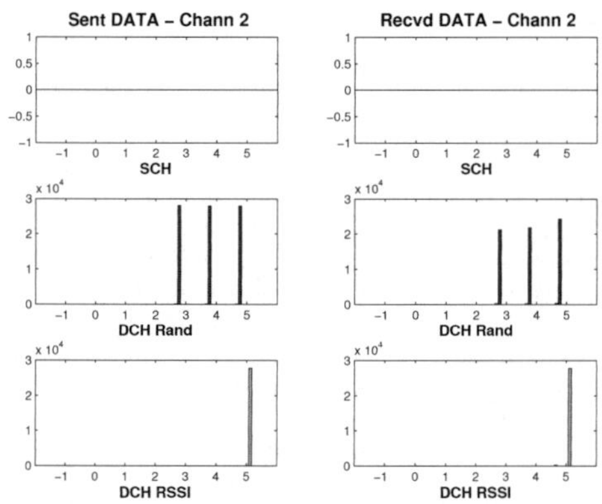

Figure 8: Sent and received MAC DATA packets on Channel 2

For SCH all DATA packets were sent on channel 1. Most DATA packets were sent from source to node 0 in one hop but there was a small amount of forwarding by other nodes as seen in the received packet counts (right-hand graph).

For both DCH Rand and DCH RSSI some packets were sent on channel 1 and some on channel 2, depending on which channel was selected (Note that both radios in a node can simultaneously send and receive packets with higher layer module operation decoupled by buffers.) For DCH Rand nearly all packets were sent in one hop to node 0. The same was true for DCH RSSI except packets from node 5 were sent to node 0 via node 3, the first hop using channel 2 and the second hop using channel 1.

We then examined how many AODV control messages (RREQ, RREP, RERR, RREPACK (denoted by RACK in the figure) and HELLO) were sent and received by nodes with message counts shown in Tables 2 and 3, respectively, for the 1400 second simulation. RERR message counts are not shown as none were detected. As a reference point the total number of application packets sent in each simulation was around 138,987. The sent message counts are the number of messages sent by a node to all other nodes and the received message counts are the number of messages received by a node from all other nodes.

Table 2: Count of AODV control messages sent from a node to all other nodes for SCH, DCH Rand and DCH RSSI AODV.

SCH (sent messages)

Ch	Pkttype	Node:0	1	2	3	4	5
1	RREQ	0	1	1	110	1	109
1	RREP	6327	33938	32058	40911	29920	40749
1	RACK	0	21802	19912	27213	17700	27056
1	HELLO	0	57	57	57	57	57

DCH Rand (sent messages)

Ch	Pkttype	Node:	1	2	3	4	5
1	RREQ	0	2	1	3	2	2
1	RREP	3	2	2	0	1	0
1	RACK	0	1	1	0	0	0
1	HELLO	0	56	57	0	0	0
2	RREQ	0	1	3	1	2	3
2	RREP	3	2	1	2	2	0
2	RACK	0	0	0	1	1	1
2	HELLO	0	0	0	57	56	56

DCH RSSI (sent messages)

Ch	Pkttype	Node:0	1	2	3	4	5
1	RREQ	0	2	1	2	3	2
1	RREP	2	2	2	4	1	1
1	RACK	0	1	1	2	1	0
1	HELLO	0	56	57	56	56	0
2	RREQ	0	2	4	2	2	3
2	RREP	5	1	0	2	1	0
2	RACK	0	0	0	0	0	1
2	HELLO	0	0	0	0	0	56

Table 3: Count of AODV control messages received by a node all other nodes for SCH, DCH Rand and DCH RSSI AODV.

SCH (received messages)

Ch	Pkttype	Node:0	1	2	3	4	5
1	RREQ	68983	55078	55068	55296	55051	55198
1	RREP	0	21802	19912	27213	17700	27056
1	RACK	6230	19680	17775	26879	15711	26558
1	HELLO	282	224	227	225	224	222

DCH Rand (received messages)

Ch	Pkttype	Node:0	1	2	3	4	5
1	RREQ	10	7	7	8	8	7
1	RREP	0	1	1	0	0	0
1	RACK	2	0	0	0	0	0
1	HELLO	113	57	56	113	113	113
2	RREQ	8	7	6	6	6	3
2	RREP	0	0	0	1	1	1
2	RACK	3	0	0	0	0	0
2	HELLO	150	152	146	98	105	91

DCH RSSI (received messages)

Ch	Pkttype	Node:0	1	2	3	4	5
1	RREQ	13	7	10	8	10	8
1	RREP	0	1	1	2	1	0
1	RACK	5	0	0	0	0	0
1	HELLO	224	168	167	168	168	223
2	RREQ	11	9	7	10	9	8
2	RREP	0	0	0	0	0	1
2	RACK	0	0	0	1	0	0
2	HELLO	56	55	56	56	56	0

The SCH case shows that significantly more RREQ, RREP and RREPACK messages were sent and received than in DCH Rand and DCH RSSI. Further analysis of the SCH case showed that the network was experiencing routing instability. The maximum RREQ message transmission rate from a node was set to 10 per second (Castalia default). At this rate not enough RREQ messages could be sent to allow convergence to occur to stable routes. As a consequence RREQ retransmission buffers became very full in some nodes that keep on transmitting large numbers of RREQs. Increasing the RREQ message transmission rate from a node to 100 per second removed the instability. We concluded that both dual-channel AODVs had much better routing convergence and stability than SCH. In summary, DCH RSSI delivered similar numbers of application packets to what SCH could deliver but needed less control messages to be sent and received (control message overhead). Although DCH Rand has a similar control message overhead to DCH RSSI, the number of application packets delivered was more with DCH RSSI. The benefits of dual channel operation appeared to come from the capacity to reduce the number nodes trying to communicate with each other, leading to less numbers of control messages being sent and better convergence.

The graphs of MAC DATA packets sent and received per node on each channel is shown in Figures 7 and 8. For SCH there were significant numbers of packets sent between a node and all the other nodes as a result of the high number of AODV control messages being broadcast and then responded to. However, the dominant number of MAC DATA packets sent from a node were to node 0, carrying AODV DATA packets. The MAC DATA packets sent in DCH Rand were nearly all carrying AODV data packets and the transmission pattern was consistent with the AODV packet transmission numbers in Figures 5 and 6. DCH RSSI was similar, except that the number of MAC DATA packets sent from node 3 to node 0 was about double that of the other nodes as it was sending its own AODV DATA packets and forwarding the AODV DATA packets of node 5 as well.

There are several parameters that need to be configured in TMAC and additional studies and analyses showed that the interaction between TMAC parameters and AODV parameters and timer time-outs could be quite complex. For example, increasing the number of allowed RREQ retries also increases the RREQ expiry time-out value. Increasing the number of RREQ retries also leads to more contention in the MAC layer. On the other hand more contention in the MAC layer leads to more failures to deliver RREQ packets and consequent time-outs. The optimum configuration of parameters in dual channel operation is an open issue.

Table 4: Comparison of total consumed energy (Joules)

	Node=0	1	2	3	4	5
SCH	52.2543	52.0576	52.0548	52.0503	52.0584	52.0559
DCH Rand	52.2583	52.1071	52.1022	52.1035	52.1075	52.1086
DCH RSSI	52.2581	52.107	52.102	51.9579	52.1073	52.1108

Table 5: Comparison of energy efficiency (nJoules/bit)

	Node=1	2	3	4	5
SCH	8109.57	7988.91	7943.16	7914.98	8028.41
DCH Rand	7858.16	7737.82	14145.5	10932.8	8075.25
DCH RSSI	7873.09	7736.83	7855.56	7878.14	8040

In terms of energy usage we found only small differences between actual energy usages in the different simulations (Table 4). However, DCH RSSI gave the best energy efficiency (nJoules per bit) of the three cases.

8. CONCLUSION

In this paper we developed a multi-channel AODV routing protocol that was implemented in the OMNet++ based Castalia WBAN simulation model. We showed that DCH RSSI gave equal performance to SCH in terms of packet delivery but with less AODV control overhead, better routing stability and slightly better energy efficiency. In future work, we will examine how node mobility affects operation and the use of energy and other metrics such as ETX (Expected Number of Transmissions) and WCETT (Weighted Cumulative Expected Transmission Time) that require additional changes to the Castalia Radio module. We also plan to investigate the use of dual-channel Radio and/or dual-channel MAC modules.

9. REFERENCES

[1] H. Cao ,V .Leung , Chow, C , H. Chan, "Enabling technologies for wireless body area networks: A survey and outlook", IEEE Communications Magazine, 47(12), 84-93, 2009.

[2] IEEE Standards Association. 802.15.6-2012 - IEEE Standard for Local and metropolitan area networks - Part 15.6: Wireless Body Area Networks. Available from https://standards.ieee.org/findstds/standard/802.15.6-2012.html.

[3] S. Movassaghi, M. Abolhasan, J. Lipman, D. Smith, and A. Jamalipour, "Wireless Body Area Networks: A Survey" IEEE Communications Survey & Tutorials, 16(3) 1658-1686, 2013.

[4] J. Buckley, B. O'Flynn, P. Angove, L. Loizou, P. Haigh, D. Boyle, J. Barton, C. O'Mathúna, E. Popovici, S. O'Connell, "A Novel and Miniaturized 433/868MHz Multi-Band Wireless Sensor Platform for Body Sensor Network Applications" Ninth International Conference on, 9-12 May 2012

[5] A. Argyriou and A. C. Breva, "Optimizing data forwarding from body area networks in the presence of body shadowing with dual wireless nodes", IEEE Trans. on Mobile Computing, 14(3), 632-645, 2015.

[6] J. Tak , K. Kwon and J. Choi, "Design of a dual band repeater antenna for medical self-monitoring applications" , In Antennas and Propagation Society International Symposium (APSURSI), IEEE, 2091-2092. 2013.

[7] K. M. S Thotahewa, J.-M. Redoute and M. R. Yuce, "Implementation of a dual band sensor node", In Microwave Workshop Series on RF and Wireless Technologies for Biomedical and Healthcare Applications (IMWS-BIO), 2013 IEEE MTT-S International, pp. 1-3, 2013.

[8] W. Yang, K. Ma, K. S. Yeo, W. M. Lim and Z. H. Kong, "A compact dual-band meander-line antenna for biomedical applications", In Microwave Workshop Series on RF and Wireless Technologies for Biomedical and Healthcare Applications (IMWS-BIO), IEEE MTT-S International, pp. 1-3. 2013.

[9] E. F. Sundarsingh, S. Velan, M. Kanagasabai, A. K. Sarma, C. Raviteja and M. G. N. Alsath, "Polygon-shaped slotted dual-band antenna for wearable applications", IEEE Antennas and Wireless Propagation Letters, 13, 611-614, 2104.

[10] H. Huang, P.-Y. Chen, M. Ferrari, Y. Hu and D. Akinwande, "Dual-band electrically small non-uniform pitch ellipsoidal helix antenna for cardia pacemakers", In Radio and Wireless Symposium (RWS), IEEE, 325-327, 2013.

[11] Perkins, Charles, Elizabeth Belding-Royer, and Samir Das. Ad hoc on-demand distance vector (AODV) routing. No. RFC 3561. 2003.

[12] Castalia A simulator for wireless sensor networks and body area networks. User's manual. Version 3.2. NICTA. March 2011.

[13] A. Varga, "The OMNeT++ discrete event simulation system." Proceedings of the European Simulation Multiconference (ESM'2001). Vol. 9. No. S 185. sn, 2001.

[14] S. Movassaghi and M. Abolhasan, "A review of routing protocols in wireless body area networks', Journal of Networks, 8(3), 559-575, 2013.

[15] J. I. Bangash, A. H. Abdullah, M. H. Anisi and A. W. Khan, "A survery of routing protocols in wireless body sensor networks", Sensors, 14, 1322-1357, 2014.

[16] M. X. Gong and S. F. Midkiff, "Distributed channel assignment protocols: a cross-layer approach", In IEEE Wireless Communications and Networking Conference, vol. 4, pp. 2195-2200. IEEE, 2005.

[17] A. Raniwala and T. Chieuh, "Architecture and algorithms for an IEEE 802.11-based multi-channel wireless mesh network", In INFOCOM 2005. 24th Annual Joint Conference of the IEEE Computer and Communications Societies. Proceedings IEEE, vol. 3, 2223-2234.2005.

[18] J. Mo, H.S. Wilson, J. Walrand, "Comparison of Multichannel MAC Protocols", IEEE Transactions on Mobile Computing 7(1), 50-65, 2008.

[19] S.-M. He, D.-F. Zhang, K. Xie, H. Qiao and J. Zhang, "Channel aware opportunistic routing in multi-radio multi-channel wireless mesh networks", Journal of Computer Science and Technology, 29(3), 487-501, 2014.

[20] C. E. Perkins and E. M. Royer. The Ad hoc On-Demand Distance Vector Protocol. In C. E. Perkins, editor, Ad hoc Networking, pages 173–219. Addison-Wesley, 2000.

[21] S. Taneja and A. Kush, "A survey of routing protocols in mobile ad-hoc networks", International Journal of Innovation, Management and Technology, 1(3), 2010-0248, 2010.

[22] IEEE P802.15-08-0780-12-0006, "Channel Model for Body Area Network (BAN)," Nov. 10, 2010.

[23] IEEE P802.15-08-0519-01-0006, "A Statistical Path Loss Model for MICS," Sept. 8, 2008.

[24] R. Chavez-Santiago, K. Sayrafian-Pour, A. Khaleghi, K. Takizawa, J. Wang, I. Balasingham and H.-B. Li, "Propagation models for IEEE 802.15.6 standardization of implant communication in body area networks", IEEE Communications Magazine, 51(8), 80-87, 2013.

[25] S. L. Cotton, R. D'Errico and C. Oestges, "A review of radio channel models for body centric communications", Radio Science, 49(6), 371-388, 2104.

[26] D. B. Smith, D. Miniutti, T. A. Lamahewa and L. W. Hanlen, "Propagation models for body area networks: A survey and new outlook", IEEE Antennas and Propagation Magazine, IEEE, 55(5), 97-117. 2013.

[27] Q. Zhang, K. Kortermand, R. H. Jacobsen and T. S. Toftgaard, "Reactive virtual coordinate routing for body sensor networks", In Communications (ICC), 2012 IEEE International Conference on, pp. 3388-3393. 2012.

[28] 'Single-Chip 2.4 GHz IEEE 802.15.4 Compliant and ZigBee™ Ready RF Transceiver http://www.ti.com/product/cc2420.

Muscle Strength Testing using Wearable Wireless Sensors

Debadri Mukherjee
Centre for Speckled Computing
School of Informatics
University of Edinburgh
D.Mukherjee@sms.ed.ac.uk

DK Arvind
Centre for Speckled Computing
School of Informatics
University of Edinburgh
dka@inf.ed.ac.uk

ABSTRACT

Manual muscle testing and its variants have a long history of use for classifying muscle strengths. For the first time, inexpensive wearable wireless sensors combined with machine learning techniques are used to classify different levels of muscle strength, which addresses some limitations of the manual method. A mean accuracy of 93% was obtained across ten subjects using gyroscope and accelerometer data in classifying four distinct levels of strengths of the biceps brachii muscle when performing muscle contraction under appropriate load. This was reduced by 2% for accelerometer-only data, thus offering a potentially inexpensive and viable solution for testing muscle strength.

Keywords

Muscle strength testing; Orient specks; Classification; *k*-nearest neighbours.

1. INTRODUCTION

Muscle strength can be reduced for a number of reasons such as the result of a stroke, Parkinson's disease or bone fracture. Patients would be required to undergo a regime of rehabilitation to improve their muscle strength. Muscle testing is important to calibrate the strength and track improvements in movement during the treatment. Accurate assessment of muscle strength is therefore central in determining the course of treatment by physiotherapists. The two common techniques for muscle testing are Manual Muscle Testing (MMT) and Handheld Dynamometry (HHD). MMT is a popular choice amongst physiotherapists where the equipment cost of the dynamometer is an issue. However, MMT has been criticised for its seeming lack of objectivity as the physiotherapist's strength is said to influence the assessment [1]. It has been suggested that MMT is more reliable when assessing heavy impairment, but equipment-based testing is preferred in the cases of moderate or mild levels of impairment [1].

This paper proposes a wireless sensor-based approach to test muscle strength accurately and objectively. The method uses an Orient speck [2], which combines a tri-axial gyroscope, accelerometer and magnetometer with wireless networking capabilities. The sensor data is analysed and supervised machine learning methods are applied to classify four distinct levels of muscle strength of the biceps brachii. Ten healthy subjects simulated these four levels of muscle strength by performing the muscle contraction under the application of an appropriate load. We present results obtained using a *k*-nearest neighbour classifier model, firstly on individual datasets corresponding to the subjects, and then on an aggregated dataset, in order to address issues of subjectivity. The features (four) in the dataset(s) were constructed using the gyroscope and accelerometer data. We show further that it is possible to use only the accelerometer data, with a small reduction (2%) in the classification performance.

2. BACKGROUND AND RELATED WORK

In MMT, the examiner (therapist) assigns a numerical (integer) grade between 0 and 5 to a muscle, based on the results of muscle-specific test procedures using the criteria listed in Table 1:

Table 1: Criteria for assigning different grades in MMT.

Grade	*Description*	*Criterion*
0	No Activity	Muscle is completely inert on palpitation or visual inspection.
1	Trace Activity	Detection of contractile activity but no resulting movement.
2	Poor	Full range of motion (ROM) only in a horizontal plane.
3	Fair	Full range of motion (ROM) against the effect of gravity.
4	Good	Full ROM against gravity and test position is held under minimum resistance
5	Normal	Full ROM against gravity and test position is held under maximum resistance.

Muscle testing has been applied in practice for around one hundred years [3], and can be traced back to the pioneering work of Wilhelmine G. Wright [4] and Robert W. Lovett [5]. This paper reports the first use of wireless inertial sensors to classify muscle strength and addresses the known deficiencies of manual muscle testing. Previous work using wireless sensors in this domain has focused mainly on fatigue detection [6][7].

BODYNETS 2015, September 28-30, Sydney, Australia

DOI 10.4108/eai.28-9-2015.2261461

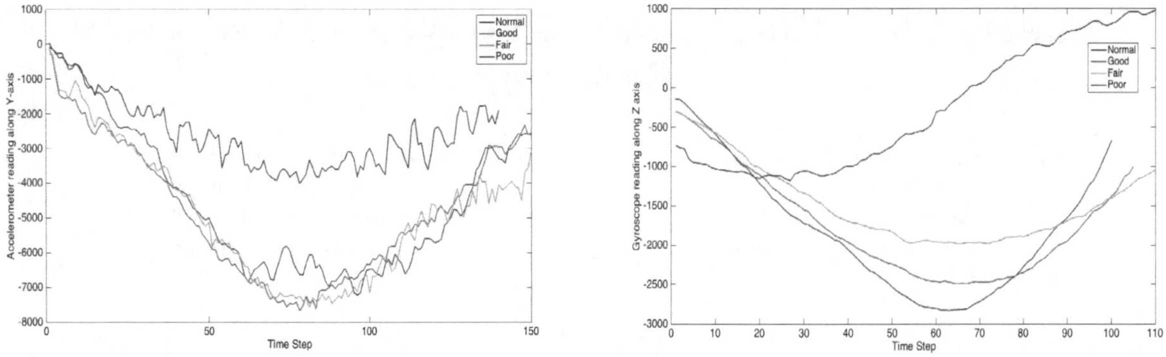

Figure 2: Sample Plots of Accelerometer data along Y-axis (left) and Gyroscope data along Z-axis (right) against time steps during the simulation of different muscle qualities.

3. METHODOLOGY

3.1 Data Collection

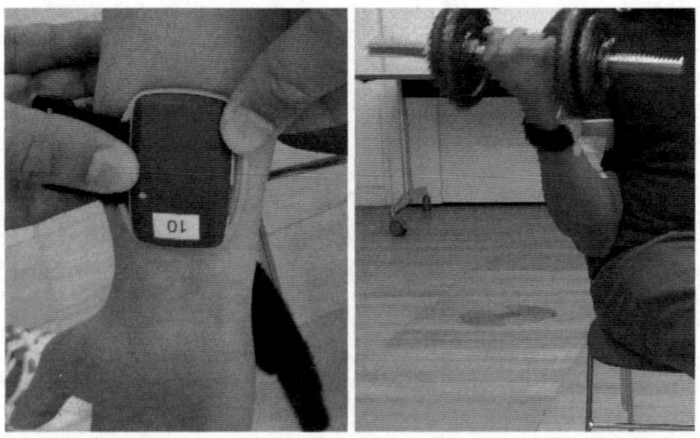

Figure 1: Placement of the Orient speck (left) during elbow flexion (right).

This work has focused on the different strength (weakness) levels of the biceps (bicep brachii), and therefore the motion studied was elbow flexion against gravity (Figure 1, right). The ten able-bodied subjects (5 female and 5 male) were in turn instructed to: "Sit up straight with the (dexterous) arm stretched out by your side and fingers pointing to the ground. The palm should be facing out. Close your grip (or hold the weight). Perform (or attempt) a smooth elbow flexion ending with your forearm touching your shoulder." An Orient speck was placed on the forearm (Figure 1, left) of the subject as close to the palm as possible, which is the point with the greatest degree of freedom with the hand behaving as a Class III lever and the elbow acting as the fulcrum. The four distinct muscle strength levels simulated by each subject have been described in Table 2, which correspond to MMT grades ranging between 2+ and 5 (Table 1).

Each subject demonstrated five instances of elbow flexion for each level (20 in total for each subject), by picking a suitable resistance in the form of weights - R_0, R_1, R_2 and R_3 – depending upon their individual strengths, which would allow them to match the description of muscle strength levels N, G, F and P, respectively:

$$R_0 = 0 \rightarrow \text{No resistance, and } R_1 < R_2 < R_3.$$

Table 2: Description of the four levels of muscle strength.

Class	*Name*	*Description*
N	Normal	Full and smooth ROM against gravity.
G	Good	Full ROM against gravity with a little difficulty.
F	Fair	Full ROM against gravity with considerable difficulty.
P	Poor	Partial (incomplete) ROM against gravity.

3.2 Data Analysis

A representative example of the accelerometer readings along the Y-axis and gyroscope readings along Z-axis is presented in Figure 2. There is a central region common to both the plots, which has a characteristic 'U' shape.

In case of the accelerometer data (Figure 2, left), there are undulations displayed as changes in the slope of the graph due to subsequent increase and decrease (or vice versa) in the acceleration due to gravity. During this full range of motion, the alignment of the Y- axis of the accelerometer changes from 90° to 0°, and then from 0° to 90° with respect to the vertical, i.e., direction of the gravitational force. Therefore, at the starting position of this motion, the gravitational force acting upon the Y-axis of the accelerometer is 0 as it is perpendicular to the vertical; it reaches its peak at the half-way point when the forearm is perpendicular to the upper arm along the elbow joint, as in this case the Y-axis of the accelerometer is along the vertical. In general, we observe different degrees of change in the slope at points in the plot (Figure 2, left) for the four muscle qualities. The direction of the slope changes more frequently and the value of the slopes is greater (on average) when simulating greater muscle weakness. On increasing the resistance, the subject faces greater difficulty in completing the motion and this is manifested in jerky movements with frequent accelerations and decelerations. The slope at the individual points of the accelerometer readings also changes direction more frequently and the rate of change of accelerometer readings (the slopes at individual points) is also greater on increasing the resistance, which corresponds to simulating greater level of muscle weakness. Therefore, the behaviour of the slope is an important factor for characterising different levels of muscle strength.

The gyroscope data along the Z-axis (Figure 2, right), also reveals information of relevance. An important observation was that the value of the minima (global) of the curves is inversely proportional to the muscle strength.

3.3 Features for Classification

Average smoothness of acceleration (JC): This was measured as the mean of the absolute value of the derivatives in the accelerometer readings at each time step for the motion. This metric, the jerk cost, was computed as follows:

$$JC = \frac{1}{n}\sum_{i=1}^{n}\left|accl_i^{read} - accl_{i-1}^{read}\right| \quad (1)$$

Directional changes in the slope (SC): The number of changes in direction of the derivative of the accelerometer readings in subsequent time steps where there was a change in acceleration was recorded. This was then divided by the number of time steps so that the value remained independent of the duration of motion.

Minimum value of the accelerometer readings (MA): In order to minimise the impact of noise on this feature, the five lowest accelerometer readings in the motion were identified and this feature was computed as its average.

Accelerometer reading at the end point (DP): This recorded the accelerometer reading at the last time step in the motion. In order to guard against the effect of noise, DP was defined as the mean of the last 5 accelerometer readings.

Range of Motion Indicator (ROM): The features MA and DP had the potential to detect partial range of motion based on the analysis of the data: the former for partial range of motion below 90°, and the latter for cases beyond 90°. They were first normalised and then combined into a binary feature, ROM, which served as an indicator for full range of motion, and was set as follows:

$$ROM = \begin{cases} 1 & DP > 0.5 \text{ or } MA < 0.5 \\ 0 & \text{otherwise} \end{cases} \quad (3)$$

The rationale for these conditions was that the normalised value of MA should be high and that of DP should be low on completing the full range of motion. Setting the threshold at a value of 0.5 also guarded against noise in the data. The replacement of the two features, MA and DP, with ROM ensured that we did not overfit to the noise present in these features.

Minimum value of the gyroscope reading (MinG): As the name suggests, the feature noted the minimum value across the gyroscope readings in the motion inspired by the specific observations made in Figure 2 (right). It was calculated exactly the same way as MA to guard against noise in the sensor data.

In summary, four features were constructed for the classification task. Three (SC, JC and ROM) of them were calculated using the accelerometer readings only, whereas the gyroscope readings were used to determine MinG. All of these features were normalised prior to their use in classification.

3.4 Classifier Model

The implementation of k-Nearest Neighbour (k-NN) classifier in the Weka tool [10] (known as '*iBk*' [9]) was used to perform the classification task using the features constructed from the sensor data. As a non-parametric classifier, k-NN does not require strong assumptions about the underlying data distributions. These models are known to be more flexible in comparison to their parametric counterparts [8]. This aspect ensured that a lower bias was introduced by not making subject-specific assumptions about the data and consequently made the analysis of the results more coherent. This model was computationally inexpensive as well, thanks to the low dimensionality of the data.

4. RESULTS

The mode of evaluation was set to 10-fold cross validation for all the cases as it is a robust way of assessing classification performance. The area under the receiver operating characteristic (ROC) curve and the F-measure along with classification accuracy (Table 3). The ROC Area reflects the classification performance without regard to class distribution and error costs [9]. A high value of F-measure (harmonic mean of precision and recall) indicates high values of both Recall and Precision that are useful measures of performance.

4.1 Individual Results

Table 3: Classification Results using four features.

Subj.	*Instances*	*k*	*Accuracy*	*F-measure*	*ROC Area*
1	19 (N:5,G:4,F:5,P:5)	3	100%	1	1
2	18 (N:5,G:4,F:4,P:5)	3	94.44%	0.94	0.99
3	18 (N:4,G:5,F:5,P:4)	3	100%	1	1
4	17 (N:3,G:4,F:5,P:5)	1	94.12%	0.94	0.96
5	17 (N:3,G:4,F:5,P:5)	1	82.35%	0.82	0.82
6	19 (N:5,G:4,F:5,P:5)	3	94.74%	0.95	0.96
7	17 (N:3,G:5,F:4,P:5)	1	82.35%	0.82	0.90
8	19 (N:4,G:5,F:5,P:5)	3	94.74%	0.95	1
9	20 (N:5,G:5,F:5,P:5)	3	95%	0.95	1
10	18 (N:3,G:5,F:5,P:5)	1	88.89%	0.88	0.89

The results for the ten subjects are presented in Table 3: the total number of instances in the dataset and their distribution across the 4 classes, Normal (N), Good (G), Fair (F) and Poor (P), are detailed in the second column. Four features were used for the classification task, namely, SC, JC, ROM and MinG. The value of parameter k for the k–NN classifier used in each case is reported in the third column. The F-Measure and ROC Area reported in each case are the weighted averages across the classes weighed by the number of instances in the class. A mean classification accuracy of 92.6 ± 6.3% was obtained in this case.

4.1.1 Assessing the contribution of the Gyroscope

The gyroscope data was used to construct only one feature in the dataset – MinG, and its impact on the classification performance was evaluated by removing this feature and measuring the classification performance based on the other three features. A mean accuracy of 90.8 ± 8.7% across the ten subjects was obtained. A detailed study of the results revealed that using only the accelerometer data improved the classification performance for three subjects and did not impact the results for another three. However, the mean accuracy decreased slightly (1.78%) when the gyroscope data was not used. This is a price worth paying given that the gyroscope is usually an order of magnitude more expensive in terms of its price and power consumption. Therefore the rest of the results in this paper do not use the 'MinG' feature.

4.2 Classification on the Full Dataset

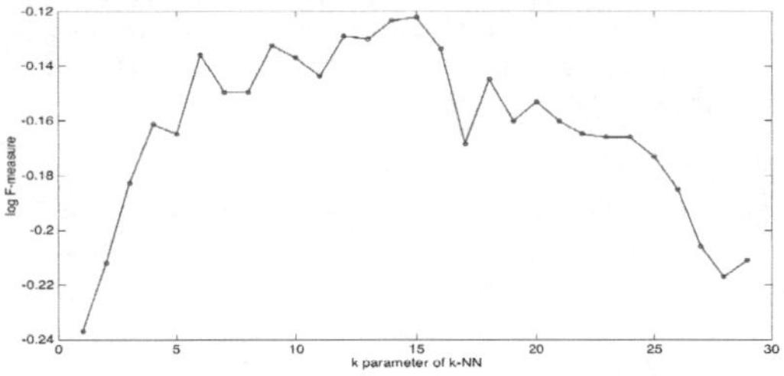

Figure 3: Plot of log F-Measure (y-axis) against *k*.

The lack of objectivity has been one of the main criticisms of MMT. In order to address this issue, results are presented in this subsection for classification on the 'full' dataset formed by aggregating the data from the 10 subjects, resulting in 182 instances. A systematic search of the state space was conducted to set the value of k for the k-NN classifier. Figure 3 shows the effect of k on performance and justifies the choice of $k = 15$. We obtained a classification accuracy of 88.46%. The weighted F-measure and weighted ROC Area were 0.89 and 0.96, respectively.

Table 4: Confusion Matrix

classified →	*N*	*G*	*F*	*P*
N	38	2	0	0
G	0	32	13	0
F	0	6	42	0
P	0	0	0	49

5. CONCLUSION

The results have highlighted the potential of using the Orient specks for testing muscle strength objectively and accurately. We were able to classify the four levels of muscle strength (weakness) with approximately 93% accuracy across the 10 subjects when using both gyroscope and accelerometer data. The use of accelerometer data alone resulted in a modest dip of only 2% in the classification performance. Thus, a 3-axis accelerometer with wireless networking capabilities could be used as a substitute. The objectivity of the approach was validated by performing classification on the full dataset (combined data of all ten subjects with varying muscularity). An accuracy of 88.5%, just 2.5% lower compared to the mean accuracy of the individual results, demonstrated that the model did not over-fit to the individual subjects.

The majority of the misclassification errors were in distinguishing between 'Good' and 'Fair' muscle strength levels. Some of the errors in distinguishing between 'Good' and 'Normal' may be attributed to noise in the data introduced by the subjects simulating weaknesses which is unlikely to be present in patients during clinical trials. Despite the presence of noise, it is encouraging to note that there were no errors in classifying 'Poor' muscle strength and all of the errors made were in distinguishing between subsequent levels of muscle strength, say between 'Good' and 'Fair'. We were able to determine perfectly whether full range of motion was completed and the errors in distinguishing between two classes occurred when these shared a boundary.

In conclusion, the work presents a possible solution to muscle strength testing, which addresses the issues of MMT, but at the same time is inexpensive and less complicated compared to approaches such as equipment based testing. In the future, this approach may be part of a self-management strategy for the patient to follow the exercise regime at home and assess improvements objectively and share a digital audit trail of progress with the remote physiotherapist.

6. ACKNOWLEDGEMENTS

We would like to thank the volunteers who participated in the study. This research was supported by the Centre for Speckled Computing (www.specknet.org), University of Edinburgh.

7. REFERENCES

[1] Helen Hislop, Dale Avers, and Marybeth Brown. Daniels and Worthingham's Muscle Testing: Techniques of Manual Examination and Performance Testing. Saunders, 9th edition, 2013.

[2] A.D. Young, M. J. Ling, D. K. Arvind, ``Orient-2 - A Wireless Real- time Posture Tracking System using Local Orientation Estimation", 4th Int. Workshop on Embedded Networked Sensors, ACM.

[3] Nancy Berryman Reese. Muscle and Sensory Testing. Elsevier Health Sciences, 3rd edition, 2013.

[4] Wilhelmine G. Wright. Muscle training in the treatment of Infantile Paralysis. Boston Medical Surgery J., 1912.

[5] Robert W. Lovett. Treatment of infantile paralysis. Preliminary Report. JAMA, 1915.

[6] Jian Zhang, Thurmon E. Lockhart, and Rahul Soangra. Classifying Lower Extremity Muscle Fatigue during Walking using Machine Learning and Inertial Sensors. Annals of biomedical engineering, 2014.

[7] Kang-Ming Chang, Shin-Hong Liu, and Xuan-Han Wu. A Wireless sEMG Recording System and its Application to Muscle Fatigue Detection. Sensors, 2012.

[8] Kevin P. Murphy. Machine Learning: A Probabilistic Perspective. MIT Press, 2012.

[9] Ian H. Witten, Eibe Frank and Mark A. Hall. "Data Mining: Practical Machine Learning Tools and Techniques". The Morgan Kaufmann Series in Data Management Systems. Third Edition, 2011.

[10] Mark Hall, Eibe Frank, Geoffrey Holmes, Bernhard Pfahringer, Peter Reutemann, Ian H. Witten (2009). The WEKA Data Mining Software: An Update; SIGKDD Explorations, Volume 11, Issue 1.

Body-IMU autocalibration for inertial hip and knee joint tracking

Sarvenaz Salehi
DFKI GmbH
Trippstadter Str. 122
67663 Kaiserslautern
sarvenaz.salehi@dfki.de

Gabriele Bleser
Technical University Kaiserslautern
Gottlieb-Daimler-Str. 48
67663 Kaiserslautern
bleser@cs.uni-kl.de

Attila Reiss
University of Passau
Innstrasse 43
94032 Passau
attila.reiss.phd@ieee.org

Didier Stricker
DFKI GmbH
Trippstadter Str. 122
67663 Kaiserslautern
didier.stricker@dfki.de

ABSTRACT
Sensor to body calibration is a key requirement for capturing accurate body movements in applications based on wearable systems. In this paper, we consider the specific problem of estimating the positions of multiple inertial measurement units (IMUs) relative to the adjacent body joints. To derive an efficient, robust and precise method based on a practical procedure is a crucial as well as challenging task when developing a wearable system with multiple embedded IMUs. In this work, first, we perform a theoretical analysis of an existing position calibration method, showing its limited applicability for the hip and knee joint. Based on this, we propose a method for simultaneously estimating the positions of three IMUs (mounted on pelvis, upper leg, lower leg) relative to these joints. The latter are here considered as an ensemble. Finally, we perform an experimental evaluation based on simulated and real data, showing the improvements of our calibration method as well as lines of future work.

Keywords
body-sensor autocalibration, wearable system, IMU, joint axes

1. INTRODUCTION
In recent years the attention towards mobile sensing for applications in sport and fitness monitoring has been drastically increasing. This is due to several factors, such as fitness awareness, the raise of motivation through gamification and competition in social networking, the proliferation of smartphones, and most importantly the advances in wearable technology and smart textiles. These wearable systems give the opportunity of self reflection to not only professional athletes but also ordinary people who are willing to pursue a healthy life and stay motivated in their training routine.

In contrast to smart watches and gadgets which contain single sensing units and mostly provide general information, such as walking speed and distance, energy expenditure, and type of activity [1, 2], smart textiles with multiple embedded sensing units can provide tracking of detailed body postures, e.g. in terms of joint angles and body segment positions [4, 18]. The latter is required during training in order to monitor and improve exercise technique and avoid injuries [5]. Moreover, body pose estimation can be used for model-based physical activity recognition, as demonstrated in [16, 23]. Such precise information, however, requires the knowledge of how the embedded sensors are mounted on each body segment when the user is wearing the textile. Using assumptions and information from anthropometric tables could result in inaccurate tracking, since there are different types of target users with different body shapes. In addition there are various types of clothing material which are used in the design of the wearables and result in varying sensor placements even for one specific individual. Manual measurements of these parameters are also cumbersome and error-prone. Therefore, an accurate, robust and autonomous sensor to body autocalibration method is required for a wearable training suit.

In [8, 14], two functional calibration procedures are proposed in order to obtain joint axes of the lower body based on fusion of the measurements of each IMU. The estimated joint axes are then used to track the joint angles in a reliable and clinically interpretable way. However, these procedures require passive and controlled movements, which are difficult to perform without supervision. Palermo et al. in [15] propose an easy and repeatable method without the need for specific and accurate movements in order to obtain the relative orientations of the IMUs with respect to the body. However, none of the above contributions provide a method for estimating the sensor positions with respect to the adjacent joints, which is a critical information in joint angle estimation using accelerometer measurements, especially during fast rotations [7] and when modeling kinematic chains [12]. In order to compensate for the resulting errors, in [14] a rotational mapping based on the integration of gyroscope measurements is used. Thus, the joint angle track-

BODYNETS 2015, September 28-30, Sydney, Australia

DOI 10.4108/eai.28-9-2015.2261522

ing accuracy is limited to time due to drift. In [10, 11], the IMU positions are used during tracking, however, these parameters are obtained through manual measurements, which is not accurate. In [24], a Kalman filter based method for minimizing the positional errors is proposed. However, this method requires multiple IMUs on each segment with controlled positional errors with respect to each other. Moreover, the large state vector, which is established for this method, is not efficient considering the computational power available in mobile applications.

In [21], Seel et al. propose a novel and practical method for estimating the joint axis of a hinge joint, as well as, the IMU positions with respect to a spheroidal joint, based on the gyroscope and accelerometer measurements of two IMUs mounted on the adjacent segments. In [20], the applicability of these methods is also discussed when considering joints with different degrees of freedom (DOF), and simple extensions are presented. In [21, 20], the method is applied to the knee and ankle joints, while in [13] it is adopted for a home-based clinical knee rehabilitation system. The methods of Seel et al. are drift-free, since they are based directly on the measurements, and work without the need for dedicated calibration movements. However, Seel et al. didn't provide an investigation of the types of movement that lead to the most accurate results. With insufficient variations in the different DOFs, the position calibration method leads to inaccurate results. This became apparent when applying the method to the hip joint, where it is difficult to perform movements with sufficient variation.

This paper builds upon the IMU position calibration method presented in [21, 20] with the goal to improve its accuracy and robustness under suboptimal movement conditions and make it applicable to the IMU-body calibration for an existing smart training pants [18], where the hip and knee joints are in focus. These are important, e.g. for monitoring exercises, such as squats [19]. We first provide a preliminary observability analysis of Seel's position calibration method (Section 3), and, based on this, propose a new calibration approach which, in contrast to Seel, considers three linked segments with IMUs (pelvis, upper leg, lower leg) and, respectively, two joints (hip, knee) in one estimation problem (Section 4). This makes it possible to benefit from an additional constraint, which is shown in experiments to provide more robust and accurate results under suboptimal movement conditions (Section 5). Note that this paper focuses on IMU position calibration, assuming the joint axes to be known, e.g. based on the method in [20].

2. PROBLEM FORMULATION

The problem of IMU position estimation can be defined as follows (cf. Figure 1) [20]: Assume two IMUs, A and B, being mounted on two segments connected via a joint m. By using sequences of measurements from A and B, the goal is to determine the two IMUs' positions, $l_{mS}, S \in \{A, B\}$, relative to the joint m. More precisely, l_{mS} denotes the vector from the joint center to the IMU center, given in the local coordinate frame of the IMU. Consider, for instance, the case where m is the knee joint. Then, IMU A is placed on the upper leg segment, IMU B is placed on the lower leg segment, and the goal is to derive the two vectors from the knee joint center to the IMUs in their respective coordinate frames.

For the above defined problem, an implicit, stochastic measurement model for timestep i can be formulated as:

$$0 = h(x_m, z_{mi}) + e_{mi}, \tag{1a}$$

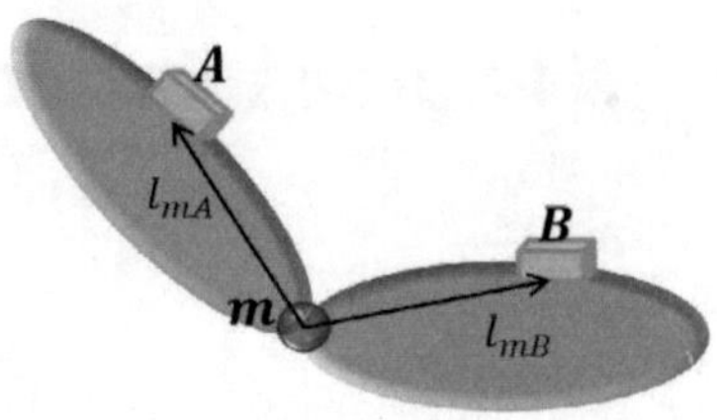

Figure 1: Illustration of the IMU position estimation problem. IMUs A and B are mounted on the adjacent segments of the joint m.

where

$$z_{mi} = [a_{Ai}, a_{Bi}, \omega_{Ai}, \omega_{Bi}, \alpha_{Ai}, \alpha_{Bi}]^T \tag{1b}$$

$$x_m = [l_{mA}, l_{mB}]^T. \tag{1c}$$

Here, z_{mi} refers to the measurement vector at timestamp $i \in 1 \dots k$. This measurement vector includes 3D acceleration, a_{Si}, angular velocity, ω_{Si}, and angular acceleration, α_{Si}, of both IMUs, $S = \{A, B\}$. Note that α_{Si} is assumed to be derived from ω_{Si}, e.g. via a third order approximation [20]. The quantity x_m refers to the parameter vector comprising the IMU positions. Finally, for simplicity, we assume additive Gaussian measurement noise $e_{mi} \sim N(0, \Sigma)$.

Given (1), a point estimate of x_m can be obtained by maximizing the maximum likelihood function:

$$\max_x \prod_{i=1\dots k} P(z_{mi}|x_m). \tag{2}$$

Using the logarithm formulation and then eliminating all constant terms from the optimization, this results in a weighted least squares problem, which can be solved with standard techniques:

$$\min_x \sum_{i=1\dots k} ||e_{mi}||^2_\Sigma. \tag{3}$$

Considering a spheroidal joint, Seel et al. introduces the following deterministic measurement model for estimating the IMU positions [21]:

$$e_{mi} = ||a_{Ai} - \Gamma_{Ai}|| - ||a_{Bi} - \Gamma_{Bi}||, \tag{4a}$$

where

$$\Gamma_{Si} = \omega_{Si} \times (\omega_{Si} \times l_{mS}) + \alpha_{Si} \times l_{mS}, \tag{4b}$$

and e_{mi} denotes the residual to be minimized. This model can be directly used in Equation (3), even if the latter reduces to a least squares formulation due to its deterministic nature.

The following section presents a preliminary observability analysis of the optimization problem (3) in combination with model (4), in which we identify major failure cases.

3. OBSERVABILITY ANALYSIS

The observability of the general optimization problem in (3) can be evaluated by computing the Fisher Information Matrix (FIM), which in our setting can be defined as [22]:

$$FIM = {J_h}^T \Sigma^{-1} J_h. \tag{5}$$

Here, J_h denotes the Jacobian of the measurement model (1) with respect to the parameter vector x_m:

$$J_h = \begin{pmatrix} \frac{\partial e_{m1}}{\partial l_{mA}} & \frac{\partial e_{m1}}{\partial l_{mB}} \\ \vdots & \vdots \\ \frac{\partial e_{mk}}{\partial l_{mA}} & \frac{\partial e_{mk}}{\partial l_{mB}} \end{pmatrix}. \quad (6)$$

If J_h has full column rank, then FIM has full rank [22], which indicates observability.

Using the measurement model (4), the partial derivatives in (6) for timestep i are:

$$\frac{\partial e_{mi}}{\partial l_{mS}} = -\frac{\tilde{a}_{Si}^T}{\|\tilde{a}_{Si}\|}([\omega_{Si}]_\times [\omega_{Si}]_\times + [\alpha_{Si}]_\times), S \in \{A, B\}, \quad (7)$$

where

$$\tilde{a}_{Ai} = a_{Ai} - \Gamma_{Ai}, \;\; \tilde{a}_{Bi} = -(a_{Bi} - \Gamma_{Bi}).$$

Here, in order to simplify, the timestep subscript is dropped and the following notations are introduced:

$$[\omega_{Si}]_\times [\omega_{Si}]_\times := W_S =$$

$$\begin{bmatrix} -(\omega_{Sz}{}^2 + \omega_{Sy}{}^2) & \omega_{Sx}\omega_{Sy} & \omega_{Sx}\omega_{Sz} \\ \omega_{Sx}\omega_{Sy} & -(\omega_{Sz}{}^2 + \omega_{Sx}{}^2) & \omega_{Sz}\omega_{Sy} \\ \omega_{Sx}\omega_{Sz} & \omega_{Sz}\omega_{Sy} & -(\omega_{Sy}{}^2 + \omega_{Sx}{}^2) \end{bmatrix} \quad (8a)$$

$$-\frac{\tilde{a}_{Si}^T}{\|\tilde{a}_{Si}\|} := [\hat{a}_{Sx}, \hat{a}_{Sy}, \hat{a}_{Sz}]^T. \quad (8b)$$

By substituting (8) in (7), we obtain:

$$\frac{\partial e_{mi}}{\partial l_{mS}} = [C_{A1}, C_{A2}, C_{A3}, C_{B1}, C_{B2}, C_{B3}], \quad (9)$$

where

$$C_{S1} = \hat{a}_{Sx} W_{S11} + \hat{a}_{Sy}(W_{S12} + \alpha_{Sz}) + \hat{a}_{Sz}(W_{S13} - \alpha_{Sy}) \quad (10a)$$

$$C_{S2} = \hat{a}_{Sx}(W_{S21} - \alpha_{Sz}) + \hat{a}_{Sy} W_{S22} + \hat{a}_{Sz}(W_{S23} + \alpha_{Sx}) \quad (10b)$$

$$C_{S3} = \hat{a}_{Sx}(W_{S31} + \alpha_y) + \hat{a}_{Sy}(W_{S32} - \alpha_x) + \hat{a}_{Sz}(W_{S33}) \quad (10c)$$

with

$$S \in \{A, B\}$$

and $W_{Spq}, p, q \in \{1, 2, 3\}$ refers to the components of W_S.

Now, in order to analyze the observability of (3), one can examine the situations, where the components in (9) are dependent. Considering each IMU (the respective blocks of J_h) separately, two cases leading to rank deficiency are:

1. When there is no rotation in at least two DOFs. For instance, assume $\omega_{Sx} = \omega_{Sy} = 0$ for a sequence of measurements, and consequently $\alpha_{Sx} = \alpha_{Sy} = 0$, which results in $C_{S3} = 0$. Then, the third column in the respective block and (measurement) rows of J_h equals zero, which reduces the rank. This is the case for the knee joint, since the dominant rotation is flexion/extension, i.e. only in one DOF.
2. When rotation appears with the same angular velocity in three DOFs for a sequence of measurements. In this situation $\omega_{Sx} = \omega_{Sy} = \omega_{Sz}$ in (10), which results in $\alpha_{Sx} = \alpha_{Sy} = \alpha_{Sz}$. By substituting these equalities, the columns in (9) are related by $C_{S1} + C_{S2} + C_{S3} = 0$.
3. Additionally, when considering both IMUs, from (9), another case leading to rank deficiency is, when two IMUs rotate with the same angular velocities in all DOFs for a sequence of measurements.

In the case of the hip joint, due to the limited movements of the pelvis, it is in fact difficult to perform movements with sufficient but different angular velocities in all the DOFs of the pelvis. Additionally, as it is discussed e.g. in [6], pelvis rotations are in-phase with upper leg swings during relatively high velocities. Such movements are typical movements performed in the calibration phase, as it was visible in our experiments. Thus, it is difficult to avoid situations (2) and (3). Note that the movements on the two segments related to a joint should be simultaneous, since otherwise situation (1) occurs.

As indicated in Section 1, Seel et al. propose a correction of the estimated positions of two IMUs B and C in the degenerate case (1) of a hinge joint n (cf. Figure 2) [20]. In this case, every point on the hinge joint axis r_n is a solution of (4). The correction of the estimated vectors, $l_{nS}, S \in \{B, C\}$ corresponds to a shift of the joint center, n, on the known joint rotation axes, $r_{nS}, S \in B, C$, as being represented in the coordinate frames of both IMUs. The shift computation is based on the assumption that the true joint center is the point on the joint axis that is closest to both IMUs. This can be formalized as:

$${}^S e_{nCoR} = \frac{1}{2}(r_{nB}^T \cdot l_{nB} + r_{nC}^T \cdot l_{nC}) r_{nS}, \;\; S \in \{B, C\}, \quad (11)$$

where ${}^S e_{nCoR}$ denotes the shift of the joint Center of Rotation (CoR) represented in the local coordinate frame of S. The latter is indicated by the left superscript. Moreover, $r_{nS}, S \in B, C$ are assumed known through calibration [20]. The corrected IMU positions are then:

$$l'_{nB} = l_{nB} - {}^B e_{nCoR}, \;\; l'_{nC} = l_{nC} - {}^C e_{nCoR}. \quad (12)$$

The above correction method has been included in the experimental evaluation in Section 5.

4. PROPOSED METHOD

The previous section describes different cases of movements, which can lead to inaccurate results when applying the IMU position calibration method of [20] to the hip and knee joint, which is considered in our work. Therefore, this section proposes a novel method, which improves upon the existing one through the following extensions: The estimation of the positions $x = [x_m, x_n]^T$ of the three IMUs $S \in \{A, B, C\}$ (on pelvis, upper leg, lower leg) with respect to the two joints m, n (hip, knee) (cf. Figure 2), from the IMU measurements $z = [z_m, z_n]^T$ is modeled jointly in one optimization problem analogously to (3), but with a new measurement model, which is introduced in the following.

4.1 Proposed measurement model

First, instead of considering only the lengths of the acceleration vectors in (4), the proposed, stochastic measurement model incorporates the relative orientations of the IMUs, leading to:

$$0 = \tilde{a}_{Ai} + R_{ABi}\tilde{a}_{Bi} + e_{mi} \quad (13a)$$

$$0 = \tilde{a}_{Ci} + R_{CBi}\tilde{a}_{Bi} + e_{ni}, \quad (13b)$$

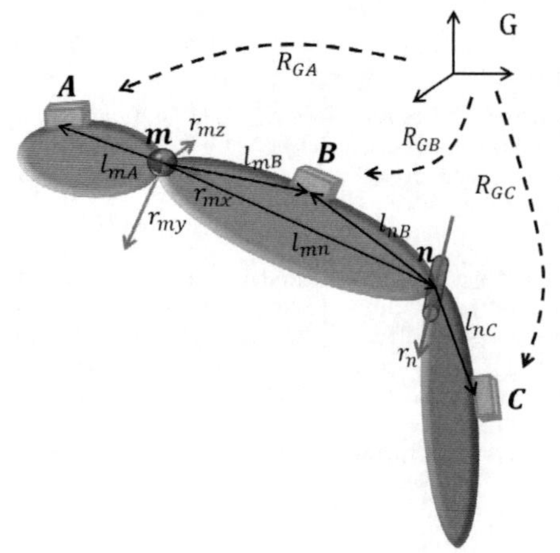

Figure 2: Illustration of the IMU position estimation problem specifically addressing the lower body. The spheroidal joint n refers to the hip (three rotation axes: r_{mx}, r_{my}, and r_{mz}), and the hinge joint n refers to the knee (one rotation axis: r_n). The two joints are linked via the upper leg segment, with a fixed length of l_{mn}. The IMUs A, B, C are mounted on the segments connected through the hip and knee joints. They are placed on the pelvis, upper leg, and lower leg, respectively. The quantities $l_{mA}, l_{mB}, l_{nB}, l_{nC}$ are the IMU position vectors to be estimated. R_{GA}, R_{GB}, R_{GC} are the orientations of the IMUs with respect to the global coordinate frame G.

where $[e_{mi}, e_{ni}]^T \sim N(0, \Sigma)$ and the relative rotation R_{YX} from X to Y can be obtained as $R_{YX} = R_{GY}^T R_{GX}$. Here, $R_{SG}, S \in \{X, Y\}$ is the orientation of IMU S with respect to a fixed global frame G, which is typically aligned with gravity and magnetic north. The global orientations can be estimated from the IMU measurements using a standard sensor fusion technique, e.g. [9]. A respective implementation is typically provided with commercially available integrated IMU sensor packages, such as the ones integrated in the smart training pants [18].

4.2 Constraints of three connected segments

We consider the hip and knee jointly in one optimization problem. This allows us to extend the measurement models in (13) with additional constraints modeling the fact that these joints, m, n in Figure 2, are linked via the upper leg segment l_{mn}.

We assume the flexion/extension joint axes of the hip and knee, r_{my} and r_n, as being approximately coplanar. In Figure 3 (left), the geometry is illustrated for an ideal coplanar case with intersecting axes, where the latter span the plane P_1 with normal vector n_{P1}. Furthermore, l_{mB} and l_{nB} are by definition coplanar, spanning the plane P_2 with normal vector n_{P2}. Assuming that r_{my} and r_n are not parallel, the normal vectors can be obtained using cross products:

$$n_{P1} = r_{my} \times r_n \tag{14a}$$

$$n_{P2} = l_{mB} \times l_{nB}. \tag{14b}$$

As is visible in the figure, in the ideal case, P_1 and P_2 intersect at a line $l_{P12} := n_{P1} \times n_{P2}$, which is parallel to $l_{mn} = l_{mB} - l_{nB}$. Moreover, n_{P1}, which is perpendicular to l_{P12}, is also perpendicular to l_{mn}. These facts can be formalized leading to the following constraints:

$$0 = (l_{mn} \times l_{P12}) + e_{mn1} \tag{15a}$$

$$0 = (n_{P1}^T \cdot l_{mn}) + e_{mn2}, \tag{15b}$$

where e_{mn1} and e_{mn1} account for the fact that the assumed coplanarity of r_{my}, r_n and l_{mn} is an approximation (cf. Figure 3).

Note, when combining (13) with (15), the respective Jacobian for one timestep i is:

$$J_{hi} = \begin{bmatrix} \frac{\partial e_{mi}}{\partial l_{mA}} & \frac{\partial e_{mi}}{\partial l_{mB}} & 0_{3\times3} & 0_{3\times3} \\ 0_{3\times3} & 0_{3\times3} & \frac{\partial e_{ni}}{\partial l_{nB}} & \frac{\partial e_{ni}}{\partial l_{nC}} \\ 0_{3\times3} & \frac{\partial e_{mn1i}}{\partial l_{mB}} & \frac{\partial e_{mn1i}}{\partial l_{nB}} & 0_{3\times3} \\ 0_{1\times3} & \frac{\partial e_{mn2i}}{\partial l_{mB}} & \frac{\partial e_{mn2i}}{\partial l_{nB}} & 0_{1\times3} \end{bmatrix} \tag{16a}$$

where

$$\frac{\partial e_{mn1i}}{\partial l_{mB}} = [l_{P12}]_\times^T + l_{mn} \times ([l_{nB}]_\times^T n_{P2}), \tag{16b}$$

$$\frac{\partial e_{mn1i}}{\partial l_{nB}} = -[l_{P12}]_\times^T + l_{mn} \times ([l_{mB}]_\times^T n_{P2}),, \tag{16c}$$

$$\frac{\partial e_{mn2i}}{\partial l_{mB}} = n_{P1}, \tag{16d}$$

$$\frac{\partial e_{mn2i}}{\partial l_{nB}} = -n_{P1} \tag{16e}$$

and $\frac{\partial e_{ni}}{\partial l_{nS}}$ is computed similarly to (7). When considering the second and third block of J_{hi}, it can be seen that the rank is not only depending on the angular velocities but also on the relative position vectors, as well as, the joint rotation axes. This gives a more complex expression, which is difficult to simplify. The rank of the first and last three columns can still be reduced as discussed in Section 3. However, by incorporating the constraint on l_{mB}, the error e_{mi} as well as the estimation error of l_{mA} are assumed to be reduced

5. EXPERIMENTAL RESULTS

The different IMU position calibration methods (Seel et al. and proposed) were first evaluated using noisy synthetic measurements simulated at 100 Hz for a setup as illustrated in Figure 2. In order to provide sufficient variations of the input data for the optimization problem, the measurements were downsampled to 10 Hz. The simulator output comprises 3D accelerometer, gyroscope and magnetometer measurements, as well as, the global orientations of each segment with respect to a fixed reference frame G. These values are calculated based on the inputs to the simulator, which include joint angles (generated from sine functions with different scales in each DOF), IMU to body poses, and also measurement noise specifications comparable to those of the IMUs used in the real data tests below.

In order to evaluate the accuracy and robustness of the different methods for different types of movements, two sets of joint angle sequences were simulated, each with 100 randomly generated IMU to body poses: Type 1 provides low variations among the DOFs of each segment, whereas the knee joint is modeled with one DOF. This resembles a natural calibration movement. Type 2 provides high variations among the DOFs and, in addition, models both joints with three DOFs. Hence, the type 1 set provides more realistic but suboptimal movement conditions, whereas the type 2 set is expected to work well with both calibration methods.

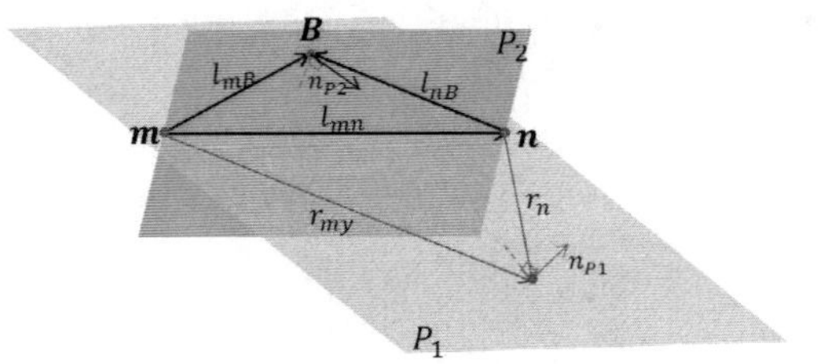

(a) Idealized geometry with intersecting joint axes at hip and knee.

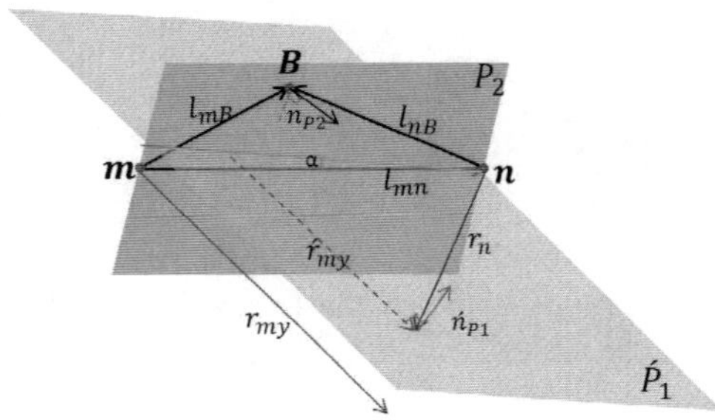

(b) Realistic geometry with skew joint axes.

Figure 3: Illustration of the constraints formulated in (15): The left figure shows the idealized geometry, which is the basis for the constraints. It approximates the more realistic setup in the right figure with skew joint axes, leading to the plane $\acute{P}1$. The latter can be assumed to have a small angle α with respect to the ideal plane $P1$.

rad/s	Type 1 [12, 13, 23]	Type 2 [12, 13, 23]	Real [12, 13, 23]
A	[0.56, 0.51, 0.13]	[3.45, 5.43, 1.67]	[0.45, 0.31, 0.57]
B	[0.8, 0.53, 2.6]	[3.62, 6.05, 7.29]	[1.56, 1.41, 1.03]
C	[3.18, 1.56, 3.7]	[7.89, 10.94, 13.38]	[2.15, 3.6, 2.9]

Table 1: The angular velocity variations for the simulated and the real IMU measurements: 12 represents the variation between the first and the second DOF for each IMU A, B, C. Each number expresses the mean of squared differences between the simulated/measured angular velocities for all the timesteps.

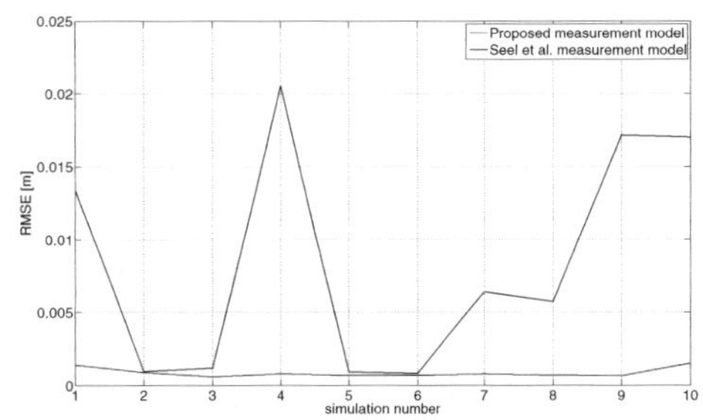

Figure 4: RMSE for 10 different IMU mounting orientations when applying the measurement model defined in (13) to type 2 movements.

In order to extract the joint rotation axes required in (14), an extra phase of movements has been added in which each segment rotates in all possible DOFs separately. More details about the simulated joint trajectories in terms of resulting angular velocity variations are provided in Table 1.

Our proposed method, as well as, the methods of Seel et al. were implemented in Matlab using *lsqnonlin* with the Levenberg-Marquardt algorithm. In the following, the behavior of these methods are evaluated through several experiments.

The effect of only introducing the relative IMU orientations as formalized in Equation (13) without coupling the two estimation problems is illustrated in Figure 4, where the Root Mean Squared Error (RMSE) for the estimated IMU positions is provided for 10 different mounting orientations using type 2 trajectories. This shows already an improvement of the proposed method with respect to accuracy and robustness under optimal movement conditions.

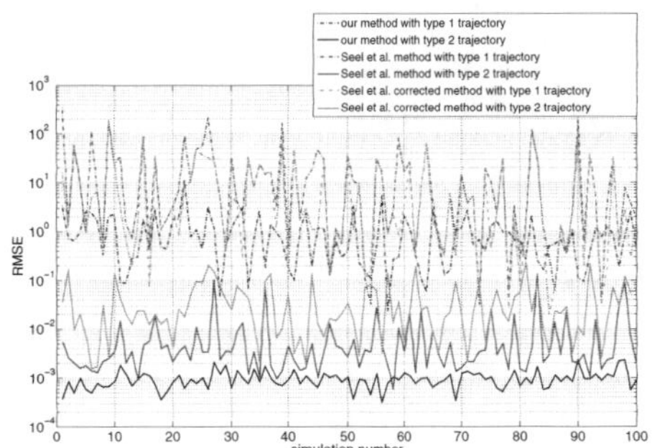

Figure 5: RMSE for 100 different IMU to body configurations when using the measurement model defined in (13) and the additional constraint in (15).

Figure 5 illustrates the RMSE when applying the different calibration methods to the two different types of movements. Here, our method includes also the constraint introduced in Section 4.2. The results show that higher movement variations during calibration improve the performance of both algorithms. However, with less variations our proposed method outperforms the ones of Seel et al.. This counts for both the original method in [21] and the correction described in Equation (12) [20].

Moreover, the convergence of both calibration methods was tested

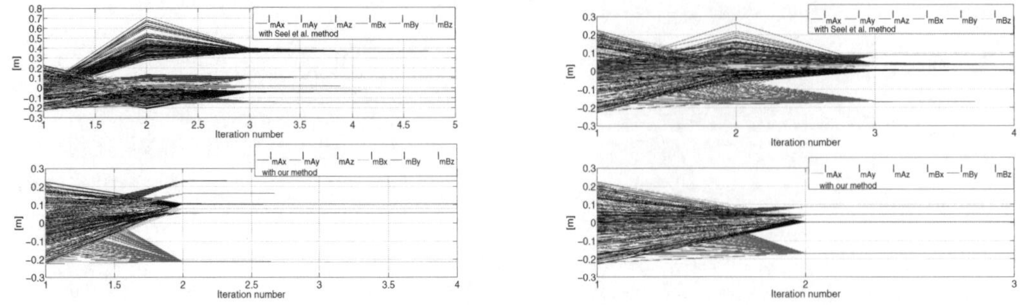

(a) Type 1 trajectory

(b) Type 2 trajectory

Figure 6: Convergence test with 100 random initial values for the IMU position. In this test the true value of l_{mA} is $[0.05, 0.09, 0.03]$ and the true value of l_{mB} is $[-0.17, 0.004, 0.03]$.

using 100 random initial values. Figure 6 presents the results of this test for measurements simulated from one IMU to body configuration. This shows that the two methods are not generally sensitive to the initial values. Nevertheless, for type 2 trajectories, both methods converge to similar results, with less than 1 cm error. However, our proposed method converges faster. With suboptimal type 1 trajectories, both methods require a higher number of iterations; however, the method of Seel et al. converges with a large error of 61 cm, while our proposed method converges with only 3 cm error.

In order to evaluate the proposed method on real measurements, we captured a dataset of 10 trials performed by one subject using a prototype wearable system [18] and an optical reference system [3]. The test setup is shown in Figure 7. In order to obtain the IMU poses, each IMU was rigidly connected with a rigid body marker. The IMUs were interconnected via textile cables and fixed to the garment using snap buttons. In order to reduce artifacts due to movement of the garment, the IMU-marker-sets were strapped firmly on the pelvis and the legs. We also used straps in order to attach marker clusters on anatomical landmarks around the hip and knee joints, from which we determined the joint CoRs. In each trial, for deducing the joint rotation axes, the subject first performed movements in each DOF of each joint separately. Then, in order to test the proposed IMU position calibration algorithm, arbitrary movements were performed simultaneously for the different segments. The resulting angular velocity variations are included in Table 1, showing that the real data corresponds to simulated type 1 movements. The global IMU orientations required in Equation (13) were calculated based on the method described in [17]. The estimated IMU position vectors were then compared with the references calculated from the optical markers. Note that errors due to marker positioning are present, however, similarly for all the tested methods. Figure 8 illustrates the RMSE when applying the different calibration methods to the real measurements. The proposed method provides more accurate or comparable results in 80 percent of the trials, while a slightly worse performance can be observed in two of the trials. The difference between the performance of the proposed method on the simulated data and the real data can be described by two factors: First, due to magnetic disturbances, the orientation estimation of the real data is erroneous. Second, the position errors for the real data are obtained by comparing the lengths of the estimated vectors and not comparing component-by-component as for the simulated data. This was mainly due to the

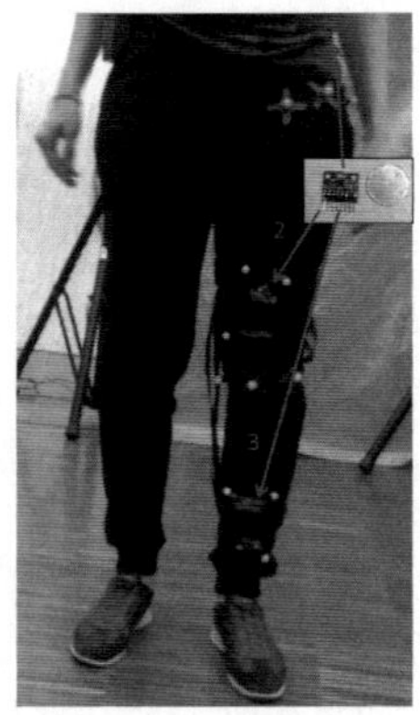

Figure 7: Real test setup. The red arrows show three IMUs which are mounted on pelvis (1, not visible), upper leg (2) and lower leg (3).

inaccuracies in finding the joint coordinates from the optical markers. A deeper analysis of the failure cases and further investigations with a higher number of subjects are required in order to draw final conclusions.

6. CONCLUSION

In this work we presented a practical IMU to body position autocalibration method, specifically developed for the lower body. The method can be used for smart training pants with multiple embedded IMUs, e.g. for application in exercise and fitness monitoring. On simulated data, the presented method shows a clear improvement in terms of accuracy and robustness compared to a previous method, in particular when it comes to suboptimal (low variation) movements during calibration. This has also been confirmed through preliminary tests with real data, though further experiments are required as part of our future work.

Another route of future work relates to the fact that the proposed method uses the global IMU orientations, which are currently estimated separately and are considered as inputs to the position calibration. Here, the results might be improved by adding, as a final step, a joint optimization of the time-varying global IMU orien-

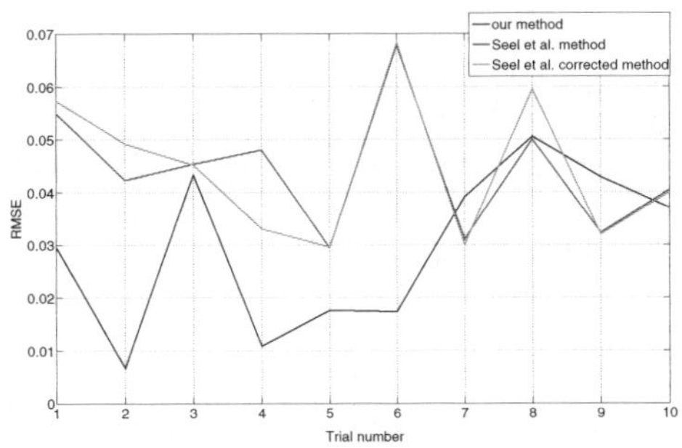

Figure 8: Results on real measurements: RMSE for one IMU to body configuration and 10 trials performed by one subject.

tations and the quasi-constant IMU positions with respect to the adjacent segments.
Moreover, using a weighted least squares estimate, the presented method could be extended to provide uncertainty measures for the estimated calibration parameters of the different IMUs, which could then be used during tracking in order to improve the results. Here, varying uncertainties could account not only for different types of movements during calibration, but also e.g. for varying amounts of garment movements or other soft tissue artifacts due to different suit material and style, or different body shapes.

7. ACKNOWLEDGEMENTS

The authors would like to thank Markus Miezal for providing the IMU simulator code.

8. REFERENCES

[1] Fitbit. `http://www.fitbit.com/uk/surge`.

[2] Jawbone upmove. `https://jawbone.com/store/buy/upmove`.

[3] Naturalpoint optitrack. `http://www.optitrack.com/products/flex-13/`.

[4] Xsens MVN. `https://www.xsens.com/products/xsens-mvn/`.

[5] G. Bleser, D. Steffen, A. Reiss, M. Weber, G. Hendeby, and L. Fradet. Personalized physical activity monitoring using wearable sensors. *Smart Health - Open Problems and Future Challenges*, pages 99–124, 2015.

[6] S. M. Bruijn, O. G. Meijer, J. H. Van Dieen, I. Kingma, and C. J. Lamoth. Coordination of leg swing, thorax rotations, and pelvis rotations during gait: the organisation of total body angular momentum. *Gait & posture*, 27(3):455–462, 2008.

[7] P. Cheng and B. Oelmann. Joint-angle measurement using accelerometers and gyroscopes, a survey. *Instrumentation and Measurement, IEEE Transactions on*, 59(2):404–414, 2010.

[8] J. Favre, R. Aissaoui, B. Jolles, J. De Guise, and K. Aminian. Functional calibration procedure for 3d knee joint angle description using inertial sensors. *Journal of biomechanics*, 42(14):2330–2335, 2009.

[9] T. Harada, T. Mori, and T. Sato. Development of a tiny orientation estimation device to operate under motion and magnetic disturbance. *The International Journal of Robotics Research*, 26(6):547–559, 2007.

[10] M. Kok, J. D. Hol, and T. B. Schön. An optimization-based approach to human body motion capture using inertial sensors. In *Proceedings of the 19th IFAC World Congress, 2014*, pages 79–85. International Federation of Automatic Control, 2014.

[11] H. Luinge, D. Roetenberg, and P. Slycke. Inertial sensor kinematic coupling, Feb. 3 2011. US Patent App. 12/534,526.

[12] M. Miezal, G. Bleser, N. Schmitz, and D. Stricker. A generic approach to inertial tracking of arbitrary kinematic chains. In *International Conference on Body Area Networks (Bodynets)*, Boston, Massachusetts, USA, 2013.

[13] R. Nerino, L. Contin, W. da Silva Pinto, G. Massazza, M. Actis, P. Capacchione, A. Chimienti, and G. Pettiti. A bsn based service for post-surgical knee rehabilitation at home. In *International Conference on Body Area Networks (Bodynets)*, pages 401–407. ICST (Institute for Computer Sciences, Social-Informatics and Telecommunications Engineering), 2013.

[14] K. J. O Donovan, R. Kamnik, D. T. O Keeffe, and G. M. Lyons. An inertial and magnetic sensor based technique for joint angle measurement. *Journal of Biomechanics*, 40(12):2604–2611, 2007.

[15] E. Palermo, S. Rossi, F. Marini, F. Patanè, and P. Cappa. Experimental evaluation of accuracy and repeatability of a novel body-to-sensor calibration procedure for inertial sensor-based gait analysis. *Measurement*, 52:145–155, 2014.

[16] A. Reiss, G. Hendeby, G. Bleser, and D. Stricker. Activity recognition using biomechanical model based pose estimation. In *Proceedings of 5th European Conference on Smart Sensing and Context (EuroSSC)*, 2010.

[17] S. Salehi, G. Bleser, N. Schmitz, and D. Stricker. A low-cost and light-weight motion tracking suit. In *International Conference on Ubiquitous Intelligence and Computing (UIC)*, pages 474–479, Vietri sul Mare, Italy, December 2013. IEEE.

[18] S. Salehi, G. Bleser, and D. Stricker. Design and development of low-cost smart training pants (stants). In *International Conference on Wireless Mobile Communication and Healthcare*, pages 51–54, 2014.

[19] B. J. Schoenfeld. Sqatting kinematics and kinetics and their application to exercise performance. *Journal of Strength and Conditioning Research*, 24(12), December 2010.

[20] T. Seel, J. Raisch, and T. Schauer. Imu-based joint angle measurement for gait analysis. *Sensors*, 14(4):6891–6909, 2014.

[21] T. Seel, T. Schauer, and J. Raisch. Joint axis and position estimation from inertial measurement data by exploiting kinematic constraints. In *Control Applications (CCA), 2012 IEEE International Conference on*, pages 45–49. IEEE, 2012.

[22] Z. Wang and G. Dissanayake. Observability analysis of slam using fisher information matrix. In *Control, Automation, Robotics and Vision, 2008. ICARCV 2008. 10th International Conference on*, pages 1242–1247. IEEE, 2008.

[23] A. Zinnen, U. Blanke, and B. Schiele. An analysis of sensor-oriented vs. model-based activity recognition. In *Proceedings of 13th Annual IEEE International Symposium on Wearable Computers (ISWC)*, pages 93–100, 2009.

[24] J. Zumer, J. Slavic, and M. Boltezar. Minimization of the positional errors for an accurate determination of the kinematic parameters of a rigid-body system with miniature inertial sensors. *Mechanism and Machine Theory*, 2014.

Toward Detection and Monitoring of Gait Pathology using Inertial Sensors under Rotation, Scale, and Offset Invariant Dynamic Time Warping

Matthew M Engelhard
Department of Systems and Information Engineering
Center for Wireless Health
University of Virginia
Charlottesville, VA, USA
mme@virginia.edu

Sriram Raju Dandu
Department of Electrical and Computer Engineering
Center for Wireless Health
University of Virginia
Charlottesville, VA, USA
sd9aj@virginia.edu

John C Lach
Department of Electrical and Computer Engineering
Center for Wireless Health
University of Virginia
Charlottesville, VA, USA
jlach@virginia.edu

Myla D Goldman
James Q. Miller MS Clinic
Department of Neurology
Center for Wireless Health
University of Virginia
Charlottesville, VA, USA
mdg3n@virginia.edu

Stephen D Patek
Department of Systems and Information Engineering
Center for Wireless Health
University of Virginia
Charlottesville, VA, USA
patek@virginia.edu

ABSTRACT

Walking ability can be degraded by a number of pathologies, including movement disorders, stroke, and injury. Personal activity tracking devices gather inertial data needed to measure walking quality, but the required algorithmic methods are an active area of study. To detect changes in walking ability, the similarity between a person's current gait cycles and their known baseline gait cycles may be measured on an ongoing basis. This strategy requires a similarity measure robust to variability encountered in an outpatient scenario, including changes in walking surface, walking speed, and sensor orientation. Here we propose rotation, scale, and offset invariant dynamic time warping (RSOI-DTW), a variant of the well-known dynamic time warping (DTW) algorithm, as a generalization of DTW appropriate for three-dimensional inertial data. RSOI-DTW is invariant under rotation, scaling, and offset, yet it preserves the salient features of gait cycles required for gait monitoring. To support this claim, gait cycles from 21 subjects walking with four different styles were compared using both DTW and RSOI-DTW. The data show that RSOI-DTW converges quickly and achieves rotation, scale, and offset invariance. Both algorithms distinguish persons and detect abnormal walking, but only RSOI-DTW does so in the presence of sensor rotation. Variations in walking speed pose a challenge for both algorithms, but performance is improved by collecting baseline information at a variety of speeds.

BODYNETS 2015, September 28-30, Sydney, Australia

DOI 10.4108/eai.28-9-2015.2261503

Categories and Subject Descriptors

I.5.3 [**Pattern Recognition**]: Clustering—*similarity measures*

General Terms

Algorithms, Experimentation, Human Factors, Measurement

Keywords

Inertial body sensors, Gait assessment, Gait recognition, Dynamic time warping

1. INTRODUCTION

Movement disorders, stroke, traumatic injury, and other pathologies can degrade walking ability. A patient's walking quality can be monitored by a care provider to guide treatment decisions, measure the effectiveness of interventions, or provide prognostic information to the patient. While personal activity tracking devices make it easy to measure the quantity of a person's walking, they are not yet equipped to measure and monitor its quality over time.

The pathology detection and monitoring problem is challenging because of heterogeneity among persons, pathologies, and devices. What is abnormal in one person might be typical in another, and two different pathologies – say, hemiparesis and Parkinsonian gait – may have little in common. Further, each personal tracking device has its own unique combination of sensors, placement location(s) on the body, and attachment method(s). If inertial signal features are used to monitor walking quality, this heterogeneity must be considered carefully: the features important in one scenario may not be important in others.

To overcome these difficulties, monitoring can be based on a similarity measure, not extracted features. In a similarity measure based strategy, rather than learning the unique set of features important for each combination of persons, pathologies, and devices, a monitoring algorithm can instead observe a person's walking at baseline, then monitor its similarity to current walking patterns as time goes on. No prior information about pathology is needed, and a person's unique walking characteristics are not a hindrance.

In rehabilitation following stroke or trauma, similarity to baseline should return as walking ability is recovered. In chronic, progressive disease – including multiple sclerosis, the focus of our clinical research – the similarity to baseline can be quantified on an ongoing basis, and new baselines can be established to detect further degradation. Current walking is compared only to baseline measurements from the same person using the same device, so observed differences may be attributed primarily to changing walking patterns.

Patients would routinely complete a self-initiated walking test at home, wearing a personal activity tracking device or smartphone able to record inertial data. Gait cycles would be compared to baseline cycles using an appropriate similarity measure. For this purpose, we propose rotation, scale, and offset invariant dynamic time warping (RSOI-DTW), a variant of the well-known dynamic time warping (DTW) algorithm. We first establish the theoretical properties of RSOI-DTW, then explore the suitability of DTW and RSOI-DTW for pathology detection and monitoring using data gathered from a walking test with 21 healthy participants.

After a brief literature review, Section 3 describes the walking test and DTW algorithm, then introduces the RSOI-DTW algorithm. Section 4 gives results from the walking test, including evidence that RSOI-DTW (1) converges quickly; (2) achieves RSO invariance in practice; (3) retains the ability to distinguish persons despite its flexibility in matching sequences; and (4) identifies simulated pathology, warranting a trial with true pathology. The last portion of Section 4 revisits these results in the presence of fast walking, highlighting the challenge posed by varying gait speed.

2. RELATED WORK

2.1 Inertial Data Processing

DTW has been used successfully for activity recognition [10] and biometric gait recognition [4][9][11][13], and several variants have been proposed. Scale and offset invariant DTW, in which one sequence can be scaled or shifted to improve similarity, has been developed by several authors, notably Chen et al., who evaluated an iterative algorithm similar to ours on a number of time series data sets [2]. When analyzing gait, scale and offset invariance may mitigate variability due to walking surface, shoe type, attachment method, and moderate changes in speed.

In addition to scale and offset invariance, RSOI-DTW incorporates rotation invariance, allowing it to match gait cycles regardless of device orientation. This is a necessity in a real world, self-testing scenario, because a particular orientation cannot be assumed. A rotation invariant DTW algorithm was used by Qiao and Yasuhara to analyze two-dimensional handwriting samples [12], and Bours et al. devised a rotation invariant algorithm based upon principal component analysis [1]. To our knowledge, no iterative, rotation invariant DTW variant appropriate for three-dimensional inertial data had been developed and tested prior to the current work.

However, a number of methods for inertial data processing not based on DTW have incorporated rotation invariance. Chien et al. corrected sensor orientation as part of model-based classification of upper limb movements and walking activities [3]. Recently, Gong et al. created a linear dynamical model based method for activity classification that is robust to sensor mounting errors, including rotation [6].

2.2 Device Based Disability Monitoring

Inertial devices have been used for disability monitoring in many different contexts. The ISway test developed by Mancini et al. uses an accelerometer to measure postural sway resulting from neurological impairment [8]. Salarian et al. created the iTug system, which uses inertial sensors to partly automate the Timed Up and Go test, a clinical measure of balance and mobility [15]. Spain et al. captured differences between multiple sclerosis subjects grouped by disability level using features derived from inertial sensors, but could not detect changes in those features over time [16]. Many studies have used daily step counts derived from inertial sensors as an outcome measure, but comparatively few have assessed features intrinsic to individual gait cycles.

3. METHODS

3.1 Data Collection and Segmentation

21 subjects participated in the walking trial. Subjects wore a single ActiGraph accelerometer on their left hip, secured using an elastic belt with a pouch for the device. All subjects wore the same device. Each subject was asked to walk down a long corridor four times to demonstrate four different styles of gait: casual walking, fast walking, ataxic walking, and right leg circumduction. Ataxic walking is seen in persons with balance difficulties, characterized by a wide base and lateral swaying. Circumduction is the outward, circular swinging of one leg in swing phase; it occurs when the leg is rigid or spastic at the knee and/or ankle joint.

Subjects walked with each style in one direction for 40 steps, then turned, paused five seconds, and walked back with the next style. Each style was demonstrated before the trial by a clinically trained research assistant, and subjects were given an opportunity to practice until comfortable.

To experimentally verify the rotation invariance of RSOI-DTW, three subjects completed a second trial where they walked casually each time, but sensor orientation was changed.

The data was manually divided by person and walking style and segmented into gait cycles, defined as the data between consecutive left heel strikes. There are prominent peaks in the acclerometer signal at the point of heel strike in all walking styles, making the heel strikes easy to identify. Subsequent processing using DTW and RSOI-DTW exploits these gait cycles.

3.2 Dynamic Time Warping

Individual gait cycles were compared using DTW and RSOI-DTW, the variant of DTW described in the next section. Here we offer a brief, formal description of DTW. A more comprehensive treatment may be found in [7].

The DTW algorithm takes two sequences $X = (x_1, ..., x_m)$ and $Y = (y_1, ..., y_n)$ as inputs and returns a measure of similarity d_{DTW}, often called the DTW distance, between them. In this work, the x_i and y_i are three dimensional acceleration vectors. Our implementation of DTW also returns warped sequences X_W and Y_W derived from X and Y by (possibly) repeating terms to improve alignment. More precisely,

$X_W = ((x_1)^{a_1}, ..., (x_m)^{a_m})$ and $Y_W = ((y_1)^{b_1}, ..., (y_n)^{b_n})$, where $(\cdot)^k$ denotes k repetitions of a term, and the a_j and b_j are positive integers found by the algorithm. Using this notation, the DTW distance d_{DTW} is the squared Euclidean distance between X_W and Y_W, defined as follows:

DEFINITION 1. *Given sequences $A = (a_1, ..., a_N)$ and $B = (b_1, ..., b_N)$, the squared Euclidean distance between A and B is:*

$$d(A, B) = \sum_{i=1}^{N} \|a_i - b_i\|^2 \quad (1)$$

where $\|\cdot\|$ is the usual Euclidean norm.

To compute d_{DTW}, X_W, and Y_W, we first construct an $(m \times n)$ matrix D, where $D_{(i,j)} = \|x_i - y_j\|^2$. Intuitively, we then find the minimum cost path through D from $D_{(1,1)}$ to $D_{(m,n)}$ subject to a path constraint. Letting w_k be the kth element of a warping path W – a possible path through D – we constrain W to allow only three moves: repeat the current point in X, repeat the current point in Y, or move to the next point in both. Formally, if $w_k = (i_k, j_k)$, then $w_{k+1} \in \{(i_k+1, j_k), (i_k+1, j_k+1), (i_k, j_k+1)\}$. The optimal path from (i, j) to (m, n) and its cost $C_{(i,j)}$ are computed using dynamic programming, where $C_{(m,n)} = D_{(m,n)}$, and the remaining $C_{(i,j)}$ are given by the following recursion:

$$C_{(i,j)} = D_{(i,j)} + min\{C_{(i+1,j)}, C_{(i+1,j+1)}, C_{(i,j+1)}\} \quad (2)$$

This recursion may be carried out row-wise or column-wise, with $C_{(i,j)} = \infty$ for $i > m$ or $j > n$. The final DTW distance is $C_{(1,1)}$, and the warping path W along with the warped sequences X_W and Y_W may be recovered from C.

In this work, we have resampled Y to be the same length as X and limited the warping path to the Sakoe-Chiba band [14] to reduce computation, so that $C_{(i,j)} = \infty$ whenever $|j - i|$ is greater than one fourth the length of X.

3.3 Rotation, Scale, and Offset Invariant DTW

RSOI-DTW is an iterative algorithm that alternates between optimizing the rotation, scaling, and offset of the sequence Y, and optimizing the warping path using DTW. The former is an instance of the Procrustes problem, which may be solved in closed form using singular value decomposition. The details of this problem are beyond the current scope, but may be found in [5].

In this application, the rotation matrices must be limited to $SO(3)$, the (3×3) orthogonal matrices of determinant 1. $SO(3)$ are the rigid rotations in $\mathbb{R}^3$, excluding reflection; they correspond with the rotations possible for a rigid physical object. These matrices form a group under multiplication: in particular, they are invertible, and the inverses and products of rigid rotations are also rigid rotations.

This section first defines the transformations allowed in RSOI-DTW – the RSO transformations – then provides the RSOI-DTW algorithm. Finally, it proves that RSOI-DTW is rotation, scale, and offset invariant under typical circumstances, and the algorithm is guaranteed to terminate.

DEFINITION 2. *An RSO transformation is an affine transformation $f : \mathbb{R}^3 \to \mathbb{R}^3$ of the form $f(x) = sRx + b$, where $s \in \mathbb{R}^+, R \in SO(3)$, and $b \in \mathbb{R}^3$.*

PROPOSITION 1. *The RSO transformations are closed under composition and inverse, thus forming a subgroup of the affine group.*

PROOF. Let $f_\alpha(x) = s_\alpha R_\alpha x + b_\alpha$, and $f_\beta(x) = s_\beta R_\beta x + b_\beta$. The inverse of f_α is given by $(f_\alpha)^{-1}(x) = \frac{1}{s_\alpha}(R_\alpha)^{-1}x - \frac{1}{s_\alpha}(R_\alpha)^{-1}b_\alpha$. By inspection, $\frac{1}{s_\alpha} \in \mathbb{R}^+$ and $-\frac{1}{s_\alpha}(R_\alpha)^{-1}b_\alpha \in \mathbb{R}^3$, and $(R_\alpha)^{-1} \in SO(3)$ because $SO(3)$ is closed under inverse. So, the RSO transformations are closed under inverse.

The composition of f_α and f_β is given by $(f_\alpha \circ f_\beta)(x) = (s_\alpha s_\beta)(R_\alpha R_\beta)x + (s_\alpha R_\alpha b_\beta + b_\alpha)$. As before, we note that $s_\alpha s_\beta \in \mathbb{R}^+$ and $(s_\alpha R_\alpha b_\beta + b_\alpha) \in \mathbb{R}^3$; and the closure of $SO(3)$ under composition guarantees that $R_\alpha R_\beta \in SO(3)$. Thus the RSO transformations are closed under composition. □

DEFINITION 3. *Given an RSO transformation f and a sequence $X = (x_1, ..., x_n)$, where $x_i \in \mathbb{R}^3$ $\forall i$, the sequence $f(X)$ is defined to be $(f(x_1), ..., f(x_n))$.*

With this background in place, we now present the RSOI-DTW algorithm:

ALGORITHM 1. *Rotation, Scale, and Offset Invariant DTW*

```
procedure RSOI-DTW(X, Y)
    X_W ← X
    Y_W ← Y
    d ← ∞
    repeat
        d_old ← d
        f* ← argmin d(X_W, f(Y_W))
                        ▷ where f is an RSO transformation
        (d, X_W, Y_W) ← DTW(X, f*(Y))
    until (d_old − d) < ε
    return d, X_W, f(Y_W)
end procedure
```

This algorithm can be restricted for a particular use case by limiting f to a subset of the RSO transformations. If rotation is not a concern, R may be held to I, the identity matrix, reducing RSOI-DTW to scale and offset invariant DTW, as developed in [2]. Similarly, if scaling is not a concern, s may be held to 1.

PROPOSITION 2. *RSOI-DTW is rotation, scale, and offset invariant. More precisely, let X, Y, and Z be sequences in $\mathbb{R}^3$ of equal length, where $Z = f_z(Y)$ for some RSO transformation f_z. If $d(X_W, f(Z_W))$ has a unique minimizer f^* at each iteration of the RSOI-DTW algorithm, then RSOI-DTW(X, Y) = RSOI-DTW(X, Z).*

PROOF. Let f_z be the RSO transformation taking Y to Z, so that $f_z(Y) = Z$, and suppose $f_z(Y_W) = Z_W$ at the beginning of the ith iteration of RSOI-DTW(X, Y) and RSOI-DTW(X, Z). We proceed by induction; note that the $i = 1$ case holds, since we initialize $Y_W \leftarrow Y$ and $Z_W \leftarrow Z$.

Given a unique RSO transformation f^* that minimizes $d(X_W, f(Z_W))$ in iteration i, the RSO transformation $(f^* \circ f_z)$ must be the unique minimizer of $d(X_W, f(Y_W))$. To see this, suppose there were some other RSO transformation g such that $d(X_W, g(Y_W)) \leq d(X_W, (f^* \circ f_z)(Y_W))$. Since $Y_W = f_z^{-1}(Z_W)$, where f_z^{-1} is the inverse of f_z, we have:

$$\begin{aligned} d(X_W, (g \circ f_z^{-1})(Z_W)) &= d(X_W, (g(f_z^{-1}(Z_W))) \\ &= d(X_W, g(Y_W)) \\ &\leq d(X_W, (f^* \circ f_z)(Y_W)) \\ &= d(X_W, (f^*(f_z(Y_W))) \\ &= d(X_W, f^*(Z_W)), \end{aligned}$$

violating our assumption that f^* is the unique minimizer.

Knowing that f^* and $(f^* \circ f_z)$ are the unique minimizers found in line 7 of the ith iteration of RSOI-DTW(X, Z) and RSOI-DTW(X, Y), respectively, we conclude that the input to the DTW subroutine is $f^*(Z_W)$ in either case. Because of this, DTW returns the same distance d and warping path W in both cases, guaranteeing $f_z(Y_W) = Z_W$ at the beginning of the $(i+1)^{th}$ iteration, completing our inductive proof. □

Intuitively, since the first step in RSOI-DTW is to optimally rotate, scale, and shift the input, the sequences Y_W and Z_W are both transformed to $f^*(Z_W)$ in the first iteration of the algorithm, and subsequent processing is identical.

PROPOSITION 3. *RSOI-DTW terminates.*

PROOF. First, notice that $f(X_W) = f(X)_W$, because applying the warping path W is a repetition of terms, and the transformation f is applied once to each term in either case.

Let d_i, W_i, and f_i be the distance, warping path, and optimal RSO transformation found in iteration i, so that $d_i = d(X_{W_i}, f_i(Y)_{W_i})$. In iteration $(i+1)$, f_{i+1} is chosen to minimize $d(X_{W_i}, f(Y)_{W_i})$, thus $d(X_{W_i}, f_{i+1}(Y)_{W_i}) \leq d_i$. And DTW finds the warping path W_{i+1} minimizing $d(X, f_{i+1}(Y))$. Together, we have:

$$d_{i+1} = d(X_{W_{i+1}}, f_{i+1}(Y)_{W_{i+1}}) \leq d(X_{W_i}, f_{i+1}(Y)_{W_i}) \leq d_i.$$

Since this holds for all i, the sequence $\{d_i\}_{i \in \mathbb{N}}$ is monotonically decreasing. Further, since the d_i are squared Euclidean distances, they are bounded below by zero. Therefore this sequence converges by the monotone convergence theorem, guaranteeing termination of the RSOI-DTW algorithm. □

4. RESULTS

4.1 Convergence and RSO Invariance of RSOI-DTW in Practice

Having established the theoretical properties of RSOI-DTW, we now show it performs as expected on our walking data. Figure 1 illustrates the use of RSOI-DTW to compare two gait cycles. Both cycles were taken from a single subject's casual walking segment. The raw cycles C_1 and C_2 are shown in the top and middle left plots, respectively. The bottom left plot shows C_2 after a randomly chosen RSO transformation f is applied. The right panel shows how RSOI-DTW alters the cycles. When running RSOI-DTW(C_1, C_2), a warped version of C_1 (top right) and a warped, transformed version of C_2 (middle right) are returned. Here the rotation, scale, and offset are small, because sensor alignment was consistent and no rotation was applied. When running RSOI-DTW$(C_1, f(C_2))$, the same two plots are returned. The warped version of C_1 (not shown) is identical to the top right plot, and the warped, rotated version of $f(C_2)$ (bottom right) is identical to the plot above it, because RSOI-DTW is invariant under f.

To verify that RSOI-DTW is invariant under a real rotation – that is, a misorientation of the sensor – three of our participants completed a second trial with the sensor in four different orientations: no rotation, a 90° rotation about the medial-lateral axis, a 180° rotation about the medial-lateral axis, and a 180° rotation about the vertical axis. The 125 rotated signals were compared to the non-rotated signals using DTW and RSOI-DTW, and the resulting distances were

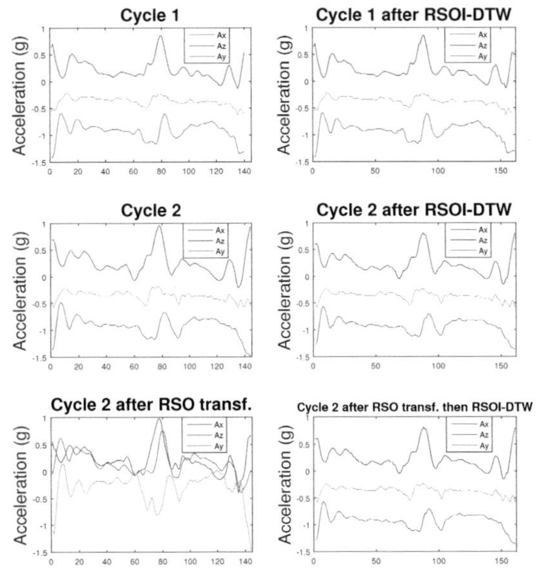

Figure 1: RSOI-DTW is rotation, scale, and offset invariant: when an RSO transformation is applied to cycle 2 (bottom left), the RSOI-DTW algorithm corrects it (bottom right).

Table 1: RSOI-DTW achieves perfect 1NN recognition of cycles collected with the sensor incorrectly oriented. The table shows the number of cycles correctly classified under DTW and RSOI-DTW distances out of the 125 cycles collected from three subjects.

	DTW	RSOI
# Correct	24	125
(%)	19.2	100.0

used to recognize subjects. 1-nearest neighbor (1NN) recognition is perfect under RSOI-DTW but worse than random under DTW (Table 1), and RSOI-DTW distances were similar for all four orientations (Figure 2).

As additional support, randomly chosen RSO transformations were applied to each of our 21 participants' 12 casual gait cycles. RSOI-DTW was used to compare the transformed cycles to the original, non-transformed cycles, for a total of $\binom{252}{2}$, or 31,626, comparisons. These distances were compared to the corresponding distances obtained without first applying a transformation. In all 31,626 cases, the RSOI-DTW distances were identical up to rounding error, never differing by more than 10^{-13}. Together with the experimental result, this suggests that RSOI-DTW is RSO invariant in practice when used on inertial time series data.

Figure 3 shows histograms of the RSOI-DTW convergence rate when comparing (a) pairs of casual walking cycles, and (b) fast walking cycles to casual walking cycles. In over 60,000 runs per plot, the algorithm most often required 7 iterations, rarely over 20, and never over 30. To ensure local optimality, we insisted that $d = d_{old}$ for convergence,

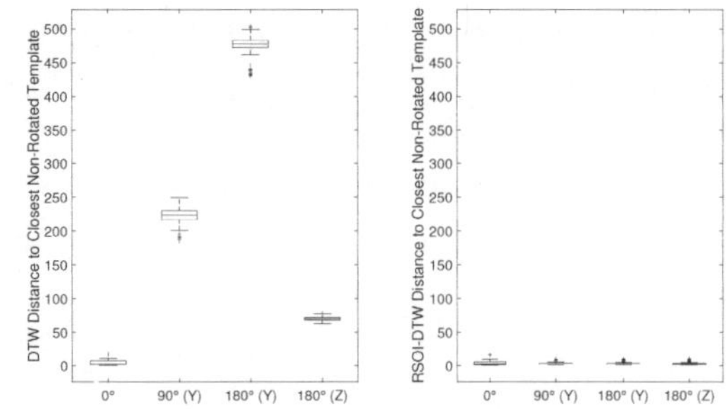

Figure 2: RSOI-DTW distances are similar regardless of sensor orientation. The figure shows DTW (left) and RSOI-DTW (right) distances between incorrectly oriented cycles and the correctly oriented cycles from the same subject.

meaning the warping path was stable. In our data, using a less strict (e.g. 10^{-5}) convergence criterion typically reduces the number of iterations by one, and never more than two.

As shown in Algorithm 1, each iteration calls DTW once and the Procrustes algorithm once. DTW involves $O(N^2)$ computations, where N is the length of the inputs: computation is proportional to the number of pairings between points in X and points in Y. However, RSOI-DTW must recover the warping path W in addition to the distance d, requiring a second trip through the cost matrix and adding a multiple of N^2 computations. Run time is increased, but not by more than a factor of two. The Procrustes problem requires only $O(N)$ computations [5], and in our data set, DTW occupies the vast majority of run time. A conservative run time estimate may be obtained by multiplying the DTW run time by $2I$, where I is the number of iterations required.

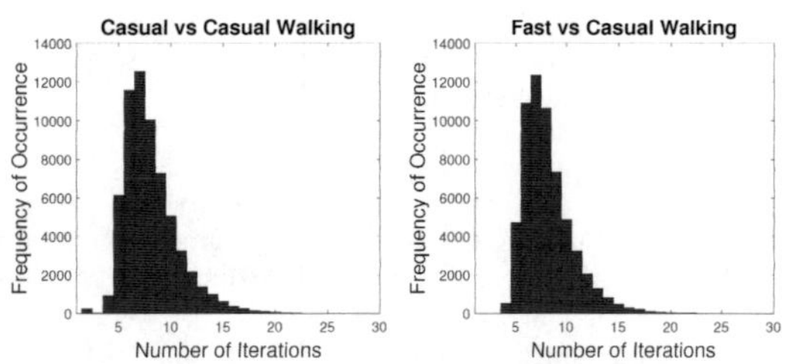

Figure 3: RSOI-DTW converges after 8 iterations on average. The figure shows histograms of the number of iterations required to compare pairs of cycles.

4.2 Distinguishing Between Persons Using DTW and RSOI-DTW

For the gait recognition problem, 1NN classification was used to match gait cycles from all 21 participants to the casual walking template cycles under DTW and RSOI-DTW distances. A test cycle Y was classified as belonging to the owner of X, where X is the template cycle minimizing DTW(X, Y) or RSOI-DTW(X, Y).

Table 2 shows that gait recognition succeeds in our data set under both DTW and RSOI-DTW distances. Out of 252 tested cycles, DTW correctly classified all of them, and RSOI-DTW misclassified only one. When distinct, randomly chosen rotations were applied to test cycles beforehand, DTW failed in most cases, but the RSOI-DTW results were unchanged due to RSO invariance.

Table 2: 1NN classification of casual gait is almost perfect under both DTW and RSOI-DTW. However, when rotations are applied to individual cycles beforehand, only RSOI-DTW succeeds. The table shows the number of cycles correctly recognized out of the 252 tested.

	Without Rotation		With Rotation	
	DTW	RSOI	DTW	RSOI
# Correct	252	251	68	251
(%)	100.0	99.6	27.0	99.6

Gait recognition may also be treated as a decision problem: the algorithm must decide (YES/NO) whether a gait cycle of unknown origin belongs to a given person. As seen in Figure 4, a threshold is set on the best match between the tested cycle and the known subject's template cycles. If best match distance is below the threshold, the cycle is accepted, otherwise it is rejected. Table 3 summarizes the decision problem results in all subjects by the equal error rate (EER), calculated by finding the threshold minimizing the difference between the false negative and false positive rates, then taking their average.

Table 3: Threshold-based gait recognition achieves an equal error rate (EER) of zero in all subjects under DTW, and all but four subjects under RSOI-DTW. The table summarizes the EER for the decision problem in all subjects.

	DTW EER (%)	RSOI EER (%)
Mean	0.0	0.5
Median	0.0	0.0
Min	0.0	0.0
Max	0.0	7.1

Figure 4 shows decision problem results for subject 8, who had the worst EER (7.1%) under RSOI-DTW among all subjects because of two unusual, poorly matching cycles. The error rates are zero in all subjects under DTW and in 17 of 21 subjects under RSOI-DTW.

4.3 Detecting Simulated Pathology

The pathology detection problem is similar to the gait recognition decision problem: the algorithm must decide (YES/NO) whether an unknown cycle represents normal gait or possible pathology. As before, a threshold is placed on the best match between the tested cycle and the known subject's template cycles. Table 4 shows that the two simulated pathologies were easily recognized in all subjects under both DTW and RSOI-DTW distances. The EER was nonzero in only one subject under RSOI-DTW. As before, only RSOI-DTW is capable of this accuracy despite the variability possible in a real-world use case.

4.4 Fast Walking

An algorithm monitoring walking ability should separate possible pathology from normal walking at any speed. Simi-

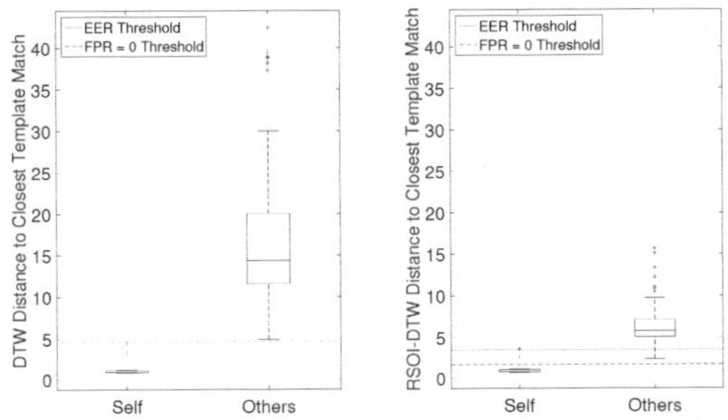

Figure 4: Threshold-based gait recognition is imperfect in subject 8 under RSOI-DTW due to two poorly matching gait cycles, but perfect in all but three of the other subjects.

Table 4: Simulated pathology can easily be distinguished from casual gait. The table summarizes the equal error rate (EER) for the decision problem with DTW and RSOI-DTW.

	DTW EER (%)	RSOI EER (%)
Mean	0.0	0.4
Median	0.0	0.0
Min	0.0	0.0
Max	0.0	8.3

larly, a gait recognition algorithm should accept cycles from a known person walking at any speed, but reject cycles from other persons. Amplitude and offset invariant DTW may mitigate variability due to gait speed by warping and scaling cycles. Unfortunately, Table 5 shows that fast walking confuses the decision algorithm even using the RSOI-DTW distance. This table summarizes the EER when distinguishing normal walking, fast or slow, from simulated pathology. Again, casual walking cycles were used as templates. RSOI-DTW tended to improve performance because it can scale fast gait cycles to match the casual cycles. Still, overall peformance is poor with both measures.

Table 5: Fast gait is hard to distinguish from pathology using the casual gait cycles as templates. The table shows the equal error rate (EER) in all subjects when distinguishing normal gait (casual or fast) from simulated pathology.

	DTW EER (%)	RSOI EER (%)
Mean	43.8	31.3
Median	50.0	39.6
Min	0.0	0.0
Max	52.3	50.0

Figure 5 illustrates this difficulty in subject 10: while RSOI-DTW dramatically lowered the distances between fast cycles and the template cycles compared to DTW, it is not enough for reliable pathology detection or gait recognition.

In light of this difficulty, either (1) walking speed must be consistent between cycles, or (2) the template set must include cycles at many speeds. To test the latter, fast walking cycles were added to the template set in each subject, with results shown in Table 6. With this modification, simulated pathology could again be distinguished from normal walking (casual or fast). Compared to the near perfect results in the previous section, however, the EER is high in several subjects. RSOI-DTW improves the EER in two subjects, but worsens it in others.

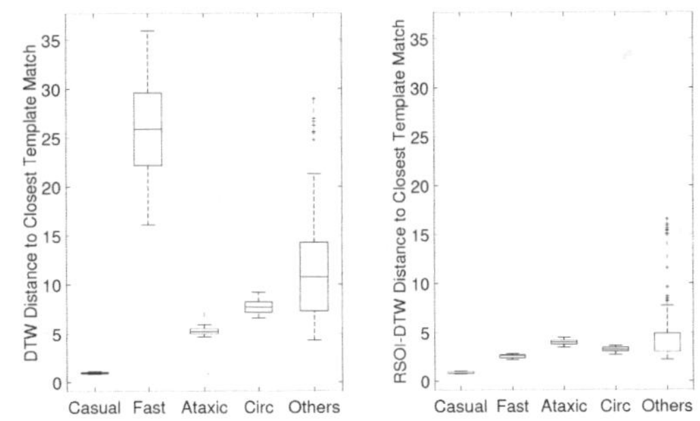

Figure 5: Fast gait confuses the pathology detection and gait recognition algorithms in subject 10 under DTW, but less so under RSOI-DTW. The figure shows distances to the closest casual gait template cycle for several groups of cycles using DTW (left) and RSOI-DTW (right).

Table 6: Including fast gait cycles in the template set dramatically improves performance when distinguishing normal gait from simulated pathology. The table summarizes the improved equal error rate (EER) in all subjects.

	DTW EER (%)	RSOI EER (%)
Mean	4.9	8.0
Median	0.0	1.1
Min	0.0	0.0
Max	31.3	33.3

5. DISCUSSION

Under the ideal conditions in our walking test, both DTW and RSOI-DTW performed well. However, only RSOI-DTW is equipped to compensate for the peculiarities of real-world gait data. Section 4 illustrates the cost of this advantage. First, in rare cases, the flexibility of RSOI-DTW allowed it to closely match cycles from different subjects. This confused the decision algorithm more than the classification algorithm, because the latter had information about the match distance to other subjects. Second, RSOI-DTW increases run time by a factor of I to $2I$, where I is the number of iterations. In this data set, I had a median value of 8. We recommend using DTW in a controlled, clinical scenario, and RSOI-DTW in real-world remote monitoring. Indeed, the RSOI-DTW algorithm can be constrained as much as the use case allows, as mentioned in Section 3.3.

RSOI-DTW solves the orientation problem, but not the gait speed problem: the distance between fast walking and casual walking was reduced, but still significant. Section 3.4 shows that increasing the size and variety of the template set improved performance substantially. We believe that further template collection may solve the problem.

Matching inertial time series can be broken into many

subproblems. One could find the gravitational vector, using it to partly correct the orientation, then adjust for sensor bias, finally running DTW to optimize alignment, and so on. RSOI-DTW is attractive partly because it solves all of these problems at once. We have not compared RSOI-DTW to another rotation invariant algorithm, because there is no clear candidate: other rotation invariant approaches use entirely different methodologies.

In our view, the RSO transformation is the most general affine transformation reasonable for inertial data; yet RSOI-DTW preserves the distinctive cycle features needed to distinguish persons and walking styles.

6. CONCLUSIONS AND FUTURE WORK

These results confirm that RSOI-DTW is an appropriate similarity measure for real-world inertial gait data, and support the proposed approach to the detection and monitoring of gait pathology. RSOI-DTW matches gait cycles despite incorrect sensor orientation, partly compensates for changes in gait speed, distinguishes our 21 participants almost perfectly, and detects the changes in walking style in this trial.

Our subsequent work will focus on using DTW and RSOI-DTW to monitor true pathology in both clinic and outpatient settings. In particular, we intend to monitor persons with multiple sclerosis while exercising to identify changes in walking patterns induced by fatigue.

Long-term monitoring will require not just a similarity measure, but also a method for clustering cycles, tracking cluster progression, and summarizing it as an outcome measure. Clustering algorithms that accept arbitrary distance metrics, such as k-medoids or affinity propagation, may be an appropriate starting point.

7. ACKNOWLEDGEMENTS

This research was partly funded by the Broadband Wireless Access and Applications Center, an NSF supported industry-university cooperative research center (NSF award #1266311).

We owe special thanks to Jiaqi Gong, Davis Blalock, and Josh Inouye for their input and guidance on this work.

8. REFERENCES

[1] P. Bours and R. Shrestha. Eigensteps: A giant leap for gait recognition. In *2010 2nd International Workshop on Security and Communication Networks (IWSCN)*, pages 1–6, May 2010.

[2] T.-W. Chen, M. Abdelmaseeh, and D. Stashuk. Affine and Regional Dynamic Time Warpng. *arXiv:1505.06531 [cs]*, May 2015. arXiv: 1505.06531.

[3] C. Chien, J. Y. Xu, H.-i. Chang, X. Wu, and G. J. Pottie. *Model Construction for Human Motion Classification Using Inertial Sensors.*

[4] M. Derawi, C. Nickel, P. Bours, and C. Busch. Unobtrusive User-Authentication on Mobile Phones Using Biometric Gait Recognition. In *2010 Sixth International Conference on Intelligent Information Hiding and Multimedia Signal Processing (IIH-MSP)*, pages 306–311, Oct. 2010.

[5] D. W. Eggert, A. Lorusso, and R. B. Fisher. Estimating 3-D rigid body transformations: a comparison of four major algorithms. *Machine Vision and Applications*, 9(5-6):272–290, Mar. 1997.

[6] J. Gong, P. Asare, J. Lach, and Y. Qi. Piecewise Linear Dynamical Model for Actions Clustering from Inertial Body Sensors with Considerations of Human Factors. In *Proceedings of the 9th International Conference on Body Area Networks*, BodyNets '14, pages 90–96, ICST, Brussels, Belgium, Belgium, 2014. ICST (Institute for Computer Sciences, Social-Informatics and Telecommunications Engineering).

[7] E. Keogh and C. A. Ratanamahatana. Exact indexing of dynamic time warping. *Knowledge and Information Systems*, 7(3):358–386, May 2004.

[8] M. Mancini, A. Salarian, P. Carlson-Kuhta, C. Zampieri, L. King, L. Chiari, and F. B. Horak. ISway: a sensitive, valid and reliable measure of postural control. *Journal of NeuroEngineering and Rehabilitation*, 9(1):59, Aug. 2012.

[9] J. Mantyjarvi, M. Lindholm, E. Vildjiounaite, S.-M. Makela, and H. Ailisto. Identifying users of portable devices from gait pattern with accelerometers. In *IEEE International Conference on Acoustics, Speech, and Signal Processing, 2005. Proceedings. (ICASSP '05)*, volume 2, pages ii/973–ii/976 Vol. 2, Mar. 2005.

[10] R. Muscillo, S. Conforto, M. Schmid, P. Caselli, and T. D'Alessio. Classification of Motor Activities through Derivative Dynamic Time Warping applied on Accelerometer Data. In *29th Annual International Conference of the IEEE Engineering in Medicine and Biology Society, 2007. EMBS 2007*, pages 4930–4933, Aug. 2007.

[11] C. Nickel, M. Derawi, P. Bours, and C. Busch. Scenario test of accelerometer-based biometric gait recognition. In *2011 Third International Workshop on Security and Communication Networks (IWSCN)*, pages 15–21, May 2011.

[12] Y. Qiao and M. Yasuhara. Affine Invariant Dynamic Time Warping and its Application to Online Rotated Handwriting Recognition. In *18th International Conference on Pattern Recognition, 2006. ICPR 2006*, volume 2, pages 905–908, Aug. 2006.

[13] L. Rong, Z. Jianzhong, L. Ming, and H. Xiangfeng. A Wearable Acceleration Sensor System for Gait Recognition. In *2nd IEEE Conference on Industrial Electronics and Applications, 2007. ICIEA 2007*, pages 2654–2659, May 2007.

[14] H. Sakoe and S. Chiba. Dynamic programming algorithm optimization for spoken word recognition. *IEEE Transactions on Acoustics, Speech and Signal Processing*, 26(1):43–49, Feb. 1978.

[15] A. Salarian, F. Horak, C. Zampieri, P. Carlson-Kuhta, J. Nutt, and K. Aminian. iTUG, a Sensitive and Reliable Measure of Mobility. *IEEE Transactions on Neural Systems and Rehabilitation Engineering*, 18(3):303–310, June 2010.

[16] R. I. Spain, M. Mancini, F. B. Horak, and D. Bourdette. Body-worn sensors capture variability, but not decline, of gait and balance measures in multiple sclerosis over 18 months. *Gait & Posture*, 39(3):958–964, Mar. 2014.

An Empirical Measurement of Signal Attenuation and BER of IEEE 802.15.6 HBC using a phantom solution

Kim Taylor
College of Engineering and Science
Victoria University
Victoria, Australia
kim.taylor4@research.vu.edu.au

Daniel Lai
College of Engineering and Science
Victoria University
Victoria, Australia
daniel.lai@vu.edu.au

ABSTRACT

The implementation of an IEEE 802.15.6 section 10 compliant human body communications (HBC) transceiver requires an understanding of the signal integrity expected at the receiver. This paper focuses on the reception of IEEE 802.15.6 compliant data packets through the human body. The experiment used a phantom solution to model the electrical characteristics of muscle tissue in a controlled environment. The prototype transmitter was able to achieve a power consumption of 4.5nJ per bit using FPGA technology at the minimum spreading factor, while a minimum channel attenuation of 11.4dB was measured at 21MHz. Further characterisation of the human body communications channel will be possible with the future development of a portable prototype, optimising the receiver design using the empirical results presented here.

Keywords

Capacitive coupling, Attenuation, IEEE 802.15.6, HBC

1. INTRODUCTION

The IEEE 802.15.6 [1] standard was introduced in 2012 to address the need for low power communications over a personal, body area network (BAN). The standard has been divided into three technologies. 802.15.6 sections 8 and 9 cover RF based approaches, using narrow band and ultra-wideband modulation schemes respectively. Section 10 describes a baseband communications technique where the transceivers are to be directly coupled to the user's skin. The subject's body tissue forms one half of the communications channel, while the ground connection is completed through the user's environment. This form of coupling is referred to as capacitive coupling in literature due to the lack of DC connection between the transmitter and the receiver.

One of the focuses of the standard is low power consumption. Many RF modulation schemes rely on accurate digital to analogue and analogue to digital conversion, combined with complex signal processing blocks, both requiring significant energy resources. For example the OFDM modulation schemes employed in IEEE 802.11 require high speed Fourier transform computation, combined with high speed digital to analogue conversion. IEEE 802.15.6 section 10 on the other hand aims to directly couple a digital logic signal to the body, via a spectrum mask, avoiding the need for digital to analogue conversion. The scheme that has been adopted has been labelled frequency selective digital transmission (FSDT).

The proposed modulation technique consists of 3 parts: A serial to parallel converter, a Walsh code modulator and a frequency spreader. For IEEE 802.15.6 compliance, the chip rate must be fixed at 42 mega chips per second (Mcps)[1]. The frequency spreader applies a frequency shift code (FSC) consisting of an alternating bit pattern XORed with the output stream of the Walsh modulator. Spreading factors nominated by IEEE 802.15.6 are 64, 32, 16 and 8. By changing the length of the spreading pattern, a constant chip rate results in four possible data rates, 164Kbps, 328Kbps, 656Kbps and 1312Kbps.

Increasing the spreading factor, increases the likelihood of the receiver correctly determining the phase of the input signal and decoding the transmitted message. This comes at the cost of increased power consumption and a slower data rate as demonstrated in this work.

While the IEEE 802.15.6 standard completely describes the transmitter requirements, the receiver implementation is left to the designer. In order for designers to develop low cost, low power receiver implementations, a knowledge of the body channel characteristics are required. While previous studies have provided an insight into the frequency response of the human body channel, it is worthwhile to observe how well the IEEE 802.15.6 modulation scheme addresses the requirements for a low power and low cost body area network.

Previous studies have been made on the characterisation of the human body channel. Choo *et al.* [2] developed a lumped element model for capacitive coupling, and did empirical testing on a human subject using a battery powered transmitter module connected to a transmitter electrode and a spectrum analyser connected to a receiver electrode. Their results demonstrated high pass filter characteristics of the

[1]A chip rate of 42Mcps corresponds to a fundamental transmission frequency of 21MHz.

BODYNETS 2015, September 28-30, Sydney, Australia

DOI 10.4108/eai.28-9-2015.2261666

human body channel, attributed to the capacitive return path.

Lucev *et al.* [4] conducted a similar experiment using a human test subject and a sinusoidal excitation source. Their results showed similar high pass characteristics to Choo's study. Interestingly they found that the receiver contact impedance varied approximately linearly from 100KΩ to 100Ω over the 100kHz to 100MHz test frequency range.

As the focus of this paper is IEEE 802.15.6 HBC transceiver implementation, the excitation source will be IEEE 802.15.6 compliant packets. This experiment aims to vary the chip rate, in order to observe changes in attenuation, power consumption and BER at the data link layer. While IEEE 802.15.6 compliance requires a transmission frequency of 21MHz, it is worthwhile measuring the performance of the scheme at other frequencies. The experiment tested transmission frequencies ranging from 300kHz to 60MHz.

In order to obtain repeatable measurements, the empirical data obtained in this paper utilised a phantom solution in place of a human test subject. The recipe for the phantom solution was based on Hagmann *et al.* [3].

2. EXPERIMENTAL SETUP

The experiment seeks to collect data on: a) transmitter power consumption, b) channel attenuation and c) bit error rate before and after demodulation. The experimental approach for each of these metrics will be discussed separately. Variables to be considered were chip rate, modulation spreading factor and transmitter, receiver separation.

2.1 Transmitter setup

A prototype IEEE 802.15.6 compliant transmitter has been implemented using a Xilinx Virtex 5 FPGA device. The transmitter design consists of a modular peripheral written in VHDL that may be interfaced with an embedded CPU. The prototype also implements this CPU on the same FPGA using the Xilinx Microblaze core, in order to create a compact transmitter design, requiring only a single FPGA. Throughout this experiment, the transmitter has been programmed to transmit the longest packet length prescribed by IEEE 802.15.6 (256 bytes). As required by IEEE 802.15.6, the transmitter includes a pseudo random sequence generator, or scrambler. The output of the scrambler is XORed with the transmit stream, resulting in a pseudo random transmit sequence.

The FPGA device used, a Xilinx Virtex 5, has a maximum logic clock frequency of 400MHz, as such the highest transmission frequency clock requirements (120MHz) fall well within the device's operating range.

In order to obtain an estimate for power consumption, a gate level simulation of the transmitter logic has been run for each transmission frequency and modulation rate. The results of the simulations provide a profile for the toggle rates of all gates involved in packet transmission. This information is then fed to the Xilinx Xpwr tool, which provides an accurate power estimate for the FPGA device. This method allows for precise measurement of transmitter power consumption, allowing for separation of dynamic power consumption from the FPGA device's static power consumption.[2] The power consumption results presented in this paper do not include static power consumption.

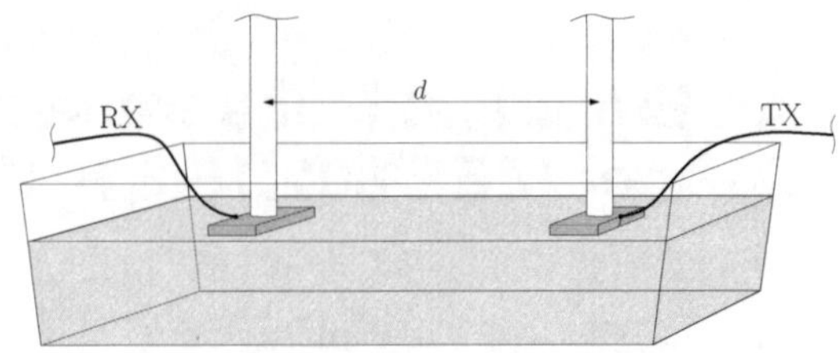

Figure 1: Experiment setup showing electrode placement and fluid. *d* denotes the distance between the centre of the electrodes.

2.2 Phantom model setup

Channel attenuation was measured using a test apparatus consisting of a transmitter electrode, a phantom solution and a receiver electrode. The phantom solutions used were based on recipes from [3] and have been reproduced in Table 1. The solutions have been designed to provide the equivalent conductivity and permittivity of human muscle tissue. In order to approximate the complex environment of muscle tissue with a homogeneous solution, it is necessary to alter the concentrations of salt and glycine for different transmission frequencies. As shown in Figure 1 the values presented are those that are available in literature. The first column of Table 1 matches the nearest transmission frequency to each published solution composition.

The electrodes were placed on top of the solution as shown in Figure 1. The horizontal spacing d between the centre of the transmitter and receiver electrodes was set at either 11.25 cm or 22.5 cm from the centre of the electrodes.

The electrodes have two copper layers, isolated by a dielectric. Closed cell rubber was used in order to prevent any of the phantom solution from occupying the space between the ground and signal copper planes. Figure 2 shows the construction of the electrodes. The dimensions were chosen to be similar to a prototype transceiver that is being developed concurrently.

An oscilloscope was connected to both the transmitter and receiver electrodes, allowing for attenuation measurements. A Tektronix MSO5204 10GS/s was used at full sampling rate. The channel 1 and channel 2 inputs were programmed for 50Ω termination. The oscilloscope has a common ground for all input channels. In practice, wireless devices will not have electrical connection and will rely on capacitive coupling between the ground layer of the electrodes. The experimental setup achieved this by separating the ground electrodes using a balun, and through the use of a battery powered transmitter. Figure 4 is a schematic of the experiment

[2]Static power consumption is device dependent and primarily consists of transistor leakage current in the FPGA device. Dynamic power is associated with the transmitter switching activity, and is a function of node capacitance, supply voltage and switching frequency [9].

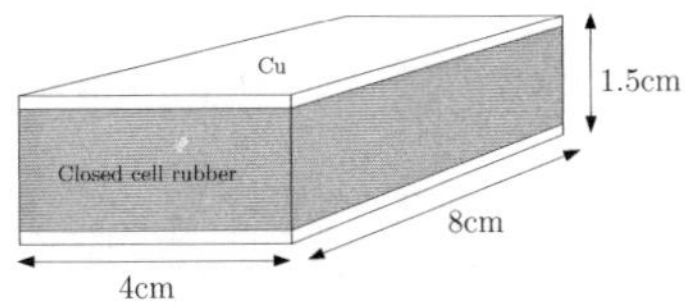

Figure 2: Electrode detail. The dimensions were chosen to approximate the prototype transciever construction.

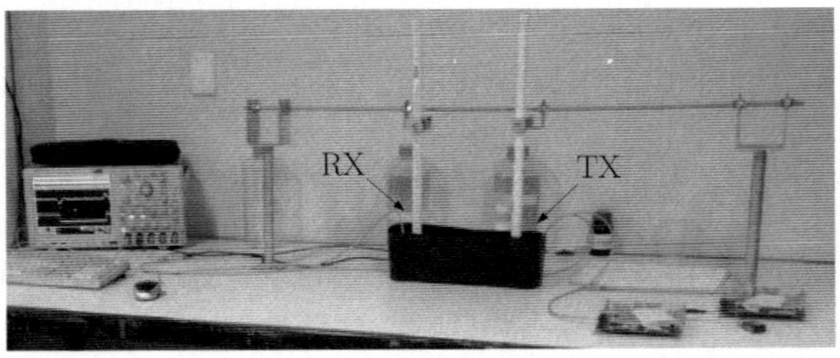

Figure 3: Photograph of experimental setup, showing the transmitter and receiver electrodes suspended in the phantom solution.

setup.

The attenuation information presented here was generated by performing a fast Fourier transform FFT on the oscilloscope PCM sample data, and normalising the results based on the received waveform on channel 2. As shown in Figure 4, the signal on the receiver electrode is connected to channel 1, while the reference signal is connected to channel 2. The attenuation was calculated as the difference between the channel 1 and channel 2 FFT coefficients at the frequency of transmission, then averaged using the two adjacent FFT coefficients.

Given the channel 1 raw real valued[3] PCM samples, $x_0, ..., x_{N-1}$ and the resultant FFT coefficients, $X_0, ..., X_{N/2}$, where the closest coefficient to the transmission frequency is X_T. The attenuation was calculated as:

[3]As the input data is real valued, $X_{N-k} = X_k^*$, thus we only require coefficients X_0(DC) to $X_{N/2}$ (the Nyquist frequency).

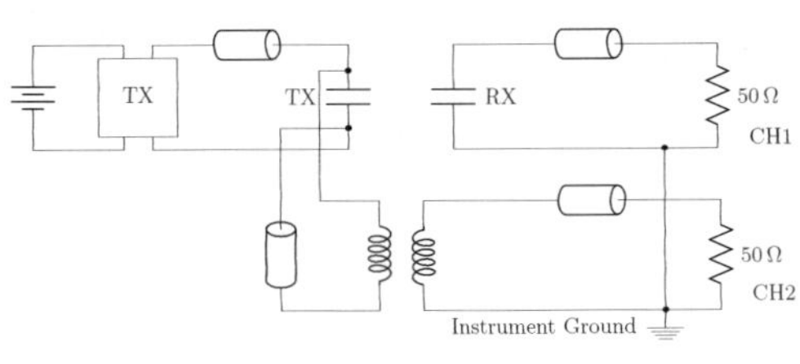

Figure 4: Experiment schematic diagram. The transmission lines shown are 50 Ω cables. Each 50Ω resistor represents the input stage of the oscilloscope.

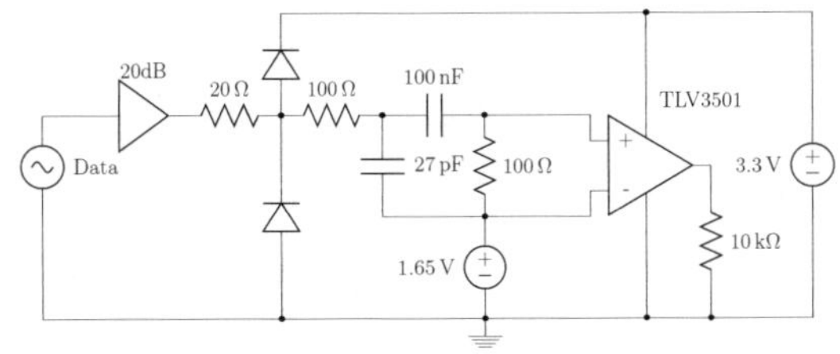

Figure 5: Receiver analogue front end spice model. The 20dB gain block and associated clamping diodes used to model an off the shelf low noise amplifier.

$$\frac{1}{3}[(Y'_{T-1} + Y'_T + Y'_{T+1}) - (X'_{T-1} + X'_T + X'_{T+1})]$$

where $Y_0, ..., Y_{N/2}$ are the FFT coefficients for channel 2, and $X'_n = 20log_{10}|X_n|$ and $Y' = 20log_{10}|Y_n|$. The coefficients X_n and Y_n were normalised such that $max(Y'_n) = 0$.

In order to compensate for transmitter to receiver coupling thought the cables and RF propagation from the electrodes, the experiment was repeated with air used in place of the phantom solution. The electrode spacing and position was the same for both the air and fluid measurements.

2.3 BER measurement

The received waveform was sampled at 10Gs/s and imported into a SPICE model for the receiver analogue front end. The analogue component of the receiver consists of filtering and hard decision detection using a Texas Instruments TLV3501 comparator. The analogue front end schematic is shown in Figure 5. This data was then imported into VHDL test bench for the receiver logic which, like the transmitter, has been implemented on a Xilinx Vertex-5 FPGA device.

The receiver architecture was then simulated and the demodulated data exported. The demodulation procedure includes data recovery, phase alignment, comma detection, packet rate detection, serial to parallel conversion, Walsh code detection based on hamming distance, and descrambling. A graphical depiction of the designed receiver architecture is shown in Figure 6 The demodulated packets were then compared with the transmitted packets in order to calculate BER at the data link layer. In order to demonstrate effectiveness of the Walsh coding scheme for error correction, the received chips after hard decision detection were also compared to the transmitted data and presented as raw BER.

The first stage of the receiver, data recovery, consists of a 4x oversampling stage and edge detection logic. 4x oversampling is a result of using four phases of a clock signal set at twice the transmission frequency. The structure of this data recovery block closely follows that presented by Xilinx in their application note 225 [6].

Receiver synchronisation is achieved in the phase alignment stage. An IEEE 802.15.6 packet starts with a preamble of a known sequence repeated 4 times. The receiver checks for

Table 1: Formulations for muscle simulating phantoms matched to transmission frequencies.

Transmission Frequency (MHz)	Solution Frequency (MHz)	Weight Percent			Dielectric Properties	
		Water	Glycine	NaCl	ϵ'	σ (S/m)
0.300, 2.000, 5.000, 13.00	13.56	79.4	20	0.58	145	0.6
21.00, 30.00	27.12	88.5	11	0.49	112	0.6
42.00, 55.00, 60.00	40.68	93.5	6.0	0.52	93.5	0.7

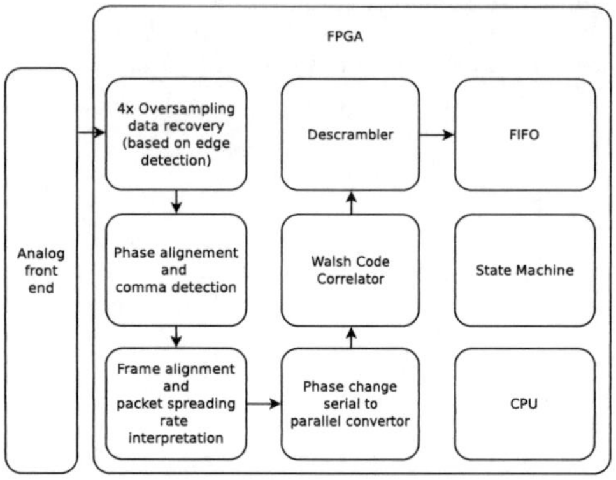

Figure 6: Prototype receiver architecture, as implemented in hardware using a Xilinx Virtex-5 FPGA device. A simulation of this hardware was used in order to allow detailed analysis of operation.

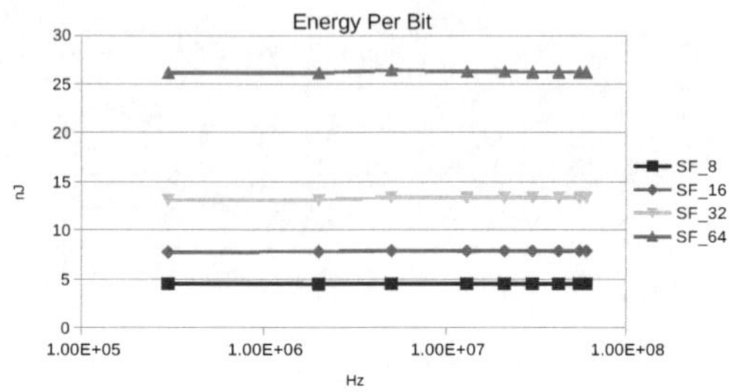

Figure 7: Transmitter power consumption vs frequency for each IEEE 802.15.6 spreading factor (SF)

this known sequence by calculating the hamming distance between the input data and the packet preamble. This is done for each possible phase alignment. IEEE 802.15.6 stipulates that a spreading factor of 8 is used for the preamble. Consequently there are 8 possible phase alignments. Once the preamble sequence has been detected, the best phase is selected based on hamming distance and detection of phase transitions on the input stream. An earlier receiver design used detection of phase transitions only, however this was found to be inadequate when phase transitions are distorted by the communications channel. Efficient calculation of hamming distance is achieved using look up tables LUTs based on the methods published by Sklyarov *et al.* [7].

Once the receiver has been synchronised, the VHDL test bench then prints both the raw data stream and the demodulated data to file for comparison with the original transmitted message.

3. RESULTS AND DISCUSSION

3.1 Transmitter power consumption

The results of the Xilinx Xpwr simulations for the transmitter hardware are presented in Figure 7. The maximum variation in power consumption for each spreading factor was less than 2%.

This result is consistent with the modulation scheme's implementation of spreading factor. Doubling the spreading factor approximately doubles the packet length. For spreading factors of 8, 16, 32 and 64 chips per bit, the transmitter power requirements are approximately 4.5nJ, 7.9nJ, 13.4nJ and 26.3nJ per bit respectively. The IEEE 802.15.6 transmit spectral mask will require further power, however the prototype transmitter achieves this using analogue filtering, offering an improvement in power consumption over the approach of digital filtering followed by a digital to analogue converter [5].

3.2 Channel attenuation

Figure 8 plots the channel attenuation at each transmission frequency and electrode separation. Also included are the results with the phantom solution replaced with air. The results are consistent with those produced by Choo *et al.* [2] and Lucev *et al.* [4] in that the channel exhibits high pass characteristics initially, although no substantial low pass effect was observed above 45MHz. As the communications channel relies on capacitive coupling for the ground path, the experiment environment will have significant influence on the results.

Looking at the air coupling results, it can be seen that generally, RF coupling of the signal increases with frequency. Within the environmental conditions of this experiment, the largest difference between RF coupled reception and capacitively coupled reception occurs at 21 MHz.

For comparison with the RF based approach presented in IEEE 802.15.6 section 9, Wang *et al.* demonstrate that over a similar distance, ultra wideband (UWB) communications show losses closer to 60dB [8].

As shown in Table 2 the difference between attenuation for

	11.25cm Attenuation (dB)	22.5cm Attenuation (dB)	Attenuation Difference (dB)
300kHz	46.5	46.8	0.3
2MHz	29.6	29.5	-0.2
5MHz	21.9	22.3	0.4
13MHz	10.1	11.9	1.8
21MHz	9.8	11.4	1.6
30MHz	16.6	18.4	1.8
42MHz	12.8	13.6	0.8
55MHz	12.5	11.0	-1.5
60MHz	10.8	12.9	2.1

Table 2: Channel attenuation in phantom solution for each transmission frequency. Attenuation difference shown is the difference in attenuation for $d = 11.25cm$ and $d = 22.5cm$.

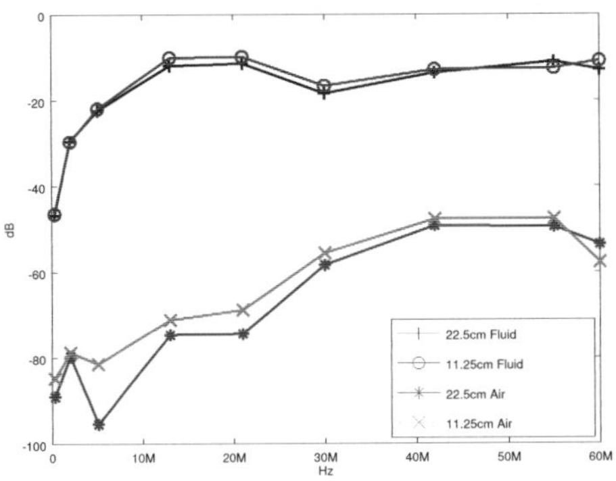

Figure 8: Channel attenuation in phantom solution and in air for $d = 11.25cm$ and $d = 22.5cm$.

$d = 11.25cm$ and $d = 22.5cm$ averages 1.7 dB from 13MHz to 30MHz. At higher frequencies, increased air coupling makes it difficult to isolate the effect of the increased spacing. This experiment does not take into account variations in environment, which may have more significant impact on attenuation than electrode separation. The relationship between environment and channel attenuation will be further investigated in future experiments.

Figures 9 and 10 show the spectrum of the transmitted signal (in green, normalised) and the received signal (in blue) at 30MHz, with $d = 22.5cm$ and spreading factor 8 though the phantom solution and a male test subject's arm respectively. While there is a 6dB difference in attenuation at the peak frequency of 30MHz between the two mediums, the channel frequency characteristics are similar, demonstrating the feasibility of the use of a phantom solution to model the human body channel in a controlled environment.

The experimental setup allows complete contact between the electrodes and the phantom solution, while contact with the subject's arm is often degraded. The difference in attenuation is consistent with variations in attenuation due to electrode contact degradation seen by Lucev *et al.* [4]. The relationship between channel attenuation and electrode contact will be further investigated using the prototype transceiver in real world applications.

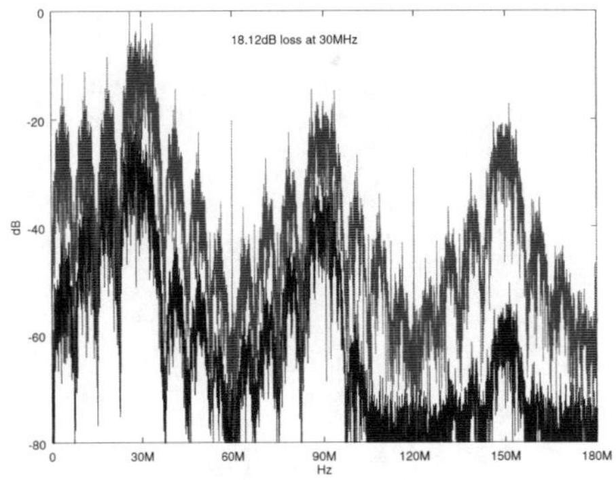

Figure 9: Spectrum plot of received signal (blue) and reference signal (green) at 30MHz through the phantom solution with $d = 22.5cm$.

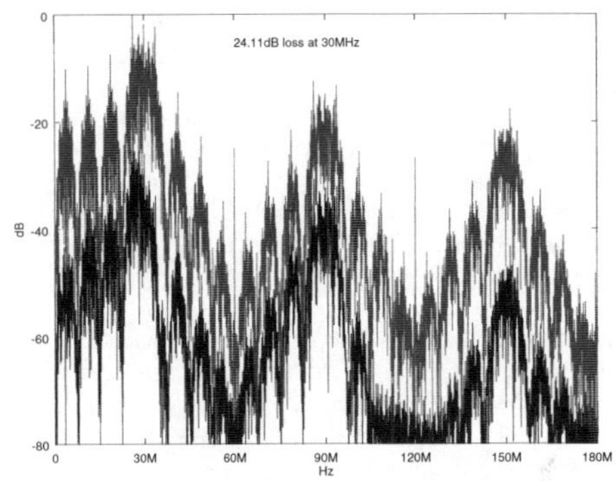

Figure 10: Spectrum plot of received signal (blue) and reference signal (green) at 30MHz through a male test subject's arm with $d = 22.5cm$.

Figure 11 is a time-domain plot of the transmitted signal (in green) and the received signal (in blue) at 21MHz with a spreading factor of 8. The effect of the capacitive coupling can be most easily observed at each phase transition where the received signal decays towards zero during the two simultaneous chips. It is here that incorrect hard decision results at the output of the comparator in Figure 5 are most likely.

One of the consequences of sampling the data with a fixed clock frequency occurs when there is drift in clock frequency. In such cases, the receiver may for example move from sampling at 180°to 90°to 0°to 270°. In this case the receiver must "wrap" to the previously sampled chip. The sensitivity to clock jitter is then proportional to the size of the input

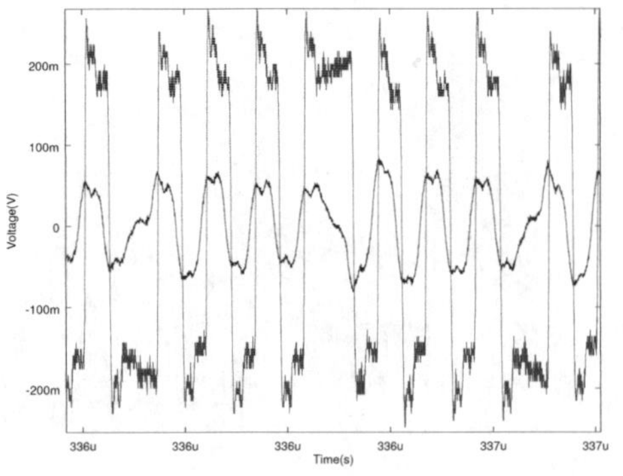

Figure 11: Time domain plot of received signal (blue) and reference signal (green) at 21MHz, spreading factor 8 with $d = 22.5cm$

sample buffer. The sample buffer has been set to 64 in the prototype receiver design.

The presence of noise, combined with the transient response of the input filter would occasionally cause the receiver data recovery stage to incorrectly "wrap", leading to an extra chip detected and a corresponding loss of synchronisation. This was the case with the 5MHz BER measurements presented below.

The lower incidence of phase changes with higher spreading factors helps to alleviate this. With higher spreading factors, the channel tends to stabilise on the current phase, allowing the receiver to more easily detect the phase information, in the presence of noise.

3.3 Bit error rate performance

With a maximum sample duration of 2ms for the oscilloscope, it was not possible to demodulate packets at 300kHz or 2MHz with a spreading factor of 64. For all other packet types, Figures 12 and 13 show the raw and demodulated bit error rates respectively. Note that for all spreading factors, at 5MHz, the receiver was unable to correctly synchronise. Similarly at a spreading factor of 8 synchronisation was not achieved at 21 and 42MHz. For all other frequencies and spreading factors the receiver was able to synchronise with correct demodulation except at 42MHz, spreading factor 16.

The number of chips captured during the 2ms sampling interval varied from 4096 chips at 300MHz to 233474 chips at 60MHz. Incorrect chip detection around the phase transitions was the largest contributing factor to the raw BER. This can be seen in 12 where the BER improves for larger spreading factors. The compromise between energy per bit requirements and BER performance may be seen by comparing figures 7 and 12.

Achieving reliable synchronisation at the intended operating frequency requires customisation of the analogue front end filter to the transmission frequency. Further work to improve

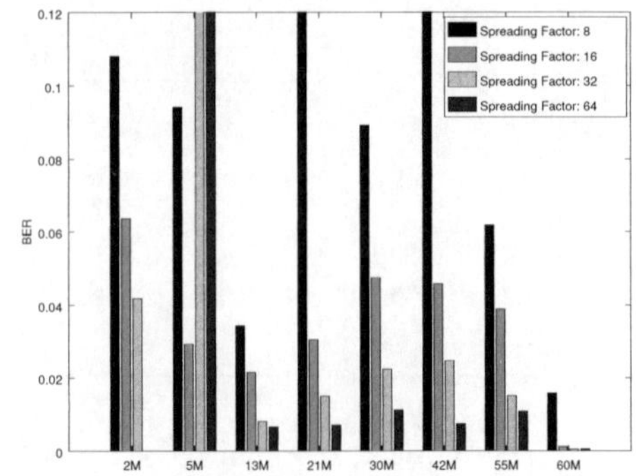

Figure 12: Plot of BER at the receiver before after hard decision detection.

the receiver's data recovery stage will be investigated.

The use of Walsh coding provides effective error correction over the channel under consistent environmental conditions. For example, at a spreading factor of 8 at 30MHz, the receiver was able to correct 5940 hard decision bit errors and correctly reconstruct the packet. A comparison of Figures 12 and 13 demonstrates the effectiveness of the error correction scheme. The Walsh coding algorithm presented in IEEE 802.15.6 allows for a low complexity receiver through the use of LUTs [7], reducing the logic requirements of the receiver. The 64 bit hamming distance LUT implemented in the prototype receiver requires 17 6 bit LUTs. Future testing of environmental fading found in real world applications will be undertaken in order to characterise the performance of the error correction scheme.

Figure 12 demonstrates improvements in raw BER with frequency. While this might suggest that higher frequencies will be more attractive for capacitively coupled human body communications, the increase in air coupling shown in Figure 8 suggests that RF propagation is becoming more dominant at high frequencies.

4. CONCLUSION

This experiment has shown that reliable communications using capacitive coupling with the IEEE 802.15.6 protocol may be achieved using low cost FPGA technology combined with simple analogue interfacing. With channel attenuation as low as 11.4dB over 22.5cm, capacitive coupling offers significantly lower attenuation than an RF based approach. As seen in this study, transmitter power consumption may be as low as 4.5 nJ per bit, using FPGA technology. Development of a portable prototype transceiver will allow for rapid channel attenuation measurement in variety of environments, including those typically experienced by an end user. This information will be used in future assessment of the efficacy of the modulation scheme proposed by IEEE 802.15.6.

5. REFERENCES

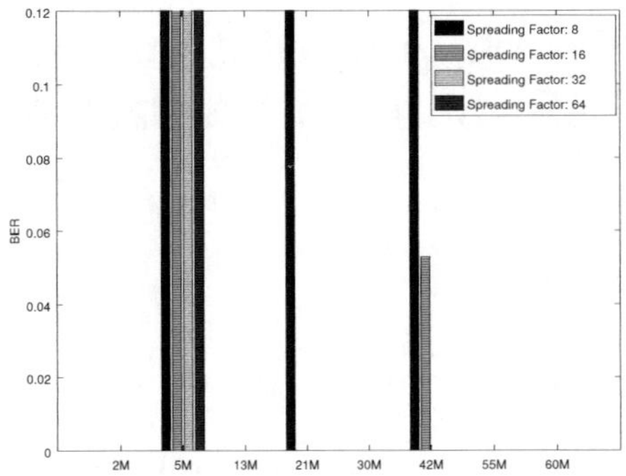

Figure 13: Plot of BER demodulation by the prototype receiver. Loss of synchronisation is the cause of the large BER seen at 5MHz.

[1] IEEE Standard for Local and metropolitan area networks - Part 15.6: Wireless Body Area Networks. *IEEE Std 802.15.6-2012*, pages 1–271, Feb. 2012.

[2] N. Cho, J. Yoo, S.-J. Song, J. Lee, S. Jeon, and H.-J. Yoo. The Human Body Characteristics as a Signal Transmission Medium for Intrabody Communication. *Microwave Theory and Techniques, IEEE Transactions on*, 55(5):1080–1086, May 2007.

[3] M. Hagmann, R. Levin, L. Calloway, A. Osborn, and K. Foster. Muscle-equivalent phantom materials for 10-100 MHz. *Microwave Theory and Techniques, IEEE Transactions on*, 40(4):760–762, 1992.

[4] Z. Lucev, I. Krois, and M. Cifrek. A Capacitive Intrabody Communication Channel from 100 kHz to 100 MHz. *Instrumentation and Measurement, IEEE Transactions on*, 61(12):3280–3289, Dec. 2012.

[5] G. Makkena, K. Abhilash, and M. Srinivas. Gaussian filter approximation using Levin's transformation for implementation in analog domain. In *Microelectronics and Electronics (PrimeAsia), 2013 IEEE Asia Pacific Conference on Postgraduate Research in*, pages 204–207, Dec. 2013.

[6] Nick Sawyer. XAPP225: Data to Clock Phase Alignment, Feb. 2009.

[7] V. Sklyarov and I. Skliarova. Digital Hamming weight and distance analyzers for binary vectors and matrices.

[8] J. Wang and Q. Wang. *Body Area Communications: Channel Modeling, Communication Systems, and EMC.* Wiley-IEEE Press, 2012.

[9] Xilinx Inc. UG733: Xilinx Power Tools Tutorial, Mar. 2010.

Simultaneous Estimation of WCE Moving Distance and Heading Direction Based on RSSI-based Localization

Takahiro Ito, Daisuke Anzai and Jianqing Wang
Graduate School of Engineering
Nagoya Institute of Technology
Gokiso-cho, Showa-ku, Nagoya, Aichi 466-8555, Japan
t.ito.436@stn.nitech.ac.jp, {anzai,wang}@nitech.ac.jp

ABSTRACT

In this paper, we propose a simultaneous moving distance and heading direction estimation method for wireless capsule endoscope (WCE) system only with RSSI measurement data, which can be obtained as a fundamental function of wireless communications. This paper first focuses on an RSSI-based WCE location tracking method with a particle filter algorithm. Then, in order to accurately estimate the moving distance and heading direction, the proposed method detects the waypoints (pass points) based on the time-series estimated WCE location information, on which the WCE moving in gastrointestinal tract. Consequently, both estimation can be realized with connecting the estimated waypoints. From our computer simulation results, the proposed method can achieve good estimation performances of the moving distance and heading direction with the accuracies of several centimeters and several degrees, respectively, without specific additional sensor devices.

Categories and Subject Descriptors

C.2.1 [**Computer-Communication Networks**]: Network Architecture and Design—*Wireless communication*

General Terms

Measurement

Keywords

Body area network, wireless capsule endoscope, localization.

1. INTRODUCTION

Recently, body area network (BAN) technology has been widely studied and applied to medical or healthcare applications [1]. In particular, a wireless capsule endoscope (WCE) system is an important application in implant BAN technologies [2–6]. A WCE contains a color camera, a battery, lights, and a transmitter. It moves depending on peristalsis and provides videos or photographs taken in a gastrointestinal (GI) tract.

Considering a realistic situation for WCE systems, the WCE location information is convenient to doctors for diagnosis. In addition to the location information, it is important to estimate the moving distance and the heading direction as well. If we can obtain not only the location information but also the moving distance, the correctness of diagnosis in a small intestine would be improved because tumor location should be more clearly identified. Additionally, the heading direction information allows us to realize highly effective wireless power transmission, which can be expected to solve the energy consumption problem in WCE systems.

There are some ways to obtain the moving distance and heading direction of a WCE. For example, it is a simple way to equip sensor devices into the WCE, such as triaxial accelerometer sensor for moving distance measurement and gyro sensor for heading direction detection. However, it is unrealistic to add such sensor devices to the WCE due to its small size. For avoiding to introduce additional devices on the WCE, this paper aims to estimate them only with received signal strength indicator (RSSI) data, which can be measured as a fundamental function of wireless communications. As for WCE location estimation methods, some radio frequency (RF)-based localization methods have been proposed in literature [3, 4]. Also, we have so far developed an RSSI-based WCE tracking method with a particle filter algorithm, and demonstrated its localization accuracy of 7 mm [5]. In this paper, we propose a moving distance and heading direction estimation method based on the time-series location estimated by the RSSI-based localization, and evaluate its performance through computer simulations.

The rest of this paper is organized as follows: In Section 2, we introduce an RSSI-based WCE localization method with a particle filter. Section 3 proposes an estimation method of the moving distance and heading direction. The performance evaluation is performed in Section 4, and we finally conclude this paper in Section 5.

2. RSSI-BASED LOCALIZATION METHOD FOR WCE WITH PARTICLE FILTER

2.1 System model

We assume that M receivers are located on patient's body and a WCE is located inside of small intestine. The location of the m-th receiver is represented as $\boldsymbol{r}_m$ and the WCE location is represented as $\boldsymbol{r}$. We assume 400MHz medical implant communication services (MICS) band signals as transmit signals. The location information of all receivers are

BODYNETS 2015, September 28-30, Sydney, Australia

DOI 10.4108/eai.28-9-2015.2261407

known in advance, on the other hand, the WCE location is unknown. Their three-dimensional locations are defined as

$$\boldsymbol{r} = [x, y, z]^T \quad (1)$$

$$\boldsymbol{r}_m = [x_m, y_m, z_m]^T \quad (2)$$

where $(\cdot)^T$ indicates the transpose of $(\cdot)$. We also define RSSI vector as $\boldsymbol{P} = [P_1, \cdots, P_M]$. Here, $\boldsymbol{P}$ obtained on each receiver will be handed over to a localization system.

2.2 RSSI-based location tracking with particle filter

The propagation characteristic of implant BAN signals in MICS band can be well expressed with the following two-layered model [6].

$$\mu(d) = \log \overline{P_r} = \log[\alpha d^{-n}] \quad (3)$$

$$p(P_r|d) = \frac{1}{\sqrt{2\pi}\sigma P_r} \exp\left[-\frac{\{\log P_r - \mu(d)\}^2}{2\sigma^2}\right] \quad (4)$$

where P_r, d are the received power (namely, RSSI) and the distance between the transceivers, respectively. The literature [6] reported the parameters, $\alpha = 10^{-7.5}$, $n = 6.65$ and $\sigma = 5.50$.

Then, we apply the propagation characteristics shown in Eqs. (3) and (4) into a particle filter-based location tracking algorithm. The particle filter algorithm repeats the following four steps within every time interval Δt. In the prediction step of the particle filter, each particle is linearly moved to respective destination depending on random waypoint (pass point) model [5, 7] resembling intestinal peristalsis. When a particle reaches its destined waypoint, new destination will be set to it. Besides, the particle is expected to linger in intestine bends for a random amount of time, therefore it stops working for the seconds decided by the uniform distribution $\mathcal{U}(0, 20)$. The update step in the particle filter then executes that importance weight of each particle is updated based on the likelihood function derived in Eq. (4). In order to avoid significant degeneracy, resampling is performed in the particle filter algorithm. Resampling is a process that the negligible particles with low weight are eliminated and effective particles with high weight are duplicated. Finally in the estimation step, the estimated location is calculated with the weighted average of all particles.

3. ESTIMATION METHOD OF MOVING DISTANCE AND HEADING DIRECTION

3.1 Simple moving distance estimation

To simply estimate the moving distance, it can be estimated by integrate the instantaneous velocities of the WCE. In this method, the estimated moving distance $l[n]$ is expressed by

$$l[n] = \sum_{i=1}^{n} \left|\hat{\boldsymbol{r}}[i] - \hat{\boldsymbol{r}}[i-1]\right| \quad (5)$$

where $\hat{\boldsymbol{r}}[i]$ is the estimated location vector calculated by the RSSI-based localization at the time index i. However, because of the WCE forward and back movement, this simple method might not be able to perform accurate direction estimation. For this reason, we propose another method which

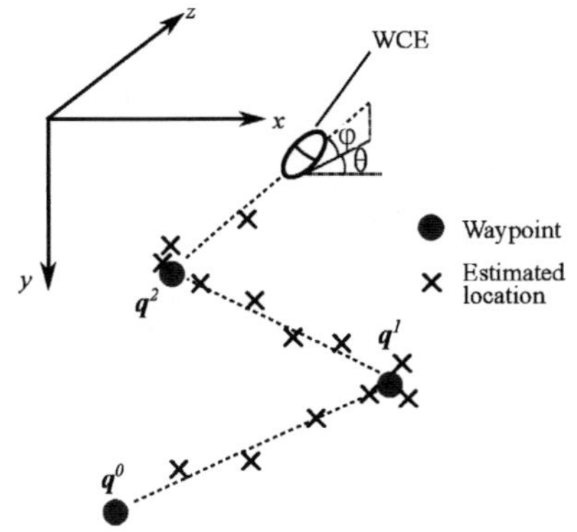

Figure 1: Example of WCE movement.

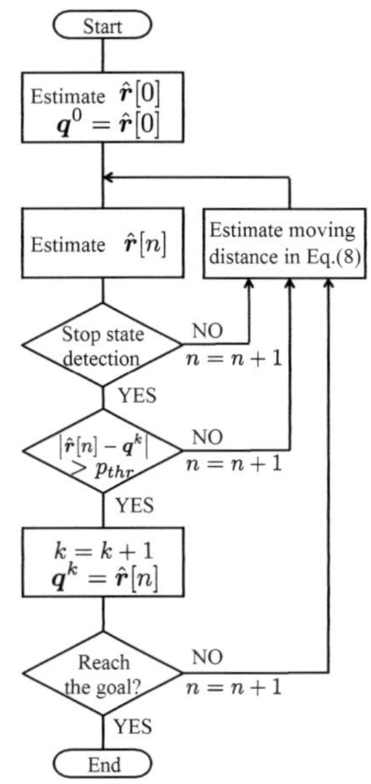

Figure 2: Flowchart of moving distance estimation.

detects the waypoints based on the time-series estimated WCE location information, on which the WCE moving in GI tract and then calculates the moving distance with connecting them.

3.2 Proposed moving distance estimation

Let us define the k-th three-dimensional location of the waypoints as $\boldsymbol{q}^k = [q_x^k, q_y^k, q_z^k]^T$. $\boldsymbol{q}^k$ should be decided as the location where the heading direction of the WCE changes. An example of WCE movement is shown in Fig. 1. In this figure, the WCE moves according to the Random Waypoint model, so it can be seen that we are able to detect the waypoints based on the time-series estimated location information. Also, the flowchart of our proposed method is shown in Fig.2. Our proposed algorithm consists of the following 5 procedures.

Initialization: At the beginning, the first estimated location

Table 1: Simulation parameters.

Number of particles	5000
Resampling threshold	0.7
Transmission interval Δt	0.1 s
Average speed of WCE moving	0.05 cm/s
Variance of the speed	0.005 $(\text{cm/s})^2$
S	20

$\hat{\boldsymbol{r}}[0]$ is calculated by the particle filter and assigned to the first waypoint $\boldsymbol{q}^0$.

Location estimation: $\hat{\boldsymbol{r}}[n]$ is estimated by the RSSI-based location tracking with the particle filter.

Stop state detection: In this step, we detect whether the WCE moves or stops. This detection is performed as follows:

$$\textit{Detect stop state if } |\boldsymbol{r}'_1[n] - \boldsymbol{r}'_2[n]| < r_{thr}$$
$$\textit{Detect moving state otherwise.}$$

where

$$\boldsymbol{r}'_1[n] = \frac{1}{S/2}\sum_{i=1}^{S/2} \boldsymbol{r}[n-S+i] \quad (6)$$

$$\boldsymbol{r}'_2[n] = \frac{1}{S/2}\sum_{i=S/2+1}^{S} \boldsymbol{r}[n-S+i] \quad (7)$$

In the above equations, S and r_{thr} are the time interval and a threshold of the detection, respectively. Here, the location with the stop state indicates the waypoint.

Waypoint update: The distance between $\hat{\boldsymbol{r}}[n]$ and $\boldsymbol{q}^k$ is calculated. If the distance is larger than p_{thr}, we update the waypoint q^k.In this case, k becomes $k+1$ and $\hat{\boldsymbol{r}}[n]$ is assigned to $\boldsymbol{q}^{k+1}$. Note that the threshold p_{thr} gives the minimum distance between each waypoint.

Moving distance estimation: Finally, using the estimated waypoint $\boldsymbol{q}^k$, the moving distance can be estimated as

$$l[n] = \left|\hat{\boldsymbol{r}}[n] - \boldsymbol{q}^k\right| + \sum_{k'=1}^{k} \left|\boldsymbol{q}^{k'} - \boldsymbol{q}^{k'-1}\right|. \quad (8)$$

3.3 Heading direction estimation

Moreover, we can simultaneously obtain heading direction information of the WCE according to the following equations:

$$\theta^k = \arctan\left(\frac{q_z^{k+1} - q_z^k}{q_x^{k+1} - q_x^k}\right) \quad (9)$$

$$\phi^k = \arctan\left(\frac{q_y^{k+1} - q_y^k}{\sqrt{(q_x^{k+1} - q_x^k)^2 + (q_z^{k+1} - q_z^k)^2}}\right) \quad (10)$$

where θ^k and ϕ^k are the k-th angle in the horizontal plane and the k-th angle of elevation/depression, respectively, as shown in Fig. 1.

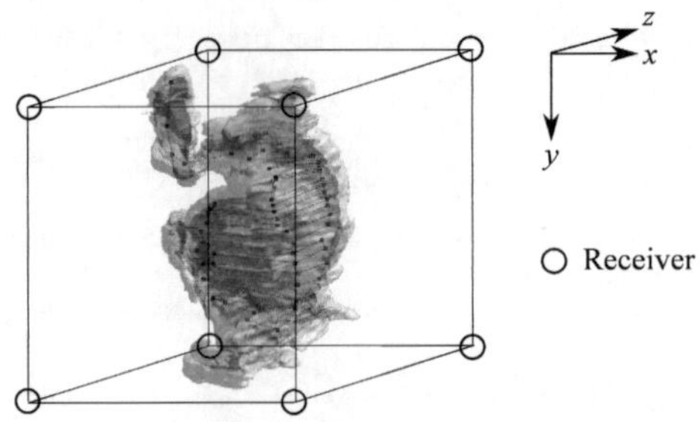

Figure 3: Locus of WCE.

4. PERFORMANCE EVALUATION

4.1 Simulation settings

In order to evaluate the performance of the proposed estimation method, we performed computer simulations. We assumed that a WCE was inside of small intestine and moves in accordance with the random way point model as shown in Fig.3. The location estimation area was a cuboid area whose sizes were 40 cm × 40 cm × 20 cm. Receivers were located on the corners of the cuboid location estimation area. The other simulation parameters are summarized in Table 1.

4.2 Performance evaluation

Fig. 4 illustrates the root mean square (RMS) location estimation error of the RSSI-based tracking with the particle filter in time domain for 10 minutes. Fig. 4 shows that particle filter-based localization can achieve the accuracy of 8.5 mm at 600 s. In contrast, the simple 40-taps FIR (finite impulse response) filter-based localization is also evaluated. The localization accuracy of FIR filter-based localization is about 15 mm, which is twice as large as that of the particle filter-based localization.

Fig. 5 shows the simulation results of the estimated moving distance against the threshold p_{thr} at 10 minutes. From the results, when p_{thr} is 0.02 or 0.03 m, the moving distance can be accurately estimated with any values of r_{thr}. For instance, the estimation error is -0.01479 m when p_{thr} = 0.03[m] and r_{thr} = 0.003[m]. Fig. 6 shows the estimated moving distance in time domain. Fig. 6 also includes the result by the simple estimation method shown in Eq.(5). As can be seen from Fig. 6, the performance of the proposed estimation method is much better than that of the simple method. This means that is difficult to estimate the moving distance by simple integration of the instantaneous velocities due to the forward and back movement of the WCE. On the other hand, the proposed method can properly estimate the moving distance by accurately detecting the waypoints.

Finally, let us discuss the performance of the heading direction estimation. Fig. 7 illustrates the RMS heading direction estimation error with r_{thr} = 0.003[m] at 10 minutes. When we use the parameter p_{thr} from 0.02 to 0.05 m, RMS heading direction estimation error converges less than 0.5 rad, therefore, the proposed method can estimated the heading direction with the accuracy of less than 10 degrees without equipping special sensor devices into the WCE.

5. CONCLUSIONS

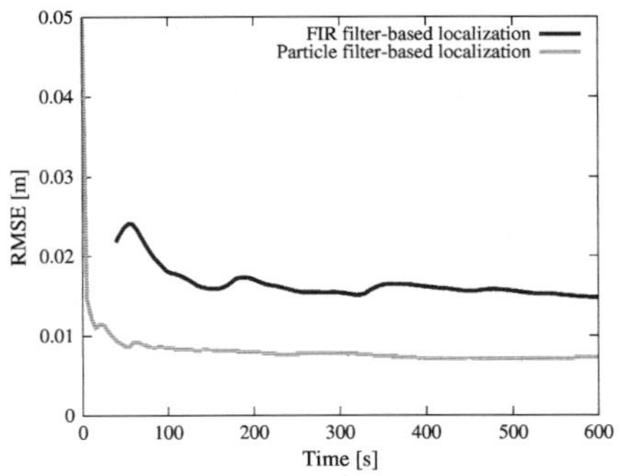

Figure 4: Location estimation accuracy.

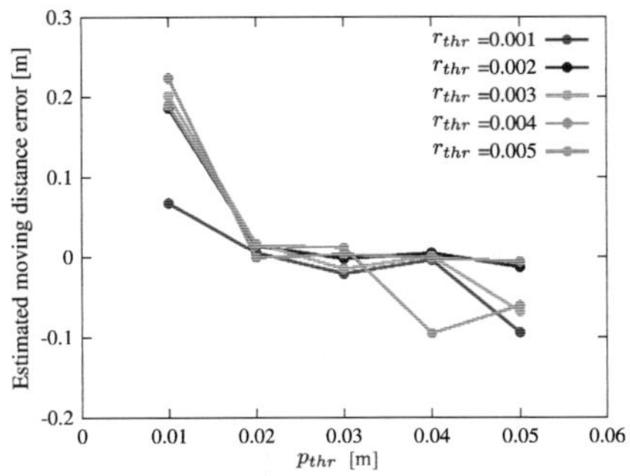

Figure 5: Moving distance estimation performance.

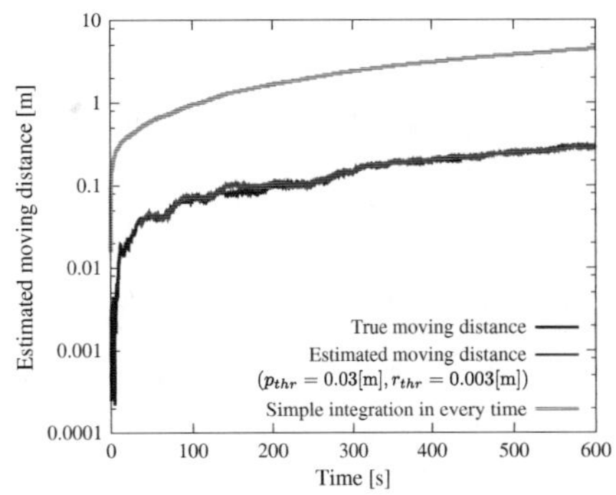

Figure 6: Estimated moving distance in time domain.

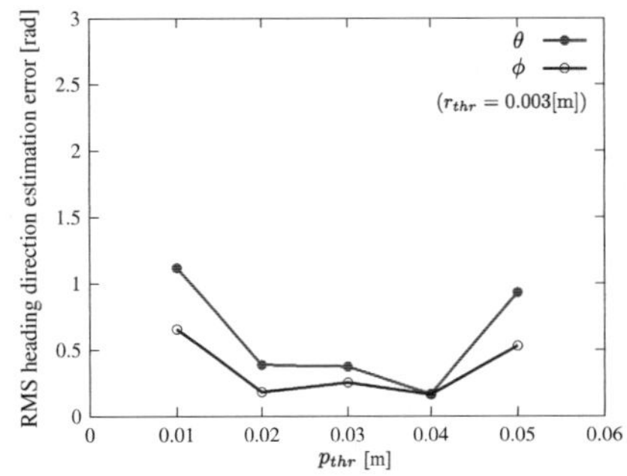

Figure 7: RMS heading direction estimation error.

This paper has proposed a method which simultaneously estimates moving distance and heading direction of a WCE from time-series estimated location information. Then we have evaluated the performances of our proposed method. From the simulation results, the moving distance and the heading direction have been estimated with high accuracies of less than 3 cm and 10 degrees, respectively, without specific sensor devices on the WCE.

6. ACKNOWLEDGMENTS

This study was supported partially by JSPS KAKENHI Grant Number 15K18063, The Telecommunications Advancement Foundation and The Naito Research Grant.

7. REFERENCES

[1] H. Li and R. Kohno, "Body area network and its standardization at IEEE 802.15. BAN," *Advances in Mobile and Wireless Communications*, pp. 223–238, 2008.

[2] M.Fischer, R.Schreiber, D.Levi, and R.Eliakim, "Capsule endoscopy: the localization system," *Gastrointestinal endoscopy clinics of north america*, vol. 14, pp. 25–31, 2004.

[3] M. Kawasaki and R. Kohno, "A TOA based positioning technipue of medical implanted devices," in *Proc. of the 3rd International Symposium on Medical Information and Communication Technology (ISMICT)*, 2009.

[4] A. Nafchi, S. Goh, and S. Zekavat, "Circular arrays and inertial measurement unit for DOA/TOA/TDOA-based endoscopy capsule localization: Performance and complexity investigation," *IEEE Sensors Jornal*, vol. 14, pp. 3791–3799, 2014.

[5] T. Ito, D. Anzai, and J. Wang, "Performance evaluation on RSSI-based wireless capsule endoscope location tracking with particle filter," *IEICE Trans. Commun.*, vol. 97, no. 3, pp. 579–586, 2014.

[6] D. Anzai, S. Aoyama, and W. Jianqing, "Performance evaluation on RSSI-based localization for capsule endoscopy systems with 400 MHz MICS band signals," *IEICE Trans. Commun.*, vol. 95, no. 10, pp. 3081–3087, 2012.

[7] B. Moussakhani, R. Chavez-Santiago, and I. Balasingham, "Multi model tracking for localization in wireless capsule endoscopes," in *Proc. of the 4th International Symposium on Applied Sciences in Biomedical and Communication Technologies (ISABEL)*, no. 159, 2011.

A smart phone based gait monitor system

Dong Qin
Department of Electrical Engineering and Computer Science
Case Western Reserve University
10900 Euclid Ave
Cleveland, Ohio
dxq21@case.edu

Ming-Chun Huang
Department of Electrical Engineering and Computer Science
Case Western Reserve University
10900 Euclid Ave
Cleveland, Ohio
ming-chun.huang@case.edu

ABSTRACT

Gait analysis is the study of human locomotion and is able to provide useful information in various areas such as health care, therapy, sports training, and characteristic recognition. This paper presents a smartphone based system to collect and calculate gait parameters. These parameters consisted of step length, velocity, cadence, motion intensity, and walking regularity are calculated from the sensor data collected by the inertial sensor of a smart-phone. A prototype of gait parameter collection and visualization system was developed on a laptop and cell phone. The proposed system collects accelerometer data from a smart-phone and calculates the gait parameters related to walking activity. All the parameters are displayed on a customized Matlab graphic user interface on the laptop. The fall detection function is also integrated into the system. Once the user fall down, an alarm message will be sent to preset contact. The experiments are carried out on 4 subjects to test the stability and accuracy of the system. The system shows high accuracy and reliability on counting steps (error<5.47%) and walking duration (error<4.55%). Based on the gait monitor system, an anomaly data detection method is presented. Four independent gait parameters include cadence, and tri-axel motion intensity parameters are chosen from previous results during normal activity. If the latest data deviates from the normal activity model too far, the data will be set as an abnormal event.

Keywords

Gait analysis, wearable computing, fall detection, gait model

1. INTRODUCTION

Gait analysis studies human locomotion in terms of gait parameters, like walking cadence, velocity and step length, augmented by measuring body movements, body mechanics, and the activity of the muscles. Gait analysis is used to assess, plan, and treats individuals with diseases that affect their ability to walk. It is also commonly used in sports biomechanics to improve athletes run in more efficiently way or to identify posture or movement related problems for injured people. Walking activities are described as gait event in the studies. The gait event or cycle begins when one heel hits the ground and ends when another heel hitting the same ground. The events consist of the stance phase (the heel-to-toe contact sequence of the foot) and the Swing phase (the foot suspending and proceeding in the air).

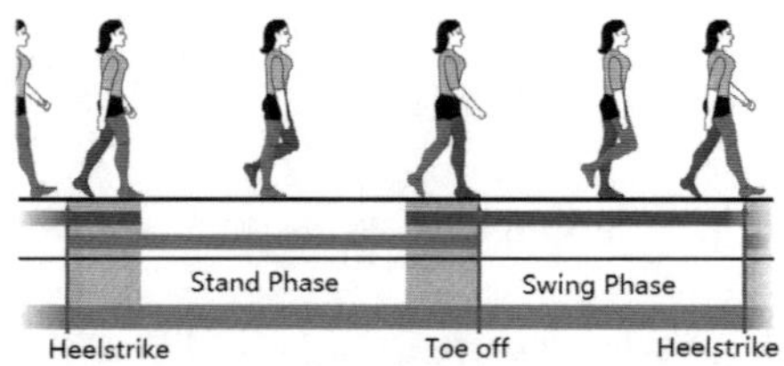

Figure 1: Gait cycle [1]

Some commonly used gait parameters are defined based on the detection of gait event. The velocity is the relation between the walking distance and duration. Step length is the tip-to-tip or heel-to-heel distance between two subsequent feet. Cadence is the number of steps the person walking per second. A search on the web for scientific articles that include "gait" in the title returned more than 3,400 publications between 2012 and 2013 [16]. All these researches are acquired quantitative measurements that characterized gait in order to apply them to various fields. Therefore, various sensors have been developed to measure data related to walking activities. These user carried sensors can be divided into three categories: imaging, floor, and body-worn sensors.

The statistical data shows that 40% of the reviewed articles published in late 2012 and 2013 are related to non-wearable systems, and 37.5% of them are proposed inertial sensor-based systems. The remaining 22.5% are from other wearable systems. An increasing number of researches indicated the fact that the body-wear based portable sensors systems are the most promising method for gait analysis [16].

Our work is focused on designing a smart-phone based gait monitor system which is easier to spread than other independent gait monitor systems. Most smart-phone has an inertial measurement unit built inside. An inertial measurement unit worked by detecting current rate of acceleration using multi-axes accelerometer and rotational attributes like

BODYNETS 2015, September 28-30, Sydney, Australia

DOI 10.4108/eai.28-9-2015.2261519

pitch, roll and yaw using multi-axis gyroscope. Some also include magnetometer mostly to assist calibration against orientation drift. For the purpose of gait analysis, these data are converted into commonly used gait parameters such as velocity, step length, and cadence.

Falling detection is an important application for inertial sensor. Falling can happen in anytime and anywhere, and may cause serious consequence especially for the older population. It is estimated that more than one third of the adults aged over 65 years fell each year [2],[17], and therefore makes it the leading cause of nonfatal injury for the age group. Recent researches on injuries in general public have shown that the fall is an increasing cause of injury, especially fractures, in elderly individuals [11].

Among older people, 55 percent of fall injuries occurred inside the home. An additional 23 percent occurred outside but near their home [19],[3]. Traditionally, placing seniors in nursing homes or care centers reduces the risk of fall. However, with wireless networks and low-power mote technology, we can now approach the problem from a different perspective [3],[4],[9]. With highly reliable fall detection system, person suffered from fall especially the aged population can be found immediately, and a real time alarm system can be build based on the architectures.

In addition to fall, similar accidents happening during daily life include slip and trip. Slip has been a research topic for a long time. Some researches focus on the relation between fall or trip accidents and build features like stairs, ladders, windows and roofs. They find fall accounted for more than 80% slip, trip and fall (STF) related fatalities, and 61.4% of these accidents are related to fall on stairs [5]. There are also some researches studied the STF accidents in work groups with reference to age. The group with age of 45 or higher has an increased rate of STF accidents in recent years [12]. Aside from occupational accidents, STF is also the second-leading reason for intentional death. It cause more than 25,000 fatalities in 2009. Elderly individuals have the highest risk, more than 3.3 million nonfatal STFs happen on elderly individuals in 2012.

2. RELATED WORKS

The following researches provide statistic references for others. Herran et al. [16] reviewed gait analysis researches, including image processing, floor sensors, and sensors placed on the body. The statistic result shows a trend that the wearable sensor are becoming more and more popular in both research field and application field. Kunze et al. [13] compared the differences among the body sensors placements such as on the head, wrist, torso, and pocket. They implanted series of experiments and the result suggested that the waist could be the most reliable choice for measuring human activity.

In order to obtain accurate gait parameters, various algorithms for converting raw sensor data to gait parameters have been developed. Trojaniello et al. [20]reviewed five methods of estimating gait event and temporal parameter from the acceleration signals of single inertial measurement unit were compared through tests. Their result indicates that their sensitivity values varies from 81% to 100% across methods. Their positive predictive values are ranged from 94% to 100%. In the estimation of step and stride durations, all methods are acceptable while in estimating swing, stance and double support time some differences were found due to the error of final contact detection. It shows the position of the IMU on the lower trunk does not affect the accuracy too much except for one method. Depending on the statistical analysis result in the previous paper. M method has a good performance in the estimation of gait parameters. In the paper of M method [15], the author presents their estimating method which is relatively better than other two methods in previous researches. They take advantages from the continuous wavelet transform which can remove extraneous signal fluctuation but preserve the underlying frequency. When combining with differentiation analysis, it shows good performance in suppressing noise, correcting baseline drift, resolving overlapping peaks. Thus, it can detect the initial contact (IC) and final contact (FC) exactly which indicates the beginning and the ending of a gait event. They also present a method to determine if the contact came from the right foot or the left foot. Except accelerometer, inertial measurement unit (IMU) also provided with gyroscope, so they can use angular velocity signal within the gyroscope to distinguish each side of contacts. In their experiment, all ICs and FCs are detected by their method and the time error was approximately 2% and 3% in each side, respectively.

Accelerometer or inertial sensor based fall detection methods have been raised in recent years. Gupta et al. [10] performed falling detection using tri-axial accelerometer. They put the accelerometer on subjects' waist combining with pressure sensor in the insole. They applied threshold based algorithm for fall detection which was similar to the algorithms from others. They also present new algorithm based on frequency analysis which used wavelet transform. It has good performance for gait classification and fall detection. Chen et al. [7]presented a fall detection method using non-invasive wearable sensor in conjunction with wireless network. They used low-power and low-cost MEMS technology based accelerometer and built a wearable circuit board for that. Then it was put on the waist for measuring the acceleration of a subject. Once the norm of the acceleration exceeds a threshold, an impact was found. If there was no impact within next several seconds, the system started to look for orientation change. If there was no orientation change from the subject, which indicated the subject was injured or even unconscious, the alarm system would send warning message to the nurse. Selvabalab et al. [18] implemented the human fall detection system using two wireless network architectures, named cross bow wireless sensor node system and PIC18LF4620 wireless module. The fall detection mechanism was conceived with two sensors including three-axes accelerometer and Passive Infrared (PIR) sensor to monitor the activities for elderly people. The resultant voltage changed because of the human activities are the targeted interest and are detected through both sensors. The real time output is compared with stored templates and the computational analysis is done within microcontroller in real time. The system informs the caretaker through the wireless architecture once any abnormal data different from the stored templates detected.

More complex activity monitor systems can identify different activities or recognize stumble rather than general fall. Lee et al. [14] implemented wireless accelerometer sensor module and algorithms to recognize wearer's posture, activities and fall. In their algorithm, activity is determined by the AC component of accelerometer signal and the posture is determined by the DC component of accelerometer signal. Those activity and posture included standing, sitting, lying, walking, running and so on. The fall detection rate of the system is 93.2% on 30 subjects. The whole system is built and tested using wireless sensor network in experimental space. This system can be applied to elders for activity monitoring, fall detection, exercise measurement, and pattern analysis. Different from looking for a specific pattern, Chehade et al. introduced a normal distribution walking model based on one feature extracted from acceleration signal during walking [6]. They tried seven different places for the tri-axes accelerometer on the human body. Finally they found the sensor on the chest had the best performance for separating stumble from normal activities. The stumble data is considered as an abnormal deviation from the normal activity model, so they trained their model through a long period of history data. The best threshold of this model was when the model reached the lowest false alarm rate. Some researchers developed a gait parameter analysis tool based on one accelerometer [23]. Yang's group designed a software program for extracting gait parameters from accelerometer signal and displaying these parameter through a graphic user interface. Their work provided a convenient tool for themselves and others. For general purpose, more complicated body sensor networks (BSNs) contain inertial, ECG, humidity, and light sensors, have been studied intensively in recent years. In the perspective of system design methodology, Fortino et al. summarized the common tasks and requirements for BSNs applications in their paper [8]. This paper presented an open-source programming framework, signal processing in node environment (SPINE), which could fulfill these requirements. Therefore, an efficient management of body sensor networks could be achieved under this architecture. In this project, several parameters like cadence, velocity, motion intensity are collected.

3. SYSTEM

3.1 Gait parameter calculation

The system collects data from the sensors in the smartphone which is clipped on the waist. The mobile device recorded acceleration data in a sampling frequency of 50Hz. Then the data is transmitted to the laptop in the Matlab where the raw sensor data is converted into gait parameters. All results and a Flash playing the walking or running cadence of the user are shown in a customized Matlab GUI. Figure 2 and 3 show the system diagram and the system flowchart.

Step counting algorithm is the core of the whole program. This self-adaptive peak-detection algorithm has following advantages comparing with other algorithms. First, it is insensitive to the peak amplitude changing. The amplitude of the peak usually changes and the main reasons can be the location changing in response to our body or motion intensity. The changes of the smart-phone placement may severely affect the peak value because it changed the orientation of the smart-phone and the distribution of the gravity in three coordinates. That is the reason that caused the in-

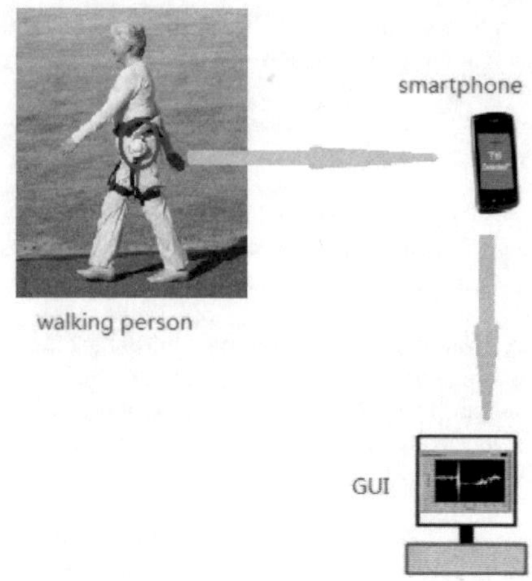

Figure 2: Gait monitor system diagram

Figure 3: System flowchart

accuracy of the threshold based algorithm. Second, since the window sizes change with fundamental frequency all the time, no matter how fast or slow the user walks or runs, it can be guaranteed that the window will not cover two true peaks in anytime while it can exclude the false peak that is closed to the true peak. Thus, this algorithm is superior comparing to other peak detection algorithms using sliding window for fixed size or using filter of fixed cut off frequency.

$$Cadence = steps/walkingduration \tag{1}$$

$$Averagesteplength = walkingdistance/steps \tag{2}$$

$$Velocity = walkingdistance/walkingduration \tag{3}$$

$$RMS = \sqrt{\sum (A_i - A_m)^2/N} \tag{4}$$

$$regularity = A_{ff}^2/\sum A_{fi}^2 \tag{5}$$

The starting and ending times for each walking activity are detected automatically through the real-time step counting algorithm so that the walking duration can be acquired in this way. Based on these information, variety of gait parameters can be calculated through these formulas above. Some of them might require walking distance information input by users. Root mean square (RMS) that related to the exercise intensity is defined by the formula 4. A_i represents i th acceleration sample in the sequence, this sequence contains all samples of a complete walking activity. A_m represents the average value of this sequence and N represents the length of this sequence. The RMS1-3 indicate the three axis of the acceleration signal individually. Regularity is defined by

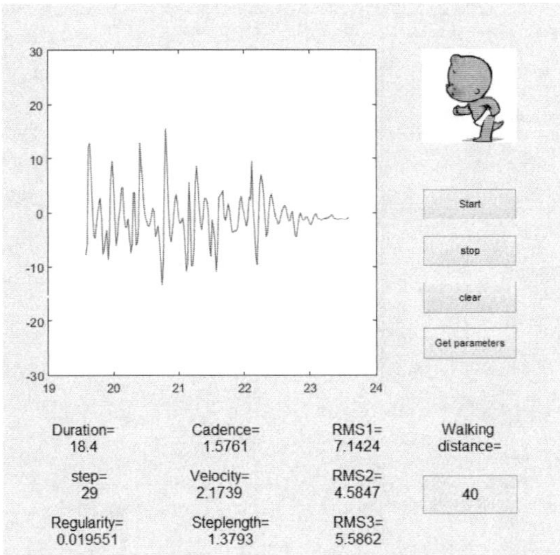

Figure 4: Matlab GUI

Algorithm 1 The gait analysis algorithm

Input: Acceleration samples
Output: Gait parameters
Part a: Dynamic window size adjustment (The system obtains a sliding window with the size equal or close to the duration of one step)
Step 1: Collecting latest post-anterior acceleration data from a fixed window with the size of 150.
Step 2: Performing FFT analysis on these 150 samples, acquiring the fundamental frequency of this sequence.
Step 3: Based on the fundamental frequency, making a new window with the size equal to one cycle of the fundamental component of the signal.
Step 4: If this window size is out of the range between 12 and 50, it is limited to the margin of this range. Which means we suppose that the gait event frequency cannot be higher than 4.16/sec or lower than 1/sec.
Part b: Window locating (In this part the system finds a peak then moves the window to the peak)
Step 5: Applying the new window on the signal sequence, finding the negative peak within the window.
Step 6: Putting the window around the negative peak, so the peak is located in the center of the window.
Part c: Peak verification (In the last the system makes sure that the peak found in last part does correspond to one step)
Step 7: Determining whether the negative peak is the lowest value within the window. If not, go back to step 1. Otherwise, go to next step.
Step 8: If it is different from the last peak value M and this negative peak value is also lower than -2.5*g (gravitation), the number of steps increases by one and the value of M is replaced by this peak value. Otherwise, go back to step 1.
Step 9: Calculating gait parameters based on formulas (1)˜(5).

---

formula 5. In the formula 5, A_{ff} represents the amplitude of the fundamental frequency and A_{fi} represents the amplitude of the i th frequency in the spectrum. The better the subject keeps in a fixed walking cadence, the higher regularity and amplitude of the fundamental frequency. All these parameters are shown in the Figure 4.

3.2 Fall detection

Fall detection and alarming functions are integrated into the system. According to the observation from related experiment [7] falling has distinct feature. The average peak of acceleration changes during siting and walking only reaches 2.5*G and 1.9*G, respectively, while falling are from 6.9*G to 12.7*G. In another experiment [10], the minimal peak value of acceleration changed during falling down is 8.4*G while the maxima values during walking, sitting and shuffle walk are 5.3*G,4.0*G and 4.9*G. These results ensured a robust methodology for threshold based fall detection. In our system, we defined the acceleration changing through the following formula.

$$A_c = \sqrt{\sum (a_{imax} - a_{imin})^2} \tag{6}$$

In this formula, A_c is the indicator of amplitude changing, a_{imax} and a_{imin} is the maximum and minimum values for the latest input acceleration signal sequence with length of 100 in i th direction.

People suffered from fall do not always need help, in most cases they can help themselves. Thus, a double check is implemented after a falling has been found. If there is no distinct acceleration changing after fall for a time period longer than 20 seconds, which means that the person cannot move himself/herself, the system will send an alarm message to another person. We use the formula below to determine if there is any movement on the subject.

$$A_d(n) = \sqrt{\sum a_i(n)^2} - \sqrt{\sum a_i(n-1)^2} \tag{7}$$

$a_i(n)$ represented the n th acceleration data in i th direction. If A_d is larger than 2, the system will take the subject as being able to help himself/herself.

3.3 Abnormal activity detection

An abnormal activity detection algorithm is presented in this work. A normal activity model is built based on several independent real-time gait parameters acquired from previous work (cadence, RMS1-3). When people suffered from accidents like fall, slip or trip, their motion intensity and walking cadence are changing rapidly. Therefore, these parameters are capable of reflecting effectively whether some accidents are happened on the user. First of all, the system collects past 2 minutes data and separates these data into 24 short segments (L,1)˜(L,24). Each segment L has a length for 5 seconds without overlapping. Second, these gait parameters are calculated for each segment. Four sequences of different parameters, (C,1)˜(C,24), (R1,1)˜(R1,24), (R2,1)˜(R2,24) and (R3,1)˜(R3,24) are extracted from (L,1)˜(L,24). These sequences correspond to cadence, RMS1-3. Third, the mean μ and standard deviation σ are calculated in each parameter sequence (C, R1, R2, R3). A normal distribution model is built as Eq.(8).

$$\frac{1}{\sqrt{2\pi}\sigma}exp(-\frac{(x-\mu)^2}{2\sigma^2}) \quad (8)$$

Fourth, a dynamic threshold τ is set based on the normal distribution model, the initial value of the threshold is plus/minus 3σ away from the mean value. Once any of these gait parameters of latest segment is out of the thresholds, an alarm message is shown on the GUI and the user can determine if the reported anomaly is true or false. The threshold in each model is modified based on the false positive and negative. If a sequence of normal walking is reported as an accident, the threshold will be modified by 0.5σ to reduce the sensitivity of alarm system. Vice versa, if an accident is missing, the sensitivity will increase by the same amount. Different from other specific pattern recognition model, the proposed model is built based on a normal walking or running activity. Four different features from the previous gait parameter calculation system are selected to build the normal activity model. This anomaly detection algorithm can find distinct abnormal gait parameters that come from an occasional accident.

4. EXPERIMENT

4.1 Experiment setup

Gait parameters acquired from our system are tested through the following experiments on 4 people. The experiment tools include experiment and control groups. Experiment group includes a smart-phone (Google Nexus6) with clip on a phone case, and a laptop. Control group contains a video recording device and a tape measure. The experiment environment is on an outdoor field with 40 meters straight line drown on the ground.

4.2 Description

During the experiment, each subject went through the calibrated line three times by slow speed walking, fast speed walking, and jogging. The whole process was recorded by video recording device. Following the experiment results, steps, cadence, average velocity, average step length were compared with the real data derived from the video record. Other results like RMS1-3 and regularity were listed individually. In the fall detection test, each subject was asked to fall down on the mattress 3 times in each direction (forward, backward, and sideward), and the number of correct detection times were recorded.

4.3 Results

Subject 1:

slow speed walking

	experimental data	real data
step	60	61
duration(s)	40.6	42.72
cadences(s^{-1})	1.4778	1.4280
velocity(m/s)	0.98522	0.93633
step length(m)	0.66667	0.65574

Fast speed walking

	experimental data	real data
step	55	54
duration(s)	30.8	28.24
cadences(s^{-1})	1.7857	1.9121
velocity(m/s)	1.2987	1.4164
step length(m)	0.72727	0.74074

Jogging

	experimental data	real data
step	44	47
duration(s)	17.6	18.15
cadences(s^{-1})	2.5	2.59
velocity(m/s)	2.2727	2.2039
step length(m)	0.90909	0.85106

Subject 2:

Slow speed walking

	experimental data	real data
step	54	54
duration(s)	32.4	33.31
cadences(s^{-1})	1.6667	1.6211
velocity(m/s)	1.2346	1.2008
step length(m)	0.74074	0.74074

Fast speed walking

	experimental data	real data
step	46	46
duration(s)	22.4	22.39
cadences(s^{-1})	2.0536	2.0545
velocity(m/s)	1.7857	1.7865
step length(m)	0.86957	0.86957

Jogging

	experimental data	real data
step	39	38
duration(s)	15.6	14.92
cadences(s^{-1})	2.5	2.5469
velocity(m/s)	2.5641	2.6810
step length(m)	1.0256	1.0526

Subject 3:

slow speed walking

	experimental data	real data
step	58	52
duration(s)	33.2	29.59
cadences(s^{-1})	1.747	1.757
velocity(m/s)	1.2048	1.3518
step length(m)	0.68966	0.76923

Fast speed walking

	experimental data	real data
step	48	45
duration(s)	22.6	2.0911
cadences(s^{-1})	2.1239	2.0545
velocity(m/s)	1.7699	1.8587
step length(m)	0.83333	0.88889

Jogging

	experimental data	real data
step	29	37
duration(s)	18.4	17.09
cadences(s^{-1})	1.5761	2.165
velocity(m/s)	2.1739	2.3406
step length(m)	1.3793	1.0811

Subject 4:

slow speed walking

	experimental data	real data
step	49	48
duration(s)	26	26.46
cadences(s^{-1})	1.8846	1.8141
velocity(m/s)	1.5385	1.5117
step length(m)	0.81633	0.83333

Fast speed walking

	experimental data	real data
step	44	43
duration(s)	19.8	19.69
cadences(s^{-1})	2.2222	2.0315
velocity(m/s)	2.0202	2.0315
step length(m)	0.90909	0.9302

Jogging

	experimental data	real data
step	41	45
duration(s)	18.2	18.76
cadences(s^{-1})	2.2527	2.3987
velocity(m/s)	2.1978	2.1322
step length(m)	0.97561	0.88889

Subject 1:

	RMS1	RMS2	RMS3	regularity
slow walking	1.9142	1.9892	2.376	0.041143
fast walking	2.492	2.8603	3.6882	0.071887
jogging	6.4425	5.0591	4.0318	0.049401

Subject 2:

	RMS1	RMS2	RMS3	regularity
slow walking	2.5243	1.7616	2.2281	0.037587
fast walking	5.1626	3.1166	3.5248	0.07455
jogging	8.2043	3.5137	4.4467	0.044224

Subject 3:

	RMS1	RMS2	RMS3	regularity
slow walking	3.3612	2.9098	2.6414	0.051346
fast walking	5.6903	4.344	4.2622	0.07823
jogging	7.1424	4.5847	5.5862	0.019551

Subject 4:

	RMS1	RMS2	RMS3	regularity
slow walking	3.8638	2.4607	2.4824	0.061895
fast walking	5.5494	3.983	4.1272	0.091909
jogging	7.026	3.0014	5.1557	0.035737

During fall detection test, falling sideward has the highest detection rate, 100%, and the detection rate of forward and backward falling are 91.7% and 83.3%, respectively.

5. DISCUSSION

The experiment results show acceptable accuracy for calculating steps, duration, cadence, average step length, and velocity. The average error for steps and duration are 5.4692% and 4.5465%, respectively. The main error comes from the jogging test of subject 3. Unlike other subjects, subject 3 did not wear leather belt on the trouser, and the smart-phone could not be placed securely on the user. It caused irregular movement of the smart-phone while jogging. The results indicate that most people have better ability to keep their gait cadence in walking than running. In addition, the comparison of the results from all subjects shows that keeping cadence during running is a challenge task. So the regularity can be used to determine how well people can control their body movement in a regular pattern. The motion intensity indicator RMS shows that in most cases people have more intense movement in vertical direction during walking and running. The limitation of the system is that the gait parameter calculation method requires manually input the walking distance. Currently, many popular commercialized sports bands from Fitbit, Jawbone, and Nike have the function of step counting while none of them has achieve the accurate calculation of walking distance. The related studies have been done in some areas like the inertial sensor based navigation system. This limitation hopefully could be addressed based on these researches. Comparing with these commercialized products, our system is more suitable for people with some abnormal walking posture. In our early research [22][21], these commercialized products were tested on old people, and found perform huge errors on cane or walker users. However, our smart-phone based system does not affected by the abnormal posture from user's arm.

The accuracy of fall detection is closely related to how people fall. Falling sideward has the heaviest impact while the impact of falling forward and backward has mitigated by arm or hip. The threshold based fall detection method could be failed in case of affecting by people's subconscious protection actions. After falling, if the subject stand up within 20 seconds, the alarm will not be triggered. The experiment has one limitation which frequently appears in similar experiments. In order to verify such kind of system, the test should be carried out on people in realistic situations. Since the falling is a rarely happened event, it is hard to collect enough data from realistic situation. Therefore, all falling events are simulated in the laboratory environment. A deliberate falling is slower and slighter than an accidental falling. Moreover, all subjects are falling on a mattress instead of the ground, and it mitigates the impact in some degree and reduces the amplitude of the signal peak during falling. The falling in the realistic situation could be more intense and the amplitude of acceleration signal will be higher as well.

The accuracy of the system has been verified by the experiments, and these gait parameters can be used to describe human activity. The normal distribution model of walking can be used to detect accidents caused by either internal or external factors. The observation and experience indicates that people tend to keep a fixed pace during normal activity. Therefore, the acceleration signal has a repeated pattern and gait parameters should be in a limited range within a short period of time. Any parameter far from this range can be caused by accidents. However, the limitation of this method is it cannot distinguish what accident it is. It requires different sensor in different places like pressure sensor in the insole or inertial sensor on the ankle to recognize some specific patterns.

6. CONCLUSION

This paper presents a convenient tool for collecting data from smart-phons, plotting real-time acceleration data and playing corresponding flash of the user's cadence in GUI, and calculating 9 different key parameters closely related to walking activity. The integrated accident detection function also protects people from injury. The smart-phone platform can be extended to other mobile devices with accelerometer and data transmission functions, and the sampling frequency can also be adjusted from 20 to 250Hz. Currently, the algorithm is designed for putting smart-phone on the waist, the future work will include improving the feasibility of the mobile device on different positions of human body. Moreover, the system performs well in different walking speeds without information from the source of the acceleration peak, and the peak caused by other activities like jumping or sitting can also be taken as a step. Thus, activity classification function can be added to the system.

7. REFERENCES

[1] Definitions of some terms in gait analysis. [online]. `http://www.optogait.com/Applications/Gait-Analysis.`

[2] M. Belshaw, B. Taati, J. Snoek, and A. Mihailidis. Towards a single sensor passive solution for automated fall detection. In *Engineering in Medicine and Biology Society, EMBC, 2011 Annual International Conference of the IEEE*, pages 1773–1776. IEEE, 2011.

[3] J. Cabestany, J. M. Moreno, C. Pérez, A. Samà, A. Catala, A. Rodriguez-Molinero, and M. Arnal. Fate: One step towards an automatic aging people fall detection service. In *Mixed Design of Integrated Circuits and Systems (MIXDES), 2013 Proceedings of the 20th International Conference*, pages 545–552. IEEE, 2013.

[4] B. Caby, S. Kieffer, M. de Saint Hubert, G. Cremer, and B. Macq. Feature extraction and selection for objective gait analysis and fall risk assessment by accelerometry. *Biomedical engineering online*, 10(1):1, 2011.

[5] S. Cayless. Slip, trip and fall accidents: relationship to building features and use of coroners' reports in ascribing cause. *Applied Ergonomics*, 32(2):155–162, 2001.

[6] N. H. Chehade, P. Ozisik, J. Gomez, F. Ramos, and G. Pottie. Detecting stumbles with a single accelerometer. In *Engineering in Medicine and Biology Society (EMBC), 2012 Annual International Conference of the IEEE*, pages 6681–6686. IEEE, 2012.

[7] J. Chen, K. Kwong, D. Chang, J. Luk, and R. Bajcsy. Wearable sensors for reliable fall detection. In *Engineering in Medicine and Biology Society, 2005. IEEE-EMBS 2005. 27th Annual International Conference of the*, pages 3551–3554. IEEE, 2006.

[8] G. Fortino, R. Giannantonio, R. Gravina, P. Kuryloski, and R. Jafari. Enabling effective programming and flexible management of efficient body sensor network applications. *Human-Machine Systems, IEEE Transactions on*, 43(1):115–133, 2013.

[9] P. Gupta. *Real-time fall detection system using wireless MEMS sensors and ZigBee protocol.* PhD thesis, Texas Tech University, 2009.

[10] P. Gupta, G. Ramirez, D. Y. Lie, T. Dallas, R. E. Banister, and A. Dentino. Mems-based sensing and algorithm development for fall detection and gait analysis. In *MOEMS-MEMS*, pages 75930U–75930U. International Society for Optics and Photonics, 2010.

[11] S. Z. Kalula. A who global report on falls among older persons.

[12] K. Kemmlert and L. Lundholm. Slips, trips and falls in different work groups with reference to age. *Safety Science*, 28(1):59–75, 1998.

[13] K. Kunze and P. Lukowicz. Sensor placement variations in wearable activity recognition. *Pervasive Computing, IEEE*, 13(4):32–41, 2014.

[14] Y. Lee, J. Kim, M. Son, and M. Lee. Implementation of accelerometer sensor module and fall detection monitoring system based on wireless sensor network. In *Engineering in Medicine and Biology Society, 2007. EMBS 2007. 29th Annual International Conference of the IEEE*, pages 2315–2318. IEEE, 2007.

[15] J. McCamley, M. Donati, E. Grimpampi, and C. Mazza. An enhanced estimate of initial contact and final contact instants of time using lower trunk inertial sensor data. *Gait & posture*, 36(2):316–318, 2012.

[16] A. Muro-de-la Herran, B. Garcia-Zapirain, and A. Mendez-Zorrilla. Gait analysis methods: an overview of wearable and non-wearable systems, highlighting clinical applications. *Sensors*, 14(2):3362–3394, 2014.

[17] J. Park and I. Yoo. Relationships of stroke patients' gait parameters with fear of falling. *Journal of physical therapy science*, 26(12):1883, 2014.

[18] V. S. N. Selvabala and A. B. Ganesh. Implementation of wireless sensor network based human fall detection system. *Procedia Engineering*, 30:767–773, 2012.

[19] S. Slaughter, C. Hilbert, N. Jouett, and M. McEwen. Quantifying and learning human movement characteristics for fall prevention in the elderly using inertial measurement units and neural networks. In *International Conference of Education, Research and Innovation, Madrid, Spain, ISBN*, pages 978–84, 2009.

[20] D. Trojaniello, A. Cereatti, and U. Della Croce. Accuracy, sensitivity and robustness of five different methods for the estimation of gait temporal parameters using a single inertial sensor mounted on the lower trunk. *Gait & posture*, 40(4):487–492, 2014.

[21] Y. Wu, W. Xu, J. J. Liu, M.-C. Huang, S. Luan, and Y. Lee. An energy-efficient adaptive sensing framework for gait monitoring using smart insole. *Sensors Journal, IEEE*, 15(4):2335–2343, 2015.

[22] W. Xu, M.-C. Huang, N. Amini, J. J. Liu, L. He, and M. Sarrafzadeh. Smart insole: a wearable system for gait analysis. In *Proceedings of the 5th International Conference on PErvasive Technologies Related to Assistive Environments*, page 18. ACM, 2012.

[23] M. Yang, H. Zheng, H. Wang, S. McClean, and D. Newell. igait: An interactive accelerometer based gait analysis system. *Computer methods and programs in biomedicine*, 108(2):715–723, 2012.

Towards Implantable Body Sensor Networks - Performance of MICS Band Radio Communication in Animal Tissue

V.R.K. Ramachandran
Pervasive Systems
Dept. of Computer Science
University of Twente,
Netherlands
v.r.karuppiahramachandran@utwente.nl

Kui Zhang
Pervasive Systems
Dept. of Computer Science
University of Twente,
Netherlands
k.zhang@utwente.nl

Nirvana Meratnia
Pervasive Systems
Dept. of Computer Science
University of Twente,
Netherlands
n.meratnia@utwente.nl

Paul J.M. Havinga
Pervasive Systems
Dept. of Computer Science
University of Twente,
Netherlands
p.j.m.havinga@utwente.nl

ABSTRACT

Reliable wireless communication inside the human body is crucial for the design of implantable body sensor networks (IBSN). The tissues in human body are heterogeneous and have different conductivity and permittivity, which make the modeling of the wireless channel challenging. The design of upper layers of the network stack requires the physical layer characteristics including the channel model. Currently, there is no unique channel model available for implant communication inside body. Various measurement campaigns of channel characteristics are underway. The channel model characteristics depends on the hardware components used such as antenna and matching circuit as well as the operating frequency, which are not taken into account by the existing channel models for implant communication. Moreover, hardware losses and different tissue characteristics have not been taken into account in the link budget of the existing channel models. The approach used in this paper pays special attention to the losses introduced by hardware components of the implant itself and the physical medium. This paper presents characteristics of radio channel using animal tissue. A comparison is made between these measured characteristics and the existing channel characteristics provided by the IEEE 802.15.6 standard. The empirical measurements are used to validate the simulations of the IEEE 802.15.6 model.

Keywords

Pathloss, Animal tissue, Channel model, MICS band radio

1. INTRODUCTION

Reliability of wireless communication largely depends on the environment and the communication medium. The medium in the case of IBSN is the body itself, which is conductive with varying permittivity and permeability and largely affects the propagation of the electromagnetic waves. The physical layer (PHY) and the medium access control layer (MAC) of implant communication are standardized by the IEEE 802.15 task group 6 [13]. A frequency band called Medical Implant Communication Service (MICS) is introduced, which operates at 402-405 MHz for implant communication [13]. MICS band is used by the U.S. Federal Communications Commission (FCC) and the European Telecommunications Standards Institute (ETSI).

The antenna used for IBSN is limited in size and the RF propagation is not trivial inside the body [18]. The communication channel inside the body is completely different from that in the free space because of the tissue properties. Furthermore, the directivity of the antenna is a challenge because the properties of the body tissues influence the antenna radiation pattern. Channel characteristics provided in the IEEE 802.15.6 standard do not clearly indicate the characteristics of the antenna in the path loss model. Furthermore, it is unclear whether antenna matching has been applied when obtaining the channel model in the IEEE 802.15.6 standard [18].

Although different works in modeling the radio propagation in computer based simulation [1, 10, 21] have been done, the amount of research work estimating the empirical path loss response of the real biological tissue in MICS band communications is not adequate. In order to evaluate these electro-magnetic (EM) parameters in *in-vitro* conditions, an environment that has a close resemblance to tissue is required. For instance, a body phantom can be used to simulate the characteristics of tissues in human body [5, 12]. However, the phantoms cannot simulate the heterogeneous layered structure of human tissue. To understand the layered characteristics of the tissue, an animal tissue, which has

BODYNETS 2015, September 28-30, Sydney, Australia

DOI 10.4108/eai.28-9-2015.2261413

close resemblance to human tissue can be used. It is known that the tissue of the pig has the closest resemblance to human tissue [19]. Hence the performance of radio communication in a layered tissue structure can be obtained from tissue extracted from a pig.

To the best of our knowledge, all existing empirical results addressing human channel modeling are related to, communication between sensors placed on the surface of the body (i.e. communication between on-body sensors) and communication between in-body and on-body sensors [8, 14, 15]. The empirical channel modeling related to the communication between in-body sensors are still in its infancy. To this end, EM properties such as relative permittivity, and conductivity of 57 different human tissues were analyzed for RF and microwave frequencies (10 Hz — 20 GHz) in [9]. A few investigations have been reported to determine the effect of human body as a radio channel in wireless medical communication [20]. There are not any empirical measurements of the channel that are made using the animal tissue in MICS band communication.

1.1 Contributions

This paper focuses on the characterization and evaluation of PHY parameters of IBSN in animal tissue. Performance of radio inside the tissue is evaluated with different PHY configurations including transmission power, transmission distance, antenna orientation, and data rate. The main contributions of this paper are:

- Investigation of relationships between operating frequency, transmission power, packet delivery ratio, and data rate with distance and antenna orientations for implant communication;
- Validation of simulations results provided by the IEEE 802.15.6 standard through experimentation with animal tissue
- Characterize the performance of the radio in terms of packet delivery ratio in animal tissue environment.

The rest of this paper is organized as follows. In Section 2 channel model proposed by the IEEE 802.15.6 standard is summarized and its characteristics are described. Section 3 explains our test environment. PHY configurations and choices of evaluation parameters are presented in Section 4 followed by results and a comparison between the simulations of IEEE 802.15.6 in Section 5. Finally the paper is concluded in Section 6 after presenting the observations made from our experiments.

2. IN-BODY COMMUNICATION CHANNEL OF THE IEEE 802.15.6 STANDARD

The human body model of IEEE 802.15.6 is based on frequency dependent biological material and is claimed to have an accuracy of 2mm in tissue properties [18]. The received signal strength is calculated for a grid of points within a cylinder area around the body. The resulting data is then filtered for 2 scenarios, i.e., (i) in-body propagation (channel model 1 (CM 1)): set of points that completely reside inside the body, (ii) in-body to on-body (body surface) propagation (CM 2): set of points that reside within a certain distance (i.e., 2mm, 10mm, 20mm, 50mm) from the body surface. In this paper, we are interested in these two sets of propagation, where the transmitting node is placed inside the body and the receiving node is either placed inside the body or outside the body. The reference path loss $PL(d_0)$ is calculated using the formula shown in Eq. 1, where G_T, P_T, P_R represent the gain of receiving antenna, the transmission power and the receiving power, respectively.

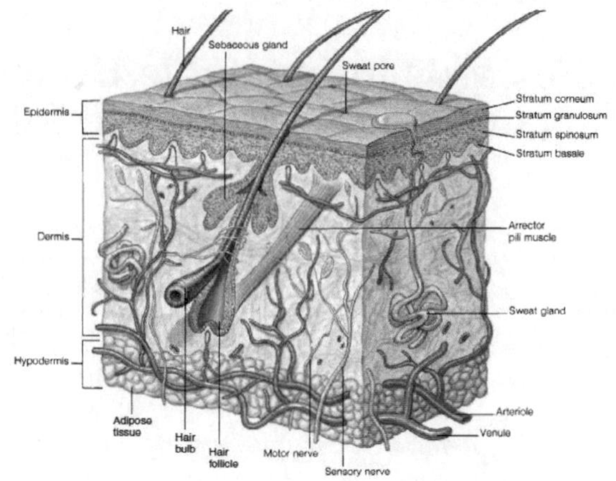

Figure 1: A cross section of animal tissue showing different layers including skin. [6]

$$PL(d_0) = \frac{G_R.P_T}{P_R(d_0)} \quad (1)$$

$$PL(d) = PL(d_0) + 10n\log_{10}(\frac{d}{d_0}) + S \quad (2)$$

The path loss is expressed in terms of log normal distance as shown in Eq. 2, where d_0, $PL(d_0)$, and n are reference distance, path loss at the reference distance d_0, and the path-loss exponent, respectively. S is a Gaussian random variable with zero mean and standard deviation of σ_s accounting for the losses due to tissue layers. When there is a direct line of sight between the sender and the receiver, a free space path loss can be added to CM 2 to account for the additional loss that the signal sent by the implant will go through once it leaves the body.

2.1 Simulation settings of the IEEE 802.15.6 model

In order to validate the simulation results of the channel model we implement the same settings that are used for the simulations. The settings of simulation are tabulated in Table 1.

Parameter	Value
Antenna position	2 cm beneath tissue surface (in-body)
	0-300 cm away from the tissue (off-body)
Transmission distance	0-16 cm (in-body), 0-300 cm (in air)
Antenna orientation	Parallel to the body surface
Transmit power	25μW EIRP (or) -15dBm
Operating frequency	403.5 MHHz center frequency with
	3 MHz bandwidth

Table 1: Simulation parameters from IEEE 802.15.6

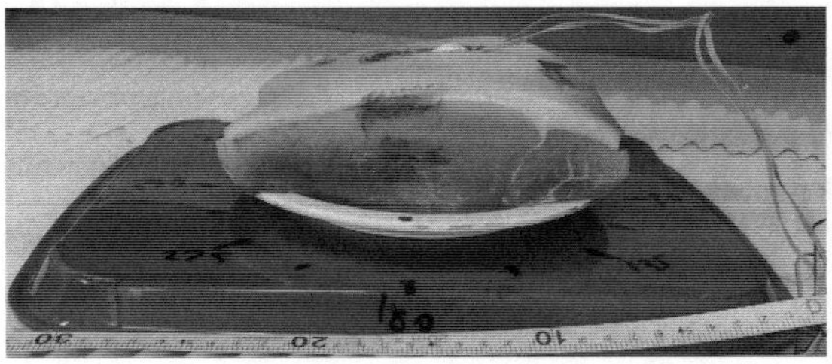

Figure 2: A dissected part of pig tissue used for experimenting with implant communication.

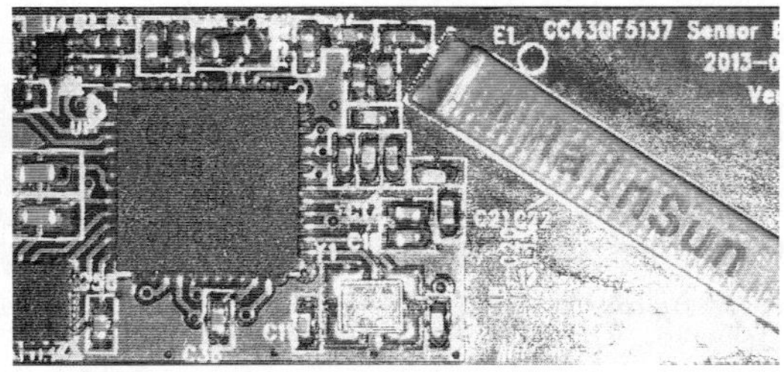

Figure 3: CC430 based implant used in experiments

A complete channel model, which includes shadowing, fading model, delay profile, and spatial properties, is not the aim of this paper. We aim to measure the deviation in path-loss model by measuring the received power at various transmission distances and power. This will ensure the reliability of the computer-simulated model by including the environmental losses which have to be considered in addition to the losses caused by the tissues.

3. EXPERIMENTAL CHARACTERIZATION OF CHANNEL MODEL USING ANIMAL TISSUE

3.1 Log-distance path loss model

In order to obtain a realistic prediction of the received signal strength of in-body communication, we employ the log-distance path loss model [18], in which the received signal strength (in dBm) at a distance d (in meters) from the transmitter $(PL_R(d))$ is expressed as:

$$PL_R(d) = PL_R(d_0) + 10n log_{10}(d) + S_R, \qquad (3)$$

where $PL_R(d_0)$ represents the mean (expected) signal strength at a distance of d_0 = 1cm from the transmitter and is calculated using Eq. 1, n is the path loss exponent. S_R represents a Gaussian random variable with zero mean and standard deviation of σ_s dB [18] contributing to the loss due to the channel characteristics. In the equation above, $PL_R(d)$ denotes a random variable. This model takes into account the different obstacles present in multiple transmitter-receiver paths having the same separation (also known as lognormal shadowing). The parameters (n, σ_s) define the statistical model and are known to be heavily dependent on the environmental characteristics. Measurements in the literature have reported empirical values for n in the range between 4.22 (near tissue implants) and 6.26 (deep-tissue implants), while values for σ_s usually fall into the [6.81,9.05] dB interval [13].

3.2 Animal tissue

Our test environment for the implant communication is a piece of muscle tissue extracted from the thigh of the pig including the (layers of) skin. Anatomically, the near-surface implantable devices are implanted in between the dermis and subcutaneous layer of the skin [2, 3, 17]. The dermis layer, as shown in Fig. 1, is just below the epidermis which forms the outer layer of the skin. From literature the most resemblance to the human tissue is found with the tissue of pigs [19]. The animal tissue is chosen for various reasons such as elimination of difficulties and complexities of test processes using real human tissue, not being dependent on the human phantoms with static EM properties, and identification of practical limitations faced using real tissues. It is important to note that different layers of skin have different conductivity (μ) and permittivity (ϵ). These values change dynamically with body mass, structure, and diet, which cannot thoroughly be validated using simulations.

Therefore, the choice of animal tissue over computer simulations or phantoms is taken to validate the performance of the radio. Fig. 2 illustrates the tissue used for experiments dissected from the thigh of a pig. It was extracted from the animal immediately after euthanization. The experiments were conducted on the tissue within 30 minutes of the euthanasia. We used a biological safety cabinet to prevent any contamination while carrying out the experiments. The ethical codes [7] were carefully followed during the experiments.

3.3 Hardware

While designing an implant two important requirements, namely longer lifetime and compactness, should be taken into account. In terms of ultra low-power radios, there are different radio chips available in the market which can comply with the requirements of the medical implant. The implant we used for experiments is shown in Fig. 3. It comprises of a CC430 chip set from Texas Instruments, a ceramic antenna matched to operate at 400 MHz band, and an accelerometer. The implant has a UART and a SPI connection through which the software is loaded and the output will be debugged. The main features making the CC430 suitable for evaluation are its ultra-low power radio operation - 160μA/MHz, its ability to operate in the MICS band (402-405 MHz), clear channel assessment, configurable access to PHY, configurable MAC layer, 16 bit CPU with 50ns instruction cycle time, memory (32 kB of flash and 4 kB of RAM).

Casing for the hardware: The purpose of casing is two-fold. One is to prevent any contact with the conductive tissue, which would cause a short circuit on the board. The other one is to ensure biocompatibility of the sensor node. The casing is made up of biocompatible ceramic, glass, or polymers [11] depending on the application. These casing provide transparent RF window and do not attenuate the signal [11]. For our experiments, it was sufficient to encapsulate the node in a paraffin cover just to prevent any contact with conductive tissues.

4. EXPERIMENTAL SETUP

The PHY parameters to be examined are transmission power, data rate, and frequency of operation. In addition to these parameters, transmission distance and antenna orientation will also have influences on the performance of in-body communication. To this end, we perform experiments with the following parameters:

1. Transmission (Tx) Power

The power at which the radio signal is delivered from the antenna. If the antenna is matched with the impedance of the channel, the power delivered at the antenna should ideally be equal to the transmission power. The PHY specification of the IEEE 802.15.6 group recommends 25μW effective isotropic radiated power (EIRP), which limits the transmission power to be at -15dBm.

2. Tx Rate

The rate at which data is sent from the transmitter to the receiver. The IEEE 802.15.6 group recommends a minimum data rate of 57.5 Kbps when operating in the MICS band of frequency.

3. Tx frequency

High frequencies have lesser the propagation inside the body. The in-body communication as mentioned earlier is standardized to operate in the MICS band.

4. Distance

The distance between Tx and Rx. This distance will change the radio performance. IEEE 802.15.6 recommended a maximum single-hop coverage distance of 3 meters in the MICS band communication.

5. Antenna orientation

The orientation of the antenna inside the tissue with respect to the receiver. The Tx antenna and Rx antenna can be placed horizontally (0° - posterior plane of the Tx antenna faces the posterior plane of the Rx antenna, 0° - posterior plane of Tx antenna faces the anterior plane of the Rx antenna) or vertically (90°) with reference to the 2D surface of the tissue. For the MICS band, the near-field of the antenna is less than 16 cm. The hardware used in our experiments has an isotropic antenna, which radiates uniformly in all directions and is affected by the near-field reflections for distances less than 16 cm. This effect may induce attenuation and signal loss, which will also be taken into account in our path-loss model. There will be no significant difference in RSSI due to antenna orientations in CM 2, because of the relatively larger distances between the transmitter and the receiver

4.1 Evaluation methodology

The values of the PHY parameters are chosen statistically as shown in Table 2. The parameters are divided into two groups, physical and network parameters. The physical parameters are directly related to the EM propagation such as transmission power, distance and orientation of the transmitting and receiving antennas, whereas the network parameters are related to the performance of the radio in terms of data rate and packet length with respect to the packet delivery ratio (PDR).

Set of parameters	Evaluating parameters
Set of physical parameters	Transmission power (dBm)
	Transmission distance (cm)
	Antenna orientation (degrees)
Set of network parameters	Data rate (Kbps)
	Packet length (bytes)

Table 2: Evaluation of hardware with two different sets of physical and network parameters.

In order to simplify the measurement process, a UART interpreter is developed. The radio has to be reset for every change in the physical parameters. Radio resets will put the radio into sleep mode [22]. Thus for every change, the implant has to be initialized with physical parameters before sending any data. In CM2 scenario, the RSSI at larger distances is limited by the receiver sensitivity of CC430 radio. Optimum values for the physical parameters are found out before experimenting with the network parameters.

Evaluation parameters	Values
Antenna orientation	0°,90°,180°
Transmission power	5, 0, -10, -15, -30 dBm
Transmission distance	CM 1 : 0, 2, 4, 8, 16 cm
	CM 2 : 0, 25, 50, 75, 100, 150, 225, 300 cm

Table 3: Set of physical parameters. Repeated for CM 1 and CM 2

4.2 Setting the physical parameters

Table 3 shows different configurations of set of experiments with CM 1 and CM 2. In case of CM 1, the nodes are placed within the tissue at a distance of at-most 16 cm. The characterization of the channel when devices communicate in such close distance is crucial for the design of the topology of an IBSN [16]. In case of CM 2, larger distances are used, where an implant could communicate to a device placed outside the body. We increase the distance gradually from 25cm to 3m to understand the channel characteristics through RSSI information varying in distance. The values of the physical parameters are shown in Table 3.

4.3 Setting the network parameters

The set of network parameters used for the evaluation are data rate, packet length. We vary the network parameters and measure the packet delivery ratio for each possible combination of parameter values. This will help in finding the optimum settings for network parameters. The values of the network parameters are shown in Table 4.

Evaluation parameter	Values
Packet length	5, 20, 40, 60, 80, 100 bytes
Data rate	5, 20, 40, 60, 80, 100, 150 Kbps

Table 4: Set of network parameters. Repeated for CM 1 and CM 2

The network parameters are set through the UART interpreter of the implant. Received packet information is read back through the UART interpreter and stored in a local PC for further analysis with MATLAB. The results from that data analysis are discussed in Section 5.

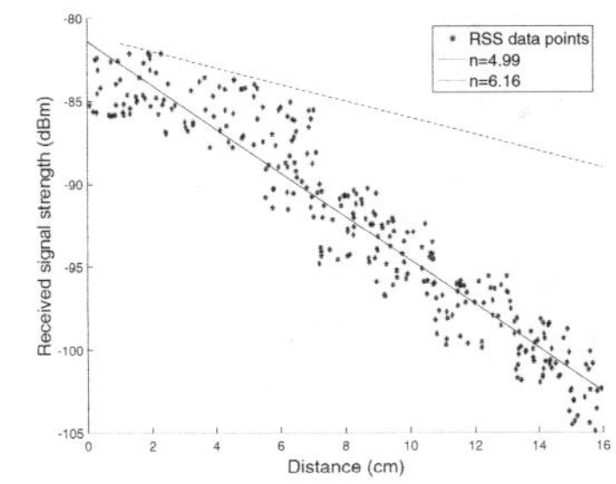

Figure 4: RSSI as a function of distance (Tx=-15dBm) CM 1

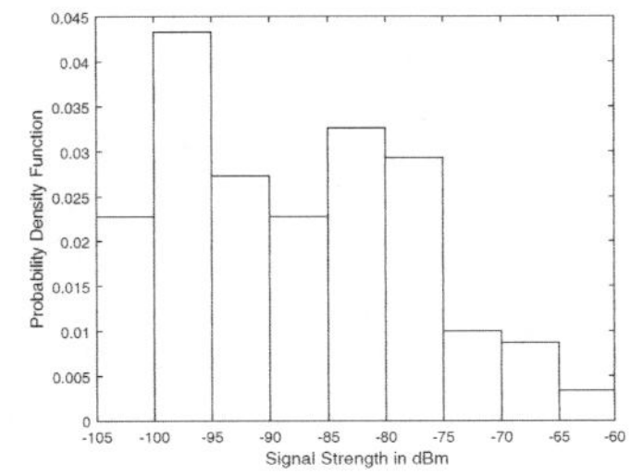

Figure 5: Probability density of RSSI(CM 1 and CM 2 combined) Tx=-15dBm

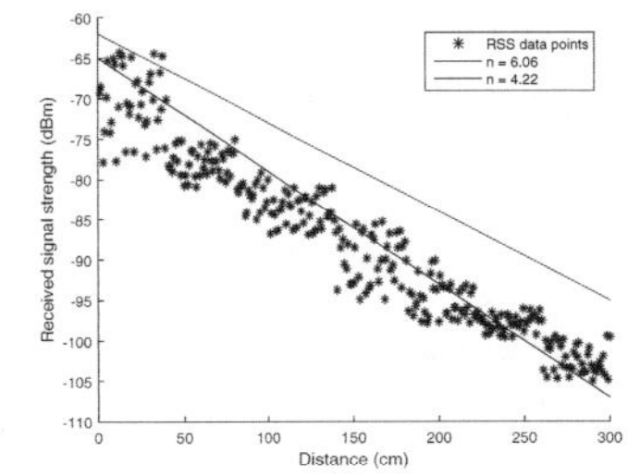

Figure 6: RSSI as a function of distance (Tx=-15dBm) CM 2

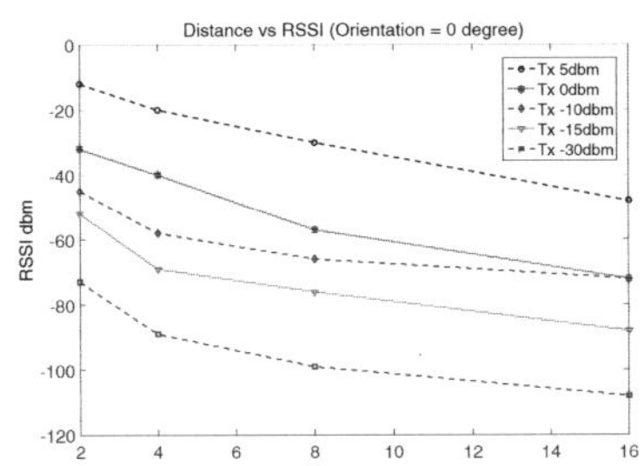

Figure 7: RSSI vs Distance at 0 degree antenna orientation

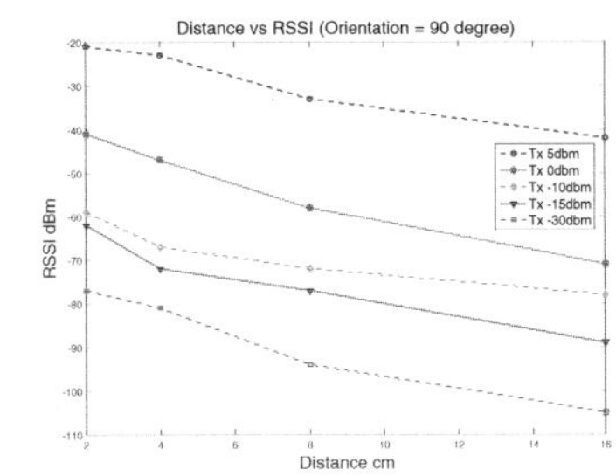

Figure 8: RSSI vs Distance at 90 degree antenna orientation

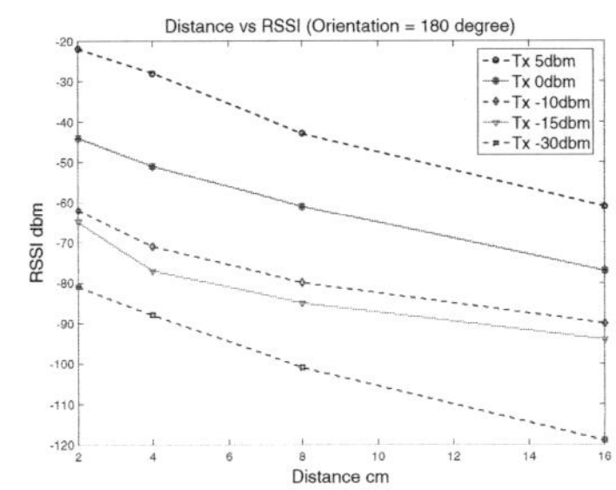

Figure 9: RSSI vs Distance at 180 degree antenna orientation

5. RESULTS AND DISCUSSIONS

In our experiments, we collected 150 data points for each step of the parameters which are shown in Fig. 4 - Fig. 6. The scatter plot of CM 1 shows how RSSI information varies with the transmission distance. The mean value of the received power has an impact over the path loss exponent (n) which is shown in a regression line in the scatter plot. The value of path loss exponent (n) from the IEEE 802.15.6 simulation model is expressed in a regression line, which has n=4.22 [13]. Whereas the empirical estimation of the path-loss exponent $(n)$is 6.16 which is much higher than the estimated value from path loss model of IEEE 802.15.6. The CM 2 scenario also has variation as shown in the Fig. 6. The deviation in CM 2 is not as much as when the communication takes place completely inside the meat.

Fig. 5 shows the probability density of RSSI of CM 1 and CM 2 combined, which indicates that the received signal strength will be close to -105 dbm at most of the times. In such situations, the receiver has to operate at high sensitivity by consuming more power. When operating at high sensitivity the radio receiver provides reduced data rate [22].

5.1 Evaluation of the physical parameters

Validation results of the set of physical parameters are shown in Fig. 7 - 9. Generally speaking, RSSI is linearly decreasing with distance. This can be formulated as:

$$RSSI \propto \log\left(\left(\frac{k}{Distance}\right) \cdot (\mu \cdot Tx\ power)\right), \qquad (4)$$

where k and μ are statistical constants. In order to match the standards of the MICS band, the transmission power should not be higher than 25μW. By referring to the datasheets of antenna and CC430 radio chip [22], we found out that at a transmitting power of -15dBm, the EIRP of the node will not exceed $25\mu W$. However, no hardware measurement is made in order to verify the EIRP. Additionally, by lowering down the power further below -15dBm, we were not able to communicate at distances larger than 5cm with a packet delivery ratio higher than 95%. Experimenting with larger distances resulted in very low signal strengths as shown in Fig. 6. Having lower RSSI values may result in higher error rates in data transmission, which is not desirable for in-body communication.

As far as CM 1 model is concerned, the attenuation of signal is very high even for short distances. The plot shown in Fig. 7 illustrates that with 0 degree antenna orientation (which implies that the antennas are placed facing each other in line of sight), even at 2cm separation, a transmission sent by 5 dBm is received as -20 dBm. This attenuation is persistent in all the set of repeated experiments, which indicates the presence of large reflection of signals in the near field of the antenna.

A linear decrease in RSSI is expected as the distance increases. However, experimental results show that the decrease in RSSI is not linear at larger distances. An additional path-loss due to NLOS communication is also accounted together with the statistical path-loss model in our experiments. Based on our experiments, the optimum physical and network parameters are presented in Table 5.

5.2 Evaluation of the network parameters

Both CM 1 and CM 2 models were used to evaluate the set of network parameters. The data rate is varied from the minimum of 2 Kbps to 150 Kbps and the corresponding PDR is measured. The PDR indicates how many packets are successfully received. For most of the application in CM 1 and CM 2 scenarios, the tolerable packet error rate has been set to atmost 10% for a 256-byte payload with a packet delivery ratio of 95% [4, 23]. Different packet sizes will help to identify the number of re-transmissions required in case of larger packet lengths. Upon exceeding the maximum number of re-transmissions, the receiver will ignore the packet. However, in our experiments, we do not use any re-transmission and as soon as a packet fails, it is considered as a dropped packet.

Parameter	Value
Tx power	-15 dBm
Tx distance	CM 1 :16 cm
	CM 2 :100 cm
Packet length	20 bytes
Data rate	40 kbps
Modulation	BPSK

Table 5: Optimum values of physical and network parameters obtained from experiments

Using the CM 1 model, as the packet length increases, the packet delivery ratio decreases even for higher data rates as shown in Fig. 11. This indicates that large packet length allows the implant to communicate for a longer time. The failure of a packet can also occur if a frame is corrupted due to very low RSSI. It is also conversely found that higher data rates will not increase the packet delivery ratio, in case of large packet length. For a fixed packet length, the PDR increases as the data rate increases. An important observation is that the PDR is almost constant at higher data rates for a fixed packet length.

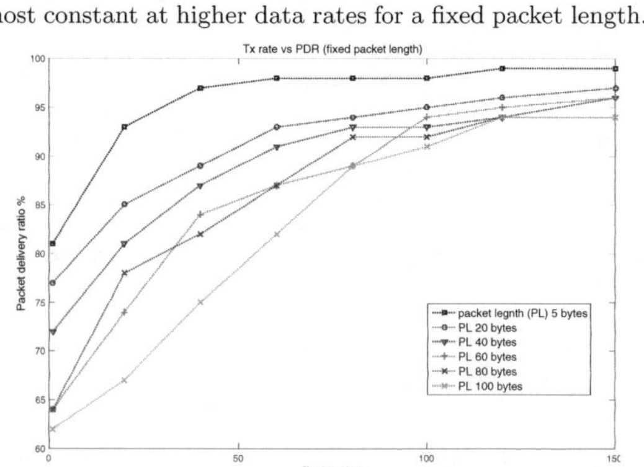

Figure 10: Tx Rate vs Packet delivery ratio evaluated with fixed packet length. Measured in CM2

Using the CM 2 model, as the packet length increases, the packet delivery ratio is decreased even for higher data rates as shown in Fig. 10. This behavior is similar to that of the CM 1. The data rate is directly proportional to the packet delivery ratio; however it changes with that of the packet length. As the packet length increases, PDR is decreased. PDR increases, as the data rate is increases. This indicates that small packet length and higher data rates are required to maintain the reliability of the network.

Small packet length with twice the data rate will have better performance while using both CMs. Sending packets at a faster rate will reduce the congestion in the network.

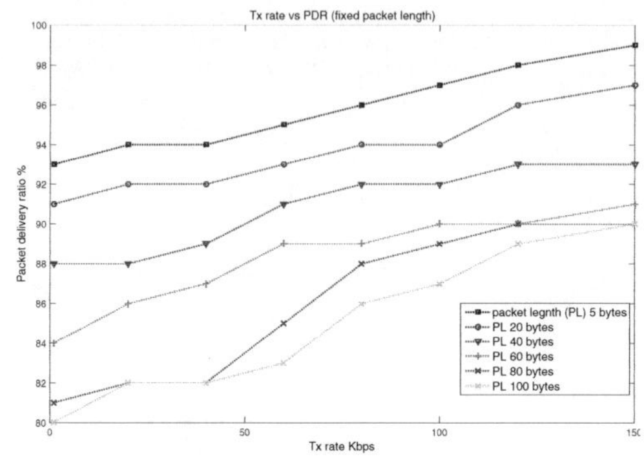

Figure 11: Tx Rate vs Packet delivery ratio evaluated with fixed packet length. Measured in CM1

5.3 Comparison of empirical results and simulation models for IEEE 802.15.6

The deviations in the simulated model and the empirical results are shown in Table 6. The differences in the statistical constants are large and is not in line with the values from the computer simulated models of IEEE 802.15.6. Even though simulations may exhibit a good network performance, this does not guarantee good performance of the radio in a network setup under practical scenarios.

PL parameters	CM 1		CM 2	
	simulation	empirical	simulation	empirical
$PL(d_0)$dB	40.94	56.65	49.81	61.32
n	4.99	6.18	4.22	6.06
σ_s	9.05	10.65	6.81	9.56

Table 6: Comparision of our empirical results and simulation results from [18]

It can be seen that the path loss from our measurements includes the additional losses, which can be due to the indoor propagation losses and multipath effects. In addition to the free space path loss, indoor path loss has to be accounted for. From the results, it can be assumed that the radio waves are partially scattered to the air medium when a transmitting from inside the body. The scattered signal is picked up by the receiver has multipath characteristics such as fading and a delay profile which are not explicitly shown in the results. More experiments are needed to create an appropriate model of the in-body channel with additional losses. This study shows that the existing channel model from computer simulations is not accurate and cannot be applied for the development of network protocols for IBSN.

6. CONCLUSION

Two different CMs were chosen for evaluation of PHY parameters and characterization of the performance of radio in animal tissue. From the results, it is shown that the attenuation of radio communication is very high inside the tissue. The path loss exponent inside the animal tissue deviates from that of the IEEE 802.15.6 results. Moreover, additional path loss has to be accounted for the in-body to off-body communication, which includes the indoor propagation losses. To compensate for the losses induced by the animal tissue, the settings of PHY parameters can be adjusted such as transmission power, antenna orientation and transmission distance. In order to characterize the channel, it is necessary that rigorous experiments are carried out with different parameters as explained in this paper. These channel model parameters will be used also in our future experiments and simulations when validating the network performance of IBSN.

7. ACKNOWLEDGMENTS

This research is funded by the STW project Cyber Physical Systems (CPS).

8. REFERENCES

[1] A. Alomainy, Y. Hao, Y. Yuan, Y. Liu, "Modelling and Characterisation of Radio Propagation from Wireless Implants at Different Frequencies," The 9th European Conference on Wireless Technology, 2006.

[2] M. Bagary, "Epilepsy, Consciousness and Neurostimulation", Behavioural Neurology, vol. 24, no. 1, pp. 75-81, 2011.

[3] R. Bolash, N. Mekhail, "Intrathecal Pain Pumps: Indications, Patient Selection, Techniques, and Outcomes", Neurosurgery Clinics of North America, Volume 25, Issue 4, October 2014, Pages 735-742.

[4] C. A. Chin, G.V. Crosby, T. Ghosh, R. Murimi, "Advances and challenges of wireless body area networks for healthcare applications", in: IEEE International Conference on Computing, Networking and Communications (ICNC), 2012.

[5] Z.N. Chen; G.C. Liu; T.S.P. See, "Transmission of RF Signals Between MICS Loop Antennas in Free Space and Implanted in the Human Head," IEEE Transactions on Antennas and Propagation, vol.57, June 2009

[6] Dermis anatomy of the skin. Accessed online May 2015. URL:http://www.naturallyhealthyskin.org

[7] Federation of Laboratory Animal Science Associations, Europe, 2014. URL accessed on February 2014. http://www.felasa.eu/

[8] P.A. Floor, R. Chavez-Santiago, S. Brovoll, O. Aardal, J. Bergsland,O. Grymyr, P.S Halvorsen, R. Palomar, D. Plettemeier, S.E. Hamran, T.A. Ramstad, I. Balasingham, "In-Body to On-Body Ultrawideband Propagation Model Derived From Measurements in Living Animals," IEEE Journal of Biomedical and Health Informatics, vol.19, May 2015

[9] C. Gabriel, "Compilation of the dielectric properties of body tissues at RF and microwave frequencies." Defense Technical Information Center, Tech. Rep., 1996.

[10] J. Gemio, J. Parron, and J. Soler, "Human body effects on implantable antennas for ISM bands applications: models comparison and propagation losses study," Progress In Electromagnetics Research, Vol. 110, 437-452, 2010

[11] H. Higgins, "Chapter 4: Wireless Communications, Body Sensor Networks" pp.155-180. Springer-Verlag London, Edition 2, ISBN 978-1-4471-6373-2,

[12] H. Higgins, "In-body RF Communications and The Future of Healthcare", ARMMS, RF and Microwave Society. Access online May 2015. URL:http://www.armms.org

[13] IEEE Computer Society, "IEEE Standard for Local and metropolitan area networks: Part 15.6 Wireless Body Area Networks", IEEE Standards Association, 29, Feb., 2012.

[14] T. Karacolak, R. Cooper, E.S. Unlu, E. Topsakal, "Dielectric Properties of Porcine Skin Tissue and In Vivo Testing of Implantable Antennas Using Pigs as Model Animals," IEEE Antennas and Wireless Propagation Letters, vol.11, 2012

[15] S.H. Lee, J. Lee, Y.J. Yoon, S.P.C. Cheon, K. Kim, S. Nam, "A Wideband Spiral Antenna for Ingestible Capsule Endoscope Systems: Experimental Results in a Human Phantom and a Pig" , IEEE Transactions on Biomedical Engineering , vol.58, no.6, pp.1734,1741, June 2011.

[16] V.R.K. Ramachandran, B.J. van der Zwaag, N. Meratnia, P.J.M. Havinga, "Evaluation of MAC protocols with wake-up radio for implantable sensor networks", in: First International Workshop on Wireless Solutions for Healthcare Applications (Concerto), 2014.

[17] A. G. Rapsang, P. Bhattacharyya, "Pacemakers and implantable cardioverter defibrillators - general and anesthetic considerations", Brazilian Journal of Anesthesiology (English Edition), Volume 64, Issue 3, May-June 2014, Pages 205-214.

[18] K. Sayrafian-Pour, W. B Yang, J. Hagedorn, J. Terrill, K.Y. Yazdandoost, "A statistical path loss model for medical implant communication channels", IEEE 20th International Symposium on Personal, Indoor and Mobile Radio Communications, Sept. 2009.

[19] C. P. Smith, "Information Resources on Swine in Biomedical Research", United States Department of Agriculture, February 2014. URL:http://www.nal.usda.gov/

[20] A. Taparugssanagorn, A. Rabbachin, M. Hamalainen, J. Saloranta, J. Iinatti et al., "A review of channel modelling for wireless body area network in wireless medical communications", Citeseer, 2008.

[21] H. Terchoune, D. Lautru, A. Gati, A. Cortel Carrasco, M. Fai Wong, J. Wiart, and V.F. Hanna, "Onbody radio channel modeling for different human body models using FDTD techniques," vol. 51, no 10, Oct. 2009, pp. 2498-2501.

[22] Texas instruments, " CC430 Sub-Ghz radio for ISM band applications" (June 2014). URL:http://www.ti.com

[23] S. Ullah, H. Higgins, B. Braem, B. Latre, C. Blondia, I. Moerman, S. Saleem, Z. Rahman, K.S. Kwak, "A comprehensive survey of wireless body area networks", Journal of medical systems, 2012.

Transmission Policies for Energy Harvesting Sensors Based on Markov Chain Energy Supply

Wenxiang Zhu, Pingping Xu,
Maozong Zheng, Guilu Wu
National Mobile Communications Research Laboratory,Southeast University
Nanjing, China
{zwx,xpp}@seu.edu.cn

Honglei Wang
School of Information and Electrical Engineering
Xuzhou College of Industrial Technology
Xuzhou, China
wanghl@mail.xzcit.cn

ABSTRACT

Due to the small energy harvesting rates and stochastic energy harvesting processes, energy management of energy harvesting senor is still crucial for body network. Transmission polices for energy harvesting sensors with Markov chain energy supply over time varying channels is formulated as an infinite discounted reward Markov Decision Problem under the assumption of geometric distribution of sensors' lifetime. In this paper, we firstly propose a low-storage transmission policy based on probability of successful transmission for body network. Then we narrow the feasible region of parameters in our policies from the real domain to a discrete set with limited number, which makes the method of combing optimal equations and enumeration algorithm to obtain optimal parameters workable. Finally, numerical results show that our presented transmission policies can achieve a good approximated performance of optimal policies, which can be derived by policy iteration algorithm. Compared with the optimal policies, our presented policies has the advantage of low storage.

Keywords

Energy Harvesting, Wireless Sensor Networks, Energy Management, Markov Decision Process

1. INTRODUCTION

With the development of energy harvesting techniques, harvesting energy from the environment has received increasing attention in wireless sensor networks. Wireless sensor networks with energy harvesting nodes can operate for long periods. However, due to the low replenishing rate and the stochastic energy renewal process, energy management is still crucial [1].

Many previous works have been conducted in the optimization of a point-to-point energy harvesting communication system in which the transmitter is equipped with an energy harvesting device. They can be categorized into two classes based on the assumption of whether or not the source knows the information about the energy and data arrival processes. The review about optimization in energy harvesting communication system has been conducted in [2]. Our paper mainly focuses on online scheduling.

Online scheduling assumes that the source contains statistical information about the energy harvesting processes[3]-[7]. In [3], a threshold algorithm is proposed for utilizing available energy to transmit packets with different rewards based on a memoryless Markov chain for battery state, and time correlation in the energy supply is introduced in [4]. In [5], energy management polices for energy harvesting sensor nodes to maximize the date rate while the data queue stays stable are proposed. An online heuristic policy[6] that performs closely to the online optimal is proposed for the finite horizon optimal packet scheduling problem. In [7], a Markov Decision Problem(MDP) is formulated to maximize the number of successfully delivered packets per time slot for an energy harvesting node with infinite capacity. It is proved that the optimal policy is a threshold policy depending on the state of the channel and the length of the energy queue.

However, on one hand, it is not possible to know the noncausal information before transmitting; on the other hand, the parameters of the underlying stochastic processes change over time in many practical systems. So, neither offline scheduling or online scheduling will be applicable. In [8], a learning approach is proposed to learn the optimal transmission policy that maximizes the expected sum of the data transmitted during the transmitter's life over a fixed channel.

In our paper, we consider a point-to-point communication system in a time-slot fashion with time-correlated energy supply, which is similar to [4]. However, in [4], the model did not consider the impact of limited source lifetime. In our paper, we model the lifetime of the source as a random variable, which means the source can stop its operation at any time slot with fixed probability. At the beginning of each time slot, the source node decides to transmit a packet or drop it depending on the channel state and the energy queue length. The objective for the source is to maximize the average amount of data successfully transmitted during its lifetime.

BODYNETS 2015, September 28-30, Sydney, Australia

DOI 10.4108/eai.28-9-2015.2261406

The rest of the paper is organized as follows. In section II, a system model is presented and the problem is formulated as an infinite-horizon discounted reward Markov Decision Processes(MDP). In section III, we define a low storage transmission policy and present an algorithm to find the optimal policy. Finally, numerical results are presented in section IV, followed by our concluding in section V.

2. SYSTEM MODEL

In this section, we present our system model for a point-to-point energy harvesting communication system and formulate the optimal transmission problem as an infinite-horizon discounted reward MDP. A time slotted system is considered, which the k-th time slot means $[k, k+1)$, $k \in Z$. Fig. 1 gives the model of the source node with a finite battery. The data queue is assumed to be saturated, that means there is always data to be sent at the beginning of each time slot. We use E to indicate the energy queue length.And the capacity of the battery is N units. And we also assume that the life time of source is geometric random variable with mean of $\frac{1}{1-\beta}$ $(0 < 1-\beta \leq 1)$. In other words, at each slot, the source node can terminate its operation with small probability 1-β, which is independent and identically distributed.

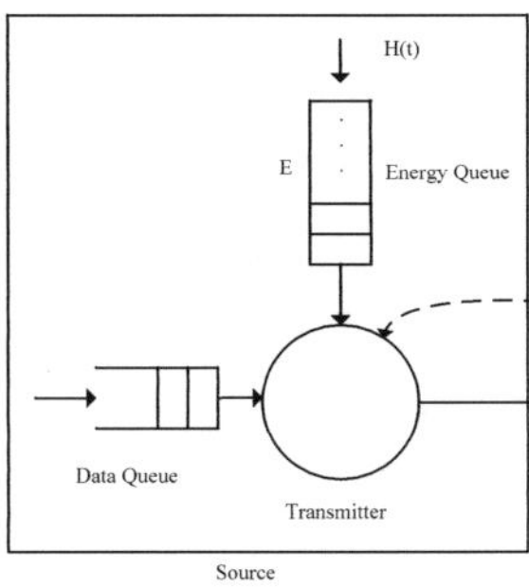

Figure 1: system model

We model the time correlation energy harvesting process $\{B_k\}$ as two-states Markov chain, as shown in Fig.2. In state 1, node can harvest one unit energy with probability λ_1, and can not harvest energy with probability $1-\lambda_1$; in state 0, node can not harvest energy. Define $p_1 = P(B_k = 1|B_{k-1} = 1)$ as transmission probability from state 1 to state 1, $p_0 = P(B_k = 0|B_{k-1} = 0)$ as transmission probability from state 0 to state 0.

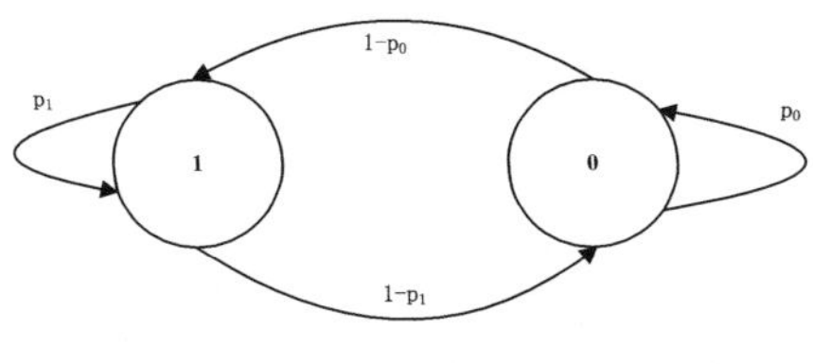

Figure 2: energy supply model

Let H_k be the channel state during the time slot k. We assume that H_k follows a Markov model and p_{lj} is the transmission probability from state l to state j. $h_k (0 \leq h_k \leq 1)$ is the successful transmission probability during slot k, which has M values. Here we assume the channel state process and energy harvesting process are independent.

At the beginning of each slot, the source node decides to either transmit a packet or discard it. One unit energy is used from the energy queue when a packet is transmitted. We assume the source node can receive the feedback from the receiver about the *CSI* at the beginning of each slot, then the action is taken by the source node based on $\{E_k, B_{k-1}, H_k\}$. We use a to indicate the action, where $a = T$ means the action is to transmit a packet and $a = D$ means the action is to discard a packet. The objective of the source node is to find the optimal policy that maximizes the expected total number of packets that are received successfully during the lifetime of the source node.

Next, define S as state space, which contains $\{E_k, B_{k-1}, H_k\}$, $A(i)$ as possible action set at state i, π as the policy used by the source node. We define $V(i, \pi)$ as the expected total reward with the initial state i at a given policy π. It can be calculated by the following expression

$$V(i,\pi) = E_i^{\pi}\left\{E_Y\left[\sum_{k=1}^{Y} r(s_k, a_k)\right]\right\}, i \in S \quad (1)$$

where k is the time slot index, s_k is the state at time slot k, a_k is the action taken at the time slot k, random variable Y is the lifetime of the source, E_Y denotes the statistical expectation and E_i^{π} denotes the expectation of total reward. The term $r(s_k, a_k)$ is reward when the state is s_k and the action is a_k, and has the following expression

$$r(s_k, a_k) = \begin{cases} h_k, a_k = T \\ 0, \ a_k = D \end{cases} \quad (2)$$

The reward represents the number of packets received correctly when the action is taken. If the source chooses action T, which means to transmit a packet, the reward will be h_k depending the channel state at time slot k. If the source choose action D, which means to discard a packet, the reward will be 0 since there is no packet to be transmitted.

Due to the geometric distribution of the lifetime Y of the source with mean $\frac{1}{1-\beta}$, equation (1) can be equal to the objective function of infinite-horizon discounted reward, which has the following expression[9]:

$$V(i,\pi) = E_i^{\pi}\left\{\sum_{k=0}^{\infty} \beta^k r(s_k, a_k)\right\}, i \in S \quad (3)$$

The optimal problem can be expressed as follows:

$$V^*(i) = \max_{\pi} V(i, \pi) \quad (4)$$

3. ONLINE TRANSMISSION POLICIES

The optimal problem is an infinite-horizon discounted reward MDP. Because in our system, state space S is countable and discrete, and the number of actions for each state is finite, there exists an optimal deterministic stationary policy. Furthermore, policy iteration algorithm(PIA)[10] can be used to solve the problem and will terminate in a finite number of iterations with an optimal stationary policy.

However, when the number of states is large, the algorithm needs a lot of calculation to solve the linear system of equations, and also needs large storage to save the optimal policy. So in this section, we present a low storage policy and an algorithm to solve the optimal parameter of the policy.

3.1 Definition of Transmission Policies

The definition of transmission policies as follows,

$$a = \begin{cases} T, E_k \geq 1 \cap h_k \geq \theta_b \\ D, E_k = 0 \cup h_k < \theta_b \end{cases} \tag{5}$$

where E_k is the energy level of k-th slot, h_k is the successful transmission probability during slot k. θ_b is a threshold of previous slot's energy harvesting state b, which b can be 1 or 0, and $\theta_0 \geq \theta_1$.

When energy queue length $E_k = 0$, the source takes action D; When energy queue length $E_k \geq 1$, the source decides action according to h_k. When $h_k < \theta_b$, the source tends to take action D to save energy; when $h_k \geq \theta_b$, the source tends to take action T to get good reward. θ_1 is threshold of $B_{k-1} = 1$, and θ_0 is threshold of $B_{k-1} = 0$. And when the energy harvesting rate is larger, more data should be transmitted, so we have $\theta_0 \geq \theta_1$.

In the optimal policy solved by PIA, source needs to store a look-up table, which contains the states and corresponding action. In our present policy, source only needs to store two thresholds θ_1 and θ_0. Our present policy has the advantages of low storage capacity.

3.2 Algorithm of Optimal Threshold

From the policy, we can see different thresholds lead to different rewards. In this section, we present an algorithm to solve the optimal threshold.

Firstly, we narrow the feasible region of the threshold from the real domain to discrete set with limited number. The range of θ_b is $[0, 1]$. Sort the channel state from small to large by the successful transmission probability, denoted by $h_1, h_2, \cdots, h_M$ with $h_0 = 0$. Assumed there is $h_i < \theta_b \leq h_{i+1}, i = 0, 1, \cdots, M-1$, then when the k-th successful transmission probability is any of $\{h_1, h_2, \cdots, h_i\}$, the source takes action D; when the k-th successful transmission probability is any of $\{h_{i+1}, h_{i+2}, \cdots, h_M\}$, the source takes action T. The effect is equal to $\theta_b = h_{i+1}$. And if $\theta_b = h_M + \varepsilon, \varepsilon > 0$, the source can only take action D. So the feasible region of threshold can be narrowed to the set $\{h_1, h_2, \cdots, h_M, h_M + \varepsilon\}, \varepsilon > 0$.

The optimal threshold can be solved by combining optimal equations [10] and enumeration algorithm. The algorithm flowchart is as follows:

1. Sort the channel state from small to large by the successful transmission probability, denoted by $h_1, h_2, \cdots, h_M$. So $\theta_b \in \{h_1, h_2, \cdots, h_M, h_M + \varepsilon\}, \varepsilon > 0, b = 0$ *or* 1, and $\theta_0 \geq \theta_1$.
2. Enumerate the possible values of θ_1, θ_0, to get policy according to equation (5). Then solve the following equation to get the rewards.The threshold, which make the reward biggest is optimal.

$$(I - \beta P(f)) V = R(f) \tag{6}$$

In equation (6), V is the expected total reward, $R(f)$ is the instant reward of each state given policy f, which can be computed according to equation (2). $P(f)$ is transmission probability matrix at given policy f. Next we introduce computational formula of $P(f)$.

The k-th state is denoted by (E_k, B_{k-1}, H_k). On one hand ,when source takes action T to transmission a packet, one unit energy is depleted. On the other hand, if $B_{k-1} = 1$, the source can harvest one unit energy by the probability λ_1, so the energy level can either remain same or decrease by one unit. If $B_{k-1} = 0$, the source can't harvest energy, so the energy level E_k will decrease one unit. Also, channel state process and energy harvesting process are independent. So we can derive the following formula.

$$\begin{aligned} & 1 \leq E \leq N \\ & P((E,1,j)|(E,1,k)) = \lambda_1 p_1 p_{kj} \\ & P((E,0,j)|(E,1,k)) = \lambda_1 (1-p_1) p_{kj} \\ & P((E-1,1,j)|(E,1,k)) = (1-\lambda_1) p_1 p_{kj} \\ & P((E-1,0,j)|(E,1,k)) = (1-\lambda_1)(1-p_1) p_{kj} \\ & P((E-1,1,j)|(E,0,k)) = (1-p_0) p_{kj} \\ & P((E-1,0,j)|(E,0,k)) = p_0 p_{kj} \end{aligned} \tag{7}$$

When source takes action D, energy level E_k will either remain same or increase one unit. However, due to the limit of battery capacity, when $E_k = N$, energy level E_k can only be N. So we can derive the following formula.

$$\begin{aligned} & 0 \leq E < N \\ & P((E+1,1,j)|(E,1,k)) = \lambda_1 p_1 p_{kj} \\ & P((E+1,0,j)|(E,1,k)) = \lambda_1 (1-p_1) p_{kj} \\ & P((E,1,j)|(E,1,k)) = (1-\lambda_1) p_1 p_{kj} \\ & P((E,0,j)|(E,1,k)) = (1-\lambda_1)(1-p_1) p_{kj} \\ & P((E,1,j)|(E,0,k)) = (1-p_0) p_{kj} \\ & P((E,0,j)|(E,0,k)) = p_0 p_{kj} \\ & E = N \\ & P((E,1,j)|(E,1,k)) = p_1 p_{kj} \\ & P((E,0,j)|(E,1,k)) = (1-p_1) p_{kj} \\ & P((E,1,j)|(E,0,k)) = (1-p_0) p_{kj} \\ & P((E,0,j)|(E,0,k)) = p_0 p_{kj} \end{aligned} \tag{8}$$

4. NUMERICAL RESULTS

In this section, we compare the performance of three transmission policies. They are optimal policies by PIA, our presented adaptive transmission policies, and greedy polices which means that source can take action T only when $B_{k-1} = 1$ and $E_k > 0$.The performance is the expected total number of packets that are received successfully during the lifetime of the source node with initial state $E_k = 0$.

We consider H_k are Gilbert-Elliot channel model[11], which has $p_{11} = 0.8, p_{01} = 0.4, h_1 = 0.5, h_0 = 0.2$. Besides, $N = 10, \beta = 0.95$.

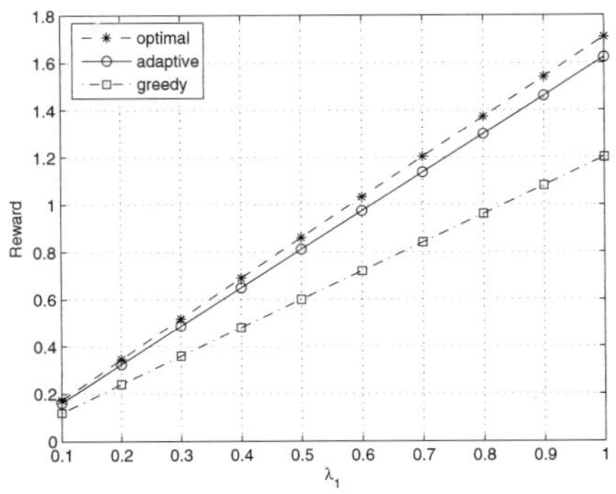

Figure 3: $p_1 = 0.2, p_0 = 0.8$

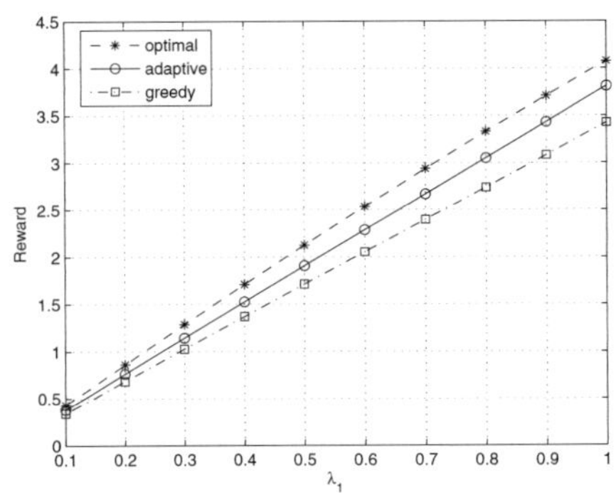

Figure 4: $p_1 = 0.5, p_0 = 0.5$

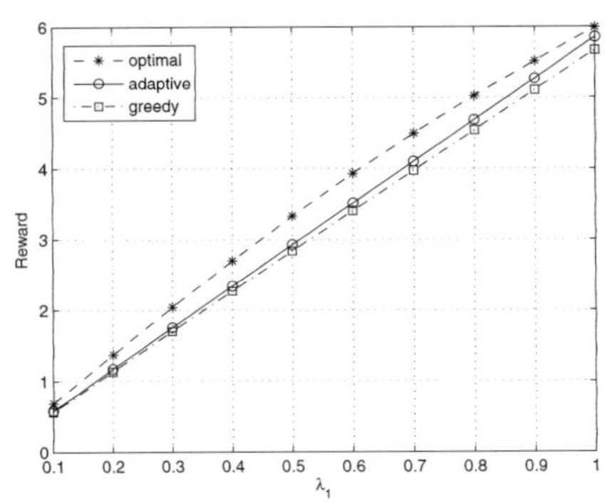

Figure 5: $p_1 = 0.8, p_0 = 0.2$

Fig. 3-5 show the performance against energy harvesting probability λ_1 over different parameters of the energy harvesting process. In Fig.3, $p_1 = 0.2, p_0 = 0.8$ means source stays on energy harvesting state 0 for a longer time; in Fig.4, $p_1 = 0.5, p_0 = 0.5$ means source stays on energy harvesting state 0 and 1 for the same time; in Fig.5, $p_1 = 0.8, p_0 = 0.2$ means source stays on energy harvesting state 1 for a longer time. First of all, from the three figures, we can see that the performance of transmission policies increases with the increasing of energy harvesting probability λ_1. This is due to the fact that the bigger energy harvesting probability is , more energy can be used to transmit data. Secondly, the performance of our presented adaptive policy is larger than that of Greedy policies, but smaller than that of optimal policies. However, when energy harvesting probability is lower than a threshold, the performance of our presented adaptive policy is a good approximation of optimal polices's performance. Finally, the difference of performance between optimal polices and adaptive polices increases with the increase of energy harvesting probability λ_1. This is because in our presented adaptive policies, we only consider different thresholds for different energy harvesting states. However, the thresholds have nothing to do with energy level.

5. CONCLUSIONS

In this paper, we have considered a point-to-point energy harvesting system with time-correlated energy supply and limited lifetime of source over time varying channel in a time slot system. Our goal is to find optimal transmission policies to maximize the expected sum of successfully transmitted data during the lifetime of the source. First, assumed that the life time of source is geometric random variable, we formulated above problem as an infinite-horizon discounted reward MDP. Then we presented a low storage transmission policies and introduced an algorithm to solve the optimal parameter in our present policies. Also, numerical results show that when the energy harvesting is lower than a threshold, the performance of our presented policies can be a good approximation of that of optimal polices, which can be derived through policy iteration algorithm.

6. ACKNOWLEDGMENTS

This work is supported by the National Natural Science Foundation of China (No.6504030000), Research Fund of National Mobile Communications Research Laboratory, Southeast University (No.2014A03) and 2013 Xuzhou science and technology development fund plan (No.XF13C035).

7. REFERENCES

[1] Seah, Winston KG, Zhi Ang Eu, and Hwee-Pink Tan. "Wireless sensor networks powered by ambient energy harvesting (WSN-HEAP)-Survey and challenges." Wireless Communication, Vehicular Technology, Information Theory and Aerospace & Electronic Systems Technology, 2009. Wireless VITAE 2009. 1st International Conference on. IEEE, 2009.

[2] Gunduz D, Stamatiou K, Michelusi, Zorzi M. "Design intelligient energy harvesting communication systems[J]." IEEE Communications Magazine, 2014, vol 52(1), pp:210-216.

[3] Jing Lei and Yates, R. and Greenstein, L.,"A generic model for optimizing single-hop transmission policy of

replenishable sensors", Wireless Communications, IEEE Transactions on Feb 2009, vol 8(2), pp.547-551.

[4] Michelusi, N. and Stamatiou, K. and Zorzi, M.,"Transmission Policies for Energy Harvesting Sensors with Time-Correlated Energy Supply",Communications, IEEE Transactions on July, 2013, vol 6(7),pp.2988-3001.

[5] Sharma, V. and Mukherji, U. and Joseph, V. and Gupta, S.,"Optimal energy management policies for energy harvesting sensor nodes", Wireless Communications, IEEE Transactions on April 2010, vol 9(4), pp.1326-1336.

[6] Bacinoglu, B.T. and Uysal-Biyikoglu, E. "Finite horizon online packet scheduling with energy and delay constraints", Communications and Networking (BlackSeaCom), 2013 First International Black Sea Conference on July, 2013, pp. 191-195.

[7] Kashef, M. and Ephremides, Anthony,"Optimal packet scheduling for energy harvesting sources on time varying wireless channels",Communications and Networks, Journal of April 2012, vol 14(2), pp.121-129.

[8] Blasco, P. and Gunduz, D. and Dohler, M.,"A learning theoretic approach to energy harvesting communication system optimization",Globecom Workshops (GC Wkshps), 2012 IEEE, pp.1657-1662.

[9] M. L. Puterman, "Markov Decision Processes: Discrete Stochastic Dynamic Programming", New York,NY:John Wiley and Sons, 2005.

[10] Liu Ke, "Applied Markov Decision processes", Tsinghua University Press, 2004.

[11] Wang H.S., Moayeri N. "Finite-State Markov Channel: A Useful Model for Radio Communication Channels[J]." Vehicular Technology, IEEE Transcation on 1995, VOL 44(1), PP:163-171.

Diagnosing Bipolar Disorders in a Wearable Device

Chao Gui[1], Jie Zhu[2]
Department of Electronic Engineering
Shanghai Jiao Tong University
Shanghai, 200240, China
gl0901@126.com[1], zhujie@sjtu.edu.cn[2]

ABSTRACT

Bipolar disorder, also known as a manic-depressive illness, is a common chronic recurrent psychosis and it mainly relies on doctors' experience to determine the patient's condition currently. Internationally, the doctor or mental health professional conduct a complete diagnostic evaluation by combining their auditory sense with YMRS (Young Mania Rating Scale). However, YMRS have significant limitations, e.g. extensive medical experience, Subjectivity, Misjudgment. For overcoming the traditional limitations, we aimed to find a useful methodology to diagnose the mental state and guide medical treatment by using speech signal processing.

The structure of the mania speech processing in this paper is depicted in Figure 1.

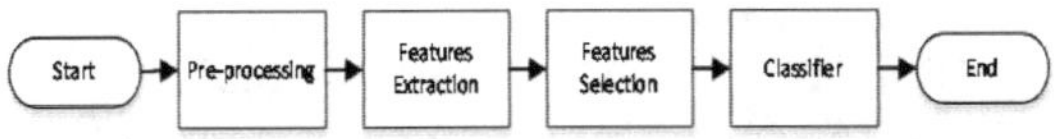

Figure 1. Structure of the Mania Speech Processing

The core issues of this paper are the feature extraction and classifier. In our research, we extract the six feature classes: pitch, formant, LPC, LSF, MFCC, PLPCC, GT filter. LPC is the most important feature of this article. In order to intuitively compare the assorted ability of different features, the features of Between-class Variance and Within-class Variance are calculated which shows in Figure 2.

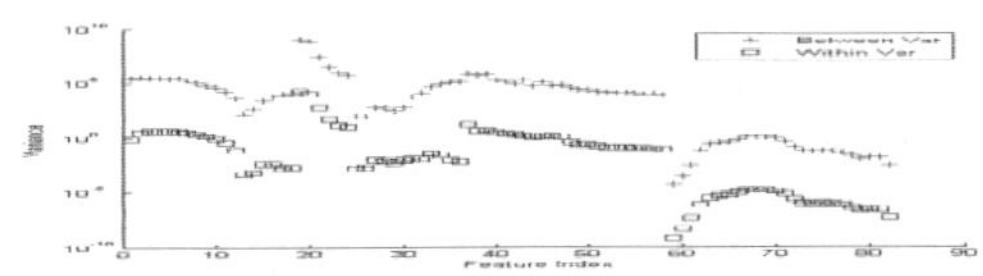

Figure 2. Feature assessment.

And then, we use SVM to classify the single patient and use GMM-UBM to classify multi patients whose processing could be seen in Figure 3.

In our system, we use genetic algorithm to select feature for SVM/GMM; and obtain optimal c and g for SVM. The classification accuracy is shown in Tables.

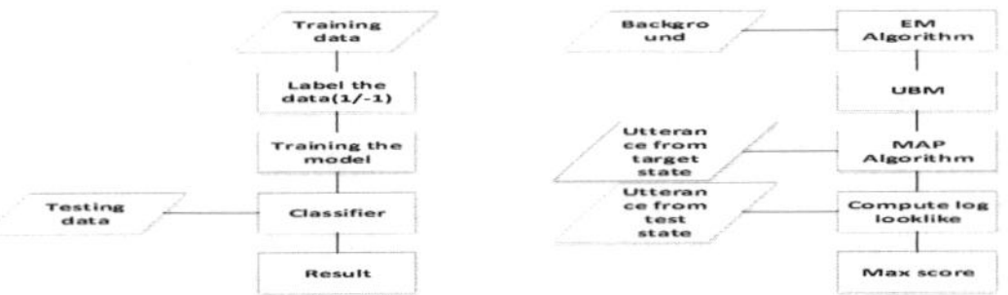

Figure 3. SVM/GMM processing.

Table 1. Result of Classification (N: Normal M: Manic)

SVM for signal patient			SVM for multi patients			GMM for multi patients	
	N	M		N	M		
N	86.00	7.60	N	58.53	39.42	N	81.00
M	14.00	92.40	M	41.47	60.58	M	72.00

According to the experiment, we have found that the recognition rate of SVM classifier for a single patient were up to 90% and multi patients' rate of 50%. The GMM classifier yields the better performance than SVM with a classification rate of 72%.

The project's ultimate vision is develop a wearable device for diagnosis of affective disorders. As long as we set the parameters on the device in advance, patients could master their own mental state in real time by connecting the Bluetooth. As the Figure 4, we could get state when the speech data is upload to the Smart Bracelet.

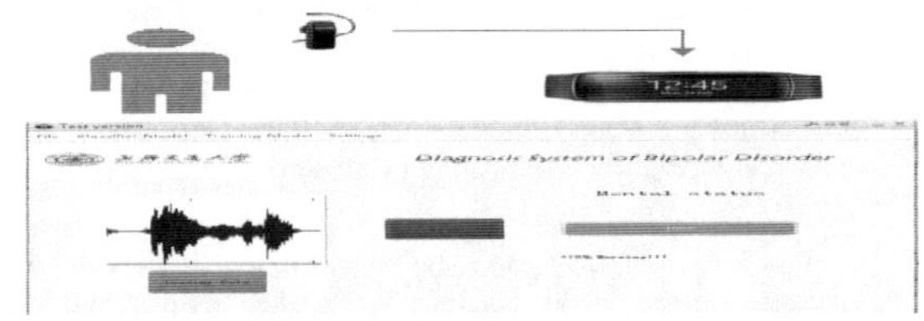

Figure 4. Wearable Device.

In our future works, the improvement of classifiers (SVM and GMM) will still be the core work in the next stage, and then, the all work will be fulfilled to provide a useful diagnostic tool for doctors.

Keywords

Bipolar Disorder, Support Vector Machine (SVM), Gaussian Mixture Model (GMM), Wearable Device.

This work was supported by the National Natural Science Foundation of China (NSFC) under Grants No. 61271349, 61371147and 11433002, the Shanghai Jiao Tong University joint research fund for Biomedical Engineering under Grant No. YG2012ZD04.

BODYNETS 2015, September 28-30, Sydney, Australia

DOI 10.4108/eai.28-9-2015.2261428

Multilayered Phantom for Input Impedance Evaluation of Human Body Communication Electrodes

Dairoku Muramatsu
Graduate School of Frontier Sciences, The Univ. of Tokyo
5-1-5 Kashiwano-ha, Kashiwa, Chiba 277-8563, JAPAN
+81-4-7136-4618, JP
muramatsu@ems.k.u-tokyo.ac.jp

Fukuro Koshiji
Faculty of Engineering, Tokyo Polytechnic University
1583 Iiyama, Atsugi, Kanagawa, 243-0297, JAPAN
+81-3-3372-1321, JP
koshiji@gen.t-kougei.ac.jp

Kohji Koshiji
RIST, Tokyo University of Science
12641 Yamazaki, Noda-shi, Chiba 278-8510, JAPAN
+81-4-7124-1501, JP
koshiji@rs.noda.tus.ac.jp

Ken Sasaki
Graduate School of Frontier Sciences, The Univ. of Tokyo
5-1-5 Kashiwano-ha, Kashiwa, Chiba 277-8563, JAPAN
+81-4-7136-4621, JP
ksasaki@k.u-tokyo.ac.jp

ABSTRACT
This paper presents the input impedance measurement of a human body communication electrode by using newly developed multilayered phantom. Based on the comparison between analysis and measurement values, it was found that the multilayered phantom can be used for accurate evaluation.

Keywords
Human body communication, Biological tissue, Phantom, Electrode, Input impedance

1. MEASUREMENT AND ANALYSIS
Human body communication (HBC) is one of the physical layers of IEEE802.15.6, which utilizes a part of the human body as a transmission medium. In HBC, radio frequency signal is excited or received through the electrodes attached to the human body. In order to evaluate the input impedance characteristics of the electrodes (antennas), multilayered tissue structure phantom is needed because the human body consists of many different biological tissues which have different electrical properties [1]. In this paper, the input impedance characteristics of a transmitter electrode were measured by using the multilayered phantom and compared with the analyzed value obtained from a detailed model.

Figure 1 shows the configuration of a multilayered phantom mimicking the human arm and a transmitter. Table 1 shows the relative permittivity and conductivity of the each phantom layer at 10, 20 and 30 MHz. These electrical properties were measured by the transmission method using a coaxial line. Figure 2 shows the input impedance characteristics of the transmitter electrode. Solid lines show the value measured by the multilayered phantom. Broken lines show the value analyzed by a detailed human arm model including seven different biological tissues using FDTD method. Circle markers show the value obtained from the FDTD simulation with the phantom model which has the shape shown in Fig. 1 and electrical properties shown in Table 1.The black and red line shows the real and imaginary part of the input impedance respectively. These differences in the input impedance between the measurement and analysis shown in Fig. 2 are within an acceptable range considering individual differences of real bodies.

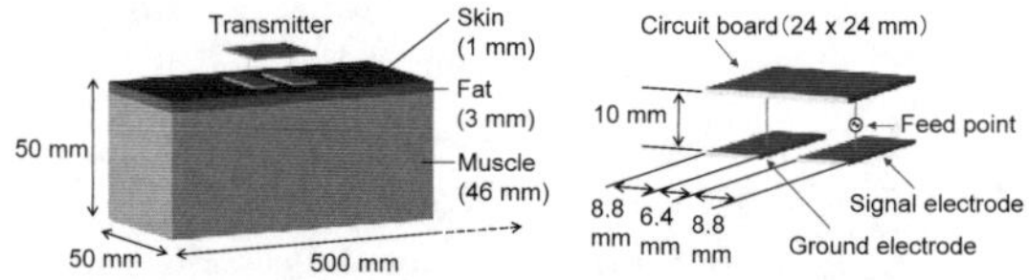

Figure 1. Configuration of phantom and transmitter electrode.

Table 1. Electrical properties of each phantom layer

Tissue	10 MHz		20 MHz		30 MHz	
	ε_r	σ [S/m]	ε_r	σ [S/m]	ε_r	σ [S/m]
Skin	421	0.17	283	0.36	196	0.50
Fat	71	0.028	39	0.060	26	0.076
Muscle	184	0.67	141	0.75	111	0.78

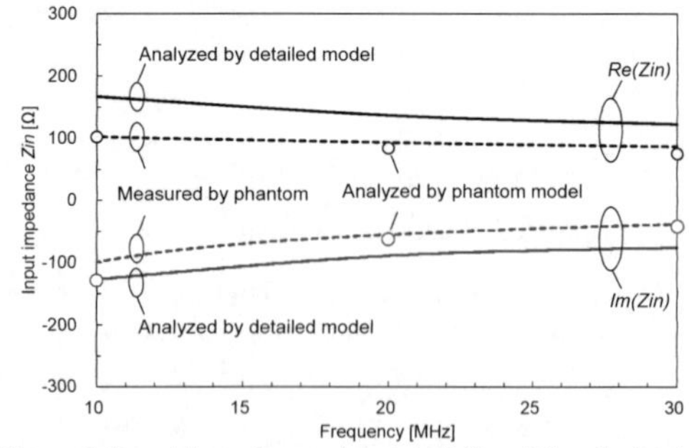

Figure 2. Input impedance characteristics of the electrode.

2. ACKNOWLEDGMENTS
A part of this research was carried out through a Grant-in-Aid for JSPS Fellows (25-5924).

3. REFERENCES
[1] D. Muramatsu, et al., *Trans of JIEP*, Vol. 16, No. 7, pp. 528-534, 2013.

BODYNETS 2015, September 28-30, Sydney, Australia

DOI 10.4108/eai.28-9-2015.2261486

Modeling and Experimental Analysis of an In-body Area Nanonetwork

Valeria Loscrí[*]
FUN Team
INRIA Lille-Nord Europe
Lille, France

Ladislau Matekovits[†]
Department of Electronics and Telecommunications
Politecnico di Torino
Torino, Italy

Ildiko Peter[‡]
Department of Applied Science and Technology
Politecnico di Torino
Torino, Italy

Anna Maria Vegni[§]
Department of Engineering
Roma TRE University
Rome, Italy

ABSTRACT

Nanotechnology is gaining more and more consensus in several application fields, comprised in-body applications. Innovative therapies and diagnostic approaches are based on the use of injections or oral delivery of nanoparticles. The acceleration of this type of development makes very urgent a deeply and accurate analysis of the interaction between the nanoparticles and the biological fluid where the nanoparticles are immersed.

In this paper, we focus on Titanium (Ti and its alloy ($e.g., TiO_2$) systems, given their specific features in terms of density, lack of cytotoxic effects, etc.. Specifically, we design and study an in-body system by characterizing the emission and diffusion processes. Further, we propose an experimental study of the morphology and other important characteristics ($e.g.$ the pH of the particles, and the dielectric constant of the solution) of nano-TiO_2 systems when immersed in a Ringer solution, in order to derive important information related to their potential toxicity inside the human body.

[*]Valeria Loscrí is with INRIA Lille-Nord Europe, France. Email: *valeria.loscri@inria.fr*

[†]Ladislau Matekovits is with the Department of Electronics and Telecommunications, Politecnico di Torino, 24, C.so Duca degli Abruzzi, 10129 Torino, Italy. Email: *ladislau.matekovits@polito.it*

[‡]Ildiko Peter is with the Department of Applied Science and Technology, Politecnico di Torino, 24, C.so Duca degli Abruzzi, 10129 Torino, Italy. Email: *ildiko.peter@polito.it*

[§]Anna Maria Vegni is with the Department of Engineering, COMLAB Telecommunication Lab, Roma TRE University, Via Vito Volterra, 62, 00146 Rome, Italy. Email: *annamaria.vegni@uniroma3.it*

Categories and Subject Descriptors

I.6 [**Simulation and Modeling**]: Miscellaneous; I.6.5 [**Model Development**]: Modeling methodologies—*complexity measures, performance measures*

General Terms

Theory, Experimentation

Keywords

In-body area nanonetwork, titanium nanoparticles, Ringer solution, nanoparticle emission and diffusion

1. INTRODUCTION

Nanotechnology is a new research field that finds applications in several areas. In nanomedicine, the use of nanodevices (*i.e.* nanorobots and nanosensors, opportunely functionalized or inner drugged with medicament) may not only improve the therapeutic index of drugs by improving their effectiveness, and increasing their tolerability in the body by interfering at a minimum level with the immune system [1], but also for diagnostic purposes [2, 3, 4] even if the related security and privacy issues present very important challenges [5].

Different types of nanoparticles can be exploited for nanomedicine applications, and are constructed from a huge range of organic and inorganic materials, such as emulsions, Solid Lipid Nanoparticles (SLNs), gold nanoparticles, silver nanoparticles, titanium dioxide $Ti0_2$ nanoparticles, dendrimers, Carbon Nano-Tubes (CNTs), etc. just to mention the main types [6]. All these materials can be used as carriers for localized Drug Delivery Systems (DDSs) and for diagnostic scopes when opportunistically functionalized. In the first case, the aim is to provide a locally controlled drug concentration, where the medication is needed [2]. The second case is to provide information about in-body conditions,

BODYNETS 2015, September 28-30, Sydney, Australia

DOI 10.4108/eai.28-9-2015.2261435

by opportunistically measuring specific parameters and/or chemical concentrations, etc. [3].

Noble metals, like silver and gold, are largely used for the design of nanoparticles in the field of sensing applications, as well as acting as carriers of medicament molecules. Particularly, colloidal silver has been used as an antibacterial agent by weakening DNA replication and inactivating proteins, while gold has low toxicity to biological systems, and so results inefficient for antibiotic therapy [7].

In addition, nanoparticles are also engineered to provide sustained drug release [8, 9], especially beneficial for chronic therapies. In [10], the authors use gold nanoparticles for diagnostic and drug delivery applications by exploiting chitosan, with the dual purpose of (*i*) acting as a reducing agent in the synthesis of gold nanoparticles, and also (*ii*) promoting the penetration and uptaking the peptide hormone insulin across the mucosa.

For both DDS and diagnostic applications, common methods adopted include (*a*) inhalation, (*b*) intravenous and intramuscular injection and (*c*) ingestion/oral [11]. In all these methods, the most important thing is to characterize the interaction between the in-body solution and the specific nanoparticles.

The contribution of this paper is twofold: (*i*) the characterization of the $Ti0_2$ nanoparticles emission, and diffusion processes, and (*ii*) an experimental analysis of the $Ti0_2$ nanoparticles in a biologic-like fluidic medium, in order to infer main features as pH, diffraction patterns and dielectric constant.

Notice that the choice of $Ti0_2$ nanoparticles is due to their benefits for biomedical applications. Indeed, among other existing systems, because of their low density, excellent corrosion resistance, lack of cytotoxic effects, good mechanical properties, Ti and its alloys, $Ti0_2$ are well established materials for biomedical application as orthopedic and dental implants, cardiovascular stents, joint replacement [12], [13, 14, 15, 16]. Addition of a controlled drug delivery characteristic to TiO_2 nanoparticles could enlarge its potential use in biomedical fields.

This paper is organized as follows. In Section 2 we present our general (and not specific to materials discussed later in the paper) nanoparticulate model suitable both for injection of tablets and liquids containing nanoparticle concentration. We highlight the main processes that occur when a concentration of nanoparticles (*i.e.* $Ti0_2$ nanoparticles in our case) is introduced in what we name here "*compartment*" to indicate a closed volume containing a biological fluid. Specifically, we detail the laws characterizing the emission/ transmission [1] and diffusion processes. In Section 3 we describe the details of the experiment we dealt in order to infer the main characteristics of the interactions between the nanoparticles and the biological fluid. Finally, conclusions are drawn at the end of the paper.

[1]In this paper, the terms emission and transmission are interchanged.

2. CHARACTERIZATION OF THE IN-BODY PHASES

In this section, we describe the two main processes that characterize the pharmacokinetics model we considered in this work, namely the *emission* and the *diffusion*.

2.1 Nanoparticle emission process

In our model, we rely on the *pharmacokinetics* laws, which provide a mathematical basis for analyzing how the human body reacts to the administration of "external substances" (*i.e.* a fluid with a given nanoparticle concentration). Pharmacokinetics considers the rate at which drug concentrations change in the body, and includes the kinetics of absorption, distribution, metabolism and excretion of a drug.

There exist three approaches of pharmacokinetics modeling *i.e.*, (*i*) compartmental, (*ii*) physiological, and (*iii*) model-independent. The first is an empirical approach, where the compartment can represent a body/organ volume. Usually one or two compartments are used. The physiological model identifies the compartments with actual body spaces. The model is more complex than the compartmental models; it is largely used for predictions, and is more suitable for clinical therapy, and when changing situations like alterations of flow rates due to conditions such as swelling, or fever occur. Finally, the model-independent approach is the most recent, but does not provide any specific information about how the drug is distributed.

In this paper, we rely on *one compartment model* for oral drug administration, so that we can model a compartment with a biological fluid (*e.g.* the Ringer solution as described in Section 3) into which a flow of nanoparticles is added by a rapid single dose. Notice that the multi-particulate DDSs show reproducible pharmacokinetics behavior than conventional (monolithic) formulations; this means that after disintegration, which occurs within a few minutes (often even within seconds), the individual nanoparticles are released within the "compartment".

After such a period (*i.e.*, t_1 [s]), we assume that the nanoparticle concentration *i.e.*, $C_{NP}(t_1)$, is uniform in the "compartment", and has reached a maximum value. The analysis of this model relies on a simple mass balance compliant with the dissolution kinetics of $Ti0_2$ nanoparticles [17] that have been used in the experiments described in Section 3.

The mass balance model that provides the *nanoparticle transmission rate* in the compartment model is expressed as

$$r_{Tx}(t) = \frac{dC_{NP}(t)}{dt} = k_d c_{in} - k_e C_{NP}(t), \qquad (1)$$

where $C_{NP}(t)$ is the nanoparticle concentration behavior along time, c_{in} is the initial nanoparticle concentration, k_d [min^{-1}] and k_e [h^{-1}] are the first-order dissolution and elimination rate constants, respectively. The solution of (1) is obtained by integration:

$$C_{NP}(t) = \frac{k_d}{k_d - k_e} \cdot C_0 \left[\exp(-k_e t) - \exp(-k_d t)\right], \qquad (2)$$

where C_0 [L^{-1}] represents the amount of nanoparticles (dose) at zero concentration. The peak of nanoparticle concentration in the compartment corresponds to $C_{NP}(t = t_1)$, *i.e.*,

$$C_{NP}(t_1) = \frac{NNP}{V}, \tag{3}$$

with NNP as the quantity of nanoparticles in the volume V. Notice that V has no direct physiological meaning, but corresponds to the apparent volume of distribution, defined as that volume of plasma in which the total amount of nanoparticles in the compartment would be required to be dissolved in order to reflect the nanoparticles concentration attained in plasma.

Fig. 1 depicts the behavior of nanoparticles in the compartment *i.e.*, the nanoparticle concentration versus time. We assumed $C_0 = 100$ $[\text{L}^{-1}]$, $k_e = 0.0578$ $[\text{h}^{-1}]$, and different values of dissolution constant *i.e.*, $k_d = (0.03, 0.05, 0.07)$ $[\text{min}^{-1}]$. The value of $k_d = 0.03$ corresponds to the dissolution kinetics constant of the $Ti0_2$ nanoparticles [18]. We notice that the concentration increases faster for higher values of dissolution constant, while it decreases very slowly due to typical value of elimination constant, that is

$$k_e = \frac{\ln(2)}{t_{1/2}}, \tag{4}$$

where $t_{1/2}$ [h] is the elimination half-life, that is the time required for the concentration of the nanoparticles to reach half of its original value (*i.e.*, $t_{1/2} = 12$ h).

Notice that the behavior of nanoparticle concentration in the compartment reflects that of a pulse-based modulation scheme [19], where a transmitter nanomachine instantaneously releases a pulse of molecules. Indeed, due to the nano-scale size of nanoparticles approximable to that of molecules, we can consider the nanoparticle concentration behavior as a spike, followed by a slow decrease of concentration, as depicted in Fig. 1.

The time instant when the nanoparticle concentration reaches the peak is t_1 [min], and the analytical expression can be obtained by derivation of (2), posed equal to zero, such as

$$\frac{dC_{NP}(t)}{dt} = \frac{k_d C_0}{k_d - k_e} \cdot \frac{d\left[\exp(-k_e t) - \exp(-k_d t)\right]}{dt} = 0, \tag{5}$$

from which follows that

$$t_1 = \frac{1}{(k_d - k_e)} \cdot \ln\left(\frac{k_d}{k_e}\right), \tag{6}$$

where $k_d \neq k_e$. This expression represents the time instant for which the concentration of emitted nanoparticles reaches its global maximum, and can be interpreted as the *nanoparticle concentration delay* [min], depending on the values of dissolution and elimination constants. Notice that this delay represents the time for the whole dose of nanoparticles to be emitted outside the tablet; for higher values of the dissolution constant k_d, the delay decreases, meaning that the nanoparticle concentration reaches the peak faster.

Fig. 2 depicts the nanoparticle transmission delay, versus the dissolution constant. It is intuitive that higher the dissolution rate (*i.e.*, k_d), lower will be the transmission delay occurring from the emission process at the transmitter (*i.e.*, the tablet) up to the diffusion process, where the maximum nanoparticle concentration has been delivered.

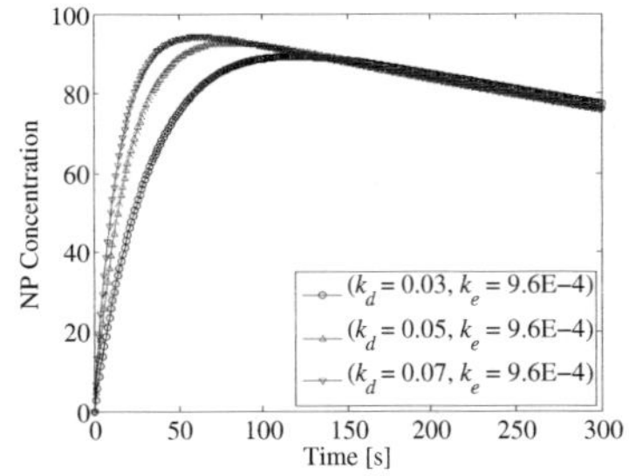

Figure 1: Nanoparticle concentration within the compartment model, for different values of the dissolution constant. Higher the dissolution constant, faster the increase of concentration.

Another feature is the *nanoparticle concentration width* t_w [min] that represents the time interval from t_1 up to t_2, where t_2 is that value corresponding to an amplitude of NP concentration greater than half of its maximum value, that is:

$$C_{NP}(t_2) = \frac{C_{NP}(t_1)}{2}, \tag{7}$$

which becomes

$$\frac{NNP}{2V} = \frac{k_d}{k_d - k_e} C_0 \left[\exp(-k_e t_2) - \exp(-k_d t_2)\right], \tag{8}$$

and simplified provides the value of t_2 [min], that is

$$t_2 = -\frac{1}{k_e - k_d} \ln\left(\frac{NNP}{2V} \cdot \frac{k_d - k_e}{k_d C_0}\right). \tag{9}$$

From (9), we can obtain the expression of the nanoparticle concentration width t_w [min] as

$$t_w = t_2 - t_1, \tag{10}$$

where by substituting (6) and (9), we obtain:

$$t_w = -\frac{1}{k_e - k_d} \ln\left(\frac{NNP}{2V} \cdot \frac{k_d - k_e}{k_d C_0}\right) - \frac{1}{k_d - k_e} \ln\left(\frac{k_d}{k_e}\right), \tag{11}$$

which becomes

$$t_w = \frac{1}{(k_d - k_e)} \cdot \ln \frac{NNP}{C_0 V}. \tag{12}$$

2.2 Nanoparticle diffusion process

The diffusion process can be studied by distinguishing two cases *i.e.*, (*i*) the ideal, and (*ii*) non-ideal case. In the first scenario, the nanoparticle concentration is assumed as homogeneous and no nanoparticle is lost during the diffusion. On the other hand, in the non-ideal case a portion of nanoparticles is lost and cannot reach a destination point.

In an *ideal case*, the concentration is assumed homogeneous and the residence time attains a mean reference value. Unfortunately, in a real reactor the nanoparticle fluid spends a different time inside the reactor, depending on specific characteristics of the compartment. The ideal case that models the compartment can be represented through a bioreactor. A bioreactor is a reactor that utilizes either a living organism

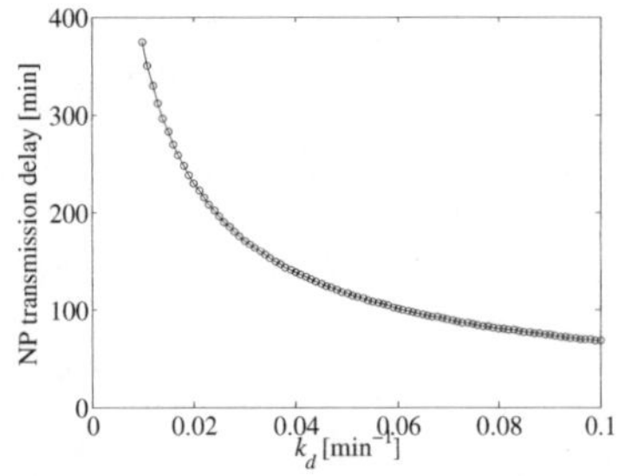

Figure 2: Transmission delay of nanoparticle concentration within the compartment model, versus different values of the dissolution constant. Higher the dissolution constant, lower the nanoparticle transmission delay.

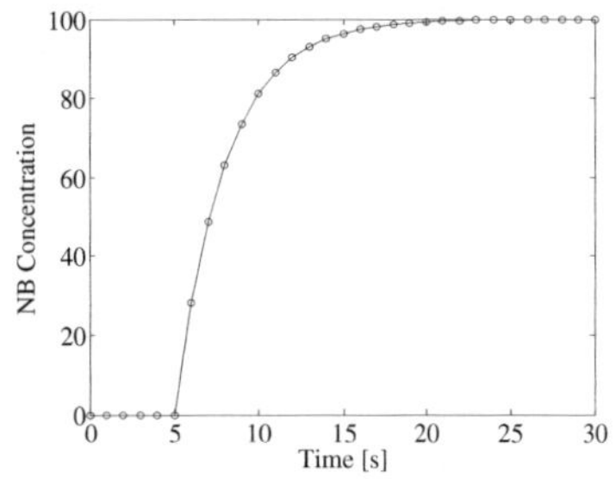

Figure 3: Binding concentration within the compartment model, which occurs for $t > 5$ s, and increases until reaching the maximum value NB.

or one or more enzymes from a living organism to accomplish a certain chemical transformation.

For the *non-ideal case*, from (1), the nanoparticle transmission rate $r_T(t)$ can be identified with the nanoparticle concentration flux $J_T(x,t)$ at the output of the tablet *i.e.*, for $x = x_T$. The particle concentration flux $J_T(x,t)$ is dependent on the nanoparticle concentration gradient at time t and position x through the Fick's first law, as follows

$$J_T(x,t) = -D\nabla C_{NP}(x,t), \tag{13}$$

where D [cm^2/s] is the diffusion coefficient, assumed as a constant value for a given fluidic medium, and depending on the size and shape of nanoparticles, as well as the interaction with the solvent and viscosity of the solvent. Unfortunately, the Fick's first law works when applied to steady state systems, namely the concentration will keep constant both along the space and in the time. In our application, the concentration changes during the time, since nanoparticles diffuse along the space by determining different levels of concentrations. For that, we need to consider the Fick's second law. In practice, the diffusion associated with the degradation kinetics yields to the following mass balance:

$$\frac{\delta C_{NP}(x,t)}{\delta t} = D\frac{\delta^2 C_{NP}(x,t)}{\delta x^2} + b' \cdot C_{NP}(x,t), \tag{14}$$

where b' is a kinetic rate constant, and C_{NP} is the drug concentration as transmitted from the previous phase. Due to the thinness of the wall as compared to the overall "compartment" radius, we can use Cartesian coordinates as approximation instead of cylindrical coordinates.

We consider our compartment with a total volume V, and a flux going through the two reactors (*i.e.*, F). Then, we can apply and solve the mass balances that follow directly from (14). The concentration of magnitude C_{NP} corresponds to the nanoparticle dose in the tablet. The mass balance on the first reactor can be modeled as a first order differential equation, that is

$$\frac{dC_1(t)}{dt} = -\left(\frac{2F}{V} + k\right)C_1(t) + \left(\frac{2F}{V} + k\right)C_{input}(t), \tag{15}$$

with the following conditions

$$C_1(t=0) = 0, \quad C_{input}(t) = C_{NP} \cdot \delta(t). \tag{16}$$

This leads to the solution for $C_1(t)$ as

$$C_1(t) = C_{NP} \cdot \exp\left[-(k + 1/\tau)t\right], \tag{17}$$

where $\tau = \frac{V}{2F}$. The quantity $(C_{NP} - C_1(t))$ corresponds to the portion of nanoparticle concentration that will be directly eliminated by the body, without reaching the receiver.

As an analogy to (15), we can write the following mass balance equation:

$$\frac{dC_2(t)}{dt} = -\left(\frac{2F}{V} + k\right)C_2(t) + \left(\frac{2F}{V} + k\right) \cdot \exp\left[-(k + 1/\tau)t\right], \tag{18}$$

whose solution is

$$C_2(t) = \frac{C_{NP} \cdot t}{\tau} \cdot \exp\left[-(k + 1/\tau)t\right], \tag{19}$$

which represents the *concentration of dissolved nanoparticles* in the compartment.

As we modelled a scenario as a fluidic medium where nanoparticles are free to move following the diffusion laws until reaching the target cells [2], they are able to form chemical *bindings* with them. Thus, from (19), we can obtain the *concentration of bindings i.e.*, $C_b(t)$, formed due to the dissolved nanoparticles bound with the receptors, which can be described by the following formula:

$$C_b(t) \cdot u(t - \delta) = \begin{cases} NB \cdot \left[1 - \exp\left(-\frac{t-\delta}{\tau}\right)\right], & t > \delta \\ 0, & t \leq \delta \end{cases} \tag{20}$$

where NB is the maximum number of bindings that can occur *i.e.*, $NB = \max C_2(t)$, τ [s] is the delay necessary for the binding formation, δ [s] is the start time of the reception process that is related to the diffusion delay of the nanoparticles, and $u(t)$ is the Heaviside step function. Figure 3 shows the trend of binding concentration, obtained under the assumption that $NB = 100$, $\delta = 5$ s, and $\tau = 3$ s.

[2]As an instance, a target cell is a tumor cell that has been previously detected.

3. IN-BODY MODELING: EXPERIMENTAL EVALUATION AND CHARACTERIZATION

In this section we will describe the details and features of the nanoparticles, and the solution considered to infer the main features of the interaction between nanoparticles and body-like fluid solution. Specifically, we will study the morphology of the nanoparticles and any pH variations, as well as the dielectric constant of the considered solutions.

$Nano - TiO_2$ (anatase, nanopowder, 99.99% purity; Sigma-Aldrich) and an aqueous solution of chlorides of sodium, potassium and calcium in the same concentrations as normal body fluids (Ringer solution, 7.5 ml lactic acid, 5.85 g NaCl, 300 ml H_2O di grade 2 purity, and 700 ml H_2O and regulation of the pH to $6.9 - 7.0$) were used for the experiments. This solution is often used as a physiological solution for *in vitro* study of biomaterials due to its similarity to the body environment.

Two different TiO_2 particle sizes have been selected for the experiments, with the aim to assess how this parameter can guide the interactions between the biological system and specific therapeutic nanostructure. Static immersion test has been performed at 37°C (± 0.4° C) by adding the nanoparticles by a rapid single dose. The study has been carried out monitoring the following parameters:

1. the structure and the morphology of the nanoparticles before and after their permanence in the physiological solution for 14 days by SEM (Scanning Electron Microscope) observation and X-ray diffraction analysis;

2. the pH of the solution containing the nanoparticles at a prefixed time and comparing them to the pH of the physiological solution maintained in the same condition without any nanoparticles inside. Moreover, experimental determination of the complex dielectric constant of the physiological solutions with different concentrations of nanoparticles (*i.e.* loadings), comparing the results to the un-loaded physiological solution.

The size of the particles has been measured by Small-angle X-Ray scattering technique, as depicted in Figure 4. According to this study the most frequent radius of the particles is (i) $40.0A°$ (Sample type 1) with a surface-to-volume ratio [3] equal to $0.1003(A°)^{-1}$, and (ii) $44.0A°$ (Sample type 2) with a surface-to-volume ratio equal to $0.1422(A°)^{-1}$. A non-homogeneous particles size has a positive effect during the reactions that occur at the surface of the nanoparticles during the bonding of the drugs and consequently during their distribution and transport.

The particle shape and their surface reactivity can influence the transport properties of other particles in the body environment, and thus affecting the adhesion kinetics of the therapeutic particles loaded on and their transfer to the favorite position. Figure 5 (a) and (c) confirm the previously obtained results, that is, the TiO_2 nanoparticles used for this study are not perfectly homogeneous as their size concerns, and additionally, because their non-spherical shape can be beneficial to improve drug transport and delivery efficiency as compared to the identical spherical particles.

[3] Also called surface-area-to-volume ratio, and represents the amount of surface area per unit volume of an object or collection of objects. It is frequently used to characterize materials with very small diameter (powder), or very porous or that are otherwise not compact.

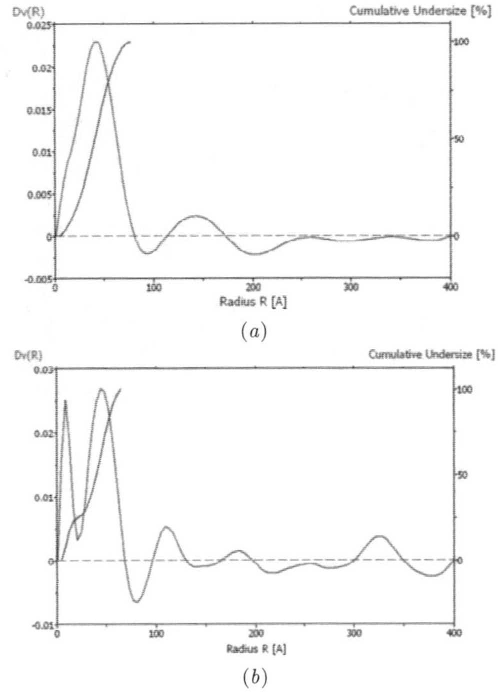

Figure 4: Size distribution by volume of (a) $40\mu m$, and (b) $44\mu m$ TiO_2 nanoparticles.

In such conditions, the difference in curvature between nanoparticles favours an increased loading efficiency and leads obtaining higher attachment to the specific therapeutic particles and a vascular barrier. The nanoparticles show a slightly different microstructure following their permanence in the physiological solution. Indeed, the agglomeration of the nanoparticles takes place (Figure 5 (b) and (d), and the enhancement of their surface area occurs.

The surface area-to-volume ratio influences the reactions, which occur at the surface; it derives that the particles with a higher surface area have a higher number of reaction sites compared to the particles with a lower surface area, thus resulting in enhanced chemical reactivity. In addition, both TiO_2 surfaces show a high tendency to be wetted by the aqueous solution, due to a strong affinity for water.

Apart from the presence of tetragonal Titanium Oxide in both X-ray diffraction spectra, the presence of monoclinic Titanium Hydrogen Oxide has been detected, as shown in

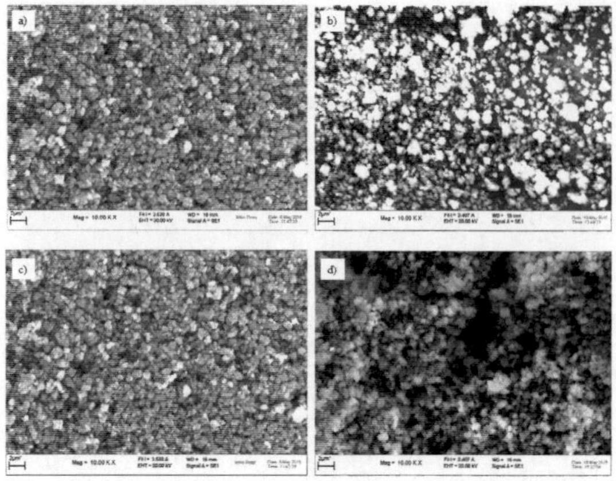

Figure 5: SEM microstructure of the TiO_2 nanoparticles at the beginning of the analysis for (a) $40\mu m$, and (c) $44\mu m$ size, and following the extraction from the physiological solution after 14 days, for (b) $40\mu m$, and (d) $44\mu m$ size.

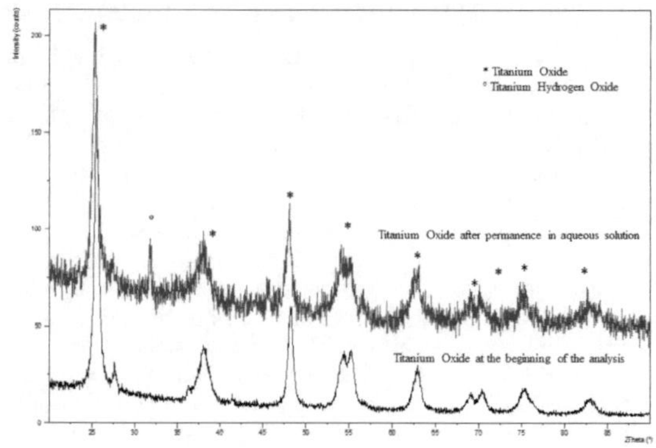

Figure 6: X-Ray diffraction patterns for the starting TiO_2 and following the extraction from the physiological solution after 14 days

Figure 6, following their permanence in the physiological solution. The chemical bond established between the TiO_2 nanoparticles and O, and H atoms coming from the aqueous solution, is an un-stable configuration and confers a hydrophilic character to the nanoparticles, independently form their size, which results to be more reactive towards any chemical compounds.

Finally, by checking the pH of the solutions for 14 days, no any modification of this parameter was obtained *i.e.*, the pH value of the simulated body environment remains the same during the experiment (pH= $6.9-7.0$). This corresponds to the absence of any release of Ti ions in the physiological solution and indicates a non-toxic character of the considered system.

Experimental characterization of the complex dielectric constant of solutions with different TiO_2 concentrations [20, 21] has been carried out using 85070D Dielectric Probe Kit (Agilent, now Keysight Technology) attached to a E8361A PNA Network Analyzer (10 MHz to 67 GHz), and compared with the Ringer solution and distilled water reference cases.

A $f_{step} = 10$ MHz frequency step between $f_{min} = 60$ MHz and $f_{max} = 8$ GHz has been considered. Real and imaginary parts are reported in Figure 7 and 8 in the considered frequency band. The values are shown splitting the overall considered frequency band in the interval $[60, 200]$ MHz, and from 100 MHz to 8 GHz. For the sake of completeness the measured values of the distilled water (also used for the calibration) are also reported.

The dispersion in the considered wide frequency band is basically determined by the Ringer solution's characteristics. A high value of losses in the low frequency range can be observed, that has a minimum around the $f \approx 2{\div}3$ GHz range. Above this frequency the imaginary part of ε_{eff} asymptotically approaches the reference (*i.e.*, distilled water curve). The real part of the doped liquid has a more significative variation with respect to the imaginary part that is not influenced by the presence of the TiO_2 nanoparticles. On the other hand, the real part feels both the concentrations and dimensions of the nanoparticles. This observation allows envisaging changes of the concentration and/or dimensions of the TiO_2 nanoparticles based on other considerations depending on the thought-out applications, as for example quantity of the drug to be delivered, characteristics of the targeted organs, etc.

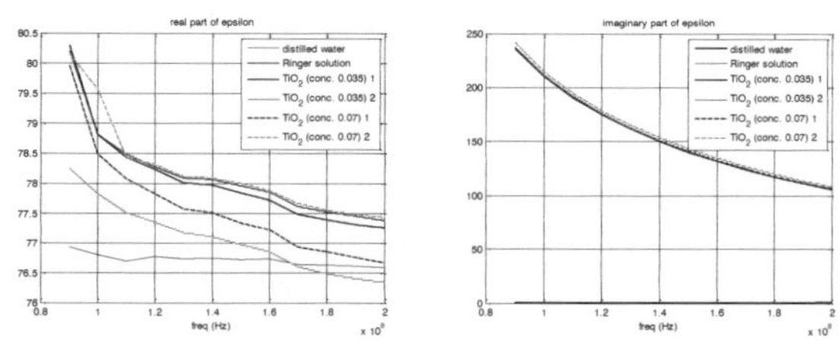

Figure 7: Variation of the real (*left*) and imaginary (*right*) part of the complex dielectric constant in the range $[60, 200]$ MHz for different solutions.

4. CONCLUSIONS AND FUTURE DIRECTIONS

In this paper, we investigated how nanoparticles are injected in the human body for nanomedicine applications. The behavior at the nano-scale is described by means the modeling of the emission, and diffusion processes. Specifically, the one compartment model for oral drug administration is presented and discussed. TiO_2 nanoparticles and a biological fluid system as possible carriers to sustain drugs have been studied.

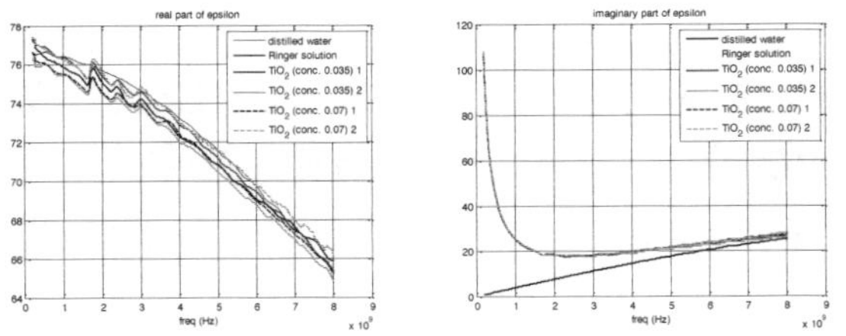

Figure 8: Variation of the real (*left*) and imaginary (*right*) part of the complex dielectric constant in the range from 100 MHz to 8 GHz for different solutions.

This research shows the possibility of combining the biocompatibility of TiO_2 to the drug delivery features and their use in biomedical field. We observed the complete absence of any release of Ti ions in the physiological solution demonstrating, once again, a non-toxic character of the considered system. The particles with a high surface area show a higher tendency to be wetted by the aqueous biological solution and they can support more efficiently any drug loaded on their surfaces.

As future work, we will consider the morphological differences in such a way to match them with specific and different tasks, *e.g.* based on their properties they can be more suitable for drug delivery or for diagnostic purposes. For the last aspects is of paramount importance to take into account all the specific features and then the specific requirements needed. Furthermore, we are planning to investigate deeply the interactions between the *signalling* features with the specific system introduced in this work, namely the "*in-vivo*-like" environment with nano-TiO_2 particles immersed in the Ringer solution.

5. REFERENCES

[1] V. Loscrí and A. M. Vegni, "On the affection of the human immune system on a nanoparticulate nanomedicine system," in *Proceedings of the 9th International Conference on Body Area Networks - BODYNETs*, 2014.

[2] S. Svenson and R. K. Prud'homme, *Multifunctional Nanoparticles for Drug Delivery Applications: Imaging, Targeting, and Delivery*, Springer, Ed., 2012.

[3] R. A. Freitas, "What is nanomedicine?" *Nanomedicine: nanotechnology, biology, and medicine*, vol. 1, no. 1, pp. 2–9, March 2005.

[4] V. Loscrí and A. M. Vegni, "An acoustic communication technique of nanorobot swarms for nanomedicine applications," *NanoBioscience, IEEE Transactions on*, vol. PP, no. 99, pp. 1–1, 2015.

[5] V. Loscrí, C. Marchal, N. Mitton, G. Fortino, and A. V. Vasilakos, "Security and privacy in molecular communication and networking: Opportunities and challenges," *IEEE Transactions on NanoBioscience*, vol. 13, no. 3, pp. 198–207, 2014.

[6] N. Kumar, *Handbook of Particulate Drug Delivery*, A. S. Publishers, Ed., 2008.

[7] Y. Zhou, Y. Kong, S. Kundu, J. Cirillo, and H. Liang, "Antibacterial activities of gold and silver nanoparticles against escherichia coli and bacillus Calmette-Guérin," *Journal of Nanobiotechnology*, vol. 10, 2012.

[8] M. Hossen, K. Kajimoto, H. Akita, M. Hyodo, and H. Harashima, "Vascular-targeted nanotherapy for obesity: Unexpected passive targeting mechanism to obese fat for the enhancement of active drug delivery," *J. Control. Release*, vol. 163, pp. 101 – 110, 2012.

[9] D. Vllasaliu, C. Alexander, M. Garnett, M. Eaton, and S. Stolnik, "Fc-mediated transport of nanoparticles across airway epithelial cell layers," *J. Control. Release*, vol. 158, pp. 479–486, 2012.

[10] D. Bhumkar, H. Joshi, M. Sastry, and V. Pokharkar, "Chitosan reduced gold nanoparticles as novel carriers for transmucosal delivery of insulin," *Pharmaceutical Research*, vol. 24, 2007.

[11] J. Cleland, A. Daugherty, and R. Mrsny, "Emerging protein delivery methods," *Curr. Opin. Biotechnol.*, vol. 12, pp. 212–219, 2001.

[12] M. Long and H. Rack, "Titanium alloys in total joint replacement - a materials science perspective," *Biomaterials*, vol. 19, no. 18, pp. 1621 – 1639, 1998.

[13] M. N. Helmus, D. F. Gibbons, and D. Cebon, "Biocompatibility: Meeting a key functional requirement of next-generation medical devices," *Toxicologic Pathology*, vol. 36, no. 1, pp. 70–80, 2008.

[14] E. Gultepe, D. Nagesha, S. Sridhar, and M. Amiji, "Nanoporous inorganic membranes or coatings for sustained drug delivery in implantable devices," *Advanced Drug Delivery Reviews*, vol. 62, no. 3, pp. 305 – 315, 2010.

[15] I. Peter and M. Rosso, "Study of Ti-enriched CoCrMo alloy for dental application," *Access, IEEE*, vol. 3, pp. 73–80, 2015.

[16] I. Peter, M. Rosso, A. Toppi, I. Dan, and B. Ghiban, "Investigation on cobalt based alloy modified by titanium for dental application," *Archives of Materials Science and Engineering*, vol. 61, no. 2, pp. 62–68, June 2013.

[17] W. Utembe, K. Potgieter, A. B. Stefaniak, and M. Gulumian, "Dissolution kinetics of titanium dioxide nanoparticles: the observation of an unusual kinetic size effect," *Particle and Fibre Toxicology*, vol. 12, no. 11, pp. 1–12, 2015.

[18] J. Schmidt and W. Vogelsberger, "Dissolution kinetics of titanium dioxide nanoparticles: the observation of an unusual kinetic size effect," *J Phys Chem B.*, vol. 110, pp. 3955–3963, 2006.

[19] I. Llatser, E. Alarcon, and M. Pierobon, "Diffusion-based channel characterization in molecular nanonetworks," in *Proc. of the 1st IEEE International Workshop on Molecular and Nano Scale Communication (MoNaCom), in conjunction with IEEE INFOCOM*, Shanghai (China), April 2011.

[20] J. Bao, C. Davis, and M.Swicord, "Microwave dielectric measurements of erythrocyte suspensions," *Biophysical Journal*, vol. 66, pp. 2173–2180, 1994.

[21] U. Kaatze, "Complex permittivity of water as a function of frequency and temperature," *Journal Chemical Engineering Data*, vol. 34, pp. 371–374, 1989.

Estimating Calorie Expenditure from Output Voltage of Piezoelectric Energy Harvester - an Experimental Feasibility Study

Guohao Lan[1,2], Sara Khalifa[1,2], Mahbub Hassan[1,2], and Wen Hu[1,2]

[1]School of Computer Science and Engineering, University of New South Wales, Sydney, NSW, Australia

[2]National ICT Australia, Alexandria, NSW, Australia

{glan, sarak, mahbub, wenh}@cse.unsw.edu.au

ABSTRACT

There is a growing interest in developing energy harvesting solutions for wearable devices so they can self-power themselves without relying on batteries. Piezoelectric energy harvesters (PEHs) can convert kinetic energy released from human activities into usable electrical energy for powering various electronic circuits inside the wearable device. Intuitively, the kinetic energy is produced because the user expends some calories during the physical activities. We therefore postulate that the voltage output of a PEH in a wearable device should contain information that can be used to estimate the amount of calorie expended. If this is true, then the PEH can be used as a new source for calorie estimation. Unlike conventional sensors, such as accelerometers, a PEH does not consume any power, which would make this new source very attractive. In this paper, using real PEH hardware and the data collected from ten real subjects, we conduct an experimental study to assess the suitability of PEH voltage in estimating calorie expenditure for two different activities, walking and running. We find that, for most subjects, the calorie estimations obtained from the output voltage of PEH is very close to those obtained from a 3-axial accelerometer.

Categories and Subject Descriptors

J.3 [**Computer Applications**]: Life and medical sciences

General Terms

Experimentation

Keywords

Piezoelectric Energy Harvester, Accelerometer, Calorie Expenditure Estimation

1. INTRODUCTION

Calorie expenditure estimation (CEE) is valuable in monitoring many health problems, such as obesity, an epidemic which is predicted to be the most preventive health problem in the future [25]. A large number of works in the literature have been devoted to estimate the calorie expenditure based on the output signals of accelerometers [3, 4, 5, 16] available in wearable devices. By combining acceleration data with anthropometric features, such as weight, height, age, etc., these algorithms can accurately estimate calorie expenditure of a user. These advancements have resulted in many popular wearable products in the market, such as Fitbit, Apple Watch, and Jawbone, that can collect and analyse human acceleration to estimate, display, or upload calorie expenditure on a continuous basis.

Accelerometers consume power. At the moment, most wearable devices are powered by batteries. There is, however, a growing interest in developing energy harvesting solutions for wearable devices so they can self-power themselves without relying on batteries [8, 17, 23, 24, 26]. Although there are several choices for energy harvesting, such as solar [10], wind [19], thermal [21], kinetic, etc., piezoelectric energy harvester (PEH) is known to generate the most significant power by converting human motion to electricity [17]. If PEH is used, then it can be used to power the accelerometers and other circuits in a wearable device.

In this paper we seek to find a new use of PEH for CEE. Intuitively, the kinetic energy is produced because the user expends some calories during the physical activities. We therefore postulate that the voltage output of a PEH in a wearable device should contain information that can be used to estimate the amount of calorie expended. If this is true, then the PEH can be used as a new source for calorie estimation. Unlike conventional sensors used in CEE, such as accelerometers, a PEH does not consume any power, which would make this new source very attractive.

Using real PEH hardware and the data collected from ten real subjects, we conduct an experimental study to assess the suitability of PEH voltage in estimating calorie expenditure for two different activities, walking and running. We find that, for most subjects, the calorie estimations obtained

BODYNETS 2015, September 28-30, Sydney, Australia

DOI 10.4108/eai.28-9-2015.2261453

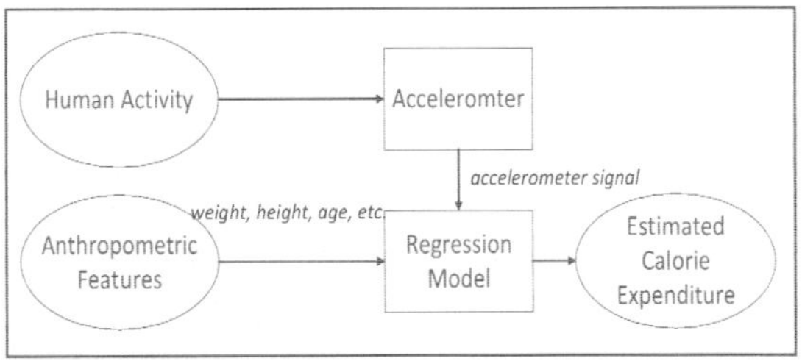

Figure 1: Architecture of the accelerometer based calorie expenditure estimation.

from the output voltage of PEH is very close to those obtained from a 3-axial accelerometer. The main contributions of this paper can be summarized as follows:

- We propose the use of output voltage of PEH as a new source of realising CEE for kinetic-powered devices, which is the first of its kind in the CEE literature.
- We propose a linear regression model based on PEH voltage data collected from ten subjects and show that, for most subjects, the calorie estimations obtained from the output voltage of PEH is very close to those obtained from a 3-axial accelerometer.

The rest of the paper is organised as follows. In Section 2, we explain the accelerometer-based CEE method we used in this study for comparison. We present our experimental hardware, our data collection and the proposed PEH-based CEE method in Section 3, followed by the performance evaluation in Section 4. Related work is reviewed in Section 5. We conclude our work in Section 6.

2. ACCELEROMETER-BASED CEE

Accelerometer based calorie expenditure estimation highly relies on the accelerometers to frequently sample the human activities. The architecture of the conventional accelerometer based CEE is shown in Figure 1. In order to estimate the calorie expenditure, accelerometer outputs are combined with the anthropometric features of the subjects to perform regression analysis [4, 5].

In this paper, we apply the popular method proposed in [4] to estimate the calorie expenditure base on the signal from a 3-axis accelerometer and the anthropometric features of the subjects. The regression model is given as follows:

$$\overline{CEE}_{acc} = a \times H(k) + b \times V(k) \tag{1}$$

where, $\overline{CEE}_{acc}$ represents the estimated calorie expenditure at the kth minute. $H(k)$ was defined as the square root of the sum of squared of the accelerometer signals on the x and y-axes ($H(k) = \sqrt{Acc_x^2 + Acc_y^2}$). $V(k)$ was defined as the accelerometer signal on the z-axe ($V(k) = \sqrt{Acc_z^2}$). Parameters a and b represent the coefficients of the regression model (1), and are generalized by stepwise multiple-linear regression based on the anthropometric features of 125 subjects in study [4]:

$$a = \frac{5.78 \times Mass + 11.95 \times Height + 6.89 \times Age - 2001}{1000} \tag{2}$$

$$b = \frac{5.96 \times Mass + 349.5}{1000} \tag{3}$$

It has been reported that this regression model can achieve 60-95% correlation [4, 18] in estimating the calorie expenditure for walking and running.

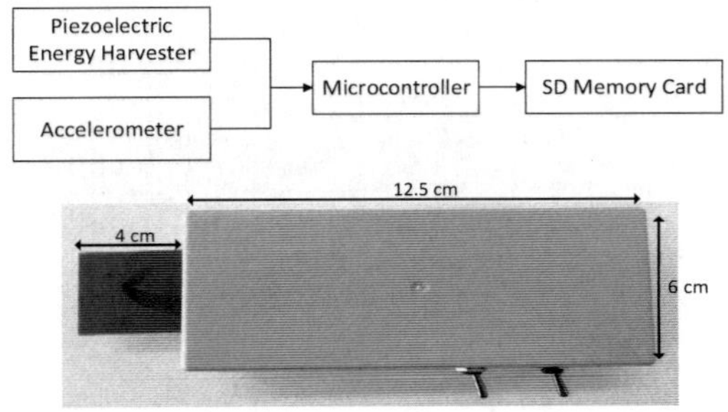

Figure 2: The hardware platform.

3. PEH-BASED CEE

Pizoelectric energy harvester, which harvests energy from the vibration generated by the human motion, has been regarded as a promising energy source to power future wearable sensors. Unfortunately, a recent study [14] has shown that the amount of power that can be harvested from the energy harvester through the body motion can hardly be sufficient to power the accelerometers at a high sampling rate, thus, it results in poor accuracy for the upper layer applications, such as activity recognition and calorie expenditure estimation.

Instead of using the signals from the accelerometers to estimate the calorie expenditure, or using the energy harvested by the energy harvester to power the accelerometer, the primary idea of our method is to develop an regression model based on the output voltage signals from the pizoelectric energy harvester directly. Prior to presenting the proposed method, we introduce the hardware we designed for this study and our data collection method.

3.1 Hardware setup

We designed and built a data logger for this study. The data logger includes a vibration energy harvesting product from the MIDÈ Technology called Volture, which implements the transducer to provide AC voltage as its output. Our hardware also includes a 3-axis accelerometer (MMA7361LC) to record the acceleration signals, simultaneously with the voltage signal. An Arduino Uno has been used as a microcontroller device for sampling the data from both the Volture and the accelerometer. A sampling rate of 1 KHz has been used for data collection. The sampled data has been saved on an 8GB microSD card which has been equipped to the Arduino using microSD shield. A 9 volts battery has been

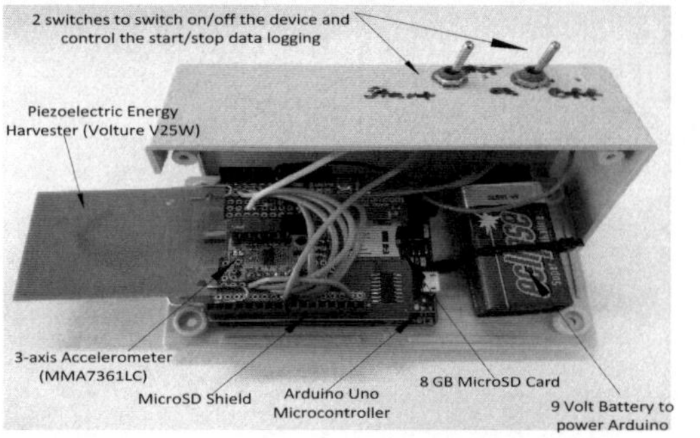

Figure 3: The internal appearance of the data logger.

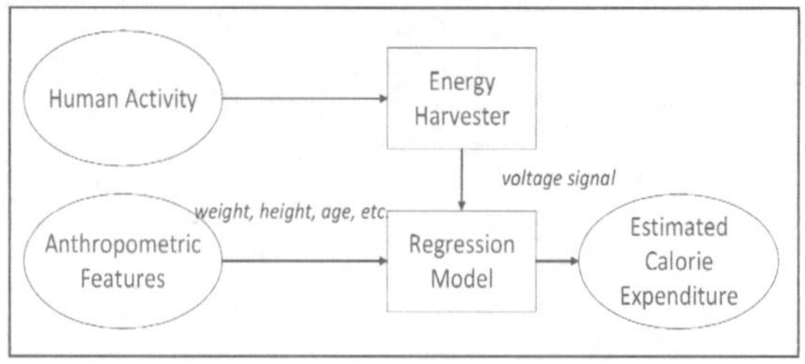

Figure 4: Architecture of the PEH based calorie expenditure estimation.

used to power the Arduino. To control the data collection, our data logger also includes two switches, one to switch on/off the device and the other to control the start and stop of data logging. The hardware platform and the internal appearance of the data logger are shown in Figure 2 and Figure 3, respectively.

3.2 Data collection

Ten healthy subjects (4 male, and 6 female) of different ethnic backgrounds from our lab volunteered to participate in this research study. The participants were asked to hold the data logger in either their left or right hand and perform two different activities: walking and running. The details of the anthropometric features of the subjects are as follows: Age (26-35 years, μ = 29, and σ = 3.06), Weight (58-91 Kg, μ = 69.3, and σ = 10.21), Height (154-185 cm, μ = 168.5, and σ = 9.98).

All subjects performed walking and running with their natural speed, i.e., there was no special speed control, thus, the step frequencies of walking and running vary among different subjects. To avoid mislabeling, the switch on the data logger has been used to control the start and stop of data collection at the beginning and end of each activity. Subjects were asked to stop and wait a few seconds after an activity and before starting the next activity. The data collected between the start and stop times of an activity were labeled with the name of that activity. Each subject provided between 25 and 35 seconds of data for both walking and running.

3.3 Proposed Calorie Expenditure Estimation using Harvested Voltage Signal

The architecture of the proposed pizoelectric energy harvester based method is shown in Figure 4. The system contains a kinetic energy harvester which harvests energy directly from human activity. Instead of using the harvested energy to power the accelerometer, the output voltage is used as the input signal, together with the subject's anthropometric features, to generate a regression model for calorie expenditure. No acceleration data is used in the proposed architecture comparing with the accelerometer based architecture given in Figure 1.

3.4 Regression Model

We performed a regression analysis to generate the generalized regression model. The linear regression model can be represented as follows:

$$\overline{CEE}_{volt} = X\beta + \varepsilon \tag{4}$$

where, $\overline{CEE}_{volt}$ indicates the estimated calorie expenditure at the kth minute. X denotes the vector of input signals, including the anthropometric features of the subjects (weight, height, and age), and the output voltage signals from the energy harvester. The β and ε are the vector of coefficients and residual error, respectively.

Without the ground truth from the indirect calorimeter, we applied the accelerometer based method proposed given in Equation (1) to estimate the calorie expenditure of the collected activity traces. The estimated results are used as the ground truth to train and calibrate our regression model. Note that, because Equation (1) is a generalized model, our regression model will not specify the activity type.

For each subject, S_i, in our subjects set, we have collected two acceleration signal traces, one for walking, and one for running. Using those two signal traces as inputs, we apply Equation (1) to get the acceleration based calorie expenditure estimations, $\overline{CEE}_{acc\_walk}$, and $\overline{CEE}_{acc\_run}$, for walking and running activity of subject S_i, respectively. These two acceleration based CEE results are synchronized with the recorded output voltage signal from the PEH during S_i's walking and running.

As an example, Figure 5 exhibits the output signals of the 3-axis accelerometer for both walking and running of subject 2. Together with the anthropometric features of subject 2, the acceleration signals are used to estimate the calorie expenditure (apply Equation (1), (2), and(3)). The results $\overline{CEE}_{acc\_walk}$ and $\overline{CEE}_{acc\_run}$ of subject 2 are given in Figure 6(a), which clearly indicates that running can expend more calories than walking. Correspondingly, Figure 6(b) shows the synchronized output voltage signals of the PEH recorded by our data logger for the same subject. Expectedly, PEH can harvest more energy from running than walking.

In order to generate the regression Equation (4), for each subject, S_i, we used the rest 9 subjects as the training set to train the linear regression model, and applied the Leave-one-out cross-validation to evaluate the performance of the

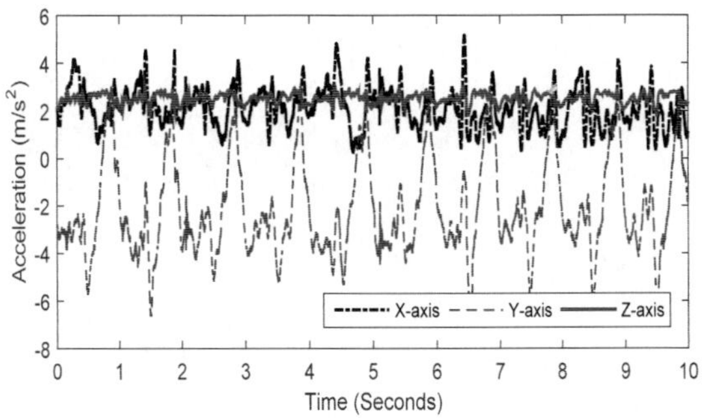

(a) Accelerometer Output for walking

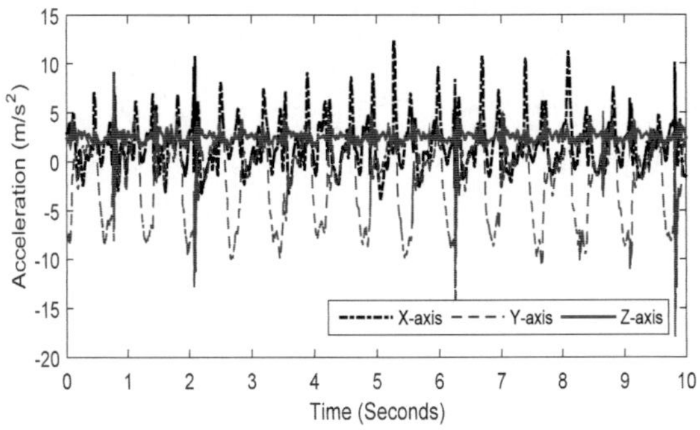

(b) Accelerometer Output for running

Figure 5: The output signal of the 3-axis accelerometer for both walking and running of subject 2.

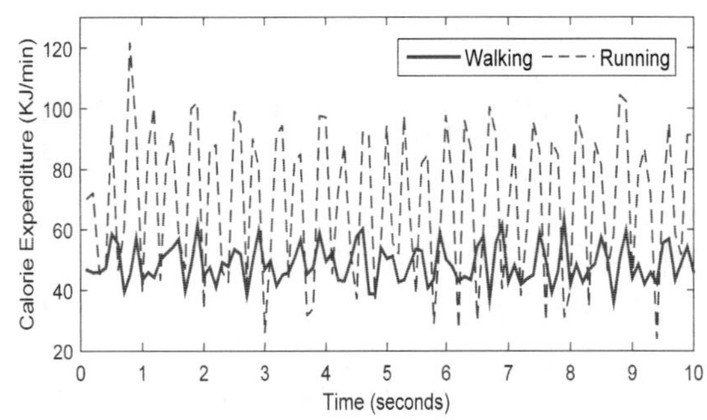

(a) Plot of the $\overline{CEE}_{acc\_walk}$ and $\overline{CEE}_{acc\_run}$ of subject 2, using the regression model given in Equation (1)

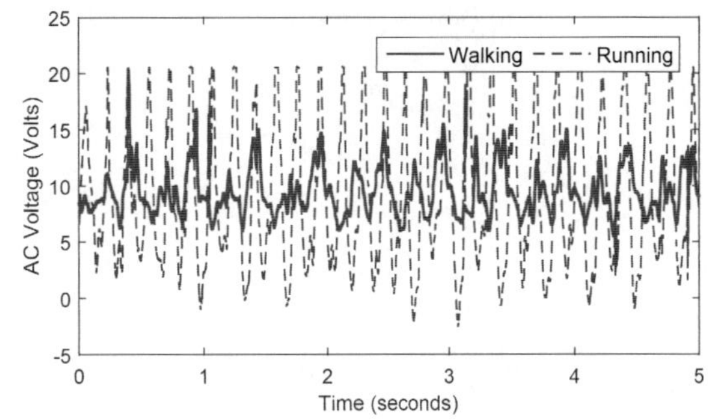

(b) Plot of the output voltage signals of pizoelectric energy harvester

Figure 6: Plot of the output voltage and calorie expenditure for subject 2.

generated regression model on S_i. The Pearson's correlation coefficients of the linear correlation between the estimated calorie expenditure, $\overline{CEE}_{volt}$, and the input signal vector, X, for all the ten subjects are given in Figure 7. In case of walking, the Pearson's r is 0.78 on average, and in case of running, we achieved a value of 0.71 on average, which indicates a strong positive correlation between the voltage signals and calorie expenditure for both walking and running.

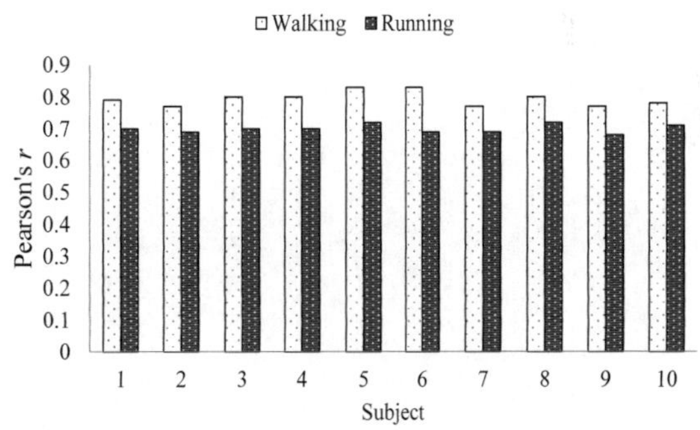

Figure 7: The Pearson's correlation coefficients of the linear correlation between the estimated results $\overline{CEE}_{volt}$ and the input signal vector X for all ten subjects.

4. EXPERIMENTS RESULTS

The instantaneous estimations of the PEH-based CEE and the ACC-based CEE, of walking and running, for all the ten subjects are given in Figure 8. Every second includes 1000 estimations. The results show that although the instantaneous estimations of our proposed PEH-based method are different from that of the ACC-based method, the averages of the PEH-based CEE over a period of time (one second or longer), are very close to that of the ACC-based methods. The average value over longer terms is more useful in practical applications, comparing with the instantaneous measurements for every second. In addition, Figure 9 plots the mean of the estimated calorie expenditure over one second of the PEH-based and ACC-based methods. Figure 9(a) compares the $\overline{CEE}_{volt}$ of the PEH-based method with the $\overline{CEE}_{acc}$ of the ACC-based methods for walking. The Mean Absolute Percentage Error (MAPE) is 0.12 in case of walking. Similarly, Figure 9(b) shows the results for running and the MAPE is 0.16. However, which is indicated in Figure 8(o) and Figure 9(a), the PEH-based method will overestimate the calorie expenditure for walking. In addition, Figure 8(f)(l)(t) expose that the PEH-based method

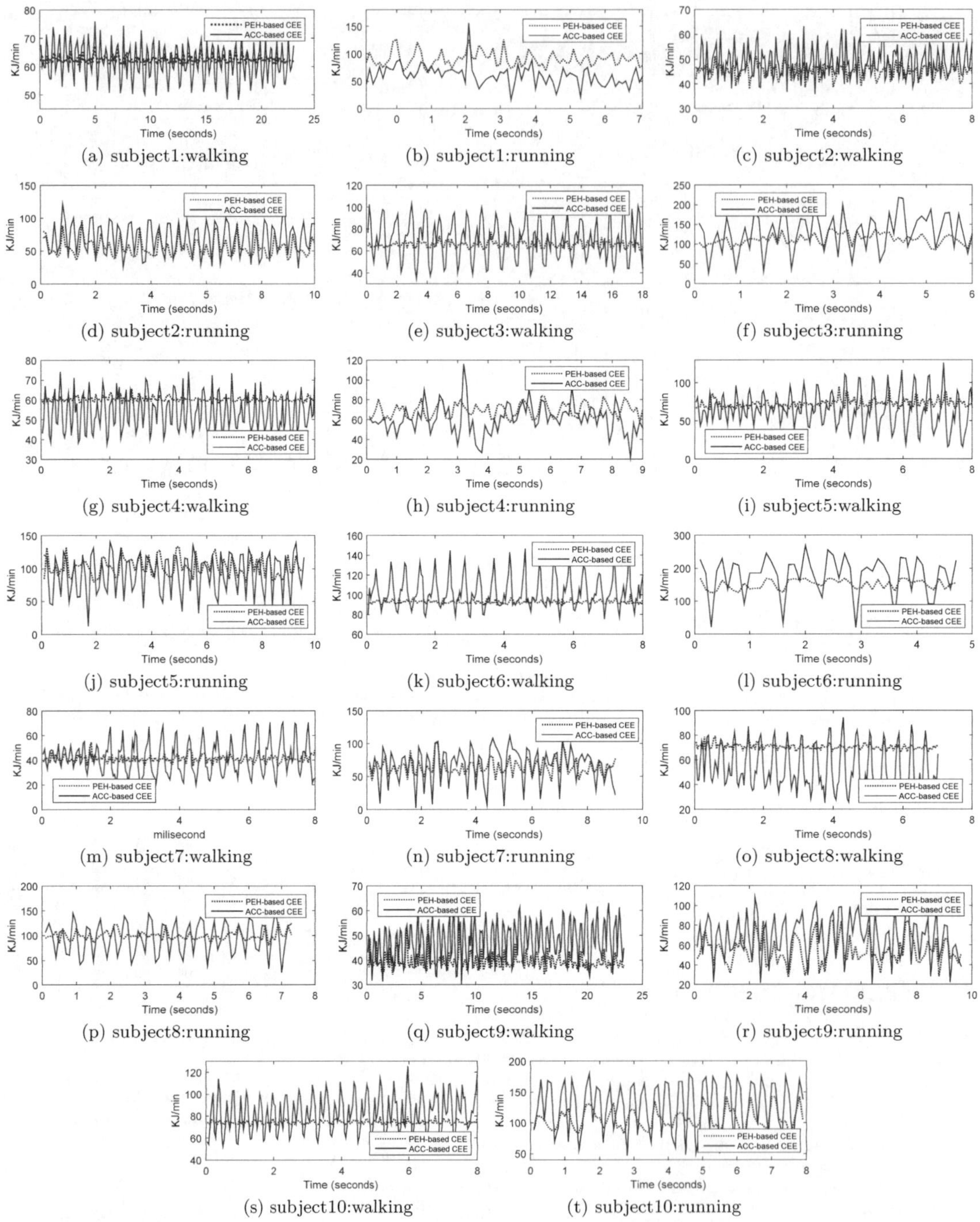

(a) subject1:walking (b) subject1:running (c) subject2:walking
(d) subject2:running (e) subject3:walking (f) subject3:running
(g) subject4:walking (h) subject4:running (i) subject5:walking
(j) subject5:running (k) subject6:walking (l) subject6:running
(m) subject7:walking (n) subject7:running (o) subject8:walking
(p) subject8:running (q) subject9:walking (r) subject9:running
(s) subject10:walking (t) subject10:running

Figure 8: The instantaneous estimation results of the PEH-based and ACC-based CEE for all the ten subjects, for both walking and running.

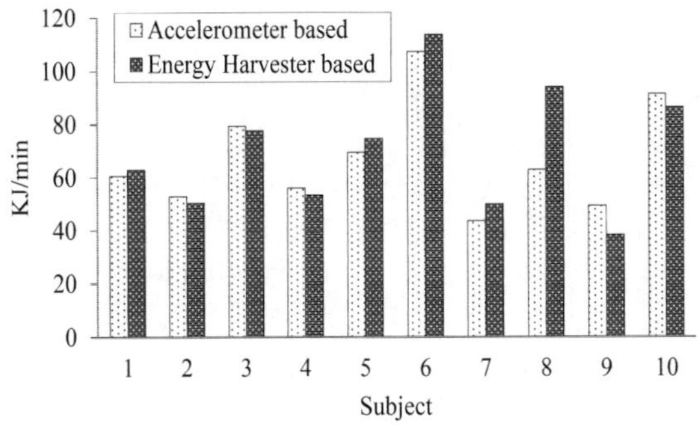

(a) Plot of the $\overline{CEE}_{volt}$ and $\overline{CEE}_{acc}$ for walking

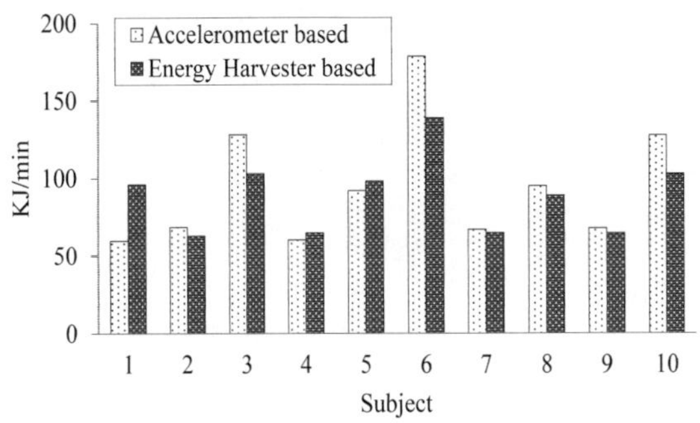

(b) Plot of the $\overline{CEE}_{volt}$ and $\overline{CEE}_{acc}$ for running

Figure 9: The average CEE per second of the ACC-based and proposed PEH-based method.

will underestimate the calorie expenditure for running. We investigated that this results from the uncontrolled intensity and step frequency of the subjects' activity during our data collection. We will improve this by collecting more reliable data in our future work.

5. RELATED WORK

In the laboratory environment, the most accurate way of calorie expenditure estimation is to use the indirect calorimeters. Indirect calorimeter, such as the *COSMED k4b2*, estimates the amount of energy expenditure by measuring the consumption of oxygen and the production of carbon dioxide. Although it has been reported that using the indirect calorimeter can achieve a very high correlation with the actual calorie expenditure [6, 20], it is impractical for everyday calorie estimation, due to its inconvenience.

Outside the laboratory, wearable sensors are widely used as the alternatives to capture the information of daily activities and estimate the energy expenditure [1, 3, 5, 16, 18]. Early studies [7, 22] used accelerometer signals to generate a generalized regression model for the CEE of different activities. However, a study [1] has shown that, due to the variety of the activity intensities, methods using a single regression model will underestimate the expenditure of the high intensity activities, but overestimate that of the low intensity activities. To resolve this shortcoming, algorithms for human activity recognition (HAR), which have been widely used in the indoor positioning and smart living [9, 11, 12, 13], have also been applied in CEE. Recent studies have proposed the activity-specific CEE, which first recognizes the activity, and then generates an activity specific regression model [5], or assigns the Metabolic Equivalent of Task (MET, is a measurement of the calorie expenditure of a physical activity) to that activity [1, 2]. Their results [1, 3] shown that the activity specific CEE methods can greatly improve the accuracy of CEE.

Unfortunately, the shortcoming of those methods is the power consumption of the wearable sensors, especially the accelerometers, used in the activity recognition is relatively high [14, 15]. To achieve continuous calorie estimation, we either need to instrument the wearable devices with large batteries, or frequently replace the batteries. Obviously, neither of these choices is desirable for future body area wearable devices. Compared to the literature, our work in this paper is unique in the sense that we do not use accelerometer at all to estimate calorie expenditure. PEH-based CEE is a totally new concept to the best of our knowledge. It opens the door to a completely new direction for calorie estimation. The fact that it can estimate calorie simply from the PEH data makes this method more competitive than the conventional accelerometer-based techniques for the realisation of battery-less wearables.

6. CONCLUSION AND FUTURE WORK

We have conducted the first experimental study to estimate calorie expenditure from the voltage output of PEH. We have used real PEH hardware and collected voltage data from 10 different subjects performing two different activities, walking and running. We have found that, for most subjects, the calorie estimations obtained from the output voltage of PEH is very close to those obtained from a 3-axial accelerometer. The result of this study shows the feasibility of estimation the calorie expenditure from the output signal of PEH in kinetic-powered wearable devices, which provides opportunities to develop new wearable devices for calorie estimation.

Motivated by the results of this paper, we plan to extend the current experimental study by collecting more data from a larger subject set, and studying a variety of activities with different intensities, including standing, walking, running, and biking. Moreover, instead of applying the estimated results from the accelerometer based method as the ground truth, we will use the indirect calorimeters, *COSMED k4b2*, to measure the actual calorie expenditure and train our regression model. Another direction of our future work would be generating activity-specific regression model for PEH based CEE. For activity recognition, we would like to apply the method proposed in [15] to achieve accelerometer-free activity recognition.

7. ACKNOWLEDGEMENT

We would like to thank all the participants for their help in the data collection. We also appreciate the anonymous reviewers for their detailed comments, which helped improving the final version of this paper.

8. REFERENCES

[1] F. Albinali, S. Intille, W. Haskell, and M. Rosenberger. Using wearable activity type detection to improve physical activity energy expenditure estimation. In *Proceedings of the 12th ACM international conference on Ubiquitous computing*, pages 311–320. ACM, 2010.

[2] M. Altini, J. Penders, and O. Amft. Energy expenditure estimation using wearable sensors: a new methodology for activity-specific models. In *Proceedings of the conference on Wireless Health*, page 1. ACM, 2012.

[3] M. Altini, J. Penders, R. Vullers, and O. Amft. Estimating energy expenditure using body-worn accelerometers: a comparison of methods, sensors number and positioning. *Biomedical and Health Informatics, IEEE Journal of*, 19(1):219–226, 2015.

[4] K. Y. Chen and M. Sun. Improving energy expenditure estimation by using a triaxial accelerometer. *Journal of applied Physiology*, 83(6):2112–2122, 1997.

[5] S. E. Crouter, K. G. Clowers, and D. R. Bassett. A novel method for using accelerometer data to predict energy expenditure. *Journal of applied physiology*, 100(4):1324–1331, 2006.

[6] R. Duffield, B. Dawson, H. Pinnington, and P. Wong. Accuracy and reliability of a cosmed k4b 2 portable gas analysis system. *Journal of Science and Medicine in Sport*, 7(1):11–22, 2004.

[7] P. S. Freedson, E. Melanson, and J. Sirard. Calibration of the computer science and applications, inc. accelerometer. *Medicine and science in sports and exercise*, 30(5):777–781, 1998.

[8] M. Gorlatova, J. Sarik, G. Grebla, M. Cong, I. Kymissis, and G. Zussman. Movers and shakers: Kinetic energy harvesting for the internet of things. In *The 2014 ACM international conference on Measurement and modeling of computer systems*, pages 407–419. ACM, 2014.

[9] M. Hassan. A performance model of pedestrian dead reckoning with activity-based location updates. In *Networks (ICON), 2012 18th IEEE International Conference on*, pages 64–69. IEEE, 2012.

[10] X. Jiang, J. Polastre, and D. Culler. Perpetual environmentally powered sensor networks. In *Information Processing in Sensor Networks, 2005. IPSN 2005. Fourth International Symposium on*, pages 463–468. IEEE, 2005.

[11] S. Khalifa and M. Hassan. Evaluating mismatch probability of activity-based map matching in indoor positioning. In *Indoor Positioning and Indoor Navigation (IPIN), 2012 International Conference on*, pages 1–9. IEEE, 2012.

[12] S. Khalifa, M. Hassan, and A. Seneviratne. Adaptive pedestrian activity classification for indoor dead reckoning systems. In *Indoor Positioning and Indoor Navigation (IPIN), 2013 International Conference on*, pages 1–7. IEEE, 2013.

[13] S. Khalifa, M. Hassan, and A. Seneviratne. Feature selection for floor-changing activity recognition in multi-floor pedestrian navigation. In *Mobile Computing and Ubiquitous Networking (ICMU), 2014 Seventh International Conference on*, pages 1–6. IEEE, 2014.

[14] S. Khalifa, M. Hassan, and A. Seneviratne. Pervasive self-powered human activity recognition without the accelerometer. In *IEEE International Conference on Pervasive Computing and Communications (PerCom)*. IEEE, 2015.

[15] S. Khalifa, M. Hassan, A. Seneviratne, and S. K. Das. Energy harvesting wearables for activity-aware services. *Internet Computing, IEEE*, 20(5):2–10, 2015.

[16] J. Lester, C. Hartung, L. Pina, R. Libby, G. Borriello, and G. Duncan. Validated caloric expenditure estimation using a single body-worn sensor. In *Proceedings of the 11th international conference on Ubiquitous computing*, pages 225–234. ACM, 2009.

[17] P. D. Mitcheson, E. M. Yeatman, G. K. Rao, A. S. Holmes, and T. C. Green. Energy harvesting from human and machine motion for wireless electronic devices. *Proceedings of the IEEE*, 96(9):1457–1486, 2008.

[18] A. Pande, Y. Zeng, A. K. Das, P. Mohapatra, S. Miyamoto, E. Seto, E. K. Henricson, and J. J. Han. Energy expenditure estimation with smartphone body sensors. In *Proceedings of the 8th International Conference on Body Area Networks*, pages 8–14. ICST, 2013.

[19] C. Park and P. H. Chou. Ambimax: Autonomous energy harvesting platform for multi-supply wireless sensor nodes. In *Sensor and Ad Hoc Communications and Networks, 2006. SECON'06. 2006 3rd Annual IEEE Communications Society on*, volume 1, pages 168–177. IEEE, 2006.

[20] H. C. Pinnington, P. Wong, J. Tay, D. Green, and B. Dawson. The level of accuracy and agreement in measures of f e o 2, f e co 2 and vĬĞ e between the cosmed k4b 2 portable, respiratory gas analysis system and a metabolic cart. *Journal of Science and Medicine in Sport*, 4(3):324–335, 2001.

[21] M. Strasser, R. Aigner, M. Franosch, and G. Wachutka. Miniaturized thermoelectric generators based on poly-si and poly-sige surface micromachining. *Sensors and Actuators A: Physical*, 97:535–542, 2002.

[22] A. M. Swartz, S. J. Strath, D. R. Bassett, W. L. O Brien, G. A. King, and B. E. Ainsworth. Estimation of energy expenditure using csa accelerometers at hip and wrist sites. *Medicine and Science in Sports and Exercise*, 32(9; SUPP/1):S450–S456, 2000.

[23] T. Von Büren, P. D. Mitcheson, T. C. Green, E. M. Yeatman, A. S. Holmes, and G. Tröster. Optimization of inertial micropower generators for human walking motion. *Sensors Journal, IEEE*, 6(1):28–38, 2006.

[24] R. Vullers, R. van Schaijk, I. Doms, C. Van Hoof, and R. Mertens. Micropower energy harvesting. *Solid-State Electronics*, 53(7):684–693, 2009.

[25] Y. Wang, M. A. Beydoun, L. Liang, B. Caballero, and S. K. Kumanyika. Will all americans become overweight or obese? estimating the progression and cost of the us obesity epidemic. *Obesity*, 16(10):2323–2330, 2008.

[26] J. Yun, S. N. Patel, M. S. Reynolds, and G. D. Abowd. Design and performance of an optimal inertial power harvester for human-powered devices. *Mobile Computing, IEEE Transactions on*, 10(5):669–683, 2011.

Cloud Based Software Defined Wireless Body Area Networks Architecture for Virtual Hospital

Md Al Shayokh
Department of IT Convergence Engineering
Kumoh National Institute of Technology
Gumi, South Korea
shayokh@kumoh.ac.kr

Jin Woo Kim
Department of IT Convergence Engineering
Kumoh National Institute of Technology
Gumi, South Korea
rerua@kumoh.ac.kr

Soo Young Shin
Department of IT Convergence Engineering
Kumoh National Institute of Technology
Gumi, South Korea
wdragon@kumoh.ac.kr

ABSTRACT
Recent developments in wireless communication inflate a new area of research named as Wireless Body Area Networks. WBANs enhance the concept of virtual hospital with the help of cloud computing (CC) technology. Still numerous technical challenges could be found to integrate Cloud Computing (CC) and WBANs. From networking perspective, Software Defined Networking (SDN) becomes popular for its centralized nature to manage complex network infrastructure. In this paper, the concept of cloud enabled virtual hospital architecture based on software defined networking has been proposed and studied for wireless body area networks. This paper highlights a new, simplified architecture for virtual hospital concepts harnessing the benefits of software defined networking to mitigate the complexity of cloud architecture and its integration with WBAN.

Categories and Subject Descriptors
B.7.1 [**Types and Design**]: Advanced Technologies; C.2.3 [**Network Operations**]: Network Management

General Terms
Management, Design, Security, Theory.

Keywords
WBAN, Cloud Computing, SDN, Virtual Hospital, e-health monitoring

1. INTRODUCTION
Advancements in the field of wireless and mobile communication technologies especially in low powered communication devices make the concept of virtual hospital or e-healthcare and management system very popular. Data management for the collected data from numerous WBAN devices in large scale still remains as a matter of concern and research. Having standards such as low power, limited memory, energy and computational time, the requirement of powerful and scalable high performance computing immense storage infrastructure for data processing and storage become a vital point in terms of medical data analysis. With the growth of internet in today's world the concept of virtual hospital become very popular [1]. This concept is basically an integration of multi discipline such as network technologies, information technologies, clinical medicines etc. Network technologies play a significant role in virtual hospital system. Cloud computing (CC) is one of the emerging technologies which provide tremendous computing flexibility, storage and software services in a virtual platform. Cloud can manage large scale server cluster, storage server and other virtualized resources at low cost. Cloud computing could be described as the virtualized computational resource pool which could calculate and expand to more computation resources [2]. As technologies expands through time, the networking infrastructure becoming complex and hard to manage. For that, new idea came up to pull out computational and memory intensive network management operation which also gives hope to change the limitations of current network infrastructure. This concept is widely known as Software Defined Networking (SDN). SDN divides vertical integration by separating control plane from the routers which forwards the data plane. By separating control and data plane, networking devices' design become simple and using control logic with the help of a centralized controller makes network reconfiguration easier than before. Data and computational modules storage facility as well as processing facility in cloud make cloud computing devices reasonably cheap [3]. It could be predicted that the integration of cloud computing and WBANs is going to facilitate a new cost effective and data driven system which would be able to boost up the concept of virtual hospital for the upcoming days. Integration of these technologies will include advantages such as higher functionalities and services, increased efficiency, higher reliability etc. Although cloud based WBAN platforms are still in its outset stage, there would be several technical issues and challenges to intensify this platform into the research area [4]. In this paper, an architecture for the virtual hospital has been proposed with the integration of software defined networking in the cloud computing and WBANs to augment the storage and computational capability of cloud computing with the simplicity and flexibility of SDN which is crucial to implement the pervasive hospital system. The remainder of this paper is organized as follows. Section 2 will discuss about the integration of cloud computing with WBANs having SDN capabilities. Section 3 provides an architectural overview of the proposed architecture with functionalities. Finally, section 4 will present possible research directions with concluding remarks.

BODYNETS 2015, September 28-30, Sydney, Australia

DOI 10.4108/eai.28-9-2015.2261508

2. INTREGATION OF SOFTWARE DEFINED CLOUD COMPUTING WITH WBANs

WBANs have gained popularity as an imperative technology for remote healthcare system as well as for the virtual hospitalization sector also. Miniaturized wearable devices used for WBANs are able to collect vital signals and movements and could forward them to dedicated medical servers. As cloud computing has advantage in terms of scalability, elasticity and cost efficiency, it could be a better choice to use these advantages with the integration of WBANs [5]. Moreover, SDN which renowned as an emerging architecture could add another dimension with cloud computing in terms of adaptability, high bandwidth capability as well as manageability. As different mobile applications in healthcare system getting popular day by day and medical video streaming become prime concern, cloud computing enabled SDN could be a part of solution to this concern in terms of QoS and other functionalities. The necessity of cloud computing having SDN capabilities in WBANs could be benefited as following aspects:

- *Data Handling:* Continuous data generated by the WBANs sensors have to be collected, stored and processed efficiently. Data management system has to be distributed in terms of space and time. Cloud computing could make possible this management system by enabling a seamless access to a massive scale storage.
- *Data Analysis:* Collected data could be imported for analyzing and modeling as well as making medical decision based on medical decision management (MDM) system.
- *Centrally Manageable System:* By using SDN in networking, network intelligence is going to be centralized with the help of SDN controllers which maintain a global view of network. Moreover, QoS mechanism could be programmed by using OpenFlow.
- *Cloud Computing Applications:* Developing massive scale WBAN application seems to be a complex task which includes large scale programming capability where coordination of collecting, storing and processing of distributed wearable body sensors data are prime concern. Due to these issues, software as a service (SaaS) approaches has proposed for further exploiting with the integration of WBAN frameworks.

Here, a SDN based conceptual architecture has been demonstrated with the integration of CC and WBANs in figure 1. In this figure, mobile devices will act as a gateway for the WBANs and could access the unified SDN network via Wi-Fi or cellular networks for coordinating with cloud. Later, requested tasks would be performed in cloud with the help of virtual machine (VM) as per the request of the patients or stake holders.

3. PROPOSED ARCHITECTURE

The prime goal of this paper is to design software based cloud enabled architecture for WBANs in different environments where the virtual hospital concept concerned. In this part, the proposed framework for the virtual hospital based on software defined networking for cloud computing will be discussed briefly with system functionalities.

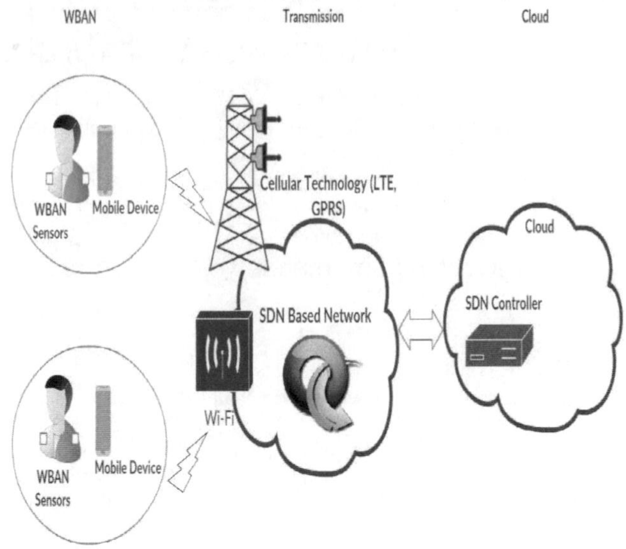

Figure 1: Conceptual architecture for WBAN with SDN based Cloud

3.1 SDN Based Cloud Integrated WBAN Architecture

Figure 2 illustrates a general architectural framework for virtual hospital in which SDN based cloud computing has been integrated in WBANs. The system can be viewed as the collaboration of WBANs, virtualized cellular/wireless networks, cloud services and Users. WBANs are deployed on human body to collect details of quantitative real-time body signs such as heart rate, blood pressure, temperature, etc. extending the health care beyond the confines of limited geographical area. With the existence of WBANs, a huge amount of medical data is sent to be stored in cloud knowledge base via mobile device used as a gateway. The cloud infrastructures have the necessary resources such CPU power, memory space and bandwidth to provide services including medical video streaming, alarming system, GPS and GIS services and decision support system from the knowledge base. The knowledge base stores the raw data captured from wearable body area network devices and exchanges its data with data mining module for knowledge discovery. The large data generated and collected from body area networks can be analyzed by exploiting data mining techniques to uncover meaningful and important knowledge for decision making. The discovered knowledge daily increases to help in fostering hospital operations and enhance quality of services for patients, as well as helps researchers for medical innovation. For instance, urgent health concerns can be handled based on the information extracted from knowledge base. A number of techniques and methods such as classification, cluster analysis, sequential data mining, association rule mining, clinical pathways analysis and other sophisticated approaches can be used to mine valuable knowledge from medical data for decision-making activities. The integration of WBAN technology enabled by cloud computing can also increase the quality of service for virtual hospitals, particularly in reducing errors by learning from previous error patterns and responding fast for urgent cases. Different users such as hospital staff, families and government can access the cloud data on web and from mobile entities. It has been found after a rigorous and extensive research that few research works such as [7-9] have been found in literature to investigate the integration of WBAN and cloud for an

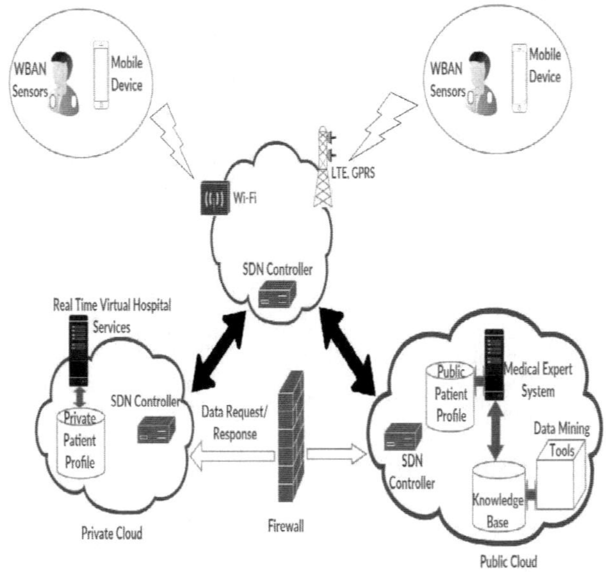

Figure 2: Framework for SDN enabled Cloud based Virtual Hospital Systems

optimized, pervasive health care systems but none of them focused open, programmable, flexible, QoS-aware system that can guarantee quality of service requirements which is necessary for health information. In this paper, prime aspects and vital issues has been suggested for virtual hospital services and applications to exploit SDN capabilities..

3.2 Standards and Technologies as an Enabler for large-scale Virtual hospital

For the proposed architecture, appropriate WBANs standards, benefits of cloud computing integrated with WBANs, Data Mining and the innovation that SDN leverages with cloud services has been discussed and pinpointed.

- *WBAN standards:* low power consumption remains a critical issue in WBANs which has its root in communication standards and protocols. Nowadays, many protocols and standards has been introduced for WBANs such as IEEE 802.15.1, IEEE 802.15.4, IEEE 802.15.6, Insteon, Z-Wave, ANT, RuBee and radio frequency identification (RFID). It has been found that IEEE 802.15.4 standard is suitable for WBANs due to low-power consumption, fast and scalable capability [6].
- *Cloud:* A combination of 2 or more cloud forms hybrid clouds where the entities remain unique. A hybrid cloud deployment will share technology but the information, applications, etc. will be kept apart. Healthcare providers deploy a hybrid cloud for disaster recovery of diagnostic images or clinical systems. Important medical data and applications such as GIS deployment can be deployed on a local private cloud to guarantee security while operations related to system development, upgrade, and testing can be carried out on a public cloud. Increased levels of control over the data are more apparent in a hybrid model, as applications keep a degree of separation between facilities while utilizing economies of scale in the infrastructure.
- *Data mining:* From figure 2, the data mining module in the cloud performs data mining techniques and algorithms to extract meaningful data stored in cloud, which is utilized in medical guidelines, resource management, and decision making. The system helps in automatic data gathering from body via WBANs devices to make data available in cloud for users and various stake holders and help in managing hospital resources and increase the quality of health care services [6].The health employees can predict the symptoms and effects of certain health problems of the patient based on the knowledge contained in the knowledge base. *SDN:* SDN accelerates innovation by breaking the bond between proprietary hardware and control/application software. Coupled with Network Function Virtualization (NFV), SDN seek to leverage automation and virtualization to achieve greater agility while reducing both OPEX (Operational Expenditure) and CAPEX (Capital Expenditure) [7]. Whereas NFV is intended to optimize the deployment of network functions, OpenFlow-based SDN is focused on optimizing the underlying networks. In our system, various cellular and wireless networks such as LTE, 3G, Wi-Max, Wi-Fi and GPRS share the same underlying physical infrastructure by network function virtualization (NFV) under SDN/OpenFlow. The SDN/OpenFlow provides with a system that is programmable, flexible and multi-protocol, hiding the heterogeneity (LTE, 3G, Wi-Max, Wi-Fi and GPRS), complexity and flow behaviors.

3.3 QoS Support and Functionalities in SDN based Cloud Enabled WBANs

From figure 2, the medical situation of patient could be followed up on a regular basis by WBAN, virtualized cellular/wireless networks and successfully stored in cloud based on the location of patient and urgency of the case. The patient can directly communicate with caregivers or relatives over video conference. The profile and medical data of patient is stored on public or private cloud according to their sensitivity. Different kinds of users like families and doctors can view patient's data using web or mobile devices according to service priority or alarming system. With cloud support, the mobile devices of medical staff will easily exhibit richer mobile video streaming from remote cameras. The cloud services also provide GIS deployment for patient location tracking. The flowchart of a virtual hospital system with SDN based mobile cloud capability is given in Fig. 3. QoS supporting functionalities has been focused from WBAN to users via cloud for patients in different locations and using different virtual services. As figure 3 flow chart shows, the cluster head of body sensors collect data and send to mobile gateway, which classify the flows according to the QoS classes. Based on the mobile QoS classification, the network allocates the bandwidth differently to handle each classified flow. For simplicity, we defined the category as urgent and non-urgent flows. Urgent flows are flows related to abnormal values of heart beat, blood pressure and etc measures reported by sensors while normal readings of sensors are categorized under non-urgent flows. Each body sensor is predefined with ID, type, normal and abnormal reading ranges. If the abnormal reading is encountered while mobile device checks the incoming date from sensors against its defined threshold, it invokes QoS mechanism. Assume that B is the total bandwidth, and C is the sub-bandwidth of the total. Urgent packets use the exclusively allocated bandwidth B-C, but shares C with non-urgent packets. For the indoor patients such as at home and hospital, various wireless technologies can help us for locating the real and exact location. For instance, time difference of arrival (TDOA) and time of arrival (TOA) and other location based technology could be implemented for further determine patient activity by data fusion technology. For outdoor patients, mobile device could be used to collect and submit the patient's data to the cloud. The alert messaging system immediately informs various medical stakeholders and families in the time of emergency according to GPS or GIS location information.

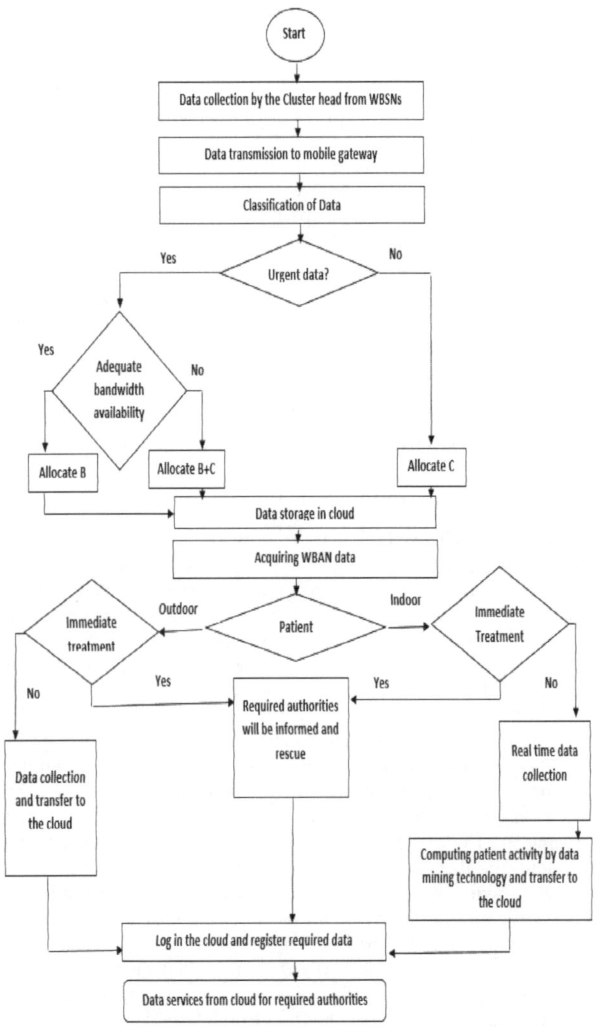

Figure 3: Logical flowchart for proposed virtual hospital with the integration of SDN based CC

4. OPEN RESEARCH ISSUES IN WBAN AND CONCLUSION

Integration of BAN with Cloud Computing emerges as recent research area where various research issues do still exist. Cloud resource allocation mechanisms as well as cloud security remains an issue for research where adaptation of WBAN with CC could be a great challenge in terms of methodologies and tools development. In this paper, generalized software defined cloud based architecture for virtual hospital has been proposed. Specifically, functionality, reliability and uniqueness of knowledge based data mining technology has been provided in this paper. Finally, future possible open research issues and challenges have been discussed to provide an interesting and enormous research effort for near future.

5. ACKNOWLEDGEMENTS

This research was supported by the MSIP (Ministry of Science, ICT and Future Planning), Korea under the CITRC (Convergence Information Technology Research Center) support program (IITP-2015-H8601-15-1011).

6. REFERENCES

[1] Ghada Almashaqbeh, Thaier Hayajneh, Athanasios, Bassam J. Mohd. *"QoS Aware Health Monitoring System using Cloud based WBANs"*. Journal of Medical Systems, 2014. DOI=http://dl.acm.org/citation.cfm?id=2685241

[2] C. Doukas, T. Pliakas, I. Maglogiannis. *"Mobile Healthcare information Management Utilizing Cloud Computing and Android OS". Proceedings of IEEE Eng. Med. Bio. Soc.*, 1037-1040, 2010

[3] Bruno Astuto A. Nunes, Marc Mendonca, Xuan-Nam Nguyen, Katia Obraczka, Thierry Turletti. *"A Survey of Software Defined Networking: Past, Present and Fututre programmable Networks". IEEE Communications Surveys & Tutorials,* Vol. 16, No.3, 1617-1634, 2014. DOI=http://ieeexplore.ieee.org/stamp/stamp.jsp?tp=&arnumber=6739370

[4] Gian Carlo Fortino, Giuseppe Di Fatta, Mukaddim Pathan, Athanasios V. Vasilakos. *"Cloud Assisted Body Area Networks: State of the Art and Future Challenges".* Wireless Networks, 1925-1938, 2014. DOI=http://link.springer.com/article/10.1007%2Fs11276-014-0714-1#page-1

[5] W. Yi, M.B Blake. *"Service Oriented Computing and Cloud Computing: Challenges and Opportunities".* IEEE Internet Computing, Vol. 14, No.6, 72-75, 2010. DOI=http://ieeexplore.ieee.org/stamp/stamp.jsp?tp=&arnumber=5617062

[6] Gian Carlo Fortino, Raffaele Gravina, Antonio Guerrieri, Giuseppe Di Fatta. *"Engineering Large Scale Body Area Network Applications". Proceedings of Bodynet Conference* (Boston, United States, September 30-October 2, 2013) DOI=http://dl.acm.org/citation.cfm?id=2555402

[7] G Fortino, M Pathan, G Di Fatta. *"BodyCloud: Integration of Cloud Computing and body sensor networks"*, IEEE International Conference on Cloud Computing Technology and Science (CloudCom), Dec.2012 DOI=http://dx.doi.org/10.1109/CloudCom.2012.6427537

Driver's ECG Signal Detection and Transmission by Impulse-Radio-Based Human Body Communication Technology

Jianqing Wang
Graduate School of Engineering
Nagoya Institute of Technology
Nagoya 466-8555, Japan
wang@nitech.ac.jp

Taku Kato
Graduate School of Engineering
Nagoya Institute of Technology
Nagoya 466-8555, Japan
25417509@stn.nitech.ac.jp

Daisuke Anzai
Graduate School of Engineering
Nagoya Institute of Technology
Nagoya 466-8555, Japan
anzai@nitech.ac.jp

ABSTRACT
In this study, we developed a wearable electrocardiogram (ECG) sensor with human body communication (HBC) technology for vital data transmission in a car. The ECG signals were modulated with wideband pulse signals between 10 and 60 MHz based on an impulse radio (IR) scheme, which provides a data rate as high as 1.25 Mbps. To apply the HBC-based wearable ECG in a moving car, we employed a moving average algorithm to reduce the noises produced in the received ECG signals due to the car's movement. As a result, we confirmed a real-time ECG transmission of driver in the moving car with a reasonable accuracy.

Categories and Subject Descriptors
C.2.1 [Computer-Communication Networks]: Network Architecture and Design-Wireless Communication

General Terms
Experimentation

Keywords
Human body communication, impulse radio transceiver, electrocardiogram

1. INTRODUCTION
There is a wide-scale demand for health-state monitoring in various environments [1][2]. One of them is the monitoring of driver's health-state for safe driving. In this scenario, some vital sign sensors are placed on the driver's body to collect signals such as ECG, blood presser and pulse rate. The ECG sensor may be embedded in the driver's seat belt, and the access point may be embedded in the steering wheel so that the driver unconsciously wears the sensors and send the data to an access point by a wireless or HBC technology [3]-[5]. The car's control unit can then analyze the driver's health-state data collected in the access point and generate warning signs or take automatic control of car, if necessary.

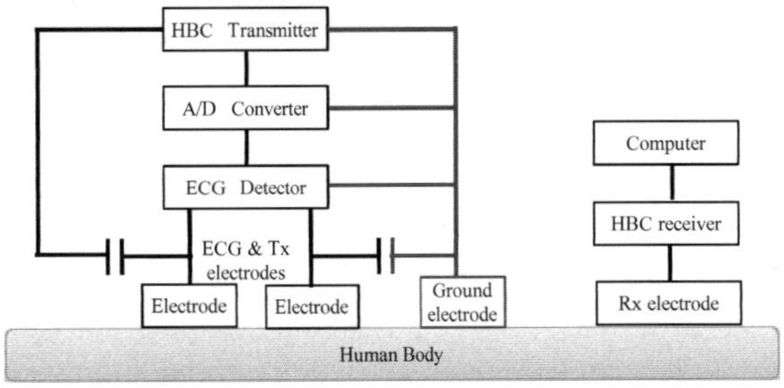

Figure 1: Structure of wearable ECG.

In this study, we develop a wearable ECG sensor with HBC technology for real time monitoring. Instead of a sinusoid signal, digitized ECG signals are modulated with wide band pulses between 10 and 60 MHz, which is known as impulse radio (IR) scheme [6]. Such a wide band transmission can provide advantages such as high data rate and anti-interference feature. Its low power consumption also contributes to a long time use. After the development of the HBC-based wearable ECG, we apply it in a moving car for real time transmission of driver's ECG signals. We introduce a moving average algorithm to reduce the noises produced in the received ECG signals due to the car's movement, and demonstrate the usefulness of the developed wearable ECG in the moving car.

2. HBC-BASED WEARABLE ECG
Fig. 1 shows the structure of our developed HBC-based wearable ECG. The ECG sensor is composited of two 3 cm × 3 cm square electrodes. The two electrodes are attached to the chest for ECG signal sensing. A ground electrode is further attached to the human body as a reference. The ECG signals acquired by the two sensing electrodes are filtered and differentially amplified in the ECG detector, and then converted to digital signals by an analog-to-digital (AD) converter. The AD-converted ECG signals are transmitted by the HBC transmitter to a HBC receiver through the hu-

BODYNETS 2015, September 28-30, Sydney, Australia

DOI 10.4108/eai.28-9-2015.2261526

Table 1: IR transceiver specifications

Frequency band	10 - 60 MHz
Modulation	IR-PPM
Data Rate	1.25 Mbps
Maximum output	-15 dBm
Demodulation	Energy detection

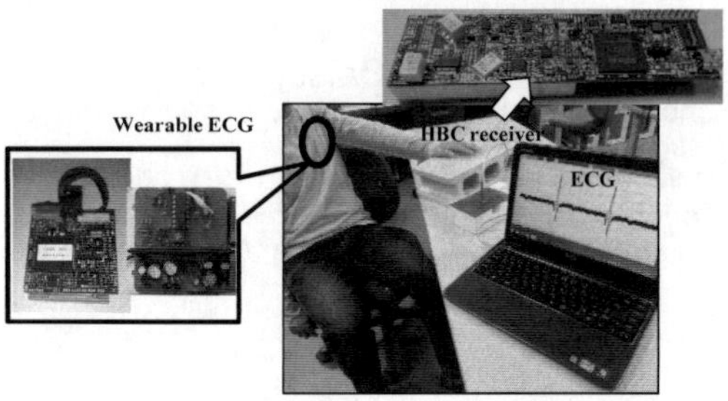

Figure 2: View of verification experiment.

man body. The two transmit electrodes are common as the two sensing electrodes. In the ECG signal sensing, the two sensing electrodes act both as the signal electrodes. However, in the HBC transmission, one of them acts as signal electrode, and the other acts as the ground electrode. To make the two electrodes be commonly used, we insert two capacitors, as shown in Fig. 1, to make their DC potential be different. Such a structure makes the two electrodes can act for not only signal sensing but also signal transmission. Moreover, the low pass filter (LPF) in the ECG detector is designed yo also avoid the mixture of the HBC pulses into the ECG signals. The ECG signals are transmitted by the two common-use electrodes along the human body to the HBC receiver. The HBC receiver has a universal serial bus (USB) interface via which the received ECG signals can be sent to a computer for further process or display.

The digitized ECG signals are modulated with wide band pulses based on IR scheme in the transmitter. The transmit pulses are produced by a 5-MHz oscillator. The XOR operation of the pulse sequence at 5 MHz and its delayed version with a delay time of 10 ns are made to produce a new pulse sequence. The pulse width in the new pulse sequence is around 10 ns and the pulse number is doubled. Its spectrum shape is formed between 10 and 60 MHz with appropriate filtering. In order to transmit the digitized data bits, we employ multiple pulse positions to represent bits " 1 " and " 0 ", which is actually a pulse position modulation (PPM) scheme at a date rate of 1.25 Mbps. The HBC receiver employs an envelope detector for demodulation. The received signal is filtered and amplified, and is then adjusted to an adequate level by an automatic gain controller for demodulation. Table 1 summarizes the basic specifications of the IR-type HBC transceiver.

3. VERIFICATION EXPERIMENT

The validity of the developed HBC-based wearable ECG was verified by comparison of the measured results between our wearable ECG and a commercial available Holter ECG

Table 2: Comparison of correlation coefficient of RRI

A	B	C	Average
0.953	0.984	0.972	0.970

Table 3: Comparison of RR50 (Sample/min)

	A	B	C	Average
Wearable	18.8	12.3	7.8	13.0
Holter	17.7	11.3	8.3	12.4
Difference (%)	5.8	8.7	6.5	7.0

(Fukuda Denshi Co. Ltd.). We set both our wearable ECG and the Holter ECG on the chest, and acquired the ECG signal simultaneously. Fig. 2 shows the view of ECG acquisition and transmission experiment. This experiment was conducted for three persons (A, B and C). For the acquired ECG signals from the three persons, we made a heart rate variability analysis, and extracted the inter-beat (RR) interval (RRI) and the number that the RR difference is larger than 50 ms per minute (RR50). Table 2 and 3 compare the RRI and RR50 between our wearable ECG and the Holter ECG. As can be seen, the correlation coefficient is higher than 0.953 for RRI, and the average difference is only 7.0% for RR50. Moreover, we also compared the low-frequency (0.05 - 0.15 Hz) to high-frequency (0.15 - 0.40 Hz) (LF/HF) ratio for the acquired ECG signals. The LF/HF ratio is usually used as an index of cardiac sympathetic modulation. Table 4 compares the LF/HF ratio between our wearable ECG and the Holter ECG. Again, the average difference is only 4.4%. Such a good correlation and low differences suggest that our wearable ECG has the same performance as commercial Holter ECG.

4. ECG TRANSMISSION IN CAR

After the performance validation for our developed wearable ECG, we applied it in a moving car to acquire and transmit the driver's ECG signal to a personal computer in the front of the car. Fig. 3 shows the view of the experiment. The wearable ECG was set on the chest of the driver. When the driver's hand touched the receiver electrodes, his ECG signal was detected and sent to the receiver and then displayed on the PC screen in a real time.

Fig. 4 shows two examples of acquired ECG signals. One is that when the car stopped, and the other is that when the car ran at a speed of about 30 km/h. As can be seen in the figures, not only the Q-, R-, S-waves but also the P- and T-waves were observed in the ECG signals even when the car was running. The results demonstrate a sufficient feasibility of our wearable ECG for driver's ECG monitoring. However, it was also found that more noise components appeared in the ECG signals when driving. The P-wave and T-wave were especially affected by the noises. By performing a Fourier

Table 4: Comparison of LF/HF

	A	B	C	Average
Wearable	0.76	1.86	1.51	1.38
Holter	0.73	1.78	1.44	1.32
Difference (%)	4.2	4.6	4.4	4.4

Figure 3: ECG acquisition and transmission in a moving car.

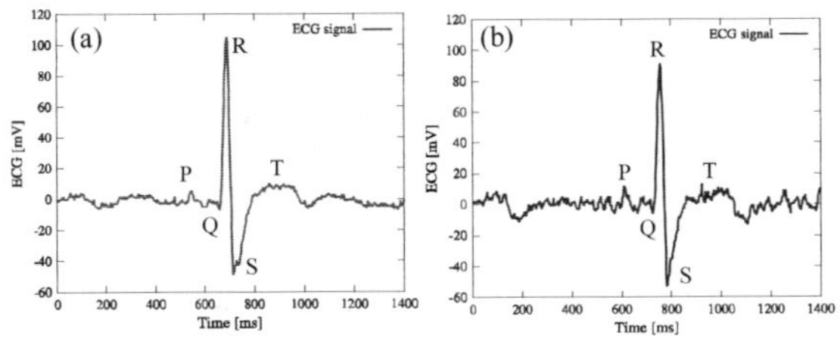

Figure 4: Acquired ECG signals. (a) Stopping, (b) driving.

transform for the noise components in the ECG signals, we found that the noise components were mainly between 30 and 50 Hz. We then introduced a moving average filter in the receiver side. The moving average filter was designed to have 10 taps for removing the frequency components from 30 to 50 Hz. As shown in Fig. 5, the noise components in driving were attenuated about 40 dB by the moving average filter. Fig. 6 shows the ECG signal after the moving average filter when driving. The ECG signal quality was significantly improved. Such a filter is easily realized in the receiver side, and it almost does not yield any obvious signal delay. In our experiment, we implemented it in PC by software.

5. CONCLUSION

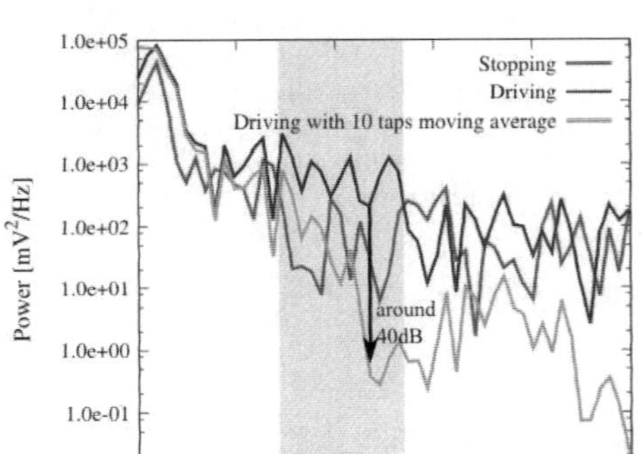

Figure 5: Frequency spectra of acquired ECG signals.

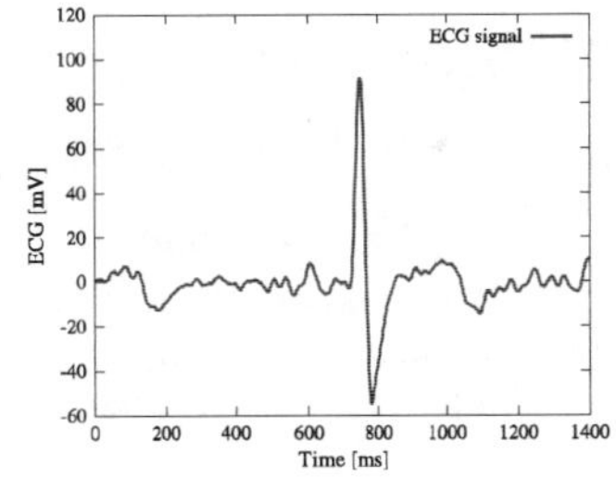

Figure 6: ECG signal processed by moving average filter when driving.

As a promising application of health-state monitoring, we have developed a wearable ECG based on HBC technology for monitoring driver's health-state in a car. The ECG signals are acquired by two signal electrodes and then modulated by a high-speed IR-PPM scheme in a wide frequency band from 10 to 60 MHz. The modulated ECG signals are transmitted by the two sensing electrodes through the human body. The common use of the two electrodes acting for both signal sensing and transmitting has largely simplified the wearable ECG structure. Moreover, we have also employed a moving average algorithm in the receiver side for removing the noises in the received ECG signals due to the car's movement. As a result, we have confirmed a real time ECG transmission of driver in the moving car with a reasonable accuracy.

The future subject is to further improve the filtering algorithm for removing various possible noises in driving.

6. ACKNOWLEDGMENTS

This study was supported in part by JSPS KAKENHI Grant Number 15H04006.

7. REFERENCES

[1] J. Wang and Q. Wang, Body Area Communications, Wiley-IEEE, 2013.

[2] IEEE Std 802.15.6-2012: IEEE Standard for local and metropolitan area networks – Part 15.6: Wireless Body Area Networks, 2012.

[3] T. G. Zimmerman, "Personal area networks: Near-field intrabody communications," IBM Syst. J., Vol. 35, No. 3&4, pp. 609-617, 1996.

[4] M. Shinagawa, M. Fukumoto, K. Ochiai, and H. Kyuragi, "A nearfield-sensing transceiver for intrabody communication based on the electrooptic effect," IEEE Trans. Instrum. Meas., vol. 53, no. 12, pp.1533-1538, Dec. 2004.

[5] J. Wang, Y. Nishikawa and T. Shibata, "Analysis of on-body transmission mechanism and characteristic based on an electromagnetic field approach," IEEE Trans. Microw. Theory Tech., vol. 57, no. 10, pp. 2464-2470, Oct. 2009.

[6] J. Wang, T. Fujiwara and D. Anzai, "Development of impulse radio HBC transceiver for vital signal monitoring of drivers", Proc. 8th Inter. Conf. on Body Area Networks, Boston, USA, Sept. 30 - Oct. 2, 2013.

Miniaturized Implantable DS-PIFA Antenna for Biomedical Applications

Farhad Gozasht
Centre for Health Technologies
School of Electrical, Mechanical and Mechatronic Systems
Faculty of Engineering and IT,
University of Technology Sydney, 2007, Australia
Farhad.gozasht@uts.edu.au

Ananda Sanagavarapu Mohan
Centre for Health Technologies
School of Electrical, Mechanical and Mechatronic Systems
Faculty of Engineering and IT,
University of Technology Sydney, 2007, Australia
Ananda.sanagavarapu@uts.edu.au

ABSTRACT
This paper presents an implantable miniaturized planar inverted-F antenna (PIFA) for biomedical applications. We propose small sized PIFA that can operate over 2.45 GHz Industrial, Scientific, and Medical (ISM) band. We have investigated the effect of antenna parameters on resonant frequencies using empirical parametric studies and achieved highly compact PIFA antenna occupies a volume of 92 mm^3 with a size of $8.1\times7.1\times1.6$ mm^3. Moreover, the effects of the variation of surrounding environment such as skin and fat thickness on the antenna performance are also considered. The impedance characteristics of the proposed antennas are measured using experimental tissue mimicking phantoms. We have also evaluated the calculated Specific Absorption Rate (SAR) by using an indirect thermal method to measure the SAR inside the mimicking phantom.

Categories and Subject Descriptors
B.4.1 – Data Communication Devices.

General Terms
Design, Experimentation, Measurement and Verification.

Keywords
Biomedical implantable antennas, Wireless Medical Telemetry, Electrically small antennas, SAR.

1. INTRODUCTION
Major challenges faced by the design of antennas for implantation inside human body include miniaturization, improved radiation performance and bandwidth enhancement [1-3]. The radiation efficiency of an implantable antenna decreases due to the high dielectric loss caused by the surrounding human tissues. The smaller size and lower efficiencies coupled with low power constraints can lead to a shorter communication range. To overcome these challenges, many improved implantable antenna designs have been proposed in the literature [2], [4]. Folded dipoles have simpler structure but their radiation efficiency is 0.14% which is quite low [2]. To improve this, a multi-layered spiral antenna was proposed in [4] with a radiation efficiency about 0.5% at 2.45 GHz, which is still low. An implantable, miniaturized annular slot antenna having size of $22\times20mm^2$ was reported in [3] with a radiation efficiency of 1.2% which is an improvement over existing works [2], [4]. It is also important to consider trade-off between antenna size and achievable radiation efficiency. In addition, impedance bandwidth is another important parameter for body-implanted antennas as larger bandwidth can accommodate possible shifts in the resonant frequency due to variation in human tissue properties or other perturbations that may occur during implantation. To satisfy these, a cavity loaded patch antenna was reported in [5], and yet, the best antenna size achieved was only $10\times10\times1.27mm^3$ at 2.45 GHz with a 7.7% impedance bandwidth.

In order to obtain improved performance, this paper proposes a miniaturized implantable Dual-Slot (DS) PIFA antenna which operates over ISM band at 2.45 GHz, and occupies a volume of only 92 mm^3 with a compact size of $8.1\times7.1\times1.6$ mm^3. The antenna has a measured bandwidth of 330MHz (13.5%) and provides a reasonably moderate radiation efficiency of 2.5% when immersed inside a human-tissue mimicking numerical phantom which is better than the reported results in the literature [2-5]. We also report measured SAR performance when the proposed antenna is implanted inside an experimental tissue mimicking phantom. The paper is organized as follows: in section 2, we present the antenna design procedure, and section 3 provides information about the human tissue mimicking phantoms. In section 4, measurements are reported and the conclusions are provided in section 5.

2. DESIGN PROCEDURE
The geometry of the proposed miniaturized implantable DS-PIFA printed on a FR-4 substrate is shown in figure 1. The antenna design procedure has been carried out in two steps: first, the dimensions of the dual slot antenna having a shorting pin and feed were obtained using empirical formulas [6] to operate at 2.45 GHz in air. Then, using FEKO™ [7], the antenna model was immersed inside a homogeneous tissue mimicking numerical phantom to obtain its geometrical dimensions for operation in the 2.45 GHz band. Next, a thin dielectric superstrate was added to the antenna and the FEKO calculations were carried out when it is embedded inside a multi-layered human tissue mimicking numerical phantom mainly to fine tune the geometrical

BODYNETS 2015, September 28-30, Sydney, Australia

DOI 10.4108/eai.28-9-2015.2261517

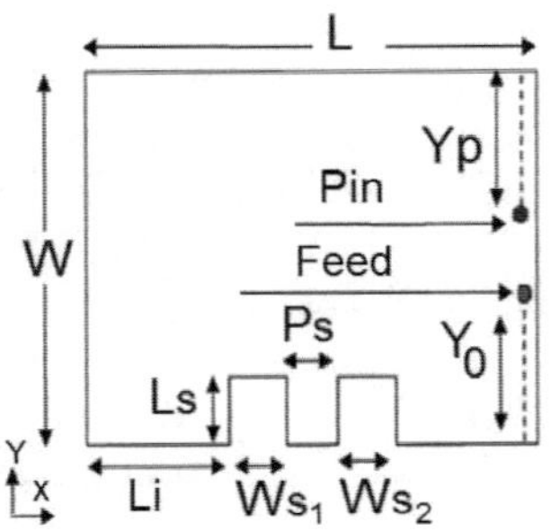

Figure 1: Geometry of proposed PIFA.

dimensions of the antenna to obtain resonance in the 2.45 GHz band. Detailed parametric studies have been conducted in order to quantify the effects of the position of shorting pin, feed point as well as different tissue parameters of the phantom to empirically optimize the antenna geometry. Referring to figure1, the dimensions of the rectangular-shaped patch as well the two radiating slots are the key parameters for antenna operation. In addition, the locations of the shorting pin and the coaxial feed are also important to obtain good matching within the chosen band. The advantage of the DS-PIFA geometry is that it could provide significantly larger bandwidths than conventional patch antennas as its structure helps to obtain antenna resonance at two close resonant frequencies thus leading to the creation of wideband operation. The calculated results on reflection coefficient showed that a ground plane that is slightly larger than the metallic patch can obtain the reflection coefficient better than -10dB within the band of interest. It has been found that the antenna can perform optimally when the feed and the shorting pin are placed on the symmetric central vertical axis with respect to the slots. The geometrical dimensions of the DS-PIFA were 19×17×1.6mm to operate at 2.45 GHz inside a lossy human tissue mimicking phantom. The antenna has a simple coaxial feeding structure. The dielectric permittivity and conductivity of the FR4 substrate are 4.4 and 0.025 respectively. The metallic patch has been covered by a superstrate having the same dielectric constant and thickness as that of the substrate.

We have conducted parametric studies to investigate the effects of each geometrical parameter of the proposed antenna on the resonant frequency and impedance bandwidth with an aim to further miniaturize the antenna. These investigations included investigating the effects of the variation of the positions of feed and shorting pin, the variation of widths and lengths of slots plus their symmetry. In each of these cases only one of the parameters was varied while keeping other antenna parameters fixed. It was found that the slot width variation contributes to variation of the antenna resonant frequency. Our investigations also highlighted that for certain feed and pin positions on the patch, the slot lengths could be reduced without affecting the resonance at 2.45 GHz. When the slot length was reduced, the area of the patch increased making the antenna to resonate at lower frequencies. By appropriately reducing the patch area and varying the pin position, we could obtain further size reduction of the antenna without affecting the resonant frequency at 2.45 GHz band. The initial size of 19×17×1.6mm has now been reduced to 8.1×7.1×1.6mm, i.e., a 58% reduction in the antenna physical size is achieved still operating at 2.45 GHz. The resultant miniaturized PIFA is quite small compared to other reported implantable antennas in the literature [2-5].

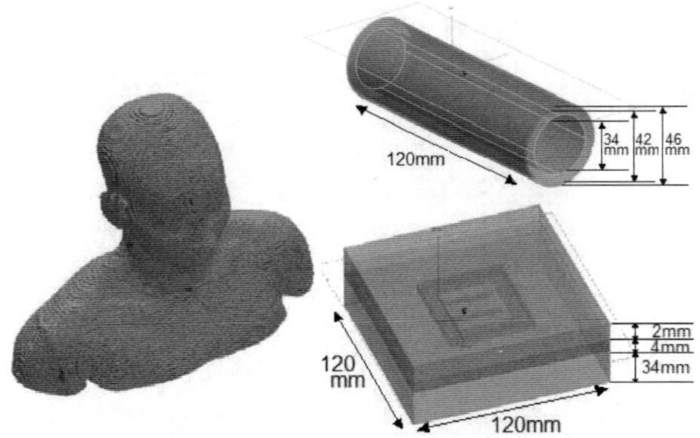

Figure 2: Multi-layered human tissue numerical phantoms. a) Complex human body phantom, b) Layered cylindrical and Layered Block phantoms.

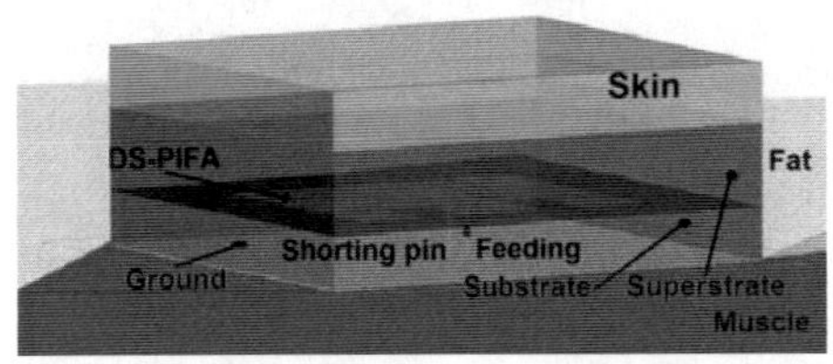

Figure 3: 3D view in Numerical Multilayered Tissue Mimicking phantom.

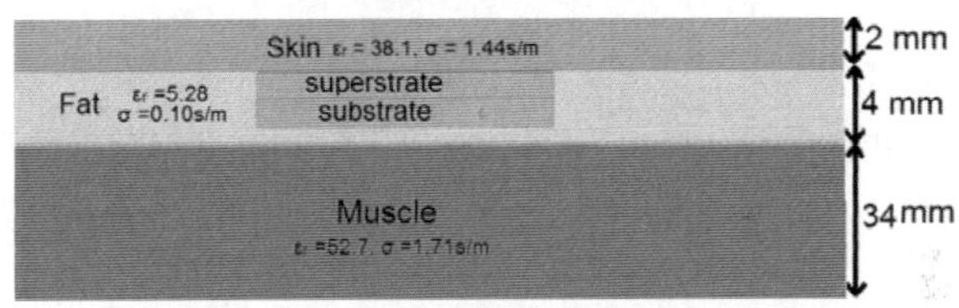

Figure 4. Side view in mimicking phantom.

3. TISSUE MIMICKING PHANTOMS

3.1 Numerical Phantoms

The numerical phantoms used in simulations are shown in figure 2 in which the DS-PIFA is immersed inside inhomogeneous multi layered complex human body model. Figure 3 and 4 show the position of the proposed implantable PIFA inside the numerical multilayered phantoms. The antenna is embedded into the fat layer under the skin and above the chest muscles. The dielectric properties [10] and the thickness of each tissue layer are shown in figure 4. The complex human body phantom provides accurate results; however, it requires a lot of computational resources for each run. So, we used alternate, smaller, multi-layered block-shaped and cylindrical shaped numerical phantoms but using the same dielectric properties for skin, fat and muscle layers as shown in figure 4(b). It is expected that the cylindrically shaped multi-layered phantom can simulate antenna implantation inside the arm whereas the layered rectangular block phantom simulates antenna implantation under the chest skin. Results obtained using FEKO on reflection coefficient and radiation efficiency using these smaller, but layered numerical phantoms demonstrate a good agreement with those obtained using complex human body numerical phantom as shown in figure 5.

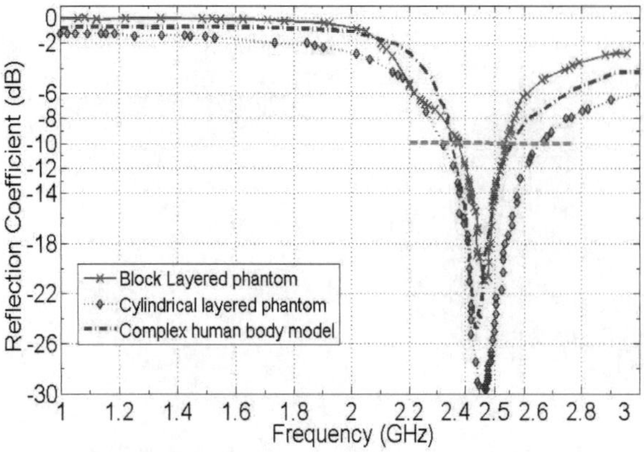

Figure 5: Calculated Reflection coefficient of Dual-slot PIFA: Layered Block and cylindrical phantoms versus Complex human body phantom.

The calculated radiation efficiency of the proposed antenna including the superstrate layer is 2.5% when immersed inside a complex human body model. As expected, the calculated efficiency is low due to the presence of lossy tissues. However, the efficiency is much better than those published for similar class of antennas in the literature [2-5].

We have also included in our simulations, other factors that may affect the antenna performance during implantation and testing in realistic scenarios. These include variations in dielectric properties and thickness of the fat and skin layers of experimental vivo models. The proposed PIFA performs well in simulations even with reasonable changes in tissue dielectric parameters and thicknesses so that the coverage of 2.45 GHz band can be guaranteed for a variety of human tissue parameters.

3.2 Experimental Mixed-Meat Phantom

To verify the numerical performance, we have conducted measurements inside an experimental phantom whose dielectric properties are close to the tissue properties. For this, we developed a mixed-meat phantom that is prepared with a mixture of lean pork and beef. The conductivity and dielectric constants of the mixture were measured by using dielectric probe kit and Agilent E5071C VNA from 100MHz to 3GHz by placing the mixture in a plastic container of size 120×120×45mm^3. A good agreement with the desired dielectric properties was observed and comparison of relative permittivity and conductivities of the mixed meat, skin, and muscle are shown in figure 6.

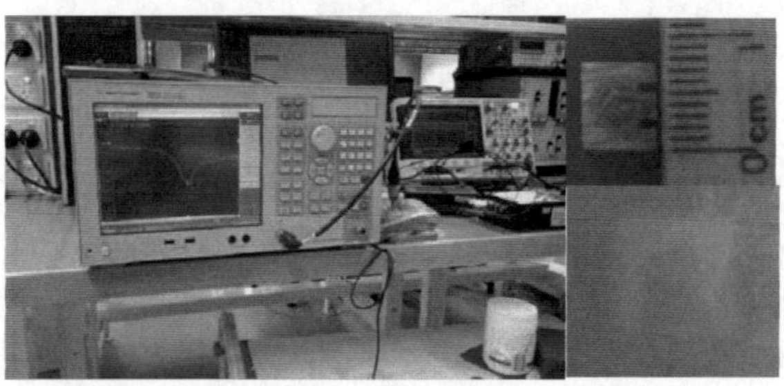

Figure 7. Measurement setup and proposed PIFA on FR4 substrate.

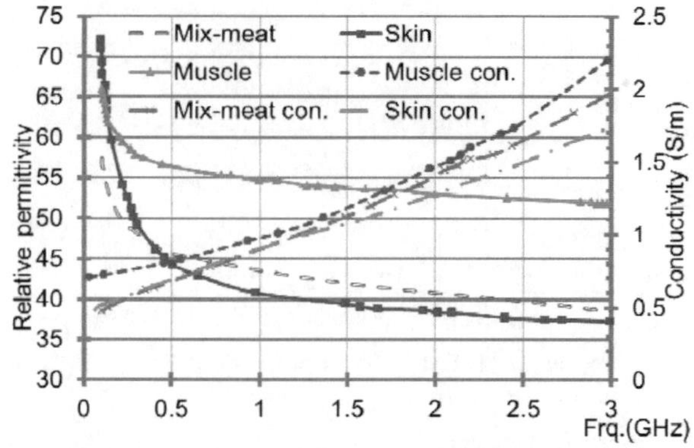

Figure 6: Comparison of relative permittivity and conductivity of the mixed-meat phantom with skin, and muscle.

It can be observed that the relative permittivity of mixed meat phantom is closer to human skin which is useful as the antenna is placed very close to the skin layer.

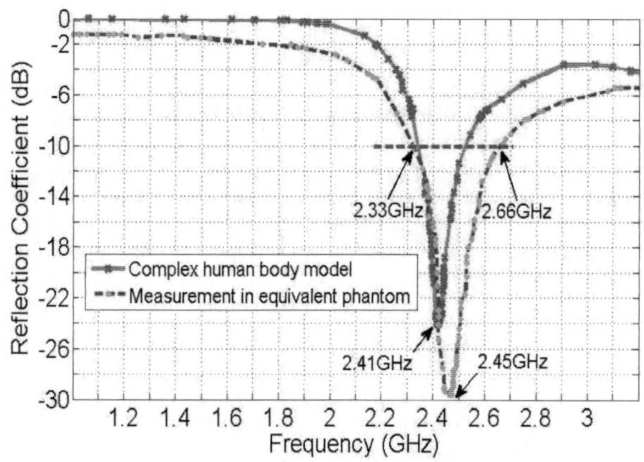

Figure 8: Reflection coefficient of Dual-slot PIFA: Measured vs. Calculated.

4. MEASUREMENT RESULTS

The miniaturized implantable DS-PIFA antenna prototype and the measurement set up are shown in figure 7. The calculated result on reflection coefficient using complex human body numerical phantom is compared in figure 8 with the measured result when the antenna (including superstrate) was immersed in the mixed-meat phantom. Figure 7 reveals good agreement between the calculated and measured results on the impedance bandwidth.

We have also measured the specific absorption rate (SAR) using an indirect thermal method [8]. SAR refers to the rate at which the human body absorbs electromagnetic energy, an essential parameter to measure the human body safety under the electromagnetic wave exposure. Generally, the electric field probe scanning technique is used as a practical method for SAR measurement. However, this measurement technique requires expensive equipment.

Table 1. Effects of variation of fat thickness and dielectric properties

variations	Fat thickness (mm)		Fat εr	
Value	**3**	**5**	**3.9**	**6.5**
Efficiency%	2.3	2.3	2.1	2.4
Bandwidth (MHZ)	260	260	280	270
Δf (MHz)	-10	20	-30	60

Δf = (f-fr) (MHz), fr = 2.45 GHz

Table 2. Effects of variation of skin thickness and dielectric properties.

variations	Skin thickness (mm)		Skin εr	
Value	**1.5**	**2.5**	**33**	**53**
Efficiency%	2.5	2.1	2	2.5
Bandwidth (MHZ)	230	290	260	280
Δf (MHz)	-30	40	-30	80

Δf = (f-fr) (MHz), fr = 2.45 GHz

Here, we used an indirect thermal method for implantable devices when the antenna is placed inside the tissue mimicking phantom. This method offers a simple procedure for measuring the temperature rise in an equivalent human tissue caused by electromagnetic energy absorption radiated by implanted antenna. To avoid field perturbation, we have employed optical fiber thermal sensors. We measured the temperature rise in the human tissue mimicking phantom at multiple locations to evaluate the average SAR [8]. From the average temperature rise, we can calculate SAR using bio-heat transfer equation knowing tissue thermal properties which are available online. To conduct SAR measurement we have employed the same mixed meat phantom that was used to test the antenna performance. Optical thermal sensors are arranged in a 3-D arrangement to measure temperature rise ΔT in the phantom which is necessary to determine the average SAR. The thermal sensors are located at 18 different measurement locations with 5mm intervals over the X-Y plane parallel with radiator surface but at two different depths (0.5mm and 1.5mm) under the skin. To measure temperature raise in phantom due to irradiation, we have used Luxtron FOT Lab Kit and optical thermal sensors. The calculated 1-g SAR for the input power level of 10dBm would be 5.2w/kg while the measured result indicates 4.8w/kg for 1-g SAR with the same input power level. As the 1-g SAR with this level of power exceeds the FCC and European standards [11], the maximum input power must be set to 3dBm (2mW) to satisfy 1-g SAR regulation.

We have also considered the effects of tissue environment variations in the calculated performance of the proposed antenna. This would be beneficial for implantation in realistic human patients as we can gain more insights about the antenna performance in such realistic situations. We anticipated the contributing factors to be the variation of dielectric properties and thickness of the fat and skin. Consequently, we varied the thickness of fat and skin layers and the dielectric properties of those tissue layers in our numerical multilayered block phantom. In each of these cases, while one of the parameters was varied, others were kept fixed. The results on impedance bandwidth, radiation efficiency and resonant frequency are tabulated in table 1 and 2. The results indicate that the proposed miniaturized PIFA antenna can cover the 2.45 GHz ISM band even when the tissue parameters vary making it very suitable for realistic implantation.

5. CONCLUSIONS

A novel miniaturized implantable PIFA antenna resonating at 2.45 GHz with a measured 330MHz bandwidth is presented for implantable biomedical applications. The antenna has a small size of $8.1\times7.1mm^2$ and occupies a volume of $92mm^3$ only, the antenna has a reasonable calculated radiation efficiency of 2.5% when the immersed in a lossy human tissue mimicking phantom. Calculations using different types of human tissue mimicking numerical phantoms were carried out and obtained good agreement with measurements made using mixed-meat phantom an indirect thermal method was used to measure SAR for the safety assessment. The effects of variation of tissue environment were also investigated.

6. REFERENCES

[1] A. Kiourti, K. Psathas, P. Lelovas, N. Kostomitsopoulos, and K.S. Nikita, In Vivo Tests of Implantable Antennas in Rats: Antenna Size and Intersubject Considerations, IEEE Antennas Wireless Propag. Lett, Vol. 12, pp. 1396-1399, 2013.

[2] M. Scarpello, et.al., Design of an Implantable Slot Dipole Conformal Flexible Antenna for Biomedical Applications, IEEE Trans. Antennas Propag., vol. 59, no.10, pp. 3556-3564, Oct. 2011.

[3] A. Rosen, et.al., Dynamic Evaluation of a Digital Wireless Intracranial Pressure Sensor for the Assessment of Traumatic Brain Injury in a Swine Model, IEEE Trans. Microw. Theory Tech., vol. 61, no. 1, pp. 316-325, Jan. 2013.

[4] F. Merli, L. Bolomey, J. Zürcher, G. Corradini, E. Meurville, and A. Skrivervik, Design, Realization and Measurements of a Miniature Antenna for Implantable Wireless Communication Systems, IEEE Trans. Antennas Propag., vol. 59, no.10, pp. 3544-3555, Oct. 2011.

[5] C. Liu, Y. Guo, and S. Xiao, Capacitively Loaded Circularly Polarized Implantable Patch Antenna for ISM Band Biomedical Applications, IEEE Trans. Antennas Propag., vol. 62, no.5, pp. 2407-2417,May 2014.

[6] D.K. Neog, S.S. Pattnaik, D.C. Panda, S. Devi, M. Dutta, and O. Bajpai, New expression for the resonance frequency of an E-shaped microstrip patch antenna, Microwave Opt Tech. Lett. 48, pp. 1561–1563, 2006.

[7] FEKO™, EM Software & Systems, http://www.feko.info

[8] Y. Okano, and H. Shimoji, Comparison Measurement for Specific Absorption Rate With Physically Different Procedure, IEEE Trans. Instrumentation and Measure., vol. 61, no.2, pp. 439-446, Feb. 2012.

[9] K. Saito, Y. Hayashi, H. Yoshimura and K. Ito, "Heating Characteristics of Array Applicator Composed of Two Coaxial-Slot Antennas for Microwave Coagulation Therapy, IEEE Trans. Microw. Theory Tech., vol. 48, no.11, pp. 1800-1806, Nov. 2000.

[10] Dielectric Properties of Body Tissues (IFAC), Available: http://niremf.ifac.cnr.it/tissprop/

[11] IEEE standard for safety levels with respect to human exposure to radio frequency electromagnetic fields, 3KHz t0 300 GHz, IEEE standard C95.1-2005 (Revision of IEEE standard C95.1-1991), 2006, pp. 0_1-238.

Frequency Modulation based Resistive Sensing for Wearable Galvanic Skin Response

Md Shamsul Arefin
Biomedical Integrated Circuits and Sensors Laboratory
ECSE Department
Monash University,
Melbourne, Australia.
md.arefin@monash.edu

Jean-Michel Redouté
Biomedical Integrated Circuits and Sensors Laboratory
ECSE Department
Monash University,
Melbourne, Australia.
jean-michel.redoute@monash.edu

Mehmet Rasit Yuce*
Biomedical Integrated Circuits and Sensors Laboratory
ECSE Department
Monash University,
Melbourne, Australia.
mehmet.yuce@monash.edu

ABSTRACT

This paper presents a frequency modulation based readout circuit for the measurement of skin conductance or resistance. A charge pump based frequency-to-voltage converter circuit with adjustable sensitivity is used to convert the frequency shifts due to skin resistance changes into voltage variations. The readout circuit improves the measurement accuracy and artifact rejection in measurements of the galvanic skin response on the skin, and can be integrated with wearable physiological monitoring systems. The readout circuit is designed and fabricated using the UMC 0.18 μm CMOS technology. It occupies an area of 0.18 mm^2 and consumes 11.7 mW.

Keywords

Galvanic skin response, Frequency modulation, Frequency-to-voltage converter

1. INTRODUCTION

For monitoring health, activity, mobility, and bio-potential continuously, extensive research has been performed in the field of wearable biosensors and physiological monitoring systems [1, 2, 3, 4, 5]. The major vital signs are electrocardiogram (ECG) for electrical activity of cardiac, heart sounds, electromyogram (EMG) for electrical activity of a muscle, electroencephalogram (EEG) for electrical activity of brain, electrical conductivity of skin, blood glucose, respiration rate, mobility for limb movement, and skin temperature [2, 4]. The sensors and low-power readout circuits with wireless are integrated to develop wearable physiological monitoring systems.

*Mehmet R. Yuce's work was supported by Australian Research Council Future Fellowships Grant FT130100430.

The galvanic skin response (GSR) is an indicator of sympathetic and parasympathetic nervous system activity that affect the skin conductivity due to the activity of sweat glands [4, 5]. Since the sweating is controlled by sympathetic and parasympathetic nervous system, skin conductance is a means for the measurement of sympathetic and emotional responses [6, 7, 8, 9]. The sympathetic response due to excitations increases sweat in sweat glands that results in parallel low-resistive pathways. As a result, the conductivity of the skin increases. The parasympathetic response due to relaxation diminishes the low-resistive pathways, and therefore, decreases the conductivity of the skin. The electrodes are positioned on the fingers and/or palm.

A readout circuit is needed to covert the skin conductance or resistance to measurable voltage levels. To measure the skin resistance, a constant current is applied across the electrodes, or a constant voltage is applied across a known resistor and the electrodes in series [1]. Amplifier based readout circuit is also utilized to measure skin resistance. These circuits provide amplified voltage change proportional to the skin resistance change [5]. Various noise sources such as flicker noise ($1/f$ noise), thermal noise, amplifier noise, and substrate-noise coupling minimize the sensor readout range and resolution of these circuits [10].

In this paper, a frequency modulation based readout circuit is used for detecting galvanic skin resistance. A frequency-to-voltage converter (FVC) is used to convert the frequency shifts due to skin resistance into voltage change with adjustable sensitivity [11]. The feedback control system minimizes the overall power consumption and presents a low power alternative for resistive readout circuits. This circuit can be integrated with wearable physiological monitoring systems. The readout circuit for galvanic skin resistance is presented in Section II. The experimental results are discussed in Section III. Section IV presents a summary of this paper.

2. INTERFACE CIRCUIT

The block diagram of the readout system for skin resistance is shown in Fig. 1. A differential crossed-coupled VCO is implemented to convert skin resistance changes (ΔR_{sen}) into frequency variation (ΔF_{vco}). A sine-to-square (STS) converter circuit converts ΔF_{vco} from the VCO into time-

BODYNETS 2015, September 28-30, Sydney, Australia

DOI 10.4108/eai.28-9-2015.2261514

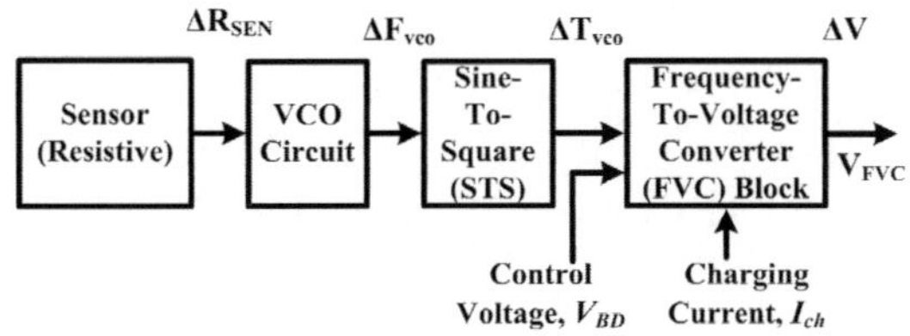

Figure 1: Block diagram of the proposed resistive sensor interface system.

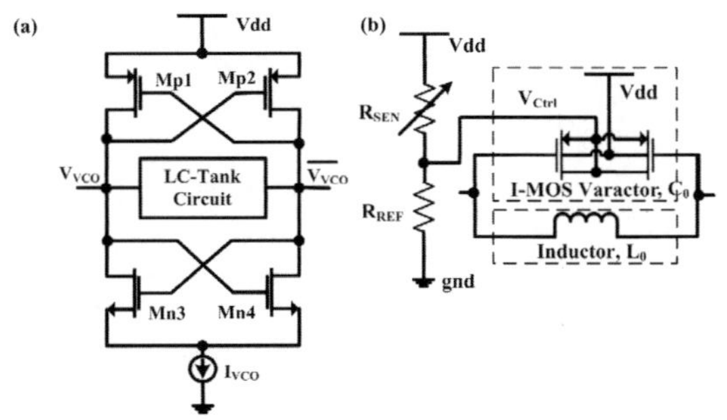

Figure 2: (a) Schematic of crossed coupled differential VCO circuit with a configurable LC-tank circuit. (b) The schematic of the LC-tank circuit for the resistive sensor system where sensor (R_{SEN}) is in series with a reference resistor (R_{REF}) to produce a varying control voltage (V_{ctrl}) with respect to R_{SEN}.

period variation (ΔT_{vco}). A frequency-to-voltage converter (FVC) circuit is designed to convert ΔT_{vco} as the voltage changes (ΔV) [11].

The schematic of a differential crossed coupled VCO employing an inversion-mode MOS (I-MOS) varactor is illustrated in Fig. 2(a). The I-MOS varactor, C_O [12] and inductor, L_O act as the LC-tank of the VCO (Fig. 2(b)). The C_O is dependent on the source-drain voltage, V_{ctrl}. The effective capacitance is modeled by $C_O(V_{ctrl}) = C_{min} + C_V(V_{ctrl})$ for $V_{ctrl} > 0$ condition [12]. Here, C_{min} is the minimum fixed capacitance of the varactor and C_V is the additive capacitance component that depends on V_{ctrl}. The skin resistance (R_{SEN}) is in series with a reference resistor (R_{REF}) to produce a varying control voltage (V_{ctrl}) with respect to R_{SEN}. The varying voltage, V_{ctrl}, resulting from skin resistance is translated to frequency variation using the VCO. The VCO oscillation frequency can be approximated for this configuration as $F_{vco} = 1/2\pi\sqrt{L_O\left(C_{min} + C_V(V_{ctrl})\right)}$. The time period of the oscillator for V_{ctrl} can be expressed as $T_{vco} = T_O\left(1 + C_V(V_{ctrl})/2C_{min}\right)$. Therefore, the change in time period is

$$\Delta T_{vco} = \frac{\Delta C_V(V_{ctrl})}{2F_O C_{min}}. \quad (1)$$

The FVC block comprising of the logic controller block and a charge pump (CP) circuit, is illustrated in Fig. 3(a). An external control voltage (V_{BD}) and a feedback voltage (V_{FVC}) from the CP circuit provide the control to translate the

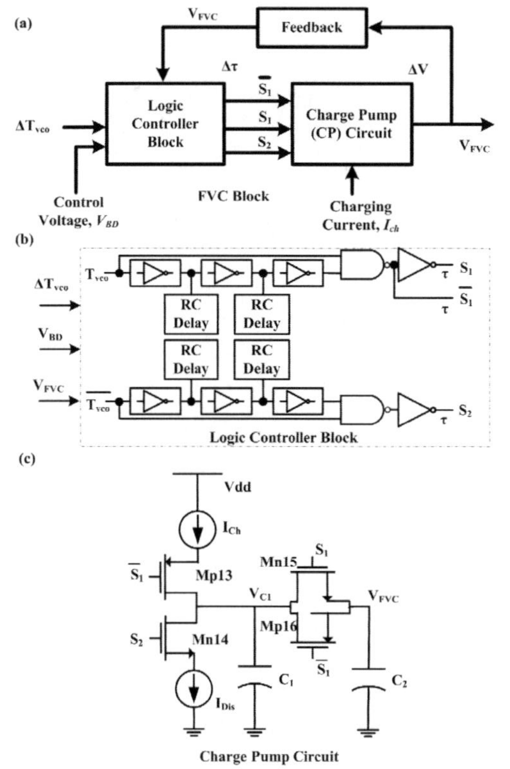

Figure 3: (a) Block diagram of the FVC circuit with feedback charge pump. (b) Schematic of logic controller circuit. (c) Schematic of the charge pump circuit.

ΔT_{vco} into pulse-width variations ($\Delta\tau$). Figure 3(b) shows the logic controller block that produces three control pulses (S_1, $\bar{S}_1$, and S_2) to control the CP circuit in response to F_{vco}, external control voltage (V_{BD}), and a feedback of FVC output voltage (V_{FVC}). Figure 3(c) shows the charge pump circuit. It is composed of two capacitors C_1 and C_2, transistors ($Mp13$, $Mn14$, $Mn15$, and $Mp16$) acting as switches, and two current sources I_{Ch} and I_{Dis}. The description and operations of the FVC block are explained in [11].

The FVC output voltage for the varactor capacitance and time-delay feedback can be approximated as

$$V_{FVC} = \frac{1}{(1+P_c K_{FD})} \begin{array}{l}[Q_c \Delta C_V(V_{ctrl}) - P_c K_{BD} V_{BD} \\ +2C_{min} Q_c - T_{ID} P_c + 1].\end{array} \quad (2)$$

where $Q_c = P_c T_O / 2C_{min}$, $P_c = I_{ch}/C_1 - 1/R_2 C_2$, and T_{ID} is the fixed delay from inverter. Here, K_{FD} and K_{BD} are the slopes of RC delay circuits. From (2), the slope of the V_{FVC} for the variation of $\Delta C_V(V_{ctrl})$ is $Q_c/(1 + P_c K_{FD})$. Since, P_c and Q_c are proportional to I_{ch}, the slope of V_{FVC} is controlled by I_{ch}. The VCO and FVC circuits are fabricated in the UMC 0.18 μm CMOS process and occupy an active area of 0.18 mm^2.

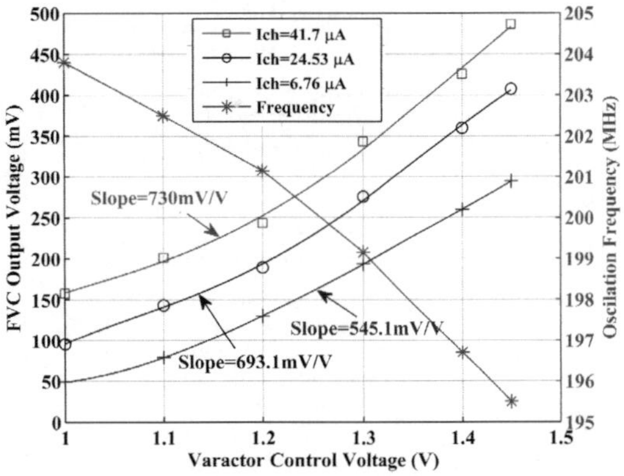

Figure 4: Experimental measurement of FVC output voltage and VCO oscillation frequency for the variation of varactor control voltage.

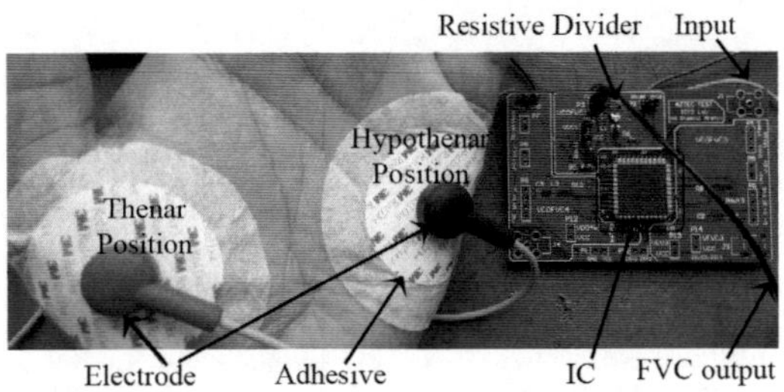

Figure 5: Experimental setup for the GSR measurement.

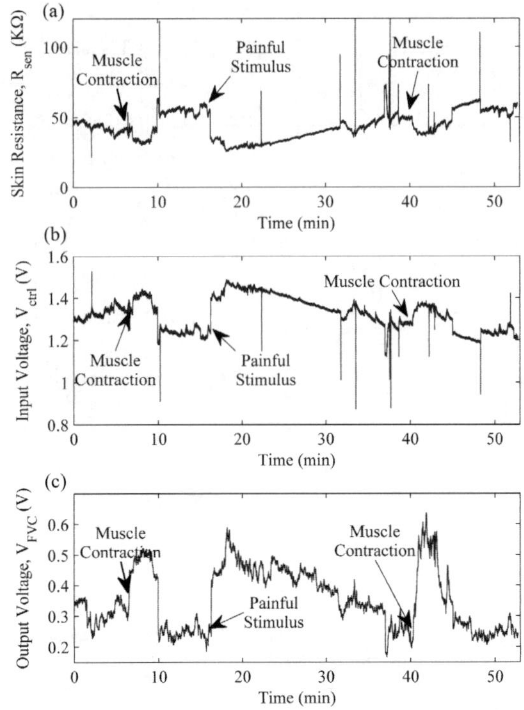

Figure 6: Time-domain plot for muscle and painful stimulus of (a) the skin resistance, (b) input control voltage from resistor divider circuit, and (c) FVC output voltage.

3. EXPERIMENTAL RESULTS

The performance of the FVC circuit is verified by applying a set of controlling parameters (I_{ch} and V_{BD}) for the variation of off-chip (SMD) resistors. Then, the readout circuit with FVC is evaluated for the measurement of GSR under the influence of controlling parameters.

The experimental measurements of the FVC output voltage for the variation of V_{ctrl} is shown in Fig. 4. The VCO circuit (L_0=15 nH) modulates from 203.8 to 195.5 MHz for the variation of V_{ctrl} from 1.0 to 1.45 V. The V_{ctrl} that changes according to the SMD resistors, is converted to frequency variations with a sensitivity of 18.44 MHz/V. The FVC translates the frequency variations to voltage variations with a sensitivity of 693.1 mV/V for I_{ch} of 24.53 μA. If I_{ch} is increased to 41.7 μA, the sensitivity increases to 730 mV/V, whereas the sensitivity decreases to 545.1 mV/V for a decreased I_{ch} of 6.76 μA. The V_{BD} is fixed at 0.4 V. As a result, the sensitivity of the output voltage is also controlled by the I_{ch}.

The GSR is measured by using two dry Ag-AgCl electrodes placed at the thenar and hypothenar positions of the palm, as shown in Fig. 5. The area of the each electrode is 1 cm^2. The range of galvanic skin resistance is 0 to 100 KΩ. The readout circuit is connected to measure skin resistance, as shown in Fig. 2(b). The reference resistor, R_{REF} is 121 KΩ and the supply voltage, Vdd is 1.8 V. The LC-tank of the VCO circuit is set by L_0 of 15 nH to convert the resistance changes to frequency shifts. The I_{ch} of 41.7 μA and V_{BD} of 0.7 V is used to convert the frequency shifts to voltage change.

The time-domain plot of the resistance (R_{SEN}) from GSR response, input control voltage (V_{ctrl}) from resistor divider circuit, and FVC output voltage (V_{FVC}) for muscle and painful stimulus are shown in Fig. 6. The acquired signals are sampled at 1000 samples/s and digitized at 12-bit resolution. The muscle contractions are performed at 6th and 39th minute of the experiment. The muscle relaxations are performed after 1 min of muscle contractions. The painful stimulus of pinprick is performed at 16th minute of the experiment. The muscle contraction and painful stimulus increases sweat secretion that in turn decreases the resistance and increases the input control voltage. The reverse events decreases the input control voltage. The input control voltage from GSR response produces noises due to the artifacts caused by motion, skin-electrode contact, and sweating. The FVC output voltage, which provides lower noises and higher temporal correlation, improves the detection of high-amplitude events compared to the simple resistor divider circuit. It also provides higher sensitivity to smaller

Table 1: Comparison of the interface circuits for GSR measurements.

Circuit Method	Implement	Sensors	Sensor Position	Applications	Ref. (Year)
Amplifier	Discrete	Ag-AgCl Electrodes	Thenar-Hypothenar (Palm)	Physiological Monitoring	[5] (2008)
Amplifier with LPF	Discrete	Ag-AgCl Electrodes	Finger	Emotion Recognition	[6] (2004)
NA	Commercial	Electrode (S220)	Finger	Driver's Emotional State	[7] (2011)
NA	Commercial	Stainless Steel	Arm	Soldier Stress Monitoring	[8] (2007)
Frequency Modulation	IC	Ag-AgCl Electrodes	Thenar-Hypothenar (Palm)	Physiological Monitoring	This Work

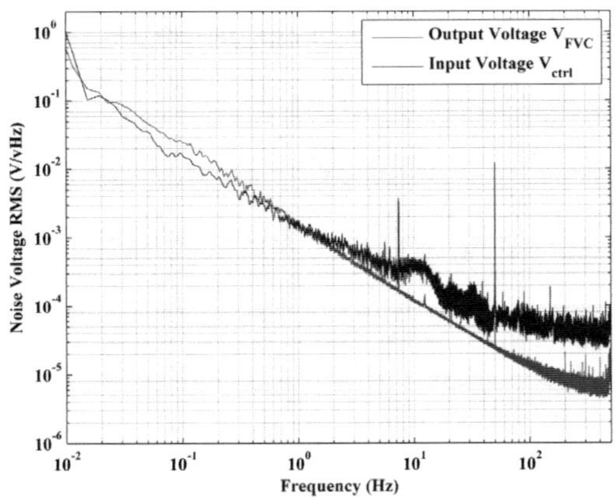

Figure 7: Measured spectral density of the FVC output voltage and the input control voltage.

amplitude events that were ignored in standard GSR recording.

Figure 7 depicts the measured spectral density of the FVC output voltage (V_{FVC}) and the input control voltage (V_{ctrl}) of the readout circuit. The signals were recorded for each 40 minutes. The $1/f$ corner frequency at the output of the circuit is 100 Hz , which is lower (around 500 Hz) than the input of the circuit. The measured thermal noise floor is 47.84 $\mu V/\sqrt(Hz)$ at the input of the readout circuit. A decrease in the thermal noise floor of 8.14 $\mu V/\sqrt(Hz)$ is observed at the output of the readout circuit. Table 1 show a comparison for the GSR measurement techniques with previous techniques in the literature.

4. CONCLUSIONS

A low noise, low power, and high resolution galvanic skin resistance readout circuit is presented. The circuit is designed using the UMC 0.18 μm technology. The changes of resistance are translated into VCO oscillation frequencies and pulse-width of control signals, which are detected using the FVC circuit as voltage outputs. The circuit has been evaluated for the events of muscle and painful stimulus. This circuit provides improved measurement accuracy and artifact rejection in measurements, higher sensitivity, and lower noise level compared to the resistor divider circuit.

5. REFERENCES

[1] U. Anliker, J. A. Ward, P. Lukowicz, G. Troster, F. Dolveck, M. Baer, et al. AMON: a wearable multiparameter medical monitoring and alert system. *IEEE Trans. Information Technology in Biomedicine*, 8:415-427, Dec. 2004.

[2] M. Chan, D. Estéve, J.-Y. Fourniols, C. Escriba, and E. Campo. Smart wearable systems: Current status and future challenges. *Artificial intelligence in medicine*, 56:137-156, Nov. 2012.

[3] M.R. Yuce. Implementation of wireless body area networks for healthcare systems. *Sensors and Actuators A: Physical*, 162(1):116-129, Jul. 2010.

[4] T. Vuorela, V.-P. Seppa, J. Vanhala, and J. Hyttinen. Design and implementation of a portable long-term physiological signal recorder. *IEEE Trans. on Information Technology in Biomedicine*, 14:718-725, May 2010.

[5] P. Pandian, K. Mohanavelu, K. Safeer, T. Kotresh, D. Shakunthala, P. Gopal, et al. Smart Vest: Wearable multi-parameter remote physiological monitoring system. *Medical engineering & physics*, 30:466-477, May 2008.

[6] K.H. Kim, S.W. Bang, and S.R. Kim. Emotion recognition system using short-term monitoring of physiological signals. *Medical and Biological Engineering and Computing*, 42(3):419427, 2004.

[7] C.D. Katsis, Y. Goletsis, G. Rigas, and D.I. Fotiadis. A wearable system for the affective monitoring of car racing drivers during simulated conditions. *Transportation research part C: emerging technologies*, 19(3):541-551, 2011.

[8] C.H. Perala and B.S. Sterling. Galvanic skin response as a measure of soldier stress. *(No. ARL-TR-4114). Army research lab*, May 2007.

[9] W. Boucsein. Physiology of the Electrodermal System. in *Electrodermal Activity*, 2nd ed. Springer US, 2012.

[10] N. Yazdi, H. Kulah, and K. Najafi. Precision readout circuits for capacitive microaccelerometers. *Proc. IEEE Sensors 2004*, pages 28-31, Vienna, Austria, 24-27 Oct. 2004.

[11] M.S. Arefin, J.-M. Redoute, M.R. Yuce. A MEMS Interface IC With Low-Power and Wide-Range Frequency-to-Voltage Converter for Biomedical Applications. *IEEE Trans. on Biomedical Circuits and Systems*, Jun. 2015.

[12] P. Andreani and S. Mattisson. On the use of MOS varactors in RF VCO's. *IEEE J. Solid-State Circuits*, 35(6):905-910, Jun. 2000.

Energy Efficient Duty Cycle Design based on Quantum Immune Clonal Evolutionary Algorithm in Body Area Networks

Jie Zhou
Department of Engineering
Macquarie University
Sydney, Australia
jie.zhou8 @students.mq.edu.au
School of Electronics Eng.
Beijing University of
Post and Telecommunications
Beijing, China

Eryk Dutkiewicz
Department of Engineering
Macquarie University
Sydney, Australia
eryk.dutkiewicz@mq.edu.au

Ren Ping Liu
Commonwealth Scientific and
Industrial Research
Organisation (CSIRO)
ren.liu@csiro.au

Gengfa Fang
Department of Engineering
Macquarie University
Sydney, Australia
Gengfa.Fang@mq.edu.au

Yuanan Liu
School of Electronics Eng.
Beijing University of
Post and Telecommunications
Beijing, China
yuliu@bupt.edu.cn

ABSTRACT

Duty cycle design is an important topic in body area networks. As small sensors are equipped with the limited power source, the extension of network lifetime is generally achieved by reducing the network energy consumption, for instance through duty cycle schemes. However, the duty cycle design is a highly complex NP-hard problem and its computational complexity is too high with exhaustive search algorithm for practical implementation. In order to extend the network lifetime, we proposed a novel quantum immune clonal evolutionary algorithm (QICEA) for duty cycle design while maintaining full coverage in the monitoring area. The QICEA is tested, and a performance comparison is made with simulated annealing (SA) and genetic algorithm (GA). Simulation results show that compared to the SA and the GA, the proposed QICEA can extending the lifetime of body area networks and enhancing the energy efficiency effectively.

Categories and Subject Descriptors

G.2.1 [**Mathematics of Computing**]: Discrete Mathematics—*Combinatorics*; F.2.2 [**Theory of Computation**]: Analysis of Algorithms and Problem Ccomplexity—*Nonnumerical Algorithms and Problems*

General Terms

Algorithms

Keywords

Wireless sensor networks, duty cycle design, evolutionary algorithm

1. INTRODUCTION

The recent advances in micro-sensor and technology growth in the field of wireless communications has facilitated the deployment of more capable body area networks to monitor and manage patients intelligently. A body area network generally consists of a number of sensor nodes for exact sensing with a wide range of potential disease. Limited by their size, small wireless sensors are generally low-cost, low-power devices with the restricted power source and limited sensing range. Due to the limited power source, Lifetime optimization through duty cycle design has always been an important issue of the body area networks. Careful duty cycle design can be an effective optimization means for achieving the maximal network lifetime with full coverage constraints. However, the computational complexity of duty cycle design problem increases exponentially with the increment of the number and the lifetime of nodes. Thus, the duty cycle design problem can be formulated as a nonlinear combinational optimization problem and its computational complexity is too high with exhaustive search algorithm for practical implementation[1].

Fortunately, the heuristic algorithms provide a perfect solution to the nonlinear combinational optimization problem, which include the particle swarm optimization (PSO), the genetic algorithm (GA) and the simulated annealing (SA). A research effort to the duty cycle design problem based on the greedy algorithm can be found in [2]. Their work focused on improving the scheduling scheme for sensor sets. The greedy algorithm is simple and fast, but it usually yields shorter network lifetime than evolutionary algorithms. GA method was first introduced in [3]. In [3], the improved GA were proposed for optimizing node scheduling in wireless sensor networks. Their algorithms have shown to perform well on a sensor networks with limited number of nodes. But it suffers from a premature convergence and low

BODYNETS 2015, September 28-30, Sydney, Australia

DOI 10.4108/eai.28-9-2015.2261427

convergence rate when the number of nodes is high. A duty cycle design scheme is proposed in [4] and PSO is used to solve the problem. However, in practice, it gets stuck into local optima and falls into evolutionary stagnation.

Based on the quantum theory, we proposed a quantum immune clonal evolutionary algorithm (QICEA) for duty cycle design in body area networks which can achieve a longer network lifetime while maintaining full coverage in the monitoring area. QICEA combines quantum computation and artificial immune clonal algorithm, where the elements of the antibody population are Q-bits. Simulation results show that this QICEA for duty cycle design problem in body area networks enjoys longer network lifetime compared to the conventional GA and SA method while maintaining full coverage in the monitoring area.

2. THE SYSTEM MODEL

This section describes the system model of the duty cycle design problem with respect to the limited sensing range, the restricted node energy, and the full coverage constraint. Cardei have used a similar model to demonstrate that the duty cycle design problem in sensor networks is NP hard[2]. In this work, a network lifetime system based on round units is employed to model the duty cycle design problem.

Consider a body area network system with M targets and N sensor nodes distributed over the monitoring area, the sensing relationship can be shown as

$$R = \begin{bmatrix} r_{1,1} & r_{1,2} & \cdots & r_{1,M-1} & r_{1,M} \\ r_{2,1} & r_{2,2} & \cdots & r_{2,M-1} & r_{2,M} \\ \vdots & & r_{n,m} & & \vdots \\ r_{N-1,1} & r_{N-1,2} & \cdots & r_{N-1,M-1} & r_{N-1,M} \\ r_{N,1} & r_{N,2} & \cdots & r_{N,M-1} & r_{N,M} \end{bmatrix} \quad (r_{n,m} \in \{0,1\}) \tag{1}$$

where $r_{n,m}$ is the sensing relationship between the m-th target and n-th sensor , $r_{n,m}$=1 stands for the m-th target is within the sensing range of the n-th sensor, and $r_{n,m}$= 0 otherwise.

Assume that the unit of lifetime is round and the maximum lifetime of each sensor node is D rounds, the duty cycle of the body area network can be represented as

$$L = \begin{bmatrix} l_{1,1} & l_{1,2} & \cdots & l_{1,N-1} & l_{1,N} \\ l_{2,1} & l_{2,2} & \cdots & l_{2,N-1} & l_{2,N} \\ \vdots & & l_{i,n} & & \vdots \\ l_{ND-1,1} & l_{ND-1,2} & \cdots & l_{ND-1,N-1} & l_{ND-1,N} \\ l_{ND,1} & l_{ND,2} & \cdots & l_{ND,N-1} & l_{ND,N} \end{bmatrix} \quad (l_{i,n} \in \{0,1\}) \tag{2}$$

where $l_{i,n} = 1$ represent the n-th sensor is in active mode in round i, and $l_{i,n} = 0$ represent the n-th sensor is in sleep mode in round i. The monitoring cycle can be formulated as the form of matrix multiplication, which can be represented as

$$LR = \begin{bmatrix} \sum_{n=1}^{N} l_{1,n}r_{n,1} & \cdots & \sum_{n=1}^{N} l_{1,n}r_{n,M} \\ \vdots & \sum_{n=1}^{N} l_{i,n}r_{n,m} & \vdots \\ \sum_{n=1}^{N} l_{ND,n}r_{n,1} & \cdots & \sum_{n=1}^{N} l_{ND,n}r_{n,M} \end{bmatrix} \tag{3}$$

where $\sum_{n=1}^{N} l_{i,n}r_{n,m} > 0$ represent the m-th target is monitored by at least one sensor in round i, and $\sum_{n=1}^{N} l_{i,n}r_{n,m} = 0$ otherwise. In order to maintain full coverage in the monitoring area in the i-th round, all elements in i-th row must be positive. Thus, from top to bottom, if all elements from row 1 to row i is positive, the network lifetime is longer than i round. So the system model of the duty cycle design problem can be represented as

Objective:

$$f(L) = row\_zero(LR) - 1 \tag{4}$$

Subject to:

$$\sum_{i=1}^{ND} l_{i,n} \leq D, n = 1 \ldots N \tag{5}$$

where row_zero is the row number for the first zero element that from top to bottom in matrix LR. The constraint $\sum_{i=1}^{ND} l_{i,n} \leq D, n = 1 \ldots N$ represent that the maximum lifetime of each sensor node is D rounds.

From the system model, we can see that the number of possible duty cycle combination increases exponentially with the sensor number and the maximum lifetime of nodes. So QICEA is proposed to solve this problem.

3. ENERGY EFFICIENT DUTY CYCLE DESIGN BASED ON QICEA

Based on the quantum and the clonal selection theory, we introduced a QICEA to enhance the performance of traditional evolutionary algorithms. Compared with the traditional iterative optimization methods, QICEA with quantum bit representation can explore the search space with a linear superposition of states. The key steps of QICEA include antibody encoding, initial antibody generation, affinity calculation, antibody selection and clonal mutation operation, etc.

3.1 Antibody Encoding

In QICEA, a Q-bit is a kind of probabilistic representation. It can be in the basis state $|0\rangle$, in the basis state $|1\rangle$, or in any superposition of the two states. As the quantum bit can represent a linear superposition of all possible solutions, its population diversity is higher than other representation. It can be defined as

$$|\psi\rangle = \alpha\,|0\rangle + \beta\,|1\rangle \tag{6}$$

where α and β denote the probability amplitudes of the $|0\rangle$ state and the $|1\rangle$ state, which satisfying

$$|\alpha|^2+|\beta|^2=1 \tag{7}$$

$|\alpha|^2$ and $|\beta|^2$ are the probability that specify the probability amplitudes of $|0\rangle$ state and the $|1\rangle$ state.

A quantum antibody, which is a form of the probabilities of states, is a Sine and Cosine representation of all binary solution states and is more straightforward than traditional Q-bits representation. A quantum antibody with N sensors and maximum lifetime of ND rounds can be represented as

$$Y = \left[\begin{array}{c|c|c|c} \cos(\theta_{1,1}) & \cos(\theta_{1,2}) & \cdots & \cos(\theta_{ND,N}) \\ \sin(\theta_{1,1}) & \sin(\theta_{1,2}) & \cdots & \sin(\theta_{ND,N}) \end{array}\right] \quad (8)$$

where the θ give the probabilities that the quantum bit exists in states $|0\rangle$ and $|1\rangle$ respectively, which must satisfy

$$\begin{cases} \cos^2(\theta) = |\alpha|^2 \\ \sin^2(\theta) = |\beta|^2 \end{cases} \quad (9)$$

3.2 Initial Antibody Generation

In QICEA, all the angles of quantum antibody are initialized with the Chebyshev map, which can be represented as

$$\theta_j = 2\pi \times |\chi_j| \quad (10)$$

where $\chi_j \in (-1, 1)$is the Chebyshev chaotic random number, which can be generated as

$$\chi_{j+1} = \cos(\phi \arccos \chi_j) \quad (11)$$

where $\phi \geq 2$ is a constant parameter. It means that all possible angles appear with a random probability at the beginning.

3.3 Affinity Calculation

For the duty cycle design problem, the quantum antibody should be converted to a binary solution for evaluation.

$$p_{i,n} = \begin{cases} 0 & random[0,1] \leq \cos^2(\theta_{i,n}) \\ 1 & random[0,1] > \cos^2(\theta_{i,n}) \end{cases} \quad (12)$$

The binary result is calculated for the affinity with formula (4). When the binary solution do not satisfy the constraint (5), we need to reduce the number of working rounds via change some 1 to 0 for the corresponding node in binary solution.

3.4 Antibody Selection and Clonal Mutation Operation

Unlike the general QEA, a clonal selection is applied in QICEA to determine the antibody with the highest affinity. We assume there are S antibodies in the population. First all antibodies are ranked in decreasing order of affinity. Then the first r antibodies with higher affinity are selected for cloning. The number of clone copies can be represented as

$$Z_k = \left\lceil \frac{\rho S}{k} \right\rceil \quad (13)$$

where Z_k is the number of copies that cloned by the k-th antibody, $\lceil\rceil$ is ceil rounding operation and ρ is a multiplying factor that is chosen empirically. In order to enlarge the population size, the total number of cloned antibody Num must satisfy

$$Num = \sum_{q=1}^{r} Z_k \geq S \quad (14)$$

Then the clonal mutation is performed on the cloned antibody population with a quantum gate. In QICEA, the state of Num quantum antibodies can be randomly converted by the a rotation gate, which can be represented as

$$\begin{bmatrix} \cos(\theta_{i,n} + \Delta\theta_j) \\ \sin(\theta_{i,n} + \Delta\theta_j) \end{bmatrix} = \begin{bmatrix} \cos(\Delta\theta_j) & -\sin(\Delta\theta_j) \\ \sin(\Delta\theta_j) & \cos(\Delta\theta_j) \end{bmatrix} \begin{bmatrix} \cos\theta_{i,n} \\ \sin\theta_{i,n} \end{bmatrix} \quad (15)$$

where $\Delta\theta_j$ is a random rotation angle for the (i, n) angle in mutation operation. In order to ensure randomness of $\Delta\theta_j$, we use the Logistic map to generate $\Delta\theta_j$, which can be represented as

$$\Delta\theta_j = \lambda(2x_{j+1} - 1) \quad (16)$$

where λ is a constant parameter that control the rotation angle, x_{j+1} is generated by the Logistic map, which can be represented as

$$x_{j+1} = \mu x_j(1 - x_j), \; j = 0, 1, 2, \cdots, ND \times N \quad (17)$$

where μ=4 is a constant parameter of the Logistic map. We use a quantum NOT gate to update the quantum antibody with a small probability, which can be represented as

$$\begin{bmatrix} 0 & 1 \\ 1 & 0 \end{bmatrix} \begin{bmatrix} \cos\theta_i \\ \sin\theta_i \end{bmatrix} = \begin{bmatrix} \sin\theta_i \\ \cos\theta_i \end{bmatrix} \quad (18)$$

We can see that probability amplitude of $|0\rangle$ state and $|1\rangle$ state exchanged. After the clonal mutation operation, the QICEA select $S - r$ antibodies from Num quantum antibodies. The combination of these $S - r$ antibodies and the original r antibodies will form a new population with S antibodies.

3.5 Basic Steps

The basic steps of QICEA for energy efficient duty cycle design are described in Algorithm 1:

Algorithm 1 The QICEA based energy efficient duty cycle design

```
1: Begin
2: Generate the initial antibodies
3: Quantum state observation for the initial antibodies
4: Evaluate the affinity for the initial antibodies
5: while Algorithm has not reached designated iterations do
6:    Antibody selection
7:    Clonal mutation
8:    Quantum state observation for the antibodies
9:    Evaluate the affinity for the antibodies
10:   Form a new population with high-affinity antibodies
11: end while
12: Output the antibody with highest affinity
13: End
```

4. SIMULATION RESULTS AND DISCUSSION

In this section, the proposed QICEA is tested with different sensors and targets deployments for the energy efficient duty cycle design problem. The monitoring area is set to 1.5×1.5m, and the sensor nodes and targets are distributed randomly in it. The sensing radius for each sensor is 0.9m and the maximum lifetime of each sensor node is 10 rounds. In QICEA, the number of antibodies is 40. Comparisons are made with GA and SA. In GA, we set the chromosome number is 40, the crossover probability to 0.9, the generation gap to 0.9, the mutation probability to 0.05. In SA, the

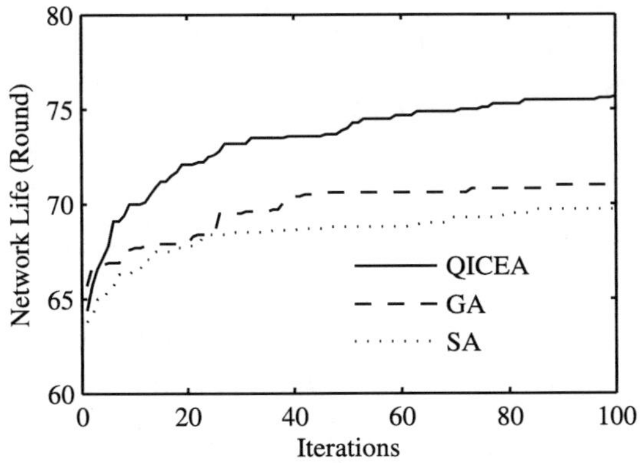

Figure 1: The network lifetime with 10 targets and 55 sensors..

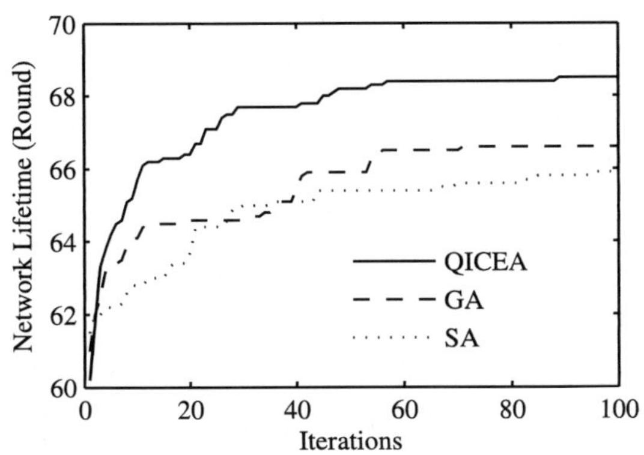

Figure 2: The network lifetime with 20 targets and 55 sensors.

initial temperature is set to 500 degrees, annealing temperature coefficient is set to 0.98. The maximum iteration of all three algorithms is set to 100.

Fig.1 to Fig.2 shows the network lifetime of QICEA, GA, and SA on the energy efficient duty cycle design problem with 10 targets, 55 sensors and 20 targets, 55 sensors respectively. From the figures, we can see that our algorithm produces a duty cycle with longer network lifetime in both conditions after 100 iterations. In the beginning, convergence rates of all three algorithms increased. However, SA gets stuck in local optima and is not able to escape it. We can see that the convergence rate is very slow after 20 iterations which mean the algorithm falls into premature convergence. The performance of GA was shown to outperform the SA most of the time in the convergence rate as well as the final network lifetime. It has fast convergence rate at the beginning but then stabilizes after 50 iterations. It can be seen that QICEA finds high-quality duty cycle scheme much faster than SA and GA. It also searches for solutions more efficiently. Simulation results show that in Fig.1 to Fig.2, the network lifetime of the proposed QICEA method is 8.61% and 3.95% longer than that of SA and 6.62% and 2.85% longer than that of GA, which means the QICEA has a higher energy efficiency.

5. CONCLUSIONS

Duty cycle design is a key problem in the operation of body area networks. In this paper, we proposed a QICEA for duty cycle design while maintaining full coverage in the monitoring area. Simulation results show that compared to the SA and the GA, the proposed QICEA can extending the lifetime of body area networks and enhancing the energy efficiency effectively.

6. ACKNOWLEDGMENTS

Jie Zhou is a recipient of a Macquarie University Research Excellence Scholarship and is under a cotutelle PhD arrangement between Macquarie University and Beijing University of Posts and Telecommunications. This work was supported in part by the National Natural Science Foundation of China (No.61170275), the National Science and Technology Major Project (No.2012ZX03001001-002), The research project of Guangdong (No.2011B090400433).

7. REFERENCES

[1] Dezun D.,Xiangke L., and Kebin L. Distributed Coverage in Wireless Ad Hoc and Sensor Networks by Topological Graph Approaches. *IEEE Transactions on Computerss*, 61(10):1417 – 1428, 2012.

[2] Cardei M., Thai M. T., and Li Y. Energy-Efficient Target Coverage in Wireless Sensor Networks. In *Proceedings of IEEE INFOCOM 05*, pages 1976–1984. IEEE, 2005.

[3] Aslanyan L.,?Aslanyan H., and?Khosravi H. Optimal node scheduling for integrated connected-coveragein wireless sensor networks. In *Proc of the Computer Science and Information Technologies (CSIT)*, pages 1–13. IEEE, 2013.

[4] Navin A. H. and Mirnia M. K. Solving coverage problem in wireless camera-based sensor networks by using a distributed evolutionary algorithm. In *Proc of the 2014 5th IEEE International Conference on Software Engineering and Service Science*, pages 1076–1079. IEEE, 2014.

Low Energy Clustering in BAN Based on Fuzzy Simulated Evolutionary Computation

Jie Zhou
Department of Engineering
Macquarie University
Sydney, Australia
jie.zhou8 @students.mq.edu.au
School of Electronics Eng.
Beijing University of
Post and Telecommunications
Beijing, China

Eryk Dutkiewicz
Department of Engineering
Macquarie University
Sydney, Australia
eryk.dutkiewicz@mq.edu.au

Ren Ping Liu
Commonwealth Scientific and
Industrial Research
Organisation (CSIRO)
ren.liu@csiro.au

Gengfa Fang
Department of Engineering
Macquarie University
Sydney, Australia
Gengfa.Fang@mq.edu.au

Yuanan Liu
School of Electronics Eng.
Beijing University of
Post and Telecommunications
Beijing, China
yuliu@bupt.edu.cn

ABSTRACT

A low energy clustering method of body area networks based on fuzzy simulated evolutionary computation is proposed in this paper. To reduce communication energy consumption, we also designed a fuzzy controller to dynamically adjust the crossover and mutation probability. Simulations are conducted by using the proposed method, the clustering methods based on the particle swarm optimization and the method based on the quantum evolutionary algorithm. Results show that the energy consumption of the proposed method decreased compared with the other two methods, which means that the proposed method significantly improves the energy efficiency.

Categories and Subject Descriptors

G.2.1 [**Mathematics of Computing**]: Discrete Mathematics—*Combinatorics*; F.2.2 [**Theory of Computation**]: Analysis of Algorithms and Problem Ccomplexity—*Nonnumerical Algorithms and Problems*

General Terms

Algorithms

Keywords

wireless sensor networks, simulated evolutionary computation, fuzzy controller

1. INTRODUCTION

With the continuous development of wireless sensor technology, more and more researchers pay attention to the high-density wireless sensor networks. High-density wireless sensor networks have a wide range of applications in the battlefield information collection, security systems, hospital theatres, office automation and target localization, etc [1]. With the improvement of intelligence and the decrease of production costs, the number of sensors in high-density wireless sensor network grows exponentially. In some networks, such as hospital theatres, there can be hundreds of sensors working simultaneously. In these applications, how to reduce the communication energy consumption by clustering is a key issue [2].

The most common clustering protocol for wireless sensor networks includes LEACH and HEED. LEACH (Low Energy Adaptive Clustering Hierarchy) [3] is a low energy consumption clustering scheme that significantly improves network lifetime. The LEACH method uses a duty cycle cluster head selection method instead of the fixed cluster heads. The HEED (Hybrid Energy-Efficient Distributed clustering approach) was first introduced in [4]. In HEED, the reserved energy and density of nodes were considered in cluster head selection.

However, both methods focus on maximizing the network lifetime instead of minimizing energy consumption. For large sensor networks, how to select a certain percentage of cluster heads with the minimum energy consumption for data collection is an important issue. In [5], a method based on the simple genetic algorithm for data collection is proposed for minimum data collection energy consumption. However, the simple genetic algorithm easily falls into local optima, and it often gets high energy consumption clustering results.

Based on the above studies, a Low Energy Clustering method of High-density wireless sensor networks based on fuzzy simulated evolutionary computation (FSEC) is proposed in this paper. In order to reduce communication energy consumption, we also designed a fuzzy controller to dynamically adjust the crossover and mutation probability. Simulations are conducted by using the proposed method, the clustering methods based on the particle swarm optimization (PSO)

BODYNETS 2015, September 28-30, Sydney, Australia

DOI 10.4108/eai.28-9-2015.2261426

and the method based on the quantum evolutionary algorithm (QEA). Results show that the energy consumption of the proposed method decreased compared to the other two methods, which means that the proposed method improves energy efficiency.

2. SYSTEM MODEL

This paper studies a class of high-density sensor network, in particular, the Wireless Body Area Networks in hospital theatres, where nodes are randomly distributed in the monitoring area. The sensor nodes within the monitoring area are divided into a number of clusters, and there is a single cluster head node within each cluster.

In the uplink transmission phase, the randomly distributed sensor nodes observe and check the targets within the monitoring area, and then send the observed data to the cluster head node. The cluster head node collects the data from sensor nodes and then uploads the data to the gateway node directly. The gateway node collects the data from the cluster head nodes and transfers the data to the user for further analysis and processing.

In the downlink phase, users allocate monitoring tasks to the cluster head nodes through the gateway node, and then the cluster head nodes assign the tasks to the sensor nodes within the cluster to complete monitoring tasks. Generally, the amount of uplink data is much larger than the downlink data in monitoring tasks.

In order to reduce the energy consumption with a node communication distance limitation, we must develop an efficient clustering scheme for high-density wireless sensor network. The energy consumption of the wireless sensor network consists of the communication energy, the sensing energy and the microprocessor energy. Studies show that the transmission radio energy and receive energy consumption accounted for more than half of the total energy consumption of wireless sensor networks. Meanwhile, the sensing energy consumption and the microprocessor energy consumption are relatively fixed, which are difficult to reduce through optimization. So we focus on how to reduce the communication energy consumption via optimal clustering in high-density sensor networks.

In high-density sensor networks, the transmission radio energy can be shown as:

$$cost_s(k,d) = E_{elec} \cdot k + \varepsilon_{amp} \cdot k \cdot d^n \tag{1}$$

where $cost_s(k,d)$ is the transmission radio energy, d is the distance between two nodes, k is the length of sending bits, ε_{amp} is the power amplification parameter, and E_{elec} is the electronics energy parameter. Depending on the communications environment, the general value of n is between 2-4. The value of n is higher when the communication environment is worse.

The receive energy of k bits data can be shown as:

$$cost_r(k) = E_{elec} \cdot k \tag{2}$$

where $cost_r(k)$ is the receiver dissipated energy for receiving k bits.

3. DESIGN OF THE FUZZY CONTROLLER

Simulated evolutionary computation specifically includes evolution programming, evolution strategies, genetic programming and genetic algorithms. As the genetic algorithm is most widely used among these numerical optimization methods, in this paper, we use fuzzy based genetic algorithm to develop an efficient clustering scheme for high-density wireless sensor networks.

3.1 Adjusting the Algorithm Parameter

Previous studies show that adaptive adjust crossover and mutation probability can significantly improve the diversity of the population and improve the convergence rate. To solve this problem, Srinivas proposed an adaptive genetic algorithm [7]. The adaptive genetic algorithm adaptively adjusts crossover and mutation probabilities with the individual fitness. The adjusting method is simple, however, the accelerating effect is not obvious.

In FSEC, a fuzzy controller is designed to automatically adjust the crossover probability and mutation probability. When the average fitness of the population is too high, the fuzzy controller adjusts crossover probability and mutation probability to a low value to avoid a population diversity decline. Similarly, when the average fitness of the population is low, the fuzzy controller adjusts the crossover probability and mutation probability to a high value to increase the population diversity.

Meanwhile, for excellent individuals, the fuzzy controller adjust its crossover probability and mutation probability to a lower value to keep the individual structure to the next iteration. Similarly, for bad individuals, the fuzzy controller will increase the crossover probability and mutation probability to improve the fitness of the individual. We should notice that for the clustering problem, individuals with low fitness have lower energy consumption, which means the individuals are better.

3.2 The Input and Output of the Fuzzy Controller

In the design of the fuzzy controller that adjusts the crossover probability and mutation probability, first we need to determine the input and output of the fuzzy controller, and design the membership function for the fuzzy input and output.

In order to adjusts the of crossover probability and mutation probability, first we need to do normalization for the average fitness of the population $\overline{f}$, the individual for mutation f_t and the individual with smaller fitness value in the crossover operation f_b. The normalization can be shown as

$$f_c = \frac{f_{\max} - f_b}{f_{\max} - f_{\min}} \tag{3}$$

$$f_m = \frac{f_{\max} - f_t}{f_{\max} - f_{\min}} \tag{4}$$

$$f_a = \frac{f_{\max} - \overline{f}}{f_{\max} - f_{\min}} \tag{5}$$

where f_c is the normalized fitness of the individual with smaller fitness value in the crossover operation, and its value range is $f_c \in [0,1]$, f_m is the normalized fitness of the individual for mutation, and its value range is $f_m \in [0,1]$. f_a is the normalized average fitness of the population, and its value range is $f_a \in [0,1]$. $f_{\max}$ is the fitness of the individual with the largest fitness value in the population, and $f_{\min}$ is the fitness of the individual with the smallest fitness value in the population.

In the high-density sensor network clustering, the individual fitness is smaller when the network communication energy is smaller. For the controller of crossover probability P_c, the fuzzy controller input parameters includes the normalized fitness of the individual with a smaller fitness value in the crossover operation f_c and the normalized average fitness of the population f_a.

When f_c is greater, it indicates that the individual with a smaller fitness value in the crossover operation is better. Similarly, when f_a is greater, it indicates that the average fitness of individuals in the population $\overline{f}$ is smaller. The output value range of the controller of crossover probability is $P_c \in [0.65, 0.95]$.

For the controller of crossover probability P_m, the fuzzy controller input parameters includes the individual in the mutation operation f_m and the normalized average fitness of the population f_a. When f_m is greater, it indicates that the individual in the mutation operation is better. Similarly, when f_a is greater, it indicates that the average fitness of individuals in the population $\overline{f}$ is smaller. The output value range of the controller of crossover probability is $P_m \in [0.05, 0.26]$.

3.3 The Membership Function

For crossover probability P_c, we use the triangular membership function and the Mamdani membership function for input value fuzzification.

For the normalized fitness of the individual with smaller fitness value in the crossover operation f_c, we choose the triangular membership function for fuzzification, and select six fuzzy sets, including very small (FVS), small (FS), relatively small (FRS), relatively big (FRB), big (FB), very big (FVB) for the of input value range $f_c \in [0, 1]$. The first letter F is used to distinguish different kinds of normalized fitness of the individuals.

$$
\begin{aligned}
FVS(f_c) &= \begin{cases} -5f_c + 1 & 0 \le f_c \le 0.2 \\ 0 & f_c > 0.2 \end{cases} \\
FS(f_c) &= \begin{cases} 5f_c & 0 \le f_c \le 0.2 \\ -5f_c + 2 & 0.2 < f_c \le 0.4 \\ 0 & f_c > 0.4 \end{cases} \\
FRS(f_c) &= \begin{cases} 0 & f_c < 0.2 \\ 5f_c - 1 & 0.2 \le f_c \le 0.4 \\ -5f_c + 3 & 0.4 < f_c \le 0.6 \\ 0 & f_c > 0.6 \end{cases} \\
FRB(f_c) &= \begin{cases} 0 & f_c < 0.4 \\ 5f_c - 2 & 0.4 \le f_c \le 0.6 \\ -5f_c + 4 & 0.6 < f_c \le 0.8 \\ 0 & f_c > 0.8 \end{cases} \\
FB(f_c) &= \begin{cases} 0 & f_c < 0.6 \\ 5f_c - 3 & 0.6 \le f_c \le 0.8 \\ -5f_c + 5 & 0.8 < f_c \le 1 \end{cases} \\
FVB(f_c) &= \begin{cases} 5f_c - 4 & 0.8 \le f_c \le 1 \\ 0 & f_c < 0.8 \end{cases}
\end{aligned} \tag{6}
$$

For the normalized average fitness of the population f_a, we choose the Mamdani membership function for fuzzification, and select six fuzzy sets, including very small (AVS), small (AS), relatively small (ARS), relatively big (ARB), big (AB), very big (AVB) for the of input value range $f_a \in [0, 1]$. For the Mamdani membership function, if the membership value is great than 1, the membership value equal to 1. The first letter A is used to distinguish different kinds of normalized fitness of the individuals.

$$
\begin{aligned}
AVS(f_a) &= 1 - e^{-\frac{0.5}{|10f_a|^{2.5}}} & 0 \le f_a \le 1 \\
AS(f_a) &= 1 - e^{-\frac{0.5}{|2-10f_a|^{2.5}}} & 0 \le f_a \le 1 \\
ARS(f_a) &= 1 - e^{-\frac{0.5}{|4-10f_a|^{2.5}}} & 0 \le f_a \le 1 \\
ARB(f_a) &= 1 - e^{-\frac{0.5}{|6-10f_a|^{2.5}}} & 0 \le f_a \le 1 \\
AB(f_a) &= 1 - e^{-\frac{0.5}{|8-10f_a|^{2.5}}} & 0 \le f_a \le 1 \\
AVB(f_a) &= 1 - e^{-\frac{0.5}{|10-10f_a|^{2.5}}} & 0 \le f_a \le 1
\end{aligned} \tag{7}
$$

For the output of the fuzzy controller that adjust P_c, we use a Gaussian fuzzy membership function for the defuzzification. The defuzzification includes seven fuzzy sets, including very small (GVS), small (GS), relatively small (GRS), medium (GM), relatively big (GRB), big (GB), very big (GVB) for the of input value range $P_c \in [0.65, 0.95]$.The first letter G is used to distinguish different kinds of normalized fitness of the individuals.

$$
\begin{aligned}
GVS(P_c) &= e^{-\frac{(P_c-0.65)^2}{2\times 0.02^2}} & 0.65 \le P_c \le 0.95 \\
GS(P_c) &= e^{-\frac{(P_c-0.7)^2}{2\times 0.02^2}} & 0.65 \le P_c \le 0.95 \\
GRS(P_c) &= e^{-\frac{(P_c-0.75)^2}{2\times 0.02^2}} & 0.65 \le P_c \le 0.95 \\
GM(P_c) &= e^{-\frac{(P_c-0.8)^2}{2\times 0.02^2}} & 0.65 \le P_c \le 0.95 \\
GRB(P_c) &= e^{-\frac{(P_c-0.85)^2}{2\times 0.02^2}} & 0.65 \le P_c \le 0.95 \\
GB(P_c) &= e^{-\frac{(P_c-0.9)^2}{2\times 0.02^2}} & 0.65 \le P_c \le 0.95 \\
GVB(P_c) &= e^{-\frac{(P_c-0.95)^2}{2\times 0.02^2}} & 0.65 \le P_c \le 0.95
\end{aligned} \tag{8}
$$

For mutation probability P_m, we also use the triangular membership function and the Mamdani membership function for input value fuzzification.

$$
\begin{aligned}
DVS(f_m) &= \begin{cases} -5f_m + 1 & 0 \le f_m \le 0.2 \\ 0 & f_m > 0.2 \end{cases} \\
DS(f_m) &= \begin{cases} 5f_m & 0 \le f_m \le 0.2 \\ -5f_m + 2 & 0.2 < f_m \le 0.4 \\ 0 & f_m > 0.4 \end{cases} \\
DRS(f_m) &= \begin{cases} 0 & f_m < 0.2 \\ 5f_m - 1 & 0.2 \le f_m \le 0.4 \\ -5f_m + 3 & 0.4 < f_m \le 0.6 \\ 0 & f_m > 0.6 \end{cases} \\
DRB(f_m) &= \begin{cases} 0 & f_m < 0.4 \\ 5f_m - 2 & 0.4 \le f_m \le 0.6 \\ -5f_m + 4 & 0.6 < f_m \le 0.8 \\ 0 & f_m > 0.8 \end{cases} \\
DB(f_m) &= \begin{cases} 0 & f_m < 0.6 \\ 5f_m - 3 & 0.6 \le f_m \le 0.8 \\ -5f_m + 5 & 0.8 < f_m \le 1 \end{cases} \\
DVB(f_m) &= \begin{cases} 5f_m - 4 & 0.8 \le f_m \le 1 \\ 0 & f_m < 0.8 \end{cases}
\end{aligned} \tag{9}
$$

For the normalized fitness of the individual in the mutation operation f_m, we choose the triangular membership function for fuzzification, and select six fuzzy sets, including very small (DVS), small (DS), relatively small (DRS), relatively big (DRB), big (DB), very big (DVB) for the of input value range $f_c \in [0, 1]$. The first letter D is used to distinguish different kinds of normalized fitness of the individuals. The fuzzification process for f_a is the same as the process in the controller for crossover probability P_c.

For the output of the fuzzy controller that adjusts P_m, we use a bell-shaped membership function for the defuzzification. The defuzzification includes eight fuzzy sets, including extremely small (OES), very small (OVS), small (OS), relatively small (ORS), medium (OM), relatively big (ORB), big (OB), very big (OVB) for the of input value range $P_m \in [0.05, 0.26]$. The first letter O is used to distinguish different kinds of normalized fitness of the individuals.

$$\begin{aligned}
OES(P_m) &= \frac{1}{1+\left|\frac{10P_m-0.5}{0.1}\right|^2} & 0.05 \le P_m \le 0.26\\
OVS(P_m) &= \frac{1}{1+\left|\frac{10P_m-0.8}{0.1}\right|^2} & 0.05 \le P_m \le 0.26\\
OS(P_m) &= \frac{1}{1+\left|\frac{10P_m-1}{0.1}\right|^2} & 0.05 \le P_m \le 0.26\\
ORS(P_m) &= \frac{1}{1+\left|\frac{10P_m-1.4}{0.1}\right|^2} & 0.05 \le P_m \le 0.26\\
OM(P_m) &= \frac{1}{1+\left|\frac{10P_m-1.7}{0.1}\right|^2} & 0.05 \le P_m \le 0.26\\
ORB(P_m) &= \frac{1}{1+\left|\frac{10P_m-2}{0.1}\right|^2} & 0.05 \le P_m \le 0.26\\
OB(P_m) &= \frac{1}{1+\left|\frac{10P_m-2.3}{0.1}\right|^2} & 0.05 \le P_m \le 0.26\\
OVB(P_m) &= \frac{1}{1+\left|\frac{10P_m-2.6}{0.1}\right|^2} & 0.05 \le P_m \le 0.26
\end{aligned} \tag{10}$$

3.4 The Fuzzy Rules and Fuzzy Implication

The previous experience for the parameter adjustment can be summarized as the following fuzzy rules [8]:

(I) "“IF f_c is bigger, THEN the crossover probability P_c is smaller"

(II) “IF f_m is bigger, THEN the crossover probability P_m is smaller"

(III) “IF f_a is bigger, THEN the crossover probability P_c is bigger"

(IV) “IF f_a is bigger, THEN the crossover probability P_m is bigger"

According to the fuzzy rule (I) and (III), we designed a double input single output (DISO) fuzzy rule table, which is shown in Table 1. As the number of the input fuzzy sets for both f_c and f_a is 6, the number of the fuzzy rules in Table 1 increases up to 36 for the output P_c.

Table 1: fuzzy rules for adjust the crossover probability P_c

	f_c					
f_a	FVB	FB	FRB	FRS	FS	FVS
AVS	1GVS	2GVS	3GS	4GRS	5GM	6GRB
AS	7GVS	8GS	9GRS	10GM	11GRB	12GB
ARS	13GS	14GS	15GRS	16GM	17GRB	18GB
ARB	19GS	20GRS	21GM	22GRB	23GB	24GB
AB	25GS	26GRS	27GM	28GRB	29GB	30GVB
AVB	31GRS	32GM	33GRB	34GB	35GVB	36GVB

The numbers in the table are used to indicate the order of rules. To assess the influence of each rule, we use the fuzzy implication $R_i(i = 1, 2, \cdots, 36)$ to express i-th rule for adjust the crossover probability P_c. Once all the contributions of the 36 implications are determined, we can aggregate these 36 fuzzy implications into one output fuzzy implication R, namely

$$R = R_1 \bigcup R_2 \bigcup \cdots R_{36} = \bigcup_{i=1}^{36} R_i \tag{11}$$

Each fuzzy implication can be expressed by the inference “IF f_c is A and f_a is B, THEN P_c is U" that is activated by the input valuef_c and f_a, namely $A(f_c) \wedge B(f_a) \to U(P_c)$. As we apply the minimum (Mamdani) implication for each $A(f_c) \wedge B(f_a) \to U(P_c)$, the text form and the corresponding activation degrees of the consequent parts of these 36 rules become:

(1)IF f_c is FVB and f_a is AVS, THEN P_c is GVS, $R_1(f_c, f_a, P_c) = FVB(f_c) \wedge AVS(f_a) \wedge GVS(P_c)$

(2)IF f_c is FB and f_a is AVS, THEN P_c is GVS, $R_2(f_c, f_a, P_c) = FB(f_c) \wedge AVS(f_a) \wedge GVS(P_c)$

...

(36)IF f_c is FVS and f_a is AVB, THEN P_c is GVB, $R_{36}(f_c, f_a, P_c) = FVS(f_c) \wedge AVB(f_a) \wedge GVB(P_c)$

According to the fuzzy rules (II) and (IV), we designed a double input single output (DISO) fuzzy rule table, which can be shown in Table 2. As the number of input fuzzy set for both f_m and f_a are 6, the number of fuzzy rules in Table 2 increases up to 36 for the output P_m.

Table 2: fuzzy rules for adjust the mutation probability P_m

	f_m					
f_a	DVB	DB	DRB	DRS	DS	DVS
AVS	1OES	2OES	3OVS	4OS	5ORS	6OM
AS	7OES	8OVS	9OS	10ORS	11OM	12ORB
ARS	13OVS	14OS	15ORS	16OM	17ORB	18OB
ARB	19OVS	20OS	21OM	22ORB	23ORB	24OB
AB	25OS	26ORS	27OM	28ORB	29OB	30OVB
AVB	31ORS	32OM	33ORB	34OB	35OVB	36OVB

To assesse the influence of each rule $G_i(i = 1, 2, \cdots, 36)$, we use the fuzzy implication $G_i(i = 1, 2, \cdots, 36)$ to express the i-th rule for adjusting the mutation probability P_m. Once all contributions of 36 implications are determined, we can aggregate these 36 fuzzy implications into one output fuzzy implication G, namely

$$G = G_1 \bigcup G_2 \bigcup \cdots G_{36} = \bigcup_{i=1}^{36} G_i \tag{12}$$

Each fuzzy implication can be expressed by the inference “IF f_m is A and f_a is B, THEN P_m is Uąś that activated by the input value f_m and f_a, namely $A(f_m) \wedge B(f_a) \to U(P_m)$. As we apply the minimum (Mamdani) implication for each $A(f_m) \wedge B(f_a) \to U(P_m)$, the text form and the corresponding activation degrees of the consequent parts of these 36 rules become:

(1)IF f_m is DVB and f_a is AVS, THEN P_m is OES, $G_1(f_m, f_a, P_m) = DVB(f_m) \wedge AVS(f_a) \wedge OES(P_m)$

(2)IF f_m is DB and f_a is AVS, THEN P_m is OES, $G_2(f_m, f_a, P_m) = DB(f_m) \wedge AVS(f_a) \wedge OES(P_m)$

...

(36)IF f_m is DVS and f_a is AVB, THEN P_m is OVB, $G_{36}(f_m, f_a, P_m) = DVS(f_m) \wedge AVB(f_a) \wedge OVB(P_m)$

3.5 Defuzzification

According to Zadeh, we use the max-min aggregation operation to get the output fuzzy set of P_c, which can be shown as

$$U^*(P_c) = (\vec{E}^*)^T \circ \bigcup_{i=1}^{36} R_i = \bigcup_{i=1}^{36} U_i(P_c) \tag{13}$$

where U^* is the membership function of the resultant output fuzzy set of P_c, the operator ąroąś means the minimum implication for the corresponding elements, and R_i is defined

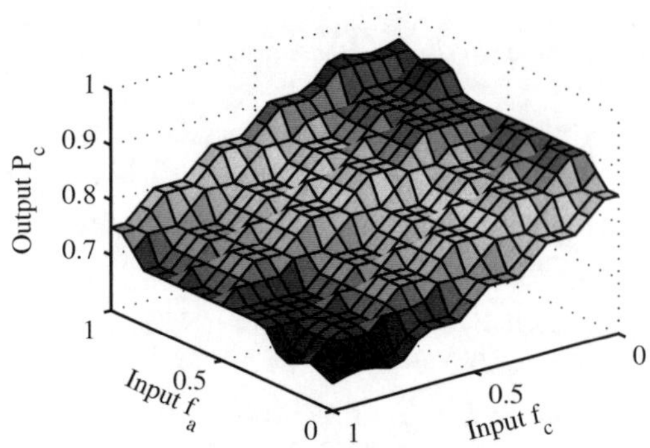

Figure 1: The output P_c

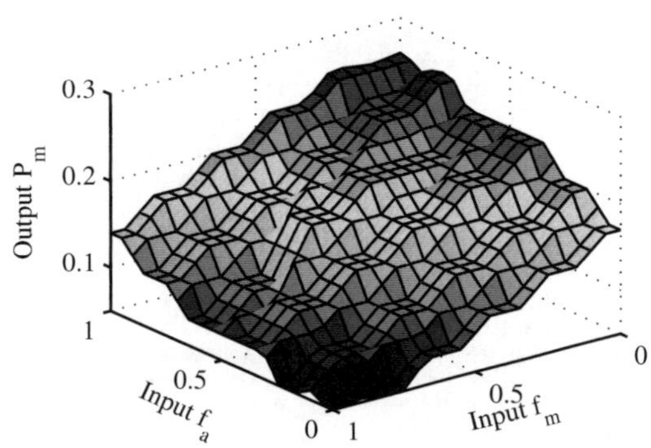

Figure 2: The output P_m

in Section 3.4. $(\vec{E}^*)^T$ is the minor premise that straightened according to the line. The fuzzy interpretation of the i-th rule can be presented as

(1) $U_1(P_c) = (FVB(f_{c0}) \wedge AVS(f_{a0})) \circ R_1(P_c)$

(2)$U_2(P_c) = (FB(f_{c0}) \wedge AVS(f_{a0})) \circ R_2(P_c)$

...

(36)$U_{36}(P_c) = (FVS(f_{c0}) \wedge AVB(f_{a0})) \circ R_{36}(P_c)$

In the defuzzification, we use the Mean of Maximum (MOM) method to calculate the control output of P_c, and the result can be shown as Fig.1.

From the figure we can see that in the input value range $f_c \in [0, 1]$ and $f_a \in [0, 1]$, the output P_c meets the previous experience (I) and (III) for the parameter adjustment, which are "IF f_c is bigger, THEN the crossover probability P_c is smaller" and "IF f_a is bigger, THEN the crossover probability P_c is bigger". Similarly, the output fuzzy set of P_m can be shown as

$$U^*(P_m) = (\vec{H}^*)^T \circ \bigcup_{i=1}^{36} G_i = \bigcup_{i=1}^{36} U_i(P_m) \tag{14}$$

where U^* is the membership function of the resultant output fuzzy set of P_m, and G_i is defined in Section 3.4. $(\vec{H}^*)^T$ is the minor premise that it is straightened according to the line. The fuzzy interpretation of the i-th rule can be presented as

(1) $U_1(P_m) = (DVB(f_{m0}) \wedge AVS(f_{a0})) \circ G_1(P_m)$

(2) $U_2(P_m) = (DB(f_{m0}) \wedge AVS(f_{a0})) \circ G_2(P_m)$

...

(36) $U_{36}(P_m) = (DVS(f_{m0}) \wedge AVB(f_{a0})) \circ G_{36}(P_m)$

In the defuzzification, we also use Mean of Maximum (MOM) method to calculate the control output of P_m, and the result can be shown as Fig.2.

From the figure we can see that in the input value range $f_m \in [0, 1]$ and $f_a \in [0, 1]$, the output P_m meet the previous experience (II) and (IV) for the parameter adjustment, which are "IF f_m is bigger, THEN the mutation probability P_m is smaller" and "IF f_a is bigger, THEN the mutation probability P_m is bigger".

3.6 Computational Complexity

For the computational complexity analysis, the two fuzzy controllers are equivalent to two dual input single output functions $g_1(f_c, f_a) = P_c$ and $g_2(f_m, f_a) = P_m$. The output P_c is calculated in advance and stored in a table for each input (f_c, f_a) that rounds to a certain precision. Similarly, the output P_m is calculated in advance and stored in a table for each input (f_m, f_a) that rounds to a certain precision. In this way, the computational complexity of both controllers is $O(1)$.

4. LOW ENERGY CLUSTERING BASED ON FUZZY SIMULATED EVOLUTIONARY COMPUTATION

In high-density WSNs, the traditional clustering methods lack an overall consideration, so there are some sensors far from the cluster head, which result in energy waste. The clustering method proposed in this paper establishes a global unity mechanism for minimizing communication energy consumption, which considers the position of the cluster heads and the sensor nodes. The main steps of our methods are individual encoding and initial population generation, design fitness function, selection, crossover and mutation, adaptive adjustment of parameters based on the fuzzy controller, etc.

4.1 Population Encoding and Initialization

In FSEC, the encoded solutions are represented by chromosomes. First, we conduct a natural number coding for all the nodes within the region with natural number 1 to L. In this way, each individual can be encoded as a vector of binary numbers, with the same length as the number of nodes L. Each bit of the individual is composed of a Boolean variable stating whether the corresponding sensor node is selected as the cluster head node or not. The "1" represents the node is selected as a cluster head node in the corresponding position, and "0" represents the node is selected as a sensor node in the corresponding position. Each sensor node only clusters with the nearest cluster head. For example, if there are 8 nodes in the region and No.3, No.5 and No.7 nodes are selected as cluster head nodes, the individuals can be represented as "00101010".

We use a population with a fixed number of individuals. The population can be shown as

$$P=\begin{bmatrix} e_{1,1} & e_{1,2} & \cdots & e_{1,L-1} & e_{1,L} \\ e_{2,1} & e_{2,2} & \cdots & e_{2,L-1} & e_{2,L} \\ \vdots & & e_{n,l} & & \vdots \\ e_{N-1,1} & e_{N-1,2} & \cdots & e_{N-1,L-1} & e_{N-1,L} \\ e_{N,1} & e_{N,2} & \cdots & e_{N,L-1} & e_{N,L} \end{bmatrix} = \begin{bmatrix} E_1 \\ E_2 \\ \vdots \\ E_{N-1} \\ E_N \end{bmatrix} \quad (e_{n,l} \in \{0,1\}) \tag{15}$$

where L is the number of nodes in sensor networks, N is the number of individuals in the population, M is the number of cluster heads. $e_{n,l}$=1 represents the n-th node of l-th individual is the cluster head node, and $e_{n,l}$= 0 otherwise.

We assume that there is a fixed number of cluster head nodes in sensor networks, so the constraint can be shown as

$$\sum_{l=1}^{L} e_{n,l}=M \quad (n \in \{1,2,\cdots,N\}) \tag{16}$$

where M is the number of cluster head nodes.

4.2 Fitness Function

Each individual in the population is awarded a score depending on the communication energy consumption. The fitness function is defined as

$$Fit(E)=\sum_{l=1}^{L}(cost_s+cost_r) \tag{17}$$

where $E_n = \begin{bmatrix} e_{n,1} & e_{n,2} & \cdots & e_{n,L-1} & e_{n,L} \end{bmatrix}$ is the fitness of the n-th individual of the population, and the fitness value equals to the communication energy consumption of the n-th clustering scheme. By this definition, the individuals with smaller fitness in the population are the better ones and are more likely to be parents in the next generation.

4.3 Selection

We use the roulette wheel proportionate selection strategy for the selection operator. The selection operator selects an individual from the current population for the next population with the probability inversely proportional to its fitness value, which can be shown as

$$P_{SELECT}(E_n)=\frac{\frac{1}{Fit(E_n)}}{\sum_{n=1}^{N}\frac{1}{Fit(E_n)}} \tag{18}$$

In this way, the individuals that have a lower communication energy consumption will have a higher probability to be selected as parents.

4.4 Crossover

In the crossover operation, two new offspring individuals are generated from each pair of selected parent individuals. In order to keep the number of cluster head nodes fixed, we designed a crossover operator based on Boolean operation.

Firstly, we apply the logical AND operation to each pair of selected parent individuals, and obtain an intermediate binary vector E'. The length of binary vector E' is equal to the number of sensor nodes L. For example, when parent individuals are E_1= [00101010] and E_2= [00100101], the intermediate binary vector is E' = [00100000].

Secondly, we apply the logical XOR operation to each pair of selected parent individuals, and obtain another intermediate binary vector E''. The length of binary vector E'' is equal to the number of sensor nodes L. For example, when the pair of selected parent individuals are E_1= [00101010] and E_2= [00100101], the other intermediate binary vector is E''= [00001111].

Finally, we average random assign the "1" in individual E'' to the corresponding position of E' to generate two new offspring individuals. The ąřaverageąś means the number of "1" assigned to each individual is equal, and the ąřrandomąś means the possibilities of the distribution being equal. For example, when E' = [00100000] and E''= [00001111], the possible two new offspring individuals can be E_1^{new}= [00101100] and E_2^{new}= [00100011].

4.5 Mutation Operation

In order to add some diversity to the population and keep the number of cluster head nodes fixed, some random mutations are applied to the individuals in the population. The mutation operation is done by randomly exchanging the position of "1" and "0" in an individual with a certain probability. For example, the individual E= [00101100] can be mutated to E= [00101001], which means the "1" in the 6th bit and the "0" in 8th bit exchanged.

4.6 Fuzzy Adjust the Algorithm Parameters

In the traditional genetic algorithm, crossover and mutation probabilities of selection have a great influence on the performance of the algorithm. We use the adjust method presented in Section 3.

5. SIMULATION RESULTS AND DISCUSSION

In this section, the proposed FSEC is tested with different sensor nodes and cluster head proportions to investigate the low energy clustering problem in high-density WSNs. Simulation experiments were conducted to verify the communication energy reduction of the proposed clustering method. In the simulations, the monitoring area is 100m $\times$ 100m, and nodes in high-density sensor network are randomly distribute within the simulating hospital floor area. The gateway node is located at $(50, 50)$. As the communication energy consumption of uplink is much larger than downlink in most WSNs, we only consider the uplink communication energy consumption. In the simulations, we set k = 1Mbps, $n = 3$, E_{elec} = 50nJ/bit, ε_{amp} = 100pJ/bit/m^2[6].

Comparisons are made with PSO and QEA by only considering the best solution in each iteration. In QEA, we use the same lookup table as [9]. In PSO, the cognitive and social parameters are set to 2, and the maximum velocity is set to 6.

Fig.3 and Fig.4 show the communication energy consumption of the high-density WSN using FSEC, the PSO and QEA with 300 and 400 nodes respectively, where the energy consumption is obtained directly from the formula (1) and (2). The cluster head proportion is 10%. The results are the average over 10 runs with different random nodes distributions. According to these comparisons, the proposed FSEC

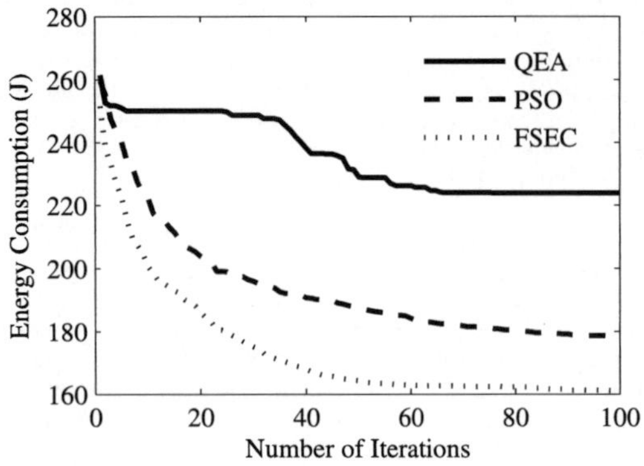

Figure 3: The communication energy consumption by iteration with 300 nodes and cluster head proportion of 10%

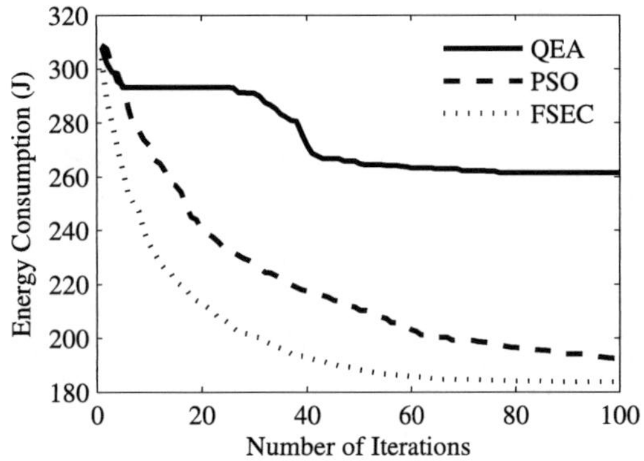

Figure 4: The communication energy consumption by iteration with 400 nodes and cluster head proportion of 10%

has a lower communication energy consumption than that of PSO and QEA methods with different numbers of nodes after 100 iterations.

As it may be observed in these figures, in the beginning, communication energy consumption of all the algorithms decreased. However, after only few iterations the QEA fall into evolutionary stagnation. From the figures, we can also see that PSO is much slower in convergence compared with F-SEC. More specifically, the communication energy consumption of FSEC is 9.78% and 4.57% less than that of PSO, and 28.08% and 29.69% less than that of QEA for 300 and 400 nodes respectively.

6. CONCLUSION

In this paper, we propose a fuzzy simulated evolutionary computation clustering method to reduce communication energy consumption for body area networks. In order to reduce communication energy consumption, we also designed a fuzzy controller to dynamically adjust the crossover and mutation probability. Simulation results show that the communication energy consumption of the proposed method decreased compared to the other two methods, which means that the proposed method significantly improves the energy efficiency.

7. ACKNOWLEDGMENTS

Jie Zhou is a recipient of a Macquarie University Research Excellence Scholarship and is under a cotutelle PhD arrangement between Macquarie University and Beijing University of Posts and Telecommunications. This work was supported in part by the National Natural Science Foundation of China (No.61170275), the National Science and Technology Major Project (No.2012ZX03001001-002), The research project of Guangdong (No.2011B090400433).

8. REFERENCES

[1] M. Li, Z. Li, and A. V. Vasilakos. A survey on topology control in wireless sensor networks: Taxonomy, comparative study, and open issues. *Proceedings of the IEEE*, 101(12):2538 – 2557, 2013.

[2] O. Demigha, W. K. Hidouci, and T. Ahmed. On energy efficiency in collaborative target tracking in wireless sensor network: A review. *IEEE Communications Surveys & Tutorials*, 15(3):1210 – 1222, 2013.

[3] W. B. Heinzelman, A. P. Chandrakasan, and H. Balakrishnan. An application-specific protocol architecture for wireless microsensor networks. *IEEE Transactions on Wireless Communications*, 1(4):660–670, 2002.

[4] O. Younis and F. Sonia HEED: a hybrid, energy-efficient, distributed clustering approach for ad hoc sensor networks. *IEEE Transactions on Mobile Computing*, 3(4):366–379, 2004.

[5] X. Li. Research on clustered-network in wireless sensor networks. *Tianjin University, China*, PhD thesis, 2006.

[6] S. Lindsey and C. S. Raghavendra. Pegasis: Power-efficient gathering in sensor information systems. In *Proceedings of the Aerospace Conference*, pages 3-1125–3-1130. IEEE, March 2002.

[7] M. Srinivas and L. M. Patnaik. Adaptive probabilities of crossover and mutation in genetic algorithms. *IEEE Transactions on Systems, Man and Cybernetics*, 24(4):656–667, 1994.

[8] Q. Li, D. L. Zhen and Y. Tang A new kind of fuzzy genetic algorithm. *Journal of University of Science and Technology Beijing*, 23(1):85–89, February 2001.

[9] H. W, C. A, and B. H. Energy-efficient communication protocol for wireless microsensor networks. In *Proceedings of the 33rd Annual Hawaill International Conference on System Sciences*, pages 1–10. IEEE, January 2000.

Low-threshold CMOS Rectifier Design for Energy Harvesting in Biomedical Sensors

Ali Mohammadi
Electrical and Computer Systems Engineering, Monash University, Clayton, VIC, Australia
mohamadi@ieee.org *

Jean-Michel Redoute
Electrical and Computer Systems Engineering, Monash University, Clayton, VIC, Australia
jean-michel.redoute@monash.edu

Mehmet R. Yuce
Electrical and Computer Systems Engineering, Monash University, Clayton, VIC, Australia
mehmet.yuce@monash.edu

ABSTRACT

The power transfer efficiency of energy harvesting systems is strongly dependent on the power conditioning circuits, especially rectifiers. The voltage drop across rectifier and its leakage current can drastically influence the efficiency. The hybrid energy harvesters impose even more severe constraints on the rectifier. The low V_{th} transistors and bulk regulation technique are used in this work to mitigated the voltage drop and leakage current, respectively. It has been shown that the bulk regulation stops the current leakage through body of PMOS transistor. A near zero threshold cross connected CMOS rectifier is presented in this work using the standard 180nm UMC technology and experimental analysis are carried out to evaluate the circuit performance.

Keywords

Hybrid energy harvesting, CMOS rectifier

1. INTRODUCTION

The increasing demand for biomedical implants is triggered by numerous factors such as reducing healthcare costs, enhancing quality of human life, and understanding human anatomy and physiology [8]. Supplying the electrical power to implants, regardless of their function and specifications, is the most stringent constraint to implant functionality. The research on energy harvesting systems is targeted significantly to find autonomous energy supplies as an alternative to batteries in low power electronic devices such as wireless sensor networks and biomedical implants. Energy harvesting systems are categorized based on the transduction mechanisms into inertial mass vibrations, near/far field wireless transmission, photo-voltaic cells, etc. The efficiency of energy harvesters generally depends on transducer as well as its following power conditioning circuit. The transducer part is application dependent and its optimization depends on a very wide set of parameters such as inductive or mechanical couplings. However, power conditioning components are all in electrical domain that consist of resonance circuit, rectifier, regulator and converter [6]. Regardless of transduction mechanism the output electrical energy is in the form of alternating current or voltage. Rectifiers are needed to generate useful direct current (DC) supply for electronic circuits. Therefore rectifiers are the most essential part of power conditioning in energy harvesters. The development of hybrid structures that can combine distinctive attributes of individual energy harvesting techniques at the same time is the recent challenge in the design of high efficiency energy harvesters [3,5]. For example, piezoelectric harvesters have a higher efficiency at high frequencies, while

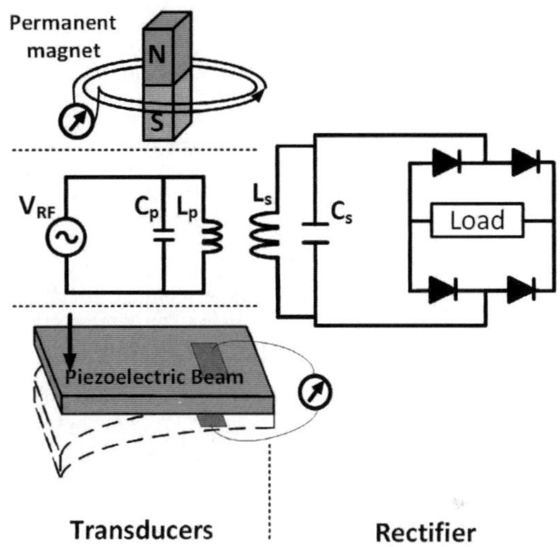

Figure 1: Hybrid energy harvesting system.

*Dr. Mohammadi, Dr Redoute and Dr. Yuce are with Biomedical Integrated Circuits and Sensors Research Lab in the Department of Electrical and Computer Systems Engineering at Monash University, Clayton (3800), VIC, Australia.

BODYNETS 2015, September 28-30, Sydney, Australia

DOI 10.4108/eai.28-9-2015.2261450

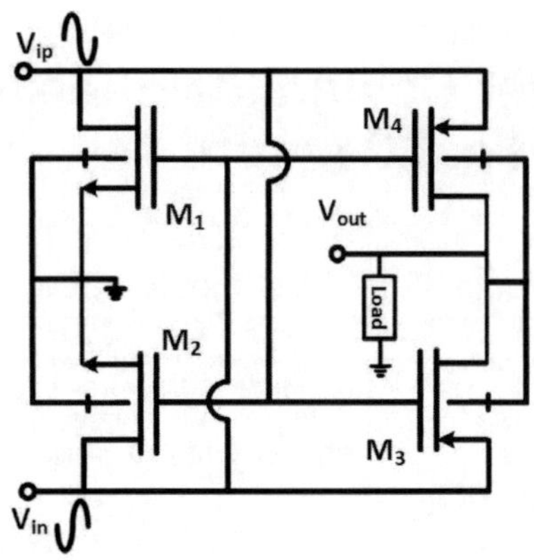

Figure 2: Differential drive (Cross-connected) CMOS rectifier

electromagnetic induction generates higher energy levels at low frequencies. Therefore combining these two techniques can lead to a broad band energy harvester. In addition, the radio frequency (RF) energy harvesters are implemented by electrical components only without any mechanical interaction, which gives a higher reliability compared with inertial counterparts. Though the inertial energy harvesters can generate higher output power compared with the RF counterparts. Therefore, in a hybrid system the RF energy scavengers could be used as a backup solution. A hybrid piezoelectric-RF energy harvester is presented in [5], where the piezoelectric output voltage is used to bias the rectifier up to the conduction point, in order to facilitate a more efficient conversion for weak RF inputs.

In this work the rectifier specification due to each energy harvesting technique is discussed and a highly efficient rectifier is implemented in CMOS. The conditions imposed on rectifier by each energy harvesting technique are discussed in Section 2. Section 3 introduces the proposed rectifier and experimental results are presented in Section 4.

2. CMOS BRIDGE RECTIFIERS

In conventional rectifier applications, Schottky diodes offer a superior performance. Their lower threshold voltage and reverse leakage results in higher conversion efficiency. However, it is impossible to implement Schottky diodes in standard CMOS processes. Popularity of CMOS rectifiers is due to their integration capability with the other electronics including sensor readout circuits, transceivers, etc. Diode connected CMOS transistor can be used as rectifier elements with minimum $1V_{th}$ voltage drop. This translates to $2V_{th}$ in a full bridge rectifier, which is more than the typical peak voltage induced in the secondary coil/antenna of RF energy harvesters. In an improved bridge rectifier for low frequency applications, i.e. inertial energy harvesters, transistors are employed in switch configuration instead of diode-connected as illustrated in Figure 2 [1]. The minimum input voltage is reduced to $1V_{th}$ that saves significant power in micro-energy harvesting. This circuit is also used for RF energy harvesting as differential drive CMOS rectifier [2] or

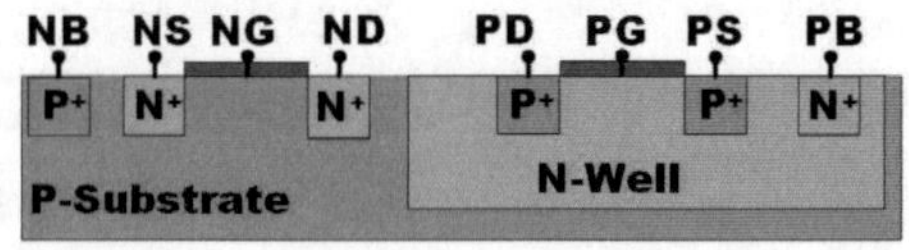

Figure 3: Cross section of standard CMOS transistor.

complementary CMOS switch rectifier [7].

Zero-threshold NMOS transistors are used in [9] to implement a voltage rectifier-doubler. In CMOS fabrication technology in order to make adjacent complementary transistors an n-well/p-well structure is needed as illustrated in Figure 3, which avoids zero-threshold p-n junction. Therefore, only one type of zero-V_{th} transistors (NMOS) is available in CMOS technology. Though, both types are needed to implement the differentially driven bridge rectifier in Figure 2. A silicon-on-saphire (SOS) fabrication technology is used in [7] to implement complementary near-zero-V_{th} transistors. However, non-standard processes result in extra fabrication costs.

3. BULK-REGULATED LOW-THRESHOLD (V_{TH}) RECTIFIER

As mentioned earlier in Section 1 hybrid energy harvesters are highly desirable for efficiency and reliability enhancement. However, hybrid transduction imposes different constraints on rectifier circuits. Several researches have been contributed in recent years to improve the efficiency of rectifiers. Though, the reported figure-of-merits fail to thoroughly describe the rectifier performance for hybrid applications. For example, the efficiency can be influenced by either reverse leakage due to high voltage outputs from piezoelectric transducers, or low voltage outputs from electromagnetic transducers that are unable to overcome the rectifier potential barrier. In addition, the high frequency outputs from RF transmitter might not be efficient due to the rectifier frequency response. In most of the researches carried out on the differentially driven CMOS rectifier, leakage currents are assumed to be ignorable. However, simulation results show that in high voltage regime, it can be even larger than the load current. In order to stop leakage current a bulk regulation technique is employed here, as shown in Figure 4.

Low-V_{th} devices are used in this design, in order to strike a compromise between the normal and zero-V_{th} transistors. Low-V_{th} CMOS transistors are available in standard fabrication technologies by low doping levels in well regions. The NMOS body (P-Substrate) in Figure 4, is connected to ground that avoids any leakage current through body. The PMOS body (N-well) should be connected to the most positive voltage of the circuit. Bulk regulation transistors (MB1-MB4) switch the body of PMOS transistors to the highest voltage, which can be either the output voltage or the input voltage. The simulation results for cross-connected rectifier with normal transistors and low-voltage transistors is compared with the bulk regulated rectifier circuit, as illustrated in Figure 8. In this simulation output load is a 10KΩ resistor in parallel with a 100nF capacitor. The negligible differ-

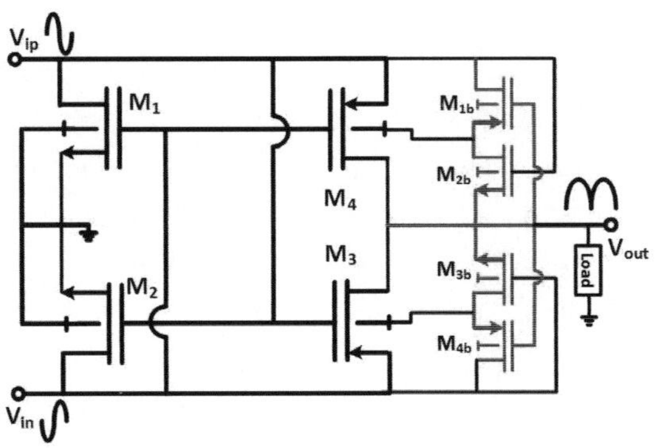

Figure 4: Bulk-regulated differential drive (Cross-connectd) CMOS rectifier

ence in the steady state load voltages is due to the different impedances seen from the rectifier inputs. The aspect ratios are the same for each transistor in corresponding circuits, though the difference is due to unequal impurity doping between normal and low-V_{th} transistor as well as added bulk regulation transistors. The bulk current of PMOS transistor M3 that is activated in the same input cycle in three different circuits is monitored in Figure 4. The bulk leakage current spikes in rectifier with normal transistor (M.b) and low-V_{th} transistor without bulk regulation (MLV.b) is much larger than load current ($\frac{V_{out}}{RL}$). However, the bulk leakage current in bulk-regulated circuit (MLVBR.b) is zero.

4. EXPERIMENTS

The proposed circuit is implemented in UMC 0.18 um CMOS technology and tested with different loads. The efficiency of the proposed circuit was shown in a previous work to be higher than Schottky diodes [4]. However adding the bulk regulation transistors influence the large signal frequency response of the circuit. The large signal frequency response of the rectifier is measured by applying sinusoidal inputs and varying the frequency. As illustrated in Figure 7, the power transfer after a certain frequency (1MH in this case) drops down significantly. This is mainly due to the wide aspect

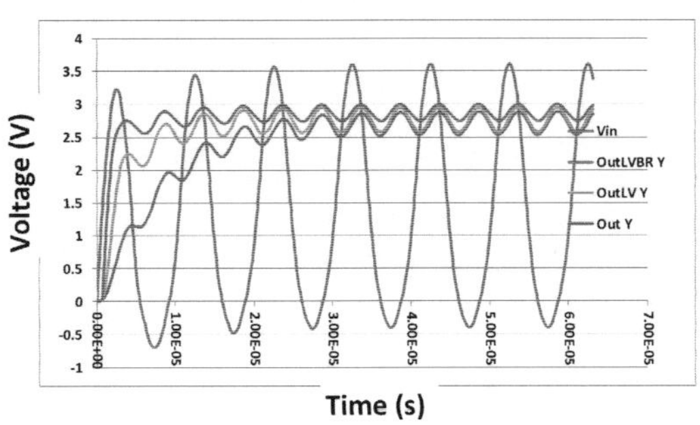

Figure 5: Transient and steady-state load voltage of CMOS rectifiers with normal and low-V_{th} transistor with and without bulk regulation.

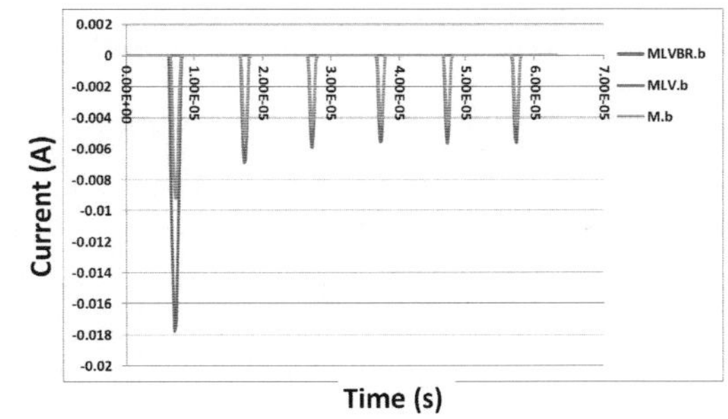

Figure 6: Transient and steady-state bulk current of CMOS rectifiers with normal and low-V_{th} transistor with and without bulk regulation.

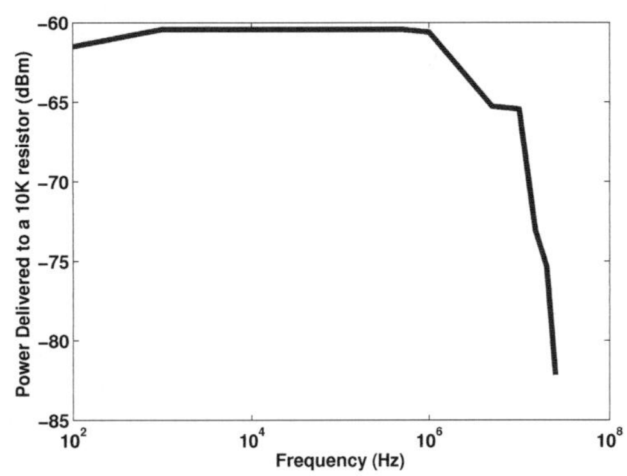

Figure 7: The large signal frequency response of CMOS rectifier

ratios of the transistors, which was selected to minimize the ohmic drop on the rectifier element.

The transfer characteristic of bulk-regulated rectifier for several load resistors is measured using X-Y mode of oscilloscope. As illustrated in Figure 8, the slope of the curve in conduction region varies with the load. The minimum voltage required to turn on the rectifier is also dependent on the load resistor.

5. CONCLUSION

The hybrid energy harvesting can boost the efficiency and reliability of autonomous sensors in applications such as biomedical implants. However, hybrid transduction mechanisms impose stringent constraints on the power conditioning circuits especially the rectifier. A CMOS rectifier with bulk regulation is designed using low-V_{th} transistors to mitigate leakage currents and voltage drop across the rectifier. The proposed circuit is implemented in 0.18um UMC CMOS technology and successfully characterized.

6. ACKNOWLEDGMENT

Mehmet R. Yuce's work was supported by Australian Research Council Future Fellowships Grant FT130100430.

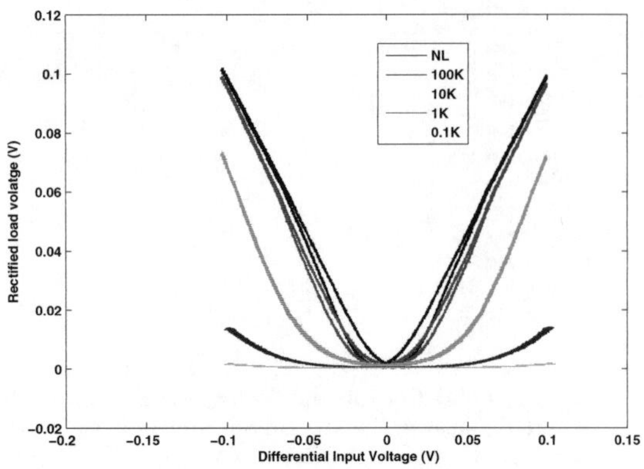

Figure 8: The rectifier input-output transfer characteristic for several ohmic loads.

7. REFERENCES

[1] M. Ghovanloo and K. Najafi. Fully integrated wideband high-current rectifiers for inductively powered devices. *IEEE Jnl. of Solid-State Circuit*, 39(11):1976–1984, 2004.

[2] K. Kotani, A. Sasaki, and T. Ito. High-efficiency differential-drive cmos rectifier for uhf rfids. *Solid-State Circuits, IEEE Journal of*, 44(11):3011–3018, Nov 2009.

[3] P. Li. An analysis of the coupling effect for a hybrid piezoelectric and electromagnetic energy harvester. *Smart Mater. Struct.*, 23(6):1–17, 2014.

[4] A. Mohammadi. Wireless power transmission for biomedical implants: The role of near-zero threshold cmos rectifiers. In *To be presented in EMBC*, 2015.

[5] T. T. Nguyen, T. Feng, P. Ha?fliger, and S. Chakrabartty. Hybrid cmos rectifier based on synergistic rf-piezoelectric energy scavenging. *Circuits and Systems I: Regular Papers, IEEE Transactions on*, 61(12):3330–3338, Dec 2014.

[6] G. Szarka, B. Stark, and S. Burrow. Review of power conditioning for kinetic energy harvesting systems. *Power Electronics, IEEE Transactions on*, 27(2):803–815, Feb 2012.

[7] P. Theilmann, C. Presti, D. Kelly, and P. Asbeck. A uw complementary bridge rectifier with near zero turn-on voltage in sos cmos for wireless power supplies. *Circuits and Systems I: Regular Papers, IEEE Transactions on*, 59(9):2111–2124, Sept 2012.

[8] A. Varpula, S. J. Lakso, and T. Havia. Harvesting vibrational energy using material work functions. *Nature, Scientific Reports*, 2014.

[9] J. Yi, W.-H. Ki, and C. ying Tsui. Analysis and design strategy of uhf micro-power cmos rectifiers for micro-sensor and rfid applications. *Circuits and Systems I: Regular Papers, IEEE Transactions on*, 54(1):153–166, Jan 2007.

Ear-Lead Multiple Smart Bio Sensor System in M-health

Numan Celik
Brunel University London
Department of Electronic and Computer Engineering
Uxbridge, UB8 3PH, London, UK
+441895 274000
numan.celik@brunel.ac.uk

Wamadeva Balachandran
Brunel University London
Department of Electronic and Computer Engineering
Uxbridge, UB8 3PH, London, UK
+441895 265774
Wamadeva.Balachandran@brunel.ac.uk

Nadarajah Manivannan
Brunel University London
Department of Electronic and Computer Engineering
Uxbridge, UB8 3PH, London, UK
+441895 274000
Nadarajah.Manivannan@brunel.ac.uk

ABSTRACT
In this paper, we present a multi-parameter wearable sensor system in conjunction with a smartphone to enable a real-time unobtrusive monitoring of core body temperature, electrocardiogram (ear-lead ECG), and blood oxygen saturation (S_pO_2) on ambulatory patients. Clinical research illustrating that continuing accurate measurements of core body temperature (CBT) are crucial to investigate human thermoregulation in ambulatory environment and during activity. On the other hand, ECG remains the mainstay test for primary diagnosis and survival analysis of heart diseases. We implement a wireless multisensory system that measures both the tympanic temperature inside the ear and ECG data from an ear and an arm. The behind-the-Ear device makes desirable to measure ECG data without any chest belt and allow the patient to move around freely. The proposed Bluetooth device has similarity of a hearing aid and is wirelessly connected to a smartphone for data transmission and displaying. This device not only gives access to the core temperature and ECG data in real time, but also the device can be controlled – removed and reapplied – by the patient at any time, thus increasing the performance of personal health applications.

Categories and Subject Descriptors
B.4 [**Input Output and Data Communications**]: Data Communication Devices; B.7 [**Integrated Circuits**]: Miscellaneous; J.3 [**Life and Medical Sciences**]: Medical Information Systems.

General Terms
Measurement, Performance, Design, Experimentation.

Keywords
Wireless Body Area Networks (WBAN), ECG, Core Body Temperature, Oxygen Saturation Level (SpO_2), Sensor Fusion, Wearable Computing.

1. INTRODUCTION
The rapid growth of wireless technologies brings new innovative ideas that enables continuous real-time remote patient monitoring of evolving healthcare services within compact wireless body sensors. The services and technologies provide relatively uncontroversial, well-communicated and monitoring devices, developed to give more affordable solutions specifically for mobile healthcare, such as daily activity monitoring, personal healthcare and monitoring systems, and body sensor systems that can alarm the clinicians via the patients' mobile phones. New trend in remote patient monitoring is moving toward the use of personal mobile devices compatible with multiple biomedical sensors using Bluetooth wireless communication [1].

In practice, this recent mobile health (m-Health) technology enables to see the people's daily activity in their smartphones. In addition, these mobile-based portable embedded devices will provide platforms to monitor their critical biological data continuously and remotely. An assessment report has been prepared for the European Union regarding the effectiveness of m-Health in biomedical applications and the diagnosis of the diseases in 2013. According to this report, m-Health could save 99 billion Euros in healthcare costs in the EU and add 93 billion Euros to the EU GDP in 2017 if its adoption is encouraged [2].

Critical body measurements such as heart rate, blood pressure, blood glucose, core temperature, ECG, EEG and oxygen saturation level (SpO_2) are truly key factors in determining the overall health of a patient. Continuous remote monitoring of these critical signs can play an important role to identify patient's disease, in particular for epilepsy, heart attack, diabetes, sleep apnea, and heart failure [3].

Electro-cardiogram (ECG) is a critical signal from the heart which may be measured from two or more sensors placed on the patient's skin. ECG monitoring is a basic diagnosis procedure to figure out whether the patients have heart diseases. Core body temperature (CBT) is a known physiological indicator of the human body. It is closely linked to a number of clinically diagnosed diseases, particularly in the characterization and diagnosis of human sleep disorders to estimate the circadian-system, which is 24-hour cycle in biological processes [4], and also CBT monitoring is a wide area of research for human thermoregulation applications. Pulse

BODYNETS 2015, September 28-30, Sydney, Australia

DOI 10.4108/eai.28-9-2015.2261544

oximetry is another vital sign for diagnosing patients' diseases such as sleep apnea and is measured using PPG (photoplethysmography) techniques (see Figure 1).

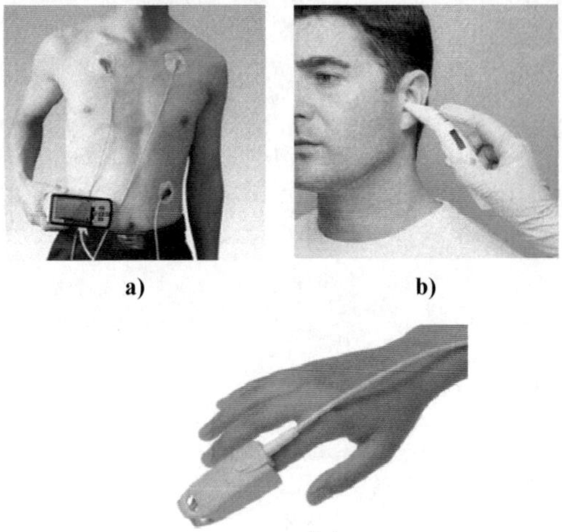

Figure 1. a) the typical 3-lead ECG monitoring system. b) ear-tympanic device to measure core body temperature. c) the reflective PPG sensor to measure blood oxygen saturation (SpO2) and heart rate.

Here, we examine a continuous, wearable and wireless critical-sign monitor worn behind the ear, combining these 3 (ECG, CBT, and PPG) sensors. The reason for choosing the ear as a location in these experiments is that it makes possible to measure ECG, CBT, and blood oxygen discreetly since the sensors can be partially hidden by hair and the ear.

This paper aims to advance the ambulatory ECG treatments by proposing a wearable behind-the-ear smart sensor that transmits integrated biological data wirelessly to a smartphone and monitors ECG, CBT and SpO_2 information in real-time. Since most conventional systems take each data separately and from different locations on the body. In contrast, we developed a smart sensor system that facilitates sensor fusion by sealing into an ear mold. Moreover, this design is less disrupted by motion artifacts. In the future, this option not only gives flexibility to the patient, but also gives the clinicians to access the physiological data in rea time.

2. RELATED WORK

When a ubiquitous smart sensor is developed, there should be basic components that should be considered: easy-for-use, mobility, accuracy, and security. There are currently many ongoing researches that investigate various solutions on the design of wireless personal healthcare monitoring devices. Lee et al. developed a mobile phone based ECG monitoring application. The system describes the design and implementation of a prototype tele-health system which monitored physiological signals of patients in real-time [5]. Sanches et al. designed an electronic temperature sensor within a headset Bluetooth device that sends the temperature measurements to a mobile phone. The proposed system measures central body temperature continuously at the ear [6]. Jung et al. proposed a wireless body sensor platform called 'Virtual Cuff' that comprises PPG and ECG sensors to estimate systolic and diastolic blood pressure (BP). The presented work fuses data from various sensors, including ECG, PPG, accelerometer, and GPS, for extrapolating BP information using signal characteristics that are derived from PPG and ECG waveforms [7]. Do Valle et al. examined [8] a behind-the-ear device that records EEG measurements on smartphone continuously and then uploads the patients' data to a secure server. Song et al. developed a body monitoring system design based on android smartphone including three main functions such as brainwave capture (EEG), ECG and temperature. These data are gathered by hardware and sent to the Bluetooth receiving device of android smartphone [9]. Boano et al. managed to measure core body temperature (CBT) on ambulatory patients and exercising athletes using a wireless wearable device that measures the tympanic temperature at the ear. The CBT data is transmitted via ATmega128RFA1 chip based on ZigBee communication which is different from other studies [10].

The brief summary of the literature review illustrate the use of modern communication technology for data exchange between ambulatory patients and mobile devices by combining several sensors in one typical system. This is one of the key factors to make m-Health platform much more desirable. However, not only for clinical purposes, but also an integrated and personalized smart sensor device, easy to use and less affected motion artifacts.

3. SYSTEM ARCHITECTURE OVERVIEW

The smart sensor platform was developed to experimentally combine 3 different body sensors and monitor vital parameters on the smartphone. The main characteristics of the proposed system are to integrate and monitor ear-lead ECG, ear-lead core temperature, oxygen saturation level (PPG from the finger) and to communicate to mobile client by using Bluetooth connection. The ECG and tympanic sensors for displaying the physiological data are integrated in the form of an earbud. PPG sensor will be attached onto the finger and it will be connected to the microcontroller unit (MCU). Each biopotentials will be experimentally examined in Subsection 3.1 and fusion of sensors will be analysed in Subsection 3.2, respectively.

3.1 Sensor Data Acquisition System

Here, each of the biosensors will be separately examined within the system design prototypes. Our system comprises both hardware and software units.

- The hardware part of the system: The single microcomputer system (Arduino UNO), a tympanic infrared sensor detecting core temperature module MLX90614, an ECG acquisition circuit module integrated with Arduino, a pulse oximeter detecting module CMS50EW, a wireless Bluetooth device, and an Android based smartphone. Figure 2 shows a block diagram to describe the multi-parameter body monitoring system using a smartphone.
- The software part of the system: Arduino IDE is used to control different hardware pieces of the sensors and communicate with Bluetooth equipment. Application programs of android platform based on the Java language were tested and implemented by using Android Studio. The installed software can begin the Bluetooth connection between the smartphone and the hardware unit, thus the biological data can be transferred to the smartphone.

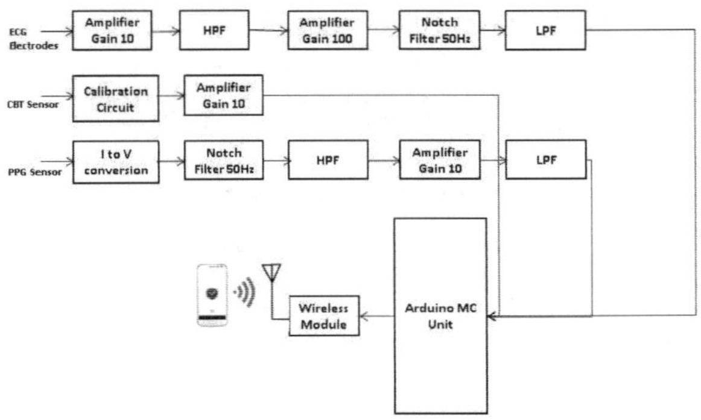

Figure 2. The block diagram of body monitoring system design

3.1.1 ECG Acquisition Platform

The core of ECG sensor platform as shown in Figure 3, is based on the e-Health sensor shield. The e-Health sensor shield allows performing in conjunction with Arduino. This enables to combine different biosignals in Arduino. The sensor shield gets ECG data and transmits through Arduino UNO. The system consists of an analog amplifier module with one differential (instrumentation) amplifier and two general purpose operational amplifiers. The signal quality is mostly determined by the instrumentation amplifier (IA) due to having low noise amplifying unit with low power dissipation. The operational amplifiers are used to forward the low voltage to a base line for signal processing with a gain of 100. The ECG signals are restricted within the range of bandwidth of 0.5 – 100 Hz. High and low pass filters were used after the first and second stages of amplification, respectively. The ECG signal is sampled at 2,048 Hz and digitized using a 16 bit ADC. The filtered digital signal is then decimated to reduce the rate of samples from 2,048 Hz down to 256 Hz and then transferred to an Android based smartphone via our Bluetooth module. The principle of data transmission has been developed in the same way after the signal processing of each sensor (CBT and PPG sensors).

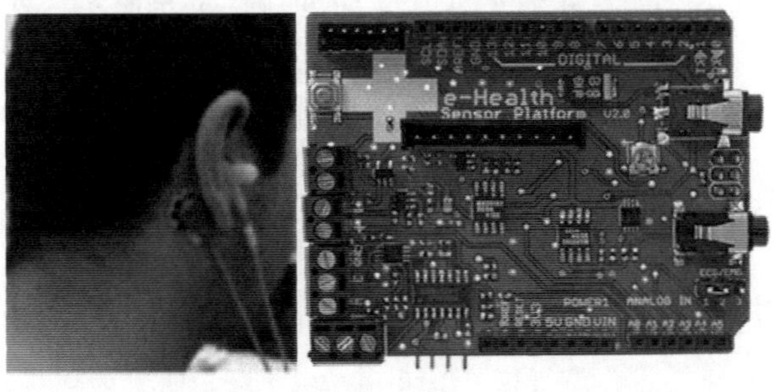

Figure 3. Earable ecg sensor placement (left); Electronic circuit for ECG amplification (right)

3.1.2 CBT Sensing Platform

In our proposed system we have used a thermopile sensor that is a non-contact sensor for measuring core temperature. Because tympanic temperature directly reflects the core temperature of the carotid artery [11], we have proposed an earbud-design infrared tympanic sensor that can continuously measure the temperature of the tympanic membrane (Figure 4). This design connects with our Arduino MCU, which is the core controller of the whole smart sensor system, to perform amplification, filtering and ADC processes. The thermopile sensor (MLX90614) gives us very sensitive information regarding the core body temperature with 17 bit resolution, thus this could be in some cases 0.0034 °C resolution.

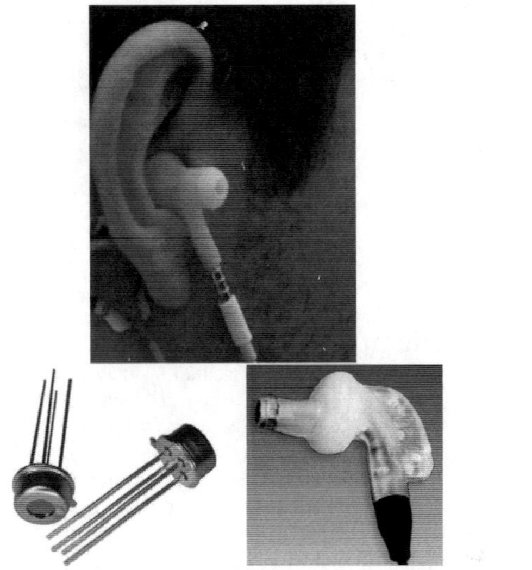

Figure 4. Our proposed earphone-type infrared sensor (above); Infrared thermopile sensor (below-left), another view of earphone-embedded thermopile sensor (below-right)

3.1.3 Pulse Oximetry Acquisition

In general, the pulse oximeter consists of a transductor which initiates two LEDs and a photodiode detector. One of the LEDs emits red light (with a wavelength of λ = 660 nm) and other LED performs an infrared light (λ = 940 nm). This technique is known as PPG (photoplethysmography) and the PPG sensor is based on the theory that the color of blood range depends on the oxygen it contains. For instance, hemoglobin particularly reflect more red lights, and PPG sensor decides oxygen saturation in the blood (SpO_2) according to this volume. For our test-bed we have performed this test using Amperor Bluetooth Finger Pulse Oximeter as that shown in Figure 5. The smart sensor system incorporates a Bluetooth connection that enables to gather PPG data from this pulse oximeter sensor. The sensor is powered with a rechargeable lithium battery lasting for about 20 hours in continuous mode. A 50 Hz notch filter is used for both ECG and PPG signals to eliminate the power line interference, thus there would not be any loss at 50 Hz component of the signals.

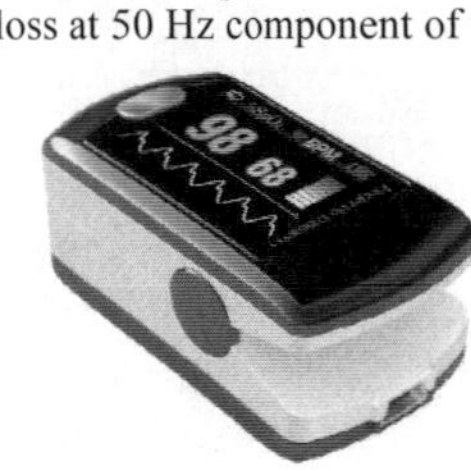

Figure 5. Bluetooth pulse oximeter

3.2 Sensor Fusion

After digitizing and conditioning the analog signals from each sensor, the suitable digital biological data are MUXed at the data acquisition hardware unit in an appropriate way. The data after being acquired by Arduino is converted in the form of packets and is wirelessly transmitted to Android based mobile phone. Figure 6 indicates ECG electrodes placement and appearance of general prototype of performed body sensors.

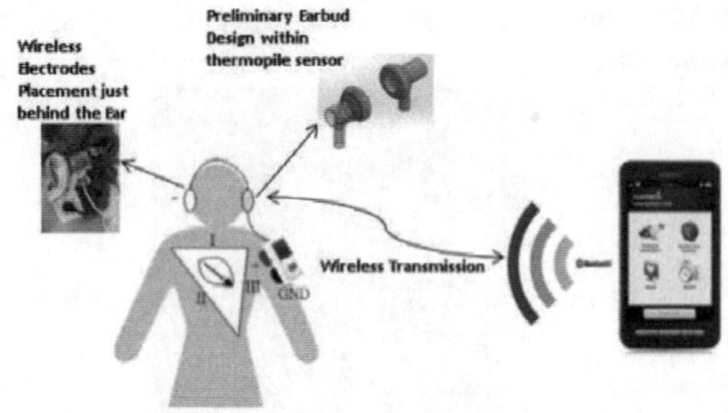

Figure 6. Ear-lead wearable multiple sensor monitoring system

3.3 Bluetooth

Bluetooth is a very useful technology to communicate wirelessly in short-range applications such as exchanging data from short distance fixed mobile devices. With the characteristic of synchronization with other Bluetooth devices, the wireless body area network can be applied successfully. Our proposed system uses HC-05 Bluetooth module that consists of different modes in its processing system. Figure 7 shows our Bluetooth serial module, which is paired to the smartphone.

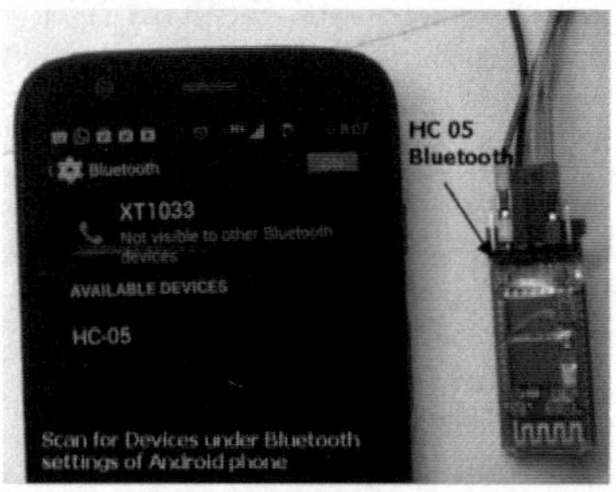

Figure 7. The view of Bluetooth module while pairing with the smartphone

As mentioned, there are different channels (ECG, CBT, and PPG) that need to be transmitted through Bluetooth communication. The communication module has the capability to transmit data over the Bluetooth with maximum baud rate of 115,200 bps. We have to calculate the overall bandwidth before transmitting the biological data. For our system, we have developed three different sensing parameters (ECG, CBT, and PPG). Core body temperature (CBT) measurement operates at 20 Hz sampling frequency (16-bit samples). ECG sensor works at 250 Hz frequency range (16-bit samples) with 3 electrodes and PPG operating at a 30 Hz (16-bit samples) with two photodiodes. Hence, the total data rate will comprise from aggregating each measured signal's bit rates. The total minimum bandwidth of the system will be:

Baud Rate = bit rate of (CBT (kbps) + ECG (kbps) + PPG (kbps))

BR = (sampling frequency of CBT) * (Nyquist-criteria) * (sampling bit number) + (sampling frequency of ECG) * (Nyquist-criteria) * (sampling bit number) * (used electrodes) + (sampling frequency of PPG) * (Nyquist criteria) * (sampling bit number) * (used electrodes)

BR = 20 * 2 (Nyquist-criteria) * 16 + 250 * 2 * 16 * 3 + 30 * 2 * 16 * 2 = 0.64 + 24 + 1.92 = 26.56 kbps.

The above number is much less than the overall Bluetooth transmission baud rate at 115,200 bps. Thus, the residue bandwidth would be enough to perform two-way handshaking and sending the data successfully.

4. EXPERIMENTS and RESULTS

Several experiments were conducted with one wireless multi-parameter body monitoring system. The analysis and display of ECG, CBT and SpO_2 was done firstly in a PC, then in a mobile phone via a Bluetooth module transmitter.

Regarding the ECG analysis, traditional Ag/AgCl electrodes (Ambu) were used to get ECG signal from the ear and the electrodes were placed just behind the ear. ECG results were displayed in a PC primarily using KST real-time data viewing plotting tool. After that, the ECG data was monitored in Android based smartphone using Android Studio software program and Arduino IDE software tools. Both results are shown together in Figure 8.

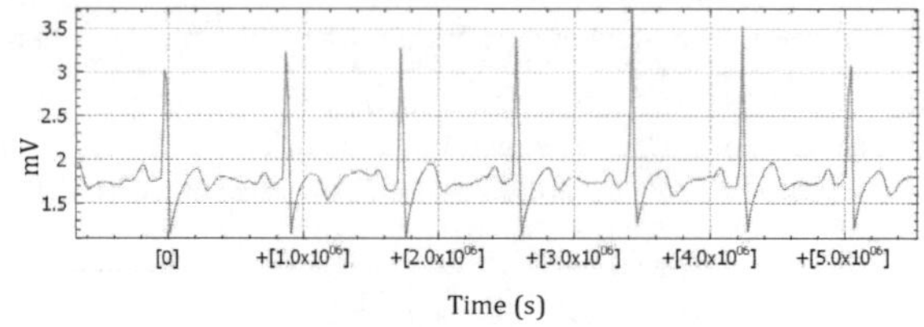

a)

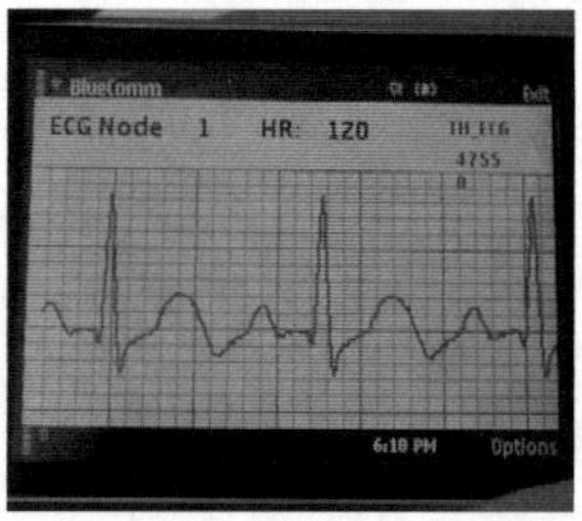

b)

Figure 8. ECG Results. a) ECG data in PC - KST platform. b) ECG data in Android based mobile phone - Samsung Galaxy Ace

The second experiment aimed at detecting core body temperature from tympanic membrane at the ear. Figure 9 illustrates the CBT monitoring in the ear for 100 seconds in Matlab environment, and mobile phone, respectively.

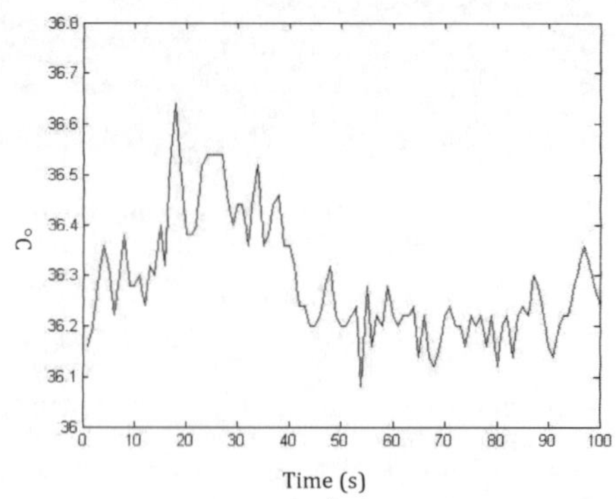

a)

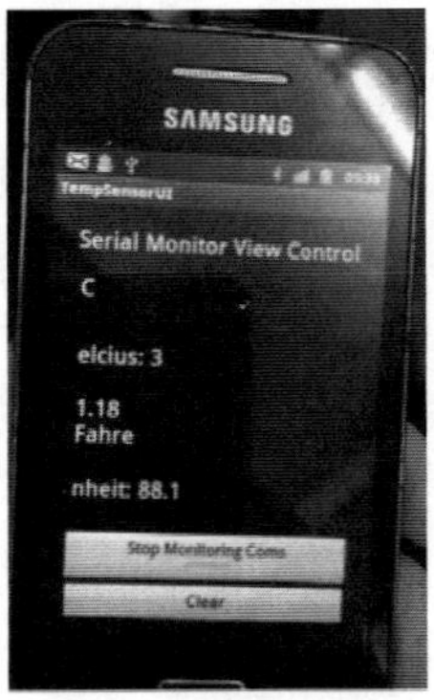

b)

Figure 9. CBT Monitoring on Matlab while plotting the data a); and on mobile device as giving Celsius and Fahrenheit degrees (b).

As can be seen in the graph, the core temperature varies between 36.1 ºC and 36.65 ºC in the ear.

The final experiment results obtained for oxygen saturation level in the blood (SpO_2) can be seen in Figure 10. The level of SpO_2 is at around 98% in the blood. The PPG data is shown in the picture as well as the SpO_2 ratio.

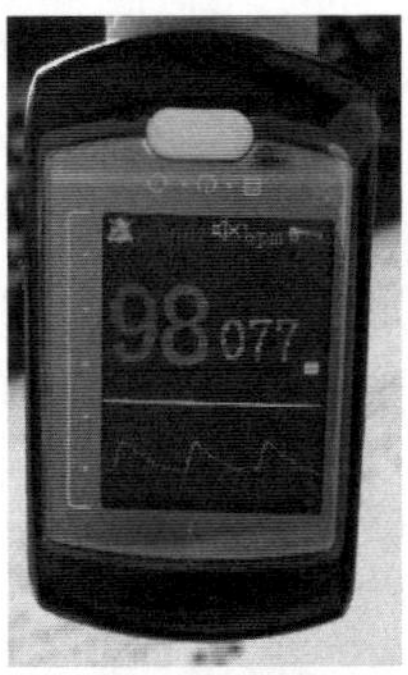

Figure 10. Oxygen saturation level in blood within PPG data using Amperor Bluetooth pulse oximeter device

5. CONCLUSION

We have proposed an ear-lead multi-parameter smart sensor system that acquires different physiological information and continuously monitor an Android based smartphone, giving patients real time control of the data. This device includes non-intrusive sensors, specifically ECG, CBT and PPG with high accuracy. Furthermore, it facilitates the difficulties of wearables giving patients significantly less restriction by eliminating the need for adapting intrusive equipment or using a laptop to see the biological data. In the future, this smart sensor system can work with a wide body area network system to offer accessing patients data by clinicians and healthcare professionals to get more accurate and quicker information for the diagnosis and treatment options.

6. REFERENCES

[1] Bifulco, P., Cesarelli, M., Fratini, A., Ruffo, M., Pasquariello, G., and Gargiulo, G. 2011. A wearable device for recording of biopotentials and body movements. In *Proceedings of the IEEE International Symposium on Medical Measurements and Applications* (Bari, Italy, May 30 – 31, 2011). DOI= http://doi.org/10.1109/MeMeA.2011.5966735

[2] "Socio-economic impact of mHealth – An assessment report for the European Union". GSMA Connected Living Programme. June 2013. Web. 21.05.2014 http://www.gsma.com/connectedliving/wp-content/uploads/2013/06/Socio-economic_impact-of-mHealth_EU_14062013V2.pdf

[3] Pierdomenico, D. S., Nicola, D. M., Esposito, L. A., et al. 2009. Prognostic value of different indices of blood pressure variability in hypertensive patients. American journal of hypertension. 22, 8 (June. 2009), 842-847. DOI= http://doi.org/10.1038/ajh.2009.103

[4] Scheer, F. A. J. L., Kenneth, P. W., Richard, E. K., Charles A. C., 2007. Plasticity of the intrinsic period of the human circadian timing system. PloS ONE, 2007. DOI= doi:10.1371/journal.pone.0000721

[5] Lee, D. H., Choi, J., Rabbi, A., Fazel-Rezai, R., 2012. Development of a mobile phone based e-Health monitoring application. International journal of advanced computer science and applications. 3, 3 (2012), 38-43. DOI= http://dx.doi.org/10.14569/IJACSA.2012.030307#sthash.fZXkf8zk.dpuf

[6] Sanches, J. M., Pereira, B., Paiva, T., Headset Bluetooth and cell phone based continuous central body temperature measurement system. In *Proceedings of the IEEE Engineering in Medicine and Biology Society* (Buenos Aires, Argentina, August 31 – Sept 4, 2010). DOI= http://doi.org/10.1109/IEMBS.2010.5626172

[7] Jung, K. H., Tran, V., Gabrielian, V., and Nahapetian, A., 2014. Virtual cuff: multisensory non-intrusive blood pressure monitoring. In *Proceedings of the 9th International Conference on Body Area Networks* (BodyNets '14). DOI= http://dx.doi.org/10.4108/icst.bodynets.2014.257046

[8] Do Valle, B. G., Cash S. S., and Sodini C. G., Wireless behind-the-ear eeg recording device with wireless interface to a mobile device (iphone/ipod touch). In *Proceedings of the IEEE Engineering in Medicine and Biology Society* (Chicago, US, August 26-30, 2014). DOI= 10.1109/EMBC.2014.6944984

[9] Song, W., Yu, H., Liang, C., Wang, Q., and Shi, Y., Body monitoring system design based on android smartphone. In *Proceedings of the 2012 World Congress on Information and Communication Technologies, WICT 2012.* DOI= http://doi.org/10.1109/WICT.2012.6409247

[10] Boano, C. A., Lasagni, M., and Romer, K., Non-Invasive measurement of core body temperature in marathon runners. In *Proceedings of the Body Sensor Networks 2013 (BSN '13)* (Cambridge, US, May 6-9, 2013). DOI= 10.1109/BSN.2013.6575484

[11] Bock, M., Hohlfeld, U., von Engleln, K., Meier, P. A., Motsch, J., Tasman, A. J., The accuracy of a new infrared ear thermometer in patients undergoing cardiac surgery, *Anesthesia & Analgesia*. 105-6, 2007. DOI= 10.1213/01.ane.0000289639.87836.79

WE-Harvest: A Wearable Piezoelectric-Electromagnetic Energy Harvester

Rawnak Hamid
Electrical and Computer Systems Engineering, Monash University, Clayton, Melbourne VIC (3800), Australia

Ali Mohammadi
Electrical and Computer Systems Engineering, Monash University, Clayton, Melbourne VIC (3800), Australia.

Mehmet Rasit Yuce
Electrical and Computer Systems Engineering, Monash University, Melbourne, VIC (3800), Australia
mehmet.yuce@monash.edu

ABSTRACT

Wearable electronics require a sustainable electrical power supply to operate. Energy harvesting techniques can be used to convert available nonelectrical energy sources into electrical energy. This paper presents WE-Harvest, a new wearable energy harvesting system that combines the piezoelectric and electromagnetic energy harvesters for wearable devices. Regular human body motions, such as moving the arm, provide the input vibrations. A two-stage modified Dickson multiplier is used to step up the output voltage. The experimental results demonstrate that the combined topology enhances the power transfer efficiency. The dependence of energy harvester output on the load and input frequency has also been investigated.

Keywords

Piezoelectric energy harvesting, magnetic energy harvesting, wearable energy harvesting, wearable sensors and devices.

1. INTRODUCTION

Wireless and portable applications provide convenience and new capabilities specifically in wireless sensors for health monitoring and wearable electronics [1]. However, the required electric power is supplied by batteries, which should be maintained frequently by changing or recharging. Chemical waste material of batteries is also an environmental threat. Recent advances in low power electronics have reduced the required electrical power for operating the sensors to several microwatts [2]. Hence, the energy generated by harvesting from ambient sources like heat, solar energy, wind, vibration and radio frequency waves can be used to power such devices [3-5].

The ubiquitous presence of vibration energy sources in our daily lives provide promising energy sources that can be harvested by micro power generators [6]. The focus of this work is on harvesting energy from low frequency vibrations like human motions. There are challenges involved due to the low repetition rates (1-30Hz), large-amplitude, aperiodicity, predominantly inconsistent and time-varying vibration signatures of the natural motions [7][8]. Mechanical vibration energy can be extracted using mechanical-to-electrical transducers. Vibration-based power generators convert the mechanical energy into electrical energy in the form of alternative current (AC). The AC power is rectified to produce a stable DC (direct current) power using a power conditioning circuit since microelectronic devices and rechargeable batteries require a DC power supply. Therefore the performance of energy harvesting systems depends on both the transducer and power conditioning electronics. The operation principle of the proposed system, the design procedure and experimental results are described in sections II, III and IV, respectively.

2. VIBRATION ENERGY HARVESTING METHODS

In inertial energy harvesting techniques, the mechanical energy available in vibrating masses is converted to electrical energy. These techniques include piezoelectric, electro-magnetic and electrostatic transductions. Some of these techniques have been applied to energy harvesting applications on the human body [8]-[11]. In piezoelectric energy harvesting, mechanical stress and strain results in structural deformation caused by human motion and movements, which is then converted to electrical energy [8]. The electromagnetic induction is based on relative motions between a magnetic field and a coil, which causes electric current flow in the coil [9]. The amount of energy that can be harvested depends on the strength of the magnetic field, the velocity of the relative motion and the number of turns in the coil. Capacitive changes of the vibration-dependent capacitors are used for electrostatic energy harvesting. Mechanical energy is converted to electrical energy when vibrations move the plates initially charged [10][11]. A separate voltage source is needed for pre-charging the capacitor plates in electrostatic energy harvesters, which adds more complication in wearable applications.

Most of energy harvesting systems is optimized to harvest energy from one of available sources on the body. Electromagnetic energy harvesters can supply higher output currents, while the piezoelectric devices generate higher voltages. A combination of piezoelectric and electromagnetic techniques is presented in this work to improve the power generation efficiency for wearable energy harvesting systems.

3. PROPOSED ENERGY HARVESTER

Typically energy harvesting systems consist of a transducer that converts non-electrical energy to electrical energy and a power conditioning circuit that converts the alternative current (AC) to direct current (DC) and adjusts the voltage level to the corresponding load. The functional block diagram in Figure 1

BODYNETS 2015, September 28-30, Sydney, Australia

DOI 10.4108/eai.28-9-2015.2261451

shows the operation principle of the energy harvester presented in this work. The proposed structure is designed to combine the electromagnetic induction and piezoelectric effect to convert the mechanical vibrations to electrical energy. The transducer and conditioning circuits for each technique are introduced next.

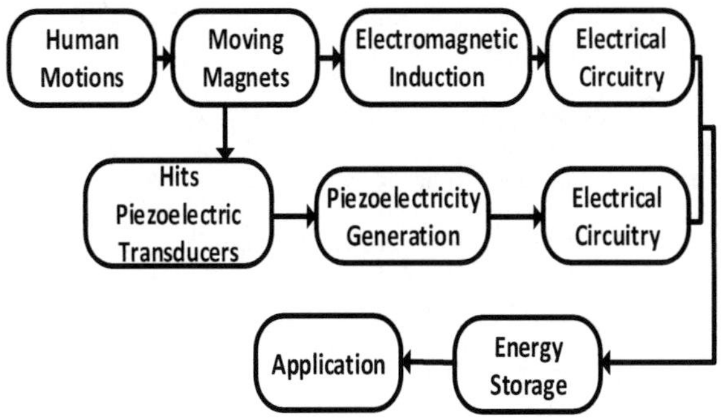

Figure 1:Functional block diagram of the energy harvesting device

3.1 Transducer Design

The mechanical structure of the proposed energy harvesting transducer is presented schematically in Figure 2, which features a pair of magnets that can slide freely inside the housing when vibrated. The copper wire is wound around the housing to convert the magnetic field changes initiated by the magnet motions to electric current. The piezoelectric transducers are fixed to the opposite walls of the housing. Human motions provide the vibration, which is needed to move the magnets back and forth, inducing current by electromagnetic induction. Simultaneously, the magnets hit the piezoelectric transducers when they reach the housing walls. Kinetic energy of the magnets applies a mechanical force to the piezoelectric layers that can be converted to electrical energy.

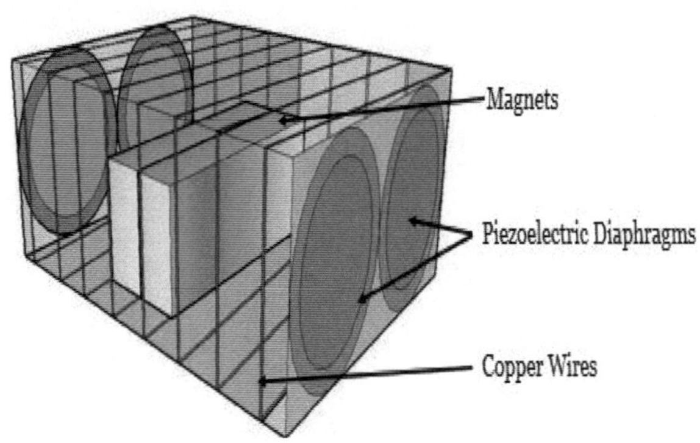

Figure 2: Schematic of the device

Four PZT (Lead Zirconate Titanate) diaphragms are electrically connected in parallel and mechanically fixed on a thin polycarbonate sheet at each side of the housing to improve the total amount of energy harvested by the PZT transducers. The parallel configuration enhance the electrical power since it increases the total output current while keeping the voltage constant. Using more than two layers of diaphragms increases the distance between the top and bottom layers and avoids the bottom layers receive enough pressure. The two sets of PZT diaphragms on opposite walls are also connected in parallel.

3.2 Power Conditioning Circuitry

A stable DC current is required in order to supply electrical power to the electronics or to charge batteries and super capacitors. Since the output power generated by both mechanisms is AC, they need to be rectified using suitable electrical circuitry. Off-the-shelf integrated circuits such as LTC3588-1 can be used to rectify the output voltages from the piezoelectric transducers [12].

The amplitude of the voltage output from electromagnetic harvester is not large enough to overcome the rectifier threshold voltage. Therefore, two cascaded voltage doubler stages are employed in the proposed system to enhance and rectify the output voltage. The cascaded stage can generate four times larger output. Figure 3 shows the two stage Dickson multiplier schematic.

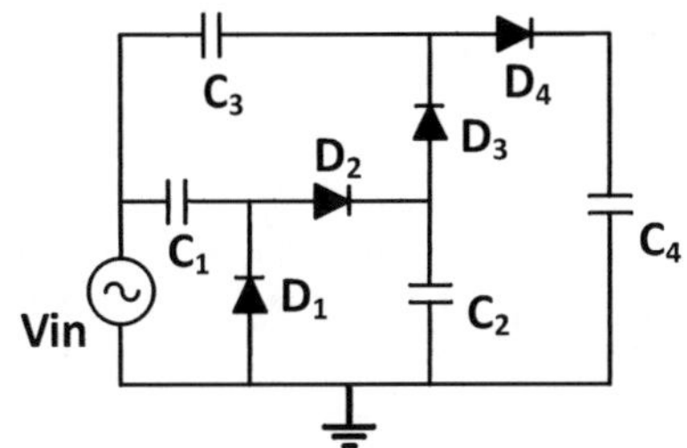

Figure 3: Two-stage Dickson multiplier

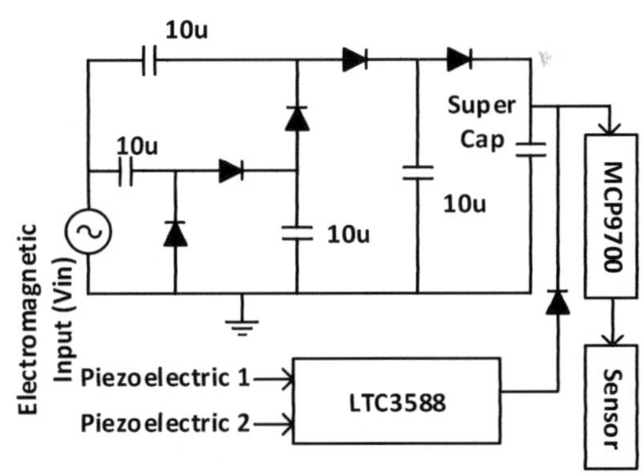

Figure 4: Power conditioning circuit, LTC3588 and MPC9700 are an off-the-shelf rectifier and a Linear Active Thermistor, respectively

The operation of voltage doubler in Figure 3 follows a certain sequence of cycles. During the input negative half cycle, D1 will charge the C1 voltage up to Vin. In the positive half cycle, the top plate of C1 is clamped to 2Vin. D1 is then turned off while D2 turns on and charge cycle for C2 starts. In the next negative half cycle D3 turns on and charges C3 to 3Vin, and in the positive half cycle the top plate of C3 is clamped to 4Vin. The combination of D2, C2, D4 and C4 act as a peak detector and smooth the ripple without increasing the multiplication. Tantalum capacitors and Schottky diodes are used to reduce the losses in the circuit. The diodes maximum voltage drop is 400mV at 10mA forward current [13]. A schematic of the overall power conditioning circuitry used to combine the electromagnetic and piezoelectric harvesters is shown in Figure 4. The output voltage of piezoelectric transducers is rectified by a power electronic module which includes a bridge rectifier and a buck converter (LTC3588). A large super capacitor is used to store the energy generated by the two harvesters. The reverse leakage of current from each harvester to the other is avoided by using diodes between harvester outputs and large capacitor. A typical application for the energy harvester is to power up low-power sensors such as temperature sensor (MCP9700). The final output of power conditioning circuitry is used to supply the sensor as a proof of concept. Further details are addressed in the experiment section.

4. EXPERIMENTS

Figure 5 shows the prototype designed in this work for integrating electromagnetic and piezoelectric energy harvesting techniques.

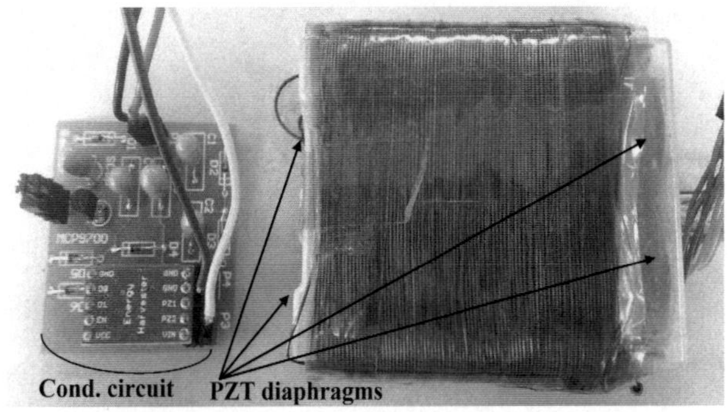

Figure 5: Prototype wearable piezoelectric-electromagnetic energy harvester.

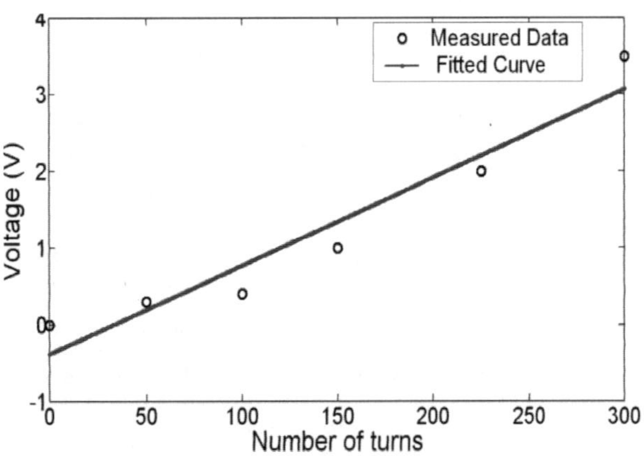

Figure 6: Plot showing the linear relationship between number of turns of coil and the output peak to peak voltage

The device was shaken manually to produce mechanical input. Experiments were repeated for each technique, individually, and their combination to show the improvements after combining the two techniques.

4.1 Electromagnetic Energy Harvester

The voltage generated at the electromagnetic energy harvester output is proportional to the number of turns in the coil. The result of experiments carried out for different number of turns in the proposed structure is illustrated in Figure 6. The energy harvester output voltage is enhanced by a Dickson multiplier. The number of multiplier stages required to achieve the desired output voltage (~3.3V) is found by simulations as shown in Figure 7. The sensor that is used in this work, as an example application, has an input impedance of 280KΩ. Therefore, the output was measured using a range of different load resistances ranging from 15kΩ to 300kΩ. Figure 8 demonstrates the output voltage with respect to the load resistances.

4.2 Piezoelectric Energy Harvester

The output voltage of a piezoelectric energy harvester is proportional to the frequency of vibration in addition to its amplitude. The frequency dependence can be explained by the capacitive structure of the piezoelectric device. Short time periods of high frequency inputs avoid the capacitive discharge on these devices. In the proposed system, a single piezoelectric diaphragm (PZT) is vibrated at varying frequencies ranging from 1Hz – 5Hz and the corresponding output voltage is recorded (See Table 1.).

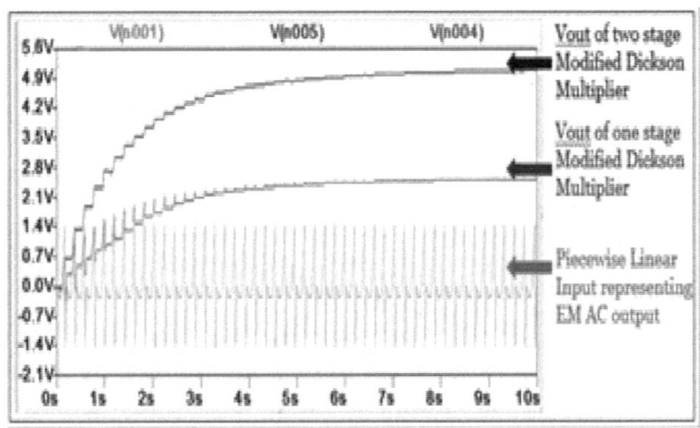

Figure 7. Simulation result for modified Dickson Multiplier

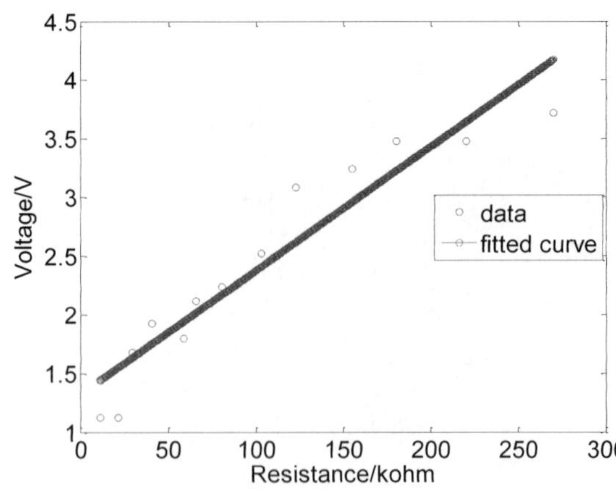

Figure 8: Plot showing the output voltage across varying load resistors

Table 1. RMS voltage obtained from a Piezoelectric diaphragm in different frequencies.

Frequency (Hz)	1	2	3	4	5
RMS Voltage (V)	1.6	2.3	3	3.1	3.2

The current output from a single PZT was about 1μA, which is very low. Connecting piezoelectric transducers in parallel increases their current output while keeping the output voltage constant. The transducer AC output voltage is rectified by an off-the-shelf circuit (LTC3588), which regulates the output voltage to 3.3 V. The rise time of a load capacitor charging curve was measured in order to evaluate the systems performance. A plot showing the comparison of the rise time of the different combinations of piezoelectric diaphragms is illustrated in Figure 9, which shows that with increased number of PZT diaphragms, the time to charge the capacitor decreases. The piezoelectric diaphragms are generally modeled as current sources. Therefore parallel configuration of piezoelectric diaphragms is expected to increase the power output and thus lead to charging the capacitor faster. The approximate input frequency is about 5Hz in the experiments.

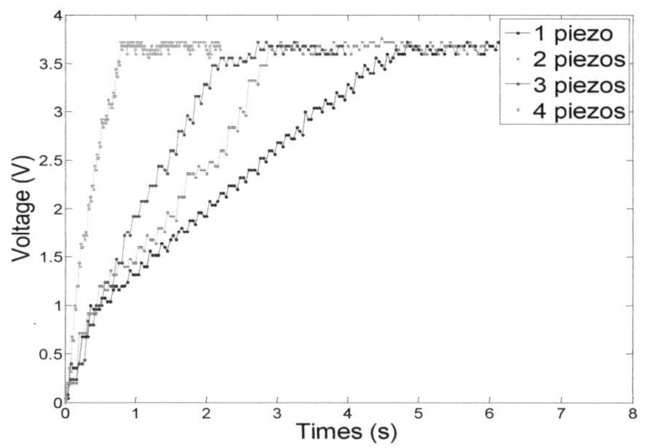

Figure 9: Plot comparing the rise time to charge a 22μF capacitor using different combinations of piezoelectric diaphragms

4.3 Electromagnetic and Piezoelectric Coupled Energy Harvester

In the integrated system, capacitors from the individual harvesters discharge into a single energy storage device through diodes. Thus they need to have comparable output voltage since the coupled device follows the output voltage of the harvester having lower output. The two individual energy harvesters and the coupled device were used to charge 10 μF capacitors.

Figure 10 illustrates that the coupled energy harvester takes less time to charge the same capacitor due to the increased output power harvested. Table 2 compares individual and coupled energy harvesting techniques. Measurement results show that the coupled energy harvester takes less than half the time to generate the same power as the individual harvesters. Hence it can be said that a coupled energy harvester is more efficient than the ones using only one harvesting technique.

5. CONCLUSION

This paper presents an energy harvesting technique that harvests energy from low frequency vibrations like human motion and stores the harvested energy to power wearable devices. Electromagnetic and piezoelectric energy harvesting techniques were combined, and the resulting energy was stored in a capacitor. It is shown that the combined system is capable of producing higher energy level for a certain amount of mechanical input. It was able to generate 45μW of power when the frequency of vibration was about 3Hz. The proposed technique was tested to power a temperature sensor, MCP9700, with a memory to store values.

6. Acknowledgment

Mehmet R. Yuce's work was supported by Australian Research Council Future Fellowships Grant FT130100430.

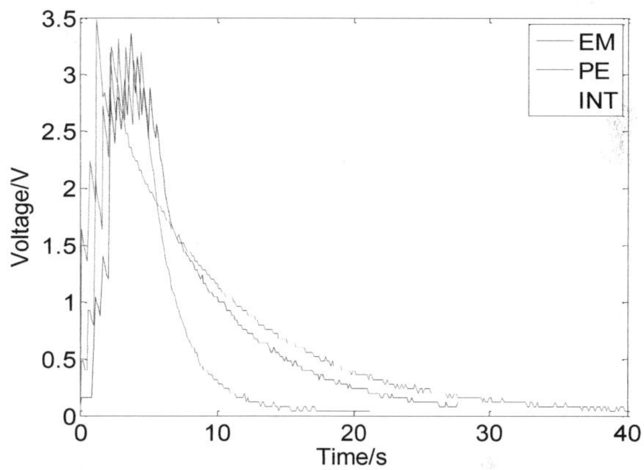

Figure 10: The output voltage from the energy harvesting device along with the individual methods, Electromagnetic, Piezoelectric and Integrated approaches.

Table 2. Comparison of individual and coupled energy harvesters

Energy Harvester	Output Power (μW)	Rise-time (s)
Electromagnetic	43.8	3.7
Piezoelectric	42.8	2.8
Coupled	44.8	1.2

7. REFERENCES

[1] M. R. Yuce, "Implementation of wireless body area networks for healthcare Systems," Sensors & Actuators: A. Physical, vol. 162, pp. 116-129, July 2010.

[2] S. Chalasani and J. M. Conrad, "A survey of energy harvesting sources for embedded systems," in Proc. IEEE Southeastcon, 2008, pp. 442-447.

[3] J. Yoo, H-J. Yoo, "Emerging low energy wearable body sensor networks using patch sensors for continuous healthcare applications," Engineering in Medicine and Biology Society (EMBC), Annual International Conference of the IEEE , pp.6381,6384, Aug. 31 -Sept. 4 2010.

[4] M. H. Ghaed, et al., "Circuits for a cubic-millimeter energy-autonomous wireless intraocular pressure monitor," IEEE Trans. Circuits Syst. I, vol. 60, no. 12, pp. 3152-3162, December 2013.

[5] J. P. Fleurial, G J Snyder, J. A. Herman, et al., "Miniaturized thermoelectric power sources," in Proc. Intersociety Energy Conversion Engineering Conference, Vancouver, BC, Canada, 1999.

[6] S. W. Liu, S. W. Lye, and J.M. Miao, "Sandwich structured electrostatic/electrets parallel-plate power generator for low acceleration and low frequency vibration energy harvesting," in Proc. IEEE 25th International Conference on Micro Electro Mechanical Systems (MEMS), pp. 1277-1280, 2012.

[7] N. Kong, D. S. Ha, A. Erturk, and D.J. Inman, "Resistive impedance matching circuit for piezoelectric energy harvesting," Journal of Intelligent Material Systems and Structures, vol. 21, pp. 1293-1302, September 2010.

[8] E. Shahhaidar, et al., "Piezoelectric and electromagnetic respiratory effort energy harvesters," 35th Annual International Conference of the IEEE Engineering in Medicine and Biology Society (EMBC), pp.3439-3442, 3-7 July 2013.

[9] B. J. Bowers and D. P. Arnold, "Spherical, rolling magnet generators for passive energy harvesting from human motion," Journal of Micromechanics and Microengineering, vol. 19, no. 9, August 2009.

[10] D. Zhu, "Vibration energy harvesting: machinery vibration, human movement and flow induced vibration," chapter 2,Sustainable Energy Harvesting Technologies - Past, Present and Future, Y. K. Tan, Ed., ed, In-Tech, 2011.

[11] Y. Zhu, S. O. R. Moheimani, M. R. Yuce, " A 2-DOF MEMS ultrasonic energy harvester," *IEEE Sensors Journal*, vol 11, pp. 155-161, January 2011.

[12] Piezoelectric Energy Harvesting Power Supply, LTC3588-1. DataSheet.: http://www.linear.com/product/LTC3588-1.

[13] P. Nintanavongsa, et al., "Design optimization and implementation for RF energy harvesting circuits," *IEEE J. Emerging and Selected Topics in Circuits and Systems*, vol. 2, pp. 24-33, March 2012.

Acu Glass: Quantifying Acupuncture Therapy using Google Glass

Haotian Jiang
Electrical and Computer Science Department
Case Western Reserve University
Cleveland, OH
hxj172@case.edu

James Starkman
Electrical and Computer Science Department
Case Western Reserve University
Cleveland, OH
jas497@case.edu

Chia-Hung Kuo
Electrical and Computer Science Department
Case Western Reserve University
Cleveland, OH
cxk78@case.edu

Ming-Chun Huang
Electrical and Computer Science Department
Case Western Reserve University
Cleveland, OH
mxh602@case.edu

ABSTRACT

Acupuncture is a therapeutic or preventative therapy through the stimulation on acupoints that located on the body surface across the anatomy to affect the functions of specific organs or soft tissues. During the acupuncture training process, mapping the acupuncture map to patients could be a challenging work since the trainees mainly rely on the instruction from experienced acupuncturists. In this study, a wearable acupuncture assistant system using augmented reality technology was introduced to record the whole treatment process with augmented information that quantified the traditional acupuncture practice. Through constructing a dynamic, personalized, and self-regulating map of virtual acupoints, the system quantified the coordinates of the acupoints to form a basic guideline to help the trainee to recall the type and location of acupuncture map. The experimental results show that the proposed system could record the coordinate of acupoints in real time and the augmented information also has the potential to be a visual guide during treatment.

General Terms

Google Glass; Augmented Reality; Acupuncture; Integrative Medicine; Training and Treatment

1. INTRODUCTION

Acupuncture is an alternative therapies practiced by inserting a fine needle at certain acupoints on the body for therapeutic purposes. Acupoints located on the body surface across the anatomy affect the functions of specific organs or soft tissues. Scientific evidence supports that acupuncture treatment can stimulate neurons under the skin and in muscle tissue for pain relieve [11, 7, 1, 2]. The training and treatment processes of acupuncture practice are still primarily and rely on instruction from the experienced acupuncturists to locate the acupoints from body acupuncture maps. The experienced-based methods is a large burden due to limited number of experienced acupuncturists and is difficult to fulfill the requirement for long-term training. An overlaid virtual acupuncture map on the acupuncturists' view of the patient's skin would improve the efficiency of their work and also the accuracy of localizing the acupoints. Augmented Reality (AR) is capable of providing the new experience by superimposing virtual information onto the real world objects. A portable hands-free Head-Mounted Displays (HMD) device that controlled by voice or hand gestures could free user's hand for acupuncture treatment. Google Glass [8] is a head-mounted wearable computer that uses a field sequential color to project rendered images through a prism and onto the retina, and could be controlled through user's voice or hand gestures. The users perceive a small translucent screen hovering at about an arms-length away, extending upward and outward from the right eye. The proposed wearable acupuncture assistant system located the coordinates of the acupoints and constructed a virtual acupuncture map according to the relative position between the user and the patient. The user performed training treatment based on viewing the superimposed acupuncture map on the patient's face through the Google Glass. In addition to the hands-free feature, the system recorded the whole treatment process with augmented information that quantified the traditional acupuncture practice, and had the potential to be a visual guide during a treatment.

2. RELATED WORK

Head-Mounted Displays have a wide range of applications in medical and health areas. Zhang et al. introduced a personalized UV monitoring and notification system using AR glasses to display augmented sunburn effects on user's body parts [13]. Yang et al. [6] reported a real-time acupuncture manipulation procession system using pattern identification of an autoregressive parameter model to identify various kinds of acupuncture manipulation. Various tracking algorithms have been developed for AR such as Scale-invariant feature transform (SIFT), Speeded Up Robust Features (SURF) [5],

BODYNETS 2015, September 28-30, Sydney, Australia

DOI 10.4108/eai.28-9-2015.2261520

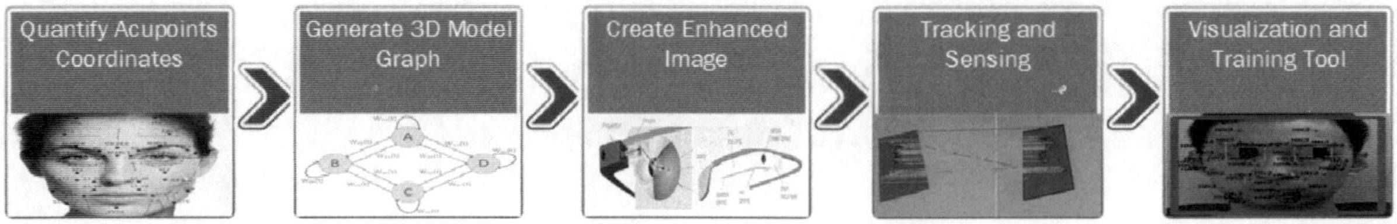

Figure 1: AcuGlass system flow

and Oriented FAST and Rotated BRIEF (ORB) [12] etc. Tracking features from frame-to-frame system gave stability to AR and the virtual object could be registered on the correct position. A study indicated that Binary Robust Independent Elementary Features (BRIEF) [3] is an efficient feature point descriptor, which only requires 256 bits or even 128 bits to obtain good matching results. The proposed work was to design an AR-based, hands-free acupuncture assistant system including face detection, image tracking and AR technology with a quantified evaluation. To the best of our knowledge, no pre-existing AR-based acupuncture training system using HMD was reported.

3. SYSTEM DESIGN

The acupuncture assistant system was designed for acupuncture training and treatment in the hospital with quantified practice approach to assist the trainee to recall the location and type of the acupoints. The acupuncture assistant system included three main components: (1) Coordinate Quantification and Map Generator (2) Tracking and Rendering (3) Visualization and Training. The Acu System flow is shown in Figure 1. The system acquired the coordinates of acupuncture points in the Cartesian coordinate system by using their relative positions on the base face. Then, the virtual acupoints were constructed as spheres and the map generator built a graph-based 3D face acupuncture point map. After getting the virtual map, rendering system put the virtual map on the real human's face over the consecutive camera frame by using the feedback from tracking system. The tracking and sensing system obtained an accurate overlay accordingly to improve the stability of performance in our AR system. Finally, the augmented reality system combined the human face in the real world with the virtual acupuncture map and displayed an enhanced view to the user through the projected screen of the Google Glass. Users could directly locate the specific acupoint according to the virtual acupoints in the AR view. If no face was detected, the system simply passed the original camera view back to the user.

3.1 Coordinate Quantification and Graph Generation

Considering a simple wire frame map with a list of nodes and edges, the proposed system visualized the spatial relationships between acupoints in a directed graph structure in which nodes represented virtual acupoints and edges represented spatial relationships between the pair of nodes (p, q). Assuming that we had N different nodes on our face, each pair of nodes had a geometric relationship that could be expressed using the standard computer graphics notation of a 4×4 homogeneous matrix. For constructing an initial virtual acupoint map, a frontal human face with standard acupuncture point map chart learned from acupuncture book was used as baseline. The geometrical relationship between each pair of $(p, q) \in N$ was scaled according to one of the specific volunteer's face, which was set as the base face. In the proposed prototype system, a simple map was preferred, and therefore, all values were expressed as a ratio to the bounding box that was returned by the face detection algorithm. For each volunteer's frontal face, the proposed system generated different referenced virtual map. For each virtual map, geometrical widths were scaled based on the distance between the centers of the user's eyes relative to the geometrical heights of the base face by calculating the height of the whole face. The scaling process could be represented by the equation (1).

$$(x' - x_o) = (x - x_o)\frac{W'}{W}, (y' - y_o) = (y - y_o)\frac{H'}{H} \quad (1)$$

where (x_o, y_o) is the origin of the coordinate system, (x, y) and (x', y') are the coordinate for each node in the image plane of base face and new face, respectively. W' and H' are the eye spacing of the new face and height of the whole new face, respectively. W and H are the corresponding value of base face. In response to the different volunteer, different referenced virtual map was used for image tracking to keep the AR system performance to be stabilized.

3.2 Tracking and Rendering

The Oriented Fast and Rotated Brief (ORB) keypoint detector and descriptor [12] were selected for the tracking system to search for the distinguishable features of the human face. ORB extended FAST [10] by efficiently computing orientations based on the intensity centroid moment and steered BRIEF according to the orientation of keypoints. Therefore, ORB was faster than SIFT or SURF and also rotation-invariant and scale-invariant. In order to find the latest relative positions relationship of corner features, the detected corner features were matched in the newly captured frame to the features in reference frame and the transformation matrix between current frame and referenced frame calculated. When the keypoints and the descriptors matched closely enough, a homography matrix could be estimated. The system crossed specific pixel to represent the virtual acupoint. With tracking, the rendering system would receive the result of a series of coordinate transformations from the tracking system and modified the relative positions of the acupoints automatically to compensate the change of view of the user. Therefore, the stability of AR system would be improved and the position bias would be reduced significantly.

3.3 Visualization and Training

3.3.1 Face Detection and Map Scaling

First, the face detection was implemented using OpenCV. The subsequent processing could be reduced to the region of interest (ROI) of the face. Before detecting both eyes, the ROI of the face could be further reduced to the approximate ROI of eyes. Then, the same OpenCV detection algorithm was used once again to detect both eyes. Note that another special haar cascade was used in this case. In this way, the distance between the two eyes was used to scale the acupoint map in the x-direction, and the height of the whole face was used to scale the acupoints map in y-direction.

3.3.2 Acupuncture Training Guide

Acupuncture Training Guide was about the interaction between the augmented information and the user. The virtual acupuncture map scaled according to the different face sizes, and the user could control the zoom level in and out via swiping the Glass's touchpad right and left. The user was able to select different labeling modes of the acupuncture assistant system for different purposes including color coded training or specific treatment sequence. The figure 2 shows training mode where the red rectangle representing ROI of face, green rectangles representing ROI of eyes, and the red line between eyes representing the eye spacing.

4. EXPERIMENTS AND RESULTS

4.1 Objective

To evaluate the usability of the system, two corresponding experiments with human subjects were conducted. The first experiment was to test the effectiveness of the tracking system for adjusting the geometrical relationship for each pair of virtual acupoints even on the different view angle of face. The second experiment was to validate if the rendering system could adjust and render the virtual acupoints map on different faces.

4.2 Experimental Setting

Six volunteers were selected for the two different experiments. The study included subjects who were more than 18 years old with normal facial features and were also willing to participate in acupoint detection by using the E-ACUPEN [4]. To verify the reasonably accuracy of the position for each virtual acupoint, E-ACUPEN was used for detecting the actual acupoints. E-ACUPEN located the acupoints through measuring the electrical resistance of the skin and indicated the major acupoints by modulating the beeping sound frequency [4, 9].

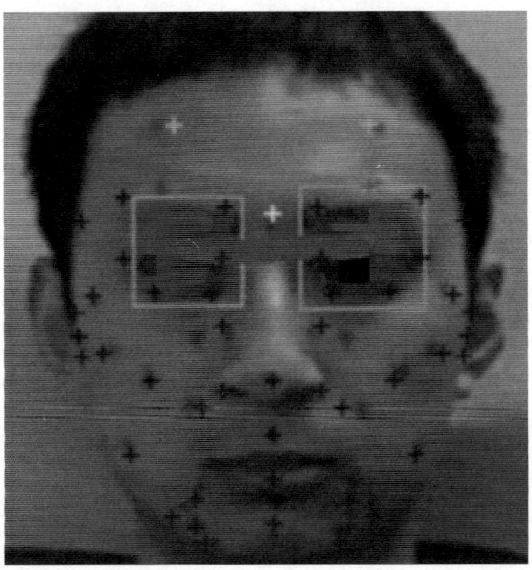

Figure 2: Virtual acupoint map on the view of frontal face in training mode.

The first experiment was to verify the effectiveness of the tracking algorithm of the system. The lighting conditions were kept unchanged because this experiment was designed to verify the basic effectiveness of face tracking. As shown in figure 3, experiment 1 was divided into two parts. First, in order to establish a basis for comparison, the position of the virtual points on the view of frontal face was used as the basic reference, and the face tracking module was temporarily removed from the proposed system while all of the other modules were retained. Then, several black plus-sign-shaped markers were drawn on the volunteer's face to save the position of the virtual acupoints. After the virtual acupoint map was overlaid on the view of the volunteer's face and the positions of the points were saved. The angle between the volunteer and Google Glass was adjusted while still kept a comfortable and roughly-fixed distance. Assuming that the initial angle $(x, y, z) = (0°, 90°, 90°)$, the volunteer moved his head to the angle of approximately $(-30°, 120°, 90°)$. For the new angle, the pixel unit distance d between plus-sign-shaped markers and virtual acupoints were processed and recorded by using Matlab. The same process was conducted again with face tracking module added back in. Let d_1 and d_2 represented the average bias between plus-sign-shaped markers and virtual acupoints under the situation of without and with tracking, respectively. If d_2 was much less than d_1 in each trial, the position bias was significantly decreased and tracking algorithm is useful and effective.

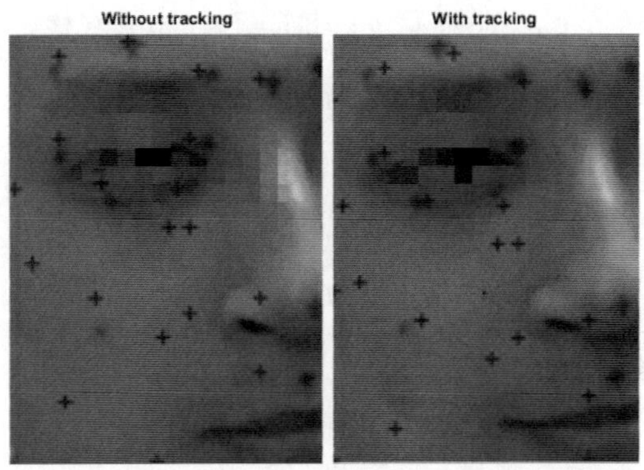

Figure 3: The comparison between non-tracking and tracking.

Table 1 summarized the average position bias for the same volunteer over 6 trials under the situation of without tracking and with tracking. The minimum value of $d_1 - d_2$ was 8.86 pixel units in the third time experiments. When position bias was more than 3 pixel unit, the jittering was obvious. In the tracking experiment, considering the minimum reduction of position bias was 8.86, which was much more than 3. Therefore, the tracking algorithm played an important role in maintaining the stability of AR and the proposed system had robust tracking result to adjust the geometrical relationship for each pair of virtual acupoints on different view angles of face.

Times	1	2	3	4	5	6
d_1	23.51	23.48	22.81	24.67	23.65	23.97
d_2	14.47	13.31	13.95	14.22	14.15	13.68

Table 1: The comparison of average position bias d in the tracking experiment

The second experiment was to test the accuracy for each virtual acupoint and its corresponding point was verified by E-ACUPEN. In conducting the experiment, the E-ACUPEN was used to find the actual acupoints and the precise positions were marked using black cross marker. Google Glass position was fixed to face directly towards the volunteer, which indicated that the angle $(x, y, z) = (0°, 90°, 90°)$. After the virtual map overlaid on the volunteer's face, the average pixel bias between each black cross marker and virtual acupoint was calculated, and the average error was represented by equation (5).

$$\sigma = \frac{1}{n} \sum_{i=1}^{n} \sqrt{(x_v - x_a)^2 + (y_v - y_a)^2} \quad (2)$$

where x_v is the virtual point's x-coordinate, and x_a the actual point's x-coordinate.

Figure 4 shows the distribution of virtual and actual acupoints on a randomly selected volunteer's face. Table 2 summarizes the average accuracy bias for three volunteers. It is more intuitive to see the acupuncture map on faces and the proposed system has reasonably rendering virtual acupoints accuracy.

Times	1	2	3
σ	7.71	8.23	8.62

Table 2: The average accuracy bias verified by E-ACUPEN

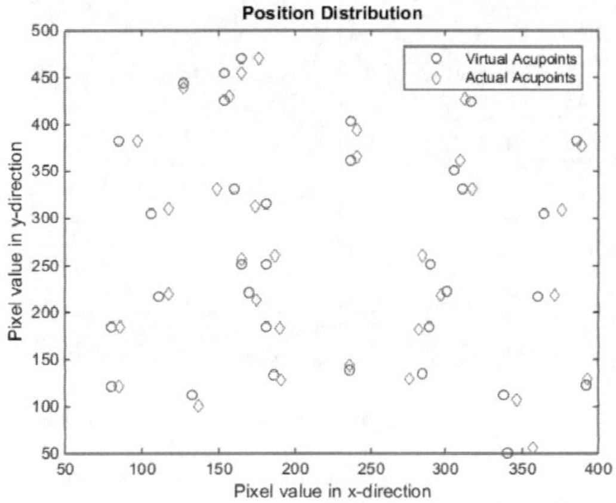

Figure 4: Position distribution from one of the volunteer

5. DISCUSSION AND FUTURE WORK

The proposed wearable acupuncture assistant system generated a virtual acupuncture map and superimposed it on patient's face on the Google glass user's view, which provided a great help on learning the relative acupoints' positions. Moreover, since the Google Glass is a head mounted AR device, it also frees the trainee's hand for practicing the acupuncture skill. The localization results obtained by the ACUPEN were served as the ground truth for verifying the accuracy for each single virtual acupoint one-by-one. The results given in this paper, although preliminary, supports that the proposed system is a feasible study.

Although slight latency occurred due to the limited calculation power from google glass, it could be improved by offloading the calculation intense task such as image processing to Android phone. The next stage of the work is to set up a client-server communication system between Google Glass and an Android phone in real time to allow multiple processors working in parallel. The whole system benefitted by letting the Android devices doing the calculation work, then the proposed work will be provided for testing by acupuncturists.

6. CONCLUSION

In this paper, we proposed an AR-based acupuncture assistant system running on Google Glass. Two experiments were carried out to verify the robustness of tracking and the rendering of the system. The experimental results showed that the AR-based system was capable of quantifying the traditional acupuncture practice and it could be applied on different objects while still preserving reasonably stability.

7. REFERENCES

[1] V. AJ, C. AM, and M. AC. Acupuncture for chronic pain: individual patient data meta-analysis. *Archives of Internal Medicine*, 172(19):396–401, 2012.

[2] B. BM, L. HM, and W. CM. Acupuncture for chronic low back pain. *New England Journal of Medicine.*, 363(5):454âĂŞ461, 2010.

[3] M. Calonder, V. Lepetit, C. Strecha, and P. Fua. Brief: Binary robust independent elementary features. In *Computer Vision–ECCV 2010*, pages 778–792. Springer, 2010.

[4] A. Comunetti, S. Laage, N. Schiessl, and A. Kistler. Characterisation of human skin conductance at acupuncture points. *Experientia*, 51(4):328–331, 1995.

[5] I. I. Eddington. Markerless affine region tracking and augmentation using mser and sift. 2011.

[6] Y. Huayuan, X. Gang, L. Jing, H. Zhuicheng, and L. Tangyi. Real-time signal procession of acupuncture manipulation and identification research on ar parameter model. *IT in Medicine and Education*, pages 86 – 90, 2009.

[7] L. K, A. G, and B. B. Acupuncture for tension-type headache. *Cochrane Database of Systematic Reviews.*, 2009.

[8] S. Mann. "glasseyes": The theory of eyetap digital eye glass. *New England Journal of Medicine.*, 31(3):10–14, 2012.

[9] M. Reichmanis, A. A. Marino, R. O. Becker, et al. Electrical correlates of acupuncture points. *IEEE Trans Biomed Eng*, 22(6):533–535, 1975.

[10] E. Rosten and T. Drummond. Machine learning for high-speed corner detection. *In ECCV*, 2006.

[11] H. RS, M. P, and P. M. Acupuncture for chronic knee pain. *A randomized clinical trial. JAMA*, 312(13):1313âĂŞ1322, 2014.

[12] E. Rublee, V. Rabaud, K. Konolige, and G. Bradski. Orb: an efficient alternative to sift or surf. *Computer Vision (ICCV)*, pages 2564 – 2571, 2011.

[13] X. Zhang, W. Xu, M.-C. Huang, N. Amini, and F. Ren. See uv on your skin: an ultraviolet sensing and visualization system. In *Proceedings of the 8th International Conference on Body Area Networks*, pages 22–28. ICST (Institute for Computer Sciences, Social-Informatics and Telecommunications Engineering), 2013.

WISEglass: Smart eyeglasses recognising context

Florian Wahl, Martin Freund, Oliver Amft
ACTLab, Chair of Sensor Technology, University of Passau, http://actlab.uni-passau.de
{wahl, freund, amft}@fim.uni-passau.de

ABSTRACT

We investigated how regular eyeglasses could be extended with multi-modal sensing and processing functions to support context-awareness applications. Our aim was to leverage eyeglasses as a platform for acquiring and processing context information according to the wearer's needs. The WISEglass architecture consists of inertial motion, environmental light, and pulse sensors, processing and wireless data transmission functionality, besides a rechargeable battery. We implemented prototypes of WISEglass and evaluated them in three application scenarios: daily activity recognition, screen-use detection, and heart rate estimation. We conducted a daily activity study with nine participants, each wearing WISEglass and recording for one day. When evaluating daily activity recognition, we obtained 77 % average accuracy for continuous recognition using Gaussian Mixture Models and classifier reject to ignore null class data. Using the light sensor for detecting screen-use, yielded 80 % accuracy. Against a chest-worn ECG reference, our heart rate estimation showed an difference below 10 beats for stationary activities across the full recording day. We concluded that smart eyeglasses provide information from a single measurement spot that is relevant in various context recognition applications.

Keywords

context inference, mobile sensing, smart glasses, activity recognition, eyewear

Categories and Subject Descriptors

I.5.m. [**Pattern Recognition**]: Miscellaneous

1. INTRODUCTION

Context awareness has opened a vast spectrum of applications that benefit from momentary information on user activity, environment, physiology, and similar. Wearable devices are often key to provide context information, as sensors could be placed comfortably at body locations such as wrist, leg, chest, or the ear. While hearing aids and Bluetooth headsets got broadly accepted as daily accessories, head-worn wearables were rarely proposed for context awareness due to potential obtrusiveness of head-attached devices. Some niche applications include ear-worn computers to manage information [17], or the ear-worn e-AR device to monitor activity and physiology [14]. There is nevertheless substantial context information available around the head [?]. Eyeglasses are regularly worn accessories that have a unique opportunity to carry sensors and process data at the head, thus fill a gap for many context-awareness applications. Moreover, eyeglasses are being worn by millions of people, for improved sight, but also as sunglasses, sports glasses, etc.

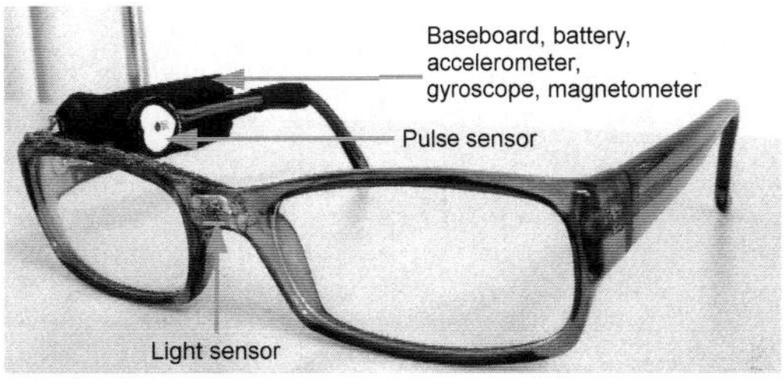

Figure 1: WISEglass prototype. Baseboard, battery, accelerometer, gyroscope, and magnetometer were mounted on the outside of a eyeglasses temple. The pulse sensor was mounted on the inside of a temple. The light sensor was integrated onto the bridge.

Substantial work has been dedicated to developing smart eyewear already. However, functionality was often centred around displaying information in front of the wearers eyes, e.g. for augmented or virtual reality applications [3, 20]. GoogleGlass and others established microinteractions as key feature of smart eyewear and focused on interaction and displaying information using glass-attachable electronics. We believe that instead of displays and direct interaction, smart eyeglasses can be built for context-aware applications, where the focus is on sensing and processing, rather than interaction. Smart eyeglasses would hence focus on acquiring and processing context information relevant to the wearer, but minimise the risk of stigmatising or raising privacy concerns.

Besides the integration of sensing and processing functions, the benefit of smart eyeglasses for different context

BODYNETS 2015, September 28-30, Sydney, Australia

DOI 10.4108/eai.28-9-2015.2261470

recognition applications needs confirmation. Previous research on head-attached devices and smart eyeglasses focused on detecting selected activities, such as walking and reading behaviour using inertial sensors and the Electrooculogram (EOG) [14, 13]. A set of daily living activities was not investigated (see related work for details). Moreover, eyeglasses could be used to acquire environmental and physiological information continuously, if a suitable smart eyeglasses implementation is found.

In this paper, we propose smart eyeglasses as a platform for a variety of context-aware applications. Our aim was to confirm that smart eyeglasses could be built and used instead of various sensors placed at different body positions. We implemented WISEglass with various sensors, including inertial motion, environmental light, and optical heart rate and investigated three application scenarios: daily activity recognition, screen-use detection, and heart rate estimation. This paper provides the following contributions:

1. We present our WISEglass eyeglasses architecture, integrating multi-modal sensing functions corresponding to frequent context types, including user activity, environmental state, and user physiology. We detail the embedded design in regular eyeglasses and data processing.
2. We evaluate WISEglass prototypes in a daily life study with nine individuals that did not wear eyeglasses regularly, including a programme of 20 daily living activities. Based on the study data, we confirm that the sensor placement and wearing across a day is suitable to implement the context recognition tasks for each application scenario.

Towards smart, regular eyeglasses there are many challenges to resolve. Our aim in this work is to establish that context recognition - and thus assistance to wearers - benefits from using smart eyeglasses due to their position at the head. Earlier work on smart eyewear primarily considered interaction and conveying visual information to the wearer. Devices often clipped onto eyeglasses only. Our approach is different, as we focus on single-point, multi-modal sensing and processing, integrated into a typical accessory, and serving different applications. We expect that in a subsequent step, continuous miniaturisation will allow us to even further integrate functionality into unobtrusive eyeglasses.

2. RELATED WORK

Head mounted sensors were considered for context awareness before. Aziz et al. [2] first used e-AR, an ear-worn sensor, for monitoring patients after abdominal surgery. In a study with 20 users they investigated motion patterns in data obtained from two dual-axis accelerometers. They used a pulse oximeter clipped to the users earlobe to monitor heart rate and oxygen saturation. No performance analysis was provided. Atallah et al. [1] compared seven different on-body motion sensor locations while grouping the activities by physical intensity level. At the head, they used e-AR and found that the ear location delivers good results for 4 out of 5 activity levels. In contrast to e-AR, our sensors are worn as eyeglasses. WISEglass features a 3-axis accelerometer, 3-axis gyroscope, 3-axis magnetometer, a RGB light sensor, and a pulse sensor, used to detect a wide range of activities of daily living.

Ishimaru et al. [12] used built-in proximity sensor and accelerometer of Google Glass to classify 5 different activities in a laboratory setting. For user dependent models they achieved an average accuracy of 67 % using blink frequency alone, and 82 % in combination with the accelerometer. Ishimaru et al. [13] used EOG and acceleration signals to classify reading, typing, eating, and talking activities, recorded from two users. They achieved an average of 70 % accuracy using user independent models. In our work, we investigate a full set of 20 activities of daily living grouped into 9 clusters in a field study rather than a laboratory setting. Moreover, our approach yielded comparable performance using user-independent models. Hernandez et. al [10] used the accelerometer, gyroscope, and camera to obtain heart and respiration rate from Google Glass, while participants were asked to remain still. They also attempted to detect emotion of the wearer in combination with an arm-worn sensor [11]. In contrast to Google Glass, which was focussed on micro-interactions and displaying information, we aim at integrating sensing and processing capabilities into regular eyeglasses. We avoid the use of a camera in order to preserve privacy. Furthermore, we gathered measurements in the field instead of a controlled a environment, e.g. heart rate is estimated during different activities.

Previous works often used multiple on-body sensing locations. Bao and Intille [4] used bi-axial accelerometers in five different body locations. They detected a set of 20 different daily living activities and achieved accuracies of up to 84 % in 20 participants. Measuring in multiple sensing locations complicates the setup process. In contrast, we propose a sensor system integrated into an accessory, thus minimising the required setup to putting on a pair of eyeglasses.

Exposure to light entrains our circadian clock, but requires light measurements close to the eye. Figueiro et al. [8] compared three different wearable sensor systems for light exposure measurement. Besides a wrist-worn device and a button worn at the collar, they found that a head-worn solution performs best as the sensor is close to the eyes. For WISEglass, we integrated a light sensor into the bridge of the glasses, thus optimising placement for light exposure measurement. As blue light is dominant in the entrainment of the circadian clock, it is of interest to know the time and duration of screen use that emits elevated blue light levels.

In the past, a variety of sensors have been placed around the head for different applications. WISEglass integrates existing sensors into *one* wearable accessory that allows wearers to benefit from smart eyeglasses in a wide range of applications, which previously required separate sensing systems.

3. WISEGLASS ARCHITECTURE

WISEglass is an approach to retrofit regular eyeglasses with a multi-modal sensor system for different context-aware applications. WISEglass could be used as a everyday accessory, just as regular eyeglasses are used today, or as a special-application device. For our design investigations, we specifically chose standard of-the-shelf eyeglasses and avoided designing the device from scratch, as to ensure that the typical eyeglasses form factor was maintained.

Processor, flash memory, communications interfaces, power controller, as well as inertial sensors were integrated onto a baseboard, the central unit of WISEglass. In our first prototypes, battery and baseboard were bound together using shrink tubing, however we consider that the units could be embedded in opposite ends of the eyeglasses frame in future versions.

With the light sensor, we investigated the embedding of components into the glasses' bridge. The light sensor magnet wiring was routed through miniature holes in the bridge into a milled channel along the top rim over the end pieces ending at the baseboard. We picked the bridge location as it is closest to the eyes and allows us to obtain most accurate light exposure measurements. Environmental light entrains our circadian clock and measuring light exposure is relevant for circadian phase guidance [18]. Another use for light sensor data could be in indoor/outdoor detection.

The pulse sensor was linked to a cable tie to enable users to customise the wearing position. The end of the cable tie was fixed to the temple tip using shrink tubing. A small block of foam was placed between the pulse sensor and the temple of the frame to ensure enough fixation to obtain a relevant signal while maintaining wearing comfort. In further versions, the implementation could be embedded directly into the temple, thus avoiding manual adjustments. Our prototype of WISEglass is depicted in Figure 1. Figure 2 depicts the WISEglass hardware architecture.

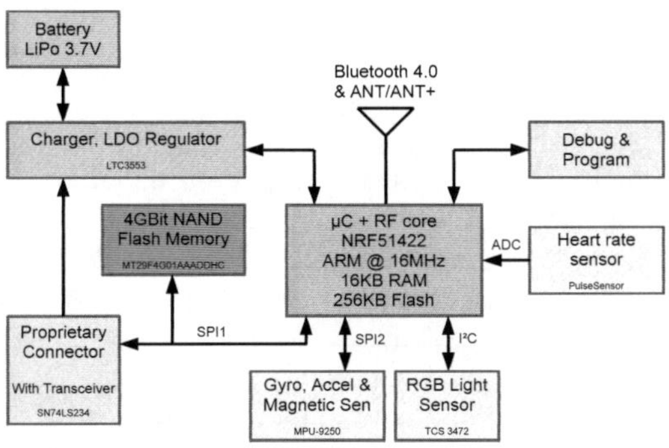

Figure 2: WISEglass hardware architecture. Separate SPI busses are used for communication of the main controller unit (MCU) with the flash memory and the inertial measurement unit to optimise data throughput.

The main controller unit (MCU) was a nRF51422 from Nordic Semiconductor that provides a 32 bit ARM Cortex-M0 core running at 16 MHz with a Bluetooth Low Energy and ANT+ wireless module as a System on Chip. We added a 512 MByte NAND flash to complement on-chip memory when storing sensor data. WISEglass is powered by a 3.7 V, 330 mAh Lithium Polymer battery.

For motion and orientation estimates, a MPU-9250 from InvenSense was used. The MPU-9250 provides accelerometer, gyroscope, magnetometer, all 3-axis inertial sensors, and a digital motion processor in a single package. The inertial sensors were AD-converted into 16 bits. Sensitivity can be configured to optimise accuracy depending on the application. For the accelerometer the ranges ± 2 g, 4 g, 8 g, and 16 g can be selected. The gyroscope offers ± 250 dps, 500 dps, 1000 dps, and 2000 dps. The magnetometer range is fixed to $\pm 4912\,\mu$T.

For light intensity measurements, a TCS3472 from ams was used. The TCS3472 senses light intensities for the red, green, blue, and clear light spectra separately. The sensor has an integrated IR filter and was connected to the MCU through the I^2C interface.

To obtain heart rate we added a PulseSensor [9] which is based on the reflexive photoplethysmography (PPG) principle. We found the temple to be a good location for measuring pulse as it eliminated the need for an ear clip.

4. DATA COLLECTION

4.1 Study methodology

To evaluate our approach, we conducted a study with nine participants (3 female, 6 male, between 20 and 27 years). Participants either did not require prescription glasses or wore contact lenses. Each participant was given a pair of smart glasses. For heart rate reference measurements, participants were fitted with a CamNtech Actiwave Cardio ECG device. Annotations were performed by an observer using the ACTLog application for Android [16]. Figure 3 shows the sensor setup for a sample of the activities considered.

Figure 3: WISEglass worn during a subset of the activities considered in our full-day study protocol. In the protocol a variety of daily activities were covered and subsequently grouped into nine activity clusters for the recognition analysis. During our study we collected 66.08 hours of data from nine participants.

We recorded up to two participants per day. Participants received three complimentary meals during the recording day and a 25 Euro Amazon voucher as compensation.

During recordings we configured the accelerometer to a range of ± 4 g and the gyroscope to a range of ± 500 dps. Accelerometer, gyroscope, and magnetometer were sampled at a a rate of 50 Hz. Light measurements were integrated with a time constant of 154 msec yielding a sampling rate of 6.5 Hz and were upsampled to 50 Hz using a latest value strategy. The pulse sensor voltage was sampled at a rate of 50 Hz. The ECG reference was sampled at 200 Hz. From the study, we acquired a total 66.08 hours of data.

4.2 Study protocol

Participants were first introduced to the study protocol and signed an informed consent form. Participants then performed a scripted study protocol as shown in Figure 4. During the exit interview, participants evaluated their experience using the system usability scale (SUS) [6]. The protocol was designed to cover typical daily activities. Table 1 shows how activities were combined to activity clusters for further evaluation.

5. EVALUATION METHODOLOGY

5.1 Data preprocessing

Data streams from the WISEglass, ECG device, and smartphone were aligned according to their time stamps, merged,

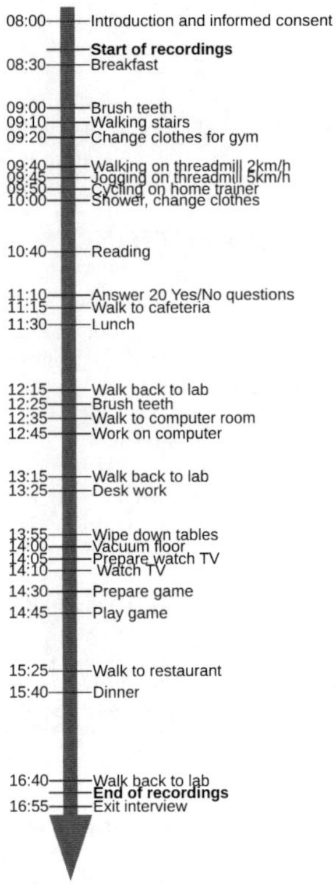

Figure 4: Protocol of the daily activity study. Recordings started before breakfast and ended before the exit interview. Sensors were temporarily removed while participants were in the gym locker room.

resampled to 50 Hz, and cropped to a common time axis. Subsequently, annotations were post-processed by visual inspection using the ACTLab MARKER toolbox for MATLAB.

5.2 Feature extraction

Features were extracted using pandas [15] and numpy [19] libraries of Python. For recognition of daily activities and the detection of screen-use, a sliding window over data samples with a window size of $n = 1500$ sa (30 s) and a step size of $s = 50$ sa (1 s) was used. Feature vectors were standardised and normalised before further processing. The sliding windows were assigned to the class that was most represented in the window. Motion features were computed over each of the three axis of the accelerometer (a_x, a_y, and a_z) and the gyroscope (g_x, g_y, and g_z). We computed the L^2 norm for the acceleration axis a_{norm} for each sample. Features listed in Table 2 were subsequently calculated for a_{norm}, a_x, a_y, a_z, g_x, g_y, and g_z per window.

In order to detect screen-use based on light sensor data, we derived features on the RGB and clear light intensity values named r, g, b, and c respectively. We calculated the median med() and number of median crossings mcr() for each color channel per window. To express spectral com-

Table 1: Activity clusters and total duration.

No	Cluster	Activity & total duration [min:sec]
1	Eat	Breakfast [84:43]
		Lunch [156:49]
		Dinner [181:53]
2	Walk	Lab to Bathroom [17:37]
		Lab to gym [36:27]
		On treadmill 2km/h [47:06]
		Gym to lab [35:56]
		Lab to cafeteria [20:11]
		Queuing for lunch [6:28]
		Picking up lunch [13:20]
		Cafeteria to lab [25:28]
		Lab to restaurant [58:36]
		Restaurant to lab [55:26]
3	Brush	Teeth [39:17]
4	Stairs	Walking [19:49]
5	Jog	On treadmill 5km/h [45:27]
6	Cycle	On gym trainer [91:14]
7	Read	A book [276:31]
		Desk work [273:34]
8	Screen	Computer work [253:50]
		Watching movie [187:56]
9	Cleaning	Vacuuming [45:22]
		Wiping tables [45:02]

Table 2: Motion features calculated for a vector of data samples w with the window size n with elements $1 \dots N$, where w_i is the i-th sample in the window. w' and w'' are the first and second derivative of w determined between two neighbouring samples. zcr() **denotes the number of zero crossings.**

1. $\bar{w}$	2. $\sum_{i=1}^{n} w_i$, if $w_i > 0$	3. $\sum_{i=1}^{n} w_i^2$
4. $\sigma^2(w)$	5. $\sum_{i=1}^{n} w_i$, if $w_i < 0$	6. $\sum_{i=1}^{n} w_i$
7. $\max(w)$	8. $\sum_{i=1}^{n} w_i'$, if $w_i' > 0$	9. $\sum_{i=1}^{n} \lvert w_i \rvert$
10. $\min(w)$	11. $\sum_{i=1}^{n} w_i'$, if $w_i' < 0$	12. $\mathrm{zcr}(w)$
13. w_1	14. $\sum_{i=1}^{n} w_i''$, if $w_i'' > 0$	15. $\sum_{i=1}^{n} \lvert w_i \rvert'$
16. w_N	17. $\sum_{i=1}^{n} w_i''$, if $w_i'' < 0$	18. $\frac{\bar{w}}{\sigma(w)}$
19. $w_N - w_1$	20. $\max(w) - \min(w)$	21. $\sqrt{\sum_{i=1}^{n} w_i^2}$
22. $\sum_{i=1}^{n} w_i'$	23. $\sum_{i=1}^{n} \lvert w_i' \rvert$	24. $\sum_{i=1}^{n} \lvert w_i'' \rvert$
25. $\sum_{i=1}^{n} w_i''$		

position of light, we computed the median of the ratio for each combination of two color channels c_1, c_2 defined as $\mathrm{crm}(c_1, c_2) = \mathrm{med}(\frac{c_1}{c_2})$.

Heart rate estimation was performed by counting the number of positive peaks in the raw voltage signal of the pulse sensor. For peak detection, we used an existing peak detector [7]. We experimented with different minimum peak distances, ranging from 0 to 25 sa in steps of 5 sa, but found 20 sa to be the best for our needs. As reference heart rate, the estimate provided by the ECG sensor was used. We computed the mean of the heart rate estimate from the ECG sensor per window. The calculation of the heart rate error was performed on windows with no overlap using window size $n = 1500$ samples.

5.3 Feature selection

We applied principle component analysis (PCA) to reduce the number of features. We configured the PCA algorithm to select the minimal number of features, such that at least 99.9 % of the variance in the training data was explained resulting in the selection of 78 out of 175 features for recognising daily activities. For screen-use detection, 9 out of 14 features were selected.

5.4 Cross-validation

To ensure generality and stability of our statistical model, we used Leave-One-Out (LOO) cross-validation on a per-participant basis. In every cross-validation fold the classifier was trained on all available feature instances from eight participants. To evaluate model performance the data of the remaining participant was used.

5.5 Classification with reject option

Classification of the motion-based activity and light-based screen detection was performed using a Gaussian Mixture Models (GMM) classifier as described in [5]. After training one GMM for each class, we computed the probabilities for each test sample. The classifier then selected the class for which the highest probability occurred. To also predict unlabelled data we implemented classifier reject to avoid making assumptions on the data in the null class. First we obtained the likelihoods for each test sample from the GMM model. If the maximum likelihood for a test sample was below the threshold, the classifier rejected it as a null class instance and otherwise selected the class of the GMM yielding the maximum likelihood. A sweep search was performed to find the optimal threshold. We used all maximum likelihoods, which occurred during training in each LOO cross-validation fold and picked the threshold yielding the best F1 score. Results per fold were averaged to show the performance for an optimal F1 score.

5.6 Heart rate estimation performance

To validate heart rate estimation from the pulse sensor, we computed the root-mean-square error (RMSe) between the ECG reference and the pulse sensor. Both signals were filtered using a bandpass filter before peak detection was applied. RMSe computation was limited to data samples, where the ECG heart rate was between 40 bpm and 150 bpm according to the reference estimate. We calculated RMSe for three data subsets to investigate the effect of motion artefacts: (1) All available data. (2) Data from stationary clusters eat, read, and screen. (3) Data from classes stairs, walking, and jogging on treadmill where the participant is assumed to be moving.

6. RESULTS

Here we show the results for recognising user activities using inertial sensor data, detecting screen-use using environmental light, and estimating heart rate using the WISEglass pulse sensor.

6.1 Daily activity recognition

We evaluated the recognition of the activity clusters (Tab. 1) using the GMM classifier and LOO cross-validation. GMM performance was analysed by varying the number of Gaussian mixture components between $c = \{1, 3, 5, 7\}$ per class, as well as analysing the covariance matrix configuration (full or diagonal). All configurations using diagonal covariance matrix yielded similar accuracies, except for the configuration with one mixture only. The full covariance matrices generally perform marginally better (3 %) than diagonal, for the same number of mixture components. For our further analysis, we resided on using a diagonal covariance matrices due to the increased modelling and computation complexity that a full covariance matrix would introduce. Using diagonal covariance matrices, highest accuracy was 77 % using 3 GMM mixture components. The lowest performance was 70 % using 1 GMM mixture component. Based on the results, we used 3 GMM mixture components per class for all subsequent analyses.

Daily activity recognition varied in accuracy between 70 % and 84 % depending on the participant considered for testing. The confusion matrix shown in Figure 5 depicts the class assignment averaged over all participants. For the confusion analysis LOO cross-validation results were averaged across folds. The confusion results indicate per-class performances between 80 % and 90 %, except for "cycle". The performance of the cycle cluster was only 50 % due to confusions with "eat", "walk", "brush", and "clean" clusters. As "cycle" took place at slow pace on a gym trainer (see Fig. 3), only minor head motion occurred, thus resulting in motion patterns similar to other classes. The activity clusters "read" and "screen" show the largest confusions. Based on motion data it seems plausible that "read" and "screen" clusters were confused as they showed similar head motions.

At a first glance, the classifier reject yields a null class accuracy of only 20 % and several confusions with other activity clusters. We found that the performance is related to our recording protocol and the diversity of motion in the activity clusters. Our activity clusters were comprehensive on the activities contained in it, thus there was simply not much unlabelled data left with other motion patterns than what was represented in the activity clusters. In the unlabelled episodes, participants were, e.g., walking, sitting at a desk, or remained in another state that often matched a modelled activity cluster.

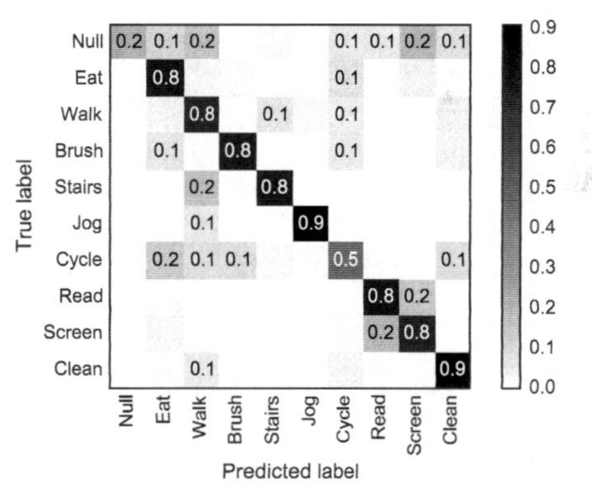

Figure 5: Daily activity recognition: confusion matrix across cross-validation folds. With the exception "cycle" cluster, all activity cluster perform at an accuracy of at least 80 %. Null class performance was low due to the nature of the study protocol, where many modelled activities occurred also as unlabelled data, thus resulting in confusions.

6.2 Screen-use detection

We detected screen-use from the light sensor data. Screen-use and its timing are important factors in circadian rhythm entrainment, as light emitted from screens and received through eyes at night may hamper falling asleep later.

Figure 6 shows mean accuracies for the light-based screen detection per participant using LOO cross-validation and a GMM classifier with diagonal covariance matrices using 3 mixtures per class. An accuracy between 64 % and 93 % was obtained here, with a mean of 80 %. While most folds achieve performance around the mean score, evaluation for participant 4 showed as an outlier.

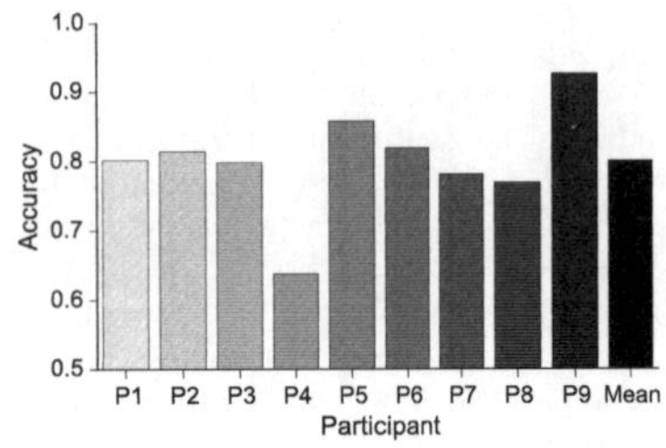

Figure 6: Screen-use detection: Normalised accuracy per participant (cross-validation fold). Mean accuracy was 80 %. Results for participant 4 seems to be an outlier.

6.3 Heart rate estimation

Heart activity was measured in WISEglass using a optical pulse sensor worn at the temple. Similar to the daily activity recognition, there are many context applications that benefit from physiological estimates. Here we focus on heart rate as one important indicator. Figure 7 shows the RMSe for all recordings as well as activity subsets "motion" and "stationary" per participant and averaged. For all activities combined, heart rate estimation RMSe varied between 10 bpm and 19 bpm with a mean of 13 bpm. Motion artefacts contributed to an increased RMSe. For motion activities the mean RMSe increases to 14 bpm while for stationary activities it is reduced by 40 % compared to motion activities, to 9 bpm. Motion artefacts were prominent in the heart data from both WISEglass pulse sensor and the ECG reference. During motion it could not be determined which of the systems (WISEglass or ECG reference) provides more accurate data. Thus during motion, the error reported here must be considered as a difference between the two systems only.

6.4 Usability evaluation

The SUS evaluation of all nine participants yielded a mean score of 66.4 of 100. Participants found the system easy to use with 4.1 of 5.0 points on average. The overall score may be negatively biased due to the experiment process (e.g. placing ECG electrodes) and hence consider the easy to use question the most relevant result of the SUS evaluation.

7. DISCUSSION

The results of this work clearly confirm idea behind WISEglass: smart eyeglasses can provide multi-purpose sensing functions for different context recognition applications. Instead of clip-on designs, as Google Glass and others, we emphasise that eyeglasses could integrate sensing and processing functions into typical eyeglasses frames. The per-

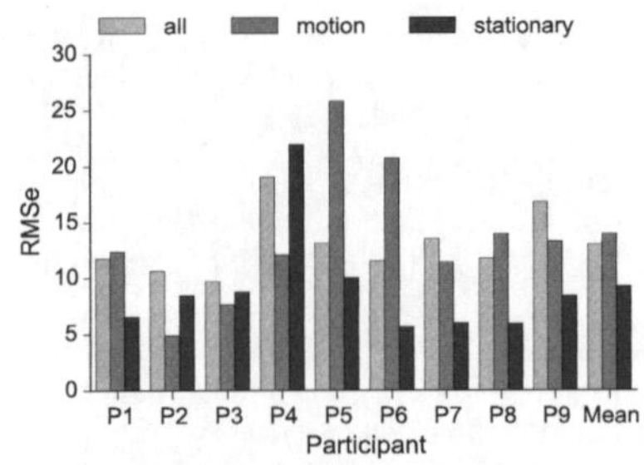

Figure 7: Heart rate estimation: RMSe analysis per participant, where the reference heart rate was between 40 and 150 bpm. RMSe was analysed for three activity clusters: all, motion ("stairs", "walk", and "jog"), and stationary ("eat", "read", and "screen").

formance for activity recognition, screen-use detection, and heart rate estimation in this work show that the head-worn measurement positions and the used pattern processing methods are adequate. Compared to a phone, the smart eyeglasses are always at the same body position and in addition can measure HR continuously. Compared to a watch-like devices, smart eyeglasses can measure the light shining into the users eyes. Another advantage is that the activities a watch can detect must somehow include the arm (e.g. watching TV might be difficult to detect), so eyeglasses can cover a broader spectrum of activities. Nevertheless, for daily activity recognition improvements of the null class modelling seem necessary. It is clear that our recordings, although made over full days and including diverse activities do not reflect all conditions under which smart eyeglasses could be used. As a consequence, we had little data that was not already modelled by the activity clusters and thus unknown activities were under-represented in the dataset. This effect shows that activity clusters are robust enough to generalise onto unknown data. In a next step, WISEglass could be used in free living conditions. Then however, less accurate annotations must be expected.

The GMM classification approach demonstrated that user-independent models with good average performance (approx. 80 %) can be obtained. Additional GMM parameter selection could be performed on a per class basis to further improve the model fit. Specifically, for the screen-use detection improvements could be realised by combining light and motion data. While we intended to span a wide range of possible applications of smart eyeglasses, improvements to the heart rate estimation method should be investigated, too. Here, a more controlled setting may be helpful to provide detailed RMSe for different movements. The ECG reference data showed motion artefacts due to insufficient electrode attachment. The present work presents a pilot study to confirm benefit of smart eyeglasses. In further investigations, additional participants and additional scenarios and applications for smart eyeglasses shall be investigated to further expand the use cases for smart eyeglasses.

We are aware that our current WISEglass prototype is yet not fully resembling the vision of regular eyeglasses. While we made important steps, e.g. by integrating the light sensor and wiring into the eyeglasses frame, further miniaturisation and integration work is necessary. Moreover, to improve unobtrusiveness, the baseboard and battery could be moved to the temple hinges. The pulse sensor could be made smaller and integrated in the temple such that the foam block disappears. Given the reliable data from the pulse sensor, we are confident that such improvements are feasible.

8. CONCLUSION

WISEglass is the first multi-modal sensor system retrofitted to off-the-shelf eyeglasses. The platform offers motion, light, and pulse sensors for use in a wide range of context-aware applications. All sensor modalities were successfully evaluated in three application scenarios, demonstrating that the smart eyeglasses serve as single-position context measurement device. For daily activity recognition, an average accuracy of 77 % for distinguishing 9 activity clusters using LOO cross-validation was achieved. The recognition rate is comparable to previous work [12, 13], while in our work more activities and user-independent models were considered. However, most importantly, WISEglass integrates all sensors into one commonly used accessory, thus does not require to wear head-mounted displays, cameras, etc. Screen-use detection achieved a mean accuracy of 80 %. Heart rate estimation was evaluated against a chest-worn ECG reference with an average RMSe of 13 bpm for all available data and 9 bpm RMSe during stationary activities confirming that the temple-worn sensor provides an adequate wearing position.

Acknowledgements

We thank Timo Spinde and Christoph Weidemeyer for collecting the dataset, Jakob Kasbauer for contributing to the light data analysis, and all study participants. This research was supported by the Dutch Technology Foundation STW under grant number 12184.

9. REFERENCES

[1] L. Atallah, B. Lo, R. King, and G.-Z. Yang. Sensor placement for activity detection using wearable accelerometers. In *Body Sensor Networks (BSN), 2010 International Conference on*, pages 24–29. IEEE, 2010.

[2] O. Aziz, B. Lo, R. King, A. Darzi, and G.-Z. Yang. Pervasive body sensor network: an approach to monitoring the post-operative surgical patient. In *Wearable and Implantable Body Sensor Networks, 2006. BSN 2006. International Workshop on*, pages 4–pp. IEEE, 2006.

[3] R. T. Azuma et al. A survey of augmented reality. *Presence*, 6(4):355–385, 1997.

[4] L. Bao and S. S. Intille. Activity recognition from user-annotated acceleration data. In *Pervasive computing*, pages 1–17. Springer, 2004.

[5] C. M. Bishop. *Pattern recognition and machine learning*. springer, 2006.

[6] J. Brooke. Sus-a quick and dirty usability scale. *Usability evaluation in industry*, 189(194):4–7, 1996.

[7] M. Duarte. Notes on scientific computing for biomechanics and motor control. https://github.com/demotu/BMC, 2015.

[8] M. Figueiro, R. Hamner, A. Bierman, and M. Rea. Comparisons of three practical field devices used to measure personal light exposures and activity levels. *Lighting Research and Technology*, 45(4):421–434, 2013.

[9] Y. Gitman and J. Murphy. Pulse sensor-a wearable device to give your projects a live heartbeat. *Make-Technology on Your Time*, 29:52, 2012.

[10] J. Hernandez, Y. Li, J. M. Rehg, and R. W. Picard. Bioglass: Physiological parameter estimation using a head-mounted wearable device. In *Wireless Mobile Communication and Healthcare, EAI 4th International Conference on*, pages 55–58. IEEE, 2014.

[11] J. Hernandez and R. W. Picard. Senseglass: Using google glass to sense daily emotions. In *Proceedings of the adjunct publication of the 27th annual ACM symposium on User interface software and technology*, pages 77–78. ACM, 2014.

[12] S. Ishimaru, K. Kunze, K. Kise, J. Weppner, A. Dengel, P. Lukowicz, and A. Bulling. In the blink of an eye: combining head motion and eye blink frequency for activity recognition with google glass. In *Proceedings of the 5th Augmented Human International Conference*, page 15. ACM, 2014.

[13] S. Ishimaru, Y. Uema, K. Kunze, K. Kise, K. Tanaka, and M. Inami. Smarter eyewear: using commercial eog glasses for activity recognition. In *Proceedings of the 2014 ACM International Joint Conference on Pervasive and Ubiquitous Computing: Adjunct Publication*, pages 239–242. ACM, 2014.

[14] D. Jarchi, B. Lo, E. Ieong, D. Nathwani, and G.-Z. Yang. Validation of the e-ar sensor for gait event detection using the parotec foot insole with application to post-operative recovery monitoring. In *BSN 2014: Proceedings of 11th International Conference on Wearable and Implantable Body Sensor Networks*, pages 127–131. IEEE, 2014.

[15] W. McKinney. pandas: a foundational python library for data analysis and statistics. *Python for High Performance and Scientific Computing*, pages 1–9, 2011.

[16] G. Spina, F. Roberts, J. Weppner, P. Lukowicz, and O. Amft. Crntc+: A smartphone-based sensor processing framework for prototyping personal healthcare applications. In *Pervasive Computing Technologies for Healthcare, 7th International Conference on*, pages 252–255. IEEE, 2013.

[17] E. Tamaki, T. Miyaki, and J. Rekimoto. Brainy hand: An ear-worn hand gesture interaction device. In *CHI '09 Extended Abstracts on Human Factors in Computing Systems*, CHI EA '09, pages 4255–4260, New York, NY, USA, 2009. ACM.

[18] F. Wahl, T. Kantermann, and O. Amft. How much light do you get? estimating daily light exposure using smartphones. In *Proceedings of the 2014 ACM International Symposium on Wearable Computers*, pages 43–46. ACM, 2014.

[19] S. v. d. Walt, S. C. Colbert, and G. Varoquaux. The numpy array: A structure for efficient numerical computation. *Computing in Science & Engineering*, 13(2):22–30, 2011.

[20] F. Zhou, H. B.-L. Duh, and M. Billinghurst. Trends in augmented reality tracking, interaction and display: A review of ten years of ismar. In *Proceedings of the 7th IEEE/ACM International Symposium on Mixed and Augmented Reality*, pages 193–202. IEEE Computer Society, 2008.

The Speckled Cellist

Classification of Cello Bowing Techniques using the Orient Specks

Debadri Mukherjee
Centre for Speckled Computing
School of Informatics
University of Edinburgh
D.Mukherjee@sms.ed.ac.uk

D K Arvind
Centre for Speckled Computing
School of Informatics
University of Edinburgh
dka@inf.ed.ac.uk

ABSTRACT

Cello bowing techniques are classified by applying supervised machine learning methods to sensor data from two inertial sensors called the Orient specks – one worn on the playing wrist and the other attached to the frog of the bow. Twelve different bowing techniques were considered, including variants on a single string and across multiple strings. Results are presented for the classification of these twelve techniques when played singly, and in combination during improvisational play. The results demonstrated that even when limited to two sensors, classification accuracy in excess of 95% was obtained for the individual bowing styles, with the added advantages of a minimalist approach.

Keywords

cello bowing; wearable sensors; wireless inertial-magnetic sensors; Orient specks; SVM classifier.

1. INTRODUCTION

Stringed instruments by definition produce sounds from vibrating strings, and can be characterised by the way the strings are made to vibrate: by plucking them (harp, mandolin, sitar), by bowing (violin, cello, sarangi), or by striking them (piano, santoor). This paper is concerned with the cello – a stringed instrument played with a bow (which is a stick with many hairs stretched between its ends). Advanced string competency involves mastering different bowing techniques. The automatic classification of the bowing techniques has attracted interest due to its technical complexity, for its possible future applications in musical pedagogy and its use in the hypercello, in triggering and modifying synthesised sounds that accompany the acoustic cello.

Previous research in this topic has been limited to a small number of bowing techniques, using special bows embedded with sensors, and restricted to classification of techniques singly, or in a pre-determined order, without tackling combinations during improvisational play. The proposed approach uses the Orient specks [13], which combines a 3-axis accelerometer, gyroscope and magnetometer, and wireless communication in a single unit measuring 36x28x11 mm and weighing 23 grams (including the battery). Orients have the advantage of being unobtrusive when worn on the playing wrist, and can be attached to the frog in the bow without affecting its balance during playing. A novel set of *d*-attributes was constructed from the sensor data for this task with the aim of making the data separable in *d*-dimensional space. Results are presented using a classifier based on a Support Vector Machine (SVM) model for three data captures sessions following the minimalist approach, which included twelve bowing techniques and addressed the aspect of string-crossings and improvisational playing by experienced cellists each with more than fifteen years of experience.

In the rest of this paper, Section 2 gives a short introduction to different bowing techniques and previous research in this area with an analysis of their strengths and weaknesses; Section 3 sets out the methodology adopted in this paper; Sections 4 and 5 present results and conclusions, respectively.

2. BACKGROUND AND RELATED WORK

2.1 Background

The drawing of the hair of the bow across the strings produces vibrations due to the spontaneous jerking motion called the stick-slip phenomenon. Different bowing techniques [7][8][9] produce characteristic sounds and the following were considered in this work:

- *Legato*: smoothly connected, without interruption between the notes, whether in one or several bow strokes.
- *Staccato*: a non –legato *martelé* type of short bow stroke played with a stop; a detached well articulated stroke.
- *Martelé*: percussive bow-stroke characterised by its sharp initial accent and post-stroke articulation.
- *Spiccato*: In the eighteenth century terminology, a style of bowing which produces a dry, detached sound, not necessarily executed off the string. In the nineteenth century, it came to mean a relatively slow, bouncing stroke.
- *Tremolo*: a rapid repetition of notes played with quickly alternating up and down bow strokes.

BODYNETS 2015, September 28-30, Sydney, Australia

DOI 10.4108/eai.28-9-2015.2261477

- *Col legno*: to strike the strings with the stick of the bow as opposed to sliding the bow across the string.
- *Ricochet*: involves at least two notes being played in the same 'bow-stroke' (either up or down).

Each of the bowing techniques (except *Col legno* and *Ricochet* – only the single string variant was considered) was treated to two variants:

1. *Single*: the techniques were applied on a single string of the cello.
2. *Crossing*: the bow moved over multiple strings of the cello, *i.e.*, the bow "crossed" strings.

2.2 Related Work

The CyberViolin project [1] presented real-time classification of violin bow strokes such as *détaché*, *martelé*, *staccato*, *spiccato*, and *legato*, using an electromagnetic motion tracking system to capture raw gesture data. The data was analysed to extract stroke features and fed to a decision tree for training and classification. An accuracy of 73% was achieved using a set of sparse features such as the length of the bow stroke and its average speed. The accuracy was improved by adding new features such as frequency of bow change, acceleration or deceleration within a stroke, continuity of motion between strokes, bow position (middle, upper, lower), number of changes in a single coordinate (stroke similarity), and the lack of movement within a stroke (stoppage).

Schedel and Fiebrink [2] constructed a real-time cello bow articulation classification system for using a bow instrumented with sensors. The commercial K-Bow [5] measures bow acceleration and tilt, bow hair tension, grip pressure and surface area, horizontal distance between frog and tip, vertical distance between fingerboard & bridge, and the tilt of the bow relative to instrument. A total of eighty features were extracted from the following sensor data for classification of *legato*, *marcato* (*martelé*), *tremolo*, *battuto* (*col legno*), *ricochet*, *hook* and *spiccato* bowing styles. The Wekinator software tool was used for real-time, interactive machine learning [6] with the following inputs: each K-Bow sensor's mean, minimum, and maximum value over a sliding window; the mean, minimum, and maximum of the first- and second-order differences within the same window; and the raw sensor value sampled once per window.

Bevilacqua *et al* at IRCAM in Paris developed the augmented violin which was an acoustic violin with added sensing capabilities to measure the bow acceleration. A k-NN (k-Nearest Neighbour) clustering technique was used to recognise *détaché*, *martelé* and *spiccato* bowing styles. Young [4] used a carbon fibre violin bow augmented with force, inertial, and position sensors to record bowing gestures on an electric violin. Principal components were computed for the data set comprising of the downward and lateral forces; x, y, z acceleration; and angular velocity about the x, y, and z axes. A k-NN classifier was employed, using the principal components as inputs to classify six different common bowing techniques: accented *détaché*, *détaché*, *lancé*, *louré*, *martelé*, *staccato* and *spiccato*.

The research presented in this paper pushes the state-of-the-art in a number of ways. Firstly, a wider variety of bowing techniques are classified including the *legato*, *staccato*, *spiccato*, *tremolo*, *martelé*, *col legno* and *ricochet*. Furthermore, the "crossing" of strings is also considered, *i.e.*, the single string and crossing string variants are considered separately for the different bowing techniques where applicable. The classification of such a comprehensive list of bowing articulations has not been attempted before.

Secondly, the approach adopted in this paper is the least intrusive to date compared to other methods; two wearable Orient wireless sensors are used – one on the wrist of the playing hand and the second attached under the frog of the bow, *i.e.*, this could be any bow and does not require a specially adapted one. Such a minimalist approach is in sharp contrast to the K-Bow which is festooned with a number of sensors: a three-axis accelerometer located inside the frog senses tilt and acceleration of the bow; changes in the grip pressure and surface area of the cellist's bow hand are sensed; an angle sensitive pressure sensor located in the junction between the bow hair and the frog measures changes in the tension of the bow hair as the cellist plays; a small circuit board beneath the fingerboard of the instrument creates an RF field and an infrared modulated wide field light cone, whose interactions with the loop antennas inside the bow stick and with the infrared detector inside the frog allow the measurement of the bow position and angle relative to the instrument.

Thirdly, despite the minimalist approach, the classification method adopted in this paper yields an impressive accuracy of up to 98.33% for the individual bowing techniques, and furthermore the method has been applied for the first time towards classifying the bowing techniques in improvised pieces: for constrained improvisation and free improvisation.

3. METHODOLOGY

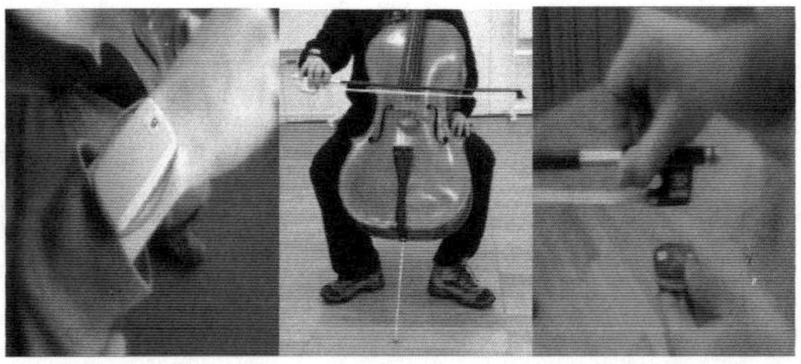

Figure 1: Cellist (Centre) with an Orient Speck attached to the wrist (Left) and another one attached to the frog of the bow (Right).

3.1 Data Capture Sessions

The cellist participating in the data capture session wore an Orient speck on the wrist of the playing hand and another speck was attached to the frog of the bow. The motion of the bow as the playing hand manoeuvres it, is central in characterising the bowing technique. This determined the placement of specks on the bow and on the playing hand (as close as possible to the point of contact with the bow). The exact position of the specks, as shown in Figure 1, was fine-tuned by the cellists to minimise any interference when playing the instrument. Each data capture session consisted of three parts: each of the twelve bowing techniques ('Single' and 'Crossing' techniques for each of Legato, Staccato, Martelé, Tremolo, and Spiccato, and 'Single' only for Col legno and Ricochet.) was played continuously for a period ranging between 20 to 25 seconds; next, a constrained improvisation piece was played which contained a random concatenation of the twelve bowing techniques, which is not a recognisable musical piece; finally, the cellist was asked to play freely an improvised piece of music which was chosen to contain the bowing techniques. The latter two sessions lasted between 120 and 150 seconds. The constrained improvisation piece is a half-way house between the individual bowing styles where the playing is well pronounced and the freely improvised musical piece in which the demarcations between the techniques are fluid, wherein one technique smears into another. The three data capture sessions considered in this paper were also videotaped for future reference. The cellists participating in the study were categorised as an expert (Subjects 1 and 2), and at intermediate level (Subject 3), to validate the robustness of the method for different playing abilities and styles.

Table 1: The twelve bowing techniques and their mnemonics.

Abbreviation	*Bowing Technique*
LS	*Legato Single*
LC	*Legato Crossing*
SS	*Staccato Single*
SC	*Staccato Crossing*
MS	*Martelé Single*
MC	*Martelé Crossing*
TS	*Tremolo Single*
TC	*Tremolo Crossing*
SPS	*Spiccato Single*
SPC	*Spiccato Crossing*
C	*Col legno*
R	*Ricochet*

3.2 Data Pre-processing

The Orient data stream contains sensor values from three-axis gyroscope, accelerometer and magnetometer produced at a sample rate of 100 Hz. As a first step in the pre-processing stage, the magnetometer data was removed because the direction of the magnetic field or changes to it does not add any relevant information for describing the movement of the bow. Next, outlier values were removed manually by visual inspection. The data from all the Orients were packed into a vector for each segment so as to represent it as an n x d data matrix[1]. This is a standard representation of datasets for data mining tasks and is suitable for use with the Weka tool [10]. When sensor values were missing, they were ignored but a segment was only considered as long as no more than 25% of the data was missing from either of the two Orients. It was established empirically that segments with 75% of the sensor values from each of the Orients encoded sufficient information for classifying the segment correctly using the methodology described in this paper.

3.3 Segmentation

For each capture, the Orient sensor data and its corresponding video were aligned with a precision of 0.05 seconds using their respective timestamps. The Orient data was next divided into segments based on a time window, which is termed as the 'segment duration' (*sd*). For example, *sd* = 1.5 corresponds to dividing the actions into 1.5 second segments. The impact of *sd* on the classification accuracy (%) was studied and the results summarised in Figure 2. The value of *sd,* ranging between 1 and 2 seconds does not have a significant effect on the accuracy. The final choice of 1 second was a compromise between the ability to pick out events of short duration of interest during the improvised pieces and in being able to encode as much of the macroscopic information in the pieces as possible. For example, *sd* = 1 will result in 25 training examples for a 25 second capture for LS (*Legato* on a single string).

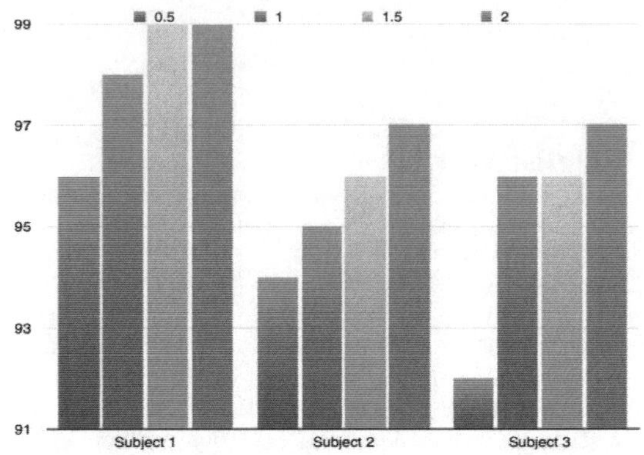

Figure 2: Impact of segment duration (*sd*) on accuracy (%).

3.4 Choice of Classifier

The choice of SVM with a normalised polynomial kernel was based on a systematic comparison of different classifier models using the Weka tool [10]. Table 2 summarises the evaluation results using 10-fold cross validation for an artificially shuffled dataset produced by randomly concatenating 1-second segments of individual bowing techniques. It was observed across all the artificially shuffled datasets using tuned versions of the classifiers, that SVM with a normalised polykernel was consistently the best performer.

Table 2: Comparison of performance for different classification methods

Classifier Model	*Accuracy*
NaiveBayes	93.75%
k-NN	93.75%
Decision Tree (J48)	90.83%
Logistic Regression	97.5%
MultiLayer Perceptron	98.33%
SVM with a Normalised PolyKernel	98.33%

3.5 Choice of Features

Six features were selected and their values calculated along the three axes using the sensor data from the two Orient specks, resulting in thirty-six (6 x 3 x 2) attributes. Given the variety of techniques including on-the-string and off-the-string bowing and those involving bow tilts, it was important to consider sensor data in all the three dimensions. The absolute values of the accelerometer and gyroscope readings were used as the bowing

[1] n is the number of segments and d is the number of attributes.

technique may be applied either in an Up-Bow ('Pushing' the bow so that its point of contact with the string moves from the tip towards the frog), or in a Down-Bow fashion (drawing the bow so that its point of contact with the string moves from the frog end towards the tip). The features were selected based on published sources on bowing techniques ([8][9][12]) and actual observations, and are listed below:

1. Average acceleration.
2. Variance in the acceleration.
3. Average smoothness of acceleration (mean of the first derivative of the accelerometer readings in a segment)
4. Average angular velocity (mean of the gyroscope readings in a segment).
5. Variance in angular velocity (variance in the gyroscope readings in a segment).
6. Average angular acceleration (mean of the first derivative of the gyroscope readings in a segment).

The utility of each feature was tested by plotting specific parts of the data, *e.g.*, variance in the acceleration was hypothesised to distinguish between *Legato* and *Martelé* as these techniques have different acceleration profiles due to their articulation. The scatter plot in Figure 3 shows the normalised values of variance in acceleration[2] plotted along the y-axis for segments of *Legato Single* (LS), *Legato Crossing* (LC), *Martelé Single* (MS) and *Martelé Crossing* (MC). The *Legato* segments have much lower values of variance, as it is a non-articulated and smoothly connected stroke, as opposed to *Martelé* which is characterised by its articulation.

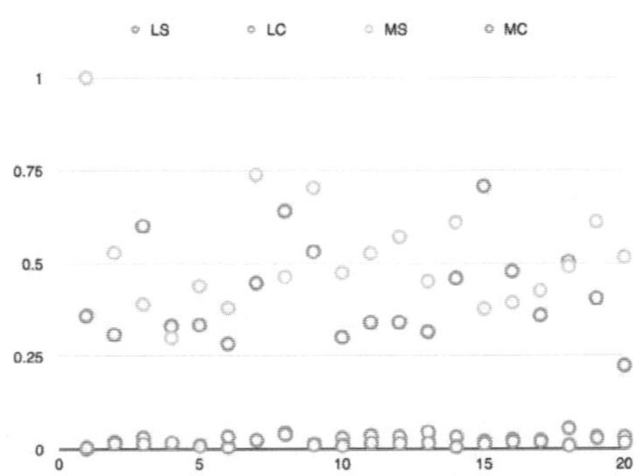

Figure 3: Plot showing normalised variance in acceleration ($m.s^{-2}$) along y-axis for *Legato* and *Martelé* segments.

Furthermore, a Voronoi tessellation[3] of the attribute space was induced by applying a 1-NN classifier model. The minimum classification accuracy on 10-fold cross validation was 90% which indicates that the data was indeed well separated in the attribute space. SVMAttributeEvaluation was used in Weka for understanding better the relative importance of the six features. Based on the results, one could infer that different features were useful for distinguishing between different types of bowing techniques and it was inconclusive in determining which one or two of these features had greater importance overall. Also, it was possible to choose a subset of attributes by not calculating some features along a specific axis without compromising on classification performance. However, such attribute selection techniques did not generalise well as an optimal subset of attributes in the case of one cellist was not necessarily the optimal one for the others.

4. RESULTS

4.1 Artificially Shuffled Datasets

We considered two "artificially shuffled" datasets for each of the three subjects: 'only single string variants' containing the 7 styles that were executed on a single string and 'full dataset' containing all of the 12 styles (Table 1). Each of these datasets had 36+1 attributes including the class label. The mode of evaluation was set to 10-fold cross validation in all cases as this is one of the most robust techniques to evaluate a classification algorithm. The two parameters of the Support Vector Machine with a Normalised PolyKernel, *viz.* the complexity parameter (c) and the order of the PolyKernel (e) were set for each dataset after performing a grid search and the pair (c,e) which resulted in the best classification performance was selected. Ties were resolved by taking the lower value in order to guard against overfitting the training data. A weighted average is reported of the Receiver Operating Characteristic (ROC) curve area across the classes in the dataset weighted by the number of instances in each class and gives the performance of a classifier without regard to class distribution or error costs [11]. The weighted average of the F-measure (the harmonic mean of recall and precision) is also reported across the classes weighed by the number of instances in each class – a high value of F-measure indicates high values of both recall and precision which are important measures of evaluating classification performance.

4.1.1 Only Single String Variants

Table 3: Classification performance on Single String Variants

Subject	*#Instances*	*Parameters*	*Accuracy*	*ROC Area*	*F-measure*
1	140	c = 2, e = 5	99.29%	0.99	0.993
2	166	c = 3, e = 7	98.19%	0.99	0.982
3	175	c = 1, e = 2	100%	1	1

[2] These were calculated using the accelerometer readings along Z-axis obtained from the Orient speck attached to the frog.

[3] This is a partition of space which associates a region $V(x_i)$ with each point x_i in such a way that all points in $V(X_i)$ are closer to x_i than any other point.

The distribution of the instances across the 7 classes (single string bowing techniques) for each subject were as follows[4]:

- Subject 1: 20 each from the 7 classes.
- Subject 2: LS – 17, MS – 24 and 25 each from the remaining 5 classes.
- Subject 3: 25 each from the 7 classes.

There was only one misclassification for Subject 1– a *staccato* was classified as a *martelé*. This can be explained as these two styles are quite similar: *staccato* is essentially a version of *martelé* executed with separation but with a less aggressive articulation [12]. In case of Subject 2, there were three errors - all of which were in distinguishing *staccato* and *legato* (2 *staccatos* were classified as *legato* and 1 *legato* was classified as a *staccato*). *Legato* and *staccato* are both on-the-string bowing techniques. However, the key difference is that the former is non-articulated whereas the latter is a well-articulated technique. Thus, in absence of the part of the articulation/non-articulation in the segment, it may be quite difficult to distinguish between these two styles. Finally, there were no errors observed for Subject 3. Overall, the classification performance as indicated by the three metrics (Accuracy, ROC Area and F-measure) was impressive and the small number of errors was explainable.

4.1.2 Full Dataset (both single and crossing string variants)

Table 4: Classification performance on Full Dataset

Subj.	*#Instances*	*Parameters*	*Accuracy*	*ROC Area*	*F-measure*
1	240	c = 3, e = 7	98.33%	0.99	0.983
2	281	c = 3, e = 7	95.02%	0.98	0.951
3	300	c = 4, e = 5	95.67%	0.95	0.992

The distribution of the instances across the 12 classes (single and crossing string bowing techniques) for each subject were as follows:

- Subject 1: 20 each from the 12 classes.
- Subject 2: LC – 18, LS – 17, MC – 22, MS – 24 and 25 each from the remaining 8 classes.
- Subject 3: 25 each from the 12 classes.

The results presented in Table 4 illustrates the fact that detecting string-crossings is challenging; however, there have been notable results. The errors for each subject have been summarised below:

- Subject 1: We observed 4 misclassifications in this case – a *staccato* crossing was classified as a *martelé* crossing; a *spiccato* crossing was classified as a *spiccato* single and the error is due to wrongly classifying a crossing; and the other two errors are inexplicable and perhaps caused by noise in the sensor data.
- Subject 2: There were fourteen errors, most of which (ten) are related to detecting string-crossings. Staccato and Spiccato share quite a few similarities especially in terms of articulation and this is likely to have been the cause for confusion. Explanation for the misclassification of the Staccatos as Legato was provided earlier in this section. Finally, the error in classifying a Spiccato Crossing as a Legato Crossing is inexplicable and may be attributed to the noise in the data.
- Subject 3: There were thirteen errors in this case mainly due to string-crossings. The other errors were in distinguishing between non-articulated (Legato) and articulated strokes (*Staccato* and *Martelé*). There was also 1 error in distinguishing between *Spiccato* and *Martelé* These two styles have similar forms of articulation giving rise to the confusion.

In summary, the string-crossings results in greater misclassifications and could possibly be due to the segmentation procedure. In the absence of the part of the act where the bow "crossed" strings in the segment, it would be virtually impossible to detect the crossing variants. Also, dealing with both these variants introduces more noise in the data which may also lead to a dip in the performance.

4.2 Improvised Playing

The SVM with a normalised PolyKernel was trained on the corresponding 'Artificially Shuffled' dataset for Subject 2 and Subject 3. The parameter setting used was the one that worked best in case of the corresponding 'Artificially Shuffled' dataset using a 10-fold CV approach. The "Improvised" dataset was loaded as the test set in Weka and had no class labels. The classifier output was obtained, and the prediction for each segment and the probability distribution among classes for that segment, were stored. Using the classifier output, "soft" predictions were made, *i.e.*, mark the segment with the class as predicted by the classifier; and, the second most likely class based on the probability distribution for that segment. A threshold t is set such that for each segment, a class label which has a probability $p > t$, is produced as an output. The threshold t is controlled in such a way that in most (or all) cases, only two predictions are allowed, *i.e.*, the actual prediction produced by the classifier and the second most likely class label based on the probability distribution for the segment which is obtained from the classifier output in Weka. The reason for making "soft" predictions is due to the inherent subjective nature of the domain, *i.e.*, the boundaries and definitions can often be fluid and the annotations rely on interpretation by musicians, which is subjective. The ground truth for assessing the accuracy on improvised pieces was obtained from the cellists themselves. A segmented version of the video of the improvised piece was provided to the cellist who was then asked to annotate each segment. The cellists were advised to mention both the techniques in case a combination was observed in a segment or if in any doubt about the exact bowing technique applied in the segment.

[4] Refer to Table 1.

Table 5: Performance on the Improvised Pieces for Subject 2

Piece	*#Segments*	*Accuracy*	*Accuracy (ignoring string-crossings)*
Constrained Improvised	154	85.71%	88.46%
Free Improvised	119	68.90%	78.15%

Table 6: Performance on the Improvised Pieces for Subject 3

Piece	*#Segments*	*Accuracy*	*Accuracy (ignoring string-crossings)*
Constrained Improvised	113	68.14%	80.53%
Free Improvised	125	68.00%	83.20%

Tables 5 and 6 show that majority of the errors were made in detecting string-crossings and the classification performance increases significantly on ignoring this by verifying that the main technique was classified correctly, *e.g.*, LS and LC are both *Legatos* and so LS and LC are treated as being the same. There were certain errors that were not observed in the artificially shuffled datasets such as detecting *Ricochet* and *Col legno.* These may be mitigated by using a larger training set to capture the fluidity and different varieties of the same technique. The other errors have either already been explained in the earlier subsection or were inexplicable, perhaps due to noise in the data. The results for Subjects 2 and 3 are summarised in Figure 4.

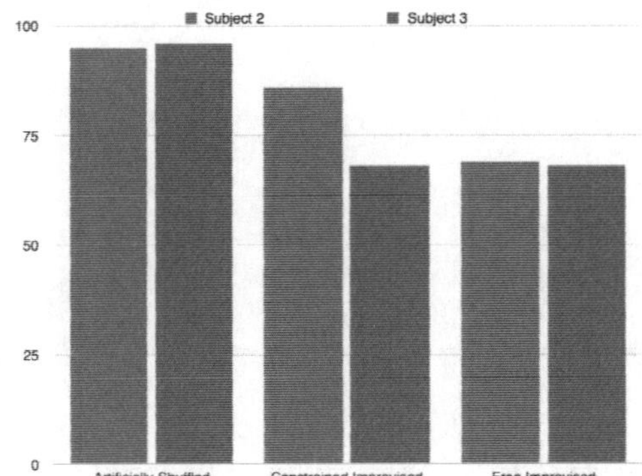

Figure 4: Classification accuracy (%) shown along the y-axis in the three distinct scenarios for Subjects 2 and 3.

5. DISCUSSION

The approach adopted in this paper is a minimalist one, identifying the lowest number of easy-to-use, wearable sensors which can be used to classify successfully twelve bowing styles. The classification based on SVM has for the first time been extended to classifying bowing styles in improvisational playing of the cello. The similarity between the results obtained in case of the expert (Subject 2) and those for the intermediate level cellist (Subject 3) validates to a limited extent the robustness of the method and indicates the generalisability of the approach. We also evaluated the performance on datasets obtained from the same cellist but in different scenarios such as playing with a different bow and in these cases as well, the results remained consistent.

The task of identification of bowing techniques is a challenging one because of the fluid nature of music in general. The differences between the individual bowing techniques may not be concrete and a certain degree of overlap is expected to be present among the various techniques. Therefore, methodologies designed to identify bowing techniques are expected to be plagued by limitations to varying degrees. The evaluation of such methods also poses a challenge because purely data-driven approaches are not terribly well suited as they fail to capture the subjective nature of musical evaluation. In light of this observation, we adjusted our evaluation procedure on the improvised pieces. One must realise that in such a domain, absolute precision, even if achievable, may not be desirable. Alternative measures of performance such as inter-annotator agreement may serve to assess the quality of such methods more accurately.

The main limitation of this work is the segmentation procedure. However, an automatic segmentation procedure would require accurate velocity readings along the axes. Bow strokes start and end at velocity zero crossings and not at acceleration zero crossings. Hence, it is not possible to segment accurately the bow strokes based on accelerometer readings alone. The approach of using the zero- crossings in accelerometer readings to segment the individual strokes has not been entirely successful. The large variety of bowing techniques considered in this work (both on-the-string and off-the-string bowing techniques) also poses a challenge for automatic segmentation, *e.g.*, *spiccato* (off-the-string) will not have velocity zero crossings along the same axis as *legato* (on the string). Hence, this approach would also have to be modified to account for such variability.

In conclusion, twelve bowing styles have been classified with above 95% accuracy for each of the three subjects despite adopting a minimalist approach. The results and its analysis in case of the improvised pieces also demonstrate the potential of this methodology especially for use in real world applications such as data-driven pedagogical approaches to support learning of stringed instruments.

Future work may involve developing an automated segmentation procedure, which would significantly improve the accuracy of this system based on our observations and conducting a deeper investigation on the generalisability of the approach to other stringed instruments using bowing. The advantages of this method may then fully be realised in applications such as interactive musical performances and on-the-fly musical compositions.

6. ACKNOWLEDGEMENT

We would like to thank cellists Nicola Baroni, Clea Friend and Oliver Perkins for their generous help during data collection and their musical knowledge in interpreting the results. This research was supported by a grant from the Centre for Speckled Computing (www.specknet.org), University of Edinburgh.

7. REFERENCES

[1] Chad Peiper, David Warden and Guy Garnett. 2003. "An Interface for Real-time Classification of Articulations Produced by Violin Bowing." In Proc. of 2003 International Conference on New Interfaces for Musical Expression (NIME03), Montreal, Canada, May 2003.

[2] Margaret Schedel and Rebecca Fiebrink. 2011. "A Demonstration of Bow Articulation Recognition with Wekinator and K-Bow". In Proc. of 2011 International Computer Music Conference (ICMC2011), July 31 – Aug 5, 2011, Huddersfield, England.

[3] Frederic Bevilacqua, Nicolas Rasamimanana, Emmanuel Flety, Serge Lemouton and Florence Baschet. 2006. "The augmented violin project: research, composition and performance report." In Proc. of 2006 International Conference on New Interfaces for Musical Expression (NIME06), Paris, France, June 2006.

[4] Diana Young. 2008. "Classification of Common Violin Bowing Techniques Using Gesture Data from a Playable Measurement System." In Proc. of 2008 International Conference on New Interfaces for Musical Expression (NIME08), Genvoa, Italy, June 2008.

[5] McMillen, K. A. 2008. "Stage-worthy sensor bows for stringed instruments." In Proc. Intl. Conf. on New Interfaces for Musical Expression (NIME08), Genvoa, Italy, June 2008.

[6] Fiebrink, R., Trueman, D., and Cook, P. R. 2009. "A meta-instrument for interactive, on-the-fly machine learning." In Proc. 2009 Intl. Conf. on New Interfaces for Musical Expression (NIME09), Pittsburg PA, USA, June 2009.

[7] Barbara G. Jackson Joel Berman and Kenneth Sarch. Dictionary of Bowing and Pizzicato terms. Tichenor Publishing, 1999.

[8] Louis Potter Jr. The Art of Cello Playing. Alfred Music, 1995.

[9] Robin Stowell. The Cambridge Companion to the Cello. Cambridge University Press, 1999.

[10] Mark Hall, Eibe Frank, Geoffrey Holmes, Bernhard Pfahringer, Peter Reutemann, Ian H. Witten (2009); The WEKA Data Mining Software: An Update; SIGKDD Explorations, Volume 11, Issue 1.

[11] Ian H. Witten, Eibe Frank and Mark A. Hall. "Data Mining: Practical Machine Learning Tools and Techniques". The Morgan Kaufmann Series in Data Management Systems. Third Edition, 2011.

[12] James Kjelland. "Orchestral Bowing: Style and Function". Alfred Publishing. 2004.

[13] A.D. Young, M. J. Ling, D. K. Arvind, ``Orient-2 - A Wireless Real-time Posture Tracking System using Local Orientation Estimation", 4th Int. Workshop on Embedded Networked Sensors, pp. 25 - 26 June, Cork, Ireland, July 2007, ACM.

mBeacon: Accurate, robust proximity detection with smart phones and smart watches using low frequency modulated magnetic fields

Gerald Pirkl
DFKI GmbH

Peter Hevesi
DFKI GmbH

Jingyuan Cheng
DFKI GmbH

Paul Lukowicz
DFKI GmbH, Technical
University of Kaiserslautern
Trippstadter Str. 122, 67663
Kaiserslautern, Germany
firstname.lastname@dfki.de

ABSTRACT

We describe a proximity detection method that leverages the internal magnetic field sensors in smart phones and smart watches to allow reliable, robust detection of proximity to predefined regions of interest within a 30-50cm radius. For marking the regions, low cost, unobtrusive, easily deployable magnetic field beacons have been implemented. We evaluate our system in 5 different use cases in semi-naturalistic lab experiments inspired by different application domains.

Categories and Subject Descriptors

I.5.4 [**PATTERN RECOGNITION**]: Signal processing systems; I.5.4 [**PATTERN RECOGNITION**]: Applications ; I.5.5 [**Implementation**]: Interactive systems

General Terms

Applications

Keywords

signal processing, static magnetic fields, smart watches, mobile phones, regions of interest ,magnetic field encoding,NFC

1. INTRODUCTION

Proximity is a key piece of information in ubiquitous computing applications. As a consequence much research has been devoted to gather this information (see related work below). In this paper we focus on the question how to detect the proximity of *a mobile consumer device such as a smart phone or a smart watch* to a predefined region of interest such as a certain table, part of a workspace, shelve in a cupboard or part of a clothes rack.

Current state of the art in proximity detection *with mobile consumer devices* are Bluetooth 4.0 (Bluetooth Low Energy) beacons (e.g. iBeacons). While the detailed accuracy of such systems depends on the specific setup and the environment, it is in general well above 1 m and thus unsuitable for higher precision applications such as distinguishing between neighboring desks or doors, detecting which shelve someone is reaching for, or tracing hand positions when browsing through a rack of clothes.

Motivated by such application scenarios, in this paper we describe a solution based on low frequency ($\simeq$ 10Hz) modulated magnetic fields with the following properties:

- It leverages the internal magnetic field sensors in smart phones and smart watches and performs all necessary processing on the device.
- It allows highly reliable, robust detection of proximity within a 30-50cm radius.
- The regions of interest can be marked using cheap, unobtrusive, easily deployable hardware.

Our approach is based on the insight that the limitations of state of art Bluetooth beacons based proximity detection systems can be traced to the physical principle behind radio frequency (RF) signals. By virtue of being electro-magnetic waves they are susceptible to reflections and refractions. In addition the 2.4GHz frequency band used by Bluetooth is strongly absorbed by the human body. By contrast, static magnetic fields are neither reflected nor refracted, and are hardly absorbed by human body. While massive metal objects can significantly disturb magnetic fields such disturbances are localized (essentially bending of field lines within the object) and have little effect on the signal further away (as opposed to reflections and refraction of RF signals). Using modulated rather than static fields allows us to deal with magnetic noise that is nearly always present in the environment. The above considerations are well known and have previously driven the development of different magnetic positioning and tracking systems mentioned in related work. The contribution of this paper is to show how to leverage them for proximity detection within the limitation of the magnetic field sensors typically found in smart phones and smart watches and practical considerations related to the generation of the field with easily deployable, low cost setups.

BODYNETS 2015, September 28-30, Sydney, Australia

DOI 10.4108/eai.28-9-2015.2261515

2. RELATED WORK

Our work is related to several research directions. First, is the general area of indoor localization [4], where however only systems that rely on the built-in sensors of a popular consumer wearable products like smart phone or a smart watch (which is a focus of this paper) are relevant. This includes WiFi based systems [17], Bluetooth beacons [19], and inertial navigation [10]. While much progress has been made in all of these technologies (including the fusion of all three above modalities [6]), reliable recognition of proximity within a range of 30 cm-50cm is still beyond the state of art. This is particularly true in dynamic environments where people and objects influence the RF signal propagation (while having less effect on static or ultra low frequency magnetic fields).

Second, there is a considerable amount of research on using magnetic fields for object tracking, positioning, and proximity detection. Again, vast majority of work to date is not applicable to smart watches and smart phones. This includes passive tag tracking as proposed e.g. by [12], a broad range of approaches based on standard passive RFID tags (which require a dedicated RFID reader) [2],[14], as well as various systems that use oscillating magnetic fields for positioning [16] or [15]. The latter use field frequencies in the range of kHz, which the sensors in smart phones cannot detect. For example in [9] a 125kHz oscillating magnetic field is used to detect proximities to given beacon emitters using magneto inductive coils. The Location-log system described in [18] is also based on 125kHz magnetic fields. The authors use a special purpose NFC hardware at 125kHz to measure the induced voltage in a receiver coil which is attached to the mobile phone. The external coil allows to measure magnetic fields with lower field strength values but requires more space and is not IC based and, therefore not as wide spread as electronic compass sensors which are basically in every smart phone. In order to retrieve information about objects persons currently interact with, a sensor modality attached to the hand or close to it is necessary. Gloves with integrated sensors (survey of this technology can be found for example in [5]) or skeleton models [11] allow to gather this information, the additional hardware typically reduces social acceptance of these approaches. Sensor integrated in watch-like devices as in Activity Trackers or Smart Watches are more and more common and therefore a good starting point.

In [13] the fields generated by power lines embedded in walls are used for proximity estimation with special purpose sensors.

Closest to our work are approaches that rely on ambient magnetic field strength distributions for indoor localization as presented in [7]. The authors use the magnetic compass sensor attached to a robot to generate a map of the ambient magnetic field. In contrast to our proposed system the authors use the ambient magnetic field and the magnetic field anomalies arose due to disturbances. The accuracy was around 30 cm. The authors of [3] also use the ambient magnetic field to achieve a localization accuracy below 1 m. Both approaches require elaborate fingerprinting and assume a static magnetic environment, which is a significant practical difference to our system.

On a technical level similar to our approach is the work by Jiang described in [8]. The authors use magnetic fields to transfer data between a computer and a mobile phone using the on-board compass sensor. The system covers data transfer in close range below 1 cm with a data rate of 44 bits per second. Similar range limitation applies to NFC technology included in many modern smart phones. By contrast, we consider proximity detection on the range of 50 cm.

3. SYSTEM DESIGN AND IMPLEMENTATION

Our system consists of three components: an RF based iBeacon for rough proximity detection to reduce the overall power consumption of the magnetic field coils, a magnetic field coil with attached driving hardware to modulate the id of the region of interest, and a mobile device (either smart watch or mobile phone equipped with a magnetic field sensor) sampling the environmental magnetic field to enable the demodulation of the id of the region of interest embedded in the artificial magnetic field.

3.1 Basic Principle

The basic idea behind our approach is to mark the relevant regions of interest with magnetic beacons that are modulated with a region specific ID-code. Whenever the user's phone or smart watch comes within a predefined range it receives and recognizes the code. The range is determined by the peak strength of the magnetic field $\mathbf{B}(d)$ and its strength drops as the distance to the coil drops.

The design space of our system is given by the limitations of the magnetic field sensors incorporated in mobile consumer devices such as smart phones and smart watches (e.g. compass sensor AKM AK8963). Typically, such sensors have a sampling rate of 10-20Hz and a measurement range between $\pm 1mT$ and $\pm 5mT$. The base signal that they continuously detect is the earth magnetic field ($30\mu T$ at the equator, $49\mu T$ in Europe).

To determine the sufficient number of windings, current and the shape of the magnetic field coil, we implemented a python script which allows to simulate the magnetic field behavior of the coil. The script supports 2 coil shapes, a circular shaped coil and a frame shaped coil. Using a finite element approach, the field fraction of the positions on the coils are calculated for a given position around the coil in 3d space. To accurately determine the id of a coil, the artificial magnetic field strength at any supported position around the coil should be at least as high as the natural magnetic field. The script is available at www.dfki.de/ei/mBeacon/script.py.

3.2 Hardware

From the above considerations the magnetic beacon utilizes a rectangular $40cm \times 30cm$ coil with 20 windings, which can be easily integrated in the environment. As magnetic fields permeate most materials, the coils can be hidden for example under a table, behind a cupboard or within a door frame. The coil is driven by a current limited power supply which is able to deliver a peak current of about 4A at 15V. Figure 2 depicts the field strength trajectory of a frame shaped coil with $40 \times 30cm$ area to which a current of I=4A is applied[1]. Using this approach also assures that the generated magnetic field is not overdriving the compass sensors.

The current is modulated by a simple relay (or an appropriate transistor) controlled by a micro-controller. In our experiments we use an off the shelf power supply (Grauppner 6458), a Songle SRD-05vdc relay and an Arduino micro-controller board. The total cost of the components as we bought them is 75 Euro. If implemented

[1] Due to the temperature rise, the resistance of the coil rises, the applied current drops from 3.6A to 3.3A depending on the used coil at a voltage of 15 V.

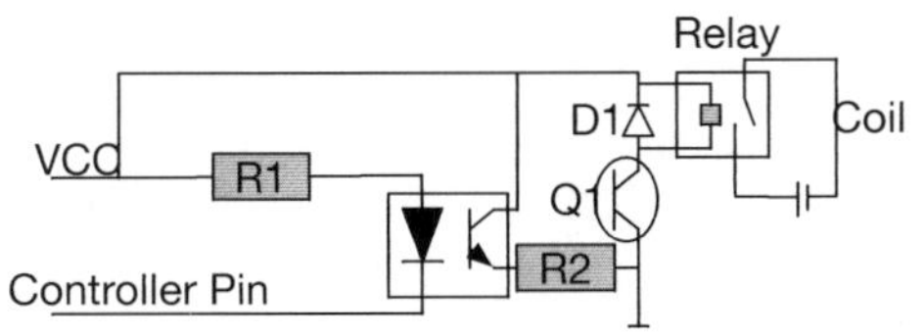

Figure 1: Schematics of the used coil driving circuit.

as a special purpose hardware this could easily be reduce to a range of 20-30 Euro. Note that although the peak power consumption is 60W, since the system is not transmitting the whole time, the average value is close to 20W. To further reduce the power consumption we use Bluetooth beacons to determine when the user is in the rough proximity and only then switch on the magnetic beacon.

3.3 Mobile Device Detection Method

The ID-Code is modulated in the magnetic field using pulse width modulation (PWM). Taking the sampling rate of compass sensors of smart watches and mobile phones into account, the minimum length of a magnetic field pulse should be around 150 ms. Notice that this interval also covers the transient oscillation of the coil. The modulated values are a multiple of the minimum pulse length ($l = n \times 150ms$).

The magnetic field strength is sampled using the on board Hall effect based compass sensors of mobile phones and smart watches. In our case these were the Nexus 5 and One Plus One mobile phones (compass sensor AKM AK8963) running under Android 5.0.1 and 4.4. Both phones supported a sampling rate of 17 Hz, for initial test the measurement vector $\mathbf{B}(x) = (m_x, m_y, m_z)$ was transfered to a computer using Wifi communication. The used smart watch was the LG Watch R with similar performance. For the experiments, the processing sequence (as described in figure 3) was implemented on the watch and the phones.

We transform the measurement vectors $\mathbf{B}_i$ into squared vector magnitudes , which automatically weights measurements with higher axis field strength (compared to the earth magnetic field vectors). The first order derivate of this parameter gives a good indication about the presence of artificial magnetic sources as the activation and deactivation process of the coil results in sharp edges. To suppress signal changes of the environmental magnetic field caused by movements, a median based sliding window is applied to the sensor values. A peak detector finds the exact time when the coil is turned on and off. After detecting when the artificial field is applied, we can use the direction change of the magnetic field vector to determine on which side of the coil the sensor is. Therefore we compute at first the median of the magnetic field vector on each axis during the artificial signal and also in the interval of 100 ms before the signal was applied. Then the difference of these two vectors is calculated. The sign of the largest component of the difference vector, defines the side of the coil. The entire detection runs on the mobile device.

4. EXPERIMENTS

We evaluated our system in 5 different use cases in semi-naturalistic lab experiments inspired by different application domains (Figure 5). The first two (Figure 5 B) and D)) are motivated by a task tracking scenario where the top level task is determined by the table region at

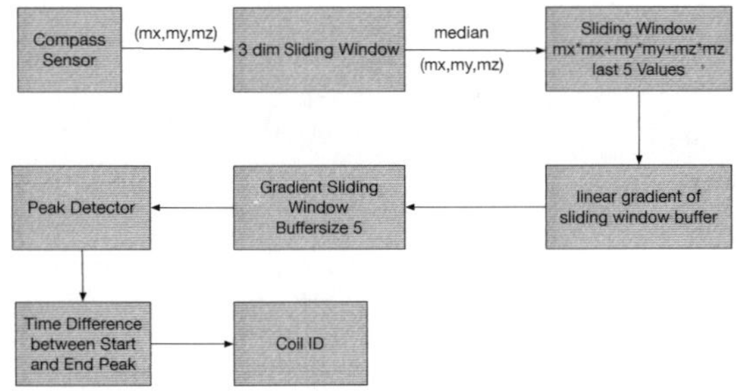

Figure 3: Processing sequence on the mobile device (smart watch or cellphone).

which a student is sitting while the individual steps involve interaction with devices placed at different regions on the table. The third use case (Figure 5 A)) is devoted to recognizing with a smart watch from which shelve of a cabinet an object is taken. It is relevant for a variety of applications, from task tracking through shopping to the recognition of various activities of daily life. Along the same lines the fourth use case (Figure 5 E)) deals with tracking user's hands when browsing through clothes hanging on a clothing rail. Finally the fifth use case ((Figure 5 C)) shows that with the magnetic beacon embedded in the door or the door frame we can detect which door the user is opening with a key, even if the doors are just next to each other.

4.1 Workbench Sitting Location

We attached 4 magnetic beacons below two workbenches (Figure 5 D)) to identify 4 different places next to each others where students can work or perform experiments. Each workbench has the dimension of 220 $cm \times 120$ cm. We split each workbench into two workplaces (each of size 110×120 cm). The experiment is motivated by a task tracking scenario where the top level task is determined by the table region at which a student is sitting. While the individual steps involve interaction with devices placed at different regions on the table. Notice that it is a typical hardware workplace which includes machines, metal tools, power supplies and a large anti-static work mat. These influence the AC magnetic field either by reflection, absorption or generate electromagnetic field by itself.

The experiments involved 5 student volunteers. Each subject was asked to sit down at one of the locations and perform a task of their choice for 10 seconds. This was repeated 15 times with a random selection from the four locations.

4.2 Interaction with Workbench Regions in a Soldering Task

The workbench (Figure 5 B)) has been equipped with 4 coils, each coil covering a specific object or region which is used in a soldering task. The subjects were asked to solder a surface mounted device (SMD) resistor to a printed circuit board (PCB). This involves 1) placing a PCB on the workbench at location 2, 2) finding a specific resistor in the resistor set placed at position 3, 3) reaching for the soldering iron and changing the tip from big tip to small tip at location 1, and 4) adjust the multimeter to check the resistor value and test if the two contacts are connected at location (taking place at location 4). Five students volunteers wearing a LG Watch R smart watch each performed the above tasks 5 times with no constraints except the above described positions. The activities/positions were

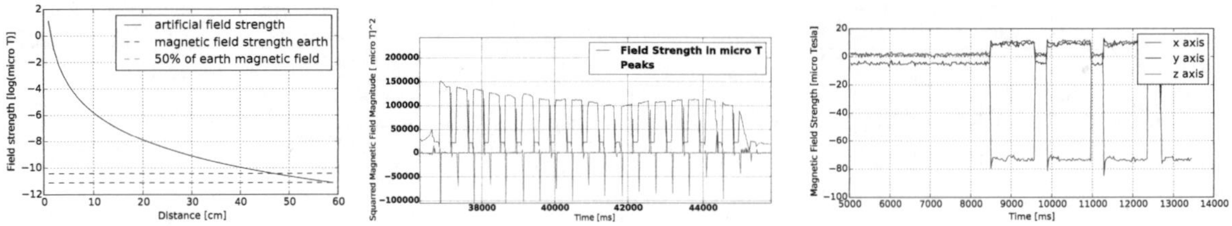

Figure 2: Left: Theoretical field strength trajectory along the norm vector of the coil plain perpendicular to the diagonal intersection with distance d to the plain. Notice the logarithmic scale. It also includes the level of the earth magnetic field strength in Europe. The intersection of earth field strength level and the trajectory is seen as maximum range. (Model values: N=20, a = 0.3m,b=0.4m, I = 5A, frame shaped coil); Middle: Squared magnetic field strength with modulated coil id. The green peaks indicate the edges of the artificial magnetic fields. Right: Superposition of earth magnetic field and artificial magnetic field measured with a mobile phone.

Id	Locations		Cabinet Shelves		Cloth Rail		Opening Doors		Work Bench, Soldering			
	FbF	Event	FbF	Event	FbF	Event	FbF	Event	FbF	Event	Events longer than 3 Seconds	missed Events
1	99.64	100	99.6	100	76.3	82.7	98.9	100	99.09	100	100	0 of 12
2	95.22	100	99.8	100	94.5	100	99.5	100	72.4	75	100	3 of 12
3	94.12	95.45	100	100	96.3	100			83.3	85	100	1 of 7
4	92.25	100	99.37	100	72.3	84.2			41.33	43	100	4 of 7

Table 1: Results of the different experiments. FbF - Frame by Frame. Notice that in the location experiment, there is one event in id 3 where a bluetooth burst disturbed the timing and therefore the length of the artificial magnetic field readings couldn't be correctly be determined.

labeled manually by an observer. For the recognition algorithm the wrist worn smart watch is of high importance as it retrieves the magnetic field information close to the hand. A drawback is that the hand typically moves fast from one location to the other and therefore either magnetic field information is missed or the magnitude trajectory is mutilated resulting in invalid information.

4.3 Taking Objects from Cabinet Shelves

A cabinet with 4 shelves (Figure 5 A)) was equipped with 4 magnetic beacons (one for each shelve). Initially we planed to equip the metal shelves of the cabinet but the magnetic field was misshaped and measurements were hardly possible. This scenario also shows the advantage of magnetic fields, it is possible to adjust the applied current so that the magnetic field of a single coil only covers the corresponding bookshelf and does not influence the neighboring compartments. We randomly chose the shelf number and 4 subjects wearing a LG Watch R smart watch were asked to reach for it. Each person reached 20 times for a randomly chosen shelf.

4.4 Cloth Rail

We attached two coils to a 120 cm cloth rail (Figure 5 E)) and thus segmented the rail into 4 sections (on the left end right sides of the coils). 11 winter jackets were distributed randomly between the 4 sections. 5 participants were then asked to browse through the jackets checking the price (attached in the inner side of the jacket). An observer manually annotated when which participant was browsing through which section of the rail.

4.5 Opening doors

In this scenario (Figure 5 C)) we attach two coils at two opposing doors that are 1.0 m apart. Within such a tight spacing, standard indoor location algorithms have very often problems in deciding in front of which door a person is standing. In the experiment one door is surrounded by a metal frame, the other door opens into a meeting room which is completely surrounded by metal frames (Resulting in anomalies of the natural environmental earth magnetic field). Two subjects were asked to open a door 20 times. In each instance the door is randomly chosen.

5. RESULTS, CONCLUSIONS AND FUTURE WORK

All of the experiments were evaluated on frame by frame and event basis. Frame by frame evaluation refers to every single cycle in which the mobile device tries to decode an ID. Event evaluation was based on the majority of IDs recognized within the window labeled as belonging to a certain location.

As it can be seen in table 1 with three exceptions the frame by frame results are well over 90% and the event based results are 100% correct. The first exception are the areas 2,3, and 4 of the workbench soldering experiment. The errors concern instances where the hand quickly reaches for an object without remaining in the area long enough for the ID to be correctly recognized. If we constrain the evaluation to events that are longer the 3 s then 100% are correct. The second exception are the first and last region in the clothes rail experiment. The errors occur when the user's hand is closer to the massive metal vertical tail than to the mBeacon. In those cases the ID is correctly recognized, however the algorithm for recognizing which side of the coil the hand is on fails and returns the wrong side. Further improvements in the orientation algorithm are needed to address this problem. The third exception is class 3 in the workbench sitting experiment. Here the error is due to timing problems resulting caused by the task manager on the phone, the magnetic sensor readout is randomly interrupted by the mobile phone scheduler resulting in missing sensor values.

In this paper, we have shown that inexpensive, unobtrusive magnetic beacons allow mobile consumer devices such as smart watches and smart phone to detect proximity to predefined regions of interest within a range that lies between Bluetooth beacons (in general more then 1 sm range) and standard NFC (a few centimeters). Key

Figure 4: Upper left picture: Transmitter coil attached and coiling frame to easily create a coil. Lower left picture: transmitter coil attached to metal door, right picture: Rack with 4 transmitter coils, the current of each coil has been tuned so that the magnetic fields do not influence each other.

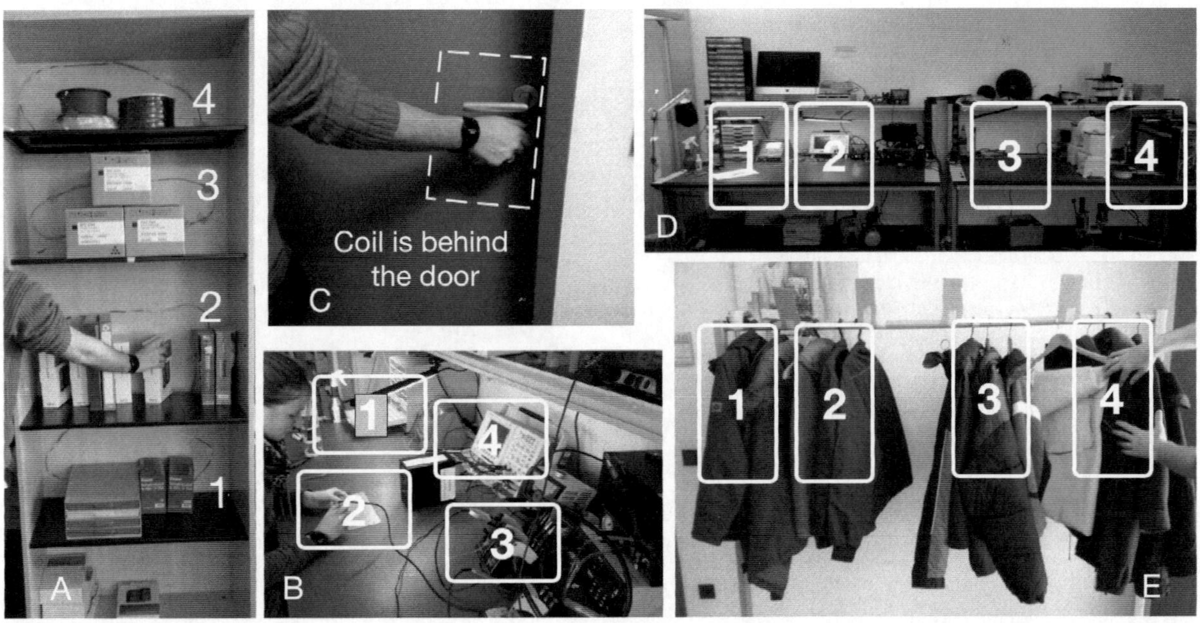

Figure 5: Different experimental setups. A) Picking equipment from different shelves B) A soldering task with different areas on the desk. C) Distinguishing between different doors. D) Estimating the position of a person at desks E) Finding a specific winter jacket at a cloth rail.

limitations are the temporal resolution and the power consumption of the beacons. Both are related to limits of the sampling frequency of the smart phone magnetic sensors (with higher temporal resolution shorter pulses are possible resulting in a lower power consumption). Future work needs to address intelligent power management of the mBeacons (e.g. synchronization with motion sensors of the mobile devices), more elaborate analysis of the orientation algorithms and investigation of more divers coil setups (e.g. using more windings to reduce the current).

6. HEALTH CONSIDERATIONS

As the system can be used in real world applications, we also consider the influence of the magnetic field on the environment. According to measurements with the mobile phone, the maximum field strength is 0.0012 T (1.2mT). The guidelines for electro magnetic fields (see [1] for details) limit the magnetic field strength to $800\mu T$ for a frequency of $7Hz$ (the duty cycle is 150 ms for a bit, therefore less than 7Hz is assumed for the field frequency) for general public exposure, occupational exposure is at $4081\mu T$. The magnetic field drops with $\frac{1}{d^3}$, therefore it is sufficient to place the coil in a box to prevent persons from touching the coil but still support magnetic field measurements. Figure 2 (right) depicts the influence of the generated artificial magnetic field of the transmitter coil at a distance of around 30 cm. The superposition results in a field strength of roughly $75\mu T$ which is in the safe field strength interval.

7. REFERENCES

[1] A. Ahlbom, U. Bergqvist, J. Bernhardt, J. Cesarini, M. Grandolfo, M. Hietanen, A. Mckinlay, M. Repacholi, D. Sliney, J. Stolwijk, et al. Guidelines for limiting exposure to time-varying electric, magnetic, and electromagnetic fields (up to 300 ghz). international commission on non-ionizing radiation protection. *Health Phys*, 74(4):494–522, 1998.

[2] M. Bouet and A. L. Dos Santos. Rfid tags: Positioning principles and localization techniques. In *Wireless Days, 2008. WD'08. 1st IFIP*, pages 1–5. IEEE, 2008.

[3] J. Chung, M. Donahoe, C. Schmandt, I.-J. Kim, P. Razavai, and M. Wiseman. Indoor location sensing using geo-magnetism. In *Proceedings of the 9th international conference on Mobile systems, applications, and services*, pages 141–154. ACM, 2011.

[4] G. Deak, K. Curran, and J. Condell. A survey of active and passive indoor localisation systems. *Computer Communications*, 35(16):1939–1954, 2012.

[5] L. Dipietro, A. M. Sabatini, and P. Dario. A survey of glove-based systems and their applications. *Systems, Man, and Cybernetics, Part C: Applications and Reviews, IEEE Transactions on*, 38(4):461–482, 2008.

[6] F. Evennou and F. Marx. Advanced integration of wifi and inertial navigation systems for indoor mobile positioning. *Eurasip journal on applied signal processing*, 2006:164–164, 2006.

[7] J. Haverinen and A. Kemppainen. Global indoor self-localization based on the ambient magnetic field. *Robotics and Autonomous Systems*, 57(10):1028–1035, 2009.

[8] W. Jiang, D. Ferreira, J. Ylioja, J. Goncalves, and V. Kostakos. Pulse: low bitrate wireless magnetic communication for smartphones. In *Proceedings of the 2014 ACM International Joint Conference on Pervasive and Ubiquitous Computing*, pages 261–265. ACM, 2014.

[9] X. Jiang, C.-J. M. Liang, K. Chen, B. Zhang, J. Hsu, J. Liu, B. Cao, and F. Zhao. Design and evaluation of a wireless magnetic-based proximity detection platform for indoor applications. In *Proceedings of the 11th international conference on Information Processing in Sensor Networks*, pages 221–232. ACM, 2012.

[10] F. Li, C. Zhao, G. Ding, J. Gong, C. Liu, and F. Zhao. A reliable and accurate indoor localization method using phone inertial sensors. In *Proceedings of the 2012 ACM Conference on Ubiquitous Computing*, pages 421–430. ACM, 2012.

[11] S. S. Mourkani, G. Bleser, N. Schmitz, and D. Stricker. A low-cost and light-weight motion tracking suit. In *IEEE International Conference on Ubiquitous Intelligence and Computing . International Conference on Ubiquitous Intelligence and Computing (UIC-2013), December 18-20, Vietri sul Mare, Italy*. o.A., 12 2013.

[12] J. A. Paradiso, K.-y. Hsiao, and A. Benbasat. Tangible music interfaces using passive magnetic tags. In *Proceedings of the 2001 conference on New interfaces for musical expression*, pages 1–4. National University of Singapore, 2001.

[13] S. N. Patel, K. N. Truong, and G. D. Abowd. Powerline positioning: A practical sub-room-level indoor location system for domestic use. In *UbiComp 2006: Ubiquitous Computing*, pages 441–458. Springer, 2006.

[14] D. J. Patterson, D. Fox, H. Kautz, and M. Philipose. Fine-grained activity recognition by aggregating abstract object usage. In *Wearable Computers, 2005. Proceedings. Ninth IEEE International Symposium on*, pages 44–51. IEEE, 2005.

[15] G. Pirkl and P. Lukowicz. Robust, low cost indoor positioning using magnetic resonant coupling. In *Proceedings of the 2012 ACM Conference on Ubiquitous Computing*, pages 431–440. ACM, 2012.

[16] E. A. Prigge and J. P. How. Signal architecture for a distributed magnetic local positioning system. *Sensors Journal, IEEE*, 4(6):864–873, 2004.

[17] P. R. Rao and P. L. Siccardo. Location determination using rf fingerprinting, July 31 2001. US Patent 6,269,246.

[18] B. Zhang, K. Chen, Y. Cheng, C.-J. M. Liang, X. Jiang, and F. Zhao. Location-log: bringing online shopping benefits to the physical world with magnetic-based proximity detection. 2012.

[19] X. Zhao, Z. Xiao, A. Markham, N. Trigoni, and Y. Ren. Does btle measure up against wifi? a comparison of indoor location performance. In *European Wireless 2014; 20th European Wireless Conference; Proceedings of*, pages 1–6. VDE, 2014.

Mauka-Mauka : Measuring and Predicting Opportunities for Webcam-based Heart Rate Sensing in Workplace Environment

Mridula Singh, Abhishek Kumar, Kuldeep Yadav, Himanshu Madhu, Tridib Mukherjee
Xerox Research Centre, India
{mridula.singh, abhishek.kumar2, kuldeep.r, himanshu.madhu2, tridib.mukherjee} @xerox.com

ABSTRACT

Prolonged sitting and physical inactivity at workplace often lead to various health risks such as diabetes, heart attack, cancer etc. Many organizations are investing in wellness programs to ensure the well-being of their employees. Generally wearable devices are used in such wellness programs to detect health problems of employees, but studies have shown that wearables do not result in sustained adoption. Heart rate measurement has emerged as an effective tool to detect various ailments such as anxiety, stress, cardiovascular diseases etc. There are pre-existing techniques that use webcam feed to sense heart rate subject to some experimental constraints like stillness of face, light illumination etc. In this paper, we show that in-situ opportunities can be found and predicted for webcam based heart rate sensing in the workplace environment by analyzing data from unobtrusive sensors in a pervasive manner.

Categories and Subject Descriptors

J.3 [**Computer Applications**]: Life and Medical Sciences—*Health*; I.4.9 [**Image Processing and Computer Vision**]: [Applications]; C.4 [**Performance of Systems**]: [Modeling techniques, Performance attributes]

Keywords

Webcam based Heart Rate Sensing, Pervasive and unobtrusive sensing, wellness programs, workplace environment

1. INTRODUCTION

People are spending increasing amount of time in workplace environments. With the evolution of computers, the number of desk jobs have increased phenomenally in the last few decades worldwide. In the United States, less than 20% of private sector jobs have moderate levels of physical activity, decreasing by nearly 30% compared to the early 60*s*. Nearly 4 out of 5 people have desk jobs in the United Kingdom [1]. Inactivity in workplace environment is becoming a high risk factor for health problems such as diabetes, heart attack and stroke, and increased mortality, among others [2, 3]. These health problems need to be detected early and prescriptive messaging is required to be put in place for affected employees.

Organizations are investing in wellness programs to improve social, mental, and physical health of their employees. These programs aim to improve quality of life, reduce the medical expenditure, and improve the productivity of the employees [4, 5]. Currently, wellness programs have started incorporating emerging wearable devices such as Fitbit, Nike+ FuelBand, Jawbone UP, etc for activity and physiological sensing in workplaces. It is estimated that more than 13 million wearable devices will be part of employee wellness programs by 2018 [5]. Wellness program use these devices to sense physical activity, sleeping patterns, heart rate, etc and afterwards, employees are encouraged to be more active in their day-to-day life by generating personalized recommendations/prescriptions, gamification, and various incentives programs. However, many recent studies have shown that wearable devices do not result in sustained adoption and many people stop using them after sometime. For example, a study in US shows that more than half of those who have bought a wearable device stopped using it [6]. Some of the known problems with wearable devices are that they are obtrusive and users often forget to wear them. Therefore, there is a need of non-obtrusive and pervasive sensing techniques which can drive sustained adoption in modern workplace environment. We envision that these pervasive sensing techniques can prove to be a low-cost alternative to wearable devices or they could be complementary to existing solutions and there by increasing sensing coverage.

Recently, there have been some research efforts to develop non-invasive and non-obtrusive sensing techniques using opportunistic use of computing devices and peripherals used as part of day-to-day life [7]. Among these techniques, webcam has been used to estimate the heart rate of a person, which is an important vital parameter to detect various ailments such as anxiety, stress, cardio-vascular disease, etc. The key idea behind webcam-based heart rate sensing involves tracking tiny changes in color of the face due to blood flow through the vessels and subsequently, estimating the heart rate of a person [8, 9]. Similarly, there have been advancements to

BODYNETS 2015, September 28-30, Sydney, Australia

DOI 10.4108/eai.28-9-2015.2261492

track respiratory rate too using video feed captured using webcam.

Due to easy availability of webcam equipped personal computing devices in workplaces, heart rate sensing could be very effective in early detection of various ailments . Though, there have been advancements in building mathematical and physiological models to increase the accuracy of heart rate sensing from webcam-based video feed [10]. There are some practical challenges associated with webcam-based heart rate sensing approaches i.e. they require face region to be detected, does not work in presence of motion, and require sufficient light/illumination on the facial region. Also, there is little known about their applicability in typical workplace environment i.e. how many opportunities exist in day-to-day life of an employee where heart rate tracking is feasible. In essence, there can be three different sensing approaches to perform regular heart rate measurements in workplace environment.

1. **Always-on Sensing:** In this approach, webcam is always ON and continuously recording the user. In the continuous video feed, sessions with minimal motion w.r.t. facial region are detected and further processed to estimate heart rate.
2. **Manually-triggered Sensing:** It prompts user once in a while to switch on the webcam and directs her to be static for some time to estimate the heart rate.
3. **Opportunity-based Sensing:** This approach tries to identify/predict the time intervals where user is likely to have limited motion w.r.t. facial region and trigger webcam to record a video feed. This video feed is processed to estimate the heart rate.

Among different approaches described above, 1 & 2 are obtrusive because they may change the user behavior and could be intrusive in her day-to-day activities. For example, a continuous-recording webcam could make users conscious where as a notification sent to manually trigger the webcam recording could create interruption for the user. There is a requirement of *pervasive* and *non-obtrusive* system that can identify/predict sensing opportunities and subsequently, automatically record the video feed to estimate heart rate in workplace environments.

To study the feasibility, we recruited 16 participants from a corporate organization. We deployed a system to perform continuous webcam-based video recording and subsequent sensing of heart rate for nearly a week across all the participants. An external off-the-shelf webcam was mounted on their laptop and participants were asked to go about their normal work. We logged their system usage history (i.e. applications, number of keys pressed, number of mouse clicks) along with heart rate measurements. Our user study was guided with following research questions:

1. How many in-situ opportunities of webcam-based heart rate sensing exist in a typical workplace environment where measurement can be performed automatically without involving the participants?
2. Do these sensing opportunities vary across different participants? What is the impact of motion and illumination on heart rate sensing?
3. Is there any correlation of these sensing opportunities with the system usage logs? Can these opportunities be predicted in advance using system usage patterns?

Contributions of the Paper: This paper answers above research questions using the data collected by a user study. Our findings suggest that nearly 120 in-situ opportunities per hour per user for webcam-based heart rate sensing exists in workplace environment. We characterized the number of sensing opportunities w.r.t. motion and found that whenever, there is limited motion, the number of opportunities are much higher at 86% compared to 50% while not considering motion. These opportunities can be predicted with the help of alternate unobtrusive sensing mechanism such as mouse, keyboard, system usage etc with an accuracy of 81%.

2. RELATED WORK

We characterize the related work in three directions i.e. invasive sensing, non-invasive but obtrusive sensing, and pervasive sensing. A similar characterization is also presented in taxonomy of wearable devices on the basis of deployment of sensors on the human body [11]. Observe that term *invasive* in the context of this paper refers to sensors, which need to be in physical contact of human body, while obtrusive is used to describe the discomfort or intrusiveness associated with the sensing techniques.

2.1 Invasive Sensing

Invasive sensing techniques use sensors that touch the skin, penetrate, or implanted inside to collect physiological measurements. A typical medical ECG equipment is an example of invasive sensing [12]. These sensing techniques are highly accurate at the same time highly obtrusive for the subject being monitored. It utilizes external devices for sensing vital parameters such as heart rate. It is not feasible to use these senors to monitor physiological parameters in day-to-day life.

2.2 Non-invasive but Obtrusive Sensing

Non-invasive sensing can be performed with sensors that may or may not be in physical contact with the body [13]. Commercial wearable devices like Fitbit, Nike+ FuelBand, Moto360, Samsung Gear are examples of non-invasive wearable sensors with physical contact. These approaches require use of an extra device for heart rate and activity monitoring, which is considered to be an overhead by many people because they are not habitual to wear them. Also, these devices are obtrusive and many people stop wearing them after sometime resulting in high drop-out rates [6].

Similarly, there are many smartphone based non-invasive techniques which are dependent on the users to initiate the heart sensing by placing their fingertip onto the camera with in-built LED (flash) switched on to detect photoplethysmograph signal from the fingertip and thereby sense the heart rate [14, 15, 16]. This methodology is an example of non-invasive sensing with physical contact, and the user has to explicitly place his finger tip on to the camera making it obtrusive. Other video-recording based heart rate sensing techniques described in [8, 9] can be classified in the category of contact-less and non-invasive sensing methods. Although, in these techniques the heart rate is sensed by capturing the users' face remotely, still it requires the user to launch the application explicitly and place the camera accurately to capture static face, again making it obtrusive for the user. Our goal in this paper is to spell out the feasibility of a non-obtrusive system to sense heart rate with little/no intervention from user.

2.3 Pervasive Sensing

These approaches include the sensing methodologies that uses existing sensors in daily use computing systems (i.e keyboard, mouse, webcam), mobile devices (acclerometers, location, camera), and objects of daily use (chair, drinkware, etc) to sense physiological signals such as heart rate. These sensing approaches are non-invasive as well as non-obtrusive because they do not require any user intervention. For instance, authors in [7, 17, 18] describes mechanisms to detect stress using non-obtrusive sensors such as keyboard and mouse. Even though, there is a direct contact with human body in aforementioned approaches, this interaction is not forced on the user compared to others described in section 2.2. However, these approaches are limited to sensing stress only whereas heart rate sensing is an important vital parameter to detect other health risks such as cardiovascular diseases too.

Recently, there have been new developments where pervasive devices or objects are augmented with extra hardware to measure physiological attributes un-obtrusively. For instance, authors in [19] proposed an mobile electrocardiogram (ECG) monitoring system that monitors the users' *ECG* opportunistically during the use of sensor-augmented smartphone. Erin et al [20] instrumented a general sitting chair with the conductive fabric on the armrests to sense heart rate and pressure sensors on the back of the chair to sense respiratory rate. In controlled-trails, instrumented chair was able to determine heart rate nearly 32% of the time and respiratory rate at nearly 52% of the time. Similarly, authors in [21] uses the surface of a drinkware to monitor the heart rate of a person and Ravicharan et al [22] uses WiFi signals with a set of dedicated transmitter and receiver to estimate breathing rate.

As described above, most of previous research in vital parameter sensing using pervasive technologies requires augmenting objects of every-day use, which is not scalable as well as is cost expensive. Our paper tries to explore feasibility of a *pervasive* and *contact-less* webcam-based heart rate sensing mechanism in day-to-day environment without any user intervention/attention.

3. PRELIMINARIES: HEART RATE ESTIMATION USING WEBCAM-BASED VIDEO FEED

As discussed in earlier sections, there have been existing research work which has focused on building techniques to improve the heart rate measurements by minimizing impact of motion artifacts and improving the accuracy to the level

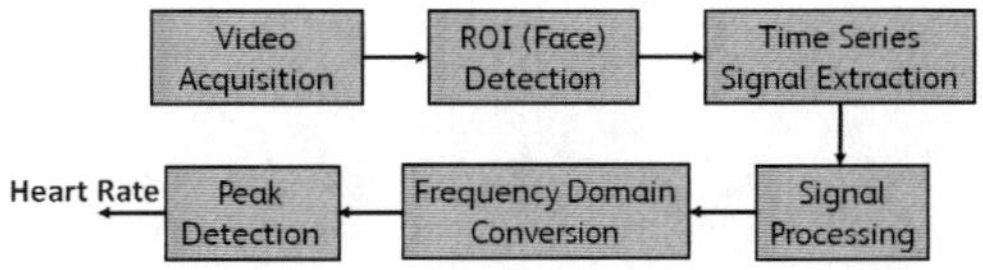

Figure 1: Process diagram depicting different steps of extraction of heart rate using the webcam feed.

of wearable physiological sensors [23, 8]. However, the focus of this paper is not on improving existing heart rate measurement techniques, rather it aims to discover and predict existing opportunities of heart rate sensing in day-to-day life. This section provides a brief introduction of the underlying approach to extract heart rate from a video feed captured using webcam [23].

Figure 1 presents a block diagram which highlights the different steps involved in extraction of heart rate using a webcam-based video feed. In the first step, webcam-based video feed is captured and automatic face tracker based on Viola-Jones face detection algorithm is used to detect the region of interest (ROI) for subsequent frames. The resultant ROI pixels are spatially averaged to create time-series signals for a batch. Batches are created by sliding a window of 15 seconds in which 1 second of frames from previous batch is replaced to provide heart rate values every second. The batch size of 15 seconds is the adopted length for most of the medical instruments. At the end of each batch, the face tracker is used to detect whether the face of the subject is still or not present in the video feed. The extracted time series signal of a batch is then subjected to series of signal preprocessing steps which includes de-trending the signal to remove low frequency components; bandpass filtering in a specified frequency range to retain the cardiac frequencies; and normalizing the signal. The pre-processed signal is then converted to frequency domain using FFT and a power spectral density (PSD) curve is obtained, which is similar to one shown in Figure 2. The peak frequencies in the PSD curve gives the estimated heart rate value. SNR (Signal to Noise ratio) as shown in Equation 1 of the signal is calculated for finding the accuracy of heart rate value calculated by this extraction process.

$$SNR = \frac{\text{The power of the region around highest point}}{\text{The Power of entire signal}} \tag{1}$$

The approach for heart rate extraction as explained above give heart rate of user and SNR to validate the heart rate but it does not validate the feasibility of webcam based heart rate sensing in workplace environment.

4. USER STUDY

The user study is focused on assessing the feasibility and effectiveness of webcam-based heart rate sensing in the workplace environment. Firstly, we provide some statistics to show that opportunity of heart rate sensing exists, when we record video continuously, i.e. user is detected still in some instances in front of camera. Then we show that

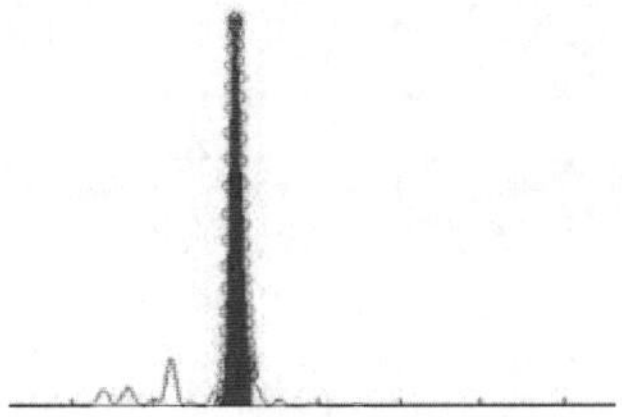

Figure 2: Power Spectral Density (PSD) of video feed, the peak frequencies in the curve gives the estimated heart rate value and noise around signal is used to calculate SNR.

information-rich data for the heart rate detection can be predicted in advance. By information-rich data, we mean the video in which user is present and is still with high probability.

4.1 Data Collection Setup

We designed our data collection application for training as well as validating our system. It collects continuous video feed with the system usage logs. The continuous video feed is captured with the help of an external off-the-shelf Logitech webcam, which records at 30 fps with a resolution of 1600X1200. We used an external webcam to bring uniformity in the video data collection and to minimize any biases occurring due to heterogeneous hardware. Further, the application collects system usage logs, including activity on keyboard/mouse and the foreground application information. The system usage logs are sampled cumulatively at an interval of 10 seconds [1].

The data collection application is developed in Microsoft.NET framework and runs as a background service in Windows OS based desktops/laptops. The video feed is saved every half an hour in AVI format where system usage logs are captured in JSON object format as shown in sensing module.

For data collection, we recruited 16 users (Female: 5, Male: 11) from a corporate organization through email asking for voluntary participation. The average age of female participants was 25 years (SD: 3.5) whereas it was 24 years for male participants. The only criteria used for the selection was possession of a Windows machine. The participants were not paid anything in return for their efforts and were given a choice to opt-out from the study or temporarily stop the data collection service anytime.

The participants were told that goal of this study was to collect facial videos and usage logs to better understand their behavior with the computer. All the participants signed an informed consent before participating in the study. The participants were instructed to carry out their usual work without getting disturbed from the mounted webcam device. We distributed external webcam devices to all the participants and asked them to mount it on their laptop in office hours for a duration of one week. All the participants had their own sitting space and there were no changes made to lighting conditions or sitting pattern. The data collection service was installed in their laptop and system usage logs and videos were collected manually due to their large size. Figure 3 shows picture of our data collection setup, when the webcam was mounted on a laptop. For participants who use external monitor, a webcam was mounted on their monitors to capture the frontal face. The data collection application was configured to run in office working hours only, i.e. 9:00 AM -6:00 PM.

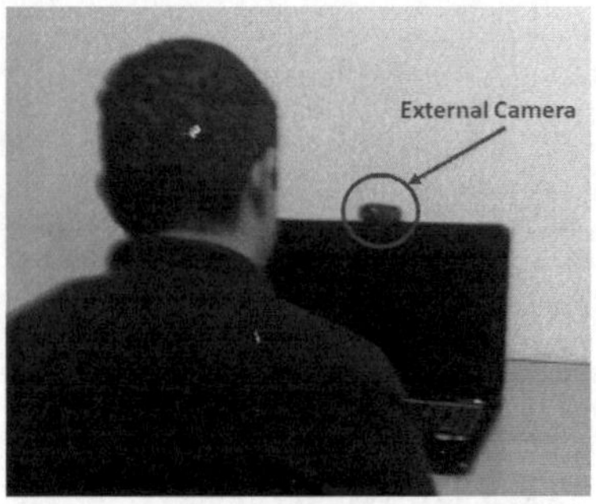

Figure 3: Setup for data collection, depicting that an external webcam is mounted on laptop to collect video feeds when user is working.

The user study ran for a week and in total, we were able to collect about 168 hours of data from all the participants. On an average, participants contributed 10 hours (SD: 6.0) of data with a minimum of 2 hours and maximum of 23 hours of data. The size of data collected was more than 200 GB. Few participants contributed very less data due to reasons such as frequent movement to meeting rooms, forgetting to switch on the data collection service after stopping it temporarily, etc. Data is filtered out from our evaluation if multiple faces are detected by the face detection algorithm or no face is detected in the video.

4.2 Analysis of Opportunity Sensing

The validity factor of the heart rate as discussed in Section 3 is SNR above some threshold and presence of single face. In our analysis we have fixed SNR threshold to 0.6. The part of the video which satisfies these constraints, we call it information-rich data. This data is information rich as it has high SNR, which show that heart rate calculated is valid and presence of the face show that the user is present in front of the webcam.

Data is split into two categories, i.e. when the user is detected still or in motion. The user is considered still if less or no motion is detected in video and in motion otherwise. In the overall data collection, the 64% of data belongs to still category. User specific distribution of data in these categories is shown in Figure 5.

To verify our hypothesis that heart rate validity is dependent on user's motion we calculated distribution of valid heart rate while the user is static and in motion. The results prove this hypothesis, showing that 86% of still data has SNR value above threshold. The user specific distribution

[1]It is a configurable parameter and can be tuned according to application requirements

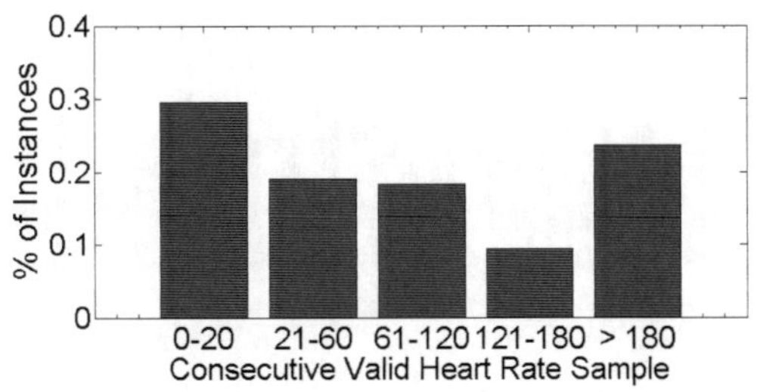

Figure 4: Distribution of consecutive valid heart rate samples. The distribution shows that 70% of data have more than 20 consecutive valid heart rate values.

5

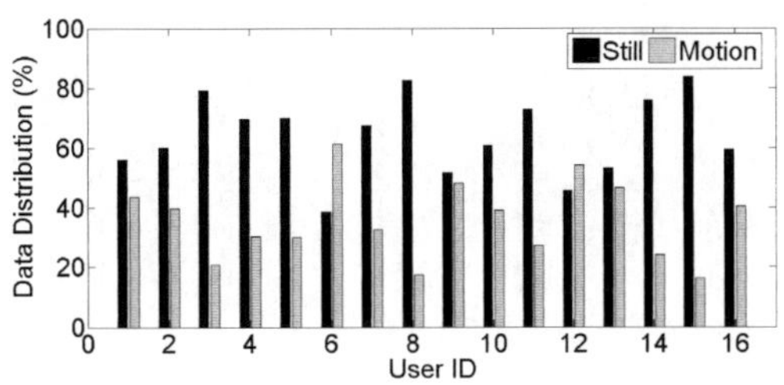

Figure 5: The distribution of the amount of time the user is still or in motion while recording video feeds.

of valid heart rate given user is still or without considering motion is presented in Figure 6 which shows that, the 55% of data collected is information rich.If we consider that window of 15 seconds as an indicator of valid heart rate value, the approach is detecting valid heart rate 30-175 times per hour per user. On an average, we could detect heart rate 120 times per hour, which shows that opportunity for extracting heart rate using webcam based approach exists. The consecutive values of SNR and motion give high confidence and validate heart rate value. The distribution of consecutive instances with valid heart rate is shown in Figure 4.

4.3 User Survey

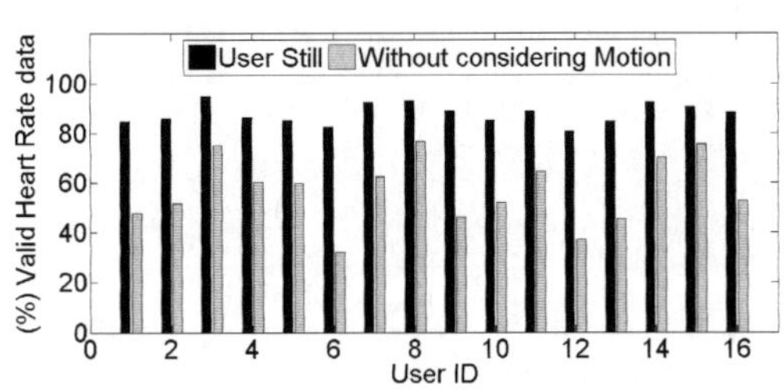

Figure 6: The data distribution when the SNR is above threshold given user is still or without considering the motion.

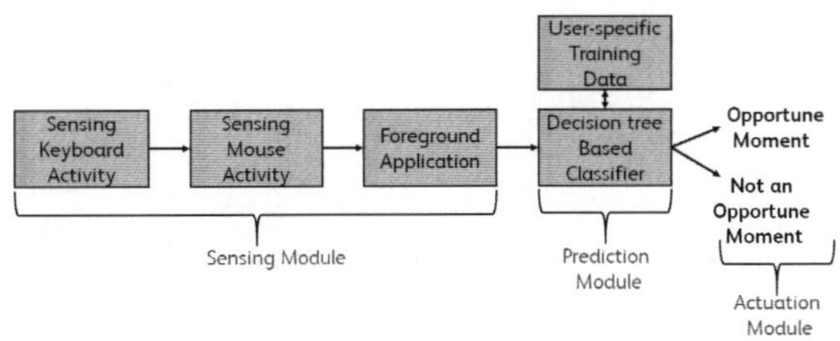

Figure 7: Flow diagram of the system depicting key components.

To further evaluate the feasibility of using our opportunistic heart rate prediction system and to validate our assumption of sustainable adoption of such a system, we conducted a small survey among the participants. We asked them their preference for using the three types of systems as described in Section 1 namely the Always-on Sensing, Manually triggered sensing and Opportunity-based sensing. The users were made to mark their preference for each of the three categories of system on a Likert scale of 1 to 5, 1 being the least preference and 5 being the most preferred. The average preference recorded for Always on sensing was 2.3 while it was 1.9 for Manual-triggered sensing. The opportunity-based sensing came out as the most preferred mechanism with an average score of 4.

5. SYSTEM FOR OPPORTUNITY PREDICTION

The focus here is to provide information-rich video as an input to the heart rate extraction algorithm. The key component of the system is sensing, classifying and actuation of webcam for video recording. The sensing and prediction module will justify the fact that the system uses unobtrusive sensors in a pervasive manner. The recorded video is used to extract heart rate information. The Figure 7 presents a flow diagram of key components of the system.

5.0.1 Sensing Module

In this module, a program running on the user's laptop/desktop collects usage statistics in a given time interval (say 10 seconds). It includes activity on keyboard, activity on the mouse, and name of the foreground application. Specifically, for the keyboard, it logs whether the user has been active on the keyboard (0/1) as well the number of keys pressed in the past 10 seconds. Similarly, user's activity on the mouse is tracked with a number of left and right clicks pressed during 10 seconds. The system program keeps track of the foreground application being run by the user. A snapshot of a JSON object generated by sensing module is presented in Figure 8. The collection of this data is both pervasive as well as unobtrusive as the data comes from sources (keyboard, mouse applications) which are implicitly present in workplace environments.

5.0.2 Iterative Classification and Prediction Module

The intent of this module is to predict the still moments, so that information-rich data can be collected for heart rate extraction. The usage logs (mouse/key characteristics, active

```
{
  "user": "[redacted]",
  "activeOnMouse": 1,
  "noOfMouseClicks": 5,
  "activeOnKeyboard": 0,
  "noOfKeyEvents": 0,
  "openApplicationTitle": "Google Chrome",
  "timestamp": "2015-02-19 11:57:20"
}
```


Figure 8: The data sensed from the unobtrusive sensors in a pervasive manner to associate with heart rate validity.

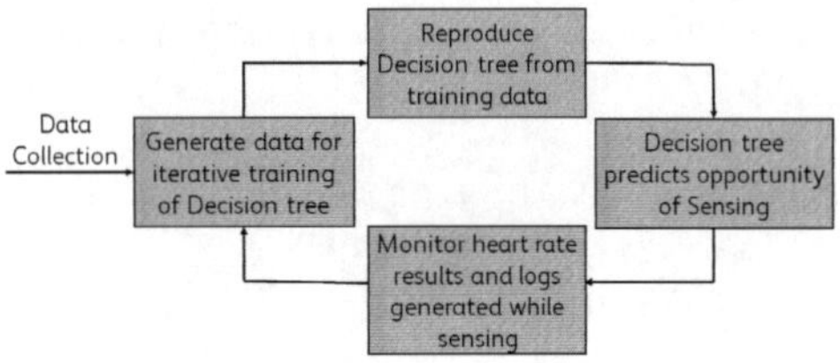

Figure 9: Classification module showing the iterative training of decision tree using data collected in prediction phase.

foreground application) generated in sensing module and validity of heart rate value in a given instance is input to prediction module. The data sensed in given 10-20 seconds is used to predict stillness of user in consecutive 10-20 seconds. Training data for the classification is generated by mapping usage logs of each 10-20 seconds with the opportunity of sensing in a near future of 10-20 seconds. Supervised binary classifier is used to generate predictive models (decision tree). This model is applied on usage logs to predict opportunity of heart rate sensing.

To improve the sensitivity of the system, the predictive model is trained iteratively. The iterative training generates more rules to take care of a new type of application or changed user behavior. The steps mentioned in Figure 9 show the process of generating predictive model iteratively by using newly collected data.

5.0.3 Opportunity prediction

The focus here is to predict the opportunity of heart rate sensing using unobtrusive sensors. We have used J48 classifier using WEKA [24], which is implementation of C4.5 decision tree algorithm. 10 fold cross validation is used to find and evaluate our model. Sensing and prediction intervals are varied to see feasible sensing and predicting interval. For instance in 10-20 scheme, 10 represents sensing time, using data of these 10 seconds decision tree predicts the opportunity to switch on the webcam in the next 20 seconds to record and calculate heart rate. On an average, proposed system was able to predict an opportunity correctly in nearly 81% of instances where sensing interval of 10 seconds was used and nearly 79% of the time whenever the sensing interval of 20 seconds was used. Sensitivity of the system on average to predict opportunity is 86% and 79% for the sensing interval of 10 and 20 respectively. Each user has different decision tree according to usage patterns and thus different sensitivity as shown in Figure 10.

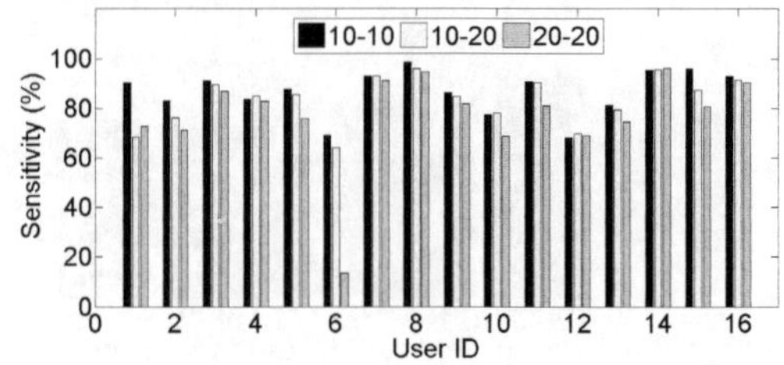

Figure 10: Sensitivity across all participants with different variants. First number (i.e. 10) means the period of sensing data (in seconds) used for prediction whereas the next number (i.e. 10) means the prediction period.

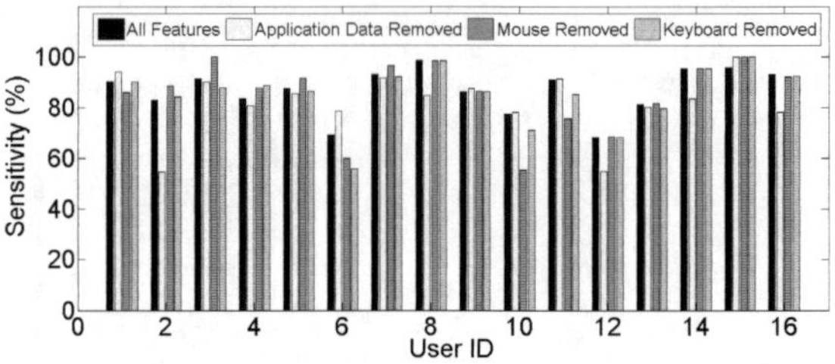

Figure 11: Sensitivity across all participants on removing a feature. Only one feature is removed at a time. The significance of each feature is different for each user

It is important to train a decision tree for each user independently as each user has a different pattern of using a keyboard and mouse and even the applications vary with users. If we train Decision tree with the data of $n-1$ users in our user set and try to apply it on n^{th} user, the accuracy on average degrades to 44% and prediction for all users is penalized. With the proper system deployment this is helpful, as data for each each user is independent, the decision tree can be trained on user machine and privacy of the user can be preserved as the user specific data remains local only.

All features, i.e. keyboard, mouse and foreground applications are equally essential for the prediction. For all users the decision tree model may or may not have all features. But Figure 11 shows that each feature contribute to the study of one user or another

We segregated the applications used by users into 4 major categories i.e. coding (Eclipse, Visual Studio etc.), Document (Word, Notepad, Excel, etc.), PDF (Adobe, Foxit etc.), Internet (IE, Chrome etc.). Correlating this data, we found that some people are still while coding while others are still during Internet surfing. Similarly, each user has a different style of using a keyboard/mouse. And the way they interact with any application can be used to determine its usefulness for predicting.

6. CONCLUSION

In this paper, we gave a proof-of-concept of a system which can predict in-situ opportunities for webcam based heart rate sensing in the workplace environment by analyzing unobtrusive sensors in a pervasive manner. We did a user study with 16 participants for a week to capture and analyze their video feed (while working) and found out that on an average we can detect heart rate 120 times per hour per user. Also, we correlated the heart-rate sensing interval with the usage patterns and predicted the opportunity of webcam based heart rate sensing with accuracy of 81%

7. REFERENCES

[1] Having desk job doubles risk of heart attack, http://www.nhs.uk/news/2012/10October/Pages/Having-desk-job-doubles-risk-of-heart-attack.aspxs

[2] Staiano AE1, Harrington DM, Barreira TV, Katzmarzyk PT., Sitting time and cardiometabolic risk in US adults: associations by sex, race, socioeconomic status and activity level, British Journal of Sports Medicine http://www.ncbi.nlm.nih.gov/pubmed/23981954

[3] Chau, Josephine Y., Anne Grunseit, Kristian Midthjell, Jostein Holmen, Turid L. Holmen, Adrian E. Bauman, and Hidde P. van der Ploeg. "Cross-sectional associations of total sitting and leisure screen time with cardiometabolic risk in adults. Results from the HUNT Study, Norway." Journal of Science and Medicine in Sport 17, no. 1 (2014): 78-84.

[4] Employee Wellness Program, https://hbr.org/2010/12/whats-the-hard-return-on-employee-wellness-programs

[5] Wellness program and wearable devices, https://www.abiresearch.com/press/corporate-wellness-is-a-13-million-unit-wearable-w

[6] Wearables and Science of Human Behavior Change, https://fortunedotcom.files.wordpress.com/2014/04/wearables-and-the-science-of-human-behavior-change-ep4.pdf

[7] Paredes, Pablo, David Sun, and John Canny. "Sensor-less sensing for affective computing and stress management technology." In Pervasive Computing Technologies for Healthcare (PervasiveHealth), 2013 7th International Conference on, IEEE, 2013.

[8] Poh, Ming-Zher, Daniel J. McDuff, and Rosalind W. Picard. "Non-contact, automated cardiac pulse measurements using video imaging and blind source separation." Optics express 18, no. 10 (2010).

[9] Measuring Heart and Respiratory Rate. http://www.techhive.com/article/244211/app_uses_your_webcam_to_detect_your_heart_and_breathing_rates.html

[10] Wei, Lan, Yonghong Tian, Yaowei Wang, Touradj Ebrahimi, and Tiejun Huang. "Automatic webcam-based human heart rate measurements using laplacian eigenmap." In Computer VisionâĂŞACCV 2012, Springer Berlin Heidelberg, 2013.

[11] Wearable Sensors: Fundamentals, Implementation and Applications : Book by Dr. Edward Sazonov, Michael R. Neuman

[12] Practice Standards for Electrocardiographic Monitoring in Hospital Settings http://circ.ahajournals.org/content/110/17/2721.full

[13] Pantelopoulos, A., & Bourbakis, N. G. (2010). A survey on wearable sensor-based systems for health monitoring and prognosis. Systems, Man, and Cybernetics, Part C: Applications and Reviews, IEEE Transactions on, 40(1), 1-12.

[14] Grimaldi D., Kurylyak Y., Lamonaca F., Nastro A., âĂIJPhotoplethysmography Detection by SmartphoneâĂŹs Videocamera,âĂİ in Proc. IEEE International Conference IDAACSâĂŹ2011

[15] Pal A., Sinha A., Choudhary A., Chattopadyay T., Visvanathan A. âĂIJA robust heart rate detection using smart-phone videoâĂİ,MobileHealth '13 In Proceedings of the 3rd ACM MobiHoc workshop on Pervasive wireless healthcare Pages 43-48

[16] Scully C. G, Lee J., MeyerJ., Gorbach A.M., Granquist-Fraser D., Mendelson Y., Chon K.H., âĂIJPhysiological Parameter Monitoring from Optical Recordings With a Mobile Phone,âĂİ IEEE Trans. on Biomedical Engineering

[17] Sun, David, Pablo Paredes, and John Canny. "MouStress: detecting stress from mouse motion." In Proceedings of the 32nd annual ACM conference on Human factors in computing systems, pp. 61-70. ACM, 2014.

[18] Hernandez, Javier, Pablo Paredes, Asta Roseway, and Mary Czerwinski. "Under pressure: sensing stress of computer users." In Proceedings of the 32nd annual ACM conference on Human factors in computing systems, pp. 51-60. ACM, 2014.

[19] Kang, S., Kwon, S., Yoo, C., Seo, S., Park, K., Song, J., and Lee, Y. Sinabro: Sinabro: Opportunistic and unobtrusive mobile electrocardiogram monitoring system. Proc. Of HotMobile, Santa Barbara, CA, 2014

[20] Griffiths, E., Saponas, T. S., & Brush, A. J. (2014, September). Health chair: implicitly sensing heart and respiratory rate. In Proceedings of the 2014 ACM International Joint Conference on Pervasive and Ubiquitous Computing, ACM. Chicago

[21] Chigira, H., Ihara, M., Kobayashi, M., Tanaka, A., & Tanaka, T. (2014, September). Heart rate monitoring through the surface of a drinkware. In Proceedings of the 2014 ACM International Joint Conference on Pervasive and Ubiquitous Computing, ACM.

[22] Ravichandran, R., Saba11, E., Chen, K. Y., Goel, M., Gupta, S., & Patel, S. N. WiBreathe: Estimating Respiration Rate Using Wireless Signals in Natural Settings in the Home. In Proceedings of the 2015 ACM International Conference on Pervasive Computing, ACM.

[23] Mestha, Lalit K., Survi Kyal, Beilei Xu, Leslie Edward Lewis, and Vijay Kumar. "Towards continuous monitoring of pulse rate in neonatal intensive care unit with a webcam." In Engineering in Medicine and Biology Society (EMBC), 2014 36th Annual International Conference of the IEEE, IEEE, 2014.

[24] WEKA J48 Decision tree, http://docs.ochem.eu/pages/viewpage.action?pageId=7013031

Analysis of Indoor Rowing Motion using Wearable Inertial Sensors

Stephan Bosch
Department of Computer Science
University of Twente
The Netherlands
s.bosch@utwente.nl

Muhammad Shoaib
Department of Computer Science
University of Twente
The Netherlands
m.shoaib@utwente.nl

Stephen Geerlings
s.a.geerlings@student.utwente.nl

Lennart Buit
l.j.buit@student.utwente.nl

Nirvana Meratnia
Department of Computer Science
University of Twente
The Netherlands
n.meratnia@utwente.nl

Paul Havinga
Department of Computer Science
University of Twente
The Netherlands
p.j.m.havinga@utwente.nl

ABSTRACT

In this exploratory work the motion of rowers is analyzed while rowing on a rowing machine. This is performed using inertial sensors that measure the orientation at several positions on the body. Using these measurements, this work provides a preliminary analysis of the differences between experienced and novice rowers, or between a good and a bad technique. The analysis shows that the measured postural angles show no clear trend that would set apart experienced and novice rowers or a bad and a good technique. However, there are clear differences in absolute postural angle's consistency and timing consistency of strokes between novice and experienced rowers. We also applied a machine learning technique to the data to find the similarities between different rowers and an experienced reference rower. The results can be used to compare the quality of the rowing technique with respect to a reference. In this paper, we present our initial results as well as the challenges that need to be further explored.

Keywords

Rowing, inertial motion capture, body sensor network, machine learning

1. INTRODUCTION

Rowing is a sport in which performance is determined by technique and strength. While building strength is relatively simple, novice rowers need a great amount of guidance from a coach to learn the proper technique and optimize their performance. Normally, most of the technique is learned on dry land using a rowing machine (ergometer). A coach can then clearly see what aspects of the technique need improvement. However, guidance from a coach is not always readily available, for example in a regular gymnasium. Volunteer coaches are a scarce resource for many rowing associations. Therefore, it would be nice to have a system with which a rower can get real-time feedback on his performance without a coach present or a coach can later on analyze the rowing motion, for example, for consistency in postural angles and timing.

To solve these issues, rowers could be monitored with a sensor system. With the sensor measurements, the system can provide information about a rower's motion during rowing activity. Using this information, the coach can better evaluate the crew's performance. When there is no coach, the system could provide that information directly to the athletes, possibly accompanied with suggestions on how performance could be improved. Alternatively, the data could be recorded for evaluation by a coach at a later time.

The performance of a rower can be assessed in a number of ways. For rowing exercise on the water, the movement of the boat and the oars can be monitored using sensors [5]. For indoor rowing, the rowing machine can be instrumented to measure various parameters of the rower's activity, such as power output, exerted force and the position of the slide and handle bar [3]. Alternatively, the posture of the rower can be measured using cameras or on-body sensors [17] .

There are proprietary systems to measure the behavior and performance of rowers in a boat. These systems are very costly and are mostly designed for professional athletes [19]. They consist of many different sensors that generate information mostly about power output and stroke rate. However, the sensors often cannot detect errors in rowing posture or timing. Rowing technique is largely composed of posture and timing and this work aims to explore these aspects further.

The goal of this research is to measure and analyze rowing motion and to develop a method to give feedback for the

BODYNETS 2015, September 28-30, Sydney, Australia

DOI 10.4108/eai.28-9-2015.2261465

rowers or coaches. Information on the posture of a rower can provide insight in flaws in the rower's technique that directly influence performance [17]. Moreover, bad posture can lead to injury [6, 24]. In this work, we compare the motion characteristics of experienced rowers to novice rowers, to determine what constitutes a correct rowing technique. We compare the posture of the rowers and the timing of their strokes. Analysis of the measured movement could be used to advise a rower what needs to be improved. Timing and posture information will be essential to advise the rower properly. This system can assist the rowers and trainers if it is easy to use and if it gives real-time feedback.

Our goal is to eventually build a system that can assess posture correctness during training on the water. However, for simplicity, we limit our experiments outlined in this paper to the rowing machine. We use on-body inertial motion sensors, because the alternative camera-based motion tracking systems are not suitable for measurement on the water and they would be prohibitively expensive for most amateur rowing associations. The disadvantage of using motion sensors is that this technique provides less accurate and less reliable measurements in most cases.

Our contributions are as follows:

- We provide a preliminary exploration of the differences in posture and timing between experienced and novice rowers. A similar approach can be used for differentiating between a good and an inferior rowing technique.
- We apply machine learning to assess the similarity between the rower's movements.
- We make our data set and videos publicly available for future research in this domain [22].

This work is explicitly limited to determining the distinction between experienced and novice rowers. This is based on the assumption that experienced rowers will have better technique than novice rowers. This is not necessarily true however, since an experienced rower can have a bad day for instance. We aim to extend this work for determining what can be improved in the rower's technique. Using expert supervision, data on good rowing technique can be collected for a large set of athletes, making this work suitable for determining whether rowers use the correct technique, irrespective of whether they are experienced or not. The system could also be personalized by using an expert to determine a good rowing technique for one particular rower. This way, the performance variation of one rower can be measured relative to the personal reference obtained with expert guidance. This could be very useful for subsequent unsupervised training.

The rest of the paper is organized as follows. In Section 2, we briefly describe related work. Some background regarding rowing technique is provided in Section 3. Subsequently, we describe our experimental setup in Section 4 and we describe the results in Section 5. Finally, we describe our conclusions and future work in Section 6.

2. RELATED WORK

Wearable sensors are extensively used in sports research, especially for analyzing the performance of elite athletes [2, 11, 16]. For rowing, most research focuses either on the athlete's force or power output [2–5, 8] and the optimal movement of the oars [1, 5, 12, 18, 19] and the boat [18, 19]. The posture of the athlete received less attention so far, while it does provide deeper insight in flaws in the rower's technique that directly influence performance. Moreover, bad posture can lead to injury [6, 24].

Hawkins et al. [14], use electrogoniometers to capture the joint angles during indoor rowing experiments similar to ours. Since these mechanical devices need to be strapped along the joints, these can constrain the rower's movements. A similar setup by Page et al. [21] uses a mechanical system involving potentiometers to measure the angles. Using an on-body network of wearable sensors to track the rower's posture can be less obtrusive, and more importantly it can be used on the water. A usability study by Franke et al. [9] demonstrates that wireless body sensors similar to ours do not constrain the rower in any way.

King et al. [17] perform experiments very similar to ours using a rowing machine and three wireless inertial sensor nodes. Although King et al. demonstrate examples of what bad technique looks like, they mainly investigate the feasibility of the measurement setup and they do not compare measurements between rowers. Tanaka et al. [24] perform posture comparisons between experienced and novice rowers, but they don't use on-body sensors and they focus entirely on preventing injury.

3. BACKGROUND

A rowing stroke has roughly two fundamental reference points: the *catch* is the moment at which the oar blade enters the water and the *finish* (also known as the *extraction*, *release*, or *tapping down*) is the moment at which the blade is finally removed from the water. At the catch position, the rower is fully bent towards the back of the boat. While the oar is in the water, the rower applies force to the oar, thereby pushing the boat forward. This is called the *drive* phase of the stroke. Once the oar is lifted above the water, the rower moves from the finish position back to the catch position, which is called the *recovery* phase of the stroke.

Much of the rowing technique revolves around timing and posture. For example, the rower needs to lean forward by the appropriate amount, needs to pull back on the oar at the correct time, the rower should keep his back straight, should pull backwards with his upper body at the correct time, etc. Therefore, when we compare experienced and novice rowers, we expect to see differences in the measured posture and the timing of the various steps in the rowing stroke.

4. EXPERIMENTS

All experiments are performed on dry land with indoor rowing machines (ergometers). Figure 1 shows an overview of the experimental setup. The rower subjects are equipped with three inertial sensor modules located at one lower leg, the lower back and the upper back. These locations are chosen based on expert knowledge. The placement of the

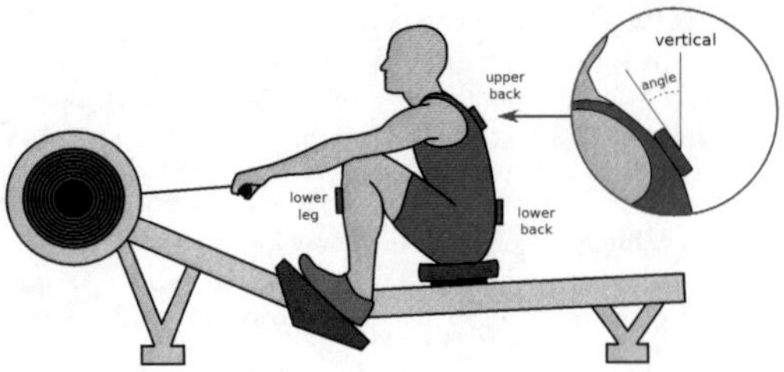

Figure 1: An overview of the experiment with the locations of the sensor modules.

sensors allows measurement of the main posture angles during the rower's motion; i.e., the angle of the lower leg and the angle of the torso. The two sensors on the back provide a measurement of the extent at which the back is curved.

The sensor modules use accelerometer and gyroscope sensors to measure the module's own acceleration and rotational velocity respectively. Using these measurements, we determine the orientation of the sensors during the experiment using the algorithm by Madgwick et al. [20]. This yields the orientation of the sensors represented in quaternions.

Using these orientation measurements, we determine the angle of each sensor relative to the vertical, as shown in Figure 1. We only evaluate the motion in a two-dimensional fashion, meaning that we assume that there is no significant sideways motion at the sensor positions [24]. With this assumption, we can use the shortest angle between the sensor orientation and the vertical. To verify the angle measurements, we made video recordings [22] of the experiments from a perspective similar to Figure 1.

We use the ProMove-3D [15] system from Inertia Technology for this work. A ProMove-3D sensor node features a 3-D accelerometer, a 3-D gyroscope and a 3-D digital compass. The accelerometer has a measurement range of up to $\pm$ 6 g and the gyroscope has a measurement range of up to $\pm 2000\,^{\circ}\,s^{-1}$. The nodes form a network using a 2.4 GHz radio. The wireless network is used to transmit sensor measurements to a computer for recording and to synchronize measurements from multiple sensor nodes within 10 µs.

The sample frequency for all sensors was set to 200Hz. The wireless transmission of the data caused a sample loss of up to 2 %, which is compensated for by means of linear interpolation.

For this work we evaluate the motion characteristics of both experienced rowers (rowing for three years or more) and novice rowers (rowing for a few months at most). Since this is only a preliminary study, we perform experiments with a limited set of only seven subjects, of which three are experienced and four are novice rowers. The characteristics of our subjects is shown in Table 1.

To determine whether the rowing speed is a factor, the rowers all perform successive experiments with 20 and 30 strokes

	Height (cm)	Weight (kg)	Age (years)
Experienced 1	196	71	23
Experienced 2	183	81	25
Experienced 3	191	93	21
Novice 1	180	70	24
Novice 2	184	74	19
Novice 3	180	72	20
Novice 4	185	67	20

Table 1: Experiment subject characteristics

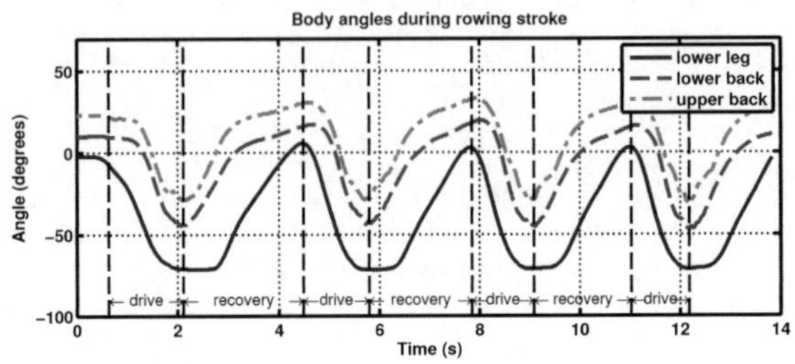

Figure 2: Example of the sensor angles during rowing at 20 strokes per minute.

per minute. The rowers use feedback from the rowing machine to maintain the requested stroke rate. Each experiment involves approximately 20 strokes, all of which are used in our evaluation (whole session). Each experiment at a specific stroke rate is performed only once by each individual rower.

5. RESULTS

For part of this analysis, we choose one experienced rower as a reference, which we label as **Exp. 1**. This is the rower with the most average physique, which means that he matches best with all the other experienced and novice rowers. The other experienced rowers are labeled with successive numbers and the novice rowers are labeled as e.g. **Nov. 1**. Rower **Exp. 2** was female and rower **Exp. 3** was male, but with a stronger physique than our reference. Measurements at 30 strokes per minute for rower **Exp. 3** failed and were not used for this analysis.

Figure 2 shows an example of the angle measurements from our reference rower performing the first four strokes at 20 strokes per minute. The figure is annotated with the *drive* and *recovery* phases of the stroke cycle. These phases are determined automatically using a simple heuristic algorithm that bases the phase transitions on peaks in the lower leg and upper back angle signals. The drive phase starts (at the catch position) when the lower leg starts to move backwards (angle decreasing) and ends (at the finish position) when the upper back starts to move forwards (angle increasing). We use these annotations to compare the stroke phases separately and align our comparisons between rowers.

Our goal is to find measurable posture characteristics that distinguish an experienced rower from a novice rower, or rather characteristics that distinguish between a good and a bad technique. We evaluate several possibilities: we compare the absolute angles and its consistency, and the timing consistency of rowing strokes. These characteristics were selected based on expert knowledge on what constitutes a good rowing technique, which largely revolves around good posture and timing. Finally, we employ machine learning techniques to obtain a generic measure of similarity.

5.1 Absolute Angles

The most obvious way to compare rowing postures is using the absolute angles measured during the experiment. Therefore, with the help of literature and expert knowledge, we devised a simple quantitative model in which the reference angles for a certain positions in the stroke phase are defined. In an effort to determine these reference angles, we evaluated the angles from our experienced rowers.

Figure 3 shows the angle differences between our reference rower and each of the other novice and experienced rowers at the upper back sensor at a velocity of 20 strokes per minute. The results are compensated for differences in the length of the strokes by normalization; the x-axis shows the phase of the full stroke rather than an absolute time. The angle differences are only shown at the stroke phase positions of the reference angles of our quantitative model.

The results show large differences in the angles, even amongst the experienced rowers. This is a clear indication that the absolute angle has very little value for comparing rowing posture. The results for the leg and lower back positions are very similar. We speculate the measured angles do not only depend on the rower's technique, but that there are also significant dependencies on the rower's physique. The rower's length and strength are likely important factors. However, these are not the only factors, since rowers with similar physique (such as **Exp. 1** and **Exp. 2**) still show significant differences. For a stroke rate of 30 strokes per minute, we observe very similar results as for the experiment at 20 strokes per minute.

Figure 4 shows the standard deviations in the leg, lower back and upper back angles at a velocity of 20 strokes per minute. These statistics show that on average the experienced rowers have lower standard deviation values than inexperienced rowers. This standard deviation can be an indication of the angle consistency of the rowers. We expect a high standard deviation for rowers with an inconsistent, bad technique. For example, **Nov. 3** has a high standard deviation for all angles, which is a likely indicator for an inconsistent technique.

5.2 Stroke Timing Consistency

Table 2 shows the stroke timings for each rower at 20 strokes per minute. The ideal stroke at that speed lasts 3 seconds. The table shows that the experienced rowers are able to match this timing more closely. More interestingly, the standard deviation of the full stroke time is smaller for the experienced rowers, meaning that their strokes are more consistent. The results show that on average about 40 % of a stroke is spent in the drive phase, which is consistent with the stroke proportion statistics reported by Dawson et al. [7]. Judging by the standard deviation, the fraction of time spent in the drive phase is also more consistent for the experienced rowers. The results for the recovery phase are not shown in Table 2, because this is the only other phase and therefore the statistics are identical.

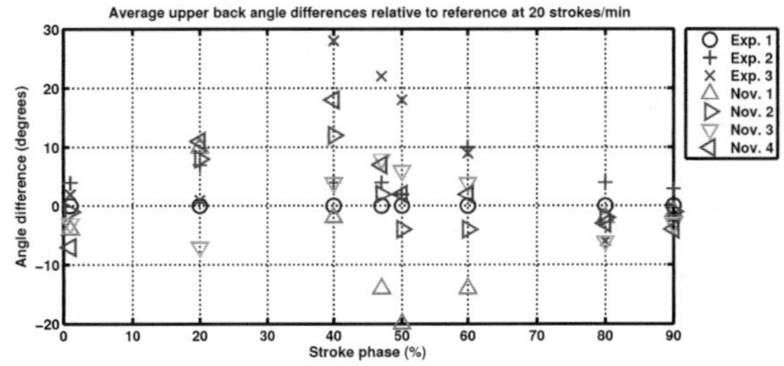

Figure 3: Average upper back angle differences at 20 strokes per minute.

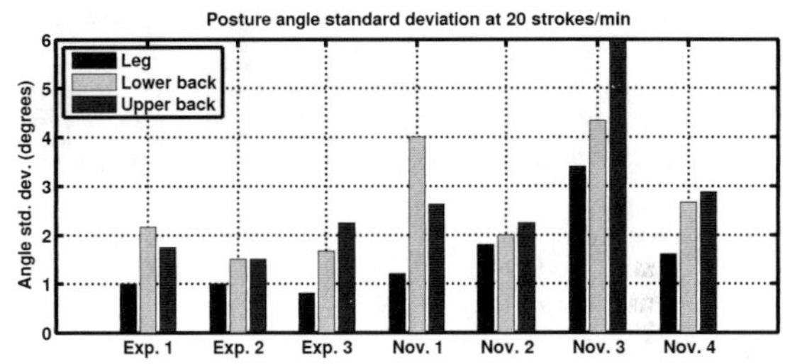

Figure 4: Posture angle standard deviation at 20 strokes/min.

	Full Stroke		Drive	
	time(s)	std.dev.(s)	time frac.(%)	std.dev.(%)
Experienced 1	3.06	0.04	40.00	2.00
Experienced 2	2.90	0.04	37.00	1.00
Experienced 3	2.95	0.07	36.00	1.00
Novice 1	2.40	0.14	44.00	2.00
Novice 2	2.87	0.17	38.00	3.00
Novice 3	2.73	0.16	35.00	5.00
Novice 4	2.92	0.11	44.00	2.00

Table 2: Stroke timing consistency for 20 strokes per minute

Table 3 shows the stroke timings for each rower 30 strokes per minute. The results show that the stroke timing consistency of experienced rowers is not noticeably affected by the stroke rate. In contrast, statistics for both the full stroke and the fraction spent in the drive phase indicate that novice rowers can maintain more consistent stroke timing at higher stroke rates. Figure 5 presents an overview of the standard deviations for the full stroke at each stroke rate for each of our subjects, which shows this stroke rate dependence more clearly. At the highest evaluated stroke rate, the standard deviation of the full stroke is for most novice rowers at the same level as the experienced rowers. Still, at that stroke rate the fraction of a full stroke spent in the drive phase still shows higher standard deviation for the novice rowers.

While a higher stroke rate may improve stroke timing con-

	Full Stroke		Drive	
	time (s)	std.dev.(s)	time frac.(%)	std.dev.(%)
Experienced 1	1.91	0.06	45.00	1.00
Experienced 2	1.97	0.06	44.00	1.00
Experienced 3	N/A	N/A	N/A	N/A
Novice 1	1.83	0.05	47.00	1.00
Novice 2	1.88	0.13	44.00	2.00
Novice 3	1.95	0.06	44.00	2.00
Novice 4	2.03	0.06	43.00	2.00

Table 3: Stroke timing consistency for 30 strokes per minute

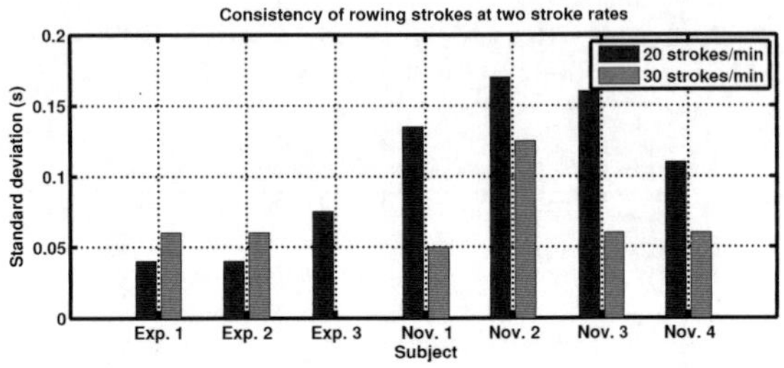

Figure 5: Overview of stroke time consistency.

sistency for novice rowers, the results in Section 5.3 indicate that the overall technique of the novice rowers becomes less similar to the experienced rowers at higher stroke rates. We speculate that it becomes more difficult to maintain correct technique at higher stroke rates.

5.3 Machine Learning

It is difficult to determine all aspects of the motion that distinguish experienced rowers from novice ones or a bad rowing technique from a good one. Therefore, we employ machine learning techniques to obtain a generic measure of similarity of the motion of subjects in our experiments relative to the motion of an experienced reference rower.

Obviously, we expect and assume that the motion of our experienced rowers will be more similar to the reference experienced rower than the novice rowers. However, if the novice rower is doing the rowing technique in the right way, then it can have a better similarity to the reference rower as well. Moreover, we also assume that the reference rower is doing the technique in the right way, which is not a very strong assumption. However, this assumption was necessary to keep the scope of this preliminary study limited. In future data collection experiments, the reference rower will be supervised by an expert where we can be sure that the reference technique is a proper one.

These machine learning results will not be useful in determining what exactly is different or wrong. However, this assessment will provide an indication of how much a rower is deviating from the reference. Such indication can be helpful for the rowers to ask for a supervised session to evaluate their technique. This approach can be very helpful in personalized training. For example, a rower can be supervised by an expert to perform the rowing technique once and use that data as a reference point, thereby training a personalized classifier. Such a personalized classifier can detect deviations from the verified technique for that specific rower, when the expert or trainer is not around. Moreover, it can help him by giving a generic feedback about such deviations. This personalized approach is more practical than the generic ones. However, we leave this for the next study as a future work.

We employ machine learning to recognize the two main phases of a rowing stroke: drive and recovery. We train our classifiers using these two stroke phases. The classifiers are trained using our reference rower, which is one of the experienced rowers, and subsequently applied to each of the other rowers as a test data. The recognition performance is used as the measure for similarity. We have used one rower as a reference because of our limited data set. In future, we are planning to cluster experienced rowers for training a classifier.

We used WEKA (version: 3.7) [13] as a machine learning tool for analysis. For our initial analysis, we selected K-nearest neighbor for finding similarities between different rowers. It uses Euclidean distance to find similarity between training data and test data. We use this classifier in its default mode in order to make our work easily reproducible, except K is chosen as 3. This specific number is chosen, because an odd number is important for breaking the possible tie in majority voting. Also, higher values of K help in avoiding the effects of noise [23].

We segmented the angle measurements into windows of 75 samples (0.375 s) with no overlap. This way, at least two window segments are fully located in either the drive or recovery phase of each stroke. Using a sliding window approach, we extracted the following features from the segmented angle measurements: the mean and the mean angular velocity. The mean angular velocity is calculated by taking the mean of the differences between each two consecutive points within each segment. Our two classes were of different sizes. Therefore, we used the *classbalancer filter* [25] on our training data in the preprocessing phase. This filter assigns the same weights to all classes, thereby avoiding bias towards the majority class by various classifiers [25].

For performance evaluation, we use accuracy, and Matthews Correlation Coefficient (MCC). MCC is considered a balanced measure for the recognition performance, because it considers all aspects of a confusion matrix [10]. These are defined as follows as per WEKA documentation:

- The **True Positive rate (TPR) or accuracy** is the proportion of examples which were classified as class x, among all examples which truly have class x, i.e. what part of the class was captured correctly.
- The **MCC** takes into account all aspects of a confusion matrix, such as true positive (TP), true negative (TN), false positive (FP), and false negative (FN) and is calculated as follows:

$$MCC = \frac{(TP * TN - FP * FN)}{\sqrt{(TP + FP)(TP + FN)(TN + FP)(TN + FN)}} \quad (1)$$

The results for the KNN classifier at 20 and 30 strokes per minute are respectively shown in Figure 6 and Figure 7. It is important to note that these results are the average of the drive and recovery phases. These results show how much the recognition performance of all rowers is lower than that of the reference rower **Exp. 1**. The reference rower is one of the three experienced rowers.

As expected, the similarity to our reference rower is consistently better for our experienced rowers than for our novice rowers with a few exceptions. In some cases, the inexperienced rowers have almost the same or better similarity to the reference rower than that of the experienced rowers. A possible explanation for this could be that the inexperienced rower is doing the technique properly at that specific time. We repeated this analysis for the other two experienced rowers (**Exp. 2** and **Exp. 3**), by taking each of them as a reference point and then evaluating the rest of the rowers with respect to them. We see similar trends.

That is one of the limitations of this study, where we assumed that inexperienced rowers will not perform the rowing technique in an optimal way compared to the experienced ones. That assumption can be wrong, so this should be explored further. One option could be to have an expert present at the data collection phase who can supervise the process and identify who is doing the technique in a proper way.

Beside this analysis, we analyzed these results in relationship with the heights of the rowers to see if it plays an important role. However, we do not see any clear connection between them.

It can also be seen that in some cases the performance drop for these rowers compared to the reference rower or compared to each other, is small. Based on expert knowledge, such small differences can be ignored by applying a threshold in comparing these performances. Because a good rowing technique does allow for different angle values within a specific range. Defining this specific range is the job of a rowing expert and it can be easily integrated with such intelligent systems.

Though this work should be further explored, we observe that different performance measures can be combined to differentiate between an experienced and inexperienced rower or a good and bad technique. As we discussed in Section 5.2, stroke timing consistency becomes better at higher stroke rates, whereas the similarity with the reference becomes worse at higher stroke rates for novice rowers. Therefore, we can combine these two factors for distinguishing experienced from novice rowers or distinguishing a bad technique from a good one, because at least one of these will likely differ.

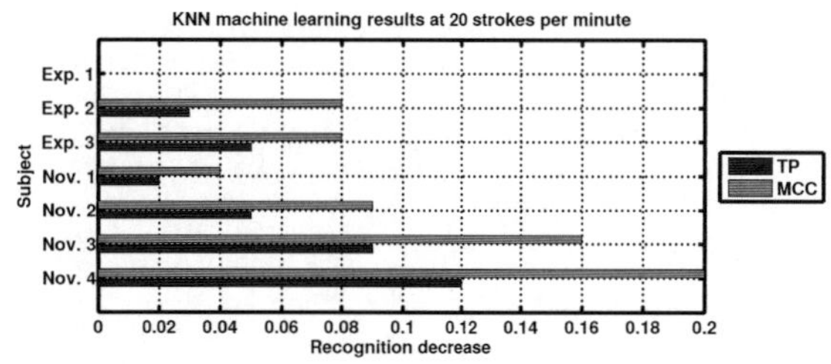

Figure 6: Machine learning results for the KNN classifier at 20 strokes per minute.

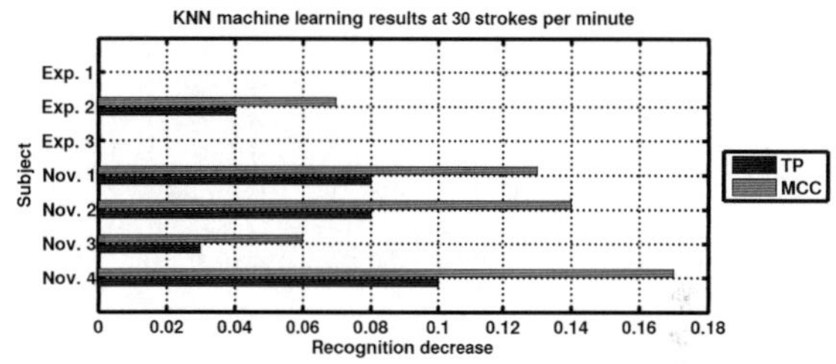

Figure 7: Machine learning results for the KNN classifier at 30 strokes per minute.

6. CONCLUSION

Our preliminary experiments show that absolute posture angles provide no direct means of distinguishing experienced and novice rowers. For the absolute posture angles, the measurements vary wildly, even amongst experienced rowers. However, the standard deviation of the absolute postural angles could be used to assess the inconsistency of the rower's technique.

In contrast, the timing consistency of the rowing strokes does show a clear difference between experienced and novice rowers. The standard deviation of the full stroke time and the fraction of the stroke spent in the drive phase is low and consistent across varying stroke rates for the experienced rowers. Novice rowers show higher standard deviation. Interestingly, the consistency of novice rowers improves with higher stroke rates.

Machine learning techniques can distinguish between experienced and novice rowers, because the recognition performance of the latter is lower compared to our reference. Unlike the stroke timing consistency, at higher stroke rates, the recognition performance using machine learning of the novice rowers becomes low compared to the experienced reference rower. Therefore, a combination of these two metrics can be used to identify a deviant rowing technique.

An important problem with using machine learning for this analysis is that it is not possible to tell exactly what an inexperienced rower is doing different from the 'good' technique. This requires further exploration. Moreover, we assumed that our inexperienced rowers would consistently perform worse than our experienced rowers. This does not account for some natural talent, which means that inexperienced rowers could perform equally well in some cases. For future experiments, we should have an expert present that can judge the technique during the experiment to make a clear assessment.

In future work, the number of subjects needs to be larger than seven and experiments need to be repeated several times. With only a few subjects each performing only a few experiments, the results can be influenced by unapparent coincidental factors, such as the participants suffering from fatigue, illness, or stress. Also, our experiments did not explicitly explore the effects of gender differences on rowing posture: most of our subjects were male, with only one exception.

Acknowledgment

This work is supported by Dutch National Program COMMIT in the context of SWELL project.

7. REFERENCES

[1] R. P. Andrews, A. P. Garcia, B. R. Dryer, S. F. Bonney, S. Badjou, and D. E. Dow. Rowing Training System for On-the-water Rehabilitation and Sport. In *Proceedings of the 8th International Conference on Body Area Networks*, BodyNets '13, pages 351–354, ICST, Brussels, Belgium, Belgium, 2013. ICST (Institute for Computer Sciences, Social-Informatics and Telecommunications Engineering).

[2] A. Baca and P. Kornfeind. Rapid Feedback Systems for Elite Sports Training. *IEEE Pervasive Computing*, 5(4):70–76, Oct. 2006.

[3] M. Bassetti, F. Braghin, F. Cheli, and S. Maldifassi. Instrumented Rowing Machine for Optimized Training. In R. Allemang, J. D. Clerck, C. Niezrecki, and J. R. Blough, editors, *Topics in Modal Analysis II, Volume 6*, Conference Proceedings of the Society for Experimental Mechanics Series, pages 499–506. Springer New York, Jan. 2012.

[4] A. Baudouin, D. Hawkins, and S. Seiler. A biomechanical review of factors affecting rowing performance. *British Journal of Sports Medicine*, 36(6):396–402, Dec. 2002.

[5] S. Bettinelli, A. Placido, L. Susmel, and R. Tovo. An Integrated Data Acquisition System for on-Water Measurement of Performance in Rowing. *Strain*, 46(5):493–509, Oct. 2010.

[6] A. M. J. Bull and A. H. McGregor. Measuring spinal motion in rowers: the use of an electromagnetic device. *Clinical Biomechanics*, 15(10):772–776, Dec. 2000.

[7] R. G. Dawson, R. J. Lockwood, J. D. Wilson, and G. Freeman. The Rowing Cycle: Sources of Variance and Invariance in Ergometer and On-the-Water Performance. *Journal of Motor Behavior*, 30(1):33–43, Mar. 1998.

[8] S. Fothergill. Examining the effect of real-time visual feedback on the quality of rowing technique. *Procedia Engineering*, 2(2):3083–3088, June 2010.

[9] T. Franke, C. Pieringer, and P. Lukowicz. How Should a Wearable Rowing Trainer Look Like? A User Study. In *2011 15th Annual International Symposium on Wearable Computers (ISWC)*, pages 15–18, June 2011.

[10] A. Gensler and B. Sick. Novel criteria to measure performance of time series segmentation techniques. In *Proceedings of the 16th LWA Workshops: KDML, IR and FGWM*, September 8-10 2014.

[11] D. Gouwanda and S. M. N. A. Senanayake. Emerging Trends of Body-Mounted Sensors in Sports and Human Gait Analysis. In D. N. A. A. Osman, D. F. Ibrahim, D. W. A. B. W. Abas, H. S. A. Rahman, and D. H.-N. Ting, editors, *4th Kuala Lumpur International Conference on Biomedical Engineering 2008*, number 21 in IFMBE Proceedings, pages 715–718. Springer Berlin Heidelberg, Jan. 2008.

[12] F. Gravenhorst, A. Muaremi, F. Kottmann, G. Troster, R. Sigrist, N. Gerig, and C. Draper. Strap and row: Rowing technique analysis based on inertial measurement units implemented in mobile phones. In *2014 IEEE Ninth International Conference on Intelligent Sensors, Sensor Networks and Information Processing (ISSNIP)*, pages 1–6, Apr. 2014.

[13] M. Hall, E. Frank, G. Holmes, B. Pfahringer, P. Reutemann, and I. H. Witten. The weka data mining software: an update. *ACM SIGKDD explorations newsletter*, 11(1):10–18, 2009.

[14] D. Hawkins. A new instrumentation system for training rowers. *Journal of Biomechanics*, 33(2):241–245, Feb. 2000.

[15] Inertia Technology. *ProMove 3D - 3D motion tracking.*

[16] D. A. James. The Application of Inertial Sensors in Elite Sports Monitoring. In E. F. Moritz and S. Haake, editors, *The Engineering of Sport 6*, pages 289–294. Springer New York, Jan. 2006.

[17] R. King, D. McIlwraith, B. Lo, J. Pansiot, A. McGregor, and G.-Z. Yang. Body Sensor Networks for Monitoring Rowing Technique. In *Sixth International Workshop on Wearable and Implantable Body Sensor Networks, 2009. BSN 2009*, pages 251–255, June 2009.

[18] J. Llosa, I. Vilajosana, X. Vilajosana, and J. Marques. Design of a Motion Detector to Monitor Rowing Performance Based on Wireless Sensor Networks. In *International Conference on Intelligent Networking and Collaborative Systems, 2009. INCOS '09*, pages 397–400, Nov. 2009.

[19] J. Llosa, I. Vilajosana, X. Vilajosana, N. Navarro, E. SuriÃśach, and J. M. MarquÃís. REMOTE, a Wireless Sensor Network Based System to Monitor Rowing Performance. *Sensors*, 9(9):7069–7082, Sept. 2009.

[20] S. Madgwick, A. Harrison, and R. Vaidyanathan. Estimation of IMU and MARG orientation using a gradient descent algorithm. In *2011 IEEE International Conference on Rehabilitation Robotics (ICORR)*, pages 1–7, June 2011.

[21] P. N. Page and D. A. Hawkins. A real-time biomechanical feedback system for training rowers. *Sports Engineering*, 6(2):67–79, June 2003.

[22] Pervasive Systems Research Data Sets. `http://ps.ewi.utwente.nl/Datasets.php`.

[23] Y. Song, J. Huang, D. Zhou, H. Zha, and C. L. Giles. Iknn: Informative k-nearest neighbor pattern classification. In *Knowledge Discovery in Databases: PKDD 2007*, pages 248–264. Springer, 2007.

[24] C. Tanaka, M. R. Ide, and R. T. Moreno. Quantitative analysis of head and trunk posture in rowers during ergonometric training. *Salusvita*, 26(1):53–64, 2007.

[25] Weka documentation for class balancer:. `http://weka.sourceforge.net/doc.dev/weka/filters/supervised/instance/ClassBalancer.html`.

Maximization of Received Signal Power by Impedance Matching in Human Body Communication Receiver

Naruto Arai　Dairoku Muramatsu　Ken Sasaki

Department of Human and Engineered Environmental Studies
Graduate School of Frontier Science, The University of Tokyo
5-1-5, Kashiwanoha, Kashiwa-shi, Chiba 277-8563, JAPAN
+81-4-7136-4618, JP

narai@ems.k.u-tokyo.ac.jp　muramatsu@ems.k.u-tokyo.ac.jp　ksasaki@k.u-tokyo.ac.jp

ABSTRACT

Human body communication (HBC) utilizes human body as part of the transmission channel. The present paper deals with HBC between a transmitter worn on the user's wrist and an off-body stationary receiver touched by the user's finger. In this configuration, transmitter-human-body system can be regarded as a signal source as viewed from the receiver. The equivalent output impedance of this signal source mainly consists of resistance of human body and capacitive reactance among the receiver, human body, and the surrounding environment. Impedance matching was achieved by inserting an inductor to cancel the capacitive reactance and adjusting the input resistor to match the resistance of the equivalent output impedance. At frequency of 10 MHz, maximum received power was obtained with 40 μH inductor and 1.5 kΩ input resistance. This suggests that the output impedance of the transmitter-human-body system is 1500-j2500 Ω.

Categories and Subject Descriptors

H.5.2 [User Interfaces]: *Input devices and strategies*

General Terms

Measurement, Experimentation

Keywords

Human Body Communication, Human Interface, Impedance Matching

1. INTRODUCTION

Human body communication (HBC) is a wireless transmission method for wearable devices which uses human body as a part of the signal transmission channel. One of the early studies on HBC is the report by Zimmerman in 1995 [1]. In 2012, IEEE 802.15.6 standard was accepted for Body Area Network, and HBC was adopted as one of the physical layers of short-range radio communication networks around human body [2]. This standard states that HBC uses electric field communication (EFC) technology and its operation is centered at 21 MHz. This standard, however, does not provide technical details on EFC technology. EFC technology is relatively new and it is not studied as much as other wireless communication technologies. Engineers who intend to use EFC technology have limited information on circuit design. The present study aims to provide some technical information for designing HBC devices.

HBC uses electrodes that are in contact with or placed close to the human body. These electrodes are the equivalent of antennas in wireless communication. The difference is that airborne antennas transmit electromagnetic wave into the air, while electrodes in HBC generate electric field around and inside the human body. One of the design parameters that we need to know for circuit design is the impedance characteristics of electrodes used in HBC. Although previous studies on electrode impedance characteristics have been studied by electromagnetic analysis and by experiments using phantoms [3, 4, 5], we need quantitative data on impedance characteristics measured by using real human body.

There are three possible forms of HBC: 1) communication among multiple devices worn by a single person, 2) communication between devices worn by two people that have physical contact such as shaking hands, and 3) communication between a wearable device and an off-body stationary device that is touched by the user. This study focuses on the third form, more specifically, data transmission from a wearable device worn on the user's wrist to an off-body stationary device touched by the user's index finger. Application examples of such data transmission are, going through a ticket gate, or payment with electronic money at vending machines.

Transmission between a transmitter worn on the user's wrist and an off-body stationary receiver touched by the user's index finger consists of current flow through the finger and arm, and current flow through capacitive coupling between human body and receiver's outer case, which is usually made of metal, and connected to the ground of the receiver circuit. Figure 1 shows the simplified equivalent circuit of this transmission. Z_r is the input impedance of receiver circuit, and Z_h is the equivalent output impedance of the signal source which is the transmitter-human-body system. The signal electrode of the receiver has physical contact with the human body, while the ground electrode, which is the outer case of the receiver, has no contact with the human body. It is electrically connected by capacitive coupling with the human body. It is known that capacitive coupling among the receiver, the human body and the surroundings affect the communication characteristic [6, 7, 8]. Therefore, we hypothesize that the equivalent output impedance Z_h is composed of capacitive reactance and some resistance of the human body.

BODYNETS 2015, September 28-30, Sydney, Australia

DOI 10.4108/eai.28-9-2015.2261445

One of the common circuit design guidelines is to maximize received signal power by matching the input impedance to the output impedance of the signal source. In the following experiments, we first insert an inductor between the receiver electrode and the input terminal of the receiver to cancel the capacitive reactance and verify that capacitive reactance exists in the transmission path. Next, the input resistance of the receiver is varied to find the resistance that gives maximum received signal power. The matched inductance and resistance corresponds to the equivalent capacitive reactance and resistance of the transmitter-human-body signal source.

2. TRANSMITTER AND RECEIVER

Figure 2 shows the experimental setup. A subject wore a transmitter on his wrist and touched the receiver electrode with his index finger. The transmitter is a battery operated Colpitts oscillator that outputs 10 MHz 1.0 Vpp sine wave across the two transmitter electrodes that are in contact with the skin of the wrist. Frequency of 10 MHz was selected according to the previous research that reported that frequency around 10MHz was suited for HBC [9]. Figure 3 shows the placement of electrodes and circuit board with respect to the arm. Three types of electrode configurations were prepared as shown in Fig. 4. All electrodes were 24 x 8 mm in size. The distances between the two electrodes were 8 mm, 24 mm, and 40 mm respectively. Circuit diagram of the receiver is shown in Fig. 5. Receiver electrode was made of stainless steel sheet and its size was 5 x 5 mm. Received signal was amplified by two-stage non-inverting amplifiers and a band pass. Total gain was 29.2 dB. Output amplitude was measured by a battery operated oscilloscope. This receiver circuit was placed in an aluminum box (200 x 150 x 40 mm), and the circuit ground was connected to this aluminum box near the receiver electrode. The receiver and the oscilloscope were placed on a wooden testing stand. Photograph of the experimental setup is shown in Fig. 6. Input impedance of the receiver circuit was first set at 4.7 kΩ, and was changed to trimmer resistor in the second experiment. In this experimental setup, shield of the coaxial cable and the oscilloscope also contribute to the capacitive coupling. It should be noted that large part of the capacitive coupling is formed around the arm and the receiver and the oscilloscope. Capacitive coupling with other parts of the body and ground loop through the floor have little contribution to the signal transmission [5]. Experiments involving measurement using human body in this study have been approved by Research Ethics Committee of the University of Tokyo.

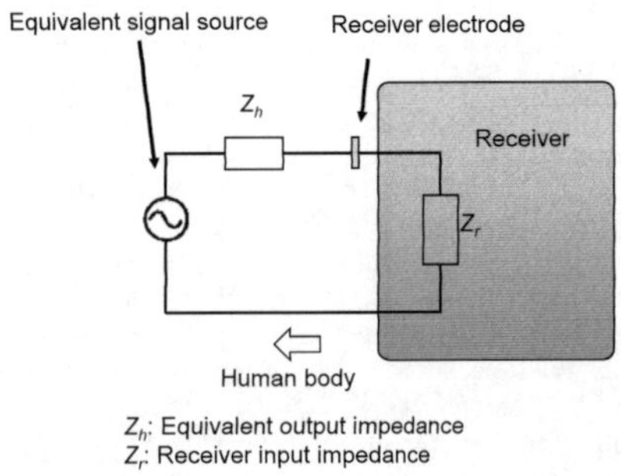

Figure 1. Equivalent circuit of HBC transmission.

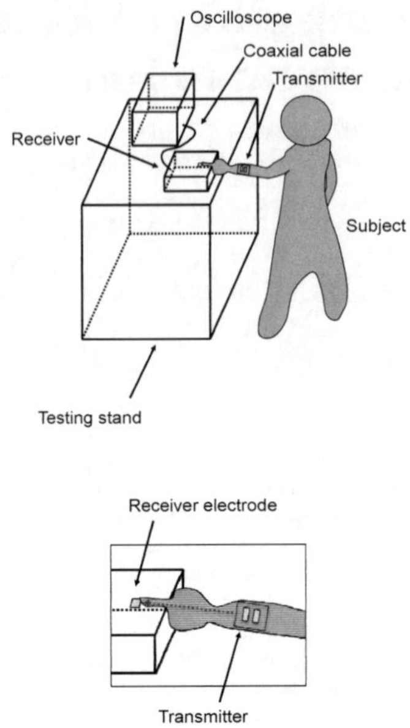

Figure 2. Experimental setup.

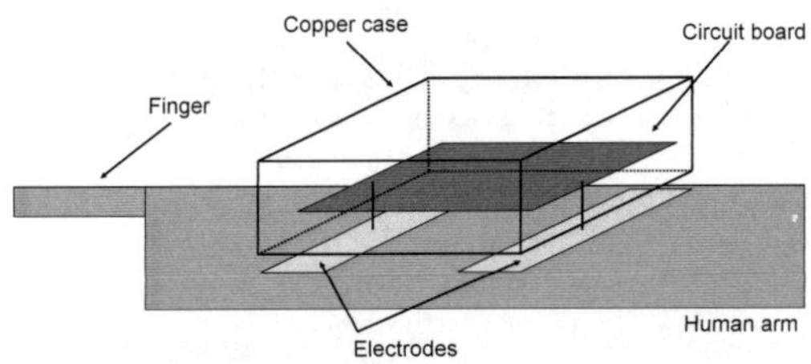

Figure 3. Placement of electrodes and circuit board.

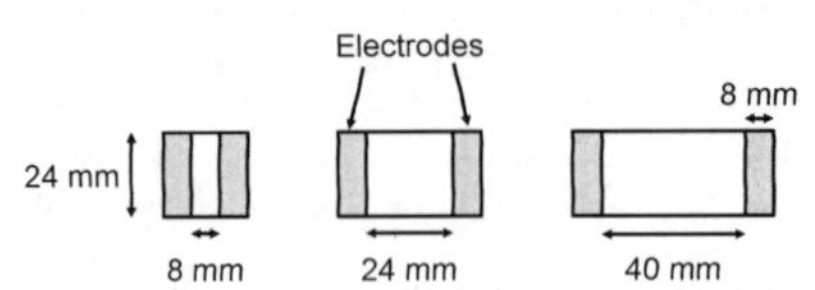

Figure 4. Configurations of transmitter electrodes.

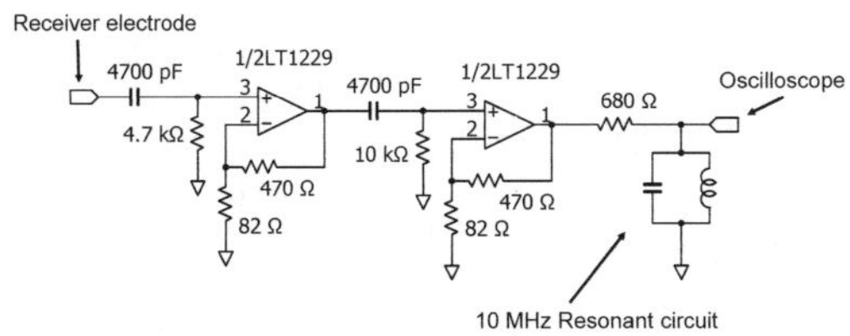

Figure 5. Circuit diagram of receiver circuit.

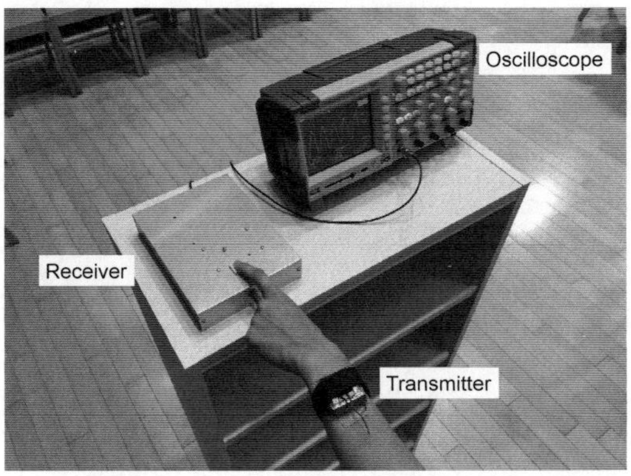

Figure 6. Experimental setup (photograph).

3. IMPEDANCE MATCHING OF REACTANCE

An inductor was inserted between the receiver electrode and the receiver circuit, and the output voltage of the receiver output was measured. The imaginary part of the equivalent output impedance was expected to be in the order of several thousands of Ohm based on our previous studies (not published). Several inductors ranging from 1 μH to 86 μH, which correspond to impedances of 63 Ω to 5400 Ω, were inserted between the receiver electrode and the input of the receiver circuit. Instead of using nominal values shown on the parts, effective inductances measured by an impedance analyzer at 10 MHz were used for calculation. For example, an inductor whose nominal value was 22 μH had an inductance of 40 μH at 10MHz. The received power was calculated from the received voltage and the input impedance (4.7 kΩ) of the receiver.

Figure 7 shows the result of this measurement. The largest received signal powers were 272 nW, 419 nW, and 485 nW, when distances between the two transmitter electrodes were 8 mm, 24 mm, and 40 mm respectively. Received signal maxima were obtained when an inductor of 40 μH was inserted for all three electrode configurations. This result suggests that capacitive reactance exists in the transmission path, and that this capacitive reactance was canceled by the inductor. Furthermore, this capacitive reactance was not affected by the transmitter electrode configuration. Impedance of 40 μH at 10 MHz is 2500 Ω. This corresponds to a capacitance of approximately 6.3pF.

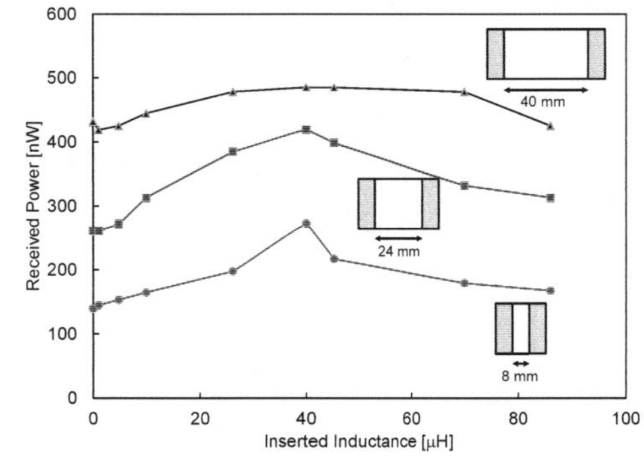

Figure 7. Relationship between inserted inductance and received power.

4. IMPEDANCE MATCHING OF RESISTANCE

In the previous experiment, the input impedance of the receiver was fixed at 4.7 kΩ. Next, this resistor was replaced by a trimmer resistor to change the input impedance of the receiver to find a resistance that gave maximum signal power. This resistance will be the resistive component of the equivalent output impedance of the signal source. An inductor of 40 μH was inserted to cancel the capacitive reactance according to the result of the previous experiment. Figure 8 shows the equivalent circuit of this impedance matching. Received voltage was measured by setting the resistance of the trimmer resistor to eleven different values ranging from 200 Ω to 4.7 kΩ. Figure 9 shows the result. The largest received powers were 337 nW, 635 nW, and 994 nW when the distances between the two transmitter electrodes were 8 mm, 24 mm, and 40 mm respectively. Received power was at its maximum when the resistance was approximately 1.5 kΩ for all three electrode configurations. This means that the real part of the equivalent output impedance is not changed by the transmitter electrode configuration. By combining the results of the two experiments, we estimated that the output impedance of the transmitter-human-body system was 1500-j2500 Ω at 10MHz. This is equivalent to 6.3 pF capacitance and 1.5 kΩ resistance in series.

This result indicates that received signal power can be maximized by setting the input impedance of the receiver to matched impedance of 1500+j2500 Ω. However, this does not mean that the actual front end of the receiver circuit should be the circuit shown in Fig. 8.

Table 1 shows comparison of received power under three conditions: 1)without impedance matching (4.7 kΩ input resistor only), 2)cancelling capacitive reactance only (inserting 40 μH inductor), and 3)matching both the imaginary and the real part (using 40 μH inductor and 1.5 kΩ resistor). The received power obtained with matched impedance was approximately twice as large as that obtained without impedance matching.

Table 1. Relationship between received power and impedance matching

	Distance between two transmitter electrodes		
	8 mm	24 mm	40 mm
Without impedance matching	140 nW	261 nW	432 nW
Cancelling capacitive reactance only	272 nW	419 nW	485 nW
Matching both the imaginary and real part	337 nW	635 nW	994 nW

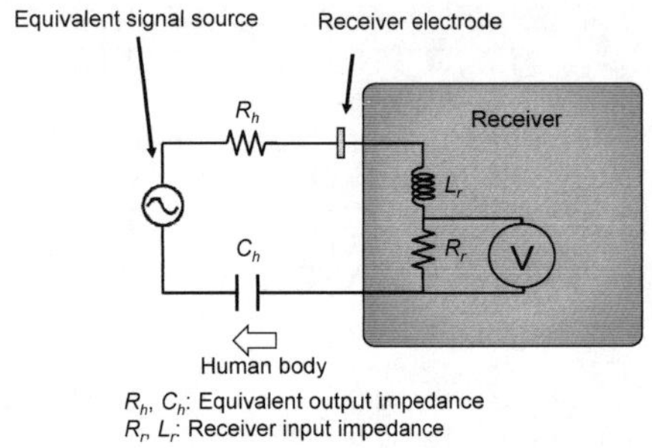

Figure 8. Equivalent circuit of impedance matching.

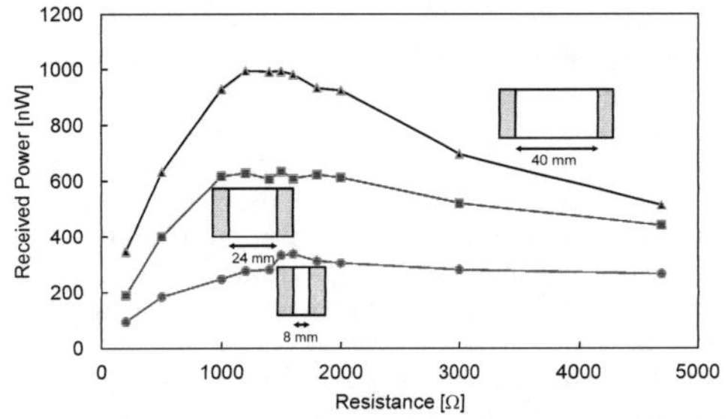

Figure 9. Relationship between input resistance and received power.

5. CONCLUSION

Impedance matching of HBC between a wearable transmitter and an off-body receiver touched by user's index finger was investigated. Transmitter-human-body system was modelled as a signal source in the equivalent circuit model of this transmission. Impedance matching of equivalent output impedance was achieved by inserting an inductor to cancel the capacitive reactance and adjusting the input resistor to match the real part of the equivalent output impedance. The equivalent output impedance was 1500-j2500 Ω at 10MHz. This value can be used to design an efficient front end circuit of the HBC receiver.

6. ACKNOWLEDGMENTS

Part of this work was supported by Japan Society for Promotion of Science (JSPS) Grants-in-Aid for Scientific Research 26420340.

7. REFERENCES

[1] Zimmerman, T.G. 1995. Personal area networks (PAN): near-field intra-body communication. *M.S. thesis*, MIT media laboratory, 1995

[2] B IEEE standard for local and metropolitan area networks-part 15.6: wireless body area networks. IEEE Computer Society, 2012.

[3] Fujii, K., Takahashi, M. and ITO, K. 2007. Electric field distributions of wearable devices using the human body as a transmission channel. *IEEE transactions on antennas and propagation*, *55* (7). 2080-2087.

[4] Fujii, K., Takahashi, M., Ito, K., Hachisuka, K., Terauchi, Y., Kishi, Y., Sasaki, K. and Itao, K. 2005. Study on the transmission mechanism for wearable device using the human body as a transmission channel. *IEICE transactions on communications*, *E88-B* (6). 2401-2410.

[5] Muramatsu, D., Koshiji, F., Koshiji, K. and Sasaki, K. 2014. Analytical and experimental studies on human body communication between wristwatch and handheld device using muscle homogenous phantom at 10 MHz. *Sensors and materials*, *26* (8). 581-589.

[6] Baldus, H., Corroy, S., Fazzi, A., Klabunde, K. and Schenk, T. 2009. Human-centric connectivity enabled by body-coupled communications. *IEEE communications magazine*, *47* (6). 172-178.

[7] Partridge, K., Dahlquist, B., Veiseh, A., Cain, A., Foreman, A., Goldberg, J. and Borriello, G. 2001. Empirical measurements of intrabody communication performance under varied physical configurations. in *The 14th Annual ACM Symposium on User Interface Software and Technology*, (Florida, U.S., 2001), Association for Computing Machinery, Inc., 183-190.

[8] Xu, R., Ng, W.C., Zhu, H., Shan, H. and Yuan, J. 2012. Equation environment coupling and interference on the electric-field intrabody communication channel. *IEEE Transactions on biomedical engineering*, *59* (7). 2051-2059.

[9] Hachisuka, K., Takeda, T., Terauchi, Y., Sasaki, K., Hosaka., H. and Itao, K. Intra-body data transmission for the personal area network. *Microsystem technologies*, *11* (8-10), 1020-1027.

Personalized neuroscience: User modeling of cognitive function and brain activity in the cloud

Teresa A. Nick
BCI, DAQRI
1201 W. 5th Street
Los Angeles, CA 90017
+1-213-375-8830
teresa.nick@daqri.com

Laura M. Berman
BCI, DAQRI
1201 W. 5th Street
Los Angeles, CA 90017
+1-213-375-8830
laura.berman@daqri.com

Arye Z. Barnehama
BCI, DAQRI
1201 W. 5th Street
Los Angeles, CA 90017
+1-213-375-8830
arye.barnehama@daqri.com

ABSTRACT
Reliable detection and prediction of neural activity and behavior requires a user model of brain activity that dynamically adapts based on known time-dependent physiological processes, as well as unknown traits of the user. We have applied wireless electroencephalography (EEG) sensors, edge devices with feedback capability, and cloud-assisted data acquisition to real-time and longitudinal brain monitoring and alerting. Toward a user model of brain function, we collected neural and behavioral data from humans in the field. The data replicate previous findings that were obtained under tight laboratory control, suggesting that the methods that we describe will be useful for user modeling of human brain activity under more natural conditions. Specifically, we report that frontal cortex oscillations reorganized with age. Focusing on time-varying aspects of behavior, we then found that performance on memory-intensive cognitive tasks declined during the day. Next, we examined interactions between neural activity and behavioral performance. We report that neural activity and performance co-varied and that this co-variation depended on the cognitive task in ways that were, again, consistent with previous laboratory studies. Lastly, we report the foundations of an adaptive model based on this system that will enable dynamic personalization tailored to each user.

Categories and Subject Descriptors
C.2.1 **[Computer-Communication Networks]**: Network Architecture and Design - *distributed networks, wireless communication*; B.4.3 **[Hardware]**: Interconnections (Subsystems) - interfaces; G.3 [Mathematics of Computing]: Probability and Statistics - *correlation and regression analysis, multivariate statistics, probabilistic algorithms, time series analysis* H.2.8 **[Information Systems]**: Database Applications - *data mining, scientific databases, statistical databases*; I.2.1 **[Artificial intelligence]**: Applications and Expert Systems - *medicine and science*

General Terms
Algorithms, Measurement, Design, Experimentation, Human Factors

Keywords
cloud, wearable, electroencephalography, EEG, cognitive game

1. INTRODUCTION
Accumulating evidence indicates that the adult brain remains somewhat plastic [1]-[4]. The adult brain also reliably expresses electrical activity patterns, enabling detection and prediction of specific states or events, such as drowsiness, seizure, and loss of focus [5], [6]. Development of a neurobehavioral user model that would enable the identification of deviations from typical patterns remains difficult due to the lack of a generic model upon which to base comparisons and build adaptive changes. In laboratory studies, large cyclic and non-cyclic changes in cognitive function and brain excitability occur reliably across time. Well-known neurobehavioral patterns are associated with age, as well as daily rhythms and other physiological cycles. For example, executive function declines with age [7] and frontal cortex brain waves in the alpha frequency band decrease with age [8], [9]. Circadian (daily) cycles and sleep pressure interact to dynamically regulate brain function [10], [11] and these changes are reflected in behavior. For example, short-term memory performance declines during the day [12]. Thus, any generic neurobehavioral user model will need to adaptively recalibrate based on these time-varying parameters.

Unfortunately, these laboratory phenomena have not been quantified in large, diverse populations with sensors that can be worn for extended time periods in a variety of environments. Further, humans in the laboratory may express different, atypical neural and behavioral patterns, suggesting that reports from laboratory studies should not be accepted at face value and, instead, will need to be retested under more natural conditions before incorporation into a user model. We have now built a system that enables minimally-obtrusive, longitudinal testing of neural and behavioral activities and compared results from this system to published laboratory-based studies.

The three main components of the system were: (1) dry electrode sensors; (2) an edge device (phone or tablet) that communicated with the sensors using Bluetooth Low Energy, engaged the user in cognitive games and other tasks, and sent data to the cloud; and (3) a cloud-based analytics and storage system that received data from the edge device, executed data-driven analytics, and presented the analyzed data back to the edge device accessible from a scalable NoSQL database. Here we report design features that enabled the integrated acquisition system and subsequent analyses.

This study evaluates the transferability of laboratory findings to the more natural conditions allowed by wearable devices.

BODYNETS 2015, September 28-30, Sydney, Australia

DOI 10.4108/eai.28-9-2015.2261443

Building on the previous laboratory work, we collected data from 848 of our users in the field. Our study differed in several important respects from these prior studies: (1) On-demand access ensured that people using the system were motivated to use it. (2) Dry electrodes in a wireless headset ensured that people were not wet, restrained, and uncomfortable. (3) The scalability of the system enabled large numbers of recording sessions that exceeded those of most other studies by at least one order of magnitude. (4) Because the user was not in the laboratory, experimental control was limited. (5) Because we did not exclude users based on any static trait, such as race, gender, or medical condition, it is likely that our recording cohort was more diverse than those of laboratory studies. (6) The use of dry electrodes necessitated limiting recordings to the forehead, which lies over the frontal cortex of the brain. The frontal cortex orchestrates executive function and plays critical roles in learning, memory, attention, and behavioral inhibition.

We provide system details on the cloud data acquisition system. Specifically, we have solved several problems regarding the recruitment and retention of users, the secure transfer and analysis of large amounts of time-series data with relatively high sampling rates, and the combination of neural and behavioral data collection in a wearable system that users carry with them.

Other contributions of this study are the novel data showing replication of highly controlled laboratory studies in the field and the descriptions of the generic and user-specific modeling approaches. The overall design is based on iterative unsupervised machine learning (*k*-means clustering) to group similar users and to mold predictive capabilities to specific users.

This integrated system enables the application of high-resolution neural and behavioral feedback to encourage user interaction in real-time and to continuously monitor user physiology in near real time. It has enabled the acquisition of large amounts of neural data and the replication of findings previously reported only in the laboratory. The development of the user model enables alerting of the user and his/her network in the event of certain medical emergencies. In case of loss of focal attention, the user can be prompted to perform an activity that enhances focus, such as breathing deeply or taking a short break. Similar non-life-threatening events can be handled with other relevant prompts.

2. SYSTEM ARCHITECTURE

2.1 Wearable EEG Hardware

Our EEG device (Figure 1, Left) is a commercially available headband with four gold-plated electrodes, 3 active and 1 passive. The headband communicates using Bluetooth Low Energy with an edge device. For the experiments described in this paper, differential recordings were made from two active electrodes placed on the left side and center of the forehead. The closest sites in the international 10-20 EEG positioning system are Fp1 and Fz, respectively. A Driven Right Leg (DRL) circuit was used to reduce common-mode interference [13]. The DRL electrode was passive. Data were sampled at 250 Hz.

The electrodes were positioned to best monitor activity of the frontal lobe of the brain, which has roles in executive function, personality, and social interactions. However, as with any EEG recording, there are other sources of voltage fluctuations that may have influenced the recordings, including brain activity in other areas, eye movements, eye blinks, and muscle activity. Movement-related artifacts were identified and removed during data processing (see below).

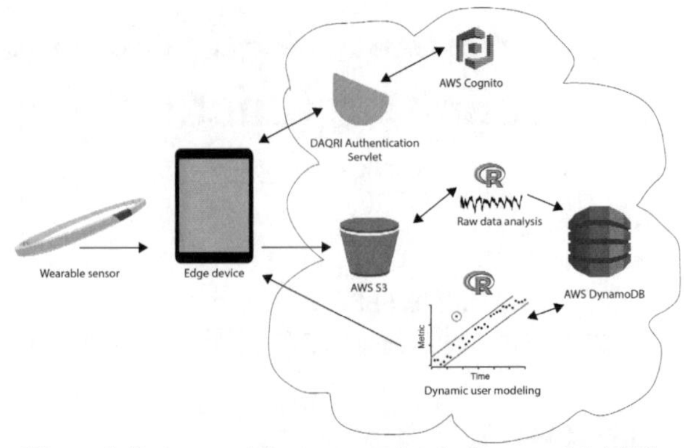

Figure 1. System architecture consisted of a wearable EEG headband (Left), an application running on an edge device (Middle), and a cloud platform built using AWS services and custom code (Right). Main cloud applications were: Authentication with Cognito (top) and storage in S3 and DynamoDB and analysis with R (bottom). Details are provided in the text.

2.2 Edge Device Application

An edge device application (Figure 1, Middle) running in iOS or Android communicated with the EEG headband. To connect to the headband, the user turned on the headband, opened the app, saw the prompt that indicated that the headband was available, and selected the headband for use. Once connected, the user could view progress on his/her "journey", play cognitive games, train focus using gaze fixation feedback, or view the filtered voltage in time or frequency domains.

Once the user selected any screen other than the journey screen, the app created an object in Amazon Web Services (AWS) S3 storage service, wrote the header in JSON, and began writing binary data from the headband. The header included various data, such as the timestamp, user identifier, the U.S. state-level location, and what screen the user was on. Moving to another screen or closing the app terminated the recording session. The file was then uploaded to S3.

For display, the time and frequency domain voltage screens relied on filtering with Infinite Impulse Response filters (1 - 50 Hz). A discrete Fourier transform was implemented to obtain power spectra for display as both meter indicators of neurally-significant frequency bands and also as a dynamic spectrogram.

Cognitive games consisted of one game that relied heavily on working memory (Pair Matching), one that relied more on focal attention (Object Mismatch), and three that relied strongly on both working memory and focal attention (Change Detection, Target Connect, and Pattern Recreation). Game scores were saved as percent correct. To encourage user retention, a journey screen was provided that allowed the user to use game achievements to earn badges and travel toward the Santa Monica Pier.

2.3 Cloud Applications

The cloud platform (Figure 1, Right) was built in AWS using Cognito, S3, DynamoDB, and Simple Workflow services. An authentication server provided tokens from Cognito to the edge device app. The edge device then used tokens to connect and put data files into S3.

The S3 data bucket was monitored by a Simple Workflow that then passed any new data files out to waiting analysis servers. The delay between the user ending the recording session and the data finishing analysis was typically less than 5 min (see Data Transfer below for file size impacts).

Data files were processed and all analyses were executed using R. Files were discarded if the timestamp had an abnormal format, the file could not be opened, the file was larger than 4 MB, the file contained < 15 seconds of data, or there was a failure in the binary read.

After conversion from binary, raw data were filtered with a 1024-order FIR filter 1-125 Hz. The trace was median subtracted and then a threshold was computed independently for each channel as mean + 8*STD of the trace. To remove large artifacts, the longest duration recording between threshold crossings was extracted for further analysis. The Fast Discrete Fourier Transform (FFT) was computed on the extracted trace. In addition, the extracted cleaned trace was analyzed with algorithms for detecting eye blinks, left and right eye movements, and facial muscle contractions. Root Mean Square (RMS) was also calculated from the clean trace to assess overall power.

Cleaned data were automatically discarded if their duration was less than 6 seconds. ~20% of incoming data were automatically rejected due to insufficient duration or file corruption. Data were marked as best quality if the maximum voltage amplitude was less than an experimentally-determined threshold. All processed data were then saved to the database and only best quality data were included in the analyses below. ~38% of data remaining after the first screen were automatically marked as best quality (see below). The power spectrum of the cleaned data was segmented into neurally-relevant frequency bands and the power in these bands was summed. In the time domain, the auto-correlations and -covariances within traces and cross-correlations and -covariances between the two channel traces were computed. Peak amplitude and lag time features were obtained from these correlation measures.

Features calculated from the cleaned data were combined with all header variables that had been converted from JSON and loaded as a single row into a DynamoDB table, with each feature constituting a separate column. Primary keys were user ID and timestamp.

3. LESSONS LEARNED

3.1 Data transfer

Given the relatively high sampling rates, we instituted a dual-buffering system. Data were stored on the device until the end of a session and then transferred to an intermediate store in S3. If the analytics pipeline backed up, the data simply sat in S3 until processing.

We found that some users recorded sessions exceeding 30 minutes, creating relatively large files that slowed down analytics because the Simple Workflow did not start a new run until all analyses from the last run were complete. To overcome this problem, we added data chunking on the edge device, such that files were closed and uploaded to S3 at faster rates. This resulted in files of standard sizes and increased analytics performance. This modification also allowed users to receive neural status updates while they were still recording.

3.2 Data quality

For our initial studies to characterize neural activity patterns, it was paramount that data be trusted. To achieve this, we marked data as best or acceptable quality and only analyzed the best quality data, with the expectation that acceptable quality data might be included once neural and behavioral patterns were identified. We have also built into the analysis system a function to keep track of the data quality from each user, so that users may be alerted to adjust their headband and/or change their recording habits when they consistently provide lower quality data.

3.3 Analysis

Due to the known contamination of neural EEG recordings with movement and muscle artifacts, we expected that we would discard large amounts of data. We found that detection of artifacts prior to filtering was not reliable, which required that we filter all incoming data. To accelerate FIR filtering and other analytics, we used AWS EC2 instances in the Compute Optimized family with high memory. Another approach would have been to use IIR filters, as we did on the edge device. However, this would have negatively impacted data quality.

4. PROOF-OF-CONCEPT

We have found that field-deployed EEG wearables and mobile apps can produce significant neural and behavioral results that are in line with previous highly-controlled laboratory studies. These wearables and apps were provided to anyone that bought the headband and data were collected without regard to any static trait, such as age, gender, profession, or race. Remarkably, in spite of the inherent variability in the data and lack of control of user behavior, results were reliable and consistent with previous findings.

4.1 Neural Activity: Frontal Activity Reorganizes With Age

Previous work indicated that brain oscillations vary with age [14]-[16]. To test the ability of the wearable EEG headband to record neural activity of humans in the field, we examined whether this phenomenon could be observed in our dataset. We had a limited number of users who had provided their age and gender, so this study was necessarily limited to those users (N = 66 users, 11 Females, 55 Males). Users younger than 20 years were compared to those 20 years and older.

The distribution of power in 5 neurally-relevant frequency bands across the two age groups were compared with a 2-way Analysis of Variance (ANOVA): delta (1 - <4 Hz), theta (4 - <7 Hz), alpha (8 - < 12 Hz), beta (15 - < 25 Hz), and gamma (30 - 125 Hz). There was a significant age x frequency band interaction, indicating that the power spectral density in these neurally-relevant bands shifts with age (Table I).

For rough visualization of these significant changes, we plotted the mean of each frequency from 1 to 40 Hz for the two groups (Figure 2).

Table I. ANOVA results for power ~ age x frequency band

	Df	Sum Sq	Mean Sq	F-value	Pr(>F)
Band	4	4.111	1.0277	534.094	< 2e-16
Age	1	0.000	0.0002	0.114	0.735419
Band x Age	4	0.046	0.0115	5.971	0.00011

Abbreviations: ANOVA: Analysis of Variance; Df: Degrees of Freedom; Sq: Squares

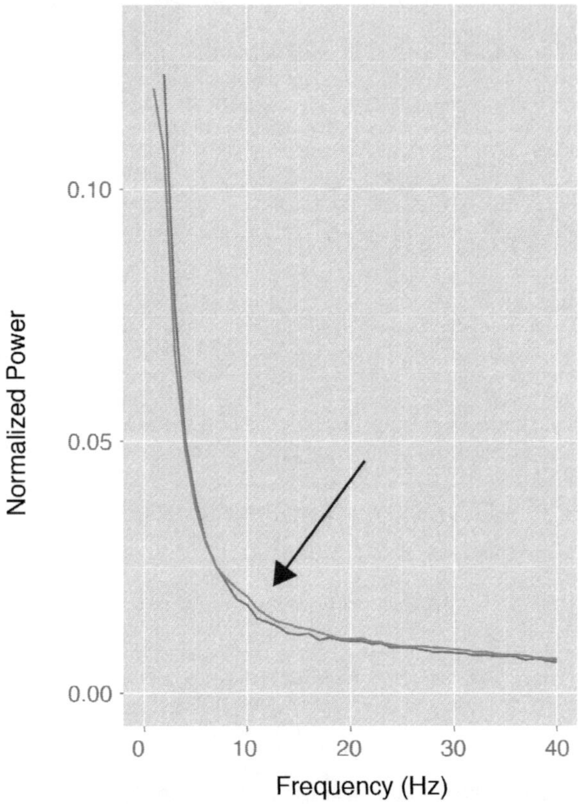

Figure 2. EEG power redistributes with age. Mean normalized power across subjects <=20 years (orange) or >20 years (cyan) is plotted relative to frequency. Frequencies in the alpha range are lower in the older subjects (arrow).

4.2 Cognitive Function: Working Memory Declines During The Day

Previous laboratory work has indicated that short-term memory declines during the day [17]. We examined whether including cognitive tasks that require working memory in our app could enable measurement of this effect in the field. We analyzed sessions during which both cognitive game scores and neural recordings were available. We found that performance on a memory-intensive task, Pair Matching (Figure 3A), declined during the day (Figure 3C). The coefficient of determination (R^2) was small, but significant, which was striking given the lack of control in these experiments.

To examine whether performance on all games, regardless of memory, might decline during the day, we also examined an Object Mismatch game (Figure 3B), which requires focal attention and little working memory. In contrast to the memory-intensive task, performance on this task was stable during the day (R2 = 0.006, p = 0.50). For Pair Matching, we obtained 70 sessions from 48 unique users. For Object Mismatch, we obtained 75 sessions from 50 unique users.

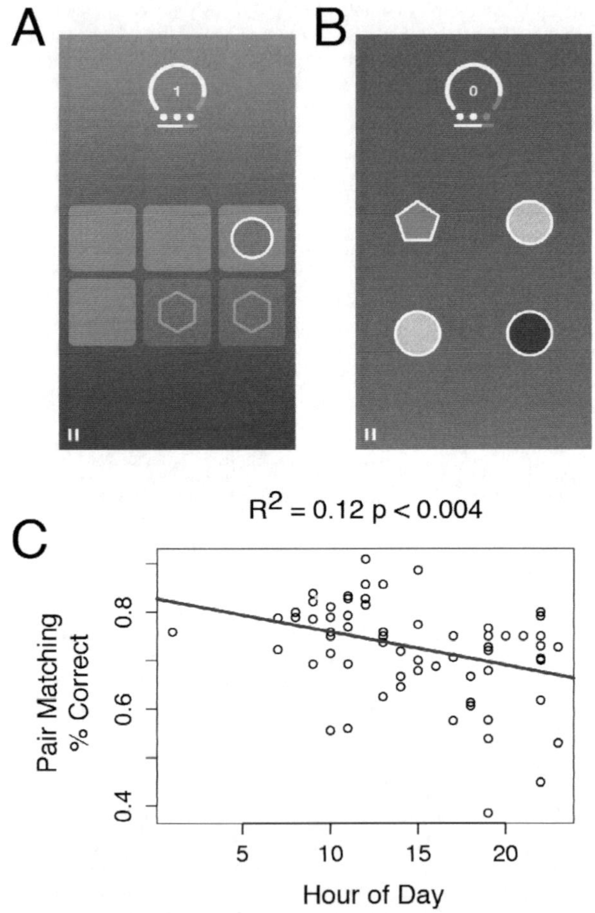

Figure 3. Performance in a working memory game, but not a focal attention game, declined with time of day. (A) The working-memory intensive Pair Matching game required the user to turn over cards and match all pairs within a 3-sec time window or a life was lost. The game ended when the user lost three lives. (B) The focal attention-intensive Object Mismatch game required the user to select the mismatched object within a 3-sec window. As with Pair Matching, the game ended when the user lost three lives. (C) Performance on the Pair Matching game declined with time of day.

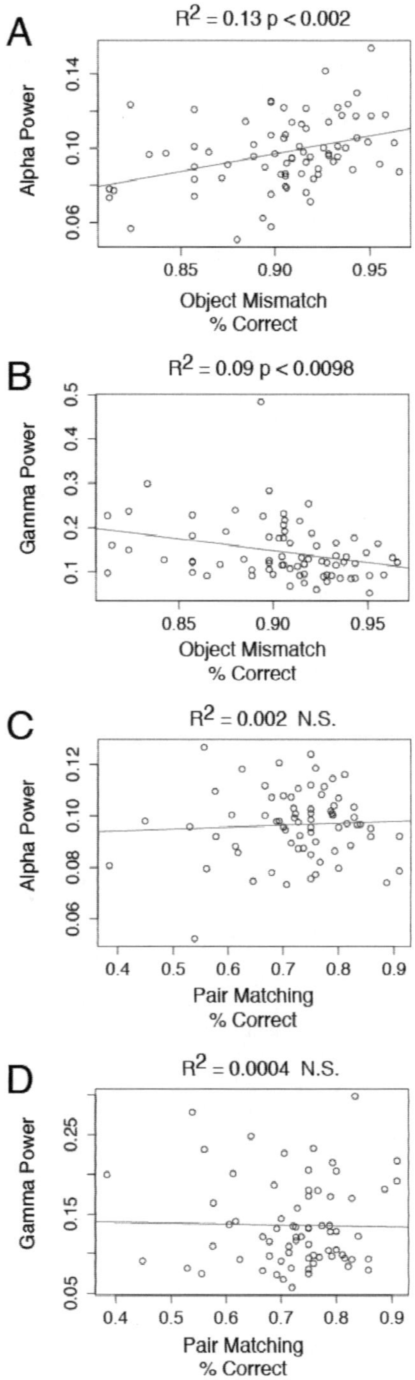

Figure 4. Alpha and gamma power varied with performance on a focal attention-intensive game, but not a memory-intensive game. (A) Alpha power increased with percent correct in the Object Mismatch game. (B) Gamma decreased with performance on Object Mismatch. (C, D) Alpha and gamma were not correlated with performance on the Pair Matching game.

4.3 Neural Activity Co-Varies With Cognitive Task

In the previous sections we showed data that indicated that the wearable headband system can measure neural and behavioral activity. We next combined neural and behavioral data in order to assess EEG power spectral changes with cognitive task. We found that EEG alpha and gamma varied with performance on a focal attention-intensive task (Object Mismatch, Figure 4A-B), but not a memory-intensive task (Pair Matching, Figure 4C-D). This finding is consistent with laboratory reports that alpha power increases with attention [18], [19]. Beta, which lies between alpha and gamma, was not significantly modulated during either task (Object Mismatch: $R^2 = 0.02$, $p = 0.23$; Pair Matching: $R^2 = 0.004$, $p = 0.57$).

These data indicate that our system can record neural performance indicators during user activity and, in the case of at least one focal attention-intensive task, predict the user's performance on that task. The fact that the neural activity varies with cognitive load also suggests that the system may be able to determine relative focal attention demand of tasks in educational, medical, and industrial settings and make that information available to users.

5. ADAPTIVE USER MODELING

Above, we present a series of small and significant findings from recordings of humans that have not been selected for any static trait. Their activity was monitored, not controlled. Using these and other data, reliable patterns in the field can be combined to learn a generic user model with a given set of static traits. Based on these traits, plus additional relevant information such as time of day, the brain activity of a given user can be predicted. Variations from this model can feed back to inform the user-specific model as well as the generic model. Alerts and triggers can then rely on deviations from the model.

5.1 A generic user modeling approach

Here we have presented data that indicate reliable patterns of brain activity and behavioral performance in terms of age, time of day, and task. However, there is much variability in the individual measures of brain activity and behavior. How does one construct a robust generic user model in spite of the variability? Below, we present an approach to forming a generic user model. We have not exhaustively tested the example model for predictive capacity, as this paper focuses on the feasibility and approach, not the model details.

We have used unsupervised machine learning, *k*-means clustering, to begin to attack the problem of generic user modeling. For our example, we show data from the Object Mismatch game discussed in the previous section. Object Mismatch neural data in the 5 frequency bands discussed earlier (delta, theta, alpha, beta, and gamma) were *k*-means clustered with a maximum cluster count of 10. 10 clusters were produced and these were sorted based on alpha power and divided in half. Next, the Object Mismatch percent correct scores were compared between the high- and low-alpha cluster groups. We found that the 5 clusters with the lowest alpha power performed significantly lower on the Object Mismatch task than the 5 clusters with the highest scores (Figure 5).

In summary, this approach uses segmentation of the data with unsupervised machine learning, potentially followed by recombination of clusters based on informed neuroscience decisions. In the example, clusters were recombined based on a simple top-bottom split based on alpha power. Next, any combined clusters should be visually inspected at least in the dimension of recombination to ensure that combined clusters remain reasonably separated (Figure 5A). Features that are not used in the clustering may be analyzed to make inferences about results one might expect in future experiments, thus forming a generic user model for neural-neural and/or neural-behavioral relationships (Figure 5B; t-test, $p < 0.043$, lowest alpha, N=31; highest alpha, N=44). Lastly, the prediction accuracy of the model should be tested regularly using post-hoc comparisons of predicted and actual data.

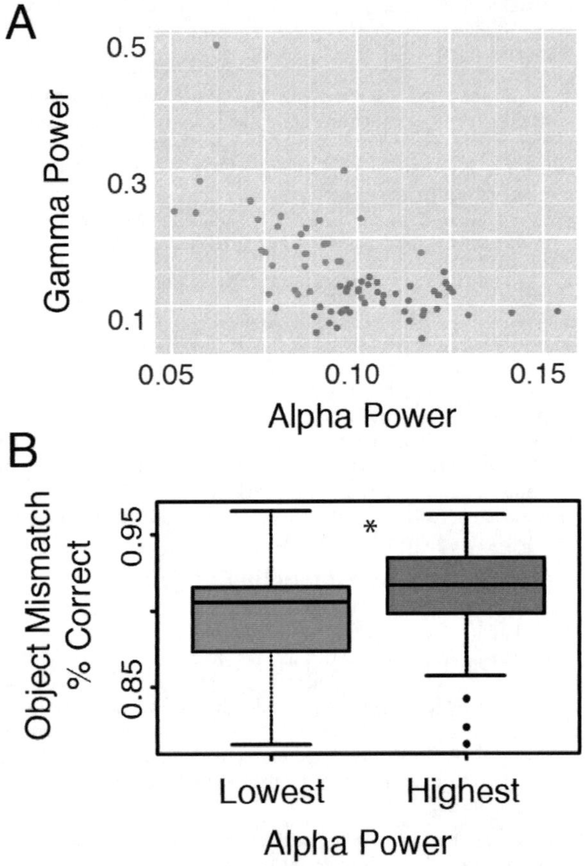

Figure 5. Unsupervised clustering of data based on neural activity results in clusters with significant differences in cognitive performance. *k*-means clustering resulted in 10 clusters that were divided in half based on mean alpha power. (A) The top (cyan) and bottom (orange) clusters visually separated in gamma and alpha dimensions. (B) The scores on Object Mismatch for the two clusters were significantly different.

5.2 A user-specific modeling approach

Once generic user models are formed, the position of specific user traits and data can be localized in multi-dimensional space. Upon initial data acquisition from a user, the generic model will provide most predictions of user behavior based on static trait alignment with existing generic clusters. As data acquisition for a given user proceeds, the generic model can be refined through an iterative approach of feeding user data into machine learning algorithms and obtaining new and/or shifting clusters. As more data from the user are acquired, the user-specific model, also created through iterative machine learning, prediction, and accuracy comparison, can begin to stand alone, becoming more and more molded to that specific user and better able to detect divergent neural or behavioral activity.

Building on this model, we have used multiple linear regression to determine the relationships (temporal and otherwise) between neural activity and behavior in each cluster, evaluated model quality based on the coefficient of determination, and calculated a user model error factor from the Mahalanobis distance of their feature vector from the center of their group's cluster. A routinely updated user model with the error factor can be automatically downloaded to the edge device to enable detection of user divergence from their own neural and behavioral baselines. The decision to alert the user upon divergence is weighted by the error factor. With large divergence, user features will likely fall into another generic cluster, potentially resulting in shifting of predictions and, subsequently, better fits.

6. CONCLUSIONS

Functional deployment of wearables for health and wellness alerting and triggering fundamentally requires dynamic user models that can provide generic multidimensional predictions of neural activity and behavior. Further, dynamic user models can enable sculpting of predictions to specific users. This requires employment of hard-core neuroscience combined with scalable recording and devices that users want to use.

We have built a scalable solution that has collected, analyzed, and stored data from over 10,000 recording sessions. Here we show analyses of these data, revealing replication of findings that have previously been observed only under highly controlled laboratory conditions. In addition, we describe a novel approach to generic and user-specific modeling utilizing iterative *k*-means clustering, quality checking, and adjustment. This system provides a mechanism for scalable personalized user neural feedback, health research, and real-time monitoring. Potential applications for this technology include a system to alert users when they are stressed based on brain hemispheric asymmetry, a system to assess the cognitive engagement of post-stroke patients in therapeutic games for rehabilitation, and a system to monitor neural correlates of focal attention of students in a classroom.

7. ACKNOWLEDGMENTS

We thank Jono Freeman and Eric Lundquist for technical assistance.

8. REFERENCES

[1] M. Merzenich, T. M. Van Vleet, and M. Nahum, "Brain Plasticity-Based Therapeutics," *Frontiers in Human ...*, vol. 8, pp. 1–16, 2014.

[2] J. Mayas, F. B. R. Parmentier, P. Andrés, and S. Ballesteros, "Plasticity of attentional functions in older adults after non-action video game training: a randomized controlled trial.," *PLoS ONE*, vol. 9, no. 3, p. e92269, 2014.

[3] J. F. Bergan, P. Ro, D. Ro, and E. I. Knudsen, "Hunting increases adaptive auditory map plasticity in adult barn owls," *J. Neurosci.*, vol. 25, no. 42, pp. 9816–9820, 2005.

[4] J. A. Anguera, J. Boccanfuso, J. L. Rintoul, O.

Al-Hashimi, F. Faraji, J. Janowich, E. Kong, Y. Larraburo, C. Rolle, E. Johnston, and A. Gazzaley, "Video game training enhances cognitive control in older adults.," *Nature*, vol. 501, no. 7465, pp. 97–101, Sep. 2013.

[5] G. R. Minasyan, J. B. Chatten, M. J. Chatten, and R. N. Harner, "Patient-Specific Early Seizure Detection From Scalp Electroencephalogram," *Journal of Clinical Neurophysiology*, vol. 27, no. 3, pp. 163–178, Jun. 2010.

[6] R. R. Johnson, D. P. Popovic, R. E. Olmstead, M. Stikic, D. J. Levendowski, and C. Berka, "Drowsiness/alertness algorithm development and validation using synchronized EEG and cognitive performance to individualize a generalized model," *Biological Psychology*, vol. 87, no. 2, pp. 241–250, May 2011.

[7] L. Nyberg, M. Lovden, K. Riklund, U. Lindenberger, and L. Backman, "Memory aging and brain maintenance," *Trends Cogn Sci*, vol. 16, pp. 292–305, May 2012.

[8] C. Richard Clark, M. D. Veltmeyer, R. J. Hamilton, E. Simms, R. Paul, D. Hermens, and E. Gordon, "Spontaneous alpha peak frequency predicts working memory performance across the age span.," *Int J Psychophysiol*, vol. 53, no. 1, pp. 1–9, Jun. 2004.

[9] W. Klimesch, "EEG alpha and theta oscillations reflect cognitive and memory performance: a review and analysis.," *Brain Res. Brain Res. Rev.*, vol. 29, no. 2, pp. 169–195, Apr. 1999.

[10] A. A. Borbély, "A two process model of sleep regulation," *Hum Neurobiol.*, vol. 1, no. 3, pp. 195–204, May 1982.

[11] L. Cummings, A. Dane, J. Rhodes, P. Lynch, and A. M. Hughes, "Diurnal variation in the quantitative EEG in healthy adult volunteers.," *Br J Clin Pharmacol*, vol. 50, no. 1, pp. 21–26, Jul. 2000.

[12] C. Schmidt, F. Collette, C. Cajochen, and P. Peigneux, "A time to think: circadian rhythms in human cognition.," *Cogn Neuropsychol*, vol. 24, no. 7, pp. 755–789, Oct. 2007.

[13] B. B. Winter and J. G. Webster, "Driven-right-leg circuit design," *IEEE Trans. Biomed. Eng.*, no. 1, pp. 62–66, 1983.

[14] T. D. R. Cummins and S. Finnigan, "Theta power is reduced in healthy cognitive aging," *International Journal of Psychophysiology*, vol. 66, no. 1, pp. 10–17, Oct. 2007.

[15] T. Kuo, J.-Y. Li, S. S. Hsieh, J.-J. Chen, C.-Y. Tsai, and C. Yang, "Effect of aging on treadmill exercise induced theta power in the rat," *Age*, vol. 32, no. 3, p. 297, Sep. 2010.

[16] E. L. Vlahou, F. Thurm, I.-T. Kolassa, and W. Schlee, "Resting-state slow wave power, healthy aging and cognitive performance," *Sci. Rep.*, vol. 4, pp. –, Jan. 2000.

[17] C. Schmidt, F. Collette, C. Cajochen, and P. Peigneux, "A time to think: circadian rhythms in human cognition.," *Cogn Neuropsychol*, vol. 24, no. 7, pp. 755–789, Oct. 2007.

[18] N. R. Cooper, A. P. Burgess, R. J. Croft, and J. H. Gruzelier, "Investigating evoked and induced electroencephalogram activity in task-related alpha power increases during an internally directed attention task.," *Neuroreport*, vol. 17, no. 2, pp. 205–208, Feb. 2006.

[19] S. M. Doesburg, J. J. Green, J. J. McDonald, and L. M. Ward, "From local inhibition to long-range integration: A functional dissociation of alpha-band synchronization across cortical scales in visuospatial attention," *Brain Research*, vol. 1303, no. C, pp. 97–110, Nov. 2009.

An analytical model of information spreading through conjugation in bacterial nanonetworks

G. Castorina L. Galluccio S. Palazzo
CNIT Research Unit at Dipartimento di Ingegneria Elettrica Elettronica e Informatica,
University of Catania, Italy
email: name.surname@cnit.it

ABSTRACT
Molecular communications are a powerful tool to implement communication functionalities in environments where the use of electromagnetic waves becomes critical, e.g. in the human body. Molecules such as proteins, DNA, RNA sequences are used to carry information. To this aim a novel approach relies on the use of genetically modified bacteria to transport enhanced DNA strands, called plasmids, where information can be encoded and then transferred among bacterial cell using the so called conjugation process. Information transfer is thus based on bacteria motility, i.e. self-propelled motion which under appropriate circumstances is exhibited by certain bacteria, which is still not completely understood. In this paper we propose an analytical model to characterize information spreading in bacterial nanonetworks by employing an epidemic approach similar to the one used to model Delay Tolerant Networks (DTNs) and we show that such modeling can be profitably used to represent information spreading in conjugation-based bacterial nanonetworks

Keywords
Information spreading, bacterial nano networks.

1. INTRODUCTION
In molecular communications information is encoded into molecules (e.g. proteins, DNA and RNA strands, pheromones, etc.) and, specifically, in their type, number, concentration or release time. In turn, molecular communications can be classified depending on the distance between sender and receiver [4] or, according to the transport mechanism used by the molecules. In the latter case we distinguish between *active* and *passive* transport techniques. Passive transport techniques do not need for external energy to move molecules and rely on diffusive phenomena (e.g. Brownian motion, diffusion theory). Active transport techniques need for external energy supply and imply the use of molecular motors, catalytic nanomotors and flagellated bacteria (suitable to transport genetic information due to the high motility given by their flagella). Several examples exist in the literature that describe architectures for active transport molecular communications based on the use of molecular motors and flagellated bacteria. Nevertheless none of these works provides a mathematical model to study information propagation in nanonetworks based on active transport techniques and, in particular, flagellated bacteria. An analytical model for delay and capacity in bacteria-based nanonetworks is derived in [2], in which bacteria are supposed to be relayed directly from nanomachine to nanomachine, but no mention to opportunistic conjugation, i.e. transfer of plasmids between bacterial cells, is available. Furthermore, in the analytical model, delay is split into a fixed delay and a stochastic propagation delay that is studied through simulations. In this paper we introduce an architecture derived from the one proposed in [4] and [5] and use an epidemic model to analytically characterize bacteria diffusion and the plasmids dissemination in molecular networks. In particular, we evaluate time delivery and loss performance in these scenarios by using epidemic approaches inherited by DTN's modeling. The rest of this paper is organized as follows. In Section 2 we describe the related work and give the necessary background to understand the proposed model. In Section 3 we describe the architecture of the proposed model and derive a mathematical description. In Section 4 numerical results are provided and discussed. In Section 5 conclusions are drawn.

BODYNETS 2015, September 28-30, Sydney, Australia

DOI 10.4108/eai.14-12-2015.151107

2. RELATED WORK
Bacteria are naturally able to spread genetic information across a colony through a process known as *conjugation*. The conjugation process takes place between pairs of bacteria that come into each other proximity and allows to exchange the genetic information contained in specific double stranded circular DNA sequences, known as *plasmids*, which are generally free to move inside the bacterial cytoplasm. A plasmid, normally, does not include functionalities necessary for the survival of the bacterium, but gives it some extra-ability (e.g. antibiotic resistance, virulence or metabolic property) useful to proliferate in particular conditions. Plasmids can be classified into incompatibility groups so that different plasmids can coexist inside the cellular body as long as they are not in the same *incompatibility group*. When a bacterium with a specific plasmid comes in proximity of another one both having no plasmids of the same incompatibility group, the conjugation process starts. As an example consider the F-plasmid (Fertility factor). The F-plasmid is responsible for the formation of a sex pilus used to initiate the conjugation process. When a bacterium pro-

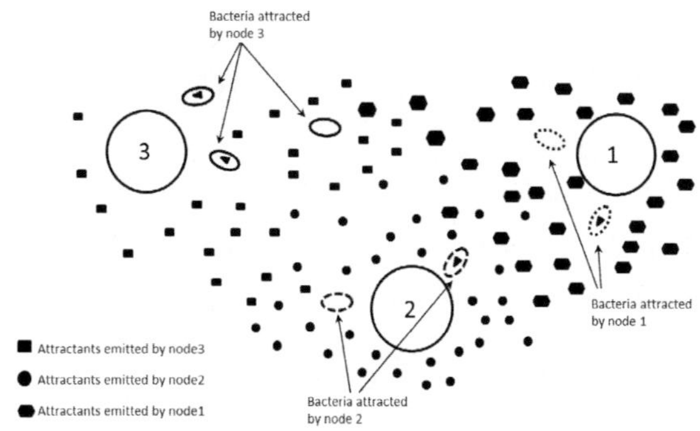

Figure 1: Example of bacterial nanonetwork

vided with the F-plasmid (F^+ bacterium) is close enough to a bacterium without the F-plasmid (F^- bacterium), a sex pilus extends from the donor (F^+ bacterium) to the recipient (F^- bacterium). Thus, due to the sex pilus contraction the two cellular membranes get in contact and a channel is opened to allow the passage of the F-plasmid from the F^+ to the F^- bacterium.
In [4] a flagellated bacteria-based paradigm was proposed to implement medium range molecular communications. Bioengineering techniques can be used to create artificial mutated bacteria with chimeric plasmids (i.e. in vitro built up plasmids) in order to form a dictionary of bacteria with a set of possible messages encoded in chimeric plasmids.
Motility of flagellated bacteria relies on helical movements of the flagella. Through several pili distributed along the cellular body, bacteria can sense concentration of nutrients in the environment and decide to move towards points with an increasing concentration level. This process is known as *chemotaxis*.
Concerning the network model in [4], it consists of several nanomachines which emit chemoattractants to attract bacteria from the environment (Figure 1). Different nodes (i.e. nanomachines) can spread different types of attractants so that they can stimulate a different bacterium. Furthermore, any node can store a set of bacteria that can carry an information packet in the form of a plasmid and can be attracted by neighbors nodes. A node that wants to send a packet to another nanomachine will release bacteria with the encoded packet into the environment. Through the chemotaxis process, bacteria will find their own way to neighbor nodes emitting the appropriate chemical compound and will deliver the packet.
An opportunistic routing scheme based on bacterial conjugation was proposed in [5]. Bacteria used to transport the information are supposed to be E. Coli and it is assumed that node-to-node paths are followed by bacteria to cross each other. If a bacterium, with a packet encoded into a plasmid, meets another one that is not carrying any message (no plasmid), conjugation will be executed so that at the end of the process both bacteria will transport the same packet. As an example consider the system shown in Figure 2: where a bacterium, sent from the nanomachine 1 (node 1) to node 2, in proximity of node 2 will eventually meet bacteria directed from node 2 to node 3; thus, by exploiting the conjugation process, the message will be relayed to node 3.

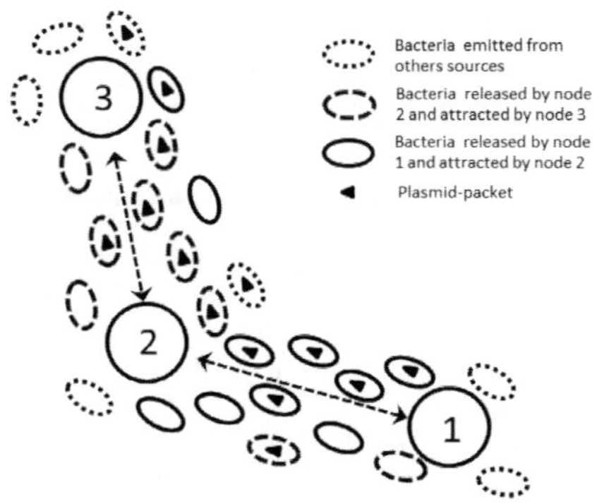

Figure 2: Opportunistic routing through conjugation

3. SYSTEM MODEL

We consider bacteria as mobile nodes that occasionally come into each other proximity and exchange information. Such a model is similar to those used for epidemic spreading in Delay Tolerant Networks (DTNs) [3], [8], [7]. In DTNs, an infection disease model, known as SIR [6], is usually exploited to describe the spreading of information among a population of mobile nodes. In the SIR models the total population is assumed constant [6] and three different classes of individuals are considered: individuals susceptible to be infected, S, infected individuals, I and recovered individuals, R (individuals that have been infected and then recovered through a vaccine or immunization process). In our model we initially consider that only one packet (i.e. plasmid) is flowing into the network issued by a source nanomachine. Each bacterium represents a mobile node (node-M). A bacterium that has no plasmid (i.e. packet) is considered susceptible (node-S) to be infected; a bacterium with a plasmid (a packet) is considered infected (node-I). Moreover, a destination node (node-D) is a nanomachine able to connect to a bacterium through a conjugation process, receive the plasmid and de-activate the bacterium that is then considered recovered (node-R). Relay nanomachines are available and can issue bacteria.
Bacteria released by the source will move randomly and eventually meet other bacteria, start conjugation and make the packet spread into the area. This process continues until one or more bacteria with the encoded plasmid reach the destination node. The destination nanomachine will be able to receive the packet and kill the bacterium. We consider a mathematical model that assigns destinations as static nodes, bacteria in the environment as mobile nodes and a static source at time $t = 0$.

3.1 Plasmid Spreading Model

We consider the case when a single plasmid can be carried by a node-M. We refer to the F-plasmid transfer model as an example and every nanomachine emits attractants, sensed by bacteria of any node-M. Attractants concentration can be approximated as uniform into the network area. Let $I(t)$ be the number of infected nodes at time t, $S(t)$ the number of susceptible nodes at time t and $R(t)$ the number of

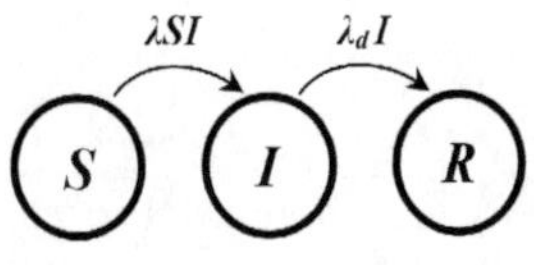

Figure 3: Markov chain of a SIR infection model

recovered nodes at time t. We assume that inter-contact time between bacteria is exponentially distributed. Let λ be the inter-contact rate between a pair of bacteria and let λ_d be the inter-contact rate between bacteria and destination nodes. Under these assumptions, the model can be described as a Markov chain where a transition occurs every time an infected node meets a non infected node (i.e. I(t) increases) or recovery occurs after an infected node reaches a node-D (I(t) decreases). If N is the average number of nodes (bacteria) and D the number of destinations, the plasmid diffusion process can be modeled as:

$$I'(t) = [N - I(t) - R(t)]\lambda I(t) - R'(t) \tag{1}$$

and

$$R'(t) = D\lambda_d I(t) \tag{2}$$

For worth of illustration we consider a static topology of nanomachines like the one plot in Figure 4: nanomachine 8 is the source node, the nano-machine 3 is the destination node.When a node needs to send a packet it will release a certain amount of bacteria (i.e. a given rate) with the same encoded message (plasmid). Due to the uniform attractants concentration, bacteria move randomly in the area with no preferential path. So they can be modeled as N nodes-M that meet each other and the destination nodes with inter-contact rates λ and λ_d, respectively. To derive the CDF of the first delivery time, we can observe that no recovery can occur until the first packet is delivered to a destination. Under this assumption eq. (1) assumes the following form:

$$I'(t) = [N - I(t)]\lambda I(t) \tag{3}$$

and eq. (3) is an ODE equation with initial condition $I(0) = 1$ that has the following solution:

$$I(t) = \frac{N}{1 + e^{-\lambda N t}(N-1)} \tag{4}$$

Furthermore, if T is the time from the generation of the packet until the first time destination receives it, by considering a single destination, the cumulative probability distribution for T, $F_T(t)$, can be computed as in [7]:

$$F_T(t) = 1 - K\left(\frac{N-1}{e^{\lambda N T} + N - 1}\right)^{\frac{\lambda_d}{\lambda}} \tag{5}$$

with $K = [\frac{N-1}{N}]^{-\frac{\lambda_d}{\lambda}}[1 - F_T(0)]$

4. NUMERICAL ANALYSIS

In this section, we illustrate the numerical results obtained by applying the proposed analytical model. We analyze the plasmid spreading model given the number of bacteria in the environment, the inter-contact rates among bacteria and the inter-contact rates between bacteria and destinations. To simplify the analysis we consider a network topology like the one plotted in Figure 2. For the plasmid model we set $N = 120$ bacteria, i.e. nodes-M, that are supposed to be uniformly distributed at random. Nanomachine 1 is assigned as the source nanomachine, nanomachine 3 as the destination nanomachine and nanomachine 2 as the relay nanomachine. Furthermore one infected bacterium is set as initial condition. The plasmid spreading model is analyzed for different values of λ and λ_d. The inter-contact rate λ is obtained from data reported in [1] and is set as $\lambda = 8 \cdot 10^{-6}$. Figure 5 shows the number of infected nodes-M (bacteria) as a function of time t. The CDF of $F_T(t)$ is computed for different values of λ_d and is plotted in Figure 6. By increasing the inter-contact rate between bacteria and destinations the delivery time decreases. In Figure 7 we report the average first delivery time versus the ratio between λ and λ_d. As expected the number of infected nodes (Figure 5) starts to increase in a non linear way and reaches a maximum value; then the recovery process becomes dominant and the number of infected nodes decreases. Note that, the maximum number of infected nodes (Figure 5) is very close to the total number of bacteria distributed in the environment; for this reason, as can be observed also in Figure 7, the recovery process immediately starts to prevail after the first delivery. This behavior

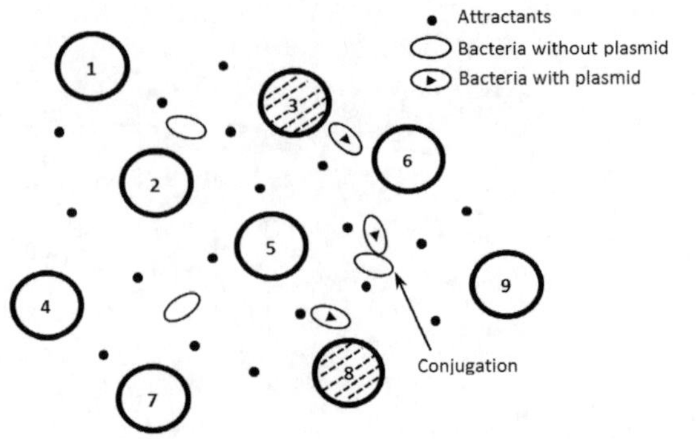

Figure 4: Static topology with a single attractants uniformly distributed at random

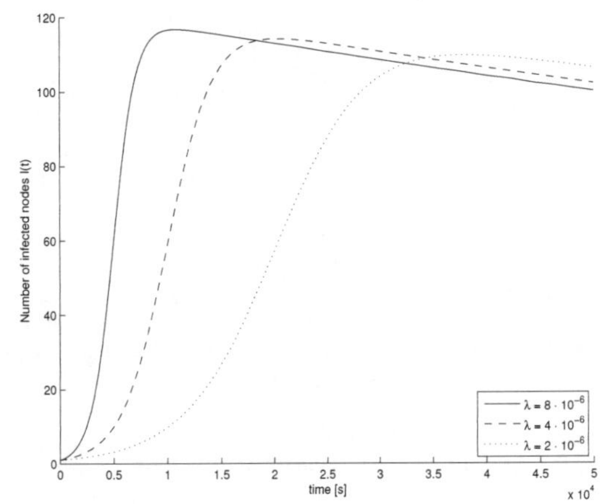

Figure 5: Number of infected nodes vs time for a single plasmid dissemination with a single attractant

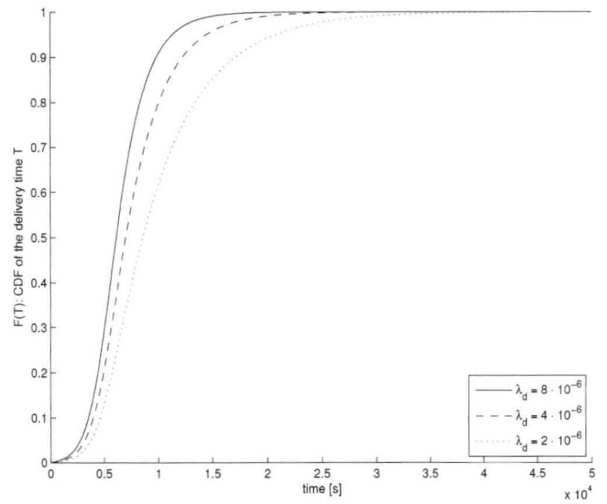

Figure 6: CDF of the delivery time T for a single plasmid dissemination with a single attractant

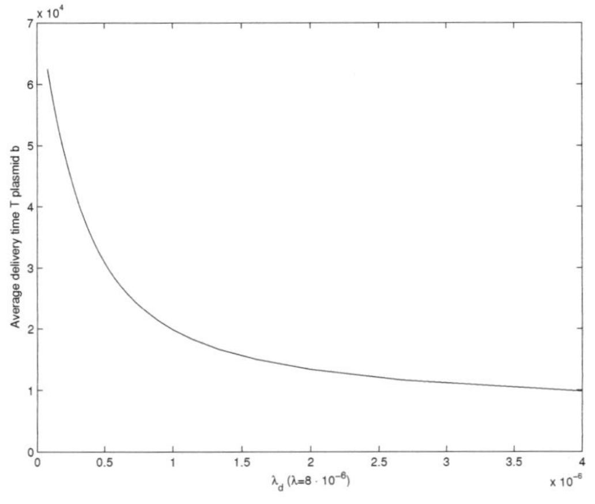

Figure 7: Average delivery time T for a single plasmid dissemination with a single attractant

suggests that the probability to deliver a packet is very low even for high number of infected nodes, but rapidly increases upon approaching the saturation of the network (number of infected nodes equal to the total number of bacteria in the environment). Finally, in Figure 8, we show the number of recovered nodes versus time. As expected the number of recovered nodes increases in a non linear way and we observe that the proposed recovery scheme is a very slow process if compared to the diffusion of the infection.

5. CONCLUSIONS

Bacteria-based communications have been recently proposed as a promising approach to implement middle range communications and support networking functionalities in molecular scenarios. In this paper we presented an analytical model to characterize the behavior of multi-hop communications in bacterial nanonetworks that take into account conjugation processes. In particular we presented a model to describe a pure epidemic routing; we set a simple test case considering a topology with 3 nodes and we derived the numerical solution. The model showed a strong dependence on the inter-contact rate among bacteria and between bacteria and destination. We think that the epidemic approach represents a simple, feasible and reliable solution for modeling of information vive spreading in conjugation-based bacterial nanonetworks.

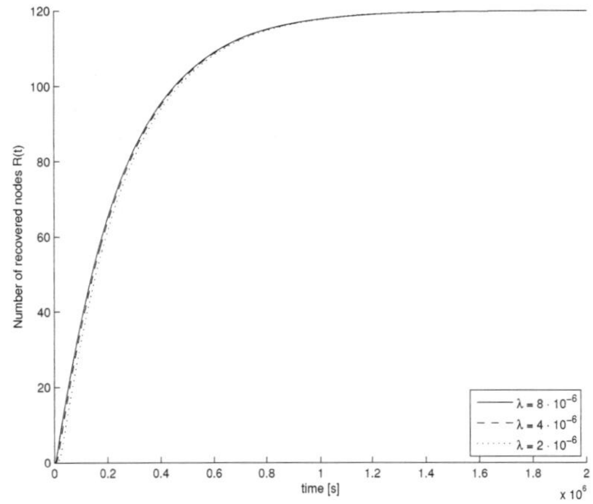

Figure 8: Number of recovered nodes vs time for a single plasmid dissemination with a single attractant

6. REFERENCES

[1] S. Balasubramaniam and P. Lio. Multi-hop conjugation based bacteria nanonetworks. *IEEE Trans. on Nanobioscience*, 12(1):47–59, March 2013.

[2] L. C. Cobo and I. F. Akyildiz. Bacteria-based communication in nanonetworks. *Nano Commun. Netw.*, 1(4):244–256, December 2010.

[3] L. Galluccio, B. Lorenzo, and S. Glisic. Sociality-aided new adaptive infection recovery schemes for multicast dtns. *Accepted for publication in a future issue of IEEE Transactions on Vehicular Technology*, 2015.

[4] M. Gregori and I. F. Akyildiz. A new nanonetwork architecture using flagellated bacteria and catalytic nanomotors. *IEEE Journal on Sel. Areas in Comm.*, 28(4):612–619, May 2010.

[5] P. Lio and S. Balasubramaniam. Opportunistic routing through conjugation in bacteria communication nanonetwork. *Nano Commun. Netw.*, 3(1):36–45, March 2012.

[6] J. Murray. *Mathematical Biology: I. An Introductioned. 3rd ed. Interdisciplinary applied mathematics, vol. 17.* Springer, New York, 2001.

[7] T. Small and Z. Haas. The shared wireless infostation model - a new ad hoc networking paradigm. In *MobiHoc*. ACM, 2003.

[8] J. K. D. T. X. Zhang, G. Neglia. Performance modeling of epidemic routing. *Computer Networks*, 51(10):2867–2891, July 2007.

AUTHOR INDEX

AUTHOR INDEX